UNDERSTANDING
HUMAN
COMMUNICATION

Third Canadian Edition

UNDERSTANDING HUMAN COMMUNICATION

Ronald B. Adler | George Rodman | Alexandre Sévigny

OXFORD
UNIVERSITY PRESS

OXFORD
UNIVERSITY PRESS

Oxford University Press is a department of the University of Oxford.
It furthers the University's objective of excellence in research, scholarship,
and education by publishing worldwide. Oxford is a registered trade mark of
Oxford University Press in the UK and in certain other countries.

Published in Canada by
Oxford University Press
8 Sampson Mews, Suite 204,
Don Mills, Ontario M3C 0H5 Canada

www.oupcanada.com

First Edition published in 2008
Second Edition published in 2011

Understanding Human Communication, 8e was originally published in English in 2003 by
Oxford University Press, Inc., 198 Madison Avenue, New York, NY 10016-4314, USA with the
ISBN 9780195219104. This adapted edition is published by arrangement. Oxford University Press Canada is
solely responsible for this adaptation from the original work. Original edition published by Oxford University
Press, Inc., 198 Madison Avenue, New York, NY 10016. Copyright © 2006 by Oxford University Press, Inc.

Library and Archives Canada Cataloguing in Publication

Adler, Ronald B. (Ronald Brian), 1946–, author
Understanding human communication / Ronald B. Adler,
George Rodman, Alexandre Sévigny. — Third Canadian edition.

Includes bibliographical references and index.
ISBN 978-0-19-900419-5 (pbk.)

1. Communication—Textbooks. 2. Communication—Canada—Textbooks.
3. Interpersonal communication—Textbooks. 4. Interpersonal communication—Canada—
Textbooks. I. Rodman, George R., 1948–, author II. Sévigny, Alexandre, author III. Title.

P90.A318 2015   302.2   C2014-907622-3

Cover image: iStockPhoto.com/SiGal

Oxford University Press is committed to our environment.
Wherever possible, our books are printed on paper which comes from responsible sources.

Printed and bound in the United States of America

1 2 3 4 — 18 17 16 15

Brief Contents

PART I   Elements of Communication   1

    1   Human Communication: What and Why   2
    2   Perception, the Self, and Communication   38
    3   Language   84
    4   Non-Verbal Communication   128
    5   Listening   166

PART II   Interpersonal Communication   209

    6   Understanding Interpersonal Relationships   210
    7   Improving Interpersonal Relationships   260

PART III   Communication in Groups   293

    8   Social Media and Communication Theory   294
    9   The Nature of Groups   338
    10   Solving Problems in Groups   368

PART IV   Persuasion and Public Communication   407

    11   Persuasion   408
    12   Writing and Delivering Speeches   430

Appendices

    I   Persuasive Professional Writing   478
    II   Communicating for Career Success   490

Contents

Preface   xv

Highlights of the New Edition   xix

PART I

Elements of Communication

1 Human Communication: What and Why   2

Communication Defined   4

Communication Is Human   5

Communication Is a Process   6

Communication Is Symbolic   6

Types of Communication   6

Intrapersonal Communication   6

Dydadic/Interpersonal Communication   7

Small-Group Communication   8

Public Communication   8

Mass Communication   9

Functions of Communication   9

Physical Needs   10

Identity Needs   11

Social Needs   13

Practical Needs   14

Modelling Communication   15

A Linear Model   15

A Transactional Model   18

Communication Competence: What Makes an Effective Communicator?   21

Communication Competence Defined   22

There Is No "Ideal" Way to Communicate   22

Characteristics of Competent Communicators   24

Clarifying Misconceptions about Communication   26

Communication Does Not Always Require Complete Understanding   26

Communication Is Not Always a Good Thing   29

No Single Person or Event Causes Another's Reaction   32

Communication Will Not Solve All Problems   32

Meanings Rest in People, Not in Words   32

Communication Is Not Simple   33

More Communication Is Not Always Better   34

Summary   34

Key Terms   35

Activities   35

Further Reading   36

Study Questions   37

2 Perception, the Self, and Communication   38

Simple Truths, Important Lessons: How Communication Shapes Perception   40

Perceiving Others   41

Narratives and Perception   41

Common Perceptual Tendencies   42

Situational Factors Influencing Perception   47

Perception and Culture   49

Empathy and Perception   51

Perceiving the Self   56

The Self-Concept Defined   56

Communication and Development of the Self   58

Culture and the Self-Concept   60

The Self-Concept, Personality, and Communication   62

The Self-Fulfilling Prophecy   64

Identity Management: Communication as Impression Management   66

Public and Private Selves   66

Characteristics of Identity Management   68

Why Manage Impressions?   73

How Do We Manage Impressions?   74

Impression Management and Honesty   78

Summary   79

Key Terms   79

Activities   79

Further Reading   81

Study Questions   82

3   Language   84

The Nature of Language   86

Language Is Symbolic   86

Meanings Are in People, Not in Words   87

Language Is Rule-Governed   87

The Power of Language   91

Language Shapes Attitudes   91

Language Reflects Attitudes   97

Troublesome Language   100

The Language of Misunderstandings   101

Disruptive Language   106

Evasive Language   108

Gender and Language   110

Content   110

Reasons for Communicating   110

Conversational Style   112

Non-Gender Variables   113

Culture and Language   115

Verbal Communication Styles   115

Language and Worldview   120

Language Use in Anglo-North American Culture   123

Summary   124

Key Terms   124

Activities   125

Further Reading   126

Study Questions   127

4   Non-Verbal Communication   128

Characteristics of Non-Verbal Communication   130

Non-Verbal Communication Exists   130

Non-Verbal Behaviour Has Communicative Value   131

Non-Verbal Communication Is Primarily Relational   132

Non-Verbal Communication Is Ambiguous   132

Non-Verbal Communication Is Different from Verbal Communication   135

Non-Verbal Skills Are Important   135

Influences on Non-Verbal Communication   136

Culture   136

Gender   138

Functions of Non-Verbal Communication   140

Repeating   140

Substituting   140

Complementing   141

Accenting   142

Regulating   142

Contradicting   142

Deceiving   142

Types of Non-Verbal Communication   147

Posture and Gesture   147

Face and Eyes   148

Voice   150

Touch   150

Physical Attractiveness   152

Clothing   153

Distance   155

Time   157

Territoriality   158

Environment   158

Social Media and Non-Verbal Communication   160

Summary   161

Key Terms   161

Activities   162

Further Reading   165

Study Questions   165

5 Listening   166

Misconceptions about Listening   169

Listening and Hearing Are Not the Same Thing   169

Listening Is Not a Natural Process   170

Listening Requires Effort   171

All Listeners Do Not Receive the Same Message   171

Overcoming Challenges to Effective Listening   172

Faulty Listening Behaviours   172

Reasons for Poor Listening   174

Personal Listening Styles   182

Content-Oriented Listening   183

People-Oriented Listening   184

Action-Oriented Listening   184

Time-Oriented Listening   184

Informational Listening   185

Don't Argue or Judge Prematurely   185

Separate the Message from the Speaker   185

Be Opportunistic   186

Look for Key Ideas   186

Ask Questions   187

Paraphrase   188

Take Notes   190

Critical Listening   190

Listen for Information before Evaluating   191

Evaluate the Speaker's Credibility   192

Examine the Speaker's Evidence and Reasoning   192

Examine Emotional Appeals   194

Empathic Listening   194

Advising   194

Judging   195

Analyzing   196

Questioning   197

Supporting   198

Paraphrasing   201

When and How to Help   204

Summary   205

Key Terms   206

Activities   206

Further Reading   207

Study Questions   208

PART II

Interpersonal Communication

6 Understanding Interpersonal Relationships   210

Characteristics of Interpersonal Relationships   212

What Makes Communication Interpersonal?   212

Interpersonal Communication and the Internet   213

Content and Relational Messages   218

Metacommunication   222

Intimacy in Interpersonal Relationships   222

Dimensions of Intimacy   222

Male and Female Intimacy Styles   224

Cultural Influences on Intimacy   227

**Relational Development and Maintenance
228**

A Developmental Perspective   228

A Dialectical Perspective   233

Characteristics of Relational Development
and Maintenance   240

**Self-Disclosure in Interpersonal
Relationships   241**

Models of Self-Disclosure   242

Characteristics of Effective Self-Disclosure   245

Guidelines for Appropriate Self-Disclosure   246

Deception, Hinting, and Equivocation   248

Summary   255

Key Terms   256

Activities   256

Further Reading   258

Study Questions   259

7 **Improving Interpersonal
Relationships   260**

**Communication Climates in Interpersonal
Relationships   262**

Confirming and Disconfirming Messages   262

How Communication Climates Develop   264

Creating Positive Communication Climates   266

Managing Interpersonal Conflict   269

The Nature of Conflict   270

Styles of Expressing Conflict   271

Characteristics of an Assertive Message   276

Gender and Conflict Style   279

Cultural Influences on Conflict   281

Methods of Conflict Resolution   282

Summary   289

Key Terms   289

Activities   289

Further Reading   291

Study Questions   291

PART III
Communication in Groups

8 **Social Media and Communication
Theory   294**

Social Media   296

Comparing Social Media and Traditional Mass Media   297

Are Social Media Completely New?   300

Types of Social Media   303

Blogs   303

Microblogs   307

Social Networking Websites   309

Wikis   311

Social News Aggregators   312

Social Bookmarking Websites   312

Social Photo and Video Sharing Websites   312

Social Media, the Self, and Society   313

Social Media and Mobility   314

**Social Media, Public Relations, and Marketing
315**

Social Media and Traditional Media   315

Newspapers   318

Television   319

Radio   320

Using Social Media Effectively   321

Dangers of Social Media   322

Protecting Yourself on Social Media   323

Key Theories of Communication   326

Harold Innis's Theory of Time-Binding and
    Space-Binding Media   326

Marshall McLuhan's Theories   328

Flow Theories   330

Social Learning Theory   331

Individual Differences Theory   331

Cultivation Theory   332

Agenda-Setting Theory   332

Cumulative Effects Theory   333

Summary   333

Key Terms   334

Activities   334

Further Reading   336

Study Questions   337

9   The Nature of Groups   338

What Is a Group?   340

Interaction   340

Interdependence   341

Time   342

Size   342

Goals   342

Goals of Groups and Their Members   342

Individual Goals   343

Group Goals   343

Types of Groups   346

Learning Groups   346

Problem-Solving Groups   347

Social Groups   348

Growth Groups   348

Characteristics of Groups   348

Rules and Norms   348

Roles   348

Patterns of Interaction   355

Decision-Making Methods   357

**Cultural Influences on Group
Communication   360**

Individualism versus Collectivism   361

Power Distance   362

Uncertainty Avoidance   363

Task versus Social Orientation   364

Short- versus Long-Term Orientation   364

Summary   365

Key Terms   365

Activities   365

Further Reading   367

Study Questions   367

10   Solving Problems in Groups   368

**Problem-Solving in Groups: When and Why
370**

Advantages of Group Problem-Solving   371

When to Use Groups for Problem-Solving   372

Group Problem-Solving Formats   372

Types of Problem-Solving Groups   373

Computer-Mediated Groups   374

**Approaches and Stages in Problem-Solving
377**

A Structured Problem-Solving Approach   378

Developmental Stages in Problem-Solving Groups
    384

Maintaining Positive Relationships   386

Basic Skills   387

Building Cohesiveness   388

Leadership and Power in Groups   390

Power in Groups   390

What Makes Leaders Effective   393

Overcoming Dangers in Group Discussion 398

Information Underload and Overload   398

Unequal Participation   399

Pressure to Conform   400

Summary   402

Key Terms   403

Activities   403

Further Reading   405

Study Questions   405

PART IV

Persuasion and Public Communication

11 Persuasion   408

Characteristics of Persuasion   410

Persuasion Is Not Coercive   411

Persuasion Is Usually Incremental   411

Persuasion Is Interactive   412

Persuasion Can Be Ethical   413

Categorizing Types of Persuasion   414

By Types of Proposition   414

By Desired Outcome   416

By Directness of Approach   418

Creating the Persuasive Message   419

Set a Clear, Persuasive Purpose   419

Avoid Fallacies   419

Interpersonal Persuasion   423

Foot-in-the-Door   423

Door-in-the-Face   423

Social Exchange   424

Low-Balling   424

That's-Not-All   425

Fear-Then-Relief   425

Summary   427

Key Terms   427

Activities   427

Further Reading   429

Study Questions   429

12 Writing and Delivering Speeches   430

Choosing a Topic   432

Defining Purpose   433

General Purpose   433

Specific Purpose   434

The Thesis Statement   435

Structuring the Speech   435

Working Outlines, Formal Outlines, and Speaking Notes   436

Organizing Your Points in a Logical Order   437

The Body of the Speech   441

The Introduction   441

The Conclusion   446

Using Transitions   448

Supporting Material   449

Types of Supporting Material   449

Styles of Support: Narration and Citation   451

Using Visual Aids   452

Holding the Audience's Attention   454

Make It Easy to Listen   454

Emphasize Important Points   456

Use Clear, Simple Language   456

Generate Audience Involvement   456

Analyzing the Audience   457

Audience Type   458

Audience Purpose   458

Demographics   458

Attitudes, Beliefs, and Values   459

Analyzing the Occasion   460

Time   460

Place   461

Audience Expectations   461

Building Credibility as a Communicator   462

Delivery   462

Types of Delivery   462

Guidelines for Delivery   464

Practising the Speech   467

Dealing with Stage Fright   467

Facilitative and Debilitative Stage Fright   467

Sources of Debilitative Stage Fright   467

Overcoming Debilitative Stage Fright   469

Sample Speech   470

Summary   474

Key Terms   475

Activities   475

Further Reading   476

Study Questions   477

Appendices

I   Persuasive Professional Writing   478

By Dr Philip Savage   478

The Purpose of Writing   479

The Process of Writing   480

Four Major Professional Writing Forms   481

Briefing Notes   483

II   Communicating for Career Success   490

The Selection Interview   490

Preparing for the Interview   490

During the Interview   495

Interviewing and the Law   497

Notes   499

Credits   519

Index   521

Preface

When I was assembling the first Canadian edition of *Understanding Human Communication* in 2006, the first thing I did was to ask the students in my Introduction to Communication course at McMaster University what their ideal introductory human communication textbook would contain. That philosophy was also reflected in the second Canadian edition, which came out in 2011. As I started research for the third Canadian edition, I became even more convinced that our pedagogy should be attuned to the evolving needs, desires, dreams, and lifestyles of our students. While preparing this edition, I spent a lot of time seeking student feedback to ensure that their first contact with the field of communication would be memorable and positive.

My students made it clear that a good textbook should spell out how theory and research relate to everyday life. The ideal text should be full of bright colours and be visually inviting, with interesting boxed features, images, and examples that help to clarify the subject matter. Its tone should be student-friendly, conversing with readers rather than talking down to them or over their heads. It should have a strong Canadian perspective, especially in its examples. For it to "feel comfortable," the content should also reflect Canadian social and cultural life in its visual elements. Some students also stated that they wanted to see more profiles of successful recent graduates. The profiles of senior and junior communicators that we introduced in the second edition have proven extremely popular among students: many told me that they found them inspiring and engaging. Above all, students have reinforced my ideas that a textbook should deliver lasting value to them, helping them grow as people while learning about how communications affects both society and themselves.

The concerns of students are vitally important, but so too are the needs of instructors. Therefore, I asked my colleagues what they think distinguishes a good textbook. They told me that a good text must present an accurate and comprehensive picture of the academic work it addresses. It should also be manageable within the length of an academic term. An ideal text would make life easier for instructors by giving students plenty of learning support.

Basic Approach

A lot of effort has gone into this third Canadian edition to help it meet the needs of both students and their instructors in the ways described above. If I have succeeded, students will find this book clear, interesting, and useful, with tools that will help them succeed in their first serious exploration of human communication. Instructors, meanwhile, will find that the book does justice to the discipline and helps render their teaching more efficient, engaging, and effective.

This edition builds on the approach that has served more than half a million students and their professors well in the past. Rather than take sides in debates on theory versus skill, *Understanding Human Communication* treats scholarship and skill development as mutually reinforcing. Its reader-friendly approach strives to present material clearly without being overly simplistic. A wealth of examples helps make concepts clear and interesting. A dynamic and inviting new design and colour scheme make the material inviting, as do a collection of stimulating photos, interesting readings, amusing and instructive cartoons, and well-chosen quotations. Key theoretical terms are defined in a running glossary, and definitions of cultural idioms help students whose first language is not English make sense of colloquial expressions.

Every chapter of this book emphasizes the influence of both culture and technology on human communication. Along with discussion in the text itself, boxed features highlight key topics in this area, many of which include thought-provoking and sometimes controversial questions that encourage students to think and talk about the role of communication in the lives of Canadians. "Understanding Diversity" boxes address subjects of interest to an increasingly diverse student audience in Canada: how French and English Canadians have different levels of self-definition and how minority languages, such as those of Canada's Aboriginal peoples, are increasingly endangered, to name just two. "Understanding Communication Technology" boxes focus on topics such as how people's relationships in their virtual lives differ from their real-world relationships, and how social media sites are changing people's lives. The "Communication On-Screen" boxes showcase examples of communication skills and processes from film and television, many made by Canadians.

Various strategies and techniques also highlight the cultural similarities and differences between Canada's founding peoples: Aboriginal peoples, French Canadians, and English Canadians, as well as Canada's diverse communities. For instance, numerous boxes draw attention to their contributions to Canada's identity, in addition to presenting insightful academic research that compares and contrasts these groups. This material, in particular, stems from a firm, personal belief that Canadians must get to know one another better for our country to continue to flourish as a beacon of hope and possibility for our own citizens, as well as for foreigners who seek peace, order, and good government. "Critical Thinking Probe" boxes pose intriguing ethical scenarios.

Third Edition: A Major Revamp

This third edition features a new structure to better suit a contemporary student audience. So much has changed in the last five years—e-mail has become a "dated technology," and social media and mobile communications have swept through the world of mediated communication, changing the cultural landscape for everyone, especially students. There is a generation of people who are growing up digital, and digital communication is becoming a core literacy. As educators, we must account for these changes in our textbooks. It is crucial that we provide critical instruction on what's out there as well as the benefits and dangers. For this reason, this edition includes a new chapter on social media and communication theory (Chapter 8), a refurbished chapter on persuasion (Chapter 11), a "condensed" discussion of speech writing and public speaking (Chapter 12) and two new appendices on the crucial skills of persuasive professional writing and interviewing.

The chapter on social media is considered a must for a book on human communication, given the overwhelming majority of students who use social media on a daily basis. Social media are becoming a huge part of the workplace as well, as organizations integrate them into normal business practices and use them to do background checks on potential employees. Understanding the opportunities and perils of this new communication landscape is of the utmost importance for students entering the workforce and wanting to make sense of the world around them. To meet this need, this chapter examines the strengths and weaknesses of various social networking media that were current at the time of this text. As part of the effort to be comprehensive and critical, the text also includes various tips and processes on how to build a personal brand, how to encourage collaboration using social media, and how to avoid the dangers of social media.

The chapter on persuasion and audiences reflects my belief that we are entering a new era of rhetoric and constant media influence through the omnipresent stream of highly tailored persuasive information which we receive through our smartphones, our tablet devices, and our computers. We are just at the beginning of this age of personally tailored persuasion—we haven't seen anything yet! Giving students the tools to identify, use, and criticize the techniques of persuasion that they will certainly face in both their private and professional lives was a serious priority in composing this chapter.

This "Age of Social Media" that is upon us is also an "Age of Writing"—especially persuasive writing. To bring in an expert voice on the topic of persuasive professional writing, I enlisted Dr Philip Savage, a colleague in the McMaster-Syracuse Master of Communications Management program, to write an appendix. Philip brings a wealth of academic and industry experience to the task, having served as the director of research for CBC Radio for many years before pursuing a career in academic research. Philip and I co-direct the COMM-Lab: McMaster Communication Metrics Laboratory, which is devoted to bringing Canadian students to the cutting edge of communication and media research.

The final chapter of the text presents a more succinct exploration of speech writing and public speaking than was offered in the previous edition, without losing any important information. This condensed chapter now introduces the necessary skills, planning, and strategies students need to compose a speech, followed by the strategic and tactical knowledge necessary for effective public speaking: overcoming stage fright, using visual aids effectively, and connecting with the audience, among many other essential skills. This chapter retains the popular sample speeches from great Canadian communicators, such as Pierre Elliott Trudeau, that were featured in the previous edition. However, they also offer the latest information on using the internet and social media to communicate effectively in a Canadian context.

Another key feature of this edition is a set of refreshed profiles of successful communicators. Each chapter contains a profile of a communications graduate who has gone on to do some fascinating things with his or her degree. These profiles are inspiring, hip, and fun; they show what amazing futures await those who invest their time, energy, and enthusiasm in becoming effective communicators. They are aspirational in tone—I want students using this book to see that others have put these ideas to work and have achieved success. Four profiles of senior Canadian communications leaders are also included. These leaders have contributed short notes to students, sharing a little wisdom and explaining what skills and attitudes students should focus on to become successful communicators.

Acknowledgements

Writing a textbook is a challenging task that would be impossible without the help and contributions of many people.

For help in finding relevant stories, profiles, and examples, I worked with David Schokking, an editorial assistant from McMaster University's Master of Arts in Communication and New Media. David was a great help in finding modern Canadian content and examples. He was a wonderful assistant who became a friend. I will miss our meandering conversations that started with the textbook and which always ended up, through many twists and turns, in the most interesting places. David was also the student editor of the 2013 edition of the McMaster Journal of Communication, of which I am faculty editor and is now a professor at Mohawk College.

I would also like to thank all the assistants who have worked on previous editions of this book: Tom Aylward-Nally and Morgan Harper on the second edition; Carolynn Conron, Jessica Foran, Melonie Fullick, and Pamela Martin on the first. I am gratified to see that they have all gone on to successful futures in law, academia, government relations, and human resources. Some even have children now. I am happy to have spent time working on *Understanding Human Communication* with each of them and even happier to see them having such fulfilled lives.

Working with the professionals at Oxford University Press Canada has been a pleasure. In particular, I am grateful to Stephen Kotowych, acquisitions editor, who nudged me into accelerating work on this textbook and meeting deadlines. I would also like to thank Meg Patterson, developmental editor, and Shelly Stevenson, copy editor, whom have both been a great pleasure to work with.

Several of my colleagues at McMaster provided valuable feedback and encouragement: Terry Flynn, Laurence Mussio, and Philip Savage of the McMaster-Syracuse Master of Communications Management program—of which I am director—who all provided excellent ideas and different points of view. I would like to express special thanks to Suzanne Crosta, our former Dean of the Faculty of Humanities, who has always seen the value of applied communications and communications management research and teaching. She was my official mentor when I began as a professor at McMaster University and was nothing but generous and visionary in her leadership and mentorship. Suzanne will be sorely missed as our Dean. I owe particular thanks to Lars Wessman, Associate Executive Director of the Ottawa Riverkeeper, who is an expert communicator, philosopher, and friend; our 23-year running conversation has inspired, shaped, and coloured many of the examples and anecdotes that have found their way into this book. Joey Coleman, an independent journalist covering the City of Hamilton, Ontario, has been a friend throughout the process of editing this book—his advice, commentary, and critique have been invaluable in keeping the examples I used relevant.

I would also like to thank some friends from the realm of industry who have given me their views on what would be practical for students to know for successful communication careers: David Estok, Vice-President of Communications, Sick Kids Foundation; Ginny Jones, President, Acuity Options; Andrew Laing, President, Cormex Research; David Scholz, Chief Marketing Officer, Leger Global; Ira Basen, Documentarian, CBC; Jessica Langer, Founder, IdeasInFlight.ca; as well as Elaine Kunda and all of the students, faculty, and alumni of the McMaster-Syracuse Master of Communications Management program who serve as a daily inspiration to me and whose friendship I treasure.

These acknowledgements would not be complete without a pat and a belly rub for my trusty research assistant Gigi, a newly slimmed down brown tabby, whose unconditional love is a comfort in lonely moments.

Highlights of the New Edition

While preparing this third Canadian edition of *Understanding Human Communication*, we kept in mind one paramount goal: to produce the most comprehensive and authoritative, yet accessible and interesting, introduction to human communication available for Canadian students.

This revision builds on the strengths of the well-received first and second Canadian editions and incorporates new features designed to enhance the book's usefulness for students and instructors alike. Using dynamic pedagogy to provide a thorough and balanced coverage of communication theory and practice, *Understanding Human Communication* covers all areas of human communication, from interpersonal communication to public speaking.

COMMUNICATING ONLINE

Ten Ways to Use LinkedIn

Creating a persuasive message extends to establishing your online presence as a professional. You want to present an image of yourself as someone others will like and want to work with. Essentially, you want to persuade someone to hire you. LinkedIn is a social media website that provides a popular way of having an up-to-date resume online at all times, while also expanding your network of professional contacts. The following tips by Guy Kawasaki provide a great base for creating an image that will persuade anyone to hire you.

1. *Fully complete your profile*: Ensuring that this contains all relevant career history and interests. LinkedIn makes this easy by displaying a percentage score to show how complete your profile is. A LinkedIn profile basically acts as an online CV, so make sure you're being honest and describing yourself and career clearly.

2. *Edit profile to claim vanity URL*: This should be set to use your name (or closest match if unavailable) within the URL, for example: www.linkedin.com/in/kevingibbons—this will help you to optimise your own name in the search engines and also makes the URL easier to remember if promoted on business cards or e-mail signatures.

3. *Make your profile publicly available*: You can set the information which is publicly available to non-members/contacts, be careful with blocking too much information as this will also be unavailable to the search engines. As a minimum, I would recommend providing enough information for the search engines to index your profile and cache the external links you have listed! In terms of optimising your profile, the main goals are normally to rank for your own name, company name and possibly industry keywords related to this.

4. *Make connections*: Increase the reach of your profile by connecting with current and former work colleagues, clients, friends, and family. I'd also recommend adding any industry contacts, perhaps from people you have met at conferences/events or are connected with on other social media sites and share a similar interest.

5. *Request recommendations*: Obviously don't ask everyone, especially if you don't know them that well. But having recommendations will help your profile to stand out and will help to build trust in your reputation to visiting users. This will help improve the visibility of your own profile within internal LinkedIn searches too.

6. *Register a company profile*: If your company doesn't already have a company listing, you should create one! If your company does have a profile, you should encourage employees to create their own individual LinkedIn profiles and ensure the current employer entry is completed. This will automatically update all employees listed on the company profile, providing the company name is exactly matched.

7. *Make use of the three website hyperlinks*: For SEO value, LinkedIn is very good—they give you the opportunity to add three hyperlinks to websites of your choice. If you're not trying to optimise your site for "My Website," "My Portfolio," and "My Blog" it might be an idea to select "Other" and choose your own anchor text instead!

8. *Join related groups*: Find groups where other industry professionals have joined and look to participate in (or at least join) these groups. Adding value to your own profile and helping you to get found by other industry contacts.

9. *Use LinkedIn Answers*: This can help to build up your reputation within a field. For SEO it also builds the number of internal links pointing to your profile from within LinkedIn, therefore helping to strengthen your profile in the search engines!

10. *Optimise your job title*: LinkedIn now includes your job title within profile title tags. I'm not saying you should lie about your job, but within reason you could include descriptive keywords which may help to attract relevant search engine traffic. For example, using "SEO Account Manager" as a job title instead of "Account Manager," if appropriate.

—Guy Kawasaki, http://blog.guykawasaki.com/2007/01/ten_ways_to_use.html, 4 January 2007

New to this edition are **"Communicating Online" boxes** that discuss effective personal and professional uses of social media, including Twitter, LinkedIn, and YouTube.

138   **PART I**   Elements of Communication

UNDERSTANDING COMMUNICATION TECHNOLOGY

Hatebase: A Crowdsourced Tool for Tracking Hate-Speech and Targeting Genocide

You may not think of interpreting nonverbal cues as a skill you use when communicating online, but there are many cues in written language that we can tune into, especially when we consider how people from varying cultural backgrounds communicate differently. In his article on hate-speech, Christopher Tuckwood, co-founder of The Sentinel Project for Genocide Prevention, discusses words that have double meanings, which can change depending on who is using them and how they are using them. As you read about Hatebase, see if you can think of other ways paying attention to what is being said online could facilitate better communication.

Co-founded by Toronto-based NGO The Sentinel Project for Genocide Prevention and Mobiocracy, Hatebase was built to assist government agencies, NGOs, research organizations, and other philanthropic individuals and groups to use hate-speech as a predictor for regional violence. Language-based classification, symbolization, and dehumanization are a few of a handful of quantifiable steps toward genocide and other mass atrocities.

Hatebase works by crowdsourcing vocabulary and real-time geo-located "sightings" of hate-speech. Essentially, users can add new terms that are not already in the database as well as log events such as incidents when they have been referred to using a certain term or heard it used against someone else. Because Hatebase is crowdsourced and therefore depends on user participation to be effective, the more people who use it in more places and languages, the more effective it will be. Not only can this data be used to establish trends and patterns but it can then be exported and used for any purpose, allowing organizations such as The Sentinel Project to leverage it and add context to existing datasets and crisis monitoring efforts, much like adding traffic congestion data to an existing street map.

Beyond crowdsourcing from human users, Hatebase also incorporates machine-driven contributions, with automated monitoring paying particular attention to open social networks like Twitter, which are constantly scanned for flagged vocabulary. Of course, many forums on the internet are filled with racist, sexist, homophobic, and other hateful language that never leads directly to violence, so a spike in hate-speech does not necessarily mean that violence is inevitable.

Although Hatebase is still in its infancy, its dataset (at www. hatebase.org.) is growing daily and currently encompasses vocabulary, sightings, and users from every corner of the world. This makes context incredibly important, as when certain, seemingly hateful, words have double meanings and can be used in benign ways. Timothy Quinn, who volunteers for Hatebase, says that the project's goal is to expand from Twitter and crawl all social media platforms. The challenge will always be in massaging their algorithm to be context-aware, knowing the slight but vast difference between, for example, "my nigga" and "you niggers." "Hate is not about vocabulary,"argues Quinn, "it's about intent."

When data from Hatebase is correlated with other indicators of the genocidal process, such as statements by nationalistic leaders or attacks on a particular minority group, then it starts to be useful for predicting and preventing atrocities. For example, statements by an inflammatory leader may inspire temporary spikes in hate-speech followed by actual violent actions. If this relationship can be established and recognized then threatened communities can be warned before words turn into violence.

Christopher Tuckwood, Co-Founder
of the Sentinel Project

QUESTIONS: How do cultural differences affect hate-speech? How does context, intention or slang change the meaning of terms?

Gender

It's easy to identify stereotypical differences in masculine and feminine styles of non-verbal communication. Just think about the exaggerated caricatures of macho men and delicate women that appear from time to time. Many humorous films and plays have been created around the situations that arise when characters try to act like members of the opposite sex.

"Understanding Communication Technology" boxes highlight contemporary issues in computer-mediated communication, such as using social media to get a job, online bullying and cyberstalking, and even using avatars to aid doctor–patient communication.

---

240   **PART II**   Interpersonal Communication

🎥 COMMUNICATION ON-SCREEN

Silver Linings Playbook (2012)
Directed by David O. Russell.

Pat Solitano (Bradley Cooper) is released from a psychiatric hospital into the care of his parents (Robert De Niro and Jackie Weaver) after a violent confrontation forces him into eight months of treatment for bipolar disorder. While at dinner with a friend, Pat meets Tiffany (Jennifer Lawrence), a woman suffering from sex addiction after the death of her husband. Pat and Tiffany strike an unusual friendship when Tiffany needs a dance partner, and Pat needs a messenger to send his ex-wife letters. Over the course of the film, Pat and Tiffany bond over their outsider status and their mutual understanding. Pat's bipolarism plays a central role in the film, as do the various mental issues of everyone, not only those who've been diagnosed, highlighting the difficulty and divides that can make interpersonal relationships in any form incredibly challenging, but ultimately rewarding.

One man all by himself is nothing. Two people who belong together make a world.
Hans Margolius, German philosopher

by sharing almost all their feelings about mutual friends with one another while keeping certain parts of their past romantic histories private.

Moderation is a sixth strategy. This strategy is characterized by compromises, in which communicators choose to back off from expressing either end of the dialectical spectrum. Adult children, for example, might manage the revelation-concealment dialectic with their inquisitive parents by answering some (though not all) unwelcome parental questions.

Communicators can also respond to dialectical challenges by reframing them in terms that redefine the situation so that the apparent contradiction disappears. Consider a couple who wince when their friends characterize them as a "perfect couple." On one hand, they want to escape from the "perfect couple" label that feels confining, but on the other hand, they enjoy the admiration that comes with this identity. By pointing out to their friends that "ideal couples" aren't always blissfully happy, they can both be themselves and keep the admiration of their friends.

A final strategy for handling dialectical tensions is *reaffirmation*—acknowledging that dialectical tensions will never disappear, accepting or even embracing the challenges they present. The metaphorical view of relational life as a kind of roller coaster reflects this orientation, and communicators who use reaffirmation view dialectical tensions as part of the ride.

Characteristics of Relational Development and Maintenance

Whether you analyze a relationship in terms of stages or dialectical dynamics, two characteristics are true of every interpersonal relationship. As you read about each, consider how it applies to your own experience.

Relationships Are Constantly Changing

Relationships are certainly not doomed to deteriorate, but even the strongest ones are rarely stable for long periods of time. In fairy tales a couple may live "happily ever after," but in real life this sort of equilibrium is less common. Consider a husband and wife who have been married for some time. Although they have formally bonded, their relationship will probably shift from one dimension of a relational dialectic to another, and forward or backward along the spectrum of stages. Sometimes the partners will feel the need to differentiate from one another, and at other times they will seek intimacy. Sometimes they will feel secure in the predictable patterns they have established, and at other times one or both will be hungry for novelty. The relationship may become more circumscribed, or even stagnant. From this point the marriage may fail, but this fate isn't certain. With effort, the partners may move from the stage of stagnating to experimenting, or from circumscribing to intensifying.

Communication theorist Richard Conville describes the constantly evolving nature of relationships as a cycle in which partners move through a series of stages,

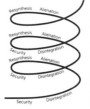

FIGURE 6.6 A Helical Model of Relational Cycles

Updated "Communication On-Screen" boxes illustrate concepts from the text found in popular culture. This edition highlights Canadian movies and television series.

Understanding Diversity

School's Playground Planning Includes Hearing-Impaired Kids

When children from Saskatoon's St. Philip School choose equipment for their community playground, they'll give some extra consideration to their playmates with hearing impairment. Pupils at the school will get to vote next month on the climbing structures, swings, and slides community members will erect this fall in the spot where aging equipment now stands.

Even the pre-readers will get to vote by placing stickers on posters with their favourite equipment, a process dubbed "dot-mocracy," said Ryan Lacoursiere, a member of the parents' committee that has been working for two years to raise money and community participation.

"It's kind of a grassroots movement. The idea is to get the community involved. Get your neighbours out helping, inspire others to realize we all have the power, we all have a voice if we work together. Hopefully we can inspire our kids to see they can achieve great things too," he said. "It will develop a sense of ownership and pride in the project to maintain it and protect it for years to come."

The school community has a heightened awareness of hearing impairment because the division's itinerant teachers, who specialize in working with deaf and hard of hearing students, make their home base at St. Philip and nine children at the school have hearing loss, said Donella Hoffman, a spokesperson for the Greater Saskatoon Catholic Schools division. "It's a new playground for the community and they want to make sure they include all the children," Hoffman said.

Lacoursiere said dry-eraser boards could be posted on the site to help with communication and steel equipment could be chosen over plastic or wood because the metal vibrates, providing another sensation and mode of communication. The St. Philip's committee got together to fill out numerous lengthy funding applications.

They were thrilled to learn their project was chosen by Let Them Be Kids, a national charity that helps fund playground construction. That application included a telephone conference call with the committee and some children who will use the park. One hearing impaired student joined the call using the Skype computer program and a local interpreter.

Let Them Be Kids will match locally raised funds for the playground, which could have a six-figure price tag, Lacoursiere said. The committee has already raised almost $24,000 and is "reaching for the stars," with a goal of $75,000 to $80,000 to be raised locally, he said. Events include bingos, a casino night, a student art auction, and steak nights. "If we wanted to make this happen, we had to take it upon ourselves."

Betty Ann Adam, *The StarPhoenix*, 23 May 2013

QUESTIONS: How does this story reflect the diverse concepts of listening described in this chapter, as well as literal issues of hearing? How are "hearing" and "listening" different?

IBRAHIM: You think I should buy it?
VESNA: I don't know. What do you think?
IBRAHIM: I just can't decide.
VESNA: [silence]
IBRAHIM: I'm going to do it. I'll never get a deal like this again.

Prompting works especially well when you can't help others make a decision. At times like this your presence can act like a catalyst to help others find their own answers. Prompting will work best when it's done sincerely. Your non-verbal behaviours—eye contact, posture, facial expression, tone of voice—have to show that you are concerned with the other person's problem. Mechanical prompting is likely to irritate instead of help.

Paraphrasing

Earlier we discussed the value of paraphrasing to understand others. The same skill can be used as a helping tool. When you use this approach, be sure to reflect both the thoughts and the

"Understanding Diversity" boxes address a range of issues relating to communicating in our diverse, multicultural society; examples include racial profiling, soft skills for immigrants, and issues for the Deaf community.

---

24   **PART I** Elements of Communication

The same principle holds true in the case of jealousy. Researchers have uncovered a variety of ways by which people deal with jealousy in their relationships.[51] These include keeping closer tabs on the partner, acting indifferent, decreasing affection, talking the matter over, and acting angry. The researchers found that no type of behaviour was effective or ineffective in every relationship, leading them to conclude that approaches that work with some people would be harmful to others. Findings like these demonstrate that competence comes from developing ways of interacting that work for you and for the other people involved.[52]

Cultural Idiom
keeping closer tabs
Paying closer attention to something or someone.

Competence Can Be Learned

To some degree, biology is destiny when it comes to communication style.[53] Studies of identical and fraternal twins suggest that traits including sociability, anger, and relaxation are partly a function of our genetic makeup. Fortunately, biology isn't the only factor that shapes how we communicate: communication is a set of skills that anyone can learn. As children grow, their ability to communicate effectively develops. For example, older children learn to use more sophisticated techniques of persuasion.[54] Along with maturity, systematic education (including classes such as the one in which you are now enrolled) can boost communicative competence. Even a modest amount of specialized training can produce dramatic results. After just 30 minutes of instruction, one group of observers became significantly more effective at detecting deception in interviews.[55] Even without systematic training, it's possible to develop communication skills through the processes of trial-and-error and observation. One study revealed that university students' communication competence increases over their undergraduate studies, regardless of whether or not they're enrolled in human communication courses.[56] Finally, we learn from our own successes and failures, as well as from observing other models—both positive and negative.

Characteristics of Competent Communicators

Cultural Idiom
common denominators
Features that are shared by all.

Although competent communication varies from one situation to another, scholars have identified several common denominators that characterize effective communication in most contexts.

A Wide Range of Behaviours

Effective communicators are able to choose their actions from a wide range of behaviours. To understand the importance of having a large communication repertoire, imagine that one of your friends repeatedly tells jokes that you find offensive. You could respond to these jokes in a number of ways. You could:

- Say nothing, figuring that the negative consequences of raising the subject would be greater than the benefits.
- Ask a third party to say something to your friend about the offensiveness of the jokes.
- Hint at your discomfort, hoping that your friend would get the point.
- Joke about your friend's insensitivity, counting on humour to soften the blow of your criticism.
- Express your discomfort in a straightforward way, asking your friend to stop telling the offensive jokes, at least around you.
- Simply demand that your friend stop.

Cultural Idiom
counting on
To depend on.

soften the blow
To ease the effect of something.

With these possible responses at your disposal (and you can probably think of others as well), you could pick the one that had the best chance of success. But if you were able to use only one or two of these responses when raising a delicate issue—always keeping quiet or always

"Cultural idiom" boxes located in the sidebars help ESL and native English speakers alike understand the meaning of figures of speech and other words and phrases commonly used in the workplace and beyond.

Appendix II

Communicating for Career Success

The Selection Interview

selection interview
An interview conducted to determine the interviewee's suitability for a post.

For many people the short time spent facing a potential employer is the most important interview of a lifetime. A selection interview may occur when you are being considered for employment, but it may also occur when you are being evaluated for promotion or reassignment. In an academic setting, selection interviews are often part of the process of being chosen for an award, a scholarship, or admission to a graduate program. Being chosen for the position you seek depends on making a good impression on the person or people who can hire you, and your interviewing skills can make the difference between receiving a job offer and being an also-ran.

Cultural Idiom
to wind up
To bring to an end, to finish.

being an also-ran
To be an unsuccessful applicant.

Preparing for the Interview

A good interview begins long before you sit down to face the other person. There are several steps you can take to boost your chances for success.

Background Research

Displaying your knowledge of an organization in an interview is a terrific way to show potential employers that you are a motivated and savvy person. Along with what you've learned from informational interviews, diligent Web browsing can reveal a wealth of information about a prospective employer and the field in which you want to work.

Most business firms, government agencies, and nonprofit agencies have websites that will help you understand their mission. If you're lucky, those websites will also contain the names of people you'll want to know about and possibly refer to during an interview.

Beyond an organization's own website, you can almost certainly find what others have published about the places where you might want to work. In your search engine, type the name of the organization and/or key people who work there. You are likely to be pleased and surprised at what you learn.

A new **appendix, "Communicating for Career Success,"** outlines how to make a good impression on a potential employer, going over details such as common questions in job interviews and how to create answers to them, how to manage anxiety and dress properly for an interview, how to follow up on an interview, and what to do about illegal interview questions.

Physical Needs

Communication is so important that it is necessary for physical health. In fact, evidence suggests that an absence of satisfying communication can even jeopardize life itself. Medical researchers have identified a wide range of hazards that result from a lack of close relationships.[8] For instance:

- People who lack strong relationships have two to three times the risk of early death, regardless of whether they smoke, drink, or exercise regularly.
- Terminal cancer strikes socially isolated people more often than it does those who have close personal relationships.
- Divorced, separated, and widowed people are 5 to 10 times more likely to need hospitalization for mental problems than are their married counterparts.
- Pregnant women under stress and without supportive relationships have three times more complications than pregnant women who suffer from the same stress but have strong social support.
- Socially isolated people are four times more susceptible to the common cold than those who have active social networks.[9]

Other studies have shown that social isolation is a major risk factor contributing to coronary disease,[10] and three recent articles in *The Globe and Mail* have discussed how loneliness has been linked to increased risk of heart attack, high blood pressure, and cancer. Not surprisingly, the quality of personal relationships has an even more significant bearing on health. This has to do with the difference between *structural support*—a person's basic network of social relationships, including friends, family, and romantic partners—and *functional support*, which refers to the quality of those relationships and whether or not a person believes,

YOUNG COMMUNICATOR PROFILE

CAROLINE GDYCZYNSKI
Producer, CBC Toronto

I realized early in my academic career that a degree in communication studies would provide me with a versatile resume of transferable skills. Since graduating, I have worked as content management specialist, a communications assistant for an NGO (non-governmental organization) with consultative status at the United Nations and most recently as a producer at the CBC.

I found each of these jobs stimulating, while presenting new challenges and opportunities. At the CBC, each day presents new stories and new ways of keeping my audience informed. In many cases, deadlines are measured in minutes and that's where research and writing are vital in ensuring news reports are factual and visually stimulating.

A newsroom can be compared to a group project—where success is achieved when each person understands their responsibilities while keeping in mind the challenges others are facing. However, at times assignments are your own responsibility and there is little collaboration.

I'm responsible for writing and research-ing, producing reporter items and finally ensuring everything gets to air on time. It's not uncommon to meet deadlines with only seconds to spare!

There are few jobs where you can see the impact of your work almost instantly—this is one of them. Each day, I'm required to put skills that have been garnered over the years to the test. As the show goes to air each evening, I'm able to sit back, critique and be critiqued on my assignments.

"Young Communicator Profile" boxes showcase young professionals who have gone on to do exciting things with their communications degrees, giving students a sense of the types of careers they can pursue with a communications degree.

PART I
Elements of Communication

PROFESSIONAL PROFILE

Rikia Saddy

Though I directed my friends in pretend television commercials as a child, and paid more attention to the ads than the programs when watching TV, I wasn't aware of the industry as a career until I landed at a graduate school with a strong advertising program.

After graduation, I joined the New York advertising world, and worked day and night to become the best in my business. The qualities it took to succeed then are the same as today: intense curiosity, a genuine interest in why people behave as they do, the ability to hold competing thoughts at the same time, lateral thinking, hard work, and an obsession with never missing a detail. None of this is taught in school, but you can learn it there.

The communications industry is the most creative field in business, and you will become part of an exciting, influential tribe. There are more media channels today, and less bureaucracy to reach them. Get to know the needs of every medium. Know which likes to launch the newest thing, which will repeat what you provide verbatim, who is overworked and will thank you for doing their job, and who needs total control. Most importantly, know your strengths and what you have to offer. Build your own brand while you build your clients'.

Do not shy away from technology. It is easy to stay current now, but in 20 years will there be a group of kids that knows more than you? The key to a successful career is to become the best at something. Choose a path that will make that journey fun.

In recent years, I've turned my attention to the world around me and grown my company to include political strategy. Like marketing strategy, it involves educating and informing the public. There is a tendency for politicians to govern by poll results, but the true path lies in finding a way to communicate the strengths and position of a leader without resorting to gimmicks.

I recently published the book *We Are Canada: A very, very short history of Canada,* designed for those of us who would like to better understand who we are and what we've built together without reading a kilo of Canadian history. Canada couldn't survive without communication and understanding. It's up to you to help move that forward.

All good marketing and communication is authentic. Your job, regardless of the field you choose, is to connect.

Rikia Saddy is a principal at Rikia Saddy Strategy, a marketing and political strategy firm in Vancouver. She has worked in Canada, the United States, and Europe.

"Professional Profiles" feature four senior Canadian communications leaders reflecting on their careers and giving advice to students beginning communication studies.

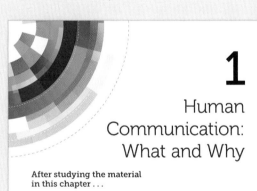

1

Human Communication: What and Why

After studying the material in this chapter . . .

You should understand:
- ✓ the working definition and characteristics of communication;
- ✓ the types of communication covered in this book;
- ✓ the needs satisfied by communication;
- ✓ the characteristics of linear and transactional communication models;
- ✓ the characteristics of competent communication; and
- ✓ the common misconceptions about communication.

You should be able to:
- ✓ define communication and give specific examples of the various types of communication introduced in this chapter;
- ✓ describe the needs you attempt to satisfy by communicating;
- ✓ judge the competence of communication (yours or others') in a specific situation and suggest ways of increasing the competence level; and
- ✓ identify how misconceptions about communication can create problems and suggest how a more accurate analysis of the situations you describe can lead to better outcomes.

Chapter Highlights

Communication, as examined in this book, possesses three important characteristics:
- It occurs between humans.
- It is a process.
- It is symbolic.

This chapter introduces several types of communication:
- intrapersonal,
- dyadic/interpersonal,
- small-group,
- public, and
- mass.

Communication helps satisfy a number of needs in our lives:
- physical needs,
- identity needs,
- social needs, and
- practical needs.

Two models of communication help us understand what is involved in this process:
- the linear model, and
- the transactional model.

Communication competence indicates a person's knowledge of how to be a good communicator. This chapter explores competence by:
- defining the nature of competence and how it is acquired; and
- outlining the characteristics of competent communicators.

The field of communications contains several misconceptions. We will consider the following clarifications:
- Communication doesn't always require complete understanding.
- Communication isn't always a good thing.
- No single person or event causes another's reaction.
- Communication won't solve all problems.
- Meanings rest in people, not in words.
- Communication isn't as simple as it often seems.
- More communication isn't always better.

Chapter openers preview the contents of each chapter through learning objectives and chapter highlights, providing a concise overview of the key concepts to be studied.

48 **PART I** Elements of Communication

CRITICAL THINKING PROBE
Perceiving Others and Yourself

1. You can gain appreciation for the way perceptual errors operate by proposing two different explanations for each of the situations that follow. First, explain the behaviour as you would if you were the person involved. Second, explain it as you would if the person involved were someone you dislike. For example:
   - dozing off in class;
   - getting angry at a customer on the job;
   - dressing sloppily in public;
   - being insensitive to a friend's distress; and
   - laughing at an inappropriate or offensive joke.

2. If your explanations for these behaviours differ, ask yourself why. Are the differing attributions justifiable, or do they support the tendency to make the perceptual errors listed on pages 42–77?

3. How do these perceptual errors operate in making judgments about others' behaviour, especially when those others come from different social groups?

Cultural Idiom
gouged by
To be charged an excessive amount.

jilted
When a person is abandoned suddenly or capriciously.

Degree of Involvement with the Other Person

We sometimes view people with whom we have (or seek to have) a close relationship more favourably than those whom we observe from a detached perspective.[18] One study revealed how this principle operates in everyday life. A group of male subjects was asked to critique presentations by women who allegedly owned restaurants. Half of these presentations were designed to be competent and half were incompetent. The men who were told they would be having a casual date with the female speakers judged their presentations—whether competent or not—more highly than did those who didn't expect any involvement with the speakers.[19]

Past Experience

What meaning do similar events hold? If, for example, you've been gouged by landlords in the past, you might be skeptical about an apartment manager's assurances that your careful housekeeping and diligence about repairs will guarantee the refund of your security deposit.

Expectations

Anticipation shapes interpretations. If you imagine that your boss is unhappy with your work, you'll probably feel threatened by a request to "see me in my office first thing Monday morning." On the other hand, if you imagine that your work will be rewarded, your weekend will probably be pleasant. As Natalia Villegas, a communications consultant based in Oakville, Ontario, describes in a recently published case study, effective internal communications can lead to more harmony in an organization by helping to manage expectations around authenticity, cultural diversity, and employee needs.[20]

Social Roles

Social relationships can influence the way we perceive others. For example, a study of communication in the workplace revealed that observers—both men and women—interpret facial expressions differently depending on their status relative to the other person.[21] Subjects were shown photos of people and asked to judge how each person was feeling. When the person pictured was described as a manager, subjects tended to see less fear than when they were told that the person pictured was an employee. Gender also makes a difference in how we perceive others. When presented with two photos, one of a woman and one of a man, both showing anger of the same intensity, subjects saw more anger and less fear in a man's expression than in a woman's, probably because gender stereotypes of emotion guided their interpretations.

Knowledge

If you know that a friend has just been jilted by a lover or been fired from a job, you'll interpret his aloof behaviour differently than you would if you were unaware of what had happened. If you work in an environment where socializing is common and colleagues have friendly

"Critical Thinking Probe" boxes located throughout the text offer students a chance to critically engage with the text.

Effective end-of-chapter pedagogy supports student learning through chapter summaries, lists of key terms, student activities, further readings, and study questions.

Summary

Perceptions of others are always selective and are often distorted. The chapter began by describing how personal narratives shape our perceptions. It then outlined several perceptual errors that can affect the way we view and communicate with others. Along with universal psychological influences, cultural factors affect perceptions. Increased empathy is a valuable tool for increasing understanding of others and hence communicating more effectively with them. Perception-checking is one tool for increasing the accuracy of perceptions and for increasing empathy.

Perceptions of one's self are just as subjective as perceptions of others, and they influence communication at least as much. Although individuals are born with some innate personality characteristics, the self-concept is shaped dramatically by communication with others, as well as by cultural factors. Once established, the self-concept can lead us to create self-fulfilling prophecies that determine how we behave and how others respond to us.

Impression management consists of strategic communication designed to influence others' perceptions. Impression management operates when we seek, consciously or unconsciously, to present one or more public faces to others. These faces may be different from the private, spontaneous behaviour that occurs outside of others' presence. Identity management is usually collaborative: communication goes most smoothly when we communicate in ways that support others' faces, and they support ours. Some communicators are high self-monitors who are highly conscious of their own behaviour, whereas others are low self-monitors who are less aware of how their words and actions affect others.

Impression management occurs for two reasons. In many cases it is designed for following social rules and conventions. In other cases it is meant to achieve a variety of content and relational goals. In either case, communicators engage in creating impressions by managing their manner, appearance, and the settings in which they interact with others. Although impression management might seem manipulative, it can be an authentic form of communication. Because each person has a variety of faces that he or she can present, choosing which one to put forth doesn't have to be dishonest.

Key Terms

empathy 51	presenting self 67
face 67	reflected appraisal 58
facework 67	self-concept 56
impression management 66	self-esteem 57
narratives 41	self-fulfilling prophecy 64
perceived self 66	self-serving bias 42
perception-checking 53	significant other 59
personality 62	sympathy 52

Activities

A. Exploring Narratives

Think about a situation where relational harmony is created because you and others involved in the situation share the same narrative. Then think of another situation where you both use different narratives to describe the same situation. What are the consequences of having different narratives in this situation?

Online Resources

Online resources provide an outstanding array of teaching and learning tools for both instructors and students. **www.oupcanada.com/AdlerSevigny3CE**

For Instructors

- A comprehensive **instructor's manual** includes lecture suggestions, discussion questions, suggested classroom activities, activities to promote critical and creative thinking, teaching activities, supplementary resources, and videos.

- An extensive **test bank** provides a comprehensive set of multiple-choice, true-or-false, short-answer, matching, and completion questions to assess students' skills.

- Hundreds of editable, vibrant **PowerPoint slides** summarize key points from each chapter and incorporate visuals drawn from the text.

For Students

- A **student study guide** features self-grading quizzes, activities, YouTube videos, and more.

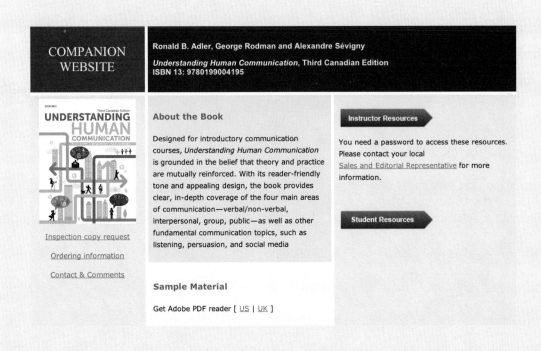

COMPANION WEBSITE

Ronald B. Adler, George Rodman and Alexandre Sévigny

Understanding Human Communication, Third Canadian Edition
ISBN 13: 9780199004195

About the Book

Designed for introductory communication courses, *Understanding Human Communication* is grounded in the belief that theory and practice are mutually reinforced. With its reader-friendly tone and appealing design, the book provides clear, in-depth coverage of the four main areas of communication—verbal/non-verbal, interpersonal, group, public—as well as other fundamental communication topics, such as listening, persuasion, and social media

Sample Material

Get Adobe PDF reader [US | UK]

Inspection copy request

Ordering information

Contact & Comments

Instructor Resources

You need a password to access these resources. Please contact your local Sales and Editorial Representative for more information.

Student Resources

PART I
Elements of Communication

PROFESSIONAL PROFILE

Rikia Saddy

Though I directed my friends in pretend television commercials as a child, and paid more attention to the ads than the programs when watching TV, I wasn't aware of the industry as a career until I landed at a graduate school with a strong advertising program.

After graduation, I joined the New York advertising world, and worked day and night to become the best in my business. The qualities it took to succeed then are the same as today: intense curiosity, a genuine interest in why people behave as they do, the ability to hold competing thoughts at the same time, lateral thinking, hard work, and an obsession with never missing a detail. None of this is taught in school, but you can learn it there.

The communications industry is the most creative field in business, and you will become part of an exciting, influential tribe. There are more media channels today, and less bureaucracy to reach them. Get to know the needs of every medium. Know which likes to launch the newest thing, which will repeat what you provide verbatim, who is overworked and will thank you for doing their job, and who needs total control. Most importantly, know your strengths and what you have to offer. Build your own brand while you build your clients'.

Do not shy away from technology. It is easy to stay current now, but in 20 years will there be a group of kids that knows more than you? The key to a successful career is to become the best at something. Choose a path that will make that journey fun.

In recent years, I've turned my attention to the world around me and grown my company to include political strategy. Like marketing strategy, it involves educating and informing the public. There is a tendency for politicians to govern by poll results, but the true path lies in finding a way to communicate the strengths and position of a leader without resorting to gimmicks.

I recently published the book *We Are Canada: A very, very short history of Canada*, designed for those of us who would like to better understand who we are and what we've built together without reading a kilo of Canadian history. Canada couldn't survive without communication and understanding. It's up to you to help move that forward.

All good marketing and communication is authentic. Your job, regardless of the field you choose, is to connect.

Rikia Saddy is a principal at Rikia Saddy Strategy, a marketing and political strategy firm in Vancouver. She has worked in Canada, the United States, and Europe.

1

Human Communication: What and Why

After studying the material in this chapter . . .

You should understand:

- ✔ the working definition and characteristics of communication;
- ✔ the types of communication covered in this book;
- ✔ the needs satisfied by communication;
- ✔ the characteristics of linear and transactional communication models;
- ✔ the characteristics of competent communication; and
- ✔ the common misconceptions about communication.

You should be able to:

- ✔ define communication and give specific examples of the various types of communication introduced in this chapter;
- ✔ describe the needs you attempt to satisfy by communicating;
- ✔ judge the competence of communication (yours or others') in a specific situation and suggest ways of increasing the competence level; and
- ✔ identify how misconceptions about communication can create problems and suggest how a more accurate analysis of the situations you describe can lead to better outcomes.

Chapter Highlights

Communication, as examined in this book, possesses three important characteristics:

» It occurs between humans.
» It is a process.
» It is symbolic.

This chapter introduces several types of communication:

» intrapersonal,
» dyadic/interpersonal,
» small-group,
» public, and
» mass.

Communication helps satisfy a number of needs in our lives:

» physical needs,
» identity needs,
» social needs, and
» practical needs.

Two models of communication help us understand what is involved in this process:

» the linear model, and
» the transactional model.

Communication competence indicates a person's knowledge of how to be a good communicator. This chapter explores competence by:

» defining the nature of competence and how it is acquired; and
» outlining the characteristics of competent communicators.

The field of communications contains several misconceptions. We will consider the following clarifications:

» Communication doesn't always require complete understanding.
» Communication isn't always a good thing.
» No single person or event causes another's reaction.
» Communication won't solve all problems.
» Meanings rest in people, not in words.
» Communication isn't as simple as it often seems.
» More communication isn't always better.

Communication Defined

Because this book is about communication, it makes sense to begin by defining that term. This task is not as simple as it might seem because people use the term in a variety of ways that are only vaguely related:

- Family members, co-workers, and friends describe their relationships in terms of communication ("We just can't communicate;" "We communicate perfectly").
- Business people talk about "office communications systems," which consist of computers, telephones, printers, and so on.
- Scientists study and describe communication among ants, dolphins, bees, and other animals.
- Companies that publish newspapers, books, and magazines or own radio and television stations may be known as "communications conglomerates."

There is clearly some relationship among such uses of the term, but we need to narrow our focus before going on. After all, a quick look at this book's table of contents will show that communication doesn't have to do with animals, computers, or newspapers. Nor is it about Holy Communion, the "bestowing of a material thing," or many of the other subjects mentioned in the *Oxford English Dictionary's* 1200-word definition of *communication*.

What, then, *are* we talking about when we use the term *communication?* A survey of the ways in which academics use the word will show that there is no one universally accepted meaning. Some definitions are long and complex, others brief and simple. This isn't the place

The Many Meanings of Communication

Few words have as many meanings as communication. *The term can refer to everything from messages on T-shirts to presidential speeches, from computer code to chimpanzee behaviour. Communication has been the professional concern of philosophers, scientists (social, biological, and physical), poets, politicians, and entertainers, to name just a few. Responding to this diversity, Brent Ruben asked, "How does being interested in communication differ from being interested in life?" There are several reasons why the term* communication *has so many different meanings. Understanding them will help explain how and why this word refers to a broad range of subjects.*

Interdisciplinary Heritage

Unlike most subjects, communication has captured the interest of scholars from a wide range of fields. Ever since classical times, philosophers have studied the meaning and significance of messages. In the twentieth century, social scientists joined the field. Psychologists examine the causes and effects of communication as it relates to individuals. Sociologists and anthropologists examine how communication operates within and between societies and cultures. Political scientists explore the ways communication influences government affairs. Engineers use their skill to devise methods of conveying messages electronically. Zoologists focus on communication between animals. With this kind of diversity, it's no surprise that *communication* is a broad and sometimes confusing term.

Field and Activity

Sometimes the word *communication* refers to a field of study (of non-verbal messages or effects of televised violence on children, for example). In other cases it denotes an activity that people do. This confusion doesn't exist in most disciplines. People may study history or sociology, but they don't "historicate" or "sociologize." Having only one word that refers to both the field of study and the activity that it examines leads to confusion.

to explore the differences among these conceptions or to defend one against the others. What we need is a working definition that will help us in our study. For our purposes we will say that **communication** is a continuous, irreversible, transactive process involving communicators who occupy different but overlapping environments and are simultaneously senders and receivers of messages, many of which are distorted by physical and psychological noise.

A point-by-point examination of this definition reveals some important characteristics of communication as we will be studying it.

Communication Is Human

In this book we'll be discussing communication between human beings. Animals clearly do communicate. Bees, for instance, instruct their hive-mates about the location of food by means of a special dance. Chimpanzees have been taught to express themselves with the same sign language used by deaf humans, and a few have developed impressive vocabularies. And on a more commonplace level, pet owners can testify to the variety of messages their animals can express. Although the subject of animal communication is fascinating and important, it goes beyond the scope of this book.[1]

> **communication**
> A continuous, irreversible, transactive process involving communicators who occupy different but overlapping environments and are simultaneously senders and receivers of messages, many of which are distorted by physical and psychological noise.

Humanities and Social Science

Unlike most disciplines, communication straddles two very different academic domains. It has one foot firmly planted in the humanities, where it shares concerns with disciplines like English and philosophy. At the same time, other scholars in the field take an approach like their colleagues in the social sciences, such as psychology, sociology, and anthropology. And to confuse matters even further, communication is sometimes associated with the performing arts, especially in the area of oral interpretation of literature.

Natural and Professional Communication

This is a natural activity that we all engage in unconsciously. At the same time, there are professional communication experts whose specialized duties require training and skill. Careers such as marketing, public relations, broadcasting, speech making, counselling, advocacy, activism, journalism, and management

all call for talent that goes far beyond what is required for everyday speaking and listening.

Communication and Communications

Even the name of the field is confusing. Traditionally, *communications* (with an "s") has been used when referring to activities involving technology and the mass media. *Communication* is typically used to describe face-to-face and written messages, as well as the field as a whole. With the growth of communication technology, the two terms are being used interchangeably more often.

Brent Ruben, *Communication and Human Behavior*

QUESTION: The author asserts that communication is a multidisciplinary field. Why do you think a professional communicator must be aware of several fields of knowledge to be effective?

Communication Is a Process

We often talk about communication as if it consisted of individual units, such as one person's utterance or a conversation between two people. In fact, communication is a continuous process. Consider, for example, a friend's compliment about your appearance. Your interpretation of those words will depend on a long series of experiences stretching far back in time: How have others judged your appearance? How do you feel about your looks? How honest has your friend been in the past? How have you been feeling about one another recently? All this history will help shape your response to the friend's remark. In turn, the words you speak and the way you say them will shape the way your friend behaves toward you and others—both in this situation and in the future.

This simple example shows that it's inaccurate to talk about "acts" of communication as if they occurred in isolation. To put it differently, communication isn't like a series of photos posted on Facebook but rather like a Twitter feed, in which the meaning comes from the unfolding of a series of interrelated microblogging messages. The fact that communication is a process is reflected in the transactional model introduced later in this chapter.

Communication Is Symbolic

Symbols are used to represent processes, ideas, or events in ways that make communication possible. Chapter 3 explores the nature of symbols in more detail, but this idea is so important that it needs an introduction now. The most significant feature of symbols is their *arbitrary* nature. For example, consider words as symbols. There's no logical reason why the letters in the word *book* should stand for the object you're reading now. French speakers call it *un livre*, and Germans call it a *buch*. Even in English, another set of letters would work just as well as long as everyone agreed to use it in the same way. We overcome the arbitrary nature of symbols by following linguistic rules and customs. Effective communication depends on agreement among people about these rules. This is easiest to see when we observe people who don't follow or aren't aware of linguistic conventions. For example, think of how unusual the speech of children sounds before they have managed to learn all the conventions.

Words are one type of symbol, but non-verbal behaviour can also have symbolic meaning. Like words, some non-verbal behaviours, though arbitrary, have clearly agreed-upon meanings. For example, to most Canadians a nod of the head means "yes." But non-verbal behaviours, even more than words, are ambiguous. Does a frown signify anger or unhappiness? Does a hug stand for a friendly greeting or a sign of romantic interest? You can't always be sure. We'll have more to say about non-verbal communication in Chapter 4.

symbol
An arbitrary sign used to represent a thing, person, idea, event, or relationship in ways that make communication possible.

Types of Communication

Within the domain of human interaction there are several types of communication. Each occurs in a different context, and, despite the features that they all share, each has its own characteristics. In the following section we'll examine the features of five different types of communication.

Intrapersonal Communication

By definition, **intrapersonal communication** means "communicating with oneself."[2] You can tune in to one way that each of us communicates internally by listening to the little voice that lives in your mind. Take a moment now and listen to what it is saying. Did you hear it? It

intrapersonal communication
Communication that occurs within a single person.

Cultural Idiom
tune in
To focus on.

may have been saying something like, "What little voice? I don't have any little voice!" This voice is the "sound" of your thinking.

We don't always think in verbal terms, but whether the process is apparent or not, the way we mentally process information influences our interactions with others. Thus, even though intrapersonal communication doesn't fit the "face-to-face" element of our definition of *communication*, it does affect those forms of interaction. You can understand the role of intrapersonal communication by imagining your thoughts in each of the following situations:

- You are about to introduce yourself to a classmate you've never spoken to.
- You scrutinize an audience of 30 strangers before beginning a 10-minute speech.
- The CEO yawns in the middle of your project proposal.
- You are defriended on Facebook.
- You wonder if you're the cause of a friend's recent irritability.

The way you handle each of these situations would depend on the intrapersonal communication that precedes or accompanies your overt behaviour. Much of Chapter 2 deals with the perception process in everyday situations.

Dyadic/Interpersonal Communication

Social scientists call two people interacting a **dyad**, and they describe this type of communication as **dyadic communication**. A dyad is the most common setting for communication. One study revealed that university and college students spend almost half of their total communication time interacting with one other person.[3] Observation in a variety of settings—playgrounds, shopping malls, railway stations—shows that most communication is dyadic in nature.[4] Even communication within larger groups (think, for instance, of classrooms, parties, and family gatherings) consists of multiple, often shifting dyadic encounters.

Dyadic interaction is sometimes considered identical to **interpersonal communication**, but as we will see in Chapter 6, not all two-person interaction can be considered interpersonal in the fullest sense of the word. At the same time, the qualities that characterize interpersonal communication aren't limited to pairs but may also be present in three-person interactions or even in small groups.

dyad
A two-person unit.

dyadic communication
Two-person communication.

interpersonal communication
Communication in which the parties consider one another as unique individuals rather than as objects. It is characterized by minimal use of stereotyped labels; unique, idiosyncratic social rules; and a high degree of information exchange.

Small-Group Communication

In **small-group communication** every person can participate actively with the other members. Small groups are common in everyday life. Your family is one. So is a collection of students or co-workers collaborating on a project. Even the players on a recreational hockey team can be considered a small group.

Whatever their makeup, small groups possess characteristics that are not present in a dyad. For instance, two or more members of a group can form a coalition to defend their position against other members, whereas in a dyad the members face each other as individuals, without support from others. In a group, the majority of members can, either consciously or unconsciously, put pressure on those in the minority to conform; in a dyad no such pressures exist. Conformity pressures can also be comforting, giving group members the confidence to take risks they would not dare to take if they were alone or in a dyad. With their greater size, groups also have the ability to be more creative than dyads. Finally, communication in groups is affected strongly by the type of leader. Groups are such an important communication setting that Chapters 9 and 10 focus exclusively on them.

Public Communication

Public communication takes place when a group becomes too large for all members to contribute. One characteristic of public communication is an unequal amount of speaking. A small number of people—sometimes even just one—will do almost all the talking, while the rest of the group becomes an audience. This leads to a second characteristic of public communication: limited verbal feedback. Audience members aren't able to respond in a two-way conversation the way they might in a dyadic or small-group setting. However, this doesn't mean that speakers operate in a vacuum when delivering their remarks. Audiences often have a chance to ask questions and make brief comments, and their non-verbal reactions offer a

wide range of clues about their reception of the speaker's remarks. This type of communication is commonly seen in talk shows, such as CBC's *The Rick Mercer Report,* hosted by Rick Mercer and Sun News Network's *The Source* with Ezra Levant.

Public speakers usually have a greater chance to plan and structure their remarks than do communicators in smaller settings. For this reason, the final two chapters of this book describe the steps you can take to prepare and deliver an effective speech.

Mass Communication

Mass communication consists of messages that are transmitted to large, widespread audiences via electronic and print media: the internet, television, radio, newspapers and magazines, and so on. Mass communication differs from interpersonal, small-group, and public communication in several ways. First, mass messages are aimed at large audiences without any personal contact between senders and receivers. Second, most of the messages sent via mass communication channels are developed, or at least financed, by large organizations. In this sense, mass communication is far less personal and more of a finished product than the other types we have examined so far.

> **mass communication**
> The transmission of messages to large, usually widespread audiences via broadcast means (such as radio and television), print (such as newspapers, magazines, and books), multimedia (such as CD-ROM, DVD, and the internet), and other forms of media such as recordings and movies.

Of course, the internet has made it possible for individuals without the backing of large organizations to broadcast their ideas on blogs and on sites like YouTube and, in this sense, has changed traditional mass communication. However, even most internet users consult sites that are produced and maintained by large organizations such as the CBC, Canada.com, *The Globe and Mail,* and the Government of Canada. As Donald Smith, director of operations, Public Affairs Branch, Canada Revenue Agency (CRA), wrote, the CRA depends on the internet to reach key audiences and stakeholders.[5] Finally, mass communication is almost always controlled by many gatekeepers who determine what messages will be delivered to consumers, how they will be constructed, and when they will be delivered. Sponsors (whether corporate or governmental), editors, producers, reporters, and executives all have the power to influence mass messages in ways that don't affect most other types of communication. Because of these and other unique characteristics, the study of mass communication raises special issues and deserves special treatment. Sometimes, mass communication can serve a very powerful democratic purpose, as Kim Morris discusses in a case study she wrote about crisis communications in rural communities in northeastern Ontario.[6]

Functions of Communication

Now that we have a working understanding of the term *communication,* it is important to discuss why we spend so much time exploring this subject. Perhaps the strongest argument for studying communication is its central role in our lives. Most of us are surrounded by others with whom we try to build understandings: family, friends, co-workers, teachers, and strangers. The amount of time we spend communicating is staggering. And many of us are replacing "face time" with social media time. One study measured the amount of time a sample group of Canadians spent communicating using social media such as LinkedIn, Instagram, Tumblr, Google+, Facebook, Twitter, and MySpace.[7] The researchers found that 49 per cent of the subjects used social media to communicate with other people or with organizations, such as companies, stores, not-for-profit agencies, or governments, at least once per day.

Whatever medium we choose to communicate through, there's a good reason why we speak, listen, read, and write so much: communication satisfies most of our needs.

Physical Needs

Communication is so important that it is necessary for physical health. In fact, evidence suggests that an absence of satisfying communication can even jeopardize life itself. Medical researchers have identified a wide range of hazards that result from a lack of close relationships.[8] For instance:

- People who lack strong relationships have two to three times the risk of early death, regardless of whether they smoke, drink, or exercise regularly.
- Terminal cancer strikes socially isolated people more often than it does those who have close personal relationships.
- Divorced, separated, and widowed people are 5 to 10 times more likely to need hospitalization for mental problems than are their married counterparts.
- Pregnant women under stress and without supportive relationships have three times more complications than pregnant women who suffer from the same stress but have strong social support.
- Socially isolated people are four times more susceptible to the common cold than those who have active social networks.[9]

Other studies have shown that social isolation is a major risk factor contributing to coronary disease,[10] and three recent articles in *The Globe and Mail* have discussed how loneliness has been linked to increased risk of heart attack, high blood pressure, and cancer. Not surprisingly, the quality of personal relationships has an even more significant bearing on health. This has to do with the difference between *structural support*—a person's basic network of social relationships, including friends, family, and romantic partners—and *functional support,* which refers to the quality of those relationships and whether or not a person believes,

YOUNG COMMUNICATOR PROFILE

CAROLINE GDYCZYNSKI

Producer, CBC Toronto

I realized early in my academic career that a degree in communication studies would provide me with a versatile resume of transferable skills. Since graduating, I have worked as content management specialist, a communications assistant for an NGO [non-governmental organization] with consultative status at the United Nations and most recently as a producer at the CBC.

I found each of these jobs stimulating, while presenting new challenges and opportunities. At the CBC, each day presents new stories and new ways of keeping our audience informed. In many cases, deadlines are measured in minutes and that's where research and writing are vital in ensuring news reports are factual and visually stimulating.

A newsroom can be compared to a group project—where success is achieved when each person understands their responsibilities while keeping in mind the challenges others are facing. However, at times assignments are your own responsibility and there is little collaboration.

I'm responsible for writing and researching, producing reporter items and finally ensuring everything gets to air on time. It's not uncommon to meet deadlines with only seconds to spare!

There are few jobs where you can see the impact of your work almost instantly—this is one of them. Each day, I'm required to put skills that have been garnered over the years to the test. As the show goes to air each evening, I'm able to sit back, critique and be critiqued on my assignments.

for example, that his or her friends will be there in a time of need.[11] A Quebec study found that psychiatric patients, in comparison with people from the general population, consistently reported less satisfaction with their social support, suggesting that functional support—that is, actual or perceived strength of social ties—is a predictor of mental health outcomes.[12]

People who have higher levels of social support are more likely to eat healthy foods, drink alcohol in moderation, and refrain from smoking. A University of Alberta study even found that adults who reported higher levels of social support expressed a greater intention to exercise.[13] A Statistics Canada study published in 2002 showed that rates of depression and alcohol dependence were lower among immigrants than among Canadian-born comparison groups, owing mainly to the strength and frequency of communication patterns within the cultural groups.[14] Another unusual fact uncovered by this study was that the "Immigrant Health Effect" was greater among more recent immigrants. Also, a study by Siavash Jafari, Souzan Baharlou, and Richard Mathias demonstrated that one of the key determinants of the mental health of Iranian immigrants to Canada was communication.[15]

Other studies suggest that high levels of humour are associated with a stronger immune system.[16] A study from the University of Waterloo found that women with high levels of humour had lower systolic blood pressure than women with low levels of coping humour. The findings differed for male subjects, however, leading the authors to surmise that female humour, which is often self-directed and better promotes social cohesion, is possibly healthier than male humour, which tends to be hostile and at the expense of others.[17] Presumably, men would derive more health benefits if their humour was more pro-social in its focus.

This research demonstrates the importance of having satisfying personal relationships. Remember, though, that not everyone needs the same amount of contact, and the quality of communication is almost certainly as important as the quantity. The main point here is that personal communication is essential for our well-being. To paraphrase an old song, "people who need people" *aren't* "the luckiest people in the world"—they're the *only* people!

Identity Needs

Communication does more than enable us to survive. Indeed, it is the only way we have to learn who we are. As you'll read in Chapter 2, our sense of identity comes from the way we interact with other people. Are we smart or stupid, attractive or ugly, talented or inept? The answers to these questions don't come from looking in the mirror. We decide who we are based on how others react to us. Deprived of communication with others, we would have no sense of identity. In his book *Bridges, Not Walls*, John Stewart dramatically illustrates this fact by citing the case of the famous "Wild Boy of Aveyron," who spent his early childhood without any apparent human contact. The boy was discovered in January 1800 while digging for vegetables in a French village garden.[18] He showed none of the behaviours that one would expect in a social human. The boy could not speak but uttered only weird cries. More significant than this absence of social skills was his lack of any identity as a human being. As author Roger Shattuck put it, "The boy had no human sense of being in the world. He had no sense of himself as a person related to other persons."[19] Only with the care and attention of a loving "mother" did the boy begin to behave—and, we can imagine, think of himself—as a human.

Contemporary stories support the essential role that communication plays in shaping identity. In 1970, authorities discovered a 12-year-old girl (they called her "Genie") who had spent virtually all her life in an otherwise empty, darkened bedroom with almost no human contact. The child could not speak and had no sense of herself as a person until she was removed from her family and "nourished" by a team of caregivers.[20] A more recent case involved a Toronto

Whether the consequence of a mental attitude or a living condition, loneliness affects millions, usually for the worse. Death certificates read heart attack, cancer, or suicide; but coroners are missing the point. With no one to love or to love us, we tend to smoke, drink, brood, or simply cry ourselves into earlier graves.

Don E. Hamachek, *Encounters with Others*

Understanding Diversity

Feeding the Need for Native News: Duncan McCue

Duncan McCue, educated as a lawyer, is a national reporter for CBC-TV News in Vancouver, and his current affairs documentaries are featured on the CBC's The National. Nominated for Gemini and Webster awards, he has received a Radio-Television News Directors Association of Canada (RTNDA) Award for investigative reporting and multiple honours from the Native American Journalists Association for investigative, news, and feature reporting. McCue is Anishinaabe and a member of the Chippewas of Georgina Island First Nations in southern Ontario. Throughout his career, he has worked diligently to bring Native stories into the mainstream media. He was recently appointed the first visiting professor in Media and Indigenous Peoples at the UBC School of Journalism.

As an Aboriginal journalist, did you face obstacles moving into the mainstream media?

The most obvious obstacle was that when I started I didn't know what I was doing. I worked for a show called *Road Movies* and for YTV News, but that was an unusual experience in that they were asking for me to do commentaries. I could write whatever I wanted, and they encouraged me to express my point of view. Journalism is a very different beast. The learning curve was huge for me, and the CBC, bless their hearts, took me on and I learned on the job. I was also the only Native reporter at CBC Vancouver for a long time. And still, there aren't many of us. Also, I had some strong views about the ways that Aboriginal communities had been covered in the mainstream media and I wanted to change that. I found that it wasn't as easy as I thought

it was going to be. It's not that there was resistance to my ideas, but the definition of what makes news and what the lead story is—that definition has been around for a long time, and my idea of what is newsworthy wasn't always what my producers thought was newsworthy.

In the first couple of years, I was racing off to blockades and things like that, which was exciting and fun. But then after a while I thought, "There's more to life in Native communities than blockades." That's when I started to pitch different ideas, and that's when it became tougher for me.

You have covered some very difficult stories addressing social and political issues. How do you balance reporting on hard issues and reporting on the positive?

I think that is partly why I have been at the CBC so long. I don't mind tackling tough issues in the Native community, whereas a lot of young Native people who come into the system want to tell positive stories. There's an old line about the "Four Ds" of news coverage for Native people. They were either "drunk, dead, or drumming or dancing." And if you are not doing one of those things then you're not going to make it on the news that night.

So there have been a lot of people who have said they want to promote more positive role models. I think there are all kinds of problems in Native communities that need to be addressed. Whether we are poaching eagles, or our kids are working the streets and being abused, or we're dealing with financial accountability—those are all tough issues that communities are

boy, Jeffrey Baldwin, who for most of his short life was confined to his room by his grandparents, unable to communicate with other children. We can only imagine how this experience affected his sense of identity and self before his tragic death at the age of six.[21]

No one is born with a ready-made sense of identity. We become aware of who we are from the ways others define us. As Chapter 2 will discuss, the messages we receive in early childhood are the strongest, but the influence of others continues throughout life. Chapter 2 also explains how we use communication to manage the way others view us.

Some scholars have argued that we are most attracted to people who confirm our identity.[22] This confirmation can come in different forms, depending on the self-image of the communicator. People with relatively high self-esteem seek out others who verify their value and, as much as possible, avoid those who treat them poorly. Conversely, people who regard themselves as unworthy may look for relationships in which others treat them badly. This principle offers one explanation for why some people stay in unsuccessful or abusive relationships. If you view yourself as worthless, you may associate with others who will confirm that self-perception. Of

grappling with. I think Native reporters have a responsibility to try to report on those, and I can put things in context in a way that non-Native reporters might not be able to.

Do you feel you are becoming a role model?

Yeah, I guess I am. But someone described me as the "first" professor of Indigenous media the other day, and I think that's an awful thing. I think of Judge Scow coming to UBC and all throughout his career being described as the "first Indian lawyer" and the "first Aboriginal judge," and I think "poor Judge Scow." First of all, being on your own for that length of time, but also that it's not a thing to celebrate [being the first]. There should be a bunch of Aboriginal journalists. There are more today, but there are still not enough, which is part of the reason I have started teaching. There are no Aboriginal students at the journalism school right now . . . and there need to be. If my going there helps some Native kid or even some middle-aged Native person think they can do it, then great.

Tell me more about what inspired you to become an educator.

CBC is a really great place to be. It is maybe not like it was 30 years ago, but it is still one of the premier training grounds for young journalists and technicians in Canada. Training has always been part of the CBC, to ensure we produce the kind of quality we expect of ourselves and that Canadians expect from us. Two or three years ago, I realized that if I am at all good at my craft, it's in part due to the training I had, and that I wanted

to pass that on—particularly because I despair about the small number of Native people who are going into journalism. There's a strong network of Native newspapers and radio stations, and now we have [Aboriginal Peoples Television Network] APTN, so there's lots of people interested in working within Indigenous media. But there are very few who want to make that crossover into the mainstream, and there needs to be Native voices in the mainstream, otherwise our voices are not being heard in the full complexity that they should be.

What is the next career step for you?

I don't know, but I am looking forward to finding out! I've always said if I get a gold watch from the CBC then I'll be disappointed with myself because at some point I'd really like to help build the Indigenous media capacity in the country, and help shape it. And I haven't done that yet, and I do feel a really strong responsibility. At some point, I would like to take some of the skills I have learned and try to blend it with my experience in the Native community and create something that would really knock the socks off of Native communities, and the rest of Canada.

UBC Alumni Profiles,
law.ubc.ca/alumni/profiles/alumni/Mccue.html

QUESTION: Professor McCue's research and writing discuss a specific demographic group: Native Canadians. How does his success story demonstrate the importance of communication to business, cultural, and political causes?

---

course, relationships can change a communicator's identity as well as validate it. Supportive relationships can transform feelings of inadequacy into self-respect, and damaging ones can lower self-esteem.

The role of communication in shaping identity works in a second way. Even as others' messages are working to shape who we think we are, we are sending messages (sometimes consciously, sometimes not) intended to shape the way others see us. For example, the choices we make about how to dress and otherwise shape our appearance are almost always attempts to manage our identity.

Social Needs

Besides helping to define who we are, communication provides a vital link with others. Researchers and theorists have identified a range of social needs that we satisfy by communicating: the need for *pleasure* (e.g., we communicate "because it's fun" or "to have a good time"); the need for *affection* (e.g., "to help others" or "to let others know I care"); the need for *inclusion* (e.g., "because I need someone to talk to or be with," "because it makes me less lonely"); the need for *escape* (e.g., "to put off doing something I should be doing"); the need for *relaxation* (e.g., "because it allows me to unwind"); and the need for *control* (e.g., "because I want someone to do something for me," "to get something I don't have").[23]

Just how vital is the need for pleasure in communication? Several Canadian researchers have investigated the benefits of humour in communication, including Rod Martin, who, with his research group at the University of Western Ontario, outlined four models that describe how humour and laughter can have a positive impact on health.[24] First, a physiological model focuses on the possibility that physiological changes associated with laughter contribute to improved health. Second, an emotion model is based on the idea that humour produces positive emotions that, in turn, contribute positively to health. Third, a stress-moderation model posits that humour, together with other processes that contribute to a positive outlook on the world, acts as a buffer to mitigate stress, thereby improving health. Finally, a social support model suggests that the benefits of humour are mediated by the increased social support that comes from being a fun-loving and outgoing individual.

As you look at the rest of the items on the list of social needs satisfied by communication, imagine how empty your life would be if these needs weren't met. Then notice that it would be impossible to fulfill these needs without communicating with others. Because relationships with others are so vital, some theorists have gone as far as to argue that communication is the primary goal of human existence. Anthropologist Walter Goldschmidt has called the drive for meeting social needs the "human career."[25]

Practical Needs

We shouldn't overlook the important everyday functions that communication serves. Communication is the tool that lets us tell the hairstylist to take just a little off the sides, explain to the police officer why we were driving 60 kilometres per hour in a 40-kilometre zone, and inform the contractor that the leaking roof needs attention right now!

Beyond these obvious needs, a wealth of research demonstrates that communication is an important key to effectiveness in a variety of everyday settings. For example, a survey of more than 400 American employers identified "communication skills" as the top characteristic that employers seek in job candidates.[26] It was rated as more important than technical competence, work experience, or academic background. A study by the Conference Board of Canada found that an employee's ability to communicate effectively is also implicitly favoured because communication skills underpin other desired skills such as teamwork.[27]

Communication is just as important outside of work. University roommates who are both willing and able to communicate effectively report higher satisfaction with one another than do those who lack these characteristics,[28] and students who demonstrate communication competence have higher grade point averages than those who do not have this skill.[29] Married couples who were identified as effective communicators reported happier relationships than did spouses with poorer communication

COMMUNICATION ON-SCREEN

The Trotsky (2009)
Directed by Robert Kevin Tierney.

Montreal high school student Leon Bronsky (Jay Baruchel) believes he is the reincarnation of Russian Bolshevik leader Leon Trotsky, much to the chagrin of his father. After trying to unionize the workers at his father's factory, he is sent to public school where he engages his dictatorial principal (Colm Feore) and vice-principal in class warfare. Through motivational rhetoric and affective communication, Leon tries to unionize and motivate his apathetic student body. For Leon (both Bronsky and Trotsky) communication is a powerful tool for affecting change in belief, freedom, oppression, and even personal identity.

skills.[30] In "getting acquainted" situations, communication competence played a major role in whether a person was judged physically attractive, socially desirable, and good at the task of getting acquainted.[31]

Modelling Communication

So far we have introduced a basic definition of *communication* and looked at the functions it performs. This information is useful, but it only begins to describe the process we will be examining throughout this book. One way to understand more about what it means to communicate is to look at some models that describe what happens when two or more people interact. As you will see, over the last half-century scholars have developed an increasingly accurate and sophisticated view of this process.

A Linear Model

Until about 50 years ago, researchers viewed communication as something that one person "does" to another.[32] In this **linear communication model**, communication is like giving an injection: a **sender encodes** ideas and feelings into some sort of **message** and then conveys them to a **receiver,** who **decodes** them (see Figure 1.1).

One important element of the linear model is the communication **channel**—the method by which the message is conveyed. For most people, face-to-face contact is the most familiar and obvious channel. Writing is another channel. In addition to these long-used forms, **mediated communication** channels include telephone, e-mail, instant messaging, faxes, voice mail, and even video conferencing. (The word *mediated* reflects the fact that these messages are conveyed through some sort of communication medium.)

The channel you choose can make a big difference in the effect of your message. For example, a typewritten love letter probably wouldn't have the same effect as a handwritten one. Likewise, ending a relationship by leaving a voice mail message would make a very different statement than delivering the bad news in person. As Table 1.1 suggests, we can improve the

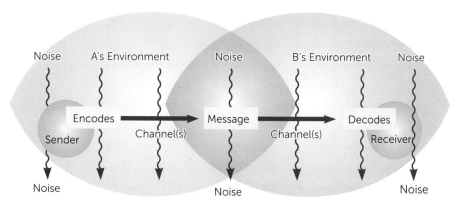

FIGURE 1.1 Linear Communication Model

---

linear communication model
A characterization of communication as a one-way event in which a message flows from sender to receiver.

sender
The originator of a message.

encode
The process of putting thoughts into symbols, most commonly words.

message
A sender's planned and unplanned words and non-verbal behaviours.

receiver
One who notices and attends to a message.

decode
The process in which a receiver attaches meaning to a message.

channel
Medium through which a message passes from sender to receiver.

mediated communication
Communication sent via a medium other than face-to-face interaction, e.g., telephone, e-mail, instant messaging, etc. Can be both mass and personal.

Marshall McLuhan

A foundational communication theorist, Marshall McLuhan was one of the most successful and prominent Canadian intellectuals of the 1960s. His theory that communication media are actually extensions of the body revolutionized the way marketers, psychologists, and public relations professionals thought of the telephone, the automobile, and many other everyday technologies. McLuhan's radical ideas such as "the wheel extends the leg" and "clothing extends the skin" made social scientists and philosophers, as well as communications professionals, rethink how to model communication. He argued that the technologies we use to communicate are just as important as the messages we send. McLuhan's legacy is an example of how Canadian communication theorists have had a huge impact on communications theory and the communications professions since World War II.

noise
External, physiological, and psychological distractions that interfere with the accurate transmission and reception of a message.

quality of our relationships by choosing the communication channel with the best chance of success in any particular situation. As Canadian communication theorist Marshall McLuhan famously claimed, "The medium is the message."[33]

The linear model also introduces the concept of **noise**—a term used by social scientists to describe any forces that interfere with effective communication. There are three types of noise—external, physiological, and psychological—and they can disrupt communication at

Table 1.1 Factors to Consider When Choosing a Communication Channel

	Time Required for Feedback	Amount of Information Conveyed	Sender's Control Over How Message Is Composed	Control Over Receiver's Attention	Effectiveness for Detailed Messages
Face-to-Face	Immediate (after contact established)	Highest	Moderate	Highest	Weak
Telephone	Immediate (after contact established)	Vocal, but not visual	Moderate	Less than in face-to-face setting	Weakest
Voice Mail	Delayed	Vocal, but not visual	Higher (since receiver can't interrupt)	Low	Weak
E-Mail	Delayed	Low (text only, no formatting)	High	Low	Better
Texting	Immediate	Low (text only, no formatting)	High	Modest	Weak
Tweeting	Immediate	Lowest (character Limit)	High	Low	Weak/Good (depends on "tweeter")
Hard Copy (e.g.,handwritten or typed message)	Delayed	Words, numbers, and images, but no non-verbal cues	Highest	Low	Good

Source: Adapted from R.B. Adler and J.M. Elmhorst, *Communicating at Work: Principles and Practices for Business and the Professions*, 8th edn (New York: McGraw-Hill, 2005): 32–3.

every stage of the process. *External noise* (also called *physical noise*) includes those factors outside the receiver that make it difficult to hear or concentrate on the message being delivered. A television switched on in a restaurant might make it hard for you to pay attention to the person sitting across the table from you, and a back-row seat in a crowded auditorium might make a speaker's remarks unclear. External noise can disrupt communication almost anywhere in our model—in the sender, in the channel, in the message, or in the receiver.

Physiological noise occurs when biological factors in the receiver or sender—illness, fatigue, and so on—interfere with accurate reception. *Psychological noise* refers to forces within a communicator that interfere with the ability to express or understand a message accurately. For instance, an angler might exaggerate the size of a catch in order to convince others of his or her talents. In the same way, a student might become so upset upon receiving a D on an essay that he or she would be unable (or perhaps unwilling) to understand clearly what went wrong.

A linear model shows that communicators often occupy different **environments**—fields of experience that help them understand others' behaviour. In communication terminology, *environment* refers not just to a physical location but also to the personal experiences and cultural backgrounds that participants bring to a conversation. Consider some of the factors that might contribute to different environments:

> **environment**
> Both the physical setting in which communication occurs and the personal perspectives of the parties involved.

- *A* might belong to one ethnic group and *B* to another;
- *A* might be rich and *B* poor;
- *A* might be rushed and *B* have nowhere to go;
- *A* might have lived a long, eventful life, and *B* might be young and inexperienced; and
- *A* might be passionately concerned with the subject and *B* indifferent to it.

Environments aren't always so obvious. Consider, for instance, the findings of an American study that showed that college students who have been enrolled in debate classes become more argumentative and verbally aggressive than those who have not been exposed to this environment.[34]

When you look at the linear model in Figure 1.1 you will see that the environments of *A* and *B* overlap. This area represents the background that the communicators must have in common. As the shared environment becomes smaller, communication becomes more difficult. Consider a few examples in which different perspectives can make understanding difficult:

- Employers who have trouble understanding the perspective of their employees will be less effective managers, and workers who do not appreciate the challenges of being in charge are more likely to be unco-operative.
- Parents who have trouble recalling their youth are likely to clash with their children, who do not yet know and may not appreciate the responsibility that comes with parenting.
- Members of a dominant culture who have never experienced being "different" may not appreciate the concerns of people from other cultures, whose own perspectives make it hard to understand the apparent cultural blindness of the majority.

Differing environments make understanding one another challenging but certainly not impossible. Hard work and many of the skills described in this book provide ways to bridge the gaps that separate all of us. For now, recognizing the challenge that comes from dissimilar environments is a good start. You can't solve a problem until you recognize that it exists.

A Transactional Model

Despite its simplicity, the linear model doesn't do a very good job of representing the way most communication operates. The **transactional communication model** in Figure 1.2 presents a more accurate picture in several respects.

Simultaneous Sending and Receiving

Although some types of mass communication flow in a one-way, linear manner, most types of personal communication are two-way exchanges.[35] The transactional model reflects the fact that we usually send and receive messages simultaneously. The roles of sender and receiver that seemed separate in the linear model are now superimposed and redefined as those of "communicators." This new term reflects the fact that at a given moment we are capable of receiving, decoding, and responding to another person's behaviour, while at the same time that other person is receiving and responding to ours.

Consider, for instance, the significance of a friend's yawn as you describe your romantic problems. Or imagine the blush you may see as you tell one of your raunchier jokes to a new acquaintance. Non-verbal behaviours like these show that most face-to-face communication is a two-way affair. The discernible response of a receiver to a sender's message is called **feedback.** Not all feedback is non-verbal, of course. Sometimes it is oral, as when you ask for clarification from an instructor who has just announced a test or when you reply to a friend who has asked what you think of her new haircut. In other cases it is written, as when you answer the questions on a mid-term exam or respond to a letter from a friend. Figure 1.2 makes the importance of feedback clear. It shows that most communication is, indeed, a two-way affair.

Another weakness of the traditional linear model is the questionable assumption that all communication involves encoding. We certainly do choose symbols to convey most verbal messages. But what about the many non-verbal cues that occur whether or not people speak: facial expressions, gestures, postures, vocal tones, and so on? Cues like these clearly do offer information

transactional communication model
A characterization of communication as the simultaneous sending and receiving of messages in an ongoing, irreversible process.

feedback
The discernible response of a receiver to a sender's message.

A new idea is delicate. It can be killed by a sneer or a yawn; it can be stabbed to death by a joke or worried to death by a frown on the right person's brow.

Charles Brower, American advertising executive and author

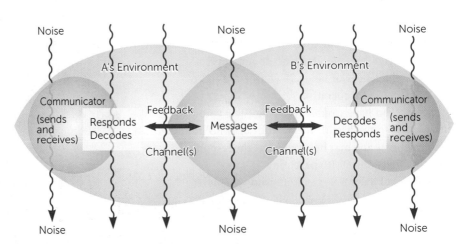

FIGURE 1.2 Transactional Communication Model

about others, although they are often unconscious and thus don't involve encoding. For this reason, the *transactional model* replaces the term *encodes* with the broader term *responds,* because it describes both intentional and unintentional actions that can be observed and interpreted.[36]

Communication Is Fluid, Not Static

Besides illustrating the simultaneous nature of face-to-face interaction, the examples we just considered show that it's difficult to isolate a single discrete "act" of communication from the events that precede and follow it. The way a friend or family member reacts to a sarcastic remark you make will probably depend on the way you have related to one another in the past. Likewise, the way you'll act toward each other in the future depends on the outcome of this conversation. Research conducted on partners in romantic relationships confirms the importance of context. As communication researcher Steve Duck put it, "Relationships are best conceived . . . as unfinished business."[37]

Communication Is Relational, Not Individual

The transactional model shows that communication isn't something we do *to* others; rather, it is something we do *with* them. In this sense, communication is rather like dancing—at least the kind of dancing we do with partners. Like dancing, communication depends on the involvement of a partner. And like good dancing, successful communication isn't something that depends just on the skill of one person. A great dancer who doesn't consider and adapt to the skill level of his or her partner can make both people look bad. In communication and dancing, having two talented partners does not guarantee success. When two talented dancers perform without coordinating their movements, the results feel bad to the dancers and look foolish to an audience. Finally, relational communication—like dancing—is a unique creation that arises out of the way in which the partners interact. The way a person dances varies depending on the partner because of its co-operative, transactional nature. Likewise, the way you communicate almost certainly varies with different partners.

Psychologist Kenneth Gergen amply captures the relational nature of communication when he points out how our success depends on interaction with others. As he says, "one cannot be 'attractive' without others who are attracted, a 'leader' without others willing to follow, or a 'loving person' without others to affirm with appreciation."[38]

Because communication is transactional, it's often a mistake to suggest that just one person is responsible for a relationship. Consider the cartoon on this page. Both of the characters had good intentions, and both probably could have handled the situation better. It would have been far better to ask, "How did we handle this situation, and what can we do to make it better?"

The transactional nature of communication shows up in school, where teachers and students influence one another's behaviour. For example, a teacher who regards some students negatively may

UNDERSTANDING COMMUNICATION TECHNOLOGY

Cyberbullying-Linked Suicides Rising, Study Says

The transactional mode of communication emphasizes that communication is a two-way channel. When you communicate with others, you are constantly sending and receiving signals. But how does this mode of communication change when you are having conversations online? The following article from CBC news considers one of the darker sides of online communication: cyberbullying. As you read, think about the relational aspect of communication and how it works for online interactions.

Cases of suicides linked to cyberbullying have grown over the past decade, but being tormented over the internet is rarely the main factor involved, a new Canadian study shows.

There have been 41 suicides since 2003 involving cyberbullying in the United States, Canada, Australia, and the United Kingdom, but most of the victims were also bullied in school and many suffered from mental illness, including depression, said John C. LeBlanc, a professor at Dalhousie University in Halifax who conducted the research.

"Although cyberbullying is a new and fairly awful modern manifestation of bullying . . . it is not a cause of suicide," he told CBC News. "It's only one factor among many . . . People who are cyberbullied have, for the most part, been bullied in more traditional manners as well."

The recent case of British Columbia teen Amanda Todd, who took her own life after posting a video on YouTube describing how she had been tormented by bullying online and struggling with depression, has shone a spotlight on the problem of cyberbullying and the tragic consequences that can result.

Her death sparked a firestorm of international attention, prompted RCMP to investigate the contributing factors, including cyberbullying, and pushed MPs to call for a national anti-bullying strategy.

There have been other high-profile cases in Canada, such as Jenna Bowers-Bryanton, a 15-year-old Nova Scotia girl who took her own life in January 2011.

John C. LeBlanc and his team of researchers analyzed English-language media reports of suicides in which cyberbullying was mentioned. They identified 41 cases, stemming as far back as 2003.

Their research showed that the incidence increased over time, with 23 cases (56 per cent) taking place between 2003 and 2010. But in 2011 and the first four months of 2012, there were 18 cases of suicides with a cyberbullying link.

"There is no clear reason why the cases appear to be growing, but exposure and use of social media has increased," LeBlanc said.

"While it is catastrophic, it is rare. These 41 cases, over four countries in eight years illustrate that . . . but it's rare and therefore very difficult to study," he said.

The vast majority of cases, 23, were in the US, followed by six in Australia, five in the UK and four in Canada.

Of the victims, 78 per cent of [those] who committed

treat them with subtle or overt disfavour. As a result, these students are likely to react negatively, which reinforces the teacher's original attitudes and expectations.[39] It isn't necessary to resolve the "who started it" issue here to recognize that the behaviours of teachers and students are part of a transactional relationship.

The transactional character of communication also figures dramatically in relationships between parents and their children. We normally think of "good parenting" as a skill that some people possess and others lack. We judge the ability of a mother and father in terms of how well their children turn out. In truth, the question of good parenting isn't quite so clear. Research suggests that the quality of interaction between parents and children is a two-way affair, that children influence parents just as much as the other way around.[40] For example, children who engage in what social scientists call "problematic behaviour" evoke more high-control responses from their parents than do co-operative children. By contrast, children with mild temperaments are less likely to provoke coercive reactions by their parents than are more aggressive children. Parents with low self-esteem tend to send more messages that weaken the self-esteem of their children, who in turn are likely to act in ways that make the parents feel even worse about themselves. Thus, a mutually reinforcing cycle arises in which parents and children shape one another's feelings and behaviour. In cases like this it is at least difficult and probably impossible to identify who is the "sender" and who is the "receiver" of messages. It's more

suicide were bullied both at school and online—with only 17 per cent targeted on the internet only, the study showed.

A mood disorder was present in 32 per cent of the teens, and another 15 per cent also had depression symptoms.

Another notable finding was that all of the victims were between the ages of 13 to 18, likely stemming from the pressures of adolescence, LeBlanc said.

"Teenagers are very vulnerable that way," he said. "Adults use social media, particularly young adults. So, it's not exposure to social media, but about being a young adolescent that is trying to form his or her identity, and cares very much about what people think."

The victims were more often female, with 24 female cases compared with 17 males, researchers found.

The researchers also catalogued the type of electronic media or social media used.

Social networking sites were used in 48 per cent of all the suicide cases, while messaging (text, pictures, or video) [was] used in 25 per cent of the cases.

Facebook was used in cyberbullying most often, cited in 27 per cent of cases, while Facebook combined with messaging of pictures, videos, and texts were used in 13 per cent.

Also, it appeared that most of the suicides took place in September and January, coinciding with the beginning of a new school semester, though there were not enough cases to be statistically significant, LeBlanc said.

The takeaway message from the study, he said, is like with traditional bullying, people must intervene when they suspect someone is being bullied.

Todd's recent suicide is a "striking example," he said, of a troubled person putting out a cry for help, but no one coming to her aid.

Because bullying usually takes places out of the view of most adults, other young people need to step in, whether online or in person, LeBlanc said.

"Youth themselves have to develop a code of ethics or civility . . . where, when things like this happen, they actually jump in to protect the other person, and they actually post things online that says this is inappropriate," he said.

CBC News, 20 October 2012, www.cbc.ca/news/technology/cyberbullying-linked-suicides-rising-study-says-1.1213435

QUESTION: The article highlights some interesting misconceptions regarding cyberbullying and shows us one of the myriad ways in which communications technology can facilitate and even extend interpersonal communications, no matter how abusive it can occasionally be. How has bullying, as well as preventative action, been effected by the increased popularity of social networking and online communications technology? How does the above article highlight the notion of relational communication in the internet age?

accurate to acknowledge that parents and children—just like husbands and wives, managers and staff, teachers and students, and any other people who communicate with one another—act in ways that mutually influence one another. The transactional nature of relationships is worth re-emphasizing: we don't communicate *to* others, we communicate *with* them.

By now you can see that a transactional model of communication should be more like a video clip than a slide show of still images. Although Figure 1.2 does a fair job of illustrating the phenomenon we call communication, an animated version in which the environments, communicators, and messages constantly change would be an even better way of capturing the process.

Communication Competence: What Makes an Effective Communicator?

It's easy to recognize good communicators, and even easier to spot poor ones. But what are the characteristics that distinguish effective communicators from those who are less successful? Answering this question has been one of the leading challenges for communication scholars.[41] Although not all of the answers are in, research has identified a great deal of important and useful information about communication competence.

Communication Competence Defined

Defining **communication competence** isn't as easy as it might seem. Although scholars are still struggling to agree on a precise definition, most would concur that effective communication involves achieving one's goals in a manner that, ideally, maintains or enhances the relationship in which it occurs.[42] This definition may seem both vague and verbose, but a closer look shows that it suggests several important characteristics of communication competence.

There Is No "Ideal" Way to Communicate

Your own experience will show you that a variety of communication styles are effective. Some very successful communicators are serious, while others use humour; some are gregarious, while others are quiet; and some are straightforward, while others hint diplomatically. Just as there are many kinds of beautiful music and art, there are many kinds of competent communication.

You will also find that the type of communication that succeeds in one situation might be a colossal blunder in another. The joking insults you routinely trade with a friend might be insensitive and discouraging if he or she has just suffered a personal setback. The language you use with your peers might offend a family member, and last Saturday night's romantic approach would probably be out of place at work or in class on Monday morning. For this reason, being a competent communicator requires flexibility in understanding what approach is likely to work best in a given situation.[43]

Cultural differences also call for different approaches to communication. What qualifies as competent behaviour in one culture might be completely inept, or even offensive, in another.[44] Habits like belching after a meal or appearing nude in public, to note two obvious examples, might be appropriate in some parts of the world but would of course be considered outrageous in others. But there are more subtle differences in competent communication. For example, such qualities as being self-disclosing and speaking clearly, which are valued among Americans and English Canadians, are likely to be considered overly aggressive and insensitive in many Asian cultures, where subtlety and indirectness are considered important.[45]

Even within a single society, people from different cultural backgrounds may have different notions of appropriate behaviour. One American study, for instance, revealed that ideas of how good friends should communicate varied from one ethnic group to another.[46] Latinos, as a group, valued relational support most highly, whereas African Americans valued respect and acceptance. Asian Americans emphasized a caring, positive exchange of ideas, and Anglo-Americans prized friends who recognized their needs as individuals.

Now, consider for a moment the cultural diversity of Canada. People of African ancestry make up a tiny fraction of the Canadian population, but they come from a very wide variety of geographic origins in Africa and the Caribbean. People of Asian descent, who make up 60 per cent of Canadian visible minorities, come from all parts of Asia, including mainland China, Hong Kong,

Taiwan, Macao, Korea, India, and Sri Lanka. And the fact that Canadians of European origin are much more likely than their American counterparts to be fluent in a language other than English makes it much more difficult to categorize them as a single group. At the same time, a recent study showed that Canadians generally feel a much stronger attachment to regional cultures, such as those of the Maritimes, the North, or Quebec, than Americans do.[47] This cultural complexity makes it difficult to generalize about cultural and communication competence in English Canada. By contrast, the identity of French Canada is relatively homogeneous, and therefore easier for most immigrants to assimilate to. Some argue that this is the reason that French-Canadian television, current affairs programs, and celebrities have relatively much higher profiles than their English-Canadian counterparts.

Findings like these mean that there can be no sure-fire list of rules or tips that will guarantee your success as a communicator. They also suggest that competent communicators are able to adapt their style to suit the individual and cultural preferences of others.[48] Throughout this book, you will be introduced to a variety of communication skills. Although all of them are likely to be effective at one time or another, they aren't meant to replace other approaches that you already use. The skills you learn from this book will broaden your repertoire of choices about how to communicate. When you combine them with other approaches, you'll be likely to recognize a change for the better in your interactions with others.

> **Cultural Idiom**
> **sure-fire way**
> A way that is certain to succeed.

Competence Is Situational

Because competent behaviour varies so much from one situation and person to another, it's a mistake to think that communication competence is a trait that a person either possesses or lacks. It's more accurate to talk about degrees or areas of competence.[49] You and the people you know are probably quite competent in some areas and less so in others. You might deal quite skilfully with peers, for example, but feel clumsy interacting with people much older or younger, wealthier or poorer, or more or less attractive than yourself. In fact, your competence with one person may vary from one situation to another. This means that it's an overgeneralization to say, in a moment of distress, "I'm a terrible communicator!" It would be more accurate to say, "I didn't handle this situation very well, even though I'm better in others." In a place as diverse as Canada it's especially important to remember that people who seem to be having difficulty communicating in one particular context may do much better in a different setting.

Competence Is Relational

Because communication is transactional, behaviour that is competent in one relationship isn't necessarily competent in others.

A fascinating study on relational satisfaction illustrates that what constitutes satisfying communication varies from one relationship to another.[50] Researchers Brant Burleson and Wendy Samter hypothesized that people with sophisticated communication skills (such as managing conflict well, giving ego-support to others, and providing comfort to relational partners) would be better than less-skilled communicators at maintaining friendships. To their surprise, the results did not support this hypothesis. In fact, friendships were most satisfying when partners possessed matching skill levels. Apparently, relational satisfaction arises in part when our styles match those of the people with whom we interact. This idea of "communication compatibility" is at the heart of eHarmony.ca, the highly successful Canadian dating website. Users of this service answer a battery of questions about themselves, the purpose of which is to determine their compatibility with other singles on the website.

The same principle holds true in the case of jealousy. Researchers have uncovered a variety of ways by which people deal with jealousy in their relationships.[51] These include keeping closer tabs on the partner, acting indifferent, decreasing affection, talking the matter over, and acting angry. The researchers found that no type of behaviour was effective or ineffective in every relationship, leading them to conclude that approaches that work with some people would be harmful to others. Findings like these demonstrate that competence comes from developing ways of interacting that work for you and for the other people involved.[52]

Competence Can Be Learned

To some degree, biology is destiny when it comes to communication style.[53] Studies of identical and fraternal twins suggest that traits including sociability, anger, and relaxation are partly a function of our genetic makeup. Fortunately, biology isn't the only factor that shapes how we communicate: communication is a set of skills that anyone can learn. As children grow, their ability to communicate effectively develops. For example, older children learn to use more sophisticated techniques of persuasion.[54] Along with maturity, systematic education (including classes such as the one in which you are now enrolled) can boost communicative competence. Even a modest amount of specialized training can produce dramatic results. After just 30 minutes of instruction, one group of observers became significantly more effective at detecting deception in interviews.[55] Even without systematic training, it's possible to develop communication skills through the processes of trial-and-error and observation. One study revealed that university students' communication competence increases over their undergraduate studies, regardless of whether or not they're enrolled in human communication courses.[56] Finally, we learn from our own successes and failures, as well as from observing other models—both positive and negative.

Characteristics of Competent Communicators

Although competent communication varies from one situation to another, scholars have identified several common denominators that characterize effective communication in most contexts.

A Wide Range of Behaviours

Effective communicators are able to choose their actions from a wide range of behaviours. To understand the importance of having a large communication repertoire, imagine that one of your friends repeatedly tells jokes that you find offensive. You could respond to these jokes in a number of ways. You could:

- Say nothing, figuring that the negative consequences of raising the subject would be greater than the benefits.
- Ask a third party to say something to your friend about the offensiveness of the jokes.
- Hint at your discomfort, hoping that your friend would get the point.
- Joke about your friend's insensitivity, counting on humour to soften the blow of your criticism.
- Express your discomfort in a straightforward way, asking your friend to stop telling the offensive jokes, at least around you.
- Simply demand that your friend stop.

With these possible responses at your disposal (and you can probably think of others as well), you could pick the one that had the best chance of success. But if you were able to use only one or two of these responses when raising a delicate issue—always keeping quiet or always hinting, for example—your chances of success would be much smaller. Indeed, many poor communicators are easy to spot by their limited range of responses. Some are chronic jokers; others are always belligerent; and still others are quiet in almost every situation. Like a pianist who knows only one tune or a chef who can prepare only a few dishes, these people are forced to rely on a small range of responses again and again, whether or not they are successful.

Ability to Choose the Most Appropriate Behaviour

Simply possessing a large array of communication skills isn't a guarantee of effectiveness. It's also necessary to know which of these skills will work

best in any particular situation. Choosing the best way to send a message is like choosing a gift: what is appropriate for one person won't be appropriate for another one at all. This ability to choose the best approach is essential because a response that works well in one setting might flop miserably in another one. Although it's impossible to say precisely how to act in every situation, there are at least three factors to consider when you are deciding which response to choose: the context, your goal, and the other person.

Skill at Performing Behaviours

After you have chosen the most appropriate way to communicate, it's still necessary to use the required skills effectively. There is a big difference between simply being aware of alternatives and skilfully putting them to work. Similarly, just reading about communication skills in the following chapters won't guarantee that you can start using them flawlessly. As with any other skills—those required to play an instrument or learn a sport, for example—the road to competence in communication is not a short one. You can expect that your first efforts at communicating differently will be awkward. After some practice you will become more skilful, although you will still have to think about the new way of speaking or listening. Finally, after practising the new skill again and again, you will find you can use it without conscious thought.

Empathy and Perspective

People have the best chance of developing an effective message when they understand the other person's point of view. And because others aren't always good at expressing their thoughts and feelings clearly, the ability to imagine how an issue might look from the other's point of view is an important skill. The value of taking the other's perspective is one reason why listening is so important. Not only does it help us to understand others, but it also gives us information to develop strategies about how to best influence them. Because empathy is such an important element of communicative competence, much of Chapter 2 is devoted to this topic.

Cognitive Complexity

Cognitive complexity is the ability to construct a variety of frameworks for viewing an issue. It is an ingredient of communication competence because it allows us to make sense of people by using a variety of perspectives. For instance, imagine that a long-time friend seems to be angry with you. One possible explanation is that your friend is offended by something you've done.

> *I witnessed recently a striking and barely believable example of such [inappropriate] behaviour at a wedding ceremony. One of the guests said loud enough for those of us on my side of the chapel to hear, "Think it through, Jerry" just at the point where the rabbi had asked Jerry if he took this woman to be his lawful wedded wife, according to (no less) the laws of Moses and Israel. So far as I could tell, the wedding guest was not drunk or embittered. He merely mistook the synagogue for Shea Stadium . . .*
>
> **Neil Postman, *Crazy Talk, Stupid Talk***

> **cognitive complexity** The ability to construct a variety of frameworks for viewing an issue.

Another possibility is that something upsetting has happened in another part of your friend's life. Or perhaps nothing at all is wrong, and you're just being overly sensitive. Researchers have found that the ability to analyze the behaviour of others in a variety of ways leads to greater "conversational sensitivity," increasing the chances of acting in ways that will produce satisfying results.[57]

Self-Monitoring

self-monitoring

The process of paying close attention to one's behaviour and using these observations to shape the way one behaves.

Psychologists use the term **self-monitoring** to describe the process of paying close attention to one's behaviour and using these observations to shape the way one behaves. Self-monitors are able to separate a part of their consciousness and observe their behaviour from a detached viewpoint, making observations such as:

- "I'm making a fool out of myself."
- "I'd better speak up now."
- "This approach is working well. I'll keep it up."

Chapter 2 explains how too much self-monitoring can be problematic. Still, people who are aware of their behaviour and the impression it makes are more skilful communicators than people who are low self-monitors.[58] For example, they are more accurate in judging others' emotional states, better at remembering information about others, less shy, and more assertive. By contrast, low self-monitors aren't even able to recognize their incompetence. One study revealed that poor communicators were blissfully ignorant of their shortcomings and more likely to overestimate their skill than were better communicators.[59] For example, experimental subjects who scored in the lowest quartile on joke-telling skill were more likely than funnier people to grossly overestimate their sense of humour.

Commitment to the Relationship

One feature that distinguishes effective communication in almost any context is commitment. People who seem to care about the relationship communicate better than those who don't.[60] This concern shows up in commitment to the other person and to the message being expressed.

Clarifying Misconceptions about Communication

Having spent time talking about what communication *is*, we also ought to identify some things it *is not*.[61] Recognizing some misconceptions is important, not only because they should be avoided by anyone knowledgeable about the subject but also because following them can get you into trouble.

Communication Does Not Always Require Complete Understanding

Most people operate on the implicit but flawed assumption that the goal of all communication is to maximize understanding between communicators. Although some understanding is necessary for us to comprehend one another's thoughts and feelings, there are some types of communication in which understanding, as we usually conceive it, is not the primary goal.[62] Consider the following examples:

- *Social rituals.* "How's it going?" you ask. "Great," the other person replies. The primary goal in exchanges like this one is mutual acknowledgement; there's obviously no serious attempt to exchange information.

- *Attempts to influence others.* A quick analysis of most TV commercials shows that they are aimed at persuading viewers to buy products, not to understand the content of the ad. In the same way, many of our attempts at persuading someone to act as we wish have little to do with getting the other person to understand what we want; they're designed to get that person to comply with our wishes.

- *Deliberate ambiguity and deception.* When you decline an unwanted invitation by saying "I can't make it," you probably want to create the impression that the decision is really beyond your control. If your goal was to be perfectly clear, you might say: "I don't want to get together. In fact, I'd rather do almost anything than accept your invitation." As Chapters 3 and 6 explain in detail, we often equivocate precisely because we want to obscure our true thoughts and feelings.

- *Coordinate action.* This term is used to *describe* situations in which participants interact smoothly with a high degree of satisfaction but without necessarily understanding one another perfectly.[63] **Coordination** without understanding can be satisfying in many important situations. Consider the many meanings of the phrases "I love you," "I admire you," "I feel great affection for you," "I want you," "I am grateful to you," "I feel guilty," "I want you to be faithful to me," or even "I hope you love me."[64] It's not hard to picture a situation in which partners gain great satisfaction—even over a lifetime—without completely understanding that the mutual love they profess is actually quite different for each of them.

> **coordination**
> Interaction in which participants interact smoothly, with a high degree of satisfaction but without necessarily understanding one another well.

At the conversational level, some scholars have compared coordinated communication to what musicians call "jamming."[65] In this sort of musical interaction, musicians play off one another, improvising melodies and riffs based on what others have contributed. There's no plan, and no attempt at understanding. Some conversations resemble this sort of jamming in several respects:

- *Coordination is more important than understanding.* Musicians in a jam session focus on and gain satisfaction from making music together, not on understanding one another. In coordinated conversations, satisfaction comes principally from being together—laughing, joking, exchanging confidences, and telling stories. The act of conversation is more important than its content.

- *Participants follow rules.* In a jam session, musicians agree on fundamentals such as the key in which they will play, the tempo, and the overall structure of the music. In coordinated communication, participants tacitly agree on things like the level of seriousness, the amount of time they will spend, and what topics are off limits. They may not understand the content of one another's messages, but they do understand how to behave with one another.

- *Everyone gets a solo.* Each musician in a jam session gets a time to take the lead, with others following. Conversations work only when the participants take turns, giving each other time to talk.
- *Sessions go to new places.* When musicians improvise, every session is unique. Likewise, no two conversations are identical in words or tone. One person's decision about what to say and how to say it triggers the other's response, which in turn results in a unique reaction. The communication is truly transactional, as described earlier.
- *Jamming builds rapport.* Musicians who jam with one another build unspoken bonds. In the same way, communicators who converse smoothly with one another feel a connection—even if the topic isn't very important or the participants don't completely understand one another.[66]

COMMUNICATING ONLINE

Effective E-mail

E-mail was one of the first killer apps of the internet. It changed the way we communicate by allowing us to use the detail of written communication and the immediacy of the spoken word. E-mail was the first tool that allowed our culture to break away from the dominance of print and toward an oral culture. In terms of formality it is somewhere between texting and a hand-written letter, but don't be fooled: the psychological impact of receiving an e-mail is very different from receiving a text message, particularly for people who grew up with print and written letters.

An e-mail has many of the features of a traditional letter. In the header, it contains all of the same information as a regular letter: address of sender and receiver and date. The content of an e-mail is also very similar to that of a letter: there is the salutation (Dear, Hello, To Whom It May Concern, etc.), the body, the closing (Yours sincerely, Yours, Kind regards, etc.), and end notations (P.S., c.c., etc.).

Many people who are very used to texting will make the error of not using complete sentences or proper punctuation in an e-mail. This is particularly annoying to those who grew up writing formal letters—it feels disrespectful to them. The minimum level of formality that you should use in an e-mail is a proper address that contains the person's name, like "Hello Alex," or "Hi Rachel," and a pleasant closing, which can be more formal like "Yours sincerely," or "Kind regards," or less formal like "Best," or "Thanks."

In terms of the content of your e-mail, bear in mind that people do not recall information they read on screens as well as they do information that is printed on paper. This means that you should keep your e-mails brief and your language punchy. Try to keep to one idea per paragraph and use numbered lists, if you have to make your e-mails longer.

A few things to avoid: using "texting talk" and short forms, using all lowercase letters, using overly familiar salutations with someone of higher rank than you, avoiding using a salutation, or not using your recipient's name in a salutation ("Hi," or "Hey there").

Ideally, you should only have one idea per e-mail, since it is asking a lot of your recipient to have them pore over their phone or their laptop screen to re-read your message to make sure they have remembered all the things you mentioned. Remember that people's online attention span is very fragmented and your e-mail is competing with texts.

Here is an example of a confusing e-mail:

Hi Simona,

Thank you for offering to help with the community workshop we're organizing this weekend. There are a few things we still need to accomplish before everyone finishes work on Friday. We need to make sure we have all the PowerPoint

Communication Is Not Always a Good Thing

For most people, belief in the value of communication rates somewhere close to loyalty, charity, or parenthood in their hierarchy of important values. In truth, communication is neither good nor bad in itself. Rather, its value comes from the way it is used. In this sense, communication is similar to fire: flames in the fireplace on a cold night keep you warm and create a cozy atmosphere, but the same flames can do serious damage if they spread into your living room. Communication can be a tool for expressing warm feelings and useful facts, but under different circumstances the same words and actions can cause both physical and emotional pain. An excellent example was recently related to one of the authors:

> Professor Sévigny, I recently met someone with whom I shared so many things in common. We loved the same cultural activities, found each other attractive, and enjoyed each other's company on the couple of dates that we went on.

presentation ready, the connector that links the computer to the digital projector, the name cards for everyone and pens for all participants.

Oh, on another note, I spoke with your little brother and he was wondering if you could ask Father David to get him out of altar boy service this Sunday at the Cathedral so that he can help us with the workshop. He can't make it to Sunday Mass, so he will be going on Saturday night.

Another thing—could you speak with our new boss and tell him that I would really like to talk to him? It's important that I meet him to explain this community workshop idea and get his approval for future workshops.

Many thanks,

Alex

Here is the same e-mail, but reorganized and easier to follow:

Hi Simona,

Thank you for offering to help with the community workshop we're organizing this weekend. There are three things we still need to accomplish before everyone finishes work on Friday.

1. We need to make sure we have:
   - the PowerPoint presentation ready;
   - the connector that links the computer to the digital projector;
   - the name cards for everyone; and
   - pens for all participants.

2. I spoke with your little brother and he was wondering if you could ask Father David to get him out of altar boy service this Sunday at the cathedral so that he can help us with the workshop. (Note: He can't make it to Sunday Mass, so he will be going on Saturday night.)

3. Could you speak with our new boss and tell him that I would really like to talk to him? It's important that I meet him to explain this community workshop idea and get his approval for future workshops.

Many thanks,

Alex

Remember Marshall McLuhan's famous adage that "the medium is the message." An e-mail is different from a text message; write e-mails with that in mind and you will advance in both your personal and professional relationships.

UNDERSTANDING COMMUNICATION TECHNOLOGY

Crisis PR: In Vancouver, Social Media Was a Riot

Social media has drastically changed both the way we report the news and the way we receive it. In his report on the role of social media in Vancouver's Stanley Cup riots, Jeff Domansky examines both the good and the bad aspects of new communication technology. As you read his article, consider whether you feel that social media's role in reporting live events and in dispensing justice is a positive or a negative development.

Social media played a huge role in the [2013] post-Stanley Cup [game] riot in Vancouver last week. It's also being used by residents to defend and restore their beautiful city's reputation. It makes a fascinating PR study of social media in a crisis.

The Vancouver Canucks had a storybook NHL season. Though they lost to the Boston Bruins, it was one of the best Stanley Cup series in years. That didn't stop crowds of drunken young people intent on creating trouble after the seventh and deciding game.

As more than 100,000 fans gathered downtown, things turned ugly fast, escalating into a terrible riot seen on newscasts, in newspapers, and on social media around the world.

After just three days, there were [nearly 23,000] news stories on Google.

Like many recent large-scale global political events and natural disasters, social media enabled live coverage of the riots. I've gathered a selection of these resources below. They tell a compelling news story both for residents and those far away.

Some of these stories and pictures will touch you deeply whether you're a Vancouver resident or just wanting insight into this news story. As in Egypt and Libya, there are tragic incidents balanced by heartwarming stories of humanity and community spirit.

Social Media during the Riot

Let's look at how social media played in the lead up to and during the riot:

- Texting, instant messaging and Tweet Ups contributed to huge post-game crowds downtown.
- Social media fanned the flames of the riot through text, video and photo sharing; instant messaging; tweets; e-mails; and live posts by citizens and journalists.
- Vancouver police used live tweets to encourage public to report crimes via Crime Stoppers and other resources.

- VPD police suggested text messages be used to report crime tips: "BCTIP" to 274637.
- Mob mentality and the presence of media, thousands of cell phone cameras, video cams and other cameras seemed to encourage escalating violence.
- Bystanders were egging on drunken youths, encouraging damage, vandalism, and looting.
- Many of the mostly-young people committing crimes seemed to be further encouraged by the celebrity; most were not concerned, or failed to recognize, they were being captured on all kinds of cameras and social media.

It was difficult not to continue watching local media coverage well into the late night and early morning hours. Coverage was shocking yet compelling whether you followed it on TV, Twitter, Facebook, e-mail or by telephone with friends living in the area.

Post-Riot Social Media

After the riots, there was fascination mixed with shock and disbelief as media and social media coverage continued nonstop.

Social media channels were being used by all kinds of individuals and organizations:

- City of Vancouver newsroom with news releases and instructions for volunteer cleanup;
- Vancouver Police Department newsroom with news releases and instructions for citizens to submit video and photos of vandalism and crime for police investigation;
- mainstream media news coverage of the riot, the cleanup and of the embarrassment playing on national and global media;
- extensive blogging and analysis by residents and bloggers near and far;
- Flickr features hundreds of dramatic photo uploads;
- Twitter coverage continues minute-by-minute and trends on several related topics;
- numerous Facebook walls suggest visitors identify pictures and video of those committing crimes;
- a lynch mob mentality seems to prevail in many comments;
- full-page newspaper ads run in both daily newspapers, by pop singer and Vancouver resident Michael Buble and

The Bay department store, each thanking volunteers and encouraging pride in the city;

- YouTube video clips of the riot are receiving tens of thousands of views; several have more than 130,000 views already;
- mainstream media and their social media sites continued coverage and post-riot analysis;
- some of the blog posts are as passionate and well-written as any journalism anywhere;
- police continue to use social media for investigations;
- some riot participants have posted online apologies publicly or anonymously and others have begun turning themselves in to police;
- The Bay department store held a free morning pancake breakfast to thank clean-up volunteers, who were invited through social media; and
- the latest development has been a series of widely-circulated public apologies, in both mainstream and social media.

The efforts have drawn applause and criticism, as well as the expected deluge of vigilante-type comments.

This is really just the tip of the iceberg in a dramatic story. It raises interesting theories and points of view about the impact, and outcomes of news and events covered and influenced by social media.

The Vancouver Sun daily newspaper reported on some of the more dramatic outcomes of social media including:

- a suburban doctor and his family forced to leave home and fearful of community backlash because of their son's actions, while their son faces losing scholarship and a position on the national water polo team;
- several employees being fired for Facebook postings;
- a University of BC donor threatening to withdraw donations unless a female student, photographed looting a tuxedo store, is expelled;
- a 20-year-old professional mountain biker losing sponsors; and
- several businesses received heavy criticism for the behavior of several of their employees identified as riot participants.

As the newspaper [*The Vancouver Sun*] noted:

Vigilante retribution delivered via social media and online "name and shame" sites is delivering what may well be life sentences to riot participants while the legal system is just beginning to work its way toward due process.

The outcome of social media and its role in this riot could have far-reaching consequences:

Christopher Schneider, a UBC sociologist and expert in criminology and social media, said the massive online reaction to the Vancouver riots is unprecedented and potentially as groundbreaking as WikiLeaks. "There will be a lot of fallout, and we will probably see a lot of case law coming out of this."

It will also, perhaps, change the way citizens move in the virtual world, forever. "The mob mentality has moved into cyberspace for the first time."

Vancouver police received more than 3500 e-mail tips from the public within three days [including]:

- 53 with videos attached;
- 676 with links to YouTube;
- 708 with images attached;
- 1011 with hyperlinks to other social media sites other than YouTube (mostly Facebook);
- 344 e-mails contain only text;
- 280 Crime Stoppers tips received; and
- 900 additional e-mails have been received by the VPD Public Affairs Section.

The riot and social media have spun off several new terms including "apoloblogs," "tweet bleats" and other random apologies.

Jeff Domansky is a writer, social media consultant, and CEO of Social Impakt Consulting Group in Vancouver, BC

QUESTION: The author discusses how social media had a special role to play in allowing the Vancouver riots to spread quickly. What are some other examples of communication technologies that are of great benefit in some circumstances but which reverse into socially destructive uses in the wrong hands?

We had exchanged over 50 e-mails, almost daily. But one night, I had had the worst day of my life—bad at work, bad at school, bad at the charity I volunteer with—and I asked her some prying, judgmental questions over text message. She was insulted and told me to go to sleep because I had a lot of work to do in the morning. I felt heartsick about having insulted her and then sent her an "'e-mail in text messages." I guess there were about 30 messages in total. My last one said: "I should really have sent this as an e-mail—all these text messages are awkward." Well, I woke up the next day to find a text message from her saying "I woke up to over 30 text messages from you! That is more than creepy to me. I would appreciate it if you didn't contact me anymore." Professor Sévigny, you don't know how much I regret sending those text messages instead of an e-mail!

No Single Person or Event Causes Another's Reaction

Although communicative skill can often make the difference between pleasant and unpleasant outcomes, it's a mistake to suggest that any single thing we say or do causes an outcome. Many factors play a role in how others will react to your communication in a given situation. Suppose, for example, that you lose your temper and say something to a friend that you regret as soon as the words escape your lips. Your friend's reaction will depend on a whole host of events besides your unjustified remark: her frame of mind at the moment (uptight or mellow), elements of her personality (judgmental or forgiving), your relational history (supportive or hostile), and her knowledge of any factors in your life that might have contributed to your unfair remark. Because communication is a transactional, ongoing, and collaborative process, it's usually a mistake to think that any event occurs in a vacuum.

Communication Will Not Solve All Problems

"If I could just communicate better . . ." is the sad refrain of many unhappy people who believe that if they could just express themselves better, their relationships would improve. Though this is sometimes true, it's an exaggeration to say that communicating—even communicating clearly—is a guaranteed remedy for relationship woes.

🎥◀ COMMUNICATION ON-SCREEN

Pontypool (2008)
Directed by Bruce McDonald.

The idea that communication isn't always desirable is taken to a rather exaggerated but entertaining end in this Canadian independent film, released under the apt tagline "Shut Up or Die." *Pontypool* reimagines the basic zombie set-up with an innovative twist. Unlike other recent portrayals (*28 Days Later, Dawn of the Dead*) where the "affliction" is treated as if it were a physical disease, the crazed hordes that overrun the town of Pontypool, Ontario, spread their infection to others through speech. Literalizing the colloquial metaphor that ideas "go viral" in our communication-rich world, the film's cast is presented with a truly unique puzzle. After all, nobody's written a survival handbook for dealing with a linguistic epidemic.

Meanings Rest in People, Not in Words

We hinted that meanings rest in people, not in words, when we said earlier that the symbols we use to communicate are arbitrary. It's a mistake to think that, just because you use a word in one way, others will do so, too.[67] Sometimes differing interpretations of symbols are easily caught, as when we might first take the statement "He's loaded" to mean that the subject has had too much to drink, only to find out that he is quite wealthy (and sober). In other cases, however, the ambiguity of words and non-verbal behaviours isn't so apparent, and thus can have more far-reaching consequences. Remember, for instance, a time when someone said to you, "I'll be honest and tell you

the truth," and only later did you learn that those words hid precisely the opposite fact. In Chapter 3 we'll look more closely at the problems that come from mistakenly assuming that meanings rest in words.

Communication Is Not Simple

Most people assume that communication is an aptitude that people develop without the need for training—rather like breathing. After all, we've been swapping ideas with one another since early childhood, and there are lots of people who communicate pretty well without ever taking a class on the subject. Though this picture of communication as a natural ability seems accurate, it's actually a gross oversimplification.[68]

Throughout history there have been cases of infants being raised without human contact. In all these cases, the children were initially unable to communicate with others when brought into society. Only after extensive teaching (and not even then, in some cases) were they able to speak and understand language in ways we take for granted. But what about the more common cases of effective communicators who have had no formal training and yet are skilful at creating and understanding messages? The answer to this question lies in the fact that not all education occurs in a classroom. Many people learn to communicate skilfully because they have been exposed to models of such behaviour by those around them. This principle of modelling explains why children who grow up in homes with stable relationships between family members have a greater chance of developing such relationships themselves. They know how to do so because they've seen effective communication in action.

Does the existence of these good communicators mean that certain people don't need courses like the one you're taking? Hardly. Even the best communicators aren't perfect: they

> **Cultural Idiom**
> **take for granted**
> To give little thought to something.

often suffer the frustration of being unable to get a message across effectively, and they frequently misunderstand others. Furthermore, even the most successful people you know can probably identify ways in which their relationships could profit by better communication. These facts show that communication skills are rather like athletic ability: even the most inept of us can learn to be more effective with training and practice, and those who are talented can always become better.

More Communication Is Not Always Better

Although it's certainly true that not communicating enough is a mistake, there are also situations when too much communication is wrong. Sometimes excessive communication is simply unproductive, as when we "talk a problem to death," going over the same ground again and again without making any headway. And there are times when communicating too much can actually aggravate a problem. We've all had the experience of "talking ourselves into a hole"— making a bad situation worse by pursuing it too far. As McCroskey and Wheeless put it, "More and more negative communication merely leads to more and more negative results."[69]

There are even times when no communication is the best course. Any good salesperson will tell you that there comes a time when it's best to stop talking and let the customer think about the product. And when two people are angry and hurt, they may say things they don't mean and will later regret. At times like these it's probably best to spend a little time cooling off, thinking about what to say and how to say it.

One key to successful communication, then, is to share an adequate amount of information in a skilful manner. Teaching you how to decide what information is adequate and what constitutes skilful behaviour is one major goal of this book.

Summary

Communication is →

This chapter began by defining communication as it will be examined in this text: a process involving communicators occupying different but overlapping environments and simultaneously sending and receiving messages, many of which are distorted by physical and psychological noise.

It introduced four communication contexts that will be covered in the rest of the book: intrapersonal, dyadic, small-group, and public. The chapter also identified several types of needs that communication satisfies: physical, identity, social, and practical.

Linear and a transactional communication models were developed, demonstrating the superiority of the transactional model in representing the process-oriented nature of human interaction.

competent communicators

The chapter went on to explore the difference between effective and ineffective exchanges by discussing communication competence, showing that there is no single correct way to behave and that competence is situational, that it is relational in nature, and that it can be learned. Competent communicators were described as those who are able to choose and perform appropriately from a wide range of behaviours; they are cognitively complex self-monitors, who can take the perspective of others and who have committed to important relationships.

After spending most of the chapter talking about what communication is, we concluded by discussing what it is not by refuting several common misconceptions. We demonstrated that communication doesn't always require complete understanding and that it is not always a good thing that will solve every problem. We showed that more communication is not always better; that meanings are in people, not in words; that no single person or event causes another's reactions; and that communication is neither simple nor easy.

Key Terms

channel   15
cognitive complexity   25
communication   5
communication competence   22
coordination   27
decode   1
dyad   7
dyadic communication   7
encode   15
environment   17
feedback   18
interpersonal communication   7

intrapersonal communication   6
linear communication model   15
mass communication   9
mediated communication   15
message   15
noise   16
public communication   8
receiver   15
self-monitoring   26
sender   15
small-group communication   8
symbol   6
transactional communication model   18

Activities

A. Analyzing Your Communication Behaviour

Prove to yourself that communication is both frequent and important by observing your interactions during a single day. Record every occasion on which you are involved in some sort of communication as it is defined on pages 4–9. Based on your findings, answer the following questions:

1. What percentage of your waking day is involved in communication?

2. What percentage of time do you spend communicating in the following contexts:
   a. intrapersonal,
   b. dyadic,
   c. small-group, and
   d. public.

3. What percentage of your communication is devoted to satisfying each of the following types of needs:
   a. physical,   *study each type in details*
   b. identity,
   c. social, and
   d. practical.

   (Note that you might try to satisfy more than one type at a time.)

   Based on your analysis, describe 5 to 10 ways you would like to communicate more effectively. For each item on your list of goals, describe who is involved (e.g., "my parents," "people I meet when I'm out") and how you would like to communicate differently (e.g., "act less defensively when criticized," "speak up instead of waiting to be approached"). Use this list to focus your studies as you read the remainder of this book.

B. Choosing the Most Effective Communication Channel

Decide which communication channel would be most effective in each of the following situations. Be prepared to explain your answer.

1. An instructor criticizes you for copying work from other sources when the work was your own. You are furious, and you don't intend to accept the charge without responding. Which approach(es) would be best for you to use?
   a. Send your instructor an e-mail or write a letter explaining your objections.
   b. Telephone your instructor and explain your position.
   c. Schedule a personal meeting with your instructor.

2. You've just returned from a semester abroad and want your grandparents to be able to view the photos you've posted to Instagram. How can you ensure that they can access the site?
   a. Demonstrate the website at an upcoming family get-together.
   b. E-mail them a link to the site.
   c. Phone them to inquire about their ability to access websites.

3. You want to be sure the members of your office team are able to use the new voice mail system. What should you do?
   a. Send each employee an instruction manual for the system.
   b. Ask employees to e-mail any questions about the system.
   c. Conduct one or more training sessions where employees can try out the system and you can clear up any questions.

4. You've just been given two free tickets to tomorrow night's concert. What is the best way to find out whether your friend can go with you?
   a. Send her an e-mail and ask for a quick reply.
   b. Leave her a voice mail asking her to phone you back.
   c. Send her a text message.

C. Increasing Your Communicative Competence

Prove to yourself that communication competence can be increased by following these steps.

1. Identify a situation in which you are dissatisfied with your present communication skill.

2. Identify at least three separate approaches you could take in this situation that might be more successful than the one you have taken in the past. If you are at a loss for alternatives, consider how other people you have observed (both real and fictional characters) have handled similar situations.

3. From these three alternatives, choose the one you think would work best for you.

4. Consider how you could become more skilful at performing your chosen approach. For example, you might rehearse it alone or with friends, or you might gain pointers from watching others.

5. Consider how to get feedback on how well you perform your new approach. For instance, you might ask friends to watch you. In some cases, you might even be able to ask the people involved how you did. This systematic approach to increasing your communicative competence isn't the only way to change, but it is one way to take the initiative in communicating more effectively.

Further Reading

Coupland, Nikolas, Howard Giles, and John M. Wiemann, eds, *Miscommunication and Problematic Talk* **(Newbury Park, CA: Sage, 1991).**
This collection of readings explores the many ways in which communication can be unsuccessful. Chapters focus on communication problems involving gender, age, physical disabilities, and culture. Other selections look at communication problems in different settings, such as medical, legal, and organizational.

McKay, Matthew, *Messages: The Communication Skills Book***, 3rd edn (Oakland, CA: New Harbinger, 2009).**
This comprehensive book on human communication (it covers listening, language, and conflict resolution, to name just a few topics) is very practical. The authors are all mental-health professionals and include exercises throughout the book to personalize the reading experience.

Rundell Carroll, Nannette, *The Communication Problem Solver* **(Washington D.C.: AMACOM, 2011).**
This book helps people discover and analyze their communication skills and provides basic problem-solving methods to resolve the issues that lessen productivity in the work environment. This book uses many relevant examples to illustrate its points.

Study Questions

1. Describe an incident that illustrates how communication is a symbolic process.

2. Using your own experiences, describe two or three examples from everyday life of each type of communication: intrapersonal, dyadic, interpersonal, small-group, public, and mass.

3. Discuss one or more typical communication transactions intended to satisfy each type of need: physical, identity, social, and practical.

4. Use an incident from everyday life to illustrate the transactional process of communication (pp. 18–21).

5. Use the characteristics of competent communication (pp. 21–6) to evaluate one transaction you have observed or experienced.

6. Show how avoiding common misconceptions about communication (pp. 26–34) can make relationships more satisfying.

7. Describe a situation in which texting has had negative consequences for a person, a company, or a government. How could these consequences have been avoided?

2

Perception, the Self, and Communication

After studying the material in this chapter . . .

You should understand:

✔ how common perceptual tendencies and situational factors influence perception;

✔ the influence of culture on perception and the self-concept;

✔ the importance of empathy in communication;

✔ the communicative influences that shape the self-concept;

✔ how self-fulfilling prophecies influence behaviour;

✔ how the process of identity management can result in presentation of multiple selves; and

✔ the reasons for and the ethical dimensions of identity management.

You should be able to:

✔ explain how the tendencies outlined in this chapter have led you to develop distorted perceptions of yourself and others;

✔ use perception-checking and empathy to be more accurate in your perceptions of others' behaviour;

✔ identify the ways you influence the self-concepts of others and the ways significant others influence your self-concept;

✔ identify the communication-related self-fulfilling prophecies that you have imposed on yourself, that others have imposed on you, and that you have imposed on others; and

✔ describe the various identities you attempt to create and the ethical merit of your identity management strategies.

Chapter Highlights

Our perceptions of others shape the way we communicate with them. Several factors influence these perceptions:

» our success at constructing shared narratives through communication;

» our tendency to make several perceptual errors;

» factors arising from our own experience and from our prior relationship with that person;

» our cultural background; and

» our ability to empathize.

The skill of perception-checking can help us clarify mistaken perceptions, leading to a shared narrative and smoother communication.

Communication depends on the way we perceive ourselves, as well as others. You will appreciate the importance of the self as you read about:

» how communication shapes the self-concept;

» the way culture shapes our self-perceptions;

» the role of personality in shaping our perceptions; and

» how self-fulfilling prophecies can lead either to more satisfying or to less productive communication.

As Chapter 1 explained, one reason we communicate is to persuade others to view ourselves as we want to be seen. To understand how this principle of identity management operates, Chapter 2 explains:

» the difference between perceived and presenting selves;

» how we communicate to manage our identities, via both face-to-face and mediated channels; and

» reasons why we communicate to manage our identities.

Simple Truths, Important Lessons: How Communication Shapes Perception

Consider the following scenarios:

- Two students, one Métis and the other English Canadian, are discussing their latest reading assignment for their Canadian history class. "Louis Riel was quite a guy," the English-Canadian student says sincerely to his classmate. "You must be very proud of him." The Métis student is offended at what sounds like a condescending remark.
- A mother and daughter are exchanging dinner plans via text. The daughter sends a message asking if her boyfriend can join but doesn't notice an awkward auto-spelling error before hitting "send." The mother doesn't comment, but cannot see her daughter or her boyfriend in the same light.
- A student is practising his first speech for a public speaking class in front of several friends. "This is a stupid topic," he laments. The others assure him that the topic is interesting and that the speech sounds good. Later in class he becomes flustered because he believes that his speech is awful. As a result of his unenthusiastic delivery, he receives a low grade on the assignment.
- In biology class, a shy but earnest student mistakenly uses the term *orgasm* instead of *organism* when answering the professor's question. The entire class breaks into raucous laughter. The student remains quiet for the remainder of the semester.
- Despite her nervousness, a graduating student does her best to look and sound confident in a job interview. Although she leaves the session convinced she botched a big chance, a few days later she is surprised to receive a job offer.
- A young woman allows a friend to take silly photos of her on a "girls' night out" at the pub and to post them to Facebook. During an interview for a teaching position in a religious school, one of her interviewers mentions the photos and questions her personal judgment. She is deeply embarrassed and messes up the interview.
- A man gets into a heated conversation with an ex-girlfriend via Twitter, in which he says some very personal and demeaning things. Feeling remorseful a few hours later, he deletes all his offensive tweets and begs her forgiveness. However, she has already posted his tweets to Facebook and to her blog. His reputation is diminished, as many of his business contacts have seen his abusive comments. He contacts her and says that he thought the tweets were "just between them." She feels bad for having posted them, but the damage is done.

You're probably familiar with stories like these, but would you believe that each of them illustrates principles that affect our communication more than almost any others we'll discuss in this book? For example:

- Two or more people often perceive the world in radically different ways, which presents major challenges for successful communication.
- The set of beliefs each of us holds about ourselves—our self-concept—has a powerful effect on our own communication behaviour.
- The messages we send can shape others' self-concepts and thus influence their communication.
- The image we present to the world varies from one situation to another.

Cultural Idiom
botched
Destroyed, ruined.

These simple truths play a role in nearly all the important messages we send and receive. The goal of this chapter is to demonstrate the significance of these truths by describing the nature of perception and showing how it influences the way we view ourselves and how we relate to others.

Perceiving Others

Suppose you woke up tomorrow in another person's body. Imagine how different the world would seem if you were 15 years older or younger, a member of the opposite sex or a different ethnic group, far more or less intelligent, vastly more attractive or ugly, more wealthy or poverty-stricken. It doesn't take much imagination to understand that the world feels like a different place to each of us, depending on our physical condition as well as our social and personal backgrounds.

Narratives and Perception

Each of us has our own story of the world, and often our stories are quite different from those of others. A family member or roommate might think your sense of humour is inappropriate, whereas you think you're quite clever. You might blame an unsatisfying class on the instructor, whom you think is an arrogant bore who likes nothing more than the sound of his own voice. On the other hand, the instructor might characterize the students as superficial and lazy and blame the class environment on them. (Chapter 3 will examine the sort of name-calling embedded in the previous sentences.)

"I know what you're thinking, but let me offer a competing narrative."

Social scientists call the personal stories that we and others create to make sense of our personal world **narratives**.[1] In a few pages we will look at how a tool called "perception-checking" can help bridge the gap between different narratives. For now, though, the important point is that differing narratives can lead to problematic communication.

> **narratives**
> The stories people create and use to make sense of their personal worlds.

After they take hold, narratives offer a framework for explaining behaviour and shaping future communication. One study of sense-making in organizations illustrates how the process operates on the job.[2] Researchers tracked down employees who had participated in office discussions about cases where a fellow worker had received "differential treatment" from management in matters such as time off, pay, or work assignments. The researchers then analyzed the conversations that employees held with their colleagues about the differential treatment. The analysis revealed that, during these conversations, employees created and reinforced the meaning of the co-worker's behaviour and management's response. For example, consider Jane, who has a habit of taking long lunches. As Jane's co-workers discuss her behaviours, they might decide that her long lunches aren't fair, or they might agree that they aren't a big deal. Either way, the co-workers' narratives of office events define those events. Once their perceptions have been defined in this way, co-workers tend to seek reinforcement for their perceptions by keeping a mental scorecard rating their fellow employees and management. ("Did you notice that Luis came in late again today?' 'Did you hear that Nadia was picked to go on that trip to Nunavut?")

COMMUNICATION ON-SCREEN

Argo (2012)
Directed by Ben Affleck.

Ben Affleck's third directed film depicts the heroic efforts of CIA operative Tony Mendez (Affleck) in rescuing six US diplomats from revolutionary Iran in the late 1970s. The film was nearly unanimously praised by American critics as a captivating thriller; however, many Canadian and international critics felt that the incredibly brave efforts of Canadians, such as Ken Taylor, were underplayed or misrepresented in order to "Americanize" the story. Furthermore, the film states that both the British and New Zealand Embassies had turned away the Americans, when this simply isn't true, as the British even housed the Americans for a time before the site was deemed too dangerous. Despite this, *Argo* took home the Best Picture Oscar at the 66th Academy Awards. Although undoubtedly an entertaining film, how does Argo and its constructed narrative effect audience perception regarding a real historical event?

Cultural Idiom
jibe
To agree.

yardsticks
Standards of comparison.

Although most of us like to think we form judgments about others on our own, the research on sense-making in organizations suggests that sense-making is an *interactive* process. And, as Western University psychologist Anne Wilson suggests, any errors of judgment we may be guilty of in the course of our sense-making do not always reflect cognitive shortcomings but the common goals and strategies we all rely on to understand our world and generate meaningful conversation.[3] In other words, reality in the workplace and elsewhere isn't "out there;" rather, we create it with others through communication.

Research on long-term happy marriages demonstrates that shared narratives don't have to be accurate to be powerful.[4] Couples who report being happily married after 50 or more years seem to collude in a relational narrative that doesn't always jibe with the facts. They might agree that they rarely have conflict even though objective analysis reveals that they do have their share of disagreements and challenges. Without overtly agreeing to do so, they choose to blame outside forces or unusual circumstances for problems instead of attributing responsibility to one another. They offer the most charitable interpretations of one another's behaviour, each believing that his or her spouse acts with good intentions when things don't go well. They seem willing to forgive, or even forget, transgressions. Examining this research, one scholar wonders:

> Should we conclude that happy couples have a poor grip on reality? Perhaps they do, but is the reality of one's marriage better known by outside onlookers than by the players themselves? The conclusion is evident. One key to a long happy marriage is to tell yourself and others that you have one and then to behave as though you do![5]

Common Perceptual Tendencies

Shared narratives may be desirable, but they can be hard to achieve. Some of the greatest obstacles to understanding and agreement arise from errors in what psychologists call *attribution*—the process of attaching meaning to behaviour. We attribute meaning to both our own actions and the actions of others, but we often use different yardsticks. Research has uncovered several perceptual errors that can lead to inaccurate attributions—and to troublesome communication.[6] By becoming aware of these errors, we can guard against them and avoid unnecessary conflicts.

We Often Judge Ourselves More Charitably than We Judge Others

In an attempt to convince ourselves and others that the positive face we show to the world is true, we tend to judge ourselves in the most generous terms possible. Social scientists have labelled this tendency the **self-serving bias**.[7] When others suffer, we often blame the problem

self-serving bias
The tendency to interpret and explain information in a way that casts the perceiver in the most favourable light.

on their personal qualities. On the other hand, when we suffer, we find explanations outside ourselves. This "cognitive conceit" occurs when we overestimate the accuracy of our beliefs and judgments, and reconstruct the memory of our past in self-serving ways. The more favourably we perceive some dimension of ourselves—our intelligence or our athletic ability, for example—the more we will tend to use that dimension as a basis for judging others.[8] Consider a few examples:

- When others botch a job, we might think they weren't listening well or trying hard enough; but when we botch a job, it's because the directions weren't clear or we weren't given enough time.
- When someone lashes out angrily, we say he or she is being moody or too sensitive; but when we lash out, it's because we're under a lot of stress at the moment.
- When someone gets caught speeding, we say she should have been more careful; but when we get caught, we deny or downplay the speeding infraction, or rhyme off a list of factors we think should have mitigated the offence under the circumstances.

> **Cultural Idiom**
> **lash out**
> To attack with words.
>
> **rhyme off**
> To recite a series of items rapidly and spontaneously.

The egocentric tendency to rate ourselves more favourably than others would has been demonstrated experimentally.[9] In one study, members of a random sample of men were asked to rank themselves on their ability to get along with others.[10] Defying mathematical laws, all subjects—every last one—put themselves in the top half of the population. Sixty per cent of the subjects rated themselves in the top 10 per cent of the population, and an amazing 25 per cent believed they were in the top 1 per cent. In the same study, 70 per cent of the men ranked their leadership skills in the top 25 per cent of the population, whereas only 2 per cent thought they were below average. Sixty per cent said they were in the top 25 per cent in athletic abilities, whereas only 6 per cent viewed themselves as below average. How could this be? In another study, researchers discovered that people tend to process and recall information about themselves more efficiently than they do information about others. As a result, they perceive themselves more favourably.[11]

This data suggests we often give ourselves more credit than we deserve. A famous example of this self-serving bias surrounds Frederick Banting and John Macleod, who shared the 1923 Nobel Prize for their role in the discovery of insulin.[12] Banting was schooled at the University of Toronto, and taught at the University of Western Ontario, before returning to his alma mater to teach Pharmacology. Macleod, a Scottish graduate of the University of Aberdeen, also taught at the University of Toronto. Each man thought the discovery of insulin was primarily his own. Banting claimed that Macleod—who headed the lab, provided one of his research assistants (Charles Best), and actively supported the research—was more of a hindrance than a help. And Macleod did not mention Banting's name, let alone his contribution to the research, when speaking in public about the discovery.

> *egotist, n.*
>
> *A person of low taste, more interested in himself than in me.*
>
> **Ambrose Bierce, *The Devil's Dictionary***

Evidence such as this suggests how uncharitable attitudes toward others can affect communication. Your harsh opinions of others can lead to judgmental messages, and self-serving defenses of your own actions can result in a defensive response when others question your behaviour.[13]

We Are Influenced by What Is Most Obvious

Every time we encounter another person, we are bombarded with more information than we can possibly take in. You can appreciate this by spending two or three minutes just reporting on what you can observe about another person through your five senses. ("Now I see you blinking your eyes;" "Now I notice you smiling;" "Now I hear you laugh and then sigh;" "Now

I notice you're wearing a red shirt.") You will find that the list seems almost endless and that every time you seem to be nearing the end, a new observation presents itself.

Faced with this tidal wave of sense data, we need to whittle down the amount of information we will use to make sense of others. There are three factors that cause us to notice some messages and ignore others: we pay attention to stimuli that are *intense* (loud music, people dressed in bright clothing), *repetitious* (dripping faucets, persistent people), or *contrastive* (a normally happy person who acts grumpy or vice versa). *Motives* help determine what information we select from our environment. If you're anxious about being late for a date, you'll notice whatever clocks may be around you; if you're hungry, you'll become aware of any restaurants, markets, and billboards advertising food in your path.

Motives also determine how we perceive people. For example, in 2013, BC Liberal Premier Christy Clark came under fire when a plan to woo ethnic voters was leaked by the competing NDP party. The plan, described by fellow Liberal party members as having made "the 'ethnic vote' a joke," seemingly condoned the use of public money to help spread political messages to targeted audiences and achieve "quick wins" by tailoring news and targeting the corrections of "historical wrongs." Norman Ruff, a University of Victoria professor described this scandal as fitting with the image of BC Liberals being out of touch. "The reason that it seems to be sticking so hard and is likely to hold right into [the election season], is that it dovetails with the image of the BC Liberal brand that has already been cemented in the public's mind . . . that's what makes it so dangerous." If intense, repetitious, or contrastive information was the most important thing to know about others, there would be no problem. But the most noticeable behaviour of others isn't always the most important. For example,

- When two children (or adults, for that matter) fight, it might be a mistake to blame the one who lashes out first. Perhaps the other one was at least equally responsible, by teasing or refusing to co-operate.
- You might complain about an acquaintance whose malicious gossiping or arguing has become annoying, forgetting that, by previously tolerating that kind of behaviour, you have been at least partly responsible.
- You might blame an unhappy working situation on your manager, overlooking factors beyond her control, such as a change in the economy, policies imposed by upper management, or the demands of customers or other workers.
- When you are working with someone who is obviously of a different ethnic or religious background from your own, you may pay more attention to superficial things, such as his or her physical appearance or manner of dress, than you do to his or her work or contribution to your common project.

We Cling to First Impressions, Even If Wrong

Labelling people according to our first impressions is an inevitable part of the perception process. These labels are a way of making interpretations. "She seems cheerful;" "He seems sincere;" "They sound awfully conceited."

If they're accurate, impressions like these can be useful ways of deciding how best to respond to people in the future. Problems arise, however, when the labels we attach are inaccurate, because after we form an opinion of someone, we tend to hang on to it and make any conflicting information fit our image.

Suppose, for instance, you mention the name of your new neighbour to a friend. "Oh, I know him," your friend replies. "He seems nice at first, but it's all an act." Perhaps this appraisal is off-base. The neighbour may have changed since your friend knew him, or perhaps your friend's judgment is simply unfair. Whether the judgment is accurate or not, once you have accepted your friend's evaluation, it will probably influence the way you respond to the neighbour. You'll look for examples of the insincerity you've heard about—and you'll probably find them. Even if the neighbour were a saint, you would be likely to interpret his behaviour in ways that fit your expectations. "Sure he seems nice," you might think, "but it's probably just a front." Of course, this sort of suspicion can become a self-fulfilling prophecy, transforming a genuinely nice person into someone who truly becomes an undesirable neighbour as he reacts to your suspicious behaviour.

Given the almost unavoidable tendency to form first impressions, the best advice we can offer is to keep an open mind and be willing to change your opinion as events prove that the first impressions were mistaken.

Cultural Idiom
a front
A pretense.

We Tend to Assume That Others Are Similar to Us

People commonly imagine that others have the same attitudes and motives that they do. For example, research shows that people with low self-esteem imagine that others view them unfavourably, whereas people who like themselves imagine that others like them, too.[14] Another study points to our tendency to arrive at a "false consensus" by believing, with certainty, that our opinions and behaviours—in particular those that are undesirable—are much more common than they are.[15] The frequently mistaken assumption that others' views are similar to our own applies in a wide range of situations. For example:

- You've heard an off-colour joke that you found funny. You might assume that it won't offend a somewhat conservative friend. It does.
- You've been bothered by an instructor's tendency to stray off topic during lectures. If you were a professor, you'd want to know if anything you were doing was creating problems for your students, so you decide that your instructor will probably be grateful for some constructive criticism. Unfortunately, you're wrong.
- You lost your temper with a friend a week ago and said some things you regret. In fact, if someone said those things to you, you would consider the relationship finished. Imagining that your friend feels the same way, you avoid making contact. However, your friend actually feels that he was partly responsible and has avoided you because he thinks you're the one who wants to end things.

Examples like these show that others don't always think or feel the way we do, and assuming that similarities exist can lead to problems. For instance, one study revealed that men consider women who initiate first dates to be more interested in sex than they (the women) actually are.[16]

How can you find out the other person's real position? Sometimes by asking directly, sometimes by checking with others, and sometimes by making an educated guess after you've thought the matter out. All these alternatives are better than simply assuming that everyone feels the same way you do.

We Tend to Favour Negative Impressions over Positive Ones

What do you think about Hector? He's handsome, hardworking, intelligent, and honest. He's also very conceited.

Did the last quality mentioned make a difference in your evaluation? If it did, you're not alone. Research shows that when people are aware of both the positive and the negative traits of another person, they tend to be more influenced by the negative. In one study, for example, researchers found that job interviewers were likely to reject candidates who revealed negative information even when the total amount of information was highly positive.[17]

Sometimes this attitude makes sense. If the negative quality clearly outweighs any positive ones, you'd be foolish to ignore it. A surgeon with shaky hands and a teacher who hates children, for example, would be unsuitable for their jobs whatever their other virtues. But much of the time it's a bad idea to pay excessive attention to negative qualities and overlook positive ones. This is the mistake some people make when screening potential friends or dates. They find some who are too outgoing or too reserved, others who aren't intelligent

Understanding Diversity

Terrorism Can Be Fought Without Racial Profiling. Train and Marathon Cases Prove It

In the chaotic minutes after two bombs tore through the crowd near the finish line at the Boston Marathon, racial discrimination turned a terror victim into a terror suspect. As a shocked world watched, media reported that a young Saudi man had been apprehended. He had been watching the race and was badly hurt by the first bomb. CBS News said a bystander saw him running and tackled him. People thought he looked "suspicious."

While doctors treated him in hospital, his apartment was searched and his roommate interrogated. His name was endlessly tweeted. Media dubbed him the "Saudi suspect." The next day, authorities cleared him. Wrong place, wrong time, said CNN. Yes, it was wrong. Racial profiling is wrong. And it's also bad policing. Research supports this. There is no evidence that racial profiling helps identify terrorists. What *can* be proven, is that profiling creates distrust and resentment among members of ethnic or religious communities. It leads them to believe they are unfairly targeted by law enforcement. Public trust is critical to combating criminal activity. We all have a civic duty to report

crime, but in practice, when trust is absent, people may fear the consequences of coming forward.

Hence my praise of how the RCMP handled the announcement of the arrest of two Muslim men allegedly connected to a plot to bomb a Toronto–New York train. The RCMP clearly invested care and thought in managing the impact of the news on Canada's Muslim communities. As reported in this newspaper last week, this approach has been years in the making. The RCMP went out of their way to credit a Toronto man for information leading to the arrests, and invited community leaders to a private briefing before breaking the news. One leader, Muhammad Robert Heft, told the Canadian Press that the briefing sent a signal: police are not targeting Muslims. It's not clear all Canadian police understand the work needed to build trust. Facts can help. Paradoxically, one important set of facts requires the collection of racial data. It may sound discriminatory, but it's actually the best way to ensure police are operating without racial bias. Starting this summer, Ottawa will be the first

enough, and still others who have the wrong sense of humour. Of course, it's important to find people you truly enjoy spending time with, but expecting perfection can lead to unnecessary loneliness.

Don't misunderstand: we don't always commit the kind of perceptual errors described in this section. Sometimes, for instance, people are responsible for their misfortunes, and sometimes our problems are not our fault. Likewise, the most obvious interpretation of a situation may be the correct one. Nonetheless, a large amount of research has proven again and again that our perceptions of others are often distorted in the ways listed here. The moral, then, is clear: don't assume that your first judgment of a person is accurate.

Situational Factors Influencing Perception

Along with the attribution errors described in the preceding pages, we consider a whole range of additional factors when trying to make sense of others' behaviour.

Relational Satisfaction

The behaviour that seems positive when you are in a satisfying relationship might seem completely different when the relationship isn't going well. For example, you might regard the quirks of a housemate with amusement when things are going smoothly but find them very annoying when you are unhappy with his or her other behaviours. In this sense, our willingness to tolerate the potentially bothersome behaviour of people we like is rather like the amusement we feel when the beloved family pet takes food while nobody is looking.

major Canadian city to do just that. Ottawa police will start collecting statistics on the race of people involved in traffic stops. This approach owes much to the experience of the Kingston police force, the first in Canada to record racial information.

Collecting racial data can show whether racial profiling is taking place. Kingston police found that it was. In some instances, officers' prejudices were getting in the way of the job. This enabled them to take corrective measures. What's more, Kingston police learned they need to be wary of the prejudices of people who report crimes. This is precisely what happened to the young man from Saudi Arabia. Wounded, scared, running for his life, a bystander accused him of wrongdoing because of how he looked. Regardless of the fact that he was cleared (and to be fair, Boston law enforcement had no option but to question him once he was turned in), false news about the Saudi man's alleged involvement continues to circulate on the internet and in social media.

Because of racial discrimination, the name of an innocent man will forever be linked to this horrific, senseless act. Some believe this kind of injustice is unavoidable. They argue that public security

and human rights are often at odds, and that in some cases we may have to give up one to have the other. The Canadian Human Rights Commission disagrees, and so does the Supreme Court of Canada. As Justices Iacobucci and Arbour wrote in a 2004 decision, "a response to terrorism within the rule of law preserves and enhances the cherished liberties that are essential to democracy." Our democratic values define us. In times of panic and confusion we must be at our most vigilant in protecting them.

David Langtry, *The Globe and Mail*, 29 April 2013, www.theglobeandmail.com/globe-debate/terrorism -can-be-fought-without-racial-profiling-train-and -marathon-cases-prove-it/article11604838/

QUESTIONS: This article focuses on reputation. Racial profiling was utilized very differently in the two examples of the averted VIA rail plot and the tragic Boston marathon bombings. In your opinion, is racial profiling a useful tool in averting tragedy, or does it cloud true objective investigation? How does stereotyping (of any kind) facilitate or undermine effective communication?

CRITICAL THINKING PROBE
Perceiving Others and Yourself

1. You can gain appreciation for the way perceptual errors operate by proposing two different explanations for each of the situations that follow. First, explain the behaviour as you would if you were the person involved. Second, explain it as you would if the person involved were someone you dislike. For example:
   - dozing off in class;
   - getting angry at a customer on the job;
   - dressing sloppily in public;
   - being insensitive to a friend's distress; and
   - laughing at an inappropriate or offensive joke.

2. If your explanations for these behaviours differ, ask yourself why. Are the differing attributions justifiable, or do they support the tendency to make the perceptual errors listed on pages 42–7?

3. How do these perceptual errors operate in making judgments about others' behaviour, especially when those others come from different social groups?

Degree of Involvement with the Other Person

We sometimes view people with whom we have (or seek to have) a close relationship more favourably than those whom we observe from a detached perspective.[18] One study revealed how this principle operates in everyday life. A group of male subjects was asked to critique presentations by women who allegedly owned restaurants. Half of these presentations were designed to be competent and half were incompetent. The men who were told they would be having a casual date with the female speakers judged their presentations—whether competent or not—more highly than did those who didn't expect any involvement with the speakers.[19]

Past Experience

What meaning do similar events hold? If, for example, you've been gouged by landlords in the past, you might be skeptical about an apartment manager's assurances that your careful housekeeping and diligence about repairs will guarantee the refund of your security deposit.

Cultural Idiom
gouged by
To be charged an excessive amount.

jilted
When a person is abandoned suddenly or capriciously.

Expectations

Anticipation shapes interpretations. If you imagine that your boss is unhappy with your work, you'll probably feel threatened by a request to "see me in my office first thing Monday morning." On the other hand, if you imagine that your work will be rewarded, your weekend will probably be pleasant. As Natalia Villegas, a communications consultant based in Oakville, Ontario, describes in a recently published case study, effective internal communications can lead to more harmony in an organization by helping to manage expectations around authenticity, cultural diversity, and employee needs.[20]

Social Roles

Social relationships can influence the way we perceive others. For example, a study of communication in the workplace revealed that observers—both men and women—interpret facial expressions differently depending on their status relative to the other person.[21] Subjects were shown photos of people and asked to judge how each person was feeling. When the person pictured was described as a manager, subjects tended to see less fear than when they were told that the person pictured was an employee. Gender also makes a difference in how we perceive others. When presented with two photos, one of a woman and one of a man, both showing anger of the same intensity, subjects saw more anger and less fear in a man's expression than in a woman's, probably because gender stereotypes of emotion guided their interpretations.

Knowledge

If you know that a friend has just been jilted by a lover or been fired from a job, you'll interpret his aloof behaviour differently than you would if you were unaware of what had happened. If you work in an environment where socializing is common and colleagues have friendly

relationships, you may be less likely to perceive a fellow worker's remark as sexual harassment than you would if you were in an unfamiliar environment.[22]

Self-Concept

When you're feeling insecure, the world is a very different place from the world you experience when you're full of confidence. For example, self-concept has proven to be the single greatest factor in determining whether people who are on the receiving end of teasing interpret the teaser's motives as being friendly or hostile and whether they respond with comfort or defensiveness.[23] And a McGill University study found that people with low self-esteem experienced significantly more difficulty processing rejection words than acceptance words, whereas people with high self-esteem showed no such difference.[24] These results are consistent with those of another Canadian study, which demonstrated that self-esteem is affected by and influences our interpersonal relationships so completely that we are often completely unaware of it.[25] Clearly, the way we feel about ourselves strongly influences how we interpret others' behaviour.

Perception and Culture

Perceptual differences make communication challenging enough between members of the same culture. But when communicators come from different cultures, the potential for misunderstanding is even greater. Culture serves as a perceptual filter that influences the way we interpret even the simplest events. A study carried out at Northwestern University and the University of Calgary, for example, found that adults of Chinese cultural background were just as likely to categorize concepts on the basis of relationship as they were on the basis of similarity; that is, given pictures of three items—a car, a bus, and a tire—they were as likely to group "car" with "tire" (a relational grouping) as they were "car" with "bus" (similarity). By contrast, English-Canadian and American adults were more likely to categorize concepts based on similarity.[26]

The same principle causes people from different cultures to interpret similar events in different ways. Blinking while another person talks may be hardly noticeable to English Canadians, but the same behaviour is considered impolite in Taiwan. A "V" sign made with two fingers means "victory" in most of the Western world—as long as the palm is facing out. But in some European countries the same sign with the back of the hand facing out means roughly "shove it." The beckoning "come-hither" finger motion that is familiar to North Americans is an insulting gesture in most Middle and Far Eastern countries.

Even beliefs about the very value of talk differ from one culture to another.[27] English-Canadian culture views talk as desirable and uses it to achieve social purposes as well as to perform tasks. Silence in conversational situations has a negative value in English- or French-Canadian culture. It is likely to be seen as evidence of a lack of interest, an unwillingness to communicate, hostility, anxiety, shyness, or interpersonal incompatibility. English and French Canadians are uncomfortable with silence, which they find embarrassing and awkward. Furthermore, the kind of talk that English Canadians admire is characterized by straightforwardness and honesty. Being indirect or vague—"beating around the bush," it might be labelled—has a negative connotation. French Canadians, on the other hand, have a significantly higher tolerance for allusion, metaphor, and indirect speech. That's why English Canadians can find French Canadians a little "flowery" in the way that they sometimes speak about relationships, using what seem to be over-the-top expressions of affection when they greet one another: "What a pleasure to find myself in the company of an old and cherished friend!" This greeting would seem a little awkward to a typical English Canadian, unless the two people truly had been best friends and hadn't seen each other for a long time.

On the other hand, most Asian cultures discourage the expression of thoughts and feelings. Silence is valued, as Taoist sayings indicate: "In much talk there is great weariness" or "One who speaks does not know; one who knows does not speak." Unlike westerners, who are uncomfortable with silence, Japanese and Chinese people believe that remaining quiet is appropriate when there is nothing to be said. To easterners, a talkative person is a show-off or is insincere. And when an Asian person does speak up on social matters, he or she is likely to phrase the message indirectly to "save face" for the recipient.

It is easy to see how these different views of speech and silence can lead to communication problems when people from different cultures meet. Both the talkative westerner and the silent easterner are behaving in ways they believe are proper, yet each views the other with disapproval and mistrust. Only when they recognize the different standards of behaviour can they adapt to one another, or at least understand and respect their differences.

Perceptual differences are just as important right at home when members of different co-cultures interact. Failure to recognize co-cultural differences can lead to unfortunate and unnecessary misunderstandings. For example, a Canadian man on a date with an Indonesian woman may interpret her silence as shyness and keep talking in an effort to put her at ease, when in fact she is behaving politely by allowing him to speak, even though she thinks he's rude for dominating the conversation.

Eye contact differs significantly between people from different cultural backgrounds. Whereas the European tradition is to look away from a partner while speaking and make eye contact when listening, the African tradition is just the reverse: looking at a partner more when talking and less when listening.[28] A speaker from Canada, therefore, might interpret a Kenyan listener's lack of eye contact as a sign of inattention or rudeness, when exactly the opposite is true.

Our perceptions of people from different cultures can lead to preferring one group over another. A cross-cultural communication study by social psychologist Wallace Lambert showed that English-Canadian women preferred English-Canadian to French-Canadian men, rating them as taller, kinder, more dependable, and more entertaining. The French-Canadian men were perceived as lacking integrity and being less socially attractive. English-Canadian men held less negative views about French-Canadian men. In the same study, French-Canadian women showed a preference for French-Canadian men and expressed admiration for English-Canadian women's assertive qualities.[29]

Along with ethnicity and nationality, geography also can influence perception. A fascinating series of studies revealed that climate and geographic latitude were remarkably accurate predictors of communication predispositions.[30] People living in southern latitudes of the United States were found to be more socially isolated, less tolerant of ambiguity, higher in self-esteem, more likely to touch others, and more likely to verbalize their thoughts and feelings. These sorts of finding help explain why communicators who travel from one part of a country to another find that their old patterns of communicating don't work as well in their new location. A southerner whose relatively talkative, high-touch style seemed completely normal at home might be viewed as pushy and aggressive to a northerner.

Empathy and Perception

By now it is clear that differing perceptions present a major challenge to communicators. One solution is to increase the ability to empathize. **Empathy** is the ability to re-create another person's perspective, to experience the world from the other's point of view.

> **empathy**
> The ability to project oneself into another person's point of view, so as to experience the other's thoughts and feelings.

Dimensions of Empathy

As we'll use the term here, *empathy* has three dimensions.[31] On one level, empathy involves *perspective-taking*—the ability to take on the viewpoint of another person. This understanding requires a suspension of judgment, so that for the moment you set aside your own opinions and take on those of the other person. Besides cognitive understanding, empathy has a second, emotional dimension that allows us to experience the feelings that others have. We know their fear, joy, sadness, and so on. When we combine the perspective-taking and emotional dimensions, we see that empathizing allows us to experience the other's perception—in effect, to become that person temporarily. A third dimension of empathy is genuine concern for the welfare of the other person. When we empathize we go beyond just thinking and feeling as others do; we genuinely care about their well-being.

COMMUNICATION ON-SCREEN

Bon Cop, Bad Cop **(2006)**

Directed by Erik Canuel.

An unlikely pairing is created as a French-Canadian police officer from the *Sûreté du Québec*, David Bouchard (Patrick Huard), joins forces with an anglophone member of the Ontario Provincial Police, Martin Ward (Colm Feore), to investigate a crime committed on the provincial border. The two must find a way to resolve their different approaches to police work and communication if they are to have any success in solving the case.

Culture isn't simply geographical. *Bon Cop, Bad Cop* is an example of the popular movie trope of "cultural misunderstandings" which is used to highlight the necessity to overcome our differences in order to work together. Other examples of cultural misunderstandings in film include *Lethal Weapon* (1987), Jackie Chan and Chris Tucker in *Rush Hour* (1998). Even animated films like *Finding Nemo* (2003) utilize this technique.

sympathy
Compassion for another's situation.

We have a marvellous gift, and you see it develop in children, this ability to become aware that other people have minds just like your own and feelings that are just as important as your own, and this gift of empathy seems to me to be the building block of our moral system.

Ian McEwan, novelist

It is easy to confuse empathy with **sympathy**, but the concepts are different in two important ways. First, sympathy means you feel compassion *for* another person's predicament, whereas empathy means you have a personal sense of what that predicament is like. Consider the difference between sympathizing with an unwed mother or a homeless person and empathizing with them—imagining what it would be like to be in their position. Despite your concern, sympathy lacks the degree of identification that empathy entails. When you sympathize, it is the other's confusion, joy, or pain; when you empathize, the experience becomes your own, at least for the moment. Both perspectives are important ones, but empathy is clearly the more complete of the two.

Empathy is different from sympathy in a second way. We sympathize only when we accept the reasons for another's pain as valid, whereas it is possible to empathize without feeling sympathy. You can empathize with a difficult relative, a rude stranger, or even a criminal without feeling much sympathy for the person. Empathizing allows you to understand another person's motives without requiring you to agree with them. After empathizing, you will almost certainly understand a person better, but sympathy won't always follow.

The ability to empathize seems to exist in a rudimentary form in even the youngest children.[32] Virtually from birth, infants become visibly upset when they hear another infant crying, and children who are just a few months old cry when they observe another child crying. Young children have trouble distinguishing others' distress from their own. If, for example, one child hurts his finger, another child might put her own finger in her mouth as if she were feeling pain. Researchers report cases in which children who see their parents crying wipe their own eyes, even though they are not crying.

While infants and toddlers may have a basic capacity to empathize, studies with twins suggest that the degree to which we are born with the ability to sense how others are feeling varies according to genetic factors. But although some people may be born with a greater potential for empathy, environmental experiences are the key to developing this skill. Specifically, the way in which parents communicate with their children seems to affect children's ability to understand others' emotional states. When parents point out to their children the distress that others feel from their misbehaviour ("Look how sad Samika is because you took her toy. Wouldn't you be sad if someone took away your toys?"), they gain a greater appreciation that their acts have emotional consequences than they do when parents simply label behaviour as inappropriate ("That was a mean thing to do!").

Total empathy is impossible to achieve. Completely understanding another person's point of view is simply too difficult a task for humans with different backgrounds and limited communication skills. Nonetheless, it is possible to get a strong sense of what the world looks like through another person's eyes.

The value of empathy is demonstrated by the results of a simple experiment in which university students were asked to list their impressions of people either shown in a videotaped discussion or described in a short story.[33] Half of the students were instructed to empathize with the person shown as much as possible, and the other half were not given any instructions about empathizing. The results were impressive: the students who did not practise empathy were prone to explain the person's behaviour in terms of personality characteristics. For example, they might have explained a cruel statement by saying that the speaker was mean, or they might have attributed a divorce to the

"Hey, YOU have got great empathy!"

partners' lack of understanding. The empathetic students, on the other hand, were more aware of possible elements in the situation that might have contributed to the reaction. For instance, they might have explained a person's unkind behaviour in terms of job pressures or personal difficulties. In other words, practising empathy seems to make people more tolerant.

An ability to empathize can make a difference in everyday disputes. For instance, in a study conducted at the Catholic University of the Sacred Heart in Milan, researchers found that empathy and forgiveness were reliable predictors of a marriage's strength. That is, partners in stronger marriages were more likely to give each other the benefit of the doubt in disagreements and were more likely to forgive. It's worth noting that the correlation between empathy and forgiveness was stronger among husbands; among wives, the severity of the blame they attributed to their husbands was a more reliable predictor of how likely they were to forgive. In other words, the milder their accusations, the more likely they were to forgive.[34]

You might argue here, "Why should I be more tolerant? Maybe the other person's position or behaviour isn't justified." Perhaps so, but research clearly shows that, as mentioned earlier, we are much more charitable when we find explanations for our own behaviour.[35] When explaining our own actions, we are often quick to suggest situational causes, such as: "I was tired," or "She started it." In other words, we often excuse ourselves by saying, "It wasn't my fault!" Perhaps becoming more empathetic can help even the score a bit, enabling us to treat others at least as kindly as we treat ourselves. The most important point to remember here is that all communication happens in a context. Just as in the examples given at the beginning of this chapter, words and pictures that seem appropriate in one context can be damning in another. While it is important to be generous in your judgment of others, it is also crucial to be aware of the context of your own communication lest you be judged yourself.

Perception-Checking

Having good intentions and making a strong effort to empathize are good ways to begin understanding others. Along with a positive attitude, however, there is a simple tool that can help you interpret the behaviour of others more accurately. To see how this tool operates, consider how often others jump to mistaken conclusions about your thoughts, feelings, and motives. We've all been addressed with questions or statements like these:

1. "Why are you mad at me?" (Who said you were?)
2. "What's the matter with you?" (Who said anything was the matter?)
3. "Come on now. Tell the truth." (Who said you were lying?)

As we'll see in Chapter 7, even if the interpretation is correct, dogmatic, mind-reading interrogations like the ones above are likely to generate defensiveness. The skill of **perception-checking** provides a better way to handle your interpretations. A complete perception check has three parts:

1. a description of the behaviour you noticed;
2. at least two possible interpretations of the behaviour; and
3. a request for clarification about how to interpret the behaviour.

> **perception-checking**
> A three-part method for verifying the accuracy of interpretations, including a description of the sense data, two possible interpretations, and a request for confirmation of the interpretations.

Perception checks for the preceding three examples would look like this:

- "When you stomped out of the room and slammed the door [*behaviour*], I wasn't sure whether you were mad at me [*first interpretation*] or just in a hurry [*second interpretation*]. How did you feel [*request for clarification*]?"

- "You've posted some pretty glum selfies to Instagram [*behaviour*]. I wonder whether something's bothering you [*first interpretation*] or whether you're just feeling quiet [*second interpretation*]. What's up [*request for clarification*]?"
- "You said you really liked the job I did [*behaviour*], but there was something about your voice that made me think you might not like it [*first interpretation*]. Maybe it's just my imagination, though [*second interpretation*]. How do you really feel [*request for clarification*]?"
- "Your last few tweets were really depressing [*behaviour*]; are you feeling sad over school [*first interpretation*] or is it just the crummy weather we've been having lately [*second interpretation*]? Is it anything serious [*request for clarification*]?"

Perception-checking is a tool for helping us understand others accurately instead of assuming that our first interpretation is correct. Because its goal is mutual understanding, perception-checking is a co-operative approach to communication. Besides leading to more accurate perceptions, it cuts down on defensiveness by allowing the other person to save face. Instead of saying, in effect, "I know what you're thinking," a perception check takes a more respectful approach that states or implies, "I know I'm not qualified to judge you without some help."

Sometimes a perception check won't need all three parts to be effective:

- "You haven't dropped by lately. Is anything the matter [single interpretation combined with request for clarification]?"

> *Retrospectively, one can ask "Who am I?" But in practice, the answer has come before the question.*
>
> **J.M. Yinger, sociologist and scholar**

Understanding Diversity

The Biggest Thing in Aboriginal Art in Ottawa

It may be the biggest piece of Aboriginal art in the nation's capital, or, at least, the biggest piece hanging on a wall.

At 3.73 metres high and six metres wide, Jessie Oonark's untitled tapestry at the National Arts Centre is just a smidgen bigger than Norval Morrisseau's grand masterpiece *Androgyny*, which hung for several years in the ballroom at Rideau Hall.

Soon, Oonark's tapestry will hang again in the foyer of the NAC, where it can be seen by all who care to visit. It'll have, says Laura Denker, a publicist for the Northern Scene cultural festival, "pride of place."

Oonark, who died in 1985, was from Baker Lake in Nunavat. She made it in 1973 for Bill and Jean Teron, the Ottawa property developers and philanthropists, and they gave it to the NAC. (Bill Teron was on the NAC's board of directors at the time, and had been instrumental in the campaign to have a national arts centre built.)

"It went up on the wall here in 1974, and it was up for approximately 20 years on and off," Denker says. In 1994 it went to Winnipeg for a retrospective of Oonark's work, then returned to the NAC where it "has been living in the archives for some time."

Now it's being readied for resurrection, with only a few weeks to go before the April 25 launch of Northern Scene, the two-week festival of arts and culture from the very top of Canada. "It's a wonderful opportunity to have it back where it belongs, and have it displayed where everyone can see it," Denker says.

Before then it must be rolled out on a large table in a work room, set deep in the rabbit warren of offices and spaces at the bottom of the NAC. Conservators Isabel Presedo and Wojciech Kulikowski have been cleaning it carefully and methodically. They have a low-suction vacuum, and what that leaves behind is plucked with tweezers.

- "I can't tell whether you're kidding me about being cheap or if you're serious [*behaviour combined with interpretations*]. Are you mad at me?"
- "Are you sure you don't mind driving? I can use a ride if it's no trouble, but I don't want to take you out of your way [*no need to describe behaviour*]."

Of course, a perception check can succeed only if your non-verbal behaviour reflects the open-mindedness of your words. An accusing tone of voice or a hostile glare will contradict the sincerely worded request for clarification, suggesting that you have already made up your mind about the other person's intentions.

Perception-checking is helpful to see what others are really thinking or feeling, but a perception check can also be usefully directed inward to see if we're presenting the thoughts and feelings we mean to. Two University of Manitoba studies showed that many people have a faulty perception of emotional transparency. The first suggested that we tend to overestimate the degree to which others can perceive our emotional states.[36] The second reinforces this idea, indicating that we are least likely to be aware of how others perceive us when we are most

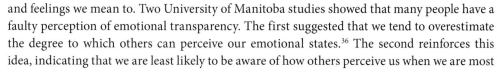

It's a daunting task. The tapestry is a vast landscape of felt, filled with a panoply of mythological and historical Inuit figures and creatures. People hunt, people travel. Some seem to be dancing, all against a horizon of turquoise and other rustic colours. It's a joyous commotion, the sort of art that makes people smile as they see it up on the wall.

The tapestry will be installed directly over the main staircase in the centre's foyer, as proud a spot as can be had in the place. It'll be difficult to hang because it's made of felt, which stretches beneath the tapestry's own weight. It can't simply be hung from the top, and must also be supported on the bottom to retain its shape.

The centre's production department is building a frame. The wardrobe department will also be involved, as will the conservators. Denker says the centre hopes to have it in place for Easter weekend.

Strangely enough, it'll be down again almost as soon as it's up, but only temporarily. Denker says it'll be removed to allow the installation of a large screen, which will roll down to protect the tapestry during public events where there's a need to project images on the wall, such as corporate logos. Jessie Oonark

was born near Baker Lake around 1906, and in the 1950s she was widowed and left with eight children. A single mother in her fifties, she turned to art to support her family. She had a successful career for the next 19 years, then surgery left her unable to draw much more. Before her death she was made a member of the Royal Canadian Academy of Arts and an officer of the Order of Canada.

There's an apocryphal story that when she saw her tapestry unveiled at the National Arts Centre, it was the first time she had seen it in its entirety. She had made it at her home in Baker Lake, and her house was so small that she could see tapestry, by some considered to be her greatest work, only in pieces.

Peter Simpson, *Ottawa Citizen*, 26 March 2013
(Photo by Julie Oliver)

QUESTIONS: Why do you think it's important to increase the visibility of Aboriginal people in the nation's capital? Is having an Indigenous-themed art festival at the National Arts Centre an effective way for promoting positive messages about Aboriginal culture? Why or why not?

immersed in what we know about ourselves. [37] In other words, the clearer our self-understanding, the more likely we are to assume that others understand us just as well, when in fact this may not be the case at all. This type of self-directed bias, where we assume that everyone sees in us what we know about ourselves, makes perception-checking a must for successful communication. You might know, for example, that you are a very joyful person but be so comfortable in your self-knowledge that you fail to be joyful with others. A quick perception check will tell you that others are not seeing your joyful self and that you should make it manifest. We'll have more to say about self-perception in the next section.

Perceiving the Self

It should be clear by now that our perceptions of others are subjective and that it takes a real effort to bridge the gap between our ideas about others and the way they view themselves. But as we've just seen, the way we perceive ourselves—and the way we think others perceive us—plays a vital role in communication. In this section we will turn our examination inward, exploring how our self-perceptions affect our communication.

The Self-Concept Defined

self-concept
The relatively stable set of perceptions each individual holds of him or herself.

The **self-concept** is a set of relatively stable perceptions that each of us holds about ourselves. The self-concept includes our conception about what makes us unique and what makes us similar to and different from others. To put it differently, the self-concept is like a mental mirror that reflects how we view ourselves: not only our physical features but also our emotional states, talents, likes and dislikes, values, and roles.

We will have more to say about the nature of the self-concept shortly, but first you will find it valuable to gain a personal understanding of how this theoretical construct applies to you. You can do so by answering the following questions: Who are you? How do you define yourself? As a student? A man, a woman, or transgendered? By your age? Your religion? Your occupation?

There are many ways of identifying yourself. Take a few minutes and list as many ways as you can to identify who you are. You'll need this list later in this chapter, so be sure to complete it now. Try to include all the characteristics that describe you:

- your moods or feelings;
- your appearance and physical condition;
- your social traits;
- your talents and limitations;
- your intellectual capacity;
- your strong beliefs; and
- your social roles.

A list of 20 or even 30 terms would be only a partial description. To make this written self-portrait complete, your list would have to be hundreds—even thousands—of words long.

Of course, not all items on such a list would be equally important. For example, the most significant part of one person's self-concept might have to do with social roles, whereas for another it might relate to physical appearance, health, friendships, accomplishments, or skills. And for some people, their self-concept might have much to do with negative qualities and skills that they lack, though many of us have difficulty identifying our less favourable traits. Two studies conducted at Concordia University showed that ego-involved people (that is, people who have high self-awareness) tended to recall a greater number of positive words about themselves, suggesting that we have a general positivity bias when we process information.[38]

Nationality or citizenship can be an important part of a person's self-concept. In Canada, most people outside Quebec identify themselves as Canadian, despite the country's emphasis on multiculturalism and the ethno-cultural mosaic. (Quebecers are more likely to identify themselves as Québécois than Canadian.) For many people, "being Canadian" means not only tolerance and respect for difference but also having the right to opt out of any cultural identity, whether mainstream French or English or one's own defined ethnic or cultural heritage.

Another factor that can determine the self-concept is race. A study conducted by Monica Das of the University of Alberta examined how four individuals of mixed race in western Canada negotiated their identities. The participants shared their life stories with Das, who uncovered five key factors that played a role in the identity development of mixed-race people: family, childhood experiences, adult experiences, physical appearance, and racism.[39]

An important element of the self-concept is **self-esteem**, our evaluations of self-worth. One person's self-concept might include being religious, tall, or athletic. That person's self-esteem would be shaped by how he or she felt about these qualities: "I'm glad that I am athletic" or "I am embarrassed about being so tall," for example.

Self-esteem has a powerful effect on the way we communicate.[40] People with high self-esteem are more willing to communicate than people with low self-esteem. They are more likely to think highly of others and expect to be accepted by others. They aren't afraid of other people's reactions and perform well when others are watching them. They work harder for people who demand high standards of performance, and they are comfortable with those they view as superior in some way. When confronted with critical comments, they are comfortable defending themselves.

By contrast, people with low self-esteem are likely to be critical of others and expect rejection from them. They are also critical of their own performances. They are sensitive to possible disapproval of others and perform poorly when being watched. They work harder for undemanding, less critical people. They feel threatened by people they view as superior in some way and have difficulty defending themselves against others' negative comments.

> **self-esteem**
> The part of the self-concept that involves evaluations of self-worth.

Communication and Development of the Self

So far we've talked about what the self-concept is; but at this point you may be asking what it has to do with the study of human communication. We can begin to answer this question by looking at how you came to possess your own self-concept.

Our identity comes almost exclusively from communication with others. As psychologists Arthur Combs and Donald Snygg put it:

> The self is essentially a social product arising out of experience with people . . . We learn the most significant and fundamental facts about ourselves from . . . "reflected appraisals," inferences about ourselves made as a consequence of the ways we perceive others behaving toward us.[41]

> **reflected appraisal**
> The theory that a person's self-concept matches the way that person believes others regard him or her.

The term **reflected appraisal**, coined by Harry Stack Sullivan,[42] is a good phrase because it captures, metaphorically, the idea that we develop an image of ourselves from the way we think others view us. This notion of the "looking-glass self" was introduced in 1902 by Charles H. Cooley, who suggested that we put ourselves in the position of other people and then, in our mind's eye, view ourselves as we imagine they see us.[43]

Understanding Diversity

Breaking Down Barriers "Shoulder to Shoulder"

When Dawn Boston enrolled in Sheridan College in January, it was a leap into the unknown. The 54-year-old Metis woman had not seen the inside of a classroom since she dropped out of school in Grade 9. "The first thing I looked for was an Aboriginal centre, to help with the transition," she says. There wasn't one. But that is about to change.

In a groundbreaking cultural collaboration, Sheridan is working with neighbouring Mohawk College to create an Aboriginal Education Centre at its Oakville Trafalgar Campus, geared to meeting the unique needs of First Nations students. If the project, set to start in the fall [of 2014], is successful, it will be expanded to Sheridan's other campuses.

Ian Marley, Sheridan's vice-president of student affairs, explains that aboriginal issues haven't received much attention in the past because—unlike Mohawk College—the Sheridan campuses do not border any Native reserves, a fact reflected in its student demographics. However, he says, "Research is showing there are a lot of urban Aboriginals who do need help."

Sheridan's aboriginal population has grown significantly over the last five years. In 2011–2012, 110 students self-identified as Aboriginal upon enrollment. But this figure does not give the complete picture; it's estimated that two to three times that number have chosen not to self-identify.

This may be a tiny percentage of Sheridan's overall student population (17,000), but as Marley points out, aboriginal education has become a priority for the provincial government. "Aboriginals are the fastest-growing group in the province [of Ontario], but are under-represented at universities and colleges," he says. "The idea is to assist these students, to give them their own place to feel comfortable in the environment." The province [of Ontario] will be funding the new centre to the tune of $180,000 annually for (at least) the next three to five years.

Boston is acutely aware of the need for a place Aboriginal students can call their own. Transitioning into a post-secondary institution, she says, is "a huge shock; the culture is so completely different. Very few First Nations people have gone to college or university, so their families don't even know how to support them."

She is the first member of her own family to pursue a college education, under a provincial government re-training program. "My 18-year-old son and I are competing for marks," she laughs. An ardent member of Sheridan's Aboriginal Awareness Committee, she sees the project as a means of breaking down these barriers to success. "Studies have shown that urban First Nations people have lost so much of their culture, it's like losing part of their identity," she says. "When they reconnect with their culture, they feel better about themselves, about who they are;

As we learn to speak and understand language, verbal messages—both positive and negative—also contribute to the developing self-concept. These messages continue later in life, especially when they come from what social scientists term **significant others**—people whose opinions we especially value. Although this term has entered colloquial usage in the past two decades with the more narrow meaning of "romantic partners," in the original academic sense significant others could be a teacher from long ago, a close friend or respected relative, or perhaps a barely known acquaintance you hold in high regard: all can leave an imprint on how you view yourself. To see the importance of significant others, ask yourself how you arrived at your opinion of yourself as a student, as a romantic partner, as an employee, and so on, and you will see that these self-evaluations were probably influenced by the way others regarded you. Jennifer Bartz and John Lydon, psychologists at McGill University, conducted two studies to examine the interaction between working self-concept and personal relationships. The studies looked at how the social interactions of participants varied depending on the nature of the relationship on which they had been "primed," in other words, whether the relationship was secure, avoidant, anxious–ambivalent, avoidant–dismissive, and so on. Their findings showed that those primed with a secure relationship increased their sense of being together, whereas those primed with less secure relationships—for instance, anxious–ambivalent or avoidant–fearful—increased the sense of having to act as an individual within the relationship.[44]

> **significant other**
> A person whose opinion is important enough to affect one's self-concept strongly.

and develop more resilience against the stresses of college life."

The new centre will have an Aboriginal adviser to assist students, and it is expected that First Nations elders will also be available to offer cultural and spiritual support. Students will have access to peer counselling and mentoring. The Aboriginal Awareness Committee will organize events, exhibits, lectures, traditional feasts, and pow-wows—designed to engage the wider student population, and spread awareness of First Nations history and culture. As Marley points out, "New immigrants to Canada are not very knowledgeable about Aboriginal culture, so it's an opportunity to educate our wider student body."

While most universities and colleges in the province [of Ontario] offer similar centres or services to their students, Sheridan has taken a unique approach in partnering with Mohawk College. "Mohawk already has a very well-developed centre," says Marley. "Why reinvent the wheel?"

Mohawk College's energetic manager of Aboriginal initiatives is Ron McLester. He runs the vibrant Aboriginal Initiatives Office and is described as "a force of nature." The agreement will see him providing guidance and day-to-day strategic support to Sheridan's new centre, while continuing to oversee the Mohawk office.

McLester points out that since Mohawk and Sheridan were already engaged in a wider partnership to facilitate delivery of some academic programs—"co-operating instead of competing"—it seemed a good idea to leverage the partnership for Aboriginal issues. Mohawk's long-standing connection to two nearby First Nations reserves has made it possible to help Sheridan's program "get up and running very quickly."

McLester believes it is important to raise the visibility of Aboriginal culture within the post-secondary context. "Aboriginal students do not lack ability," he says. "What we do lack, sometimes, is self-esteem and self-confidence." McLester contends the centre, with its emphasis on tradition, community building and experiential learning, will prime Aboriginal students for success in the wider world. "Really," McLester says, "This is about how do we go forward together, shoulder-to-shoulder, not like father and son, but like brothers."

Donna Yowching, *Toronto Star*, 27 April 2013
http://mohawkmatters.files.wordpress.com/2013/04/
toronto-star-special-report-aboriginal-student-services.pdf

QUESTIONS: How does the example of a culturally tailored program relate to perception and development of the self? Do you think Native Canadians should celebrate what defines them more? Why or why not?

As we grow older, the evaluations of others still influence beliefs about the self in some areas, such as physical attractiveness and popularity. A study out of Wilfrid Laurier and Simon Fraser universities suggests that our responses to social comparisons (for instance, when we are compared with someone more or less successful) are strongest when they come from someone with whom we share an extremely close relationship and whom we consider an important part of our identity, such as a parent or a spouse.[45] On the whole, however, the influence of significant others is less powerful as we age.[46] The looking glass of the self-concept becomes distorted, so that it shapes the input from others to make it conform with our existing beliefs. For example, if your self-concept includes the element "poor student," you might respond to a high grade by thinking "I was just lucky" or "The professor must be an easy grader."

You might argue that not every part of one's self-concept is shaped by others, insisting there are certain objective facts that are recognizable by self-observation. After all, nobody needs to tell you that you are taller than others, speak with an accent, can run quickly, and so on. These facts are obvious.

Though it's true that some features of the self are immediately apparent, the *significance* we attach to them—the rank we assign them in the hierarchy of our list and the interpretation we give them—depends greatly on our social environment. The interpretation of characteristics such as weight depends on the way people important to us regard them. Being anything less than trim and muscular is generally regarded as undesirable because others tell us that slenderness is an ideal. In one study, young women's perceptions of their bodies changed for the worse after watching just 30 minutes of televised images of the "ideal" female form.[47] Furthermore, these distorted self-images can lead to serious behavioural disorders such as depression and eating disorders. However, in cultures and societies where greater weight is considered beautiful, a Western supermodel would be considered unattractive. In the same way, the fact that one is single or married, solitary or sociable, aggressive or passive takes on meaning depending on the interpretation that society attaches to those traits. Thus, the importance of a given characteristic in your self-concept has as much to do with the significance that you and others attach to it as with the existence of the characteristic.

Culture and the Self-Concept

Canadians have long been alert to the challenges and opportunities that come from cultural diversity. But the influence of culture is far more basic and powerful than most people realize. Although we seldom recognize the fact, our whole notion of the self is shaped by the culture in which we have been reared.[48]

The most obvious expression of a culture is the language its members use. If you live in an environment where everyone speaks the same tongue, then language will have little noticeable impact. But when your primary language is not the one spoken or written by the majority, or when it is not prestigious, your sense of being a member of what social scientists call the "out-group" is likely to be strong. As a speaker of a non-dominant language, you can react in one of two ways: either you may feel pressured to assimilate by speaking the "better" language, or you may refuse to accede to the majority language and maintain loyalty to the non-dominant language.[49] In either case, the impact of language on your self-concept is powerful. On one hand, you might feel you're not as "good" as speakers of the native language; on the other, you might believe there's something unique and worth preserving in the language you use.

Cultures affect the self-concept in more subtle ways, too. Most Western cultures are highly individualistic, whereas other cultures—most Asian ones, for example—are traditionally much more collective.[50] When asked to identify themselves, Canadians, Americans,

Cultural Idiom
tongue
One's language.

Australians, and Europeans would probably respond by giving their first name, surname, street, town, and country. Many Asians would do it the other way around.[51] Steven Heine, a psychologist at the University of British Columbia, studied differences between Asian and Anglo–North American selves and found that East Asians are more likely than Anglo–North Americans to incorporate people with whom they have very close relations into the self and emphasize the distance of "outgroup" members. East Asians were also more likely to view self-criticism as an important way to motivate an individual.[52] Meanwhile, if you ask Hindus for their identity, they will give you their caste and village as well as their name. The Sanskrit formula for identifying one's self begins with lineage, goes on to family and house, and ends with one's personal name.[53]

These conventions for naming aren't just cultural idiosyncrasies: they reflect very different ways of viewing one's self.[54] In collective cultures a person gains identity by belonging to a group. This means that the degree of interdependence among members of the society and its subgroups is much higher. Feelings of pride and self-worth are likely to be shaped not only by what the individual does but also by the behaviour of other members of the community. This linkage to others explains the traditional Asian denial of self-importance—a strong contrast to the self-promotion that is common in individualistic Western cultures. In Chinese written language, for example, the pronoun "I" looks very similar to the word for "selfish."[55] Table 2.1 summarizes some differences between individualistic Western cultures and more collective Asian ones.

This sort of cultural difference isn't just a matter of anthropological interest. It shows up in the level of comfort or anxiety that people feel when communicating. In societies where the need to conform is great, there is a higher degree of communication apprehension. For example, as a group, residents of China, Korea, and Japan exhibit significantly more anxiety about speaking out than do members of individualistic cultures such as those of Canada and the United States.[56] It's important to realize that different levels of communication apprehension don't mean that shyness is a "problem" in some cultures. In fact, just the opposite is true:

In Japan, in fact, everything had been made level and uniform—even humanity. By one official count, 90 percent of the population regarded themselves as middle-class; in schools, it was not the outcasts who beat up the conformists, but vice versa. Every Japanese individual seemed to have the same goal as every other—to become like every other Japanese individual. The word for "different," I was told, was the same as the word for "wrong." And again and again in Japan, in contexts varying from the baseball stadium to the watercolor canvas, I heard the same unswerving, even maxim: "The nail that sticks out must be hammered down."

Pico Iyer, *Video Night in Katmandu*

Table 2.1 The Self in Individualistic and Collectivistic Cultures

Individualist Cultures	Collectivistic Cultures
Self is separate, unique individual; should be independent, self-sufficient.	People belong to extended families or in-groups; "we" or group orientation.
Individual should take care of self and immediate family.	Person should take care of extended family before self.
Many flexible group memberships; friends based on shared interests and activities.	Emphasis on belonging to a very few permanent in-groups, which have a strong influence over the person.
Reward for individual achievement and initiative; individual decisions encouraged; individual credit and blame assigned.	Reward for contribution to group goals and well-being; co-operation with in-group members; group decisions valued; credit and blame shared.
High value on autonomy, change, youth, individual security, and equality.	High value on duty, order, tradition, age, group security, status, and hierarchy

Source: Adapted by S. Sudweeks from H.C. Triandis, "Cross-Cultural Studies of Individualism and Collectivism," in J. Berman, ed., *Nebraska Symposium on Motivation* 37 (Lincoln, NE: University of Nebraska Press, 1990), 41–133, and E.T. Hall, *Beyond Culture* (Garden City, NY: Doubleday, 1976).

reticence is valued in these cultures. When the goal is to avoid being the nail that sticks out, it's logical to feel nervous when you make yourself appear different by calling attention to yourself. A self-concept that includes "assertive" might make a westerner feel proud, but in much of Asia it would more likely be cause for shame.

The Self-Concept, Personality, and Communication

Whereas the self-concept is an internal image we hold of ourselves, the personality is the view others hold of us. The term **personality** describes a relatively consistent set of traits people exhibit across a variety of situations.[57] We use the notion of personality to characterize others as friendly or aloof, energetic or lazy, smart or stupid, and in literally thousands of other ways. In fact, one survey revealed almost 18,000 trait words in the English language that can be used to describe a personality.[58] People do seem to possess some innate personality traits. Psychologist Jerome Kagan reports that 10 per cent of all children seem to be born with a biological disposition toward shyness.[59] Babies who stop playing when a stranger enters the room, for example, are more likely than others to be reticent and introverted as adolescents. Likewise, Kagan found that another 10 per cent of children seem to be born with especially sociable dispositions. Research with twins also suggests that personality may be at least partly a matter of genetic destiny.[60] For example, identical twins are much more similar in terms of sociability than are fraternal twins. These similarities are apparent not only in infancy but also in adulthood, and they are noticeable even when the twins have had different experiences growing up.

> **personality**
> A relatively consistent set of traits a person exhibits across a variety of situations.

Canadian researchers Kelly Schwartz and Gregory Fouts asked 164 Canadian adolescents to fill out a survey to measure personality characteristics of three groups of music listeners: those preferring light qualities of music, those preferring heavy qualities of music, and those who had eclectic preferences. They found that each of the three groups demonstrated a specific personality profile.[61]

Despite its common use, the term *personality* is often an oversimplification. Much of our behaviour isn't consistent. Rather, it varies from one situation to another. You may be quiet around strangers but gregarious around friends and family. You may be optimistic about your schoolwork or career but pessimistic about your love life. The term *easygoing* might describe your behaviour at home, whereas you might be a fanatic at work. Inconsistencies of this kind are not only common but are also often desirable. The argumentative style you use with friends wouldn't be well received by the judge in traffic court when you appeal a citation. Likewise, the affectionate behaviour you enjoy with a boyfriend or girlfriend in private wouldn't be welcomed by a stranger in public. As you read in Chapter 1, a wide range of behaviours is an important ingredient of communication competence. In this sense, a consistent personality can be more of a liability than an asset—unless that personality is "flexible."

Figure 2.1 illustrates the relationship between the self-concept and behaviour. It shows how the self-concept both shapes and is shaped by much of our communication behaviour. We can begin to examine the process by considering the self-concept you bring to an event. Suppose, for example, that one element of your self-concept is "nervous with authority figures." That image probably comes from evaluations you have received in the past from significant others— teachers, perhaps, or former employers. If you view yourself as nervous with authority figures such as these, you will probably feel nervous when you encounter them in the future, such as in a teacher–student conference or a job interview. That nervous behaviour is likely to influence how others view your personality, which in turn will shape how they respond to you—probably in ways that reinforce the self-concept you brought to the event. Finally, the responses of others will affect the way you interpret future events: other job interviews, meetings with professors, and so on. This cycle illustrates how the chicken-and-egg nature of the self-concept, which is shaped by significant others in the past, helps to govern your present behaviour and influences the way others view you.

> **Cultural Idiom**
> **chicken-and-egg**
> A reference to the philosophical question, "Which came first, the chicken or the egg?"

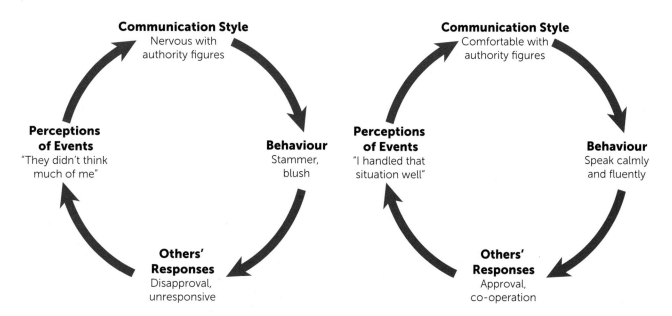

FIGURE 2.1 The Relationship between the Self-Concept and Behaviour

The Self-Fulfilling Prophecy

The self-concept is such a powerful force on the personality that it not only determines how we communicate in the present but can also actually influence our behaviour, and that of others, in the future. Such occurrences come about through a phenomenon called the self-fulfilling prophecy.

A **self-fulfilling prophecy** occurs when a person's expectation of an outcome makes the outcome more likely to occur than would otherwise have been true. Self-fulfilling prophecies occur all the time, although they might never have been labelled as such. For example, do any of the following situations sound familiar?

- You expected to become nervous and botch a job interview and ultimately did so.
- You anticipated having a good (or terrible) time at a social affair and found your expectations being met.
- A teacher or boss explained a new task to you, saying that you probably wouldn't do well at first. You did not do well.
- A friend described someone you were about to meet, saying that you wouldn't like the person. The prediction turned out to be correct.

In each of these cases, there is a good chance that the outcome happened because it had been predicted. You needn't have botched the interview; the party might have been boring only because you helped make it so; you might have done better on the new task if your boss hadn't spoken up; and you might have liked the new acquaintance if your friend hadn't planted preconceptions. In other words, what helped make each outcome occur was the expectation that it would.

There are two types of self-fulfilling prophecies. The first type occurs when your own expectations influence your behaviour. Like the job interview and the party described earlier, there are many times when an unnecessary outcome occurs because you expect it to. If you play sports you have probably psyched yourself into playing better than usual on at least one occasion, so that the only explanation for your performance was your attitude—your expectation that you would behave differently. The same principle operates for anxious public speakers: communicators who feel nervous about facing an audience often create self-fulfilling prophecies about doing poorly.[62] (Chapter 12 offers advice on overcoming this kind of stage fright.)

Research has demonstrated the power of self-fulfilling prophecies. A study of Ontarians suffering from social phobia disorder (which causes people to fear doing certain things in public, such as eating) demonstrated the debilitating effects that anticipation can have on a person, causing marked reduction in the quality of life.[63] In another study, communicators who believed they were incompetent proved less likely than others to pursue rewarding relationships and more likely to sabotage their existing relationships than did people who were less critical of themselves.[64] On the other hand, students who perceived themselves as capable achieved more academically.[65] Research conducted at the University of Waterloo demonstrated the effect of overachieving fourth-year students on the self-perception in first-year students: when first-year students read a profile of a star fourth-year student, they tended to evaluate themselves more positively because the star fourth-year student represented what they could become.[66]

In another study, subjects who were sensitive to social rejection tended to expect it, perceive it where it might not have existed, and overreact to their exaggerated perceptions in ways that jeopardized the quality of their relationships.[67]

self-fulfilling prophecy
A prophecy that causes itself to become true directly or indirectly when one's belief in the inevitable nature of the outcome causes one's behaviour to lead to fulfillment of the prophecy.

Cultural Idiom
psyched yourself
Something or someone affected your behaviour by changing your thinking.

The self-fulfilling prophecy also operates on the job. For example, salespeople who perceive themselves as effective communicators were found to be more successful than those who perceive themselves as less effective, despite the fact that there was no difference in the approach that members of each group used with customers. In other words, the apparent reason that some salespeople do well is that they expect to succeed. Self-fulfilling prophecies can be physiologically induced: putting a smile on your face, even if you're not in a good mood, can lead to a more positive disposition.[68]

A second type of self-fulfilling prophecy occurs when the expectations of one person govern another's actions. The classic example was demonstrated by Robert Rosenthal and Lenore Jacobson: 20 per cent of the children in a certain elementary school were reported to their teachers as showing unusual potential for intellectual growth. The names of these 20 per cent were drawn by means of a table of random numbers, which is to say that the names were drawn out of a hat. Eight months later these unusual or "magic" children showed significantly greater gains in IQ than did the remaining children who had not been singled out for the teachers' attention. The change in the teachers' expectations regarding the intellectual performance of these allegedly "special" children had led to an actual change in the intellectual performance of these randomly selected children.[69]

My objective is to have each student become more insightful, compassionate, introspective, and empathetic. In your case I will settle for quiet."

In other words, some children may do better in school not because they are any more intelligent than their classmates but because they learn that their teacher, a significant other, believes they can achieve.

To put this phenomenon in context with the self-concept, we can say that when a teacher communicates to students the message "I think you're bright," they accept that evaluation and change their self-concepts to include that evaluation. Unfortunately, we can assume that the same principle holds for those students whose teachers send the message "I think you're stupid."

This type of self-fulfilling prophecy has been shown to be a powerful force for shaping the self-concept, and thus the behaviour, of people in a wide range of settings beyond schools. In medicine, patients who unknowingly receive placebos—substances such as sugar pills that have no curative value—often respond just as favourably to this treatment as do people who receive the actual drug. The patients believe they have taken a substance that will help them feel better, and this belief brings about a "cure." Rosenthal and Jacobson describe several studies suggesting that psychotherapy patients who believe they will benefit from treatment do so, regardless of the type of treatment they receive. In the same vein, when a doctor expresses to a patient a belief that he or she will improve, the patient may do so precisely because of this expectation, whereas another person for whom the doctor gives little hope often fails to recover. Apparently the patient's self-concept as sick or well—as shaped by the doctor—plays an important role in determining the true state of health.

> **Cultural Idiom**
> **in the same vein**
> Something that is similar.

The self-fulfilling prophecy operates in families as well. If parents tell their children often enough that they never do anything right, the children's self-concepts will soon incorporate this idea, and they will fail at many or most of the tasks they attempt. On the other hand, if children are told they are capable, lovable, or kind, there is a much greater chance of their behaving accordingly.[70]

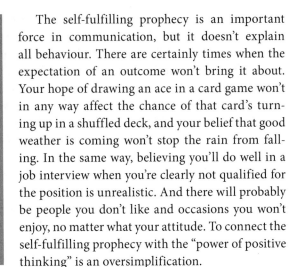

CRITICAL THINKING PROBE

Self-Fulfilling Prophecies

Explore how self-fulfilling prophecies affect your communication by answering the following questions:

1. Identify three communication-related predictions you make about others. What are the effects of these predictions? How would others behave differently if you did not impose these predictions?

2. Identify three self-fulfilling prophecies you impose on yourself. What are the effects of these prophecies? How would you communicate differently if you did not subscribe to them?

The self-fulfilling prophecy is an important force in communication, but it doesn't explain all behaviour. There are certainly times when the expectation of an outcome won't bring it about. Your hope of drawing an ace in a card game won't in any way affect the chance of that card's turning up in a shuffled deck, and your belief that good weather is coming won't stop the rain from falling. In the same way, believing you'll do well in a job interview when you're clearly not qualified for the position is unrealistic. And there will probably be people you don't like and occasions you won't enjoy, no matter what your attitude. To connect the self-fulfilling prophecy with the "power of positive thinking" is an oversimplification.

In other cases, your expectations will be borne out because you are a good predictor and not because of the self-fulfilling prophecy. For example, children are not equally equipped to do well in school, and in such cases it would be wrong to say that a child's performance was shaped by a parent or teacher even though the behaviour did match what was expected. In the same way, some workers excel and others fail, some patients recover and others don't—all according to our predictions but not because of them.

As we keep these qualifications in mind, it's important to recognize the tremendous influence that self-fulfilling prophecies play in our lives. To a great extent we are what we believe we are. In this sense we and those around us constantly create our self-concepts and thus ourselves.

Identity Management: Communication as Impression Management

So far we have described how communication shapes the way communicators view themselves and others. In the remainder of this chapter we turn the tables and focus on **impression management**—the communication strategies people use to influence how others view them. In the following pages you will see that many of our messages aim at creating desired impressions.

Public and Private Selves

To understand why impression management exists, we have to discuss the notion of self in more detail. So far we have referred to the "self" as if each of us had only one identity. In truth, each of us possesses several selves, some private and others public. Often these selves are quite different.

The **perceived self** is a reflection of the self-concept, the person you believe yourself to be in moments of honest self-examination. We can call the perceived self "private" because you are unlikely to reveal all of it to another person. You can verify the private nature of the perceived self by reviewing the self-concept list you developed while reading page 56. You'll probably find some elements of yourself there that you would not disclose to many people, and some that you would not share with anyone. You might, for example, be reluctant to share

Cultural Idiom
turn the tables
To reverse the point of view.

impression management
Strategies used by communicators to influence the way others view them.

perceived self
The person we believe ourselves to be in moments of candour. It may be identical with or different from the presenting and ideal selves.

some feelings about your appearance ("I think I'm rather unattractive"), your intelligence ("I'm not as smart as I wish I was"), your goals ("the most important thing to me is becoming rich"), or your motives ("I care more about myself than about others"). In contrast to the perceived self, the **presenting self** is a public image—the way we want to appear to others. In most cases the presenting self we seek to create is a socially approved image: diligent student, loving partner, conscientious worker, loyal friend, and so on. Social norms often create a gap between the perceived and presenting selves. Table 2.2 summarizes the results of a study of the difference between the perceived and presenting selves of male and female university students. As you will see, the self-concepts of the male and female students were quite similar, but their public selves were different in several respects both from their private selves and from the public selves of the opposite sex.[71]

Sociologist Erving Goffman used the word **face** to describe the presenting self, and he coined the term **facework** to describe the verbal and non-verbal ways we act to maintain our own presenting image and the images of others.[72] He argued that each of us can be viewed as a kind of playwright/performer who creates and then acts out roles that we want others to believe.

Facework involves two tasks: managing our own identity and communicating in ways that reinforce the identities that others are trying to present.[73] You can see how these two goals operate by recalling a time when you've used self-deprecating humour to defuse a potentially unpleasant situation. Suppose, for example, that you were late getting to a party because a friend gave you confusing directions. "Sorry I got lost," you might have said. "I'm a terrible navigator." This sort of mild, self-directed putdown accomplishes two things at once. It preserves the other person's face by implicitly saying, "It's not your fault." At the same time, your mild self-debasement shows that you're a nice person who doesn't find faults in others or make a big issue out of small problems.[74]

presenting self
The image a person presents to others. It may be identical to or different from the perceived and ideal selves.

face
The socially approved identity that a communicator tries to present.

facework
Verbal and non-verbal behaviour designed to create and maintain a communicator's face and the face of others.

TABLE 2.2 Self-Selected Adjectives Describing Perceived and Presenting Selves of College Students

Perceived Self		Presenting Self	
Men	**Women**	**Men**	**Women**
1. Friendly	1. Friendly	1. Wild	1. Active
2. Active	2. Responsible	2. Able	2. Responsible
3. Responsible	3. Independent	3. Active	3. Able
4. Independent	4. Capable	4. Strong	4. Bright
5. Capable	5. Sensible	5. Proud	5. Warm
6. Polite	6. Active	6. Smart	6. Funny
7. Attractive	7. Happy	7. Brave	7. Independent
8. Smart	8. Curious	8. Capable	8. Proud
9. Happy	9. Faithful	9. Responsible	9. Sensible
10. Funny	10. Attractive	10. Rough	10. Smart

Source: Adapted from C.M. Shaw and R. Edwards, "Self-Concepts and Self-Presentations of Males and Females: Similarities and Differences," *Communication Reports* 10 (1997): 55–62.

Characteristics of Identity Management

Now that you have a sense of what identity management is, we can look at some characteristics of this process.

We Strive to Construct Multiple Identities

In the course of even a single day, most people play a variety of roles: the respectful student, the joking friend, the friendly neighbour, and the helpful worker, to suggest just a few. We even play a variety of roles with the same person. As you grew up you almost certainly changed characters as you interacted with your parents. In one context you acted as the responsible adult ("You can trust me with the car!"), and in another context you were the helpless child ("I can't find my socks!"). At some times—perhaps on birthdays or holidays—you were a dedicated family member, and at other times you may have played the role of rebel. Likewise, in romantic relationships we switch among many behaviours, depending on the context: friend, lover, business partner, scolding critic, apologetic child, and so on.

The ability to construct multiple identities is one element of communication competence. For example, the style of speaking or even the language spoken can reflect a choice about how to construct one's identity. We recall a neuroscience professor who was always very strict and reserved with his students but who changed demeanour entirely when participating in his Catholic parish activities in Montreal. On campus or in the lab, he was quiet and demanding, whereas at church he was open, smiling, and full of jokes. In a similar vein, a University of Waterloo study looked at how bicultural Chinese Canadians who experience unfavourable circumstances in one culture (either Chinese or English Canadian) maintain their sense of well-being by shifting to their other cultural identity.[75]

Identity Management Is Collaborative

As we perform like actors trying to create a front, our "audience" is made up of other actors who are trying to create their own characters. Identity-related communication is a kind of process theatre in which we collaborate with other actors to improvise scenes in which our characters mesh.

You can appreciate the collaborative nature of identity management by thinking about how you might handle a grievance against a roommate or family member who has failed to pass along a phone message that arrived while you were out. Suppose you decide to raise the issue tactfully in an effort to avoid seeming like a nag (desired role for yourself: "nice person") and also to save the other person from the embarrassment of being confronted (hoping to avoid casting the other person in the role of "screw-up"). If your tactful bid is accepted, the dialogue might sound like this:

YOU: By the way, Dipika told me she called yesterday. If you wrote a note, I guess I missed seeing it.

OTHER: Oh . . . sorry. I meant to write a note, but as soon as I hung up, the doorbell rang, and then I had to run off to class.

YOU (in friendly tone of voice):   That's okay. Try to leave me a note next time, though.

OTHER: No problem.

In this upbeat conversation, you and the other person have accepted one another's bids for identity as basically thoughtful people. As a result, the conversation ran smoothly. Imagine, though, how different the outcome would be if the other person didn't accept your role as a "nice person":

YOU: By the way, Dipika told me she called yesterday. If you wrote a note, I guess I missed seeing it.

OTHER (defensively):   Okay, so I forgot. It's not that big a deal. You're not perfect yourself, you know!

Your first bid as "nice, face-saving person" was rejected. At this point you have the choice of persisting in your original role ("Hey, I'm not mad at you, and I know I'm not perfect!") or switching to the new role of "unjustly accused person" and giving your roommate the gears ("I never said I was perfect. But we're not talking about me here. . . .").

As this example illustrates, *collaboration* doesn't mean the same thing as *agreement*.[76] The small issue of the phone message might mushroom into a fight in which you and the other person both adopt the role of combatant. The point here is that virtually all conversations provide an arena in which communicators construct their identities in response to the behaviour of others. As we discussed in Chapter 1, communication isn't made up of discrete events that can be separated from one another. Instead, what happens at one moment is influenced by what each party brings to the interaction and by what has happened in their relationship up to that point.

> **Cultural Idiom**
> **give someone the gears**
> To pester, needle, or chastise a person.
>
> **mushroom**
> Something that escalates.

Identity Management Can Be Conscious or Unconscious

At this point you might object to the notion of strategic identity management, claiming that most of your communication is spontaneous and not a deliberate attempt to present yourself in a certain way. However, you might acknowledge that some of your communication involves a conscious attempt to manage impressions.

There's no doubt that sometimes we are highly aware of managing impressions. Most job interviews and first dates are clear examples of conscious identity management. But in other cases we unconsciously act in ways that are really small public performances.[77] For example, experimental subjects expressed facial disgust in reaction to eating sandwiches laced with a supersaturated saltwater solution only when there was another person present; when they were alone, they made no faces when eating the same sandwiches.[78] Another study showed that communicators engage in facial mimicry (such as smiling or looking sympathetic in response to another's message) in face-to-face settings only when their expressions can be seen by the other person. When they are speaking over the phone and their reactions cannot be seen, they

COMMUNICATING ONLINE

Smartphone Photography: 10 Top Tips for Better Smartphone Photography

Today's smartphone technology equips us with a handy way of capturing high-quality images wherever we go, adding another level to how we manage our identities. If you're planning to incorporate your photos into communication for others—like a business blog or a work-related Facebook posting—it pays to spend a few extra moments to make sure your photos are as effective as possible. Study technology columnist Chris Hall's "10 Tips for Better Smartphone Photography," and then see if you can make your photos create the public image you want!

1. *Clean the lens.* One of the biggest problems with smartphone pictures is fingerprints on the lens. Some phones are better designed to protect the lens, but with manufacturers producing slimmer and slimmer handsets, it's getting easier and easier to cover the lens with your fingers. Keep your lens clean.

2. *Focusing.* Give your phone the time to focus correctly and make sure that it is actually focused on what you want. Don't always rely on beeps, use your eyes. If it's not focusing correctly, try switching to touch focusing instead for more precision. If it won't focus on what you want, perhaps you're too close. Move back a little and try again, especially if you're trying to get a picture of something small.

3. *Composition.* Think about what you're looking at and what your picture is trying to show. You can very easily change the shape—also known as aspect ratio—of your photo afterwards, but if it's full of distracting background elements, or it's not clear what you're taking a photo of, then it's never going to look great. Photographers often use the rule of thirds to

get the subject into an ideal position. Imagine the scene with a tic-tac-toe grid over the top. The important things should be aligned along those lines, or at the intersection of those lines, for the greatest impact. It's simple and it works.

4. *Watch the sun.* Sunny conditions are great for taking beautiful pictures with rich blue skies and luscious greens, but think about where the sun is when you pull out your phone. In the instance of flare this is because the sun is shining right across the lens. Try using your hand to shade the lens, making sure it's not in shot, and you can get a great result. When photographing people, watch where those shadows fall and think about the best side from which to take a shot—you don't want a silhouette in front of a beautiful background because you didn't consider that the sun was behind them, for example.

5. *Consider the flash.* The flash on your smartphone isn't great. It can be harsh and in low-light conditions can result in unusual colours. But the flash can reveal shadow detail in close-up shots in sunny conditions which can be particularly useful. If you do have to use the flash indoors, it can help out dark scenes where shots would otherwise be blurry without the introduction of its additional lighting. But as flash power is tricky to control, keep an eye on the resulting shot—you wouldn't want your friend's face to be overexposed and featureless, which might mean stepping back to add some distance for a better exposure.

6. *Keep it steady.* Smartphones will often do two things to take shots in low light: one is give you a longer exposure—the

do not make the same expressions.[79] Studies such as these suggest that most of our behaviour is aimed at sending messages to others, even though reactions like the ones described are often instantaneous and unconscious. In other words, we engage in identity management even when we're not aware that we're doing it.

In the same way, many of our choices about how to act in the array of daily interactions aren't deliberate, strategic decisions. Rather, they rely on "scripts" that we have developed over time. You probably have a variety of roles for managing your identity from which to choose in familiar situations such as dealing with strangers, treating customers at work, interacting with family members, and so on. When you find yourself in such situations you probably slip into

Cultural Idiom
scripts
Practised responses.

length of time the sensor is gathering light—which can lead to blurry photos; the other is to bump up the ISO—otherwise known as sensitivity—giving you lots of image noise and making the shot look grainy or flecked with unwanted coloured spots. Often your phone will want to do both, leaving you with a blurry and noisy photo. Supporting your phone will certainly help you get a better shot. It might be a case of resting it on a table, railing, or the bar. Supporting it while you take that indoor shot gives you a better chance of getting something usable from it. In some instances you can control ISO, but not many phones will let you do this.

7. *Avoid the zoom.* Pinch zooming is all the rage on smartphones and more often than not, you'll be able to zoom digitally in the camera to get closer to your subject. However, this "i-zooming" is achieved to the detriment of quality, because what actually happens is you use a smaller area of sensor and then digitally reproduce an image at the same size as you'd normally expect. The result is that there's less information captured to put into the final image. If you need the subject to be bigger, then move closer, or try cropping the image once you've taken it to get closer to the detail, accepting you'll have a smaller overall image as a result.

8. *Turn off the shutter sound.* Some smartphones insist on using a range of beeping noises. In some cases the noises actually slow down the camera. Take a shot to see if the shutter noise really adds anything to the experience. You might find yourself waiting for the noise before you can take the next shot when you needn't. In this case you'd be best to turn it off.

9. *Vertical videos.* Hey, you're doing it wrong! As more and more people use phones to capture video, more vertical videos are starting to appear. YouTube and Facebook are filling with upright videos that perhaps make sense on your phone, but once you view them on a computer, you suddenly realize what you've done. That's right, you've created a video that's going to have huge black bars left and right, because you didn't rotate your phone. Of course you might like this effect, but as your YouTube account is probably already available on your smart TV, do you really want to waste all that screen because you didn't rotate your smartphone? No, we didn't think so.

10. *Software to the rescue.* There's a host of free applications that will tweak your photos to improve them. Your phone may well have many of the options built-in already. You can crop the photo to get closer in on the shot's main subject, or just to remove something messy from the side, but perhaps more importantly many applications will add contrast and colour that might be lacking in the original. Changing the saturation of your photo can boost colours, changing to black and white might hide image noise, adding a vignette—those darker corners and edges—might add some retro charm or impact, while helping to lead the viewer's eye on to what's important within the shot. Or there's the full retro treatment. If your shot can't be saved, why not make it worse intentionally?

—Chris Hall, Pocket-lint.com, 7 May 2013.

these roles quite often. Only when those roles don't seem quite right do you deliberately construct an approach that reflects how you want the scene to play out.

Despite the claims of some theorists, it seems like an exaggeration to suggest that all behaviour is aimed at making impressions. Young children certainly aren't strategic communicators. A baby spontaneously laughs when pleased and cries when sad or uncomfortable, without any notion of creating an impression in others. Likewise, there are almost certainly times when we, as adults, act spontaneously. But when a significant other questions the presenting self we try to put forward, the likelihood of taking actions to prop it up increases. This process isn't always conscious: at a non-conscious level, we monitor others' reactions and swing into action when our face is threatened—especially by significant others.[80]

People Differ in Their Degree of Identity Management

Some people are much more aware of their impression management behaviour than others. High self-monitors have the ability to pay attention to their own behaviour and others' reactions, adjusting their communication as necessary to create the desired impression. By contrast, low self-monitors express what they are thinking and feeling without much attention to the impression their behaviour creates.[81]

Cultural Idiom
to play out
To proceed to a conclusion.

There are certainly advantages to being a high self-monitor.[82] People who pay attention to themselves are generally good actors who can create the impression they want, acting interested when bored or friendly when they really feel quite the opposite. This allows them to handle social situations smoothly, often putting others at ease. They are also good "people-readers" who can adjust their behaviour to get the desired reaction from others. But along with these advantages are some potential drawbacks. Their analytical nature may prevent high self-monitors from experiencing events completely, because a portion of their attention will always be devoted to viewing the situation from a detached position. Their ability to perform means that it is difficult to tell how they are really feeling. In fact, because high self-monitors change roles often, they may have a hard time knowing how they really feel.

People who score low on the self-monitoring scale live life quite differently from their more self-conscious counterparts. They have a simpler, more focused idea of who they are and who they want to be. Low self-monitors are likely to have a narrower repertoire of behaviours, so that they can be expected to act in more or less the same way regardless of the situation. This means that low self-monitors are easy to read. "What you see is what you get" might be their motto. Although this lack of flexibility may make their social interaction more awkward in many situations, low self-monitors can be counted on to be straightforward communicators.

By now it should be clear that neither extremely high nor extremely low self-monitoring is the ideal. There are some situations when paying attention to yourself and adapting your behaviour can be useful, but there are other situations when reacting without considering the effect on others is a better approach. This need for a range of behaviours demonstrates again the notion of communicative competence outlined in Chapter 1: flexibility is the key to successful relationships.

Why Manage Impressions?

Why bother trying to shape others' opinions? Sometimes we create and maintain a front to follow social rules. As children we learn to act politely, even when bored. Likewise, part of growing up consists of developing a set of manners for various occasions: meeting strangers, attending school, going to religious services, and so on. Young children who haven't learned all the do's and don'ts of polite society often embarrass their parents by behaving inappropriately ("Mummy, why is that man so fat?"), but by the time they enter school, behaviour that might have been excusable or even amusing just isn't acceptable. Good manners are often aimed at making others more comfortable. For example, able-bodied people often mask their discomfort upon encountering someone with a disability by acting nonchalant or stressing similarities between themselves and the disabled person.[83]

Social rules govern our behaviour in a variety of settings. It would be impossible to keep a job, for example, without meeting certain expectations. People in sales are obliged to treat customers with courtesy. Employees need to appear reasonably respectful when talking to their managers. Some forms of clothing would be considered outrageous in the workplace. By agreeing to take on a job, you are signing an unwritten contract that you will present a certain face at work, whether or not that face reflects the way you might be feeling at a particular moment.

Even when social roles don't dictate the proper way to behave, we often manage impressions for a second reason: to accomplish personal goals. You might, for example, dress up for a visit to traffic court in the hope that your front ("responsible citizen") will persuade the judge

YOUNG COMMUNICATOR PROFILE

BIANCA FREEDMAN

Digital Account Director, Edelman Canada

While studying communications at university, I learned about the impact of technology on society, from the printing press to the internet. I never thought that after only a few years after graduating, I'd have the opportunity to help Walmart, one of the largest retailers in the world, react to a tech media revolution. E-commerce, social media, and mobile platforms have changed retail forever—it was really amazing to observe and then support that shift.

Today, I work at Edelman Worldwide—the world's largest public relations firm, building digital marketing-communications strategies for some of North America's most iconic and important companies. I manage people and resources to help bring ideas to market.

As young communicators, we have a tremendous opportunity to ride the wave of digital change and make a real impact on what's ahead for Canadian business. If you're in an Introduction to Communication course, you're already developing a valuable academic perspective. You're likely reading theorists like Marshall McLuhan; arguably the most relevant text to our generation, while gaining valuable critical thinking and presentation skills that are useful in any work environment.

Combine this knowledge with your day-to-day life: perhaps you're an app user, a Facebook addict, a Pinterest curator, a Twitter sharer, an online shopper . . . these behaviours offer an edge that is still rare in many workplaces today.

My advice to you is to have fun in class, without losing sight of how much learning goes on outside the classroom, especially in the social interactions with your friends—perhaps right now from your mobile phone.

To end with Marshall McLuhan's words, "We become what we behold. We shape our tools and then our tools shape us" (*Understanding Media*, 1964).

to treat you sympathetically. You behave affably toward your neighbours so they will respect your request that they keep their dog off your lawn. We also try to create a desired impression to achieve one or more of the social needs described in Chapter 1: affection, inclusion, control, and so on. For instance, you might act friendlier and livelier than you feel upon meeting a new person so that you will appear likeable. You could sigh and roll your eyes when arguing politics with a classmate to gain an advantage in a debate. You might smile to show the attractive stranger at a party that you would like to get better acquainted. In situations like these you aren't being deceptive as much as putting your best foot forward.

All these examples show that it is difficult—even impossible—*not* to create impressions. After all, you have to send *some* sort of message. If you don't act friendly when meeting a stranger, you may act aloof, indifferent, hostile, or other manner. If you don't act businesslike, you may act casual, goofy, or other manner. Often the question isn't whether or not to present a face to others; the question is only which face to present.

How Do We Manage Impressions?

How do we create a public face? In an age when technology provides many options for communicating, the answer depends in part on the medium of communication chosen.

Face-to-Face Impression Management

In face-to-face interaction, communicators can manage their impression in three ways: through manner, appearance, and setting.[84] *Manner* consists of a communicator's words and non-verbal actions. Physicians, for example, display a wide variety of manners as they conduct physical examinations. Some are friendly and conversational, whereas others adopt a brusque and impersonal approach. Still others are polite but businesslike. Much of a communicator's manner comes from what he or she says. A doctor who remembers details about your interests and hobbies is quite different from one who sticks to clinical questions. But along with the content of speech, non-verbal behaviours play a big role in creating impressions. A doctor who greets you with a friendly smile and a handshake comes across quite differently from one who gives nothing more than a curt nod. The same principle holds in personal relationships: your manner plays a major role in shaping how others view you. Chapters 3 and 4 will describe in detail how your words and non-verbal behaviours create impressions. Because you have to speak and act, the question isn't whether or not your manner sends messages but whether or not these messages will be intentional.

Along with manner, a second dimension of impression management is *appearance*—the personal items people use to shape an image. Sometimes appearance is part of creating a professional image. A physician's lab coat and a police officer's uniform both set the wearer apart as someone special. A tailored suit and a rumpled outfit create very different impressions in the business world. Off the job, clothing is just as important. We choose clothing that sends a message about ourselves, sometimes trendy and sometimes traditional. Some people dress in ways that accent their sexuality, whereas others hide it. Clothing can say "I'm an athlete," "I'm wealthy," or "I'm an environmentalist." Along with dress, other aspects of appearance play a strong role in impression management. Do you have any tattoos or piercings? What is your hair style?

A third way to manage impressions is through the choice of *setting*—physical items we use to influence how others view us. Consider the items that people use to decorate the space where they live. Think, for example, of how the posters and other objects a student uses to decorate her dorm room function as a kind of "who I am" statement.[85] In modern Western society the automobile is a major part of impression management. This explains why many

Cultural Idiom
putting your best foot forward
To make the best appearance possible.

Cultural Idiom
sticks to
To focus solely on something.

people lust after cars that are far more expensive and far less fuel-efficient than they really need. Whether it's a sporty red convertible or an imposing black SUV, a vehicle doesn't just get people from one place to another; it also makes a statement about the kind of person driving it.

The physical setting we choose and the way we arrange it are other important ways to manage impressions. What colours do you choose for the place you live? What artwork? What music do you play? Of course, we choose a setting that we enjoy; but in many cases we create an environment that will present the desired front to others. If you doubt this fact, just recall the last time you straightened up your home before important guests arrived. You might be comfortable with a messy place when you're "backstage," but the front you put on in public—at least to some people—is quite different.

Impression Management in Mediated Communication

At first glance, computer-mediated communication (CMC) seems to have limited potential for identity management. E-mail messages, for example, appear to lack the "richness" of other channels. They don't convey the postures, gestures, or facial expressions that are an important part of face-to-face communication. They even lack the vocal information available in telephone messages. These limitations might seem to make it harder to create and manage an identity when communicating via computer.

Recently, though, communication scholars have begun to recognize that what is missing in computer-mediated communication can actually be an advantage for communicators who want to manage the impressions they make.[86] E-mail users can edit their messages until they create just the desired impression.[87] They can choose the desired level of clarity or ambiguity, seriousness or humour, logic or emotion. Unlike face-to-face communication, electronic correspondence allows a sender to say difficult things without forcing the receiver to respond immediately, and it permits the receiver to ignore a message rather than give an unpleasant response. Options like these show that CMC can serve as a tool for impression management at least as well as face-to-face communication.

In CMC, communicators have much greater control over what kinds of information to reveal or hide. A web designer who doesn't want to be judged by his appearance (his age, his gender, his looks, etc.) can hide or manipulate these characteristics in ways that aren't possible in face-to-face settings. A telecommuter working at home can close a big deal via computer while cursing about the client, chomping on an apple, or feeding the dog—none of which is recommended in face-to-face business dealings.

In addition to providing greater control over *what* messages say, mediated channels enhance communicators' control over *how* the message is shaped, whether to enhance their own identity or to preserve the face of others. On the internet, it's possible to shape a message until it creates just the desired impression. You can edit remarks to get the right tone of sincerity, humour, irony, or concern—or not send any message at all, if that is the best way to maintain face. This kind of identity

Cultural Idiom
lust after
To strongly desire something.

Cultural Idiom
straightened up
To be cleaned and/or organized.

Cultural Idiom
richness
To have completeness.

Cultural Idiom
preserve the face of others
To protect the dignity of others.

🎥 COMMUNICATION ON-SCREEN

Being Erica (2009–11)
Created by Jana Sinyor.

This CBC show focuses on Erica Strange (Erin Karpluk), a young woman who begins seeing a therapist. Unbeknownst to her, her therapist Dr. Tom Wexlar (Micheal Riley) has the power to send Erica through time to physically relive important events throughout her life. The therapeutic tools paired with time travel and multi-dimensionality are strange and fascinating. But equally fascinating, if somewhat less befuddling, are the adjustments to verbal and non-verbal behaviours we see as Erica grows throughout her therapeutic process. When the show begins, she is brash, over-educated, and an under-achiever who lacks confidence and direction; however, as the show progresses Erica gains the skills to mediate her own shortcomings. The show, in later seasons, sees Erica undergo training in this strange time travelling therapy, eventually becoming a doctor herself. The show garnered international syndication and a fan following. The aspects of effective communication and professional/personal management of oneself were central themes for Erica to mature and succeed.

"I loved your E-mail, but I thought you'd be older."

management is important in personal communication as well as in business communication. A 2010 survey found that only 20 per cent of people said they were more truthful when communicating via text message or Twitter, while almost a third said they were more honest when speaking with another person face-to-face.[88] The CBC television program *Street Cents*, in an episode devoted to online dating, reported that more than 25 per cent of the people who have looked for dates online admit to having misrepresented themselves. The most common misrepresentations involved age, appearance, and marital status.[89]

Some statistics from a survey by the Pew Internet and American Life Project reveal how much people—especially younger ones—manage their identities on the Web. Fifty-six per cent of online teens had more than one screen name or e-mail address, and many reported that they used some of these names to hide their real identities from strangers, and even friends. Roughly a quarter of the online teens said they had given false information about themselves in emails or instant messages.[90] Despite Facebook's age limit policy requiring users

---

UNDERSTANDING COMMUNICATION TECHNOLOGY

Web 3.0

The internet has redefined the way we communicate with each other, and it's changing again with the development of Web 3.0. As you read Lars Wessman's explanation of what Web 3.0 is and how it works, think about the new ways we might use computer-mediated communication to manage our impressions.

Discussing Web 3.0 is easier if you understand what Web 2.0 is. Let's define Web 2.0.

A static web page is one where the user doesn't interact with the web page. Students who are old enough will remember a web filled with pages they read and only interacted with when they filled in forms. Web 2.0 is defined by web pages that have dynamic content. This can mean two things:

There's a social dimension to Web 2.0 as well. Web 2.0 sites are set up to take advantage of user-created content. Rather than going through the expensive and time-consuming process of creating content for a website, Web 2.0 sites concentrate on building a community on and around the website. Once the community is built, it is the members of that community who create the content for the site. In fact, one could say that the community *is* the content of the Web 2.0 site. This

model can make large websites relatively cheap to start up because most of the work is done by the users of the site. For example, Wikipedia is at the time of this writing, the fifth most popular site on the internet and has 142 full-time employees and revenues of US$48.6 million (http://en.wikipedia.org/wiki/Wikimedia_Foundation). Wikipedia employees work to support a community of about 105,000 regular content editors who volunteer their time and effort, and hundreds of millions of users every month (Wolfram Alpha).

Tim Berners-Lee (w3.org/People/Berners-Lee/) created the HTTP protocol, URL addresses, and the HTML markup language, all of which are part of the technical foundation of the internet, and he is currently the head of the W3 Consortium, which is the international organization that sets internet Standards. Berners-Lee calls static websites and Web 2.0 websites the "internet of documents." Documents are things that humans can trade, look at, and understand, so the internet of documents is where information is created, traded, and given meaning by humans.

Tim Berners-Lee talks about there being another internet, the "internet of data." In the internet of data, it is the computers themselves which trade information amongst themselves, create it, and give it meaning. It is the internet of data that we are referring to when we say "Web 3.0."

How does Web 3.0 work? Humans trade information among themselves in human languages, such as French, English, or Japanese. Computers don't understand human language very well, despite our best efforts to train them, so computer programmers need to encode information in a format that is easy for computers to deal with. To this end, programmers created various formats to do this, most of which have arcane-sounding names like RDF, OWL, or XML. These formats boil down to a simple relationship: any two objects must have a link between them and each object has a unique description that can be accessed on the internet using an URL. These descriptions of the data, if one looks at all of the descriptions linked to in a document, can often contain more information than the data being commented on by the descriptions. All this complexity is there to allow each person to describe the world the way they see it, and still have a computer be able to understand the description and have it make sense with other descriptions of the same thing, much like we can understand different descriptions of the same flower by different people.

Databases filled with information like this can be located all over the internet. A computer only needs to know where the information is located to make use of it. For example, a website that provides information about houses to prospective homebuyers might get information from databases on crime in the area where the house is located, information about the neighbors found on social networking sites, and information about building inspections from the city hall. The website could then give the buyer information about the desirability of a particular house, whether the asking price is reasonable as well as information about homes with similar profiles. The website could even provide unexpected sorts of information, such as similar homes with neighbors who have demonstrated an interest in environmental issues. If the prospective homebuyer is concerned for the environment, he or she might want to be around neighbors for whom the environment is also top of mind.

By collecting information from different sources and systematically searching and organizing the information in a process called "data-mining," computers can create new information. There are ways of analyzing relationships found in data that actually create new information about the data and about the world. Consider the website flightcaster.com. Flightcaster.com has collected information about the conditions under which flights get delayed. The website applies a proprietary method for finding patterns in that data and, on the basis of that analysis, promises to be able to predict when a plane will be delayed at least six hours before the delay will actually be announced by the airline. This sort of "intelligence" will transform our lives in the near future.

The possibilities for services built on collecting data from different sites and creating new data on-the-fly are endless. Web 3.0 is about increasing our power to know about the world around us. When Web 3.0 is coupled with mobile computing, it becomes a second nervous system and brain for each of us, connecting us together and showing us more of the world than we would be able to see without it.

The next phase in the evolution of the web will be the Internet of Things where sensors will be attached to monitor many everyday activities. Many researchers and futurists say that this new world of connected sensors, sending feedback about our daily activities to various services we subscribe to will dwarf the current internet. In this new internet, sensors will be attached to everything so that we can monitor our activity: tiny sensors in a heart patient's pacemaker to a sensor attached to the milk carton that indicates whether the carton has been opened that day; to sensors in our cars and home appliances. This web of sensors attached to our things will automatically send feedback to other machines. An early application of this technology is monitoring the health and well-being of senior citizens who live alone—sensors can indicate whether a medicine bottle has been opened, whether the toilet has been used, or whether a person has fallen down and not gotten back up. The Internet of Things will begin to realize the connected future seen in movies such as *Minority Report*, where our machines track and provide advice to us. GoodRobot is a Canadian company that has been innovating in developing medical sensors to improve quality of life for seniors who live independently (www.goodrobot.com).

Lars Wessman, Associate Executive Director,
Ottawa Riverkeeper, June 2014

QUESTIONS: The Web 3.0 revolution will make the World Wide Web much more interactive and customizable through the use of artificial intelligence. These virtual machines will do our bidding and make decisions for us about what to read and look at. What is it that makes the idea of artificial intelligence so appealing? How will impression management in the world of intelligent machines differ from the real-world kind, especially when the machines are capable of finding out all sorts of information about us?

to be at least 13 years old, in 2011, 50 per cent of British children between the ages of 9 and 12 had a Facebook account, created by lying about their age.[91]

Recent research has revealed that communicators who are concerned with impression management don't always prefer computer-mediated channels. People are generally comfortable with face-to-face interaction when they feel confident that others support the image they want to present. On the other hand, people are more likely to prefer mediated channels when their own self-presentation is threatened.[92]

Impression Management and Honesty

After reading this far, you might think that impression management sounds like an academic label for manipulation or phoniness. If the perceived self is the "real" you, it might seem that any behaviour that contradicts it would be dishonest.

There certainly are situations where impression management is dishonest. A manipulative date who pretends to be interested in a long-term relationship but is really just after a one-night stand is clearly unethical and deceitful. So are job applicants who lie about academic records or salespeople who pretend to be dedicated to customer service when their real goal is to increase their commissions. But managing impressions doesn't necessarily make you a liar. In fact, it is almost impossible to imagine how we could communicate effectively without making decisions about which front to present in one situation or another. It would be ludicrous for you to act the same way with strangers as you do with close friends, and nobody would show the same face to a two-year-old as to an adult.

Each of us has a repertoire of faces—a cast of characters—and part of being a competent communicator is choosing the best role for the situation. Consider a few examples:

- You offer to teach a friend a new skill—playing the guitar, operating a computer program, or sharpening a tennis backhand. Your friend is making slow progress with the skill, and you find yourself growing impatient.
- At a party with a companion, you meet someone you find very attractive, and you are pretty sure that the feeling is mutual. You feel an obligation to spend most of your time with the person you came with, but the opportunity here is very appealing.
- At work you face a belligerent customer. You don't believe that anyone has the right to treat you this way.
- A friend or family member makes a joke about your appearance that hurts your feelings. You aren't sure whether to make an issue of the remark or pretend that it doesn't bother you.

In each of these situations—and in countless others every day—you have a choice about how to act. It is an oversimplification to say that there is only one honest way to behave in each circumstance and that every other response would be insincere and dishonest. Instead, impression management involves deciding which face—which part of yourself—to reveal. For example, when teaching a new skill you can choose to display the patient instead of the impatient side of yourself. In the same way, at work you have the option of acting hostile or non-defensive in difficult situations. With strangers, friends, or family you can choose whether or not to disclose your feelings. Which face to show to others is an important decision, but in any case you are sharing a real part of yourself. You may not be revealing everything—but, as you will learn in Chapter 6, complete self-disclosure is rarely appropriate.

Summary

Perceptions of others are always selective and are often distorted. The chapter began by describing how personal narratives shape our perceptions. It then outlined several perceptual errors that can affect the way we view and communicate with others. Along with universal psychological influences, cultural factors affect perceptions. Increased empathy is a valuable tool for increasing understanding of others and hence communicating more effectively with them. Perception-checking is one tool for increasing the accuracy of perceptions and for increasing empathy.

Perceptions of one's self are just as subjective as perceptions of others, and they influence communication at least as much. Although individuals are born with some innate personality characteristics, the self-concept is shaped dramatically by communication with others, as well as by cultural factors. Once established, the self-concept can lead us to create self-fulfilling prophecies that determine how we behave and how others respond to us.

Impression management consists of strategic communication designed to influence others' perceptions. Impression management operates when we seek, consciously or unconsciously, to present one or more public faces to others. These faces may be different from the private, spontaneous behaviour that occurs outside of others' presence. Identity management is usually collaborative: communication goes most smoothly when we communicate in ways that support others' faces, and they support ours. Some communicators are high self-monitors who are highly conscious of their own behaviour, whereas others are low self-monitors who are less aware of how their words and actions affect others.

Impression management occurs for two reasons. In many cases it is designed for following social rules and conventions. In other cases it is meant to achieve a variety of content and relational goals. In either case, communicators engage in creating impressions by managing their manner, appearance, and the settings in which they interact with others. Although impression management might seem manipulative, it can be an authentic form of communication. Because each person has a variety of faces that he or she can present, choosing which one to put forth doesn't have to be dishonest.

Key Terms

empathy   51

face   67

facework   67

impression management   66

narratives   41

perceived self   66

perception-checking   53

personality   62

presenting self   67

reflected appraisal   58

self-concept   56

self-esteem   57

self-fulfilling prophecy   64

self-serving bias   42

significant other   59

sympathy   52

Activities

A. Exploring Narratives

Think about a situation where relational harmony is created because you and others involved in the situation share the same narrative. Then think of another situation where you both use different narratives to describe the same situation. What are the consequences of having different narratives in this situation?

B. Experiencing another Cyberculture

Spend at least an hour in an online forum that reflects a culture that is unfamiliar to you and where you are a minority. For example, visit a social gaming community such as Second Life, Call of Duty Online, or World of Warcraft and explore alternative identities where a cultural group other than your own is the majority; spend time on a discussion site with people whose political views are radically different from your own; visit an online community where people of a different age group make up the majority; or attend an online meeting of an organization or a religious group of which you are not a member. Observe how communication practices differ from those of your own culture. Based on your experience, discuss what you can do to facilitate communication with people from other cultural backgrounds whom you may encounter in your everyday life. (As you develop a list of ideas, keep in mind that what you might consider helpful behaviour could make online communicators from different cultures even more uncomfortable.)

C. Understanding Empathy

Choose a disagreement you've been having or have had with another person or group. The disagreement might be a personal one—an argument about how to settle a financial problem, for instance—or it might be a dispute over a contemporary public issue, such as what the provincial or federal government should be doing to stop climate change.

1. In 300 words or so, describe your side of the issue. State your position and explain why you believe as you do, just as if you were presenting your position to a panel of judges.

2. Now write another 300 words, in the first-person singular, to describe the position of the other person or group. For a short while get in touch with how the other person feels and thinks.

3. Show the description you wrote to your "opponent," the person whose beliefs are different from yours. Have that person read your account and correct any statements that don't reflect his or her position accurately. Remember: you're doing this so that you can more clearly understand how the issue looks to the other person.

4. Make any necessary corrections in the account you wrote and again show it to your partner. When your partner agrees that you understand his or her position, have your partner sign your paper to indicate this.

5. Now record your conclusions to this experiment. Has this perceptual shift made any difference in how you view the issue or how you feel about your partner?

D. Perception-Checking Practice

Practise your perception-checking ability by developing three-part verifications for the following situations:

1. You made what you thought was an excellent suggestion to an instructor. The instructor looked uninterested but said she would check on the matter right away. Three weeks have passed, and nothing has changed.

2. A neighbour and good friend, who is normally quite friendly, has not responded to your "Good morning" greeting for three days in a row.

3. You haven't received the usual weekly phone call from the folks back home in over a month. The last time you spoke, you had an argument about where to spend the holidays.

4. A friend with whom you have shared the problems of your love life for years has recently changed around you: the formerly casual hugs and kisses have become longer and stronger, and the occasions where you "accidentally" brush up against one another have become more frequent.

5. A person with whom you really don't have a close relationship in the real world is commenting on all of your social media posts and status updates, acting like your best friend.

E. Identifying Your Identities

Keep a one-day log of the identities you create in different situations: at school, at work, on social media, with strangers, with various family members, and with different friends. For each identity:

1. Describe the persona you are trying to project (e.g., "responsible son or daughter," "laid-back friend," "attentive student").

2. Explain how you communicate to promote this identity. What kinds of things do you say (or not say)? How do you act?

F. Honesty and Multiple Identities

This text argues that presenting different identities to the world isn't inherently dishonest. Nonetheless, there are certainly cases when it is deceitful to construct an identity that doesn't match your private self.

Explore the ethics of multiple identities by identifying a time in your life when:

1. you presented a public identity that didn't match your private self in a manner that wasn't unethical; and

2. a situation (real or hypothetical) in which you have presented or could present a dishonest identity.

Based on the situations you and your classmates present, develop a code of ethics that identifies the boundary between ethical and unethical identity management.

Further Reading

Bauby, Jean-Dominique, *The Diving Bell and the Butterfly* (London: HarperCollins, 2007).
Bauby was the publisher of *Elle* magazine in Paris until a stroke left him almost completely paralyzed; the only part of his body he could control was his left eyelid. Even though his mind remained active, his ability to communicate was restricted to blinking. Bauby's case illustrates how the "self" or mind can soar even when the body is paralyzed.

Carr, Nicholas, *The Shallows* (New York: Norton, 2011).
In this exquisitely well-written book, which had its origins in an essay published in *The Atlantic*, Carr examines how social media are rewiring our brains and changing our sense of self and others.

O'Brien, Jodi, and Peter Kollock, eds., *The Production of Reality: Essays and Readings on Social Interaction*, 3rd edn (Thousand Oaks, CA: Pine Forge Press, 2001).
Part III of this fascinating collection includes six selections describing how the self is a product of social interaction. Part IV offers five readings illustrating how the self-fulfilling prophecy operates in a variety of contexts ranging from first impressions in social situations to mental institutions.

Rapaille, Clothaire, *The Culture Code: An Ingenious Way to Understand Why People around the World Live and Buy as They Do* (New York: Broadway, 2007).
Rapaille left a successful practice as a psychologist helping autistic children, and as a psychoanalyst to troubled people, to apply his knowledge and skills to the problem of "decoding" American culture. In this book he offers insightful and convincing analyses of why people around the world relate to one another differently and why certain things make us feel comfortable and secure while others repel us. He examines the large areas of concern for most people: dating, sexuality, prestige, food, intergenerational communication, and safety, among many others.

Cunningham, Carolyn, ed., *Social Networking and Impression Management* (Plymouth, UK: Lexington Books, 2013).

This book is a collection of scholarly articles that examine how social networking is changing how we manage first impressions. The articles examine the question from social, cultural, and psychological perspectives. This collection of articles contains great insight into how to present yourself in the social media world.

Study Questions

1. Describe a situation in which an English Canadian and an immigrant from a non-European country might have incompatible narratives.

2. Discuss how common perceptual tendencies (pp. 42–7), situational factors (pp. 47–9), and cultural differences (pp. 49–51) can lead to friction. How can greater empathy help people communicate more smoothly?

3. Explain some of the factors (personal and cultural) that have helped shape your self-concept.

4. Using yourself or someone you know as an example, describe how the process of identity management operates during an average day. Discuss the ethics of presenting multiple identities.

5. Think of five ways in which social media have affected your sense of self. Now think of how social media has affected your perceptions of your friends. Discuss how social media are "rewiring" our sense of self and our perceptions of our relationships.

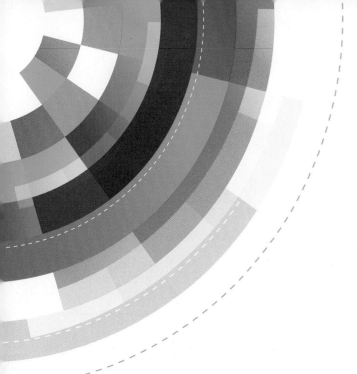

3

Language

After studying the material in this chapter . . .

You should understand:

✔ the symbolic, person-centred nature of language;

✔ the phonological, syntactic, semantic, and pragmatic rules that govern language;

✔ the ways in which language shapes and reflects attitudes;

✔ the different types of troublesome language and the skills required to deal with each;

✔ the gender and non-gender factors that characterize the speech of men and women; and

✔ the verbal styles that distinguish various cultures, and the effect that language can have on worldview.

You should be able to:

✔ discuss how you and others use phonological, syntactic, semantic, and pragmatic rules and how these rules affect the way a message is understood;

✔ identify at least two ways in which language has shaped your attitudes;

✔ identify at least two ways in which language reflects your attitudes;

✔ recognize and suggest alternatives for equivocal language, slang and jargon, relative terms, and overly abstract language;

✔ identify and suggest alternatives for fact-inference and fact-opinion confusion and for emotive statements;

✔ suggest appropriate alternatives for unnecessary or misleading euphemisms and equivocal statements; and

✔ identify the degree to which your speech reflects gender stereotypes and then reflect on the effect your cultural speech patterns have on others.

Chapter Highlights

Language has several important characteristics:

» It is symbolic.

» Its meanings reside in the minds of people, not in words themselves.

» It is governed by several types of rules, and understanding those rules helps us understand one another.

Beyond simply expressing ideas, language can be very powerful:

» It can shape our attitudes toward things and toward one another.

» It can reflect the way we feel about things and people.

Some kinds of language can create problems by unnecessarily:

» disrupting relationships,

» confusing others, or

» avoiding important information.

Gender plays an important role in the way language operates:

» The content of male and female speech varies somewhat.

» Men and women often have different reasons for communicating.

» Male and female conversational styles vary in some interesting ways.

» Gender isn't always the most important factor shaping language use.

Cultural factors can shape the way we see and understand language:

» Different cultures have different notions of what language styles are and aren't appropriate.

» The language we speak can shape the way we view the world.

At one time or another, every one of us has suffered the limits and traps of language. Even when the words we are using are familiar, it's clear that we often don't use them in ways that allow us to communicate smoothly with one another.

In the following pages we will explore the nature of linguistic communication. By the time you have finished reading this chapter, you will better appreciate the complexity of language, its power to shape our perception of people and events, and its potential for incomplete and inaccurate communication. Perhaps more important, you will be better equipped to use the tool of language more skilfully to improve your everyday interaction.

The Nature of Language

Humans speak about 10,000 language varieties.[1] Although most of these sound different from one another, all possess the same characteristics of **language**: a collection of symbols, governed by rules and used to convey messages between individuals. A closer look at this definition can both explain how language operates and suggest how we can use it more effectively.

language
A collection of symbols, governed by rules and used to convey messages between individuals.

Language Is Symbolic

There's nothing natural about calling your loyal four-pawed companion a "dog" or the object you're reading right now a "book." These two words, like virtually all language, are symbols— arbitrary constructions that represent a communicator's thoughts. Not all linguistic symbols are spoken or written words. Furthermore, speech and writing aren't the only forms of language. Sign language, as "spoken" by most deaf people, is symbolic in nature and not the pantomime it might seem. There are literally hundreds of different sign languages spoken around the world that represent the same ideas in different ways.[2] These distinct languages include Canadian Sign Language, *Langue des Signes Québécois*, British Sign Language, French Sign Language, Danish Sign Language, Chinese Sign Language—even Australian Aboriginal and Mayan sign languages.

Symbols are more than just labels: they are a way of experiencing the world. You can prove this fact by trying a simple experiment.[3] Work up some saliva in your mouth, and then spit it into a glass. Take a good look, and then drink it up. Most people find this process mildly disgusting. But ask yourself why this is so. After all, we swallow our own saliva all the time. The answer arises out of the symbolic labels we use. After the saliva is in the glass, we call it *spit* and think of it in a different way. In other words, our reaction is to the name and the concept, not the thing.

"What part of oil lamp next to double squiggle over ox don't you understand?"

The naming process operates in virtually every situation. How you react to a stranger will depend on the symbols you use to categorize him or her: gay (or straight), religious (or not), attractive (or unattractive), and so on.

Meanings Are in People, Not in Words

Ask a dozen people what the same symbol means, and you are likely to get 12 different answers. Does a Canadian flag bring up associations of peacekeeping missions around the world? Rowdy hockey fans streaming out of bars into the streets after an international victory? Inukshuks, totem poles, and other items associated with the country's Aboriginal populations? Saint-Jean-Baptiste Day parades in Montreal? How about a cross, a crescent, or a menorah: what do they represent? Sunday school? Religious imperialism? The necklace your sister always wears?

As with physical symbols, so with language: the place to look for meaning is not in words themselves but rather in the way people understand them. An unfortunate episode illustrating that truth occurred in Washington, DC, when the city ombudsman described an approach to budget-making as "niggardly" and some African-American critics accused him of uttering an unforgivable racial slur.[4] Although his defenders pointed out that the word, which means "miserly," is Scandinavian in origin and has no connection at all with the word it resembles, the incident was a reminder that, correct or not, the meanings that people associate with a word have far more significance than any dictionary definition.

Linguistic theorists C.K. Ogden and I.A. Richards illustrated the fact that meanings are social constructions in their well-known "triangle of meaning" (Figure 3.1).[5] This model shows that there is only an indirect relationship—indicated by the broken line—between a word and the thing it claims to represent. Some of these "things," or referents, do not exist in the physical world. For instance, some referents are mythical (such as unicorns), some are no longer tangible (such as Elvis, if he really is dead), and others are abstract ideas (such as love).

Problems arise when we mistakenly assume that others use words in the same way we do. It's possible to have an argument about "environmentalism" without ever realizing that you and the other person are using that term to represent entirely different things. The same goes for "conservative," "distinct society," "national health care," "rock music," and thousands upon thousands of other words and phrases. Words don't mean; people do—and often in widely different ways.

Despite the potential for linguistic problems, the situation isn't hopeless. We do, after all, communicate with one another reasonably well most of the time. And with enough effort, we can clear up most of the misunderstandings that do occur. The key to more accurate use of language is to avoid assuming that others interpret words the same way we do. In truth, successful communication occurs when we negotiate the meaning of a statement.[6] As one French proverb puts it, the spoken word belongs half to the one who speaks it and half to the one who hears.

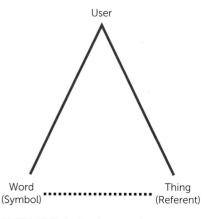

FIGURE 3.1 Ogden and Richards's Triangle of Meaning

Language Is Rule-Governed

Languages contain several types of rules. **Phonological rules** govern how words sound when pronounced. For instance, the words *champagne*, *double*, and *occasion* are spelled identically in French and English but are pronounced differently in each language. English is notable for having particularly inconsistent phonological rules, as a few examples illustrate:

phonological rules
Linguistic rules governing how sounds are combined to form words.

- He could lead if he would get the lead out.
- A farm can produce produce.

- The dump was so full it had to refuse refuse.
- The present is a good time to present the present.
- I did not object to the object.
- The bandage was wound around the wound.
- I shed a tear when I saw the tear in my clothes.

Non-native English speakers are plagued by the apparent anarchy of the language's phonological rules, especially in contrast to languages with highly regularized phonology such as Spanish and German. While those languages rigorously re-spell words as they borrow them from other tongues to ensure a word's pronounced and written form are consistent, English has compiled its vast collection of borrowed words without much concern for consistency.

Phonological rules aren't the only ones that govern the way we use language to communicate. Syntactic rules govern the structure of language—the way symbols can be arranged. For example, the rules of English syntax require that most English sentences have a subject, a verb, and an object, in that order. It also prohibits sentences such as "Have you the cookies brought?"

> **syntactic rules**
> Linguistic rules that govern the ways in which symbols can be arranged as opposed to the meanings of those symbols.

UNDERSTANDING COMMUNICATION TECHNOLOGY

First Museum in the World to Introduce an Innovative Mobile Application for BlackBerry Users

Technological advances are continually breaking down barriers that limit us from connecting to people around the world. The Canadian Museum of Civilization in Ottawa has recently introduced a mobile app that allows BlackBerry users anywhere in the world to access the museum's audio guides, floor plans, and information about exhibits. As you read the museum's press release, see if you can think of other ways institutions could use technology to broaden their audience.

The Canadian Museum of Civilization today became the first museum in the world to introduce a BlackBerry application for access to its audio guides and other museum information. This follows on a similar first for an application accessible to iPhone and iPod Touch in December 2009.

Owners of these popular handheld devices now can obtain one-stop access to museum information from anywhere in the world. They can plan a visit to the museum by accessing interactive floor maps, a calendar of events and information about hours of operation, admission fees, and public services.

"The museum is constantly looking for innovative ways to broaden its audience and reach people in Canada and around the world," said Dr Victor Rabinovitch, president and CEO of the Canadian Museum of Civilization Corporation. "We are delighted to be the first museum in the world to provide this progressive and convenient technology to the public. The Canadian Museum of Civilization strives to preserve Canadian heritage and to share our country's fabulous story with Canadians and the world."

The Museum of Civilization's Mobile Application for BlackBerry Bold 9700, developed in partnership with Tristan Interactive of Ottawa, is now available for free on BlackBerry App World in both official languages. "Tristan's support for the BlackBerry—the North American smartphone market leader—now allows millions of BlackBerry users the best access to museum multimedia. Tristan is proud to be the first in the world to build this technology," said Chris McLaren, CEO of Tristan Interactive Inc.

In addition to automatic updates about new museum programs and exhibitions, two audio guides, which were previously accessible only on museum-supplied headsets, are now available on these personal handheld devices. Visitors can use their mobile devices to visit two of the museum's largest and most popular exhibition galleries. At the touch of a button, BlackBerry owners have access to Canada Hall, which relays the history of Canada from the year 1000 to the present and the First Peoples Hall, which shares with listeners how Canada's First Peoples shaped our country as we now know it. In essence, the history of the foundation of Canada is brought to Canadians and the world through this new application.

Canadian Museum of Civilization Press Release, 29 March 2010

which is a perfectly acceptable word order in German. Although most of us aren't able to describe the syntactic rules that govern our language, it's easy to recognize their existence by noting how odd a statement that violates them appears.

Syntactic rules and pronunciation can vary even within a language. In Canada, for instance, the English language is fairly uniform except in the Atlantic provinces (Newfoundland and Labrador, Nova Scotia, New Brunswick, Prince Edward Island), where Irish, Scottish, Gaelic, and French have heavily influenced spoken English. Quebec French also shows massive regional variation in phonology and syntax. There are as many accents and dialects in the province of Quebec

as there are regions. As well, the French spoken in different provinces varies enormously: Franco-Ontarians, Franco-Albertans, Acadians, and many others have significantly different ways of pronouncing words and organizing sentences.

Technology has spawned sub-versions of English, each with its own syntactic rules.[7] For example, users of instant messaging on the internet have devised a streamlined version of English, sometimes called *leet* or *geekspeak*,[8] that speeds up typing in real-time communication (although it probably makes teachers of composition grind their teeth in anguish):[9]

A: Sup. You home?

B: yup y?

A: b/c. wnna chill?

B: nah, cant. gotta LO.

A: y?

B: i need 2 <Rup> for finals ALAP, prolly. BBM me tho, k? Im so C-P. g2g.

A: sux. kk ttyl. Zerg study later, mab, or cicyhw?

B: fersure. Lates.

Semantic rules deal with the meanings of specific words. Semantic rules are what make it possible for us to agree that "bikes" are for riding and "books" are for reading; they also help us to know whom we will and won't encounter when we open doors marked "men" or "women." Without semantic rules, communication would be impossible, because each of us would use symbols in unique ways, unintelligible to one another.

Semantic misunderstandings occur when words can be interpreted in more than one way, as the following humorous headlines prove:

- "Police Begin Campaign to Run Down Jaywalkers"
- "British Left Waffles on Falkland Islands"
- "Prostitutes Appeal to Pope"
- "Panda Mating Fails; Veterinarian Takes Over"
- "Astronaut Takes Blame for Gas in Spacecraft"
- "New Study of Obesity Looks for Larger Test Group"

Pragmatic rules govern how people use language in everyday interaction.[10] Consider the example of an employer telling a First Nations employee to "Hold down the fort while I am

semantic rules
Linguistic rules that govern the meaning of language as opposed to its structure.

pragmatic rules
Linguistic rules that govern the everyday use of language. Unlike syntactic and semantic rules, pragmatic rules are rarely written down or discussed.

Understanding Diversity

Endangered Languages

Of the six or seven thousand languages spoken in the world today, 90 per cent are in danger of extinction within the next two or three generations.

The situation in which the Mi'kmaq people of Atlantic Canada find themselves is typical of the situation facing many Aboriginal communities everywhere. The Mi'kmaq occupy a reasonably well-defined territory, exercise increasing political autonomy with respect to both the federal and provincial governments, and have a language with a number of mutually understandable dialects. Today, however, that language is perilously close to becoming extinct. Among the greatest obstacles to preserving the Mi'kmaq language is disunity: disunity among those responsible for passing it on through education, and disunity among its speakers. This is in part a systemic problem, stemming from inadequate teaching resources. But it is also a result of the way the colonial period affected Mi'kmaq perceptions, identity, and self-definition.

For centuries it was the policy first of the colonial government, then of the federal and provincial governments, to divide the First Nations by confining them to reserves, banning the celebration of their cultural traditions, and attempting to assimilate their children by placing them in residential schools. This policy served to devalue the Mi'kmaq language and culture while reinforcing the majority English or French worldview, which in many respects conflicted with the Mi'kmaq worldview. In time, the Mi'kmaq language was largely forgotten, replaced

away." It's easy to imagine how the subordinate might be offended by a cultural idiom that the boss didn't think twice about. Scholars of language have pointed out several levels at which the rules each person uses can differ. You can understand these levels by imagining how they would operate in our example:

Each person's self-concept:
> **EMPLOYER:** Views himself as a nice guy.
> **EMPLOYEE:** Self-conscious because of historical stereotypes of First Nations people.

The episode in which the comment occurs:
> **EMPLOYER:** A casual remark upon stepping out of the office.
> **EMPLOYEE:** A hurtful reminder of the era when the fort was a colonial outpost that had to be held secure against Indigenous "enemies."

Perceived relationship:
> **EMPLOYER:** Views employees like members of the family.
> **EMPLOYEE:** Depends on boss's goodwill for advancement.

Cultural background:
> **EMPLOYER:** Member of a generation in which hurtful comments about First Nations were commonplace.
> **EMPLOYEE:** Member of a generation sensitive to reminders of past wrongs against First Nations.

As this example shows, pragmatic rules don't involve semantic issues, since the meanings of the words themselves are usually understood well by almost everybody. Instead, they involve connotations—the extended meanings of those words.

by a language that was not historically linked to Mi'kmaq social life. This new language, which the Mi'kmaq had to use to organize their thoughts and perceptions of the world, was a translated worldview, a hybrid created through the imposition of English or French culture. Without a common language and culture, the people drifted apart—both linguistically and politically.

Today the situation is slowly improving. In the Canadian 2006 census, speakers of the Mi'kmaq language, as their mother tongue, was up 4 per cent to 7685 total speakers. (*Canadian Yearbook*, 2012, pg. 13). Academics, politicians, and lobbyists have all agreed that the strategies for preserving endangered Indigenous languages should come from Indigenous communities, not from non-Native "experts." There is a push toward openness and economic development, as well as better governance, education, and natural resource stewardship, in Mi'kmaq communities. Young and old alike are working to revive the old ways and adapt them to the modern realities of diverse, multicultural, information-age Canada. The Mi'kmaq are beginning to make peace with their past pains while asserting their rights and moving boldly forward as players in the Canada of tomorrow. The only question that remains is whether they will be doing it in English, French, Mi'kmaq, or a combination of all three.

QUESTION: How do you think communication technologies could help or hinder the preservation of an endangered language such as Mi'kmaq?

The Power of Language

On the most obvious level, language allows us to satisfy basic functions such as describing ideas, making requests, and solving problems. But beyond these functions, the way we use language also influences others and reflects our attitudes in more subtle ways, which we will examine now.

Language Shapes Attitudes

The power of language to shape ideas has been recognized throughout history. The first chapters of the Bible report that Adam's dominion over animals was demonstrated by his being given the power to give them names.[11] As we will now see, our speech—sometimes consciously and sometimes not—shapes others' values, attitudes, and beliefs in a variety of ways.

Naming

"What's in a name?" Juliet asked rhetorically. If Romeo had been a social scientist, he would have answered, "A great deal." Research has demonstrated that naming is more than just a simple means of identification: names shape the way others think of us, the way we view ourselves, and the way we act.

At the most fundamental level, some research suggests that even the phonetic sound of a person's name affects the way we regard him or her, at least when we don't have other information available. For example, in Canadian politics, having a name that could be either French or English, such as that of former prime minister Paul Martin, is beneficial because it allows both francophone and anglophone voters to feel comfortable with the candidate. In American politics, names that are simple, appealing, easily pronounced, and rhythmic are judged more favourably than those that are not.[12] Consider the names of the winning candidates in one series of US elections: Sanders beat Pekelis, Rielly defeated Dellwo, Grady outpolled Schumacher,

Combs trounced Bernsdorf, and Golden prevailed over Nuffer. Names don't guarantee victory, but in 78 elections studied, 48 outcomes supported the value of having an appealing name.

An excellent contemporary example of the importance of names in politics is First Lady of the United States, Michelle Obama, telling how she was surprised that this man with "a funny name" asked her out, but that she accepted him as her boyfriend anyhow. She repeated this story countless times during the Democratic nomination race and the presidential campaign in an effort to neutralize the idea that the name Barack Hussein Obama made her husband alien or threatening, especially to a public dealing with the Iraq War and terrorism. Another such example is the former president of Peru, Alberto Fujimori, who during his campaign happily adopted the nickname "El Chino" (The Chinaman) because that is how he was popularly referred to, despite actually being of Japanese origin. In Canada, which is a more multicultural nation than the United States, there are many politicians whose names indicate origins that are neither British nor French Canadian. Only one has made it to the prime minister's chair thus far—John Diefenbaker, whose name is of German origin.

The Bible's book of Proverbs (22:1) proclaims "a good name is rather to be chosen than great riches." Social science research confirms this position.[13] In one study, psychologists asked university students to rate over a thousand names according to their likeability, their masculinity or femininity, and how active or passive they seemed. The names Michael, John, and Wendy were viewed as likable and active and were rated as possessing the masculine or feminine traits of their sex. The names Percival, Isadore, and Alfreda were judged less likable, and their sexual identity was less clear.

Credibility

Scholarly speech is a good example of how speaking style influences perception. We refer to what has been called the Dr Fox hypothesis:[14] "An apparently legitimate speaker who utters an unintelligible message will be judged competent by an audience in the speaker's area of apparent expertise." The Dr Fox hypothesis got its name from one Dr Myron L. Fox, who delivered a talk followed by a half-hour discussion on "Mathematical Game Theory as Applied to Physical Education." The audience included psychiatrists, psychologists, social workers, and educators. Questionnaires collected after the session revealed that these educated listeners found the lecture clear and stimulating.

Despite his warm reception by this learned audience, Fox was a complete fraud. He was a professional actor whom researchers had coached to deliver a lecture of double-talk—a patchwork of information from a *Scientific American* article mixed with jokes, non sequiturs, contradictory statements, and meaningless references to unrelated topics. When wrapped in a linguistic package of high-level professional jargon, however, the meaningless gobbledygook was judged as important information. In other words, the reaction of Fox's audience was based more on the credibility that arose from his use of impressive-sounding language than from the ideas he expressed.

The same principle seems to hold for academic writing.[15] A group of 32 management professors rated material according to its complexity rather than its content. When a message about consumer behaviour was loaded with unnecessary words and long, complex sentences, the professors rated it highly. When the same message was translated into more readable English, with shorter words and clearer sentences, the professors judged the same research as less competent. Steven Pinker, a Canadian cognitive scientist teaching at Harvard, indicated that far more ungrammatical sentences can be found in speeches delivered at academic conferences than in the everyday speech of average people.[16]

Status

In the classic musical *My Fair Lady*, Professor Henry Higgins transforms Eliza Doolittle from a lowly flower seller into a high-society woman by replacing her cockney accent with an upper-crust speaking style. Decades of research have demonstrated that the power of speech to influence status is a fact.[17] Several factors combine to create positive or negative impressions: accent, choice of words, speech rate, and even the apparent age of a speaker. In most cases, speakers of standard language varieties are rated higher than non-standard speakers in a variety of ways: they are viewed as more competent and more self-confident, and the content of their messages is rated more favourably. The unwillingness or inability of a communicator to use the standard dialect fluently can have serious consequences. For instance, studies have shown that speakers of African-American Vernacular English (also known as "Black English")—a distinctive dialect with its own accent, grammar, syntax, and semantic rules—are rated as less intelligent, professional,

"No, this is not Mel's secretary. This is Mel."

capable, socially acceptable, and employable by speakers of standard English.[18] Another study found that some First Nations women in British Columbia felt "invalidated" by their verbal interactions with the health care system.[19]

Studies have also shown that people learning English as a second language struggle to overcome the perception that the content of their messages is less credible because they are not fluent. Suzanne Romaine, a sociolinguist, reports that when kindergarten students in Toronto were asked who was most likely to succeed and who was most likely to fail, those who had English as a second language were regarded as twice as likely to fail as native English speakers.[20] She explains that this leads to a vicious cycle where the children are less frequently encouraged to participate and thus have fewer chances to practise speaking English.

Sexism and Racism

By now it should be clear that the power of language to shape attitudes goes beyond individual cases and influences how we perceive entire groups of people. For example, Casey Miller and Kate Swift argue that some aspects of language suggest women are of lower status than men. They contend that, except for words referring by definition to females, such as "mother" and "girl," English defines many non-sexual concepts as male. Most dictionaries, in fact, define "effeminate" as the opposite of "masculine," although the opposite of "feminine" is closer to "unfeminine." They also argue that incorrect use of the pronoun "he" to refer to both men and women can have damaging results:

> On the television screen, a teacher of first-graders who has just won a national award is describing her way of teaching. "You take each child where you find him," she says. "You watch to see what he's interested in, and then you build on his interests."

A five-year-old looking at the program asks her mother, "Do only boys go to that school?"

"No," her mother begins, "she's talking about girls too, but—"

But what? The teacher being interviewed on television is speaking correct English. What can the mother tell her daughter about why a child, in any generalization, is always he rather than she? How does a five-year-old comprehend the generic personal pronoun?[21]

Although French has a separate, neutral pronoun, *on*, to refer to an individual whose sex is not known, it still offers many examples of sexist usage. Fabienne Baider, a sociolinguist, argues that in French, adjectives that would have a positive connotation when used to modify a masculine noun have a very negative connotation when used to modify a feminine noun. For example, to call a man "gallant" means that he is chivalrous and kind, whereas a "gallant" woman is one who is morally loose.[22]

Idiom-Proof

After a screening of the rough cut of *Shrek* a few years ago, it was decided there was a problem with the film's title character, a lonely ogre played by Mike Myers. The problem wasn't the dialogue or the animation; it was the accent. Myers, a native of Toronto, had delivered his lines in his regular voice, making the creature a southern Ontario ogre. That just wasn't funny.

Myers decided to re-dub the part in a Scottish brogue that reminded him of the voices his own mother, who was English, used when she read fairy tales to her children. Crowds roared at the Scottish Shrek and were forgiving of instances where the actor, according to at least one critic, lapsed into Canadian.

There are those who might take umbrage at being told their accent isn't worthy of an animated green monster. Canadians are more likely to be grateful that Mike Myers's linguistic passport was read at all. The Canadian dialect is so subtle it is routinely mistaken as non-existent, or at least as indistinguishable from generic American.

Dialects, of course, are comprised equally of accent and idioms. There isn't a uniform Canadian accent, just as there isn't a uniform British, American, or Indian accent. But there are definite characteristics to Canadian speech, and they show very little variation from the Ottawa River to the Pacific. Generally, Mainland Canadian speech is most similar to the speech of the American West. Our speech is clipped and evenly cadenced. Linguists also write about the phenomenon of "Canadian raising," whereby the initial vowel element in certain vowel clusters is spoken higher in the mouth than in American versions, with a shorter glide to the second element. We say "couch" with an

"ouch" and our "house" sounds like "lout", rather than "loud". We are rumoured to say "ah-boot" for "about," though that may simply be how others hear these high and fast diphthongs.

According to Henry Rogers, a linguist at the University of Toronto, the Canadian accent is actually moving further away from the American. "Something called the Northern Cities Vowel Shift is taking place in the US," he says. "Vowels are sort of shifting in one direction, whereas in Canada they're shifting in the other direction." And there are linguists, at the McGill Dialectology and Sociolinguistics Lab, for instance, who study regional variation in pronunciation within Canadian speech.

Still, not all experts are convinced that Canadian English is faring well. There are academic papers charting its disappearance. A few hard-headed linguists even declare the very notion of a Canadian dialect a myth, fabricated to bolster a wobbly national identity.

As for the other component of dialect, there is evidence of distinctly Canadian expressions. The most recent *Collins English Dictionary* includes some 150 new "Canadian" terms. "Status Indian" and "equalization payment" probably won't excite linguistic pride. But a "saw-off," for a compromise, and "idiot strings," for the ties that keep children's mittens attached to their coats, are lively enough. Then there are our drinking words: a "two-four" and a "twenty-sixer" and a "mickey" of rye, the latter often sipped out of a brown paper bag.

That said, Canadian English, at least from Ottawa westward, can't come close to Irish or Australian for wit and inventiveness. It can't even rival the other major Canadian dialect, the one

It's usually easy to find alternatives for sexist language. For example, the term "mankind" may be replaced by "humanity," "human beings," "human race," or "people;" the adjective "man-made" may be replaced by "artificial," "manufactured," or "synthetic;" and "manpower" may be replaced by "human power," "workers," or "workforce." Likewise:

- "Firemen" may be called "firefighters."
- "Actresses" may be called "actors."
- "Foremen" may be called "supervisors."
- "Policemen" and "policewomen" may be called "police officers."
- "Waiters" and "waitresses" may be called "servers."
- "Stewards" or "Stewardessess" may be called "flight attendants."

The use of labels for racist purposes has a long and ugly history. Names have been used to stigmatize groups that other groups have disapproved of.[23] By using derogatory terms to label some people, the out-group is set apart and pictured in an unfavourable light. In a report about

belonging to Newfoundland. Some of this, according to Charles Boberg, the director of the McGill dialectology lab, has to do with dialect variation. "Old, densely populated areas like England or the eastern US have a lot of dialect variation," he says. "More recently and sparsely settled regions, like western Canada and the western US, exhibit more homogeneity over large areas."

We drift toward the pronunciation that surrounds us, and major cities, where most Canadians now live, aren't necessarily the best places to preserve existing accents, or acquire new ones.

On Canada's East Coast, on the other hand, geographical isolation, along with deep Scottish and Irish roots, ensured that the pronunciation would remain distinct from that of the more heterogeneous middle of the country. There are entire dictionaries that catalogue the vocabularies of Prince Edward Island and Nova Scotia's Cape Breton and South Shore. And out on "The Rock," the speech remains musical and loose and nicely barbed.

An off-the-cuff remark by the Newfoundland comedian Mary Walsh, who declared someone to be "still having the mark of the bucket on her arse," started the television critic John Doyle wondering how she gets away with it. Doyle, who recalled the insult from his own Irish childhood, concluded that the line would have been unacceptable on Canadian TV "if it had been delivered in less colourful language, and without the accent."

The question is, do most Canadians want to leave such a strong impression? The linguistic impulses of most of the English-speaking nation have tended toward moderation and,

sometimes, disguise. Generations of Canadian actors and newsreaders have counted on both to launch careers in the US.

There could also be a class dimension to how the majority of us talk. Middle-class, urban societies tend to avoid strong or idiosyncratic speech, finding such verbal energy unruly. For all their appeal, regional idioms, especially those from the historically poorer "Celtic" regions of Canada, with their culturally ingrained admiration of wordplay and irreverence, have made scant impact on the wider nation. Most of the country hasn't taken into its collective mouth "having a scoff" for eating a meal, or being "stogged" for being stuffed up; it doesn't declare, about blackflies, "If you kill one, 50 more come to its funeral." Few Manitobans, say, delight in explaining that "scluttery" means fatty, or that a guy who has "chowdered it" has messed something up.

If we did, perhaps Mike Myers would have stayed with his Canadian accent. Shrek, after all, would have made a fine Newfoundland ogre.

Charles Foran, *The Walrus*, April/May 2004, http://walrusmagazine.com/articles/ 2004.04-language-accent-canadian/

QUESTIONS: Do you feel that you have an accent? How does your accent reflect your identity? Do you feel more or less Canadian because of your accent? Or does your accent make you identify more with your specific town, province, or country of origin?

Understanding Diversity

Head of Quebec Language Watchdog Resigns After "Pastagate" Controversy

The head of Quebec's language watchdog agency has resigned following a series of controversies that have created embarrassing headlines at home and abroad.

The departure of Louise Marchand, president of the *Office québécois de la langue française*, was announced by the provincial minister responsible for the agency.

Her exit follows a series of news stories that have drawn considerable ridicule upon the agency—in Quebec, the rest of Canada, and even internationally.

The first such story was about how an Italian restaurant was forced to remove the word "pasta" from its menu, and similar reports have surfaced repeatedly in recent days from other restaurant owners.

"These episodes had an undesired effect on the businesses, the Office personnel, the public, and Quebec in general," said Diane De Courcy, minister responsible for the French language.

Such stories are considered damning enough to the OQLF that some of its more nationalist defenders have even voiced theories of an Anglo plot to discredit the agency. But other OQLF defenders say its inspectors are simply doing the job politicians have asked them to do—which is to vigilantly enforce Quebec's language law.

This series of events has created a rare phenomenon in Quebec politics: the *Parti Québécois* government has been calling on the language watchdog to be less aggressive, not more.

It has also led to rare jokes in newspaper columns and cartoons, and in social media, about a 50-year-old institution that francophone Quebecers have traditionally credited as a cultural safeguard.

De Courcy announced several changes to OQLF procedures Friday. One will see the agency create a quality-control post, to keep an eye on any dispute between a business and an agency

---

racial profiling for the Ontario Human Rights Commission,[24] a young Native man, injured during an arrest, is quoted as saying:

> After that [the arrest], I grew up with a lot of hatred towards the cops, especially white cops. And I forgot to mention also that they used racial slurs against us as they were beating us against the fence.

Another young man, also injured during an arrest, said:

> It is really hard when I teach my kids to have respect and to do what is right, and then to get treated like that from the court system and put down, you know, they are not being given a fair chance.

> *The only jobs for which no man is qualified are human incubators and wet nurse. Likewise, the only job for which no woman is or can be qualified is sperm donor.*
>
> **Wilma Scott Heide, author and social activist**

The power of racist language to shape attitudes is difficult to avoid, even when it is obviously offensive. In one study, experimental subjects who heard a derogatory label used against a member of a minority group expressed annoyance at this sort of slur; despite their disapproval, the negative emotional terms did have an impact.[25] Not only did the subjects rate the minority individual's competence lower when that person performed poorly, but they also found fault with others who associated socially with the minority person—even members of the subject's own ethnic group. An excellent example of racist usage is the common practice of using expressions that are offensive to Indigenous people without even knowing it. Calling someone "Chief'" is very derogatory to an Indigenous person because it can be interpreted as a mocking reference to an Indigenous leader.

inspector. There will also be a new procedural guide, among other measures.

The so-called "Pastagate" stories are only one language headache for the government.

An even more significant problem for the PQ, in the long run, could be its difficulty to get a language bill adopted by the legislature.

Bill 14 appears on shaky ground with one opposition party saying it will reject key elements of the legislation. The leader of the Coalition for Quebec's Future says he opposes plans to make French the mandatory language in the workplace for companies with between 25 and 49 employees. He also opposes plans to make it easier to revoke the bilingual status of municipalities with dwindling English-speaking populations.

François Legault told a news conference in Quebec City this morning it is important to strike a balance between promoting French and respecting the rights of Anglophones.

The Coalition has 19 seats in the 125-member national assembly and effectively holds the balance of power.

The governing *Parti Québécois* has 54 seats and the Liberals, who have said they will vote against the language legislation, have 50. The two others are held by the left-wing sovereigntist *Québec Solidaire*. The PQ made protecting French a key issue during last year's election campaign, saying the language was threatened, particularly in Montreal and western Quebec.

The Canadian Press, 8 March 2013

QUESTIONS: How does the issue of bilingual regulation, even on an Italian restaurant menu, reflect the notions that language can shape attitude? Ought the government protect a Francophone identity, or allow multilingualism to potentially undermine a linguistic culture?

Language Reflects Attitudes

Besides shaping the way we view ourselves and others, language reflects our attitudes. Feelings of control, attraction, commitment, responsibility—all these and more are reflected in the way we use language.

Power

Communication researchers have identified a number of language patterns that add to, or detract from, a speaker's ability to influence others and that reflect how a speaker feels about his or her degree of control over a situation.[26] Table 3.1 summarizes some of these findings by listing several types of "powerless" language.

You can see the difference between powerful and powerless language by comparing the following statements:

1. Excuse me, sir, I hate to say this, but I . . . uh . . . I guess I won't be able to turn in the assignment on time. I had a personal emergency and . . . well . . . it was just impossible to finish it by today. I'll have it in your mailbox on Monday, okay?
2. I won't be able to turn in the assignment on time. I had a personal emergency, and it was impossible to finish it by today. I'll have it in your mailbox on Monday.

Although the powerless speech described in Table 3.1 can often lead to unsatisfying results, it would be a mistake to assume that it's always best to sound as powerful as you can. Along with gaining compliance, another common conversational goal is to build a supportive, friendly relationship, and sharing power with the other person can help you in this regard. For

Table 3.1 Powerless Language

Type of Usage	Example
Hedges	"I'm kinda disappointed. . . ." "I think we should. . . ." "I guess I'd like to. . . ."
Hesitations	"Uh, can I have a minute of your time?" "Well, we could try this idea. . . ." "I wish you would . . . er . . . try to be on time."
Intensifiers	"So that's how I feel. . . ." "I'm not very hungry."
Polite forms	"Excuse me, sir. . . ."
Tag questions	"It's about time we got started, isn't it?" "Don't you think we should give it another try?"
Disclaimers	"I probably shouldn't say this, but. . . ." "I'm not really sure, but. . . ."

The power which comes from names and naming is related directly to the power to define others—individuals, races, sexes, ethnic groups. Our identities, who and what we are, how others see us, are greatly affected by the names we are called and by the words with which we are labelled. The names, labels, and phrases employed to "identify" a people may in the end determine their survival.

Haig A. Bosmajian, *The Language of Oppression*

this reason, many everyday statements will contain a mixture of powerful speech and powerless speech. Our student–teacher example illustrates how combining the two can help the student get what he wants while staying on good terms with the instructor:

> Excuse me, Professor Sévigny. I want you to know that I won't be able to turn in the assignment on time. I had a personal emergency, and it was impossible to finish it by today. I'll definitely have it in your mailbox on Monday.

The Language of Oppression

Whether or not the instructor finds the excuse acceptable, it's clear that this last statement combines the best features of powerful speech and powerless speech, namely self-assurance and goodwill.

Simply counting the number of powerful or powerless statements won't always reveal who has the most control in a relationship. Social rules often mask the real distribution of power. Sociolinguist Deborah Tannen describes how politeness can be a face-saving way of delivering an order:

> I hear myself giving instructions to my assistants without actually issuing orders: "Maybe it would be a good idea to . . ." or "It would be great if you could . . .;" all the while knowing that I expect them to do what I've asked right away. . . . This rarely creates problems, though, because the people who work for me know that there is only one reason I mention tasks—because I want them done. I like giving instructions in this way; it appeals to my sense of what it means to be a good person . . . taking others' feelings into account.[27]

As this quote suggests, high-status speakers often realize that politeness is an effective way to get their needs met while protecting the face of the less powerful person. The importance of achieving both content goals and relational goals helps explain why a mixture of powerful speech and polite speech is usually most effective.[28] Of course, if the other person misinterprets politeness for weakness, it may be necessary to shift to a more powerful speaking style.

Powerful speech that gets the desired results in mainstream North American and European culture doesn't succeed everywhere with everyone.[29] In Japan, saving face for others is an important goal, so communicators from that country tend to speak in ambiguous terms and use hedge words and qualifiers. In most Japanese sentences the verb comes at the end of the sentence so the "action" part of the statement can be postponed. The traditional culture of the Mi'kmaq First Nation, with its strong emphasis on the other, makes a priority of using language to create harmony in interpersonal relationships rather than taking a firm or oppositional stance in order to make others feel more at ease. This focus on the other is so ingrained in Mi'kmaq that, as Canadian researchers Danielle Cyr and Alexandre Sévigny point out, the conventional ordering of grammatical persons in English (where the *first person* is "I," the *second person* "you") does not apply in Mi'kmaq grammar.[30] Koreans are another cultural group who prefer "indirect" to "direct" speech.

Affiliation

Power isn't the only way language reflects the status of relationships. Language can also be a way of building and showing solidarity with others. An impressive body of research has demonstrated that communicators who want to show affiliation with one another adapt their speech in a variety of ways, including their choice of vocabulary, rate of talking, number and placement of pauses, and level of politeness.[31] On an individual level, close friends and lovers often develop special terms that serve as a way of signifying their relationship.[32] Using a shared vocabulary sets these people apart from others, reminding themselves and the rest of the world of their relationship. The same process works among members of larger groups, ranging from street gangs to military personnel. Communication researchers call this linguistic accommodation **convergence**.

When two or more people feel equally positive about one another, their linguistic convergence will be mutual. But when communicators want or need the approval of others they often adapt their speech to suit the others' style, trying to say the "right thing" or speak in a way that will help them fit in. We see this process when immigrants who want to gain the rewards of material success in a new culture strive to master the prevalent language. Likewise, employees who seek advancement tend to speak more like their superiors: supervisors adopt the speech style of managers, and managers converge toward their bosses.

The principle of speech accommodation works in reverse, too. Communicators who want to set themselves apart from others adopt the strategy of **divergence**, speaking in a way that emphasizes their difference from others. For example, members of an ethnic group, even though fluent in the dominant language, might use their own language variety as a way of showing solidarity with one another—a sort of

> **convergence**
> Accommodating one's speaking style to another person, who usually is desirable or has higher status.
>
> **divergence**
> A linguistic strategy in which speakers emphasize differences between their communicative style and others' in order to create distance.

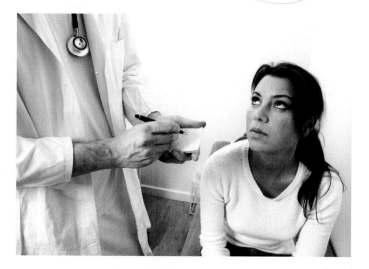

"us against them" strategy. British-born black people of Caribbean descent, for instance, have adopted a vernacular that celebrates their ancestry and separates them from the white majority.[33] Divergence also operates in other settings. A physician or an attorney who wants to establish credibility with her client might speak formally and use professional jargon to create a sense of distance. The implicit message here is "I'm different from (and more knowledgeable than) you."

Attraction and Interest

Social customs discourage us from expressing like or dislike in many situations. Only an idiot would respond to the question "What do you think of the cake I baked for you?" by saying, "It's terrible." Bashful or cautious suitors might not admit their attraction to a potential partner. Yet even when people are reluctant to speak candidly, the language they use can suggest their degree of interest in or attraction toward a person, object, or idea. Morton Wiener and Albert Mehrabian outline a number of linguistic clues that reveal these attitudes:[34]

- Demonstrative pronoun choice: Saying "*These* people want our help" (positive) versus "*Those* people want our help" (less positive).
- Negation: Saying "It's *good*" (positive) versus "It's *not bad*" (less positive).
- Sequential placement: Saying "*Dick* and Jane" (where Dick is more important) versus "*Jane* and Dick" (where Jane is more important).

It's worth noting that sequential placement isn't always significant. You may put "toilet bowl cleaner" at the top of your shopping list simply because it's in the first aisle of the grocery store, while "ice cream," further down on your list, is in the last aisle.

Responsibility

In addition to suggesting the extent of a speaker's liking or appreciation for a person or thing, language can reveal the speaker's willingness to accept responsibility for a message. Consider the following ways of accepting—or passing off—responsibility:

- "It" versus "I" statements: Saying "*It's* not finished" (less responsible) versus "*I* haven't finished it" (more responsible).
- "You" versus "I" statements: Saying "Sometimes *you* make me angry" (less responsible) versus "Sometimes *I* get angry when you do that" (more responsible); "I" statements are more likely to generate positive reactions from others.[35]
- "But" statements: Saying "It's a good idea, *but* it won't work" or "You're really terrific, *but* I think we ought to spend less time together" ("but" cancels everything that went before the word).
- Questions versus statements: Saying "Do you think we ought to do that?" (less responsible) versus "I don't think we ought to do that" (more responsible).

Troublesome Language

Besides being a blessing that enables us to live together, language can be something of a curse. We have all known the frustration of being misunderstood, and most of us have been baffled by another person's overreaction to an innocent comment. In the following pages we will look at several kinds of troublesome language, with the goal of helping you communicate in a way that makes matters better instead of worse.

The Language of Misunderstandings

The most obvious language problems are semantic: they occur when we simply don't understand others completely or accurately. Most misunderstandings arise from some common problems that are easily remedied—after you recognize them.

Equivocal Language

Equivocal words have more than one dictionary definition. Some equivocal misunderstandings are simple, at least after they are exposed. A nurse once told her patient that he "wouldn't be needing" the materials he requested from home. He interpreted the statement to mean he was near death; the nurse merely meant that he would be going home soon. A colleague once sent some confidential materials to the wrong person after his boss had instructed him to "send them to Richard"—without specifying which Richard. Some equivocal misunderstandings can be particularly embarrassing, as one woman recalls:

> In the fourth grade the teacher asked the class what a period was. I raised my hand and shared everything I had learned about girls' getting their period. But he was talking about the dot at the end of a sentence. Oops![36]

Equivocal misunderstandings can have serious consequences. Communication researchers Michael Motley and Heidi Reeder suggest that equivocation at least partly explains why men sometimes persist in attempts to become physically intimate when women have expressed unwillingness to do so.[37] Interviews and focus groups with university students revealed that women often used ambiguous phrases to say "no" to a man's sexual advances, especially when they hoped to see the man again; these phrases include "I'm confused about this," "I'm not sure that we're ready for this yet," "Are you sure you want to do this?," "Let's be friends," and even "That tickles." (The researchers found that women were more likely to give a direct response when they wanted to end the relationship.) Whereas women viewed indirect statements as equivalent to saying "no," men were more likely to interpret them as less clear-cut requests to stop. The researchers concluded that "male/female misunderstandings are not so much a matter of males hearing resistance messages as 'go', but rather their not hearing them as 'stop'." Under the law, *any instruction to stop, even an ambiguous instruction, means stop*, and anyone who argues otherwise can be in for serious legal problems.

Relative Words

Relative words gain their meaning by comparison. For example, is the school you attend large or small? This depends on what you compare it to: alongside a campus like that of the University of Toronto, with its enrollment of over 81,000 students, it probably looks small; on the other hand, compared to a smaller institution, it might seem quite large. In the same way, relative words like "fast" and "slow," "smart" and "stupid," "short" and "long" depend for their meaning on what they're compared to. (In some movie theatres, a "large" bag of popcorn is the smallest you can buy; the other sizes are "extra large" and "jumbo.")

Some relative words are so common that we mistakenly assume that they have a clear meaning. In one study, graduate students were asked to assign numerical values to terms such as "doubtful," "toss-up," "likely," "probable," "good chance," and "unlikely."[38] There was a tremendous variation in the meaning of most of these terms. For example, the responses for "possible" ranged from 0 to 99 per cent. A "good chance" meant between 35 and 90 per cent, whereas "unlikely" fell between 0 and 40 per cent.

equivocal words
Words that have more than one dictionary definition.

relative words
Words that gain their meaning by comparison.

Using relative words without explaining them can lead to communication problems. Have you ever responded to someone's question about the weather by saying it was "warm," only to find out that what was warm to you was cold to the other person? Or have you followed a friend's advice and gone to a "cheap" restaurant, only to find that it was twice as expensive as you expected? Have you been disappointed to learn that classes you've heard were "easy" turned out to be hard, that journeys you were told would be "short" were long, that "unusual" ideas were really quite ordinary? The problem in each case came from failing to anchor the relative word used to a more precise or measurable word.

Slang and Jargon

Slang is language used by a group of people whose members belong to a similar subculture or other group. Some slang is related to specialized interests and activities. For instance, cyclists who talk about "bonking" are referring to running out of energy. Fans of hip-hop and rap know that "bling" refers to jewellery and a "whip" is a nice-looking car.

Other slang consists of regionalisms—terms that are understood by people who live in one geographic area but that are incomprehensible to outsiders. This sort of use illustrates how slang defines insiders and outsiders, creating a sense of identity and solidarity.[39] For instance, many southern Ontarians spend their weekends or summers in "cottage country," but if you live in northern Ontario or Manitoba, you might call your summer retreat a "camp." Western Canadians call their cottages "cabins," while English-speaking Quebecers prefer the term "chalet." In Newfoundland and Labrador and in parts of the Maritimes, a summer residence—even a luxurious one—may be called a "shack," while the same dwelling in Cape Breton may be referred to as a "bungalow."[40]

In the East End of London, England, cockney dialect uses rhyming words as substitutes for everyday expressions: "bacon and eggs" for "legs," and "Barney Rubble" for "trouble." If you've ever referred to the derisive spitting noise made with the tongue and lips as a "raspberry," you've used rhyming slang, though you might not have known it: "raspberry" is short for "raspberry tart," rhyming slang for "fart." This sort of use also illustrates how slang can be used to identify insiders and outsiders: with enough shared rhyming, slang users can talk about outsiders without the clueless outsiders knowing that they are the subject of conversation ("Lovely set of bacons, eh?" or "Stay away from him, he's Barney").

Slang can also be age-related. Most university students know that "sick" is used to signal approval or appreciation (as in "He pulled off a 720 McTwist that was just sick"), not illness or disgust, as their parents are more likely to assume. Canadian students know that a "bird course" is one that shouldn't be too difficult to pass.

Almost everyone uses some sort of **jargon**: the specialized vocabulary that functions as a kind of shorthand among people with common backgrounds and experiences. Snowboarders have their own language to describe maneuvers: "ollie," "fakie," and "mute," to name just a few. Some jargon consists of acronyms—initials of terms that are combined to form a word. Canada's intelligence service is known as CSIS (pronounced "see-siss"); Canadian communications academics are forever pursuing grants from a government body called SSHRC (pronounced "sherk"); and English-language learners will be familiar with

slang
Language used by a group of people whose members belong to a similar co-culture or other group.

jargon
The specialized vocabulary that is used as a kind of shorthand by people with common backgrounds and experiences.

Slang is a language that rolls up its sleeves, spits on its hands, and goes to work.

Carl Sandburg, American poet and writer

"No, grandma, hashtags are not something you order with eggs."

LINC (pronounced like "link") programs offering Language Instruction for Newcomers to Canada.

The digital age has spawned its own vocabulary of jargon. For instance, computer users know that a "Wi-Fi" hotspot will give them wireless internet access. Some jargon goes beyond being descriptive and conveys attitudes. For example, cynics in the high-tech world sometimes refer to being fired from a job as being "uninstalled." They talk dismissively about the non-virtual world as the "carbon community," to books and newspapers as "treeware," and to the brain as "wetware." Some technical support staffers talk of "banana problems," meaning those that could be figured out by monkeys, as in "This is a two-banana problem at worst."[41]

Jargon can be a valuable kind of shorthand for people who understand its use. The trauma team in a hospital emergency ward can save time, and possibly lives, by speaking in shorthand, referring to "emerg" (the emergency room), "GSWs" (gunshot wounds), "chem 7" lab tests, and so on, but the same specialized vocabulary that works so well among insiders can mystify family members of the patient, who don't understand the jargon. The same confusion may be experienced by bank customers, who, on any trip to their local branch, are likely to encounter a dizzying array of acronyms, including CSB (Canada Savings Bond), GIC (Guaranteed Investment Certificate), RRSP (Registered Retirement Savings Plan), RESP (Registered Educational Savings Plan), CPP (Canada Pension Plan), and many more.

COMMUNICATION ON-SCREEN

Firefly (2002–03)
Created by Joss Whedon.

Before he directed *The Avengers* in 2013, and throughout his first two television series, *Buffy the Vampire Slayer* and *Angel*, Joss Whedon has developed a reputation for turning out scripts stuffed with his own distinctive brand of quirky dialogue. His third television series pushed into more peculiar territory still. *Firefly*—which ran just 13 episodes and prompted the follow-up feature film *Serenity*—was, put simply, a western set in outer space in the distant future. And not just any old distant future but one where China is co-dominant with America in shaping humanity's cultural melting pot. Accordingly, *Firefly's* dialogue is at times barely written in English at all but is a sort of pidgin blending hillbilly yokelisms, smatterings of Mandarin, and completely fabricated terms that are evidently period slang.

What's fascinating is how eminently comprehensible it all is. Context alone makes it quite clear what functions slang terms like "gorram," "backbirth," and "shiny" serve in this future. Whedon consciously chose not to subtitle the Mandarin so as to make its incorporation into English speech all the more seamless, and the spurts of Mandarin that do crop up—often rather colourful expletives that would make for some dicey subtitling anyway—hardly impact the overall lucidity of the on-screen communication. In making its manner of communication so exotic *Firefly* achieves that sense of "otherworldliness" so central to science fiction in a far more immersive way than any number of rubber-foreheaded extras could achieve.

Misunderstandings can arise when insiders in a particular industry use their own language with people who don't share the same vocabulary. Jeffrey Katzman of the William Morris Agency's Hollywood office experienced this sort of problem when he met with members of a Silicon Valley computer firm to discuss a joint project:

> When he used the phrase "in development," he meant a project that was as yet merely an idea. When the techies used it, on the other hand, they meant designing a specific game or program. Ultimately, says Katzman, he had to bring in a blackboard and literally define his terms. "It was like when the Japanese first came to Hollywood," he recalls. "They had to use interpreters, and we did too."[42]

Overly Abstract Language

Most objects, events, and ideas can be described with varying degrees of specificity. Consider the material you are reading right now. You could call it:

- a book,
- a textbook,

- a communication textbook,
- *Understanding Human Communication*,
- Chapter 3 of *Understanding Human Communication*,
- page 104 of Chapter 3 of *Understanding Human Communication*, and so on.

In each case your description would be more and more specific. Semanticist S.I. Hayakawa created an **abstraction ladder** to describe this process.[43] This ladder consists of a number of descriptions of the same thing. Lower items focus specifically on the person, object, or event, whereas higher terms are generalizations that include the subject as a member of a larger class. To talk about "university," for example, is more abstract than to talk about a particular school.

Higher-level abstractions are helpful because without them language would be too cumbersome to be useful. It's faster, easier, and more useful to talk about "Europe" than to list all of the countries on that continent. In the same way, using relatively abstract terms like "friendly" or "smart" can make it easier to describe people than listing their specific actions.

Abstract language—speech that refers to observable events or objects—serves a second, less obvious function. At times it allows us to avoid confrontations by deliberately being unclear.[44] Suppose, for example, your boss is enthusiastic about a new approach that you think is a terrible idea. Telling her the truth might seem too risky, but lying—saying "I think it's a great idea"—wouldn't feel right either. In situations like this, an abstract answer can hint at your true belief without a direct confrontation: "I don't know. . . . It's sure unusual. . . . It might work." The same sort of abstract language can help you avoid embarrassing friends who ask for your opinion with questions like "What do you think of my new haircut?" An abstract response like "It's really different!" may be easier for you to deliver—and for your friend to receive—than the clear, brutal truth: "It's really ugly!" We will have more to say about this strategy of equivocation later in this chapter.

Although vagueness does have its uses, highly abstract language can cause several types of problems. The first is *stereotyping*. Consider claims like "All whites are bigots," "Men don't care about relationships," "The police are a bunch of goons," or "Professors around here care more about their research than they do about students." Each of these claims ignores the very important fact that abstract descriptions are almost always too general, that they say more than we really mean.

Besides fostering stereotypes, abstract language can lead to the problem of confusing others. Imagine the lack of understanding that results from imprecise language in situations like this:

A: We never do anything that's fun anymore.

B: What do you mean?

A: We used to do lots of unusual things, but now it's the same old stuff, over and over.

B: But last week we went on that camping trip, and tomorrow we're going to that party where we'll meet all sorts of new people. Those are new things.

A: That's not what I mean. I'm talking about really unusual stuff.

B: (*becoming confused and a little impatient*): Like what? Taking hard drugs or going over Niagara Falls in a barrel?

A: Don't be stupid. All I'm saying is that we're in a rut. We should be living more exciting lives.

B: Well, I don't know what you want.

The best way to avoid this sort of overly abstract language is to use **behavioural descriptions** instead (see Table 3.2). Behavioural descriptions move down the abstraction ladder to identify

---

abstraction ladder
A range of more to less abstract terms describing an event or object.

abstract language
Language that lacks specificity or does not refer to observable behaviour or other sensory data.

Cultural Idiom
goons
Those who intimidate others.

in a rut
Having fixed and monotonous routines and habits.

behavioural description
An account that refers only to observable phenomena.

the specific, observable phenomenon being discussed. A thorough description should answer three questions:

1. *Who is involved?* Are you speaking for just yourself or for others as well? Are you talking about a group of people ("the neighbours," "classmates") or specific individuals ("the people next door with the barking dog," "Tamsin and Jenny")?

2. *In what circumstances does the behaviour occur?* Where does it occur: everywhere or in specific places (at parties, at work, in public)? When does it occur: when you're tired or when a certain subject comes up? The behaviour you are describing probably doesn't occur all the time. In order to be understood, you need to pin down what circumstances set this situation apart from other ones.

3. *What behaviours are involved?* Though terms such as "more co-operative" and "helpful" might sound like concrete descriptions of behaviour, they are usually too vague to do a clear job of explaining what's on your mind. Behaviours must be observable, ideally both to you and to others. For instance, moving down the abstraction ladder from the relatively vague term "helpful," you might come to behaviours such as "does the dishes every other day," "volunteers to help me with my studies," or "fixes dinner once or twice a week without being asked." It's easy to see that terms like these, as opposed to fuzzier abstractions, are easier for both you and others to understand.

Behavioural descriptions can improve communication in a wide range of situations, as Table 3.2 illustrates. Research also supports the value of specific language. One study found that well-adjusted couples had just as many conflicts as poorly adjusted couples, but the way the well-adjusted couples handled their problems was significantly different. Instead of blaming one another, the well-adjusted couples expressed their complaints in behavioural terms.[45]

Table 3.2 Abstract and Behavioural Descriptions

	Abstract Description	Behavioural Description			Remarks
		Who Is Involved	In What Circumstances	Specific Behaviours	
Problem	I talk too much.	People I find intimidating	When I want them to like me	I talk (mostly about myself) instead of giving them a chance to speak or asking about their lives.	Behavioural description more clearly identifies behaviours to change.
Goal	I want to be more constructive.	My roommate	When we talk about household duties	Instead of finding fault with her ideas, suggest alternatives that might work.	Behavioural description clearly outlines how to act; abstract description doesn't.
Appreciation	"You've really been helpful lately."	(Deliver to fellow worker.)	"When I've had to take time off work because of personal problems. . ."	"You took my shifts without complaining."	Give both abstract and behavioural descriptions for best results.
Request	"Clean up your act!"	(Deliver to target person.)	"When we're around my family. . ."	"Please don't tell jokes that involve sex."	Behavioural description specifies desired behaviour.

Disruptive Language

Not all linguistic problems come from misunderstandings. Sometimes people understand one another perfectly and still end up in conflict. Of course, not all disagreements can, or should be, avoided. But eliminating three bad linguistic habits from your communication repertoire can minimize the kind of clashes that don't need to happen, allowing you to save your energy for the unavoidable and important struggles.

Confusing Facts and Opinions

factual statement
A statement that can be verified as being true or false.

opinion statement
A statement based on the speaker's beliefs.

Factual statements are claims that can be verified as true or false. By contrast, **opinion statements** are based on the speaker's beliefs. Unlike matters of fact, they can never be proved or disproved. Consider a few examples of the difference between factual statements and opinion statements:

Fact	Opinion
Vancouver receives a greater accumulation of rain per year than does Winnipeg.	The climate in Winnipeg is better than in Vancouver.
Wayne Gretzky is the all-time leading goal scorer in the National Hockey League.	Gretzky is the greatest hockey player in the history of the game.
Per capita income in Canada is lower than in several other countries.	Canada is not the best model of economic success in the world.

When factual statements and opinion statements are set side by side like this, the difference between them is clear. In everyday conversation, we often present our opinions as if they were facts, and in doing so we invite an unnecessary argument. For example:

Everyone is entitled to their own opinions, but they are not entitled to their own facts.

Daniel Patrick Moynihan, academic and former US Senator

- "That was a dumb thing to say!"
- "Spending that much on _____ is a waste of money!"
- "You can't get a fair shake in this country unless you're a white male."

Notice how much less antagonistic each statement would be if it was prefaced by a qualifier like "In my opinion . . ." or "It seems to me. . . ."

Confusing Facts and Inferences

inferential statement
A conclusion arrived at from an interpretation of evidence.

Labelling your opinions can go a long way toward relational harmony, but developing this habit won't solve all linguistic problems. Difficulties also arise when we confuse factual statements with **inferential statements**—conclusions arrived at from an interpretation of evidence. Consider a few examples:

Fact	Inference
He hit a lamppost while driving down the street.	He was daydreaming when he hit the lamppost.
You interrupted me before I finished what I was saying.	You don't care about what I have to say.
You haven't paid your share of the rent on time for the past three months.	You're trying to weasel out of your responsibility.
I haven't gotten a raise in almost a year.	My employer is exploiting me.

Cultural Idiom
a fair shake
To be treated honestly.

to weasel out of
To get out of doing something.

There's nothing wrong with making inferences as long as you identify them as such: "She stomped out and slammed the door. *It looked to me as if she were furious.*" The danger comes when we confuse inferences with facts and make them sound like the absolute truth.

One way to avoid fact–inference confusion is to use the perception-checking skill described in Chapter 2 to test the accuracy of your inferences. Recall that a perception check has three parts: a description of the behaviour being discussed, your interpretation of that behaviour, and a request for verification. For instance, instead of saying, "Why are you laughing at me?" you could say, "When you laugh like that [*description of behaviour*], I get the idea you think something I did was stupid [*interpretation*]. Are you laughing at me [*question*]?"

Emotive Language

Emotive language contains words that sound as if they're describing something when they are really announcing the speaker's attitude toward something. Do you like that old picture frame? If so, you would probably call it "an antique," but if you think it's ugly, you would likely describe it as "a piece of junk." Emotive words may sound like statements of fact but are always opinions.

American singer, actor, and director Barbra Streisand once pointed out how some people use emotive language to stigmatize behaviour in women that they admire in men:

> A man is commanding—a woman is demanding.
> A man is forceful—a woman is pushy.
> A man is uncompromising—a woman is a ball-breaker.
> A man is a perfectionist—a woman's a pain in the ass.
> He's assertive—she's aggressive.
> He strategizes—she manipulates.
> He shows leadership—she's controlling.
> He's committed—she's obsessed.
> He's persevering—she's relentless.
> He sticks to his guns—she's stubborn.
> If a man wants to get it right, he's looked up to and respected.
> If a woman wants to get it right, she's difficult and impossible.[46]

Problems occur when people use emotive words without labelling them as such. You might, for

> **emotive language**
> Language that conveys the sender's attitude rather than simply offering an objective description.

CRITICAL THINKING PROBE

Emotive Language

Test your ability to identify emotive language by playing the following word game.

1. Take an action, object, or characteristic and show how it can be viewed either favourably or unfavourably, depending on the label it is given. For example:
   a. I'm casual.
      You're careless.
      He's a slob.
   b. I read adult love stories.
      You read erotic literature.
      She reads pornography.

2. Now create three-part descriptions of your own, using the following statements as a start:
   a. I'm tactful.
   b. She's a liar.
   c. I'm conservative.
   d. You have a high opinion of yourself.
   e. I'm quiet.
   f. You're pessimistic.

3. Now recall two situations in which you used emotive language as if it were a description of fact. How might the results have differed if you had used more objective language?

instance, have a long and bitter argument with a friend about whether a third person was "assertive" or "obnoxious," when a more accurate and peaceable way to handle the issue would be to acknowledge that one of you approves of the behaviour and the other doesn't.

Evasive Language

None of the troublesome language habits we have described so far is a deliberate strategy to mislead or antagonize others. Now, however, we'll consider euphemisms and equivocations, two types of language that speakers use by design to avoid communicating clearly. Although both of these have some very legitimate uses, they also can lead to frustration and confusion.

Euphemisms

A **euphemism** (from a Greek word meaning "to use words of good omen") is a pleasant term substituted for a more direct but potentially less pleasant one. We use euphemisms when we say that someone has "passed away" (as opposed to "died") or when we describe someone as being "plump" or "heavy-set" instead of "fat" or "overweight." In Canada, common euphemisms for "toilet" range from "bathroom," "restroom," "washroom," and "little boys'/girls' room" to "john," "throne," "loo," and "head." Then there are the euphemisms we substitute for swear words in polite company or in front of the children. "Fuddle-duddle," famously attributed to former Prime Minister Pierre Trudeau, is an example of this. There certainly are cases where the euphemistic pulling of linguistic punches can be face-saving. It's probably more constructive to question a possible "statistical misrepresentation" than to call someone a liar, for example. Likewise, it may be less disquieting to some to refer to people as "senior citizens" than as "old people."

Like many businesses, the airline industry uses euphemisms to avoid upsetting already nervous flyers.[47] For example, rather than saying "turbulence," pilots and flight attendants use the less frightening term "bumpy air." Likewise, they refer to thunderstorms as "rain showers" and fog as "mist" or "haze." And savvy flight personnel never use the words "your final destination."

Despite their occasional advantages, many euphemisms are not worth the effort it takes to create them. Some are pretentious and confusing, such as the renaming of one university's Home Economics Department as the Department of Human Ecology, or a junior high school's labelling of hallways as "behaviour transition corridors." Other euphemisms are downright deceptive, such as the military usage "friendly fire," which leaves one to wonder what can possibly be friendly about it if it kills people, or the term "peacemaking mission," which really means a military campaign against another country to change its political regime. Steven Pinker, in his 2001 address to incoming undergraduates at the Massachusetts Institute of Technology, warned students of the "euphemism treadmill," in which euphemisms eventually become taboo words as unpalatable as the ones they were designed to replace by taking on the negative connotations of the concepts they designate.[48] In fact, "toilet" itself is a classic example, originally used as a euphemism for earlier terms such as "lavatory" or "privy."

> **euphemism**
> A pleasant-sounding term used in place of a more direct but less pleasant one.

Euphemisms are not, as many young people think, useless verbiage for that which can and should be said bluntly; they are like secret agents on a delicate mission, they must airily pass by a stinking mess with barely so much as a nod of the head, make their point of constructive criticism and continue on in calm forbearance. Euphemisms are unpleasant truths wearing diplomatic cologne.

**Quentin Crisp,
Manners from Heaven**

"Be honest with me, Roger. By 'mid-course correction' you mean divorce, don't you."

Equivocation

It's 8:15 p.m., and you are already a half-hour late for your dinner reservation at the fanciest restaurant in town. Your partner has finally finished dressing and confronts you with the question "How do I look?" To tell the truth, you hate your partner's outfit. You don't want to lie, but on the other hand you don't want to be hurtful. Just as important, you don't want to lose your table by waiting around for your date to choose something else to wear. You think for a moment and then reply, "You look amazing. I've never seen an outfit like that before. Where did you get it?"

Your response in this situation is an **equivocation**—a deliberately vague statement that can be interpreted in more than one way. Earlier in this chapter we talked about how unintentional equivocation can lead to misunderstandings. But our discussion here focuses on intentionally ambiguous speech that is used to avoid lying on one hand and telling a painful truth on the other. Equivocations have several advantages. They spare the receiver the embarrassment that might come from a completely truthful answer, and they spare the sender the discomfort of being honest.

Despite these benefits, there are times when equivocation is used by communicators as a way to weasel out of delivering important but unpleasant messages. Suppose, for example, that you are unsure about your standing in one of your courses. You approach the professor and ask how she is doing. "Not bad," the professor answers. This answer isn't too satisfying. "What grade am I earning?" you inquire. "Oh, lots of people would be happy with it" is the answer you receive. "But will I receive an A or B this semester?" you persist. "You could" is the reply. It's easy to see how this sort of evasiveness can be frustrating.

As with euphemisms, high-level abstractions, and many other types of communication, it's impossible to say that equivocation is always helpful or harmful. As we explained in Chapter 1,

> **equivocation**
> A vague statement that can be interpreted in more than one way.

YOUNG COMMUNICATOR PROFILE

MELONIE FULLICK

York University PhD Student

My name is Melonie Fullick, and I am a York University PhD candidate researching how the governance of universities is affected by policy and by broader shifts in Canadian political and economic life. Previously I completed a BA in communication studies and an MA in linguistics.

As my background shows, the study of human communication can lead us in wide-ranging and interdisciplinary directions, bringing together many different yet interrelated phenomena around a relevant theme. For me this has meant thinking about everything from philosophies of pedagogy, to media depictions of the university's role in society. In this way I've also learned to make meaningful connections using theory from multiple "fields" such as linguistics, media theory, policy studies, and social psychology. Perhaps because of my assumption that communication is important, I've also worked to "translate" my academic research into other activities such as social media engagement, journalism, workshops, and public speaking. Studying communication has given me insight into the workings of the social world around me, from the interpersonal level to the study of institutions such as the mass media and education systems. I hope to build a career that combines research and writing, policy work, teaching, and public communication, with the goal of understanding more about how change happens in the "knowledge society"—and how we can make it a change for the better.

competent communication behaviour is situational. Your success in relating to others will depend on your ability to analyze yourself, the other person, and the situation when deciding whether to be equivocal or direct.

Gender and Language

So far we have discussed language use as if it were identical for both sexes. Some theorists and researchers, though, have argued that there are significant differences between the way men and women speak, whereas others have argued that any differences are not significant.[49] What are the similarities and differences between male and female language use?

Content

Although there is a great deal of variation within each gender, on the average, men and women discuss a surprisingly different range of topics. The first research on conversational topics was conducted over 60 years ago. Despite the changes in men's and women's roles since then, the results of more recent studies are remarkably similar.[50] In these studies, women and men ranging in age from 17 to 80 described the range of topics each discussed with friends of the same sex. Certain topics were common to both sexes: work, movies, and television proved to be frequent subjects for both groups. And men and women alike reserved discussions of sex and sexuality for members of the same gender. The differences between men and women were more striking than the similarities, however. Female friends spent much more time discussing personal and domestic subjects, relationship problems, family, health and reproductive matters, weight and food, clothing, men, and other women. Men, on the other hand, were more likely to discuss music, current events, sports, business, and other men. Men and women were equally likely to discuss personal appearance, sex, and dating in same-sex conversations. True to one common stereotype, women were more likely to gossip about close friends and family. By contrast, men spent more time gossiping about sports figures and media personalities. Women's gossip was no more derogatory than men's.

These differences can lead to frustration when men and women try to converse with one another. Researchers report that *trivial* is the word often used by both sexes to describe topics discussed by the opposite sex. "I want to talk about important things," a woman might say, "like how we're getting along. All he wants to do is talk about the news or what we'll do this weekend."

Reasons for Communicating

Research shows that the notion that men and women communicate in dramatically different ways is exaggerated. Both men and women, at least in the dominant cultures of Canada and the United States, use language to build and maintain social relationships. Regardless of the sex of the communicators, the goals of almost all ordinary conversations include making the conversation enjoyable by being friendly, showing interest in what the other person says, and talking about topics that interest the other person.[51] *How* men and women accomplish these goals is often different, though. Although most communicators try to make their interaction enjoyable, men are more likely than women to emphasize making conversation fun.

Their discussions involve a greater amount of joking and good-natured teasing. By contrast, women's conversations focus more frequently on feelings, relationships, and personal problems. In fact, communication researcher Julia Wood flatly states that "for women, talk is the essence of relationships."[52] When a group of women was surveyed to find out what kinds of satisfaction they gained from talking with their friends, the most common response was a feeling of empathy—"To know you're not alone," as some put it.[53] Whereas men commonly described conversations with other males as something they *liked*, women characterized their woman-to-woman talks as a kind of contact they *needed*. The greater frequency of female conversations reflects their importance. Nearly 50 per cent of the women surveyed said they called friends at least once a week just to talk, whereas less than half as many men did so. In fact, 40 per cent of the men surveyed reported that they never called another man just to talk.

Because women use conversation to pursue social needs, their speech typically contains statements designed to show support for the other person, demonstrate equality, and keep the conversation going. With these goals, it's not surprising that female speech typically contains statements of sympathy and empathy: "I've felt just like that myself," "The same thing happened to me!" Women are also inclined to ask lots of questions that invite the other person to share information: "How did you feel about that?" "What did you do next?" The importance of nurturing a relationship also explains why female speech is often somewhat powerless and tentative. Saying, "This is just my opinion . . ." is less likely to put off a conversational partner than a more definite "Here's what I think. . . ."

Men's speech tends to be driven by quite different goals. For instance, men are more likely to use language to accomplish the job at hand than to nourish relationships. This explains why men are less likely than women to disclose their vulnerabilities, which would be a sign of weakness. When someone else is sharing a problem, instead of empathizing, men are prone to offer advice: "That's nothing to worry about . . ." or "Here's what you need to do. . . ." Besides taking care of business, men are more likely than women to use conversations to exert control, preserve their independence, and enhance their status. Susan Sherwood writes:

"Why do we have to eat here?"
"It's convenient."
"Are there any quieter restaurants nearby?"
"Not close by."
"I wonder if this place has been inspected lately?"
"Let's go in."

In a nutshell, that conversation snippet summarizes each gender's argumentation style. Women often try to get their point across by asking many types of questions: defiant, informational, and rhetorical. The questions are designed to present an opposition or gather data.

COMMUNICATION ON-SCREEN

I Love You, Man (2009)
Directed by John Hamburg.

Peter Klaven (Paul Rudd) is pretty happy about where things stand: he has a stable—if perhaps a bit boring—job selling real estate by day and goes home to spend loving—if perhaps a bit tame—evenings with his fiancée, Zooey (Rashida Jones). A moment of unguarded frankness from Zooey, however, leads Peter to the harsh realization that he lacks any kind of strong male friendships. With his nuptials looming, Peter sets out to find himself a male best friend and, he hopes, a best man.

Although the nuances of friendship between women have been frequently explored onscreen, I Love You, Man is one of comparatively few films to tackle the nature of bond-building between males, or at least do so outside the frame of a mud-spattered warzone. As Peter strikes up a friendship with Sydney (Jason Segal), the film explores the sorts of everyday behaviour that males indulge in to meet their social needs. The nature of male-to-male communication (and miscommunication—this is a comedy, after all) features prominently.

Men's contributions to arguments are often simple and direct. They're so straightforward, in contrast to women's questions, that men might not even realize that a conflict is occurring.[54]

This explains why men are more likely to dominate conversations and one-up their partners. Men frequently interrupt their conversational partners to assert their own experiences or points of view. (Women interrupt, too, but they usually do so to offer support: quite a different goal.) But just because male talk is competitive doesn't mean it's not enjoyable. Men often regard talk as a kind of game: when researchers asked men what they liked best about their all-male talk, the most frequent answer was its ease.[55] Another common theme was appreciation of the practical value of conversation: new ways to solve problems. Men also mentioned enjoying the humour and rapid pace that characterized their all-male conversations.

Conversational Style

Women and men behave differently in conversations.[56] For example, women ask more questions in mixed-sex conversations—nearly three times as many as men do, according to one study. Other research has revealed that in mixed-sex conversations, men interrupt women far more often than the other way around. Some theorists have argued that differences like these result in women's speech being less powerful and more emotional than men's. Research has supported these theories—at least in some cases. Even when clues about the speakers' sex were edited out, researchers found clear differences between transcripts of male speech and female speech. In one study, women's talk was judged more aesthetic, whereas men's talk was seen as more dynamic, aggressive, and strong. In another, male job applicants were rated more fluent, active, confident, and effective than female applicants.

Other studies have revealed that men and women behave differently in certain conversational settings. For example, in mixed-sex dyads, women talk less than men do, whereas in situations with other women, they speak for a longer time. In larger groups, men talk more, whereas in smaller groups, women talk more. There are subtler differences, too, between men's and women's conversation: women talking with other women use more questions, justifiers, intensive adverbs, personal pronouns, and adverbials. Men talking to men use more directives, interruptions, and filler words to begin sentences.[57]

Given all these differences, it's easy to wonder how men and women manage to communicate with one another at all. One reason why cross-sex conversations do run smoothly is that women accommodate to the topics men raise. Both men and women regard topics introduced by women as tentative, whereas topics that men introduce are more likely to be pursued. In effect, women seem to grease the wheels by doing more work than men to maintain conversations. A complementary difference between men and women also promotes cross-sex conversations: men are more likely to talk about themselves with women than with other men; and because women are willing to adapt to this topic, conversations are likely to run smoothly, if one-sidedly.

An accommodating style isn't always a disadvantage for women. One study revealed that women who spoke tentatively were actually more influential with men than those who used more powerful speech.[58] On the other hand, this tentative style was

Women Communicate Better, Talk Less Than Men: Study

Women communicate better than men and actually talk less, researchers said on Friday. Men speak more words than women in a day, but have a weaker command of language in social situations, use the same words repeatedly and pay unconvincing compliments, British researchers said after studying how men and women communicate.

Manchester University researchers found that when conversation centered on serious issues such as current affairs men and women used similar language, but they differed widely when it came to chit-chat in social situations.

The women in the research commissioned by British female-friendly insurance firm Sheilas' Wheels had superior communication skills and used a wider variety of words in social situations, while men struggled with their command of language.

"It is men who are more likely to talk for the sake of talking when engaged in social chit-chat by recycling their words with ritualistic and redundant language that doesn't contain new information," Manchester University researcher Geoffrey Beattie said.

The team of researchers carried recording devices over a one-week period in order to transcribe 50 conversations, which were split between men and women in serious and social conversations. Each conversation was given to five volunteers who read five different versions with every fifth word removed and were asked to guess the missing word.

Men used a few simple words in social situations and the limited variety of their vocabulary became even more marked when it came to paying compliments, researchers said. The study showed compliments from men were 90 per cent predictable—frequently making use of words "you," "really" and "nice"—while women had more detail in their compliments, making them less predictable and more genuine-sounding.

The Manchester University team helped dispel the myth of women as chatterboxes and discovered it's men who have the tendency to blather on by analyzing supporting research into male and female communication. Only 2 out of 56 separate studies analyzing the difference in communication between men and women concluded that women use more words per day than men—while 24 concluded that men use more.

Madeleine Cowley, *Reuters Life!* 18 February 2011

less effective in persuading women. (Language use had no effect on men's persuasiveness.) This research suggests that women who are flexible in their approach can persuade both other women and men—as long as they are not dealing with a mixed-sex audience.

Gender differences are apparent not only in speech but also in writing. A study by Sarah Marinelli, a recent honours communications graduate of McMaster University, investigated the identity of op-ed writers across Canada. She found that only 20 per cent of op-eds published in major Canadian newspapers were written by women. She also found that 10 per cent of women wrote outside of their field of expertise, whereas 50 per cent of men did so. This research suggests that Canadian op-ed writing is still strongly gendered.[59]

Non-Gender Variables

Despite the differences in the ways men and women speak, the link between gender and language use isn't as clear-cut as it might seem. In fact, several research reviews have found many more similarities than differences in the ways that women and men communicate. For example, one analysis of over 1200 research studies found that only one per cent of variance in communication behaviour resulted from sex difference.[60] There is no significant difference between male speech and female speech in areas such as use of profanity, use of qualifiers such as "I guess" or "This is just my opinion," tag questions, and vocal fluency.[61] Some on-the-job research shows that male and female supervisors in similar positions behave the same way and are equally effective. In light of the considerable similarities between the sexes and the relatively minor differences, some communication scholars suggest that the *Men Are from Mars, Women Are from Venus* idea overstates the case.[62] It might be more accurate to say that men are from Vancouver and women are from Victoria.

You Just Don't Understand: Women and Men in Conversation

A growing body of research has revealed other factors that influence language use as much as, or even more than, gender does. For example, social philosophy plays a role: women who are feminists talk longer than their partners do, whereas non-feminist wives speak less than their husbands. Orientation toward problem-solving also plays a role in conversational style: the orientations of speakers—co-operative or competitive—have more influence than gender on how speakers interact.

The speaker's occupation and social role also influence speaking style. For example, the speech used by male early childhood educators to the children they're teaching resembles the language of women childcare workers more closely than it resembles the language of fathers at home. Overall, doctors interrupt their patients more often than the reverse, although male patients do interrupt female physicians more often than they do male physicians. At work, task differences exert more powerful effects on whether speakers use gender-inclusive language (such as "he or she" instead of just "he") than does biological sex.[63] A close study of trial transcripts showed that the speaker's experience on the witness stand and occupation had more to do with language use than did gender. If women generally use "powerless" language, this may reflect their social role in society at large. As the balance of power grows more equal between men and women, we can expect many linguistic differences to shrink.

Why is the research on gender differences so confusing? In some studies, male speech and female speech seem identical, whereas other studies reveal important differences. As we have already said, one reason for the confusion is that factors besides gender influence the way people speak: the setting in which conversation takes place, the expertise of the speakers, their social roles (husband/wife, boss/employee, and so on). Also, women's roles are changing so rapidly that many women simply don't use the conversational styles that characterized their older sisters and mothers. But in addition to these factors, another powerful force that influences the way individual men and women speak is their **sex role**—the social orientation that governs behaviour—rather than their biological gender. Researchers have identified three sex roles: masculine, feminine, and androgynous. These sex roles don't always line up neatly with gender. There are "masculine" females, "feminine" males, and androgynous communicators who combine traditionally masculine and feminine characteristics.

Research shows that linguistic differences are often a function of these sex roles more than the speaker's biological sex. Masculine sex-role communicators—whether male or female—use more dominant language than either feminine or androgynous speakers. Feminine speakers have the most submissive speaking style, whereas androgynous speakers fall between these extremes. When two masculine communicators are in a conversation, they often engage in a one-up battle for dominance, responding to the other's bid for control with a counter-attempt

If women speak and hear a language of connection and intimacy, while men speak and hear a language of status and independence, then communication between men and women can be like cross-cultural communication, prey to a clash of conversational styles. Instead of different dialects, it has been said they speak different genderlects.

Deborah Tannen, *You Just Don't Understand*

sex role
The social orientation that governs behaviour, in contrast to a person's biological gender.

to dominate the interaction. Feminine sex-role speakers are less predictable. They use dominance, submission, and equivalent behaviour in an almost random fashion. Androgynous individuals are more predictable: they most frequently meet another's bid for dominance with a symmetrical attempt at control, but then move quickly toward an equivalent relationship.

All this information suggests that when it comes to communicating, "masculinity" and "femininity" are culturally recognized sex roles, not biological traits. Research suggests that neither a stereotypically male style nor female style is the best choice. For example, one study showed that a "mixed gender strategy" that balanced the stereotypically male, task-oriented approach with the stereotypically female, relationship-oriented approach received the highest marks from both male and female respondents.[64] As opportunities for men and women become more equal, we can expect that the differences between male and female use of language will become smaller.

Culture and Language

Anyone who has tried to translate ideas from one language to another knows that communication across cultures can be a challenge.[65] Sometimes the results of a bungled translation can be amusing. The American manufacturers of Pet condensed milk, for instance, unknowingly introduced their product in French-speaking markets without realizing that in French the word *pet* means "fart."[66] Likewise, the naive English-speaking representative of a US soft drink manufacturer drew laughs from Mexican customers when she offered free samples of Fresca soda pop: in Mexican slang, *fresca* means "lesbian." English-Canadian food growers and canners who have to use bilingual packaging will often use the phrase *sans préservatifs* to indicate that a can of organic tomatoes (for example) contains no preservatives; in French, however, a *préservatif* is a condom.

Even knowing the right words is no guarantee that non-native speakers will use an unfamiliar language correctly. For example, Japanese insurance companies warn their policyholders who are visiting the United States to avoid their cultural tendency to say "excuse me" or "I'm sorry" if they are involved in a traffic accident.[67] In Japan, apologizing is a traditional way to express goodwill and maintain social harmony, even if the person offering the apology is not at fault. In the United States, however, an apology can be taken as an admission of guilt and could result in Japanese tourists being held accountable for accidents for which they are not responsible. Canadians, whose obliging and conciliatory culture often leads them to apologize for things they aren't directly responsible for, face the same danger when travelling in the United States.

Difficult as it may be, translation is only a small part of the communication challenges facing members of different cultures. Differences in the way language is used and the very worldview that a language creates make communicating across cultures a challenging task.

Verbal Communication Styles

Using language is more than just choosing a particular group of words to convey an idea. Each language has its own unique style that distinguishes it from others. And when a communicator tries to use the verbal style from one culture in a different one, problems are likely to arise.[68]

Direct–Indirect

One way in which verbal styles vary is in their directness. Anthropologist Edward Hall identified two distinct cultural ways of using language.[69] **Low-context cultures** use language primarily to express thoughts, feelings, and ideas as clearly and logically as possible. To low-context

**Cultural Idiom
bungled**
Something that is done imperfectly.

The whole object of travel is not to set foot on foreign land; it is at last to set foot on one's own country as a foreign land.

G. K. Chesterton, novelist and scholar

low-context culture
A culture that relies heavily on language to make messages, especially of a relational nature, explicit.

communicators, the meaning of a statement is in the words spoken. By contrast, high-context cultures value language as a way to maintain social harmony. Rather than upset others by speaking clearly, communicators in these cultures learn to discover meaning from the context in which a message is delivered: the non-verbal behaviours of the speaker, the history of the relationship, and the general social rules that govern interaction between people. Table 3.3 summarizes some key differences between the ways low- and high-context cultures use language.

Anglo–North American culture falls toward the direct, low-context end of the scale. English-speaking residents of Canada and the United States value straight talk and grow impatient with "beating around the bush." By contrast, most Asian and Middle Eastern cultures fit the high-context pattern. In many Asian cultures, for example, maintaining harmony is important, and so communicators will avoid speaking plainly if doing so would threaten another person's face. For this reason, Japanese or Korean people are less likely than English Canadians or Americans to offer a clear "no" to an undesirable request. Instead, they would probably use roundabout expressions like "I agree with you in principle, but . . ." or "I sympathize with you, but. . . ."

Low-context Anglo–North Americans may miss the subtleties of high-context messages, but people raised to recognize indirect communication have little trouble decoding them. A look at Japanese child-rearing practices helps explain why. Research shows that Japanese mothers rarely deny the requests of their young children by saying "no." Instead, they use other strategies: ignoring a child's requests, raising distractions, promising to take care of the matter later, or explaining why they cannot or will not say "yes."[70] Sociolinguist Deborah Tannen explains how this indirect approach illustrates profound differences between high- and low-context communications:

> . . . saying no is something associated with children who have not yet learned the norm. If a Japanese mother spoke that way, she would feel she was lowering herself to her child's level precisely because that way of speaking is associated with Japanese children.[71]

Tannen goes on to contrast the Japanese notion of appropriateness with the very different one held by dominant Anglo–North American society:

> Because American norms for talk are different, it is common, and therefore expected, for American parents to "just say no." That's why an American mother feels authoritative when she talks that way: because it fits her image of how an authoritative adult talks to a child.[72]

Table 3.3 Low- and High-Context Communication Styles

Low Context	High Context
Majority of information carried in explicit verbal messages, with less focus on the situational context.	Important information carried in contextual clues (time, place, relationship, or situation). Less reliance on explicit verbal messages.
Self-expression valued. Communicators state opinions and desires directly and strive to persuade others.	Relational harmony valued and maintained by indirect expression of opinions. Communicators refrain from saying "no" directly.
Clear, eloquent speech considered praiseworthy. Verbal fluency admired.	Communicators talk "around" the point, allowing others to fill in the missing pieces. Ambiguity and use of silence admired.

The clash between cultural norms of directness and indirectness can aggravate problems in cross-cultural situations. Consider, for example, encounters between straight-talking, low-context English Canadians—who value speaking clearly—and French Canadians, whose high-context culture stresses smooth interaction. It's easy to imagine how the clash of cultural styles could lead to misunderstandings and conflicts between English Canadians and their French-Canadian neighbours. English Canadians could see their French-speaking counterparts as evasive, whereas the latter could perceive the Anglophones as being insensitive and blunt.

As with the differences between English and French Canadians, subcultures within a single country can have varying notions about the value of direct speech. For example, the communication style of many Aboriginals is closer to that of high-context Japan or Korea than to low-context English Canada.[73] As a group, Aboriginal people value social harmony and avoid confrontation, which leads them to systematically speak in an indirect way to avoid giving offence. Researchers Laura Leets and Howard Giles suggest that the traditional Asian tendency to favour high-context messages sheds light on the difference: adept at recognizing hints and non-verbal cues, high-context communicators are more sensitive to messages that are overlooked by people from cultural groups that rely more heavily on unambiguous, explicit low-context messages.[74]

It's worth noting that even generally straight-talking residents of Canada raised in the low-context English-Canadian tradition often rely on context to make their point. When you decline an unwanted invitation by saying "I can't make it," it's likely that both you and the other person know that the choice of attending isn't really beyond your control. If your goal was to be perfectly clear, you might say, "I don't want to get together."

Elaborate—Succinct

Another way language styles can vary across cultures is in terms of whether they are *elaborate* or *succinct*. Speakers of Arabic, for instance, commonly use language that is much more rich and expressive than the language preferred by most

COMMUNICATION ON-SCREEN

Trailer Park Boys (2001–2009)
Directed by Mike Clattenburg.

One of the most popular Canadian series of all time, *Trailer Park Boys* extends seven seasons and two feature films, with a third on the way. The show is a mockumentary of the lives of misfits living in a trailer park in Nova Scotia, and focuses on the absurd criminal schemes of its title characters, the loser heroes—Julian, Ricky, and Bubbles. Their schemes are usually foiled by either their vindictive trailer park manager or by their own incompetence. Even when they succeed, their success is always short lived. The gang speaks in malapropisms ("what comes around is all around," "search warranty," "get two birds stoned at once"), obscenity, and mispronunciation ("merderder," "quantrintine," "distractulating"). The linguistic and communicative tropes used in the show highlight a number of social factors such as education, geography and social class, often resulting in both great laughs and a brilliant highlighting of cultural disparity and class issues.

communicators who use English. Strong assertions and exaggerations that would sound ridiculous in English are a common feature of Arabic. This contrast in linguistic style can lead to misunderstandings between people from different backgrounds. As one observer put it,

> . . . [A]n Arab feels compelled to over-assert in almost all types of communication because others expect him [or her] to. If an Arab says exactly what he [or she] means without the expected assertion, other Arabs may still think that he [or she] means the opposite. For example, a simple "no" to a host's requests to eat more or drink more will not suffice. To convey the meaning that he [or she] is actually full, the guest must keep repeating "no" several times, coupling it with an oath such as "By God" or "I swear to God."[75]

Succinctness is most extreme in cultures where silence is valued. In many Aboriginal cultures, for example, the favoured way to handle ambiguous social situations is to remain quiet.[76] When you contrast this silent style to the talkativeness common in French- and

COMMUNICATING ONLINE

Twitter Tips

The internet connects us to people of different cultures and different communication styles all across the globe. With Twitter's millions of users, it's likely that someone from a different cultural background to yours will see your tweets. Blogger and communications grad student Melanie Fullick provides her top 10 Twitter tips to help you make sure you are connecting and communicating efficiently and inoffensively with people of all backgrounds.

1. *Understand why you're there.* This helps you decide what is and isn't appropriate to post: share what fits with your purpose. It also helps you to figure out whether you want a public or private account, how much detail you want to share about your life, and whether your posts will relate primarily to personal or professional issues (or both).

2. *Don't be afraid of strangers.* Twitter is an amazing tool for starting conversations, extending your network, and making new friends. The goal is not just to post tweets, but to engage with others. While you can make all your posts "private" (other than to approved followers), in some ways you're better off not using Twitter at all if you want most people not to see what you post.

3. *Use the "grammar" of Twitter.* It will be harder to communicate with others if you don't bother to learn the language people are speaking. Use *@mentions*, *#hashtags*, and *RT* (retweets). If you alter and re-share someone else's tweet, use *MT* (modified tweet). These tools, especially hashtags, help you to join in with existing conversations and to start new ones. The best way to learn the lingo is to watch what others do, and follow their lead.

4. *Be considerate.* Thank or give credit to people who share what you post, or whose posts you re-share (use *HT*, "hat tip;" or *via @user*). If someone responds to one of your posts, try to get back to them. Try to assume the best of others; if their tone sounds "short" it might be because of the character limit on posts. If you disagree with someone, you can still express your thoughts without being insulting.

5. *It's not all about you.* Share, but not just your own material. If you have a blog, don't stick to tweeting your own blog posts or people will quickly tune out. If you're tweeting on behalf of an organization or business, share content and tweets from similar organizations, or other links and resources that are relevant. Constant self-promotion

English-Canadian cultures when people first meet, it's easy to imagine how the first encounter between an Inuit, Haida, or Mohawk and a European person might feel uncomfortable to both.

Formal–Informal

A third way languages differ from one culture to another involves *formality* and *informality*. The informal approach that characterizes relationships in countries like Canada, the United States, Australia, and New Zealand is quite different from the great concern for using proper speech in many parts of Asia and Africa. Formality isn't so much a matter of using correct grammar as of defining social position. In Korea, for example, the language reflects the Confucian system of relational hierarchies.[77] Korean has special vocabularies for both sexes, for different levels of social status, for different degrees of intimacy, and for different types of social occasions. There are different degrees of formality for speaking with old friends, non-acquaintances whose background one knows, and complete strangers. One sign of being a learned person in Korea is the ability to use language that recognizes these relational distinctions. When you contrast these sorts of distinctions with the casual friendliness many

is easily spotted and dismissed by other participants. You need to give people a reason to follow you.

6. *Be consistent.* The average tweet "disappears" after about 15 minutes. Even a single tweet posted each day is likely to be missed by those following you. So you need to post fairly often (but not too often, or other people will feel overwhelmed!). If you have a new item to share, post it more than once but at different times of the day; people aren't watching their tweet stream all the time.

7. *Think before you tweet.* This sounds basic, but it's extremely important. Check your facts—there's nothing worse than sharing information, especially about breaking news, that turns out to be incorrect or misleading. Check your grammar, spelling, and tone. If you're making a negative comment in public about an employer, client, student, or peer, you might want to stop yourself. You can also use direct messages (*DMs*) to have a private chat.

8. *Don't feed the trolls.* There are plenty of people out there who aren't going to follow tip #4. There's no need to encourage them. Remember, everything is public and others will see if you engage in or provoke a fight on-line.

Some Twitter apps will allow you to "mute" a user or a hashtag; you also have the option of "blocking" users who are consistently obnoxious.

9. *Use apps, lists, and other tools to improve your use and experience.* There are applications available that allow you to manage and enhance your experience much more effectively than you can through the Twitter website. Since app availability is changing all the time, do an on-line search for the best apps—or better yet, ask the "Twitterverse" and get some advice.

10. *Crowd source, network, [and] take it off-line.* Microblogging is a powerful means of building on-line community that extends into your "off-line" world, from making friends in a new town to organizing a "tweet-up" of like-minded colleagues at a conference. If you're good at engaging and contributing on-line, you'll find your time on Twitter is not wasted but rather leads to a larger network that becomes a means of gathering advice, answering questions, keeping up-to-date, and developing a professional profile.

—Melonie Fullick, York University PhD student

Anglo–North Americans use even when talking with complete strangers, it's easy to see how a Korean might view communicators in Canada as boorish and how a Canadian might view Koreans as stiff and unfriendly.

Language and Worldview

Different linguistic styles are important, but there may be even more fundamental differences that separate speakers of various languages. For almost 150 years, some theorists have put forth the notion of **linguistic determinism**: the theory that the worldview of a culture is shaped and reflected by the language its members speak. For instance, bilingual speakers seem to think differently when they change languages.[78] In one study, French-speaking North Americans were asked to interpret a series of pictures. When they spoke in French, their descriptions were far more romantic and emotional than when they used English. Likewise, when students in Hong Kong were asked to complete a values test, they expressed more traditional Chinese values when they answered in Cantonese than when they answered in English. In Israel, both Arab and Jewish students saw greater distinctions between their group and "outsiders" when using their native language than when they used English, a neutral tongue. Examples like these show the power of language to shape cultural identity—sometimes for better and sometimes for worse.

Exponents of linguistic determinism believe that linguistic influences start early in life. For instance, they cite the fact that English-speaking parents often label the mischievous pranks of their children as "bad," implying that there is something immoral about acting wild. On the other hand, French parents are more likely to say *Sois sage!*—"Be wise!;" the linguistic

> **linguistic determinism**
> The theory that a culture's worldview is unavoidably shaped and reflected by the language its members speak.

Understanding Diversity

Loyalists to Loonies: A Very Short History of Canadian English

Many Canadians have but one, fearful, question about their language: is it becoming more American? In light of Canadian history, this is quite ironic, since the roots of Canadian English (other than Newfoundland English, which derives from the dialects of southwest England and of Ireland) are in the speech of the United Empire Loyalists who fled the United States during and after the Revolution. At its origins, then, Canadian English *was* American English, so it is hard to know how it could become *more* American. This common origin explains why Canadians share so many words with Americans and sound more like Americans from the northern states than they sound like the British. Much of the vocabulary that distinguishes North American English from British English is an inheritance of older words that have survived over here but been superseded by other words in the UK (*fall* for *autumn*, *diaper* for *nappie*, etc.). Likewise, we retain some older pronunciations (*herb* with a silent *h*, for instance, which can be traced back to the Middle Ages). But Canadian English is different from American English, and our history accounts for that.

Ever since our arrival in Canada, English speakers have co-existed with French speakers and Aboriginal peoples. We have happily borrowed many words from both, a process that continues to this day. From early fur-trade borrowings such as *voyageur*, to nineteenth-century borrowings like *tuque* to our most recent acquisitions like *poutine*, Canadian English includes a lot of French! Words like *saskatoon* reveal our indebtedness to native languages.

In the nineteenth century, vast numbers of people from the British Isles were encouraged to settle in British North America to ward off any lurking nefarious American influence. Although their children inevitably ended up sounding like their playmates rather than their parents, some British linguistic traits managed to impose themselves. It is to this time that we owe our "British spellings," our use of "zed" rather than "zee", and the pronunciations that some (but not all) of us use, (*leftenant, shedule, herb* with an *h*). Scots in particular left their mark on Canadian English. In the Maritimes, southwestern Ontario, and the Prairies, people

implication is that misbehaving is an act of foolishness. Swedes would correct the same action with the
words *Var snall!*—"Be friendly, be kind." By contrast,
German adults would use the command *Sei artig!*—
literally, "Be of your own kind"—in other words,
get back in step, conform to your role as a child.[79]
Cognitive psychologists such as Judith Rich Harris
have persuasively challenged the "nurture hypothesis," which states that parents have a large influence
on the development of their children's cognitive
abilities and personality. Harris has demonstrated
that it is a combination of *genes* and *environment*
that shape children's identities, and that parents—
and their words—have only a very small part to play
in the process.[80] This puts her and most of cognitive neuroscience squarely at odds with those who
believe in linguistic determinism.

The best-known declaration of linguistic determinism is the **Sapir–Whorf hypothesis**,
formulated in the 1930s by anthropologist Edward Sapir and Benjamin Whorf, an amateur
linguist.[81] Following Sapir's theoretical work, Whorf suggested that the language spoken by the
Hopi, a Native American people living mainly in Arizona, represents a view of reality dramatically different from more familiar tongues. For example, he claimed that the Hopi language

> **Sapir–Whorf hypothesis**
> The theory that the structure of a language shapes the worldview of its users.

use Scottish words like *storm-stayed* and *a skiff of snow*, but other
Scottish words have made it into English across the country: *bursary* for a particular type of scholarship, *bannock* for a kind of
quick bread (this usage probably thanks to the high numbers of
"Orkneymen" in the employ of the Hudson's Bay Company).

Another phenomenon of the nineteenth century was the
hybrid language used on the west coast known as "Chinook
Jargon." This mixture of several Aboriginal languages, particularly Nuu-chah-nulth and Chinook, with English and French,
facilitated communication between the various groups. It was
widely used but has now died out, though remnants of it survive
in such words as *chum* (salmon), *Siwash sweater*, and *saltchuck*.

The twentieth century brought waves of immigrants from
non-English speaking countries, as we saw with our look at
Ukrainian and Italian words in Canadian English. As we borrow from other languages, we continue to invent new words
(*stagette*) from and apply new senses (*download*) to the existing
English vocabulary.

Canadians may be consumed by the fear of being swal-
lowed up entirely by US English, but we have already managed
to maintain our linguistic distinctiveness despite living right
next door to this behemoth for almost 250 years, with citizens
travelling back and forth freely between both countries, and
Canadians bombarded constantly by a barrage of American
publishing and media, the like of which other English-speaking
countries never experience. I believe that Canadian English will
continue to survive and thrive. Just so long, of course, as we
don't run out of loonies.

Katherine Barber, *Six Words You Never Knew
Had Something To Do with Pigs*

QUESTIONS: The author describes how Canadian English has
evolved differently from both American and British English. How
do you think Canadian English will evolve over the next 50 years?
The next hundred? What factors will influence this evolution?

makes no distinction between nouns and verbs, and therefore the people who speak it see the entire world as though it were constantly in process. The difference between the Hopi and English worldviews, according to this theory, would be similar to that between a video clip and a still photo. More recently, however, linguist and social activist Noam Chomsky and cognitive scientist Steven Pinker have argued that Whorf's methods were shoddy and his knowledge of the Hopi language non-existent.

Similarly, poor research and wishful thinking on the part of proponents of linguistic determinism are believed to be responsible for the popular myth that the Inuit have—depending on who is telling the tale—anywhere from 9 to 200 words for snow. Common Inuktitut, in fact, has only two words for snow: *aput*, meaning snow as a substance, and *qanik*, which is used most often like the verb "to snow." Like German, Inuktitut words can be extended by attaching anywhere from one to dozens of suffixes to convey more meaning, but linguists note that this practice is not substantively different from how English uses modifiers to produce compound terms like "blowing snow," "snowdrifts," or "wet snow." Inuktitut, however, is noteworthy by lacking a word for "guilt," which has contributed to some particular complexities in Nunavut's justice system.[82]

Current research in the cognitive science of language has largely discredited the Sapir–Whorf hypothesis and linguistic determinism as bad science. In fact, the links between language and thinking appear to become weaker with each passing year. But although there is little support for the extreme linguistic deterministic viewpoint that it is impossible for speakers of different languages to view the world identically, the more moderate notion of **linguistic relativism**—the idea that language exerts a strong influence on perceptions—does seem valid. As one scholar put it, "the differences between languages are not so much in what can be said, but in what it is relatively easy to say."[83] Some languages contain terms that have no exact English equivalents.[84] Consider the following, for example:

- *Nemawashi* (Japanese): The process of informally feeling out all the people involved with an issue before making a decision;
- *Lagniappe* (Louisiana Creole): An extra gift given in a transaction that wasn't expected by the terms of a contract;
- *Lao* (Mandarin): a respectful term used for older people, showing their importance in the family and in society;
- *Dharma* (Sanskrit): Each person's unique, ideal path in life and the knowledge of how to find it;
- *Schadenfreude* (German): A feeling of malicious enjoyment derived from observing someone else's misfortune; and
- *Koyaanisquatsi* (Hopi): Nature out of balance; a way of life so crazy it calls for a new way of living.

Once words like these exist and become a part of everyday life, the ideas they represent are easier to recognize. But even without such words, each of the concepts mentioned is still possible to imagine. Thus, speakers of a language that includes the notion of *lao* would probably treat older members respectfully, and those who are familiar with *lagniappe* might be more generous, but the words aren't essential to follow these principles. Although language may shape thoughts and behaviour, it doesn't dominate them absolutely.

Language Use in Anglo-North American Culture

The importance of language as a reflection of worldview isn't just a matter of interest for anthropologists and linguists. The labels we use in everyday conversation both reflect and shape the way we view others and ourselves. This explains why businesses often give employees impressive titles and why a woman's choice of the label "Ms" or "Mrs" can be a statement about her identity. Women in Western society make a conscious choice about how to identify themselves when they marry. They may follow the tradition of taking their husband's last name, hyphenate their birth name with their husband's, or keep their birth name. A fascinating study found that a woman's choice is likely to reveal a great deal about herself and her relationship with her husband.[85] Surveys suggested that women who have taken their husbands' names place the most importance on relationships, with social expectations of how they should behave placing second, and issues of self, coming last. By contrast, women who have kept their birth names put their personal concerns ahead of relationships and social expectations. Women with hyphenated names fall somewhere between the other groups, valuing self and relationships equally.

In the same way, the labels that members of an ethnic group choose to define themselves say a great deal about their sense of identity. Over the years, labels of racial identification have gone through cycles of popularity.[86] In Anglo–North America, the first freed slaves preferred to be called *Africans*. In the late nineteenth and early twentieth centuries, "coloured" was the term of choice; later Negro became the respectable word. Then, in the 1960s, the term "black" grew increasingly popular—first as a label for militants and later as a term preferred by more moderate citizens of all colours. More recently, African American and Afro-Canadian have gained popularity.[87] In Canada, the situation is a little more complicated, particularly because of the diverse origins of Canadians of African descent.[88] A recent study showed that although "black" was the most preferred label, it was but one of four identified terms (the others being Africentric, Caribbean, and Canadian). Decisions about which name to use reflect a person's attitude. For example, one survey revealed that individuals who prefer the label "black" choose it because they consider it to be "acceptable" and "based on consensus" of the larger culture.[89] They describe themselves as patriotic, accepting of the status quo, and attempting to assimilate into the larger culture. By contrast, people who choose the term Afro-American derive their identity from their ethnicity and do not want to assimilate into the larger culture, only to succeed in it. The label others choose can also be revealing. In the United States, political liberals are more likely to use the term African American than are conservatives.[90]

Canadian sociolinguists Ruth King and Sandra Clarke have identified a similar complexity surrounding the word "newfie."[91] Members of mainstream Canadian culture often use "newfie" as a derogatory and marginalizing term, but the network of its meanings is actually very complex. Originally, "newfie" denoted a happy-go-lucky fisher who didn't shoulder the cares of the world. The Newfoundland rock band, Great Big Sea, has attempted to re-appropriate the term and represent a positive and enlightened view of Newfoundland to the rest of Canada. King and Clarke cite Bob Benson, a staff reporter of *The Telegram*, a Newfoundland newspaper, who explicitly links "newfie" with the extremely derogatory term "nigger." Interestingly, when speaking amongst themselves or in their own media, Newfoundlanders are completely unselfconscious about using "newfie," even going so far as to characterize objections to the word as examples of political correctness.

Summary

Language is both one of humanity's greatest assets and the source of many problems. This chapter highlighted the characteristics that distinguish language and suggested methods of using it more effectively.

Any language is a collection of symbols governed by a variety of rules and used to convey messages between people. Because of its symbolic nature, language is not a precise tool: meanings rest in people, not in words themselves. In order for effective communication to occur, it is necessary to negotiate meanings for ambiguous statements.

Language not only describes people, ideas, processes, and events, but it also shapes our perceptions of them in areas including status, credibility, and attitudes about gender and ethnicity. Along with influencing our attitudes, language reflects them. The words we use and our manner of speech reflect power, responsibility, affiliation, attraction, and interest.

Many types of language have the potential to create misunderstandings. Other types of language can result in unnecessary conflicts. In other cases, speech and writing can be evasive, avoiding expression of unwelcome messages.

The relationship between gender and language is a confusing one. There are many differences in the ways men and women speak: the content of their conversations varies, as do their reasons for communicating and their conversational styles. Not all differences in language use can be accounted for by the speaker's gender, however. Occupation, social philosophy, and orientation toward problem-solving also influence the use of language, and psychological sex role can be more of an influence than biological sex.

Language operates on a broad level to shape the consciousness and communication of an entire society. Different languages often shape and reflect the views of a culture. Low-context cultures like that of English Canada use language primarily to express feelings and ideas as clearly and unambiguously as possible, whereas high-context cultures avoid specificity to promote social harmony. Some cultures value brevity and the succinct use of language, whereas others value elaborate forms of speech. In some societies formality is important, whereas in others informality is important. Beyond these differences, there is the controversial concept of linguistic relativism—the notion that language exerts a strong influence on the worldview of the people who speak it.

Key Terms

abstraction ladder   104
abstract language   104
behavioural description   104
convergence   99
divergence   99
emotive language   107
equivocal words   101
equivocation   109
euphemism   108
factual statement   106
high-context culture   116
inferential statement   106
jargon   102

language   86
linguistic determinism   120
linguistic relativism   122
low-context culture   115
opinion statement   106
phonological rules   87
pragmatic rules   89
relative words   101
Sapir–Whorf hypothesis   121
semantic rules   89
sex role   114
slang   102
syntactic rules   88

Activities

A. Powerful Speech and Polite Speech

Increase your ability to achieve an optimal balance between powerful speech and polite speech by rehearsing one of the following scenarios:

1. Describing your qualifications to a potential employer for a job that interests you

2. Requesting an extension on a deadline from one of your instructors

3. Explaining to a merchant why you want a cash refund on an unsatisfactory piece of merchandise when the store's policy is to issue credit

4. Asking your boss for three days off so you can attend a friend's out-of-town wedding

5. Approaching your neighbours about their dog, which barks while they are away from home

6. Tweeting to invite people to a BBQ that you and some classmates are organizing to raise money for the local Humane Society or other animal shelter

Your statement should gain its power by avoiding the types of powerless language listed in Table 3.1. You should not become abusive or threatening, and your statement should be completely honest.

B. Slang and Jargon

Find a classmate, neighbour, co-worker, or other person whose background differs significantly from yours. In an interview, ask this person to identify the slang and jargon terms that he or she finds confusing. Explore the following types of potentially baffling terms:

1. regionalisms,

2. age-related terms,

3. technical jargon,

4. acronyms, and

5. short forms used while texting.

C. Low-Level Abstractions

You can develop your ability to use low-level abstractions by following these steps:

1. Use your own experience to write each of the following:
    a. a complaint or gripe;
    b. one way you would like someone with whom you interact to change; and
    c. one reason why you appreciate a person with whom you interact.

2. Now translate each of the statements you have written into a low-level abstraction by including:
    a. the person or people involved;
    b. the circumstances in which the behaviour occurs; and
    c. the specific behaviours to which you are referring.

3. Compare the statements you have written in Step 1 and Step 2. How might the lower-level abstractions in Step 2 improve the chances of having your message understood and accepted?

D. Gender and Language

1. Note differences in the language use of three men and three women you know. (Include yourself in the analysis.) Your analysis will be most accurate if you record the speech of each person you analyze. Consider the following categories:
   a. conversational content,
   b. conversational style,
   c. reasons for communicating, and
   d. the use of powerful/powerless speech.

2. Based on your observations, answer the following questions:
   a. How much does gender influence speech?
   b. What role do other variables play? Consider occupational or social status, cultural background, social philosophy, competitive–co-operative orientation, and other factors in your analysis.

E. Sexist and Racist Language

One of the most treasured civil liberties is freedom of speech. At the same time, most people would agree that some forms of racist and sexist speech are hateful and demeaning to their targets. As you have read in these pages, language shapes the attitudes of those who hear it.

How do you reconcile the principle of free speech and the need to minimize hateful and discriminatory messages? Do you think laws and policies can and should be made to limit certain types of communication? If so, how should those limits be drafted to protect civil liberties? If not, can you justify the necessary protection of even sexist and racist language?

F. Euphemisms and Equivocations

For most people, "telling it like it is" is usually considered a virtue, and "beating around the bush" is a minor sin. You can test the function of indirect speech by following these directions:

1. Identify five examples of euphemisms and equivocations in everyday interaction.

2. Imagine how matters would have been different if the speakers or writers had used direct language in each situation.

3. Based on your observations, discuss whether equivocations and euphemisms have any place in face-to-face communication.

Further Reading

Adler, Jerry, "The War of the Words; Debate: Whether It's Climate 'Chaos,' 'Change' or 'Crisis,' Language Comes First in the Environment Fight," *Newsweek*. **16 April 2007.**
It's no surprise that politics often boils down to how words are interpreted. This article analyzes the way politicians on opposite sides of the partisan fence use language when discussing environmental issues, such as climate. For instance, one researcher says that "global warming" limits the emphasis to worldwide average temperature. A strategist believes that the term "global warming" only affects people when the weather is actually cold. A professor of linguistics asserts that "climate crisis" moves people to action, whereas "climate change" doesn't have the same urgent effect.

Kenneally, Christine, *The First Word: The Search for the Origins of Language* **(New York: Viking, 2008).**
This well-written book offers readers an accessible tour of the latest thinking on where human language came from and why it developed. The book is an exciting and engaging read that offers a window on how language—the single most defining human trait—developed.

Martel, Marcel and Pâquet, Martin, *Speaking Up: A History of Language and Politics in Canada and Quebec* (Toronto: Between the Lines, 2012).

French and English Canada have always had issues relating language culture and politics. This book captures the intricate and fascinating history of the relationship between language and politics in Canada and Quebec from 1539 to the present. Nuanced and unbiased yet empathetic, the book reveals that the language issue has been at the heart of Canada's political life for centuries.

Rheingold, Howard, *They Have a Word for It* (Los Angeles: Tarcher, 1988).

Rheingold has collected a lexicon of words and phrases from languages around the world that lend support to the Sapir–Whorf hypothesis. This entertaining 200-page compendium of "untranslatable phrases" illustrates that speaking a new language can, indeed, prompt a different worldview.

Sable, Trudy and Francis, Bernie, *Language of This Land: Mi'kma'ki* (Sidney, NB: Cape Breton University Press, 2012).

The Language of this Land, Mi'kma'ki is an exploration of Mi'kmaw worldview as expressed in language, legends, and song and dance. Using imagery as codes, these include not only place names and geologic history, but act as maps of the landscape. The authors illustrate the fluid nature of reality inherent in its expression—its embodiment in networks of relationships with the landscape integral to the cultural psyche and spirituality of the Mi'kmaq.

Smith, Neil, *Language, Bananas and Bonobos: Linguistic Problems, Puzzles and Polemics* (Oxford: Blackwell, 2002).

Smith highlights many interesting and amusing quirks of language, cognition, and the brain. This very funny and accessible book will bring you up to date on the latest linguistic and cognitive scientific theorizing.

Tannen, Deborah, *You Just Don't Understand: Women and Men in Conversation* (New York: Harper Paperbacks, 2001).

Georgetown University linguistics professor Deborah Tannen has authored seven books on language used in various interpersonal relationships. This book's focus is on the constantly perplexing communication between men and women. Tannen asserts that communication styles trump the actual words men and women use. Instead, she believes that men and women are different cultural species, meaning that each enters into a relationship with unique background in how words are used and what they mean. Readers of this perpetually popular title will learn how communication fails between men and women and how to create a more "common language" between the sexes.

Study Questions

1. Describe an incident illustrating how meanings reside in people, not words.

2. Recall incidents when (a) language shaped your attitudes, and (b) your own choice of words reflected your attitudes.

3. Explain how the types of troublesome language described on pp. 100–10 have caused problems in a situation you experienced or observed.

4. Based on your experience of English-Canadian culture, describe how the gender and non-gender variables described on pp. 110–15 affect communication.

5. Give examples illustrating which communication styles described on pp. 116–17 operate in mainstream Canadian culture.

6. Provide examples of how you think that social media and mobile computing technologies such as tablets or smartphones have changed the way you use language. Have they affected the way you write or speak? If so, how?

4

Non-Verbal Communication

After studying the material in this chapter . . .

You should understand:

- ✔ the characteristics of non-verbal communication;
- ✔ the differences between verbal and non-verbal communication;
- ✔ how culture and gender influence non-verbal communication;
- ✔ the functions that non-verbal communication can serve; and
- ✔ how the types of non-verbal communication described in this chapter function.

You should be able to:

- ✔ identify and describe non-verbal behaviour in various contexts;
- ✔ identify non-verbal behaviours that repeat, substitute for, complement, accent, regulate, and contradict verbal messages;
- ✔ recognize the emotional and relational dimensions of your own non-verbal behaviour; and
- ✔ share your interpretation of another person's non-verbal behaviour in a tentative manner when such sharing is appropriate.

Chapter Highlights

Non-verbal communication has several important characteristics:

» Unlike verbal communication, it is always present when people encounter one another and in many situations where they aren't physically present.

» It has great value in conveying information about others, and much of that information isn't something others intentionally want to reveal.

» It is especially useful in suggesting how others feel about you and the relationship, although non-verbal messages are much more ambiguous than verbal communication.

While much non-verbal communication is universal, some factors do shape the way we express ourselves and understand others:

» Culture shapes many non-verbal practices.

» Gender plays a role in the way we communicate.

Non-verbal communication serves many functions, when compared to verbal messages:

» It can repeat, complement, and accent spoken words.

» Sometimes it can substitute for speech.

» It can regulate spoken conversation.

» It can contradict spoken words, or even deceive others.

Non-verbal communication can take many forms. Some of these forms may be obvious:

» posture and gesture,

» face and eyes,

» voice,

» touch, and

» physical attractiveness and clothes.

Other forms are more subtle, involving things like:

» personal space and distance,

» use of time, and

» physical environment.

Cultural Idiom
rings hollow
Something that sounds
insincere.

There is often a big gap between what people say and what they feel. An acquaintance says, "I'd like to get together again" in a way that leaves you suspecting the opposite. (But how do you know?) A speaker tries to appear confident but acts in a way that almost screams out, "I'm nervous!" (What tells you this?) You ask a friend what's wrong, and the "Nothing" you get in response rings hollow. (Why does it sound untrue?)

Then, of course, there are times when another's message comes through even though there are no words at all. A look of irritation, a smile, a sigh—signs like these can say more than a torrent of words.

All situations like these have one point in common: the message was sent *non-verbally*. The goal of this chapter is to introduce you to this world of non-verbal communication. Although you have certainly recognized non-verbal messages before, the following pages should introduce you to a richness of information you have never noticed. And though your experience won't transform you into a mind reader, it will make you a far more accurate observer of others—and yourself.

We need to begin our study of non-verbal communication by defining this term. At first this might seem like a simple task. If non means "not" and "verbal" means "words", then "non-verbal communication" appears to mean "communication without words." This is a good starting point after we distinguish between vocal communication (by mouth) and verbal communication (with words). After this distinction is made, it becomes clear that some non-verbal messages are vocal, and some are not. Likewise, although many verbal messages are vocal, some aren't. Table 4.1 illustrates these differences.

What about languages that don't involve words? Do Canadian Sign Language and the *Langue des Signes Québécois*, for example, qualify as non-verbal communication? Most scholars would say not.[1] Keeping this fact in mind, we arrive at a working definition of **non-verbal communication:** oral and non-oral messages expressed by other than linguistic means. This rules out sign languages and written words, but it includes messages transmitted by vocal means that don't involve language—sighs, laughs, and other utterances we will discuss soon.

non-verbal
communication
Messages expressed
by other than linguistic
means.

Characteristics of Non-Verbal Communication

Our brief definition only hints at the richness of non-verbal messages. You can begin to understand their prevalence by trying a simple experiment. Spend an hour or so around a group of people who are speaking a language you don't understand. You might find such a group by visiting an area populated by an ethnic group other than your own, or by sitting in a café that caters to a cultural group different from yours, such as those in Vancouver's Chinatown or Toronto's Little India. Your goal is to see how much information you can learn about the people you're observing through means other than the verbal messages they transmit. This experiment will reveal several characteristics of non-verbal communication.

Non-Verbal Communication Exists

Your observations in the experiment show clearly that even without understanding speech it is possible to get an idea about how others are feeling. You probably noticed that some people were in a hurry, whereas others seemed happy, confused, withdrawn, or deep in thought. The point is that without any formal experience you were able to recognize, and to some degree

Table 4.1 Types of Communication

	Vocal Communication	Non-Vocal Communication
Verbal Communication	Spoken words	Written words
Non-Verbal Communication	Tone of voice, sighs, screams, vocal qualities (loudness, pitch, and so on)	Gestures, movement, appearance, facial expression, and so on

Source: Adapted from John Stewart and Gary D'Angelo, *Together: Communicating Interpersonally*, 2nd edn (Reading, MA: Addison-Wesley, 1980), 22.

interpret, messages that other people sent non-verbally. In this chapter, we want to sharpen the skills you already have and give you a better grasp of the vocabulary of non-verbal language.

Non-Verbal Behaviour Has Communicative Value

The pervasiveness of non-verbal communication brings us to its second characteristic: it's virtually impossible *not* to communicate non-verbally. Suppose you were instructed to avoid communicating any messages at all. What would you do? Close your eyes? Withdraw into a ball? Leave the room? The meaning of some non-verbal behaviour can be ambiguous, but it always has communicative value. For example, a study of bereaved First Nations family members in Canada revealed that non-verbal communication was an important part of effective palliative care for First Nations people. The study concluded that respect, communication, appropriate environments, and caregiving were necessary to ensure culturally appropriate care.[2]

Of course, we don't always intend to send non-verbal messages. Unintentional non-verbal behaviours differ from intentional ones.[3] For example, we often stammer, blush, frown, and sweat without meaning to do so. Some theorists argue that unintentional behaviour may provide information, but it shouldn't count as communication. Others draw the boundaries of non-verbal communication more broadly, suggesting that even unconscious and unintentional behaviour conveys messages and thus is worth studying as communication.[4] We take the broad view here because, whether or not our non-verbal behaviour is intentional, others recognize it and take it into account when responding to us.

Although non-verbal behaviour reveals information, we aren't always conscious of what we are communicating non-verbally. In one study, less than a quarter of experimental subjects who had been instructed to show increased or decreased approval of a partner could describe the non-verbal behaviours they used. Furthermore, just because communicators are non-verbally expressive doesn't mean that others will tune into the abundance of unspoken messages that are available. One study comparing the richness of e-mail to in-person communication confirmed the greater amount of information available in face-to-face conversations, but it also showed that some communicators (primarily men) failed to recognize these messages.[5] A study by Richard Schwier and Shelly Balbar of the University of Saskatchewan investigated the effect of face-to-face versus distant communication on learning in a graduate seminar. The study concluded that both face-to-face and non–face-to-face communication strategies worked for different sorts of learning. They found that a combination of the two appears necessary to promote the student engagement and depth required in a seminar.[6]

The fact that you and everyone around you are constantly sending non-verbal clues is important because it means that you have a constant source of information available about yourself and others. If you can tune into these signals, you will be more aware of how those around you are feeling and thinking, and you will be better able to respond to their behaviour.

Non-Verbal Communication Is Primarily Relational

Some non-verbal messages serve utilitarian functions. For example, a police officer uses hand motions to direct the flow of traffic. But non-verbal communication also serves a far more common (and more interesting) series of social functions.[7]

One of these social functions involves identity management. Chapter 2 discussed how we strive to create an image of ourselves as we want others to view us. Non-verbal communication plays an important role in this process—in many cases more important than verbal communication. Consider, for example, what happens when you attend a party where you are likely to meet strangers you would like to get to know better. Instead of projecting your image verbally ("Hi! I'm attractive, friendly, and easygoing"), you behave in ways that will present this identity. You might smile a lot, and perhaps try to strike a relaxed pose. It's also likely that you dress carefully—even if the image involves looking as if you hadn't given a lot of attention to your appearance.

Along with identity management, non-verbal communication allows us to define the kind of relationships we want to have with others. You can appreciate this fact by thinking about the wide range of ways you could behave when greeting another person. You could wave, shake hands, nod, smile, clap the other person on the back, give a hug, or avoid all contact. Each one of these decisions would send a message about the nature of your relationship with the other person.

Non-verbal communication performs a third valuable social function: conveying emotions that we may be unwilling or unable to express verbally—or ones we may not even be aware of. In fact, non-verbal communication is much better suited to expressing attitudes and feelings than ideas.[8] You can prove this for yourself by imagining how you could express each item on the following list non-verbally:

- You are bored.
- You are attracted to another person in the group.
- You are nervous about trying this experiment.
- You are opposed to stem cell research.
- You want to know if you will be tested on this material.

The first three items in this list involve attitudes. By contrast, the last two items involve ideas, and they would be quite difficult to convey without using words. The same principle

holds in everyday life: non-verbal behaviour offers many cues about the way people feel—often more than we get from their words alone. In fact, some research suggests that one important element of communicative competence is non-verbal expressiveness.[9]

Non-Verbal Communication Is Ambiguous

Before you get the idea that this book will turn you into a mind reader, it is important to realize that non-verbal communication is often difficult to interpret accurately. To appreciate the ambiguous nature of non-verbal communication, study the photo on this page. What emotions do you imagine the man is feeling? Elation? Relief? In fact, neither of these is even close. The basketball coach in this photo is reacting to a referee's call that he doesn't agree with!

Non-verbal communication can be just as vague in everyday life. For example, relying on non-verbal cues in romantic situations can lead to inaccurate guesses about a partner's interest in a sexual relationship.[10] Workers at Safeway, a chain of grocery stores in the United States and western Canada, discovered first-hand the problems with non-verbal ambiguity when they tried to follow the company's new "superior customer service" policy that required them to smile and make eye contact with customers. Twelve employees filed grievances over the policy, reporting that several customers had propositioned them after misinterpreting their actions as come-ons.[11]

Although all non-verbal behaviour is ambiguous, some emotions are easier to decode accurately than others. In laboratory experiments, subjects were better at identifying positive facial expressions—happiness, love, surprise, interest—than negative ones such as fear, sadness, anger, and disgust.[12] In real life, however, spontaneous non-verbal expressions are so ambiguous that observers are able to identify the emotions they convey no more accurately than by guessing.[13]

Some people are more skilful than others at accurately decoding non-verbal behaviour.[14] Those who are better senders of non-verbal messages also are better receivers. Decoding ability also increases with age and training, although there are still differences in ability owing to personality and occupation. For instance, extroverts are relatively accurate judges of non-verbal behaviour, whereas dogmatists are not. Women seem to be far better than men at decoding non-verbal messages. Over 95 per cent of the studies examined in one analysis showed that women are more accurate at interpreting non-verbal signals.[15] Despite these differences, even the best non-verbal decoders do not approach perfect accuracy.

When you do try to make sense out of ambiguous non-verbal behaviour, you need to consider several factors: the *context* in which it occurs (smiling at a joke and smiling at bad news reflect different feelings); the *history* of your relationship with the sender (friendly, hostile, etc.); the other's *mood* at the time; and your *feelings* (when you're feeling insecure, almost anything can seem like a threat). The important idea is that when you become aware of non-verbal messages, you should think of them not as facts but rather as clues that need to be checked out.

> *The most important thing in communication is hearing what isn't said.*
>
> **Peter Drucker, author and business guru**

'That was unkind, darling. When their mouths turn up at the corners they want to be friends.'

YOUNG COMMUNICATOR PROFILE

MILES JONES

Talks "The Jones Act (Part III)," *Succeeding In the Canadian Industry, and Making Comic Books*

One of the best things about Canada's hip-hop landscape is the sheer diversity of artists within its broad reaches. In a reflection of our multicultural country, the Canadian hip-hop scene features unique sounds from East to West Coast, and everywhere in between. One such example is Toronto-born Miles Jones. Blending futuristic beats inspired by dance and house, and infused with an ever-present boom bap quality, Jones has crafted a unique sound that reflects his musically diverse upbringing in a household with his father, Hedley Jones Jr, a longtime radio and club deejay. Most recently, Jones' efforts have culminated in the release of *The Jones Act (Part III)*, a 12-track album released on his own label, Mojo Records and Publishing. On top of that, in an equally unique endeavour, Jones has been collaborating with illustrator Ben Roboly to create comic book issues based on the songs from the album.

TCUS: Before we get into your latest album, I'd like to build towards it. You were born in Toronto, and graduated from McMaster. What did you study there?

Miles Jones: Multimedia and Communications.

TCUS: How did you get into hosting a radio show at McMaster?

Miles Jones: I basically just volunteered. It was something that I was always interested in—my dad was a broadcaster, and he used to bring me on the air when I was little, like on CFNY and Mix 99.9—and I just had this idea to host this radio show where I could [showcase] the history of breaks and things that inspired hip-hop and connect it with the current hip-hop culture. I had this idea for the show, and so I pitched it in first year, and I didn't get it. They gave me a little time slot in my second year, where I had to wake up at like 8:30 in the morning and bust my ass to get there. By the time I was in third and fourth year, I had a really cool time slot at 9:00 in the evenings, and [my co-host and I] were able to turn it into an actual show, where we were able to get guests, and started to get some really good feedback, so it kinda just escalated into that vision that I had in the beginning.

TCUS: In 2004, you started Mojo Records & Publishing. Correct me if I'm wrong, but you've described the Canadian hip-hop landscape as "prime real estate," in that it's vast and unclaimed. Can you elaborate on this?

Miles Jones: Yeah, that wasn't actually me that described that; it's in my bio. But I think what they were looking at [in that description] is there are a handful of artists that have made note of themselves in the Canadian hip-hop industry over the past few decades, but it still seems to be this fresh, young, and exciting genre. It's not completely over-saturated, and there's room for artists doing new things and creative hip-hop to find a place and establish themselves. I think it's one of those things, and it's interesting, because you see the artists that were working five years ago, ten years ago—however long any of these people have been making hip-hop music—and the ones that are still there are the ones that are doing it because they love doing it, or because it's something that they *have* to do, as opposed to just trying to make a record to make a quick buck, or because it's something cool to do. I think there's room for a lot of Canadian hip-hop still to be heard.

TCUS: What's the key to success in Canada?

Non-Verbal Communication Is Different from Verbal Communication

As Table 4.2 shows, non-verbal communication differs in several important ways from spoken and written language. These differences suggest some reasons why it is so valuable to focus on non-verbal behaviour. For example, while verbal messages are almost always intentional, non-verbal cues are often unintended, and sometimes unconscious.

Miles Jones: I don't know if you can pinpoint the key to success. It's tough to compare ourselves to the US, because hip-hop *came* from the US. It's something that has a big, huge following in the indie and the college scene, much like we do with our indie-rock scene, or our rock scene or folk scene in general—there's a huge support system of fans and audiences that build up over time. Hip-hop still has work to do in that regard, so I think it just gets frustrating for some of these really dope, talented artists, who put all this time, and energy, and money into these projects, and then they're not able to recoup them back. It's tough to go make another project if [you feel like] the first project should have been heard more, or put on a larger platform to [reach] a larger audience. If that doesn't happen, then it becomes frustrating. And for artists like D-Sisive, or Muneshine, or myself, you keep putting out projects, and you look to get a reaction, and it's one of those things where you sort of have to craft out your own niche or your own purpose of why you're actually doing it—what it means to you, what it means to the audience.

The consensus from me speaking with Mune and artists alike is that it's one thing [to say] we make hip-hop because we love it, but it doesn't mean that we can't do other things. A lot of these artists are more than just rappers, or emcees, or beatmakers. A lot of them are producers, or songwriters, or singer-songwriters, or whatever you want to call it. There's a larger scale of capabilities of what myself and all these artists can do. It's about crafting out that niche.

TCUS: Your debut album in '06, *One Chance*, was actually your graduating thesis. Tell me more about this.

Miles Jones: When I was at McMaster, I started deejaying in first and second year at this club called Quarters—I was putting out mixtapes and deejaying for like a thousand people on Thursdays and Saturdays. The deejaying led to me writing songs, and learning how to make beats, and renting an MPC when I was in second year, and starting to really dig deeper than just [deejaying]. Over the four years that I was there, I had a handful of songs and beats, and all these compositions and projects I had worked on, and the criteria for Multimedia as a thesis was that you had to come up with a project that had two different medias or more—mixed media, you could say. That's what inspired me to put together this album [and] website, and I had to write a 40-page paper about how the album got made, where all the samples came from, where all the songs came from, what the inspirations were, and that's how *One Chance* developed. And Mojo Records, which I started after I finished a graphic design class that I got an A+ on the logo, I kinda made it as a concept and then I turned it into something real and connecting all the dots together: *if I want to put out a record, what label is it going to be on? Oh, I guess it's going to be on my own.* In 2006, right when I was graduating, it was perfectly timed that I had 13 songs ready and mixed, and I had been spending the last three years working these songs into something that I wanted people to hear.

Interview by Martin Bauman, 9 January 2013, http://thecomeupshow.com/2013/01/09/ interview-miles-jones-talks-the-jones-act -part-iii-succeeding-in-the-canadian -industry-and-making-comic-books/

Non-Verbal Skills Are Important

It's hard to overemphasize the importance of effective non-verbal expression and the ability to read and respond to others' non-verbal behaviour. Non-verbal encoding and decoding skills are a strong predictor of popularity, attractiveness, and socio-emotional well-being.[16] Good non-verbal communicators are more persuasive than people who are less skilled, and they have a greater chance of success in settings ranging from careers to poker to romance. Non-verbal

Table 4.2 Some Differences between Verbal and Non-Verbal Communication

	Verbal Communication	**Non-Verbal Communication**
Complexity	One dimension (words only)	Multiple dimensions (voice, posture, gestures, distance, etc.)
Flow	Intermittent (speaking and silence alternate)	Continuous (it's impossible to avoid communicating non-verbally)
Clarity	Less subject to misinterpretation	More ambiguous
Impact	Has less impact when verbal and non-verbal cues are contradictory	Has stronger impact when verbal and non-verbal cues are contradictory
Intentionality	Usually deliberate	Often unintentional

sensitivity is a major part of what some social scientists have called "emotional intelligence," and researchers have come to recognize that it is impossible to study spoken language without paying attention to its non-verbal dimensions.[17]

Influences on Non-Verbal Communication

A lot of non-verbal communication is universal. For example, researchers have found at least six facial expressions that all humans everywhere use and understand: happiness, sadness, fear, anger, disgust, and surprise.[18] Even children who have been blind since birth reveal their feelings using these expressions. Despite these similarities, there are some important differences in the way people use and understand non-verbal behaviour. We'll look at some of these differences now.

Culture

Cultures have different non-verbal languages as well as verbal ones. For example, if you watch films of former Prime Minister Jean Chrétien's speeches with the sound turned off, you can often tell whether he's speaking English or French by the changes in his non-verbal behaviour.

The meaning of some gestures varies from one culture to another. The "okay" gesture made by joining thumb and forefinger to form a circle is a cheery affirmation to most Canadians, but it has less positive meanings in other parts of the world.[19] In France and Belgium it means "You're worth zero." In Greece and Turkey it is a vulgar sexual invitation, usually meant as an insult. Given this sort of cross-cultural ambiguity, it's easy to imagine how an innocent tourist might wind up in serious trouble.

Cultural differences also exist in other forms of non-verbal behaviour. Researchers from Queen's University and the University of Toronto in Canada and Kyoto University in Japan examined the gaze direction (where people are looking), of participants from both countries, in social and non-social contexts. There were significant differences. Canadian participants looked up while thinking only when they knew they were being observed. When they knew they couldn't be seen, Canadian participants looked down. Japanese participants looked down while they were thinking even when they were sure that they were being observed. These results confirm the view that thinking-related gaze behaviours are heavily influenced by cultural display rules and social contexts.[20]

Cultural Idiom
wind up in
To end up being in.

Less obvious cross-cultural differences can damage relationships without the parties ever recognizing exactly what has gone wrong. As anthropologist Edward T. Hall points out, people from the Middle East are likely to conduct business at a much shorter distance than most westerners would feel comfortable with.[21] It is easy to visualize the awkward advance-and-retreat dance that might occur when two diplomats or business people from those cultures meet. The Middle Easterner would probably keep moving forward to close the gap, while her Canadian colleague would keep trying to back away. Both would feel uncomfortable, probably without knowing why.

Even within a culture, various groups can have different non-verbal rules. For example, many teachers use "quasi-questions" that hint at the information they are seeking. An elementary school teacher might encourage the class to speak up by making an incorrect statement that demands refutation: "So to get six pieces we divide our pie into quarters, right?"[22] Most English-Canadian students would recognize this behaviour as a way of testing their understanding. But this style of questioning would be unfamiliar to many students raised in traditional Aboriginal cultures, who aren't likely to respond until they are directly questioned by the teacher. As a result, some teachers might view Aboriginal children as unresponsive or slow, when in fact they are simply playing by a different set of rules.

Communicators become more tolerant of others after they understand that unfamiliar non-verbal behaviours are the result of cultural differences. In one study, American adults were presented with videotaped scenes of speakers from Anglo–North America, France, and Germany.[23] When the sound was cut off, viewers judged foreigners more negatively than they did their fellow citizens. But when the speakers' voices were added (allowing viewers to recognize that they were from a different country), the critical ratings dropped.

Despite differences like these, many non-verbal behaviours have the same meanings around the world. Smiles and laughter are universal signals of positive emotions, for example, and there is a common set of sour expressions that convey displeasure in every culture.[24] Charles Darwin believed that expressions like these evolved as survival mechanisms that allowed early humans to convey emotional states before the development of language.

Although certain non-verbal expressions may be universal, the way they are used varies widely around the world. In some cultures the overt demonstration of feelings like happiness or anger is discouraged. In others the same feelings are considered perfectly appropriate. Thus a Japanese person might appear much more controlled and placid than someone from Iran, even if their feelings were identical.[25]

The same principle can be seen in action closer to home. For example, we commonly observe that French-Canadian women tend both to be non-verbally more expressive and to interrupt one another more often than is the case with English-Canadian women. This doesn't mean that French-Canadian women always feel more intensely than their English-Canadian counterparts. A more likely explanation is that the two groups follow different cultural rules. Researchers have found that in culturally mixed groups both French- and English-Canadian women moved closer to the other group's style. This non-verbal convergence shows that skilled communicators can adapt their behaviour when interacting with people from different cultural traditions in order to make the exchange more smooth and effective.[26]

> *Once identified and analyzed, non-verbal communication systems can be taught, like a foreign language. Without this training, we respond to non-verbal communications in terms of our own culture; we read everyone's behaviour as if it were our own, and thus we often misunderstand it. . . .*
>
> *The language of behaviour is extremely complex. Most of us are lucky to have under control one subcultural system—the one that reflects our sex, class, generation, and geographic region.*
>
> **Edward and Mildred Hall, authors and cultural anthropologists**

UNDERSTANDING COMMUNICATION TECHNOLOGY

Hatebase: A Crowdsourced Tool for Tracking Hate-Speech and Targeting Genocide

You may not think of interpreting nonverbal cues as a skill you use when communicating online, but there are many cues in written language that we can tune into, especially when we consider how people from varying cultural backgrounds communicate differently. In his article on hate-speech, Christopher Tuckwood, co-founder of The Sentinel Project for Genocide Prevention, discusses words that have double meanings, which can change depending on who is using them and how they are using them. As you read about Hatebase, see if you can think of other ways paying attention to what is being said online could facilitate better communication.

Co-founded by Toronto-based NGO The Sentinel Project for Genocide Prevention and Mobiocracy, Hatebase was built to assist government agencies, NGOs, research organizations, and other philanthropic individuals and groups to use hate-speech as a predictor for regional violence. Language-based classification, symbolization, and dehumanization are a few of a handful of quantifiable steps toward genocide and other mass atrocities.

Hatebase works by crowdsourcing vocabulary and real-time geo-located "sightings" of hate-speech. Essentially, users can add new terms that are not already in the database as well as log events such as incidents when they have been referred to using a certain term or heard it used against someone else. Because Hatebase is crowdsourced and therefore depends on user participation to be effective, the more people who use it in more places and languages, the more effective it will be. Not only can this data be used to establish trends and patterns but it can then be exported and used for any purpose, allowing organizations such as The Sentinel Project to leverage it and add context to existing datasets and crisis monitoring efforts, much like adding traffic congestion data to an existing street map.

Beyond crowdsourcing from human users, Hatebase also incorporates machine-driven contributions, with automated monitoring paying particular attention to open social networks like Twitter, which are constantly scanned for flagged vocabulary. Of course, many forums on the internet are filled with racist, sexist, homophobic, and other hateful language that never leads directly to violence, so a spike in hate-speech does not necessarily mean that violence is inevitable.

Although Hatebase is still in its infancy, its dataset (at www. hatebase.org.) is growing daily and currently encompasses vocabulary, sightings, and users from every corner of the world. This makes context incredibly important, as when certain, seemingly hateful, words have double meanings and can be used in benign ways. Timothy Quinn, who volunteers for Hatebase, says that the project's goal is to expand from Twitter and crawl all social media platforms. The challenge will always be in massaging their algorithm to be context-aware, knowing the slight but vast difference between, for example, "my nigga" and "you niggers." "Hate is not about vocabulary," argues Quinn, "it's about intent."

When data from Hatebase is correlated with other indicators of the genocidal process, such as statements by nationalistic leaders or attacks on a particular minority group, then it starts to be useful for predicting and preventing atrocities. For example, statements by an inflammatory leader may inspire temporary spikes in hate-speech followed by actual violent actions. If this relationship can be established and recognized then threatened communities can be warned before words turn into violence.

Christopher Tuckwood, Co-Founder of the
Sentinel Project for Genocide Prevention

QUESTIONS: How do cultural differences affect hate-speech? How does context, intention or slang change the meaning of terms?

Gender

It's easy to identify stereotypical differences in masculine and feminine styles of non-verbal communication. Just think about the exaggerated caricatures of macho men and delicate women that appear from time to time. Many humorous films and plays have been created around the situations that arise when characters try to act like members of the opposite sex.

Although few of us behave like stereotypically masculine or feminine movie characters, there are recognizable differences in the ways men and women look and act. Some of the most obvious differences are physiological: height, depth and volume of the voice, and so on. Other differences are social. For example, females are usually more non-verbally expressive, and they are better at recognizing others' non-verbal behaviour.[27]

Most communication scholars agree that social factors have more influence than biology does in shaping how men and women behave. For example, the ability to read non-verbal cues may have more to do with women's historically less powerful social status: people in subordinate work positions also have better decoding skills.[28] As women continue to gain status in the workplace and home, a paradoxical result may be less sensitivity at reading non-verbal cues.

Cultural norms in the Western world distinguish male from female behaviours.[29] For example, women make more eye contact with conversational partners than men do. They are more vocally expressive than men. Women interact at closer distances, both with men and with other women, than do men in same-sex conversations. Men are more likely to lean forward in conversations than women. They require and are given more personal space. Women are more likely to face conversational partners head-on, whereas men more typically stand at an angle. Women express more emotions via facial expressions than men. Most noticeably, women smile considerably more than men. Women gesture more frequently, whereas men use more expansive gestures.

After looking at differences like these, it might seem as if men and women communicate in radically different ways. In fact, men's and women's non-verbal communication is more similar than different in many respects.[30] Differences like the ones described in the preceding paragraph are noticeable, but they are outweighed by the similarity of our behaviour in areas such as eye contact, posture, and gestures. You can prove this by imagining what it would be like to follow radically different non-verbal rules: standing only an inch away from others, sniffing strangers, or tapping the forehead of someone when you want his or her attention. While biological sex and cultural norms certainly have an influence on non-verbal style, they aren't as dramatic as the *Men Are from Mars, Women Are from Venus* thesis suggests.

Women also have a distinctive style of speaking: "I was shopping last night? And I saw this wonderful dress?" It's hard to convey intonation in print, but the question marks indicate a rise in pitch at the end of the sentence, as in a question. Many women, especially younger women, use this intonation in declarative sentences: "This is Sally Jones? I have an appointment with Dr. Smith? And I'd like to change it to another day?"

I cringe when I hear this. The rising intonation sounds timid and lacking in self-confidence; the speaker seems to be asking for approval or permission to speak when there's no need to. And I worry that rising intonation harms women. It gets them taken less seriously than they should be . . .

Thomas Hurka, writer at University of Toronto's *Voice*.

MOM, CAN I GET A BIG TATTOO? I WANT A WINGED SERPENT COILING AROUND ONE ARM, CLUTCHING A SHIP ON MY CHEST, WITH...

.."UM... I MEAN... ...WELL...

© 1993 Watterson/Distributed by Universal Uclick

..SIGHHHH..

DID YOU KNOW MOM CAN COMMUNICATE TELEPATHICALLY?

WATTERSON 12-26

Understanding Diversity

An Expert Speaks Man to Mane

Among the swelling ranks of self-proclaimed male grooming "experts" (and there are hundreds adding their names to this dubious new form of punditry), criminal investigator Barry Ettinger is an anomaly.

The bald, fiftysomething head of security for a Yellowknife diamond mine has somehow become the unlikely face for the teen-targeted Axe hair brand that has, until now, pitched itself with images of hot women attacking unsuspecting men with lascivious intent.

At a recent Axe media launch in Toronto, Ettinger was the explanatory voice, contextualizing modern male hair peacocking through the prism of his expertise in body language and non-verbal communication. The polygraph examiner and one-time RCMP officer offers insight into male mane rituals—defined as "hair action . . . [the] surprising acts that happen when a girl can't resist getting into a guy's hair"—and how they achieve their intent.

It seems women really do want to touch before they buy.

And hair is among our most powerful symbols of personal and collective identity.

Our locks, more than even our words, contain the hidden secret to our instant attractiveness, Ettinger claims.

That means those whose flirtation strategies rely heavily on verbal communication are missing the point. All that verbiage accounts for a mere 7 per cent of communication, he says. Intonation makes up another 38 per cent. Unwittingly, the bulk of our communication—55 per cent—is body language, he says.

And hair is a key non-verbal communicator.

"Studies show that hairstyle can outweigh everything else during that first meeting," Ettinger says. "It's a sign of health, that you have something to offer. It's psychology. It can be predicted."

Functions of Non-Verbal Communication

Although verbal and non-verbal messages differ in many ways, the two forms of communication operate together on most occasions. The following discussion explains the many functions non-verbal communication can serve and shows how non-verbal messages relate to verbal ones.

Repeating

If someone asked you for directions to the nearest Tim Hortons, you could say, "Two blocks north," and repeat your answer non-verbally by pointing the way. This sort of repetition isn't just decorative: people remember words reinforced by gestures better than they do words that are merely spoken.[31]

> **emblem**
> A deliberate non-verbal behaviour with a precise meaning, known to virtually all members of a cultural group.
>
> **illustrators**
> Non-verbal behaviours that accompany and support verbal messages.

Pointing is an example of what social scientists call an **emblem**: a deliberate non-verbal behaviour with a precise meaning that is known to everyone within a particular cultural group. For example, we all know that a nod of the head means "yes," a shake of the head means "no," a wave means "hello" or "good-bye," and a hand to the ear means "I can't hear you."

Substituting

Emblems can also replace, rather than merely enhance, a verbal message. When a friend asks you what's new, you might shrug your shoulders instead of answering in words. Not all substituting consists of emblems, however. Sometimes substituting responses are more ambiguous and less intentional. A sigh, smile, or frown may substitute for a verbal answer to your question, "How's it going?" As this example suggests, non-verbal substituting is especially important when people are reluctant to express their feelings in words.

A good hair day provides a psychological image boost that invisibly broadcasts itself as irresistible confidence, he says.

But what good hair giveth, bad hair taketh away.

A bad hair day generates a kind of off-kilter inner turmoil sufficient to send the enchanting waitress at lunch running.

Ettinger recalls a distinct change in the way the world viewed him after he began losing his hair in his thirties. "Older people who lose their hair are seen as less desirable, less accepted. If I go into a room with guys who are generally the same as me, I know I'll be viewed differently."

It seems we've instinctively understood the importance of hair-based first impressions for at least 6000 years, he says.

Hieroglyphs dating back to 4000 BC reveal our ancient selves primping golden locks with animal fat in search of a date on Saturday night. Then, over thousands of years, we devised alternatives from fruit extracts, ashes, clay, and sticks. By AD 100, we'd discovered colour. Then wigs. Today, it's pomades, mousse, gels, putties, pastes, and creams. And behavioural experts.

The things we do.

Robert Cribb, *Toronto Star*, 27 March 2010

QUESTIONS: Hair is perceived by many cultures, Middle Eastern in particular, as a very sexual and alluring feature. That is why it is often covered in a shawl of some sort. Why do you think that hair is so important? What is its communication function in the classroom that you are in right now? Have you made assumptions about people based on the way they wear their hair? If so, what were those assumptions? Were they proven right when you got to know the person better?

Complementing

Sometimes non-verbal behaviours match the content of a verbal message. Consider, for example, a friend apologizing for being late. Your friend's sincerity would be reinforced if the verbal apology were accompanied by the appropriate non-verbal behaviours: the right tone of voice, facial expression, and so on. We often recognize the significance of complementary non-verbal behaviour when it is missing. If your friend's apology were delivered with a shrug, a smirk, and a light tone of voice, you probably would doubt its sincerity, no matter how profuse the verbal explanation was.

Much complementing behaviour consists of **illustrators**—non-verbal behaviours that accompany and support spoken words. Scratching your head as you search for an idea and snapping your fingers when you get it are both illustrators that complement verbal messages. Research shows that North Americans use illustrators more often when they are emotionally aroused—excited, angry, horrified, agitated, distressed—and trying to explain ideas that are difficult to put into words.[33]

COMMUNICATION ON-SCREEN

It's a Guy Girl Thing (2006)
Directed by Nick Hurran.

Body swapping comedies are a popular trope in cinema, with films like *Freaky Friday, The Change Up*, and even the third *Shrek* film; these films highlight our need to understand another person's point of view and, literally, walk in their shoes. In this fantastic Canadian film, set in the US but filmed in Ontario's Western Technical-Commercial School, two neighbours, Nell and Woody (Samaire Armstrong and Kevin Zegers, respectively) find their bodies swapped by an Aztec god at a museum. Forgive this premise, it's tough to come up with anything reasonable with this plot device. Regardless, *It's a Guy Girl Thing* highlights a number of differences in how the genders relate to each other, themselves, and their own performativity. Often it is the gendered non-verbal cues that give each of them away, resulting in the crux of the humour. Although the film does fall into clichéd plot devices, the film reflects what noted gender theorist Judith Butler argues when she describes gender performativity: "Her/his performance destabilizes the very distinctions between the natural and the artificial, depth and surface, inner and outer through which discourse about genders almost always operates."[32] With better understanding of each other's distinct perspectives, and means of communicating, both Nell and Woody are able to better understand their own strengths and vulnerabilities.

Accenting

Just as we use italics to emphasize an idea in print, we use non-verbal devices to emphasize oral messages. Pointing an accusing finger adds emphasis to criticism (and creates defensiveness in the receiver). Stressing certain words with the voice ("It was *your* idea!") is another way to add non-verbal emphasis.

Regulating

Cultural Idiom
the floor
The right or privilege to speak.

to cut off
To interrupt in order to stop someone from proceeding with their remarks.

Non-verbal behaviours can control the flow of verbal communication. For example, parties in a conversation often unconsciously send and receive turn-taking cues.[34] When you are ready to yield the floor, the unstated rule is to create a rising vocal intonation pattern; then use a falling intonation pattern or draw out the final syllable of the clause at the end of your statement; finally, stop speaking. If you want to maintain your turn when another speaker seems ready to cut you off, you can suppress the attempt by taking an audible breath, using a sustained intonation pattern (because rising and falling patterns suggest the end of a statement), and avoiding any pauses in your speech. Other non-verbal cues exist for gaining the floor and for signalling that you do not want to speak.

Contradicting

People often simultaneously express different and even contradictory messages in their verbal and non-verbal behaviours. A common example of this sort of mixed message is the experience we've all had of hearing someone with a red face and bulging veins yelling, "Angry? No, I'm not angry!"

Even though some of the ways in which people contradict themselves are subtle, mixed messages have a strong impact. Research suggests that when a receiver perceives an inconsistency between verbal and non-verbal messages, the non-verbal one carries more weight—more than 12.5 per cent more, according to some studies.[35]

Deliberately sending mixed messages might sound foolish at first, but there are times when we do just that. One deliberate use of mixed messages is to send a message politely but clearly that might be difficult or awkward to convey if it were expressed in words. For instance, think of a time when you became bored with a conversation but your companion kept rambling on. At such a time the most straightforward statement would be, "I'm tired of listening to you and want to go and do something else." Although it might feel good to be so direct, this kind of honesty is impolite for anyone over five years of age. Instead of being blunt in situations like this, a face-saving alternative is to express your lack of interest non-verbally. While nodding politely and murmuring, "Uh-huh" and "No kidding?" at the appropriate times, you can signal a desire to leave by looking around the room, turning slightly away from the speaker, or even making a point of yawning. In most cases such clues are enough to end the conversation without the awkwardness of expressing outright what's going on.

Deceiving

Cultural Idiom
a white lie
A harmless untruth.

Deception is perhaps the most interesting type of non-verbal communication, and one that social scientists have studied extensively. As Chapter 6 explains, most of the messages we exchange are not completely truthful. As you will learn, not all deception is self-serving or malicious: much of it is aimed at saving the face of the communicators involved. For example, you might tell a white lie to avoid hurting the feelings of a friend who asks your opinion: "Mmm, this casserole of yours is delicious. You'll have to give me the recipe." In a situation like this, it's easy to see how non-verbal factors can make the face-saving deception either succeed or fail.

Some people are better at hiding deceit than others. For example, most people—especially women—become more successful liars as they grow older.[36] High self-monitors are usually better at hiding their deception than are people who are less self-aware, and highly expressive liars are judged to be more honest than those who are more subdued.[37] Not surprisingly, people whose jobs may require them to behave in a certain way regardless of how they really feel, such as actors, lawyers, diplomats, and salespeople, are more successful at deception than the general population.[38]

We seem to be worse at catching deceivers when we participate actively in conversations than when we observe from the sidelines.[39] It's easiest to catch liars when they haven't had a chance to rehearse, when they feel strongly about the information being hidden, or when they feel anxious or guilty about their lies.[40] Imagine, for example, that you want to decline an unwanted invitation with a face-saving lie. Your chances of getting away with the deception are best if you have had advance notice of the invitation. If you are caught unprepared, your excuse for not attending is likely to be less persuasive. Trust (or lack of it) also plays a role in determining which deceptive messages will be successful. People who are suspicious that a speaker may be lying pay closer attention to the speaker's non-verbal behaviour (such as talking faster than normal or shifting posture) than do people who are not suspicious.[41] Still, asking questions—even if you are suspicious—isn't especially effective at uncovering deception.[42] As you read earlier, people who focus their attention on catching liars are less effective than those who are busy with other mental tasks.[43] Table 4.3 lists situations in which deceptive messages are most likely to be obvious.

Decades of research have revealed that there are no sure-fire non-verbal cues that indicate deception. Nonetheless, there are some cues that may reveal less-than-totally-honest communication. For example, deceivers typically make more speech errors—stammers, stutters, hesitations, false starts, and so on—than speakers who are telling the truth. Vocal pitch often rises when people tell lies, and liars hesitate more.[44] Deceivers tend to blink their eyes more often, fidget with their hands, and more rapidly shift their posture. Despite cues like these, it's a mistake to assume that every tongue-tied, fidgeting, eye-blinking person is a liar.

> **Cultural Idiom**
> **sure-fire**
> Certain to succeed.

Table 4.3 Leakage of Non-Verbal Clues to Deception

Deception Clues Are Most Likely When the Deceiver:	Deception Clues Are Least Likely When the Deceiver:
Wants to hide emotions being experienced at the moment.	Wants to hide information unrelated to his or her emotions.
Feels strongly about the information being hidden.	Has no strong feelings about the information being hidden.
Feels apprehensive about the deception.	Feels confident about the deception.
Feels guilty about being deceptive.	Experiences little guilt about the deception.
Gets little enjoyment from being deceptive.	Enjoys the deception.
Needs to construct the message carefully while delivering it.	Knows the deceptive message well and has rehearsed it.

Source: Based on material from Paul Ekman, "Mistakes When Deceiving," in Thomas A. Sebok and Robert Rosenthal, eds, *The Clever Hans Phenomenon: Communication with Horses, Whales, Apes, and People* (New York: New York Academy of Sciences, 1981), 269–78.

COMMUNICATING ONLINE

Top 10 Ways to Optimize Your Business

Marketing specialists understand the value of nonverbal communication. What logo design and colour will create the best brand for a business? What impression will the tone of voice, hand gestures, and clothing of the presenter in an online marketing video have on an audience of potential customers and clients? The following tips for optimizing a business YouTube channel was create by Brafton, a content marketing agency. As you consider these tips, think about which aspects you would need to consider if you were creating your own channel.

Source: www.brafton.com/infographics/
top-10-ways-to-optimize-your-business-youtube-channel

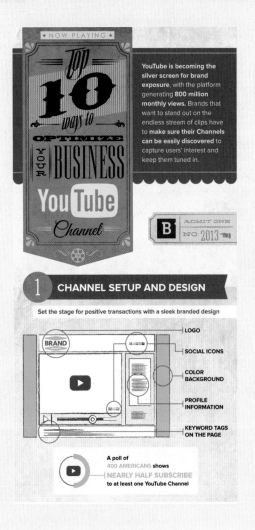

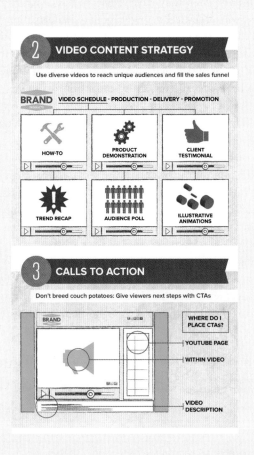

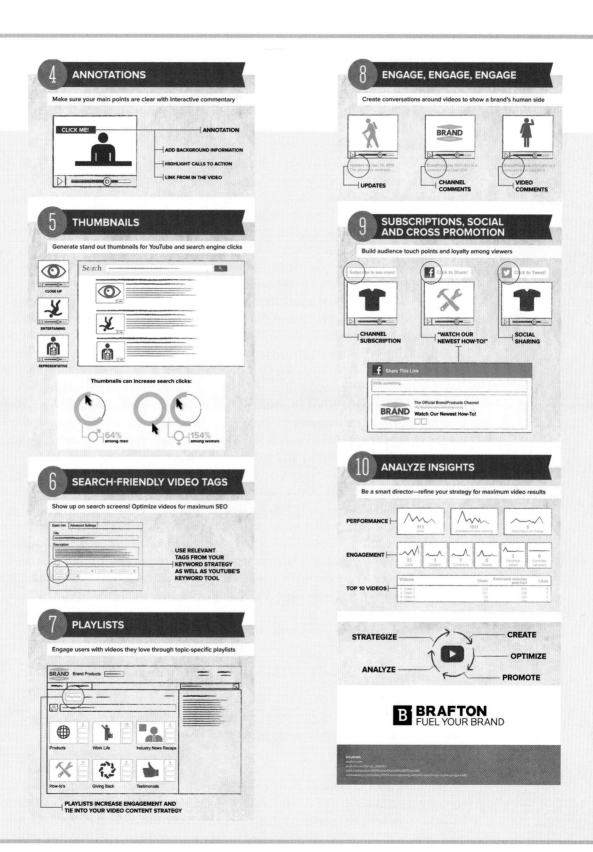

How good are people at detecting lies? The range of effectiveness in uncovering deceptive messages is broad, ranging from 45 to 70 per cent.[45] As we grow older we become better at interpreting contradictory messages. Children between the ages of 6 and 12 use a speaker's words to make sense of a message. But as adults we rely more on non-verbal cues to form many impressions.[46] Adult listeners also use non-verbal behaviours to judge the character of speakers, and differences in non-verbal behaviour influence how much listeners are persuaded by a speaker's message.[47]

Even with an awareness of non-verbal clues, it isn't always easy to detect lies. Training can improve the ability to catch deceivers.[48] Again, the range of effectiveness in uncovering deceptive messages is broad, ranging from 45 to 70 per cent.[49] Sometimes the very suspicion that someone is lying can improve the deceiver's attempts to hide the truth. Research shows that people who probe the messages of deceptive communicators are no better at detecting lies than those who don't investigate the truth of a message. One explanation for this surprising finding is that deceivers who are questioned become more careful about not revealing the truth, and their guardedness results in a better cover-up of deception cues.

<table>
<tr><td>

Cultural Idiom
cover-up
A plan to escape discovery.

</td></tr>
</table>

Some people are better than others at uncovering deception. Women, for instance, are consistently more accurate than men at detecting lying and what the underlying truth is.[50] The same research showed that as people become more intimate, their accuracy in detecting lies actually declines. This is a surprising fact: intuition suggests that we ought to be better at judging honesty as we become more familiar with others. Perhaps an element of wishful thinking interferes with our accurate decoding of these messages. After all, we would hate to think that a lover would lie to us. When intimate partners do become suspicious, however, their ability to recognize deception increases.[51] Despite their overall accuracy at detecting lies, women are more inclined to fall for the deception of their partners than are men. No matter how skilful or inept we may be at interpreting non-verbal behaviour, training can make us better.[52]

Technology may be gaining ground on deceivers. In 2002, Mayo Clinic researchers reported developing a facial imaging device capable of detecting heat patterns in the skin.[53] Apparently, as with the more familiar polygraph (or lie detector), this device does not actually measure deception but anxiety. Such devices probably have more potential uses in security contexts than in personal situations. Still, the notion of using technology to catch liars is appealing.

Before we finish considering how non-verbal behaviours can deceive, it is important to note that not all deceptive communication is aimed at taking advantage of the recipient. Sometimes deceptive behaviour is a polite way of expressing an idea that would be difficult for the listener to receive if it were expressed in words. In this sense, the ability to deliberately send non-verbal messages that contradict your words can be a kind of communication competence.

Types of Non-Verbal Communication

Now that we've seen how non-verbal messages operate as a form of communication, we can look at the various forms of non-verbal behaviour. In this section we examine how our bodies, artifacts, environments, and the way we use time all send messages.

Posture and Gesture

Stop reading for a moment and notice how you are sitting. What does your position say non-verbally about how you feel? Are there other people near you now? What messages do you get from their postures and movements? Tune your television to any program, turn off the sound, and see what messages are communicated by the movements and body positions of the people on the screen. These simple experiments illustrate the communicative power of **kinesics**, the study of body movement, posture, and gesture.

> **kinesics**
> The study of body movement, posture, and gesture.

Posture is a rich channel for conveying non-verbal information. From time to time postural messages are obvious. If you see a person drag themselves through the door or slump over while sitting in a chair, it's apparent that something significant is going on. But most postural cues are more subtle. For instance, the act of mirroring the posture of another person can have positive consequences. One experiment showed that career counsellors who used "posture echoes" to copy the postures of clients were rated as more empathic than those who did not.[54] Researchers have also found that partners in romantic relationships mirror one another's behaviours.[55]

Posture can communicate vulnerability in situations far more serious than mere social or business settings. One study revealed that rapists sometimes use postural clues to select victims that they believe will be easy to intimidate.[56] Easy targets are more likely to walk slowly and tentatively, stare at the ground, and move their arms and legs in short, jerky motions.

Gestures are a fundamental element of communication—so fundamental, in fact, that people who have been blind from birth use them.[57] One group of ambiguous gestures consists of what we usually call fidgeting—movements in which one part of the body grooms, massages, rubs, holds, pinches, picks, or otherwise manipulates another body part. Social scientists call these behaviours **manipulators**.[58] Social rules may discourage us from performing most manipulators in public, but people still do so without noticing. For example, one study revealed that deceivers bob their heads more often than truth-tellers.[59] Research confirms what common sense suggests—that increased use of manipulators is often a sign of discomfort.[60] But not all fidgeting signals uneasiness. People also are likely to use manipulators when relaxed. When they let their guard down (either alone or with friends), they will be more likely to fiddle with an earlobe, twirl a strand of hair, or clean their fingernails. Whether or not the fidgeter is hiding something, observers are likely to interpret manipulators as a signal of dishonesty; however, because not all fidgeters are liars, it's important not to jump to conclusions about the meaning of manipulators.

> **manipulators**
> Movements in which one part of the body grooms, massages, rubs, holds, pinches, picks, or otherwise manipulates another part.

> **Cultural Idiom**
> **let their guard down**
> To act or speak naturally without worrying how others will react.

Face and Eyes

The face and eyes are probably the most noticed parts of the body, and their impact is powerful. For example, smiling restaurant servers earn larger tips than unsmiling ones, and smiling nuns collect larger donations than ones with glum expressions.[61] The influence of facial expressions and eye contact doesn't mean that their non-verbal messages are always easy to read. The face is a tremendously complicated channel of expression for several reasons. One is the number of expressions people can produce; another, the speed with which they can change. For example, some videos, shown in slow motion, show expressions fleeting across a subject's face in as short a time as a fifth of a second. Finally, it seems that different emotions show most clearly in different parts of the face: happiness and surprise in the eyes and lower face, anger in the lower face and brows and forehead, fear and sadness in the eyes, and disgust in the lower face.

◀ COMMUNICATION ON-SCREEN

Monsieur Lazhar **(2011)**

Directed by Philippe Falardeau.

This fantastic Oscar-nominated Canadian film—about the difficulty in cultural communication—follows Algerian immigrant Bashir Lazhar (Mohamed Said Fellag) who is hired as a substitute teacher in Montreal after the previous teacher kills herself. Despite both Bashir and his students recovering from personal tragedy and a very evident cultural gap, he gains their trust and respect.

Bashir's precarious status as a refugee plays into the cultural divide, as does the murder of his wife and child (after she criticizes Algerian leaders in a new book). With both students and teacher devastated by confusion, guilt, and tragedy it is Bashir's understanding that uncovers the means for everyone to move beyond the tragedies in their lives and grow. The film shows that the paralanguages of grief and kindness are universal, regardless of background.

Ekman and Friesen have identified six basic emotions that facial expressions reflect—surprise, fear, anger, disgust, happiness, and sadness.[62] Expressions reflecting these emotions seem to be recognizable in and between members of all cultures. Of course, **affect blends**—combinations of two or more expressions showing different emotions—are possible. For instance, it's easy to imagine how someone would look if fearful *and* surprised or disgusted *and* angry.

Research indicates that people are quite accurate at judging facial expressions of these emotions.[63] Accuracy increases when judges know the "target" or have knowledge of the context in which the expression occurs or when they have seen several samples of the target's expressions.

The eyes themselves can send several kinds of messages. In mainstream Western culture, meeting someone's glance with your eyes is usually a sign of involvement, whereas looking away signals a desire to avoid contact. This is why solicitors on the street—panhandlers, salespeople, petitioners—try to catch our eye. After they've managed to establish contact with a glance, it becomes harder to draw away.

> **affect blends**
> Combinations of two or more expressions, each showing a different emotion.

Voice

The voice itself is another form of non-verbal communication. Social scientists use the term **paralanguage** to describe non-verbal, vocal messages. You can begin to understand the power

> **paralanguage**
> Non-linguistic means of vocal expression: rate, pitch, tone, and so on.

Understanding Diversity

Expressive Italians Let Hands Do the Talking

A recipe for trouble in Italy: make a fist, extend index finger and pinkie, thrust forward and up. A snarl is optional. The gesture—an insult suggesting an unfaithful wife—is part of the array of hand jabs, facial tics, and arm movement that add significance and sentiment to nearly every conversation among Italians.

"There are gestures for everything from making love to making dinner. The hands can often say things better than words," said Milan design artist Bruno Munari, who compiled a book illustrating some of the most popular Italian gestures. Munari's *Dictionary of Italian Gestures* contains dozens of examples stretching from early-nineteenth-century Naples to modern signals for a [cellphone] call.

Squeezing your chin between thumb and index finger signifies cuteness. Pulling slightly on the skin under the right eye with an index finger shows an agreement has been reached. Consider something foolish? Place hands together as if in prayer and then lower the pinkies.

Technology has added new gestures. The first telephone gesture was a rotating finger, simulating dialing. It was replaced by a push-button movement. Now, with [cellphones] widely popular in Italy, the latest phone gesture is a palm pressed to an ear.

With gestures, entire conversations could be conducted in silence.

"What do you want?" (Fingertips pinched together.)

"I'm hungry." (A curving motion of the hand above the top of the stomach.)

"And something to drink?" (Thumb tipped down toward the mouth.)

"No, everything's fine. It was delicious." (Shake hand with palm down. Then stick index finger in cheek and rock side to side.)

Some gestures are obvious in their intent. A threat is a thumb slashing across the neck. I'm angry: curl your index finger and bite down.

Others need translation. Rubbing two index fingers together represents an affair or secret meeting. Tapping your forehead with your finger means something is too strange to believe.

"A foreigner can come to Italy and learn the language perfectly, but without knowing the gestures you are not really fluent," said Munari.

Brian Murphy, *Associated Press*, 17 December 1994

QUESTIONS: Do you think that the sort of gestural communication that the article describes Italians using can "rub off" on other, less-gestural cultures, such as Anglos? Have you noticed that you gesture more when you are around a person who makes heavy use of gestures to communicate?

of vocal cues by considering how the meaning of a simple sentence can change just by shifting the emphasis from word to word:

- *This* is a fantastic communication text. [Not just any text but this one in particular.]
- This is a *fantastic* communication text. [This text is superior, exciting.]
- This is a fantastic *communication* text. [The text is good as far as communication goes; it may not be so good as literature or drama.]
- This is a fantastic communication *text*. [It's not a play or a CD; it's a text.]

There are many other ways the voice communicates—through tone, speed, pitch, volume, number and length of pauses, and **disfluencies** (such as stammering, use of "uh," "um," "er," and so on). All these factors can do a great deal to reinforce or contradict the message our words convey.

Sarcasm is one instance in which both emphasis and tone of voice help change a statement's meaning to the opposite of its verbal message. Experience this yourself by saying the following three statements. Say them literally first, then sarcastically.

- Thanks for waking me up.
- I really had a wonderful time on my blind date.
- I can't wait to get going on my interpersonal communication paper.

Researchers have identified the communicative value of paralanguage through the use of content-free speech—ordinary speech that has been electronically manipulated so that the words are unintelligible, but the paralanguage remains unaffected. (Hearing a foreign language that you do not understand has the same effect.) Subjects who hear content-free speech can consistently recognize the emotion being expressed, as well as identifying its strength.[64]

The impact of paralinguistic cues is strong. In fact, research shows that listeners pay more attention to the vocal messages than to the words that are spoken when asked to determine a speaker's attitudes.[65] Furthermore, when vocal factors contradict a verbal message, listeners judge the speaker's intention from the paralanguage, not from the words themselves.[66]

Paralanguage can affect behaviour in many ways, some of which are rather surprising. Researchers have discovered that communicators were most likely to comply with requests delivered by speakers whose rate—their talking speed—was similar to their own.[67] Besides *complying* with same-rate speakers, listeners feel more positive in general about people who seem to talk at their own rate. Vocal intensity also can affect how willing people are to respond to another person's requests.[68]

Vocal changes that contradict spoken words are not easy to conceal. If the speaker is trying to conceal fear or anger, the voice will probably sound higher and louder, and the rate of talk may be faster than normal. Sadness produces the opposite vocal pattern: quieter, lower-pitched speech delivered at a slower rate.[69]

Besides reinforcing or contradicting messages, some vocal factors influence the way a speaker is perceived by others. For example, communicators who speak loudly and without hesitations are viewed as more confident than those who pause and speak quietly.[70] People who speak more slowly are judged as having greater conversational control than fast talkers.[71] Research has also demonstrated that people with more attractive voices are rated more highly than those whose voice sounds less attractive.[72] Just what makes a voice attractive can vary. As Figure 4.1 shows, culture can make a difference.

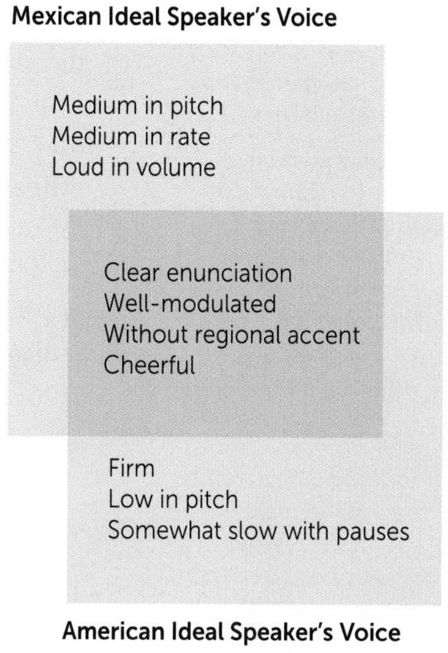

> **disfluencies**
> Non-linguistic verbalizations, such as "um," "er," and "ah."

> *At certain moments, words are nothing; it is the tone in which they are uttered.*
>
> **Paul Bouget,**
> *Cosmopolis*

Mexican Ideal Speaker's Voice

Medium in pitch
Medium in rate
Loud in volume

Clear enunciation
Well-modulated
Without regional accent
Cheerful

Firm
Low in pitch
Somewhat slow with pauses

American Ideal Speaker's Voice

FIGURE 4.1 Ideal Speaker's Voice Types in Mexico and the United States

Touch

Besides being the earliest means we have of making contact with others, touching—or haptics—is essential to our healthy development. During the nineteenth and early twentieth centuries many babies died from a disease then called *marasmus,* which, translated from Greek, means "wasting away." In some orphanages the mortality rate was quite high, but even children in "progressive" homes, hospitals, and other institutions died regularly from the ailment. When researchers finally tracked down the causes of this disease, they found that many infants suffered from lack of physical contact with parents or nurses rather than poor nutrition, medical care, or other factors. They hadn't been touched enough, and as a result they died. From this knowledge came the practice of "mothering" children in institutions—picking babies up, carrying them around, and handling them several times each day. At one hospital that began this practice, the death rate for infants fell from between 30 and 35 per cent to below 10 per cent.[73]

As a child develops, the need for being touched continues. In his book *Touching: The Human Significance of the Skin,* Ashley Montagu describes research that suggests that allergies, eczema, and other health problems are, in part, caused by a person's lack of contact as an infant with his or her mother.[74] Although Montagu says that these problems develop early in life, he also cites cases where adults suffering from conditions as diverse as asthma and schizophrenia have been successfully treated by psychiatric therapy that uses extensive physical contact.

Touch seems to increase a child's mental functioning as well as physical health. L.J. Yarrow has conducted surveys that show that babies who have been given plenty of physical stimulation by their mothers have significantly higher IQs than those receiving less contact.[75]

Touch also plays a large part in how we respond to others and to our environment.[76] For example, touch increases self-disclosure, verbalization of psychiatric patients, and the preference children have for their counsellors. Touch also increases compliance.[77] In one study, subjects were approached by a woman who asked them to return a coin left in the phone booth from which they had just emerged. When the request was accompanied by a light touch on the subject's arm, the probability that the subject would return the coin increased significantly.[78] In a similar experiment, subjects were asked to sign a petition or complete a rating scale. Again, subjects were more likely to co-operate when they were touched lightly on the arm. In the rating-scale variation of the study, the results were especially dramatic: 70 per cent of those who were touched complied, whereas only 40 per cent of the untouched subjects complied (indicating a predisposition not to comply).[79] An additional power of touch is its on-the-job utility. One study showed that fleeting touches on the hand and shoulder resulted in larger tips for restaurant staff.[80]

Touch can communicate many messages. Researchers have catalogued 12 different kinds of touches, including "positive," "playful," "control," and "ritualistic."[81] Some kinds of touch indicate varying degrees of aggression. Others signify types of relationships:[82]

- functional/professional (dental examination, haircut);
- social/polite (handshake);
- friendship/warmth (clap on back, fist bump, Spanish *abrazo,* Inuit *kunik*);
- love/intimacy (caresses, hugs); and
- sexual arousal (kisses, strokes).

You might object to the examples following each of these categories, saying that some non-verbal behaviours occur in several types of relationships. A kiss, for example, can mean

> *In our now more than slightly cockeyed world, there seems to be little provision for someone to get touched without having to go to bed with whomever does the touching. And that's something to think about. We have mixed up simple, healing, warm touching with sexual advances. So much so, that it often seems as if there is no middle way between "Don't you dare touch me!" and "Okay, you touched me, so now we should make love!"*
>
> *A nation which is able to distinguish the fine points between offensive and defensive pass interference, bogies, birdies, and par, a schuss and a slalom, a technical, a personal, and a player-control foul should certainly be able to make some far more obvious distinctions between various sorts of body contact.*
>
> **Sidney Simon, *Caring, Feeling, Touching***

anything from a polite but superficial greeting to the most intense arousal. What makes a given touch more or less intense? Researchers have suggested a number of factors:

- the part of the body that does the touching;
- the part of the body that is touched;
- the length of time the touch lasts;
- the amount of pressure used;
- whether there is movement after contact is made;
- whether anyone else is present;
- the situation in which the touch occurs; and
- the relationship between the people involved.

In traditional English-Canadian culture, touching is generally more appropriate for women than for men. Men touch their male friends less than they touch their female friends and also less than women touch their female friends. Fear of homosexuality seems to be a strong reason why many men are reluctant to touch one another. Although women are more comfortable about touching than men are, gender isn't the only factor that shapes contact. In general, the degree of touch comfort goes along with openness to expressing intimate feelings, an active interpersonal style, and satisfactory relationships.[83]

Physical Attractiveness

Most people claim that looks aren't the best measure of desirability or character, but then they typically prefer others whom they find attractive.[84] For example, women who are perceived as attractive have more dates, receive higher grades in college or university, have an easier time persuading men, and receive lighter court sentences. Both men and women whom others view as attractive are rated as being more sensitive, kind, strong, sociable, and interesting than those judged less attractive. Who is most likely to succeed in business? You can safely bet on the attractive job applicant. For example, shorter men have more difficulty finding jobs in the first place, and men over six-foot-two receive starting salaries that average 12.4 per cent higher than comparable applicants under six feet.

The influence of attractiveness begins early in life. Preschoolers were shown photographs of children their own age and asked to choose potential friends and enemies. The researchers found that children as young as three years old agreed as to who was attractive ("cute") and unattractive ("homely"). Furthermore, they valued their attractive counterparts—of both the same and the opposite sex—more highly. Also, preschool girls rated by their peers as pretty were most liked, and those identified as least pretty were least liked. Children who were interviewed rated good-looking children as having positive social characteristics ("He's friendly to other children") and unattractive children as having negative ones ("He hits other children without reason").

Teachers also are affected by students' attractiveness. Physically attractive students are usually judged more favourably—seen as more intelligent, friendly, and popular—than their less attractive counterparts.[85] Fortunately, attractiveness is something we can control without having to call a plastic surgeon. We view others as beautiful or ugly not just on the basis of the features they're born with but on how they present those features. Posture, gestures, facial expressions, and other behaviours can increase the attractiveness of a person who is otherwise physically unremarkable. Exercise can also improve the way each of us looks. Finally, the way we dress can make a significant difference in the way others perceive us, as we'll see in the next section.

Clothing

Besides protecting us from the elements, clothing is a means of non-verbal communication, providing a relatively straightforward (if sometimes expensive) method of impression management. Clothing can be used to convey economic status, educational level, social status, moral standards, athletic ability and/or interests, belief systems (political, philosophical, religious), and level of sophistication.

Research shows that we do make assumptions about people based on their clothing. Communicators who wear special clothing often gain persuasiveness. For example, experimenters dressed to resemble police officers were more successful than those dressed in civilian clothing in requesting pedestrians to pick up litter and in persuading them to lend a quarter to an over-parked motorist.[86] Likewise, solicitors wearing sheriff's and nurse's uniforms gained greater contributions to law enforcement and health-care campaigns than campaigners in "plain clothes."[87]

Uniforms aren't the only kind of clothing that carries influence. In one study, a man and woman were stationed in a hallway so that anyone who wished to go by had to avoid them or pass between them. In one condition, the conversationalists wore "formal daytime dress;" in the other, they wore "casual attire." Passersby behaved differently toward the couple depending on the style of clothing: they responded positively with the well-dressed couple and negatively when the same people were casually dressed.[88] Similar results in other situations show the influence of clothing. We are more likely to obey people dressed in a high-status manner. Pedestrians were more likely to return lost coins to well-dressed people than to those dressed in low-status clothing.[89] We are also more likely to follow the lead of high-status dressers even

UNDERSTANDING COMMUNICATION TECHNOLOGY

Computer Can Judge Human Attractiveness

Whether we like it not, physical attractiveness is an important non-verbal cue that influences how we react to others and how they react to us. Technology today has become sophisticated enough that a computer can accurately rate human attractiveness, as Andreas Janus explains in the article below. While the computer Janus is describing assesses facial features in particular, is it only a matter of time before computers are sophisticated enough to judge attractiveness based on posture, gestures, facial expressions, or even clothing choices?

University of Windsor undergraduate student Joshua Chauvin has found that a computer can be trained to rate human facial attractiveness the same way that people rate the looks of others.

For his research, Chauvin trained a computer program called a neural network—which is essentially a pattern recognition program loosely based on the human brain—to mimic how humans assess attractiveness.

He had 100 people rate images of 100 others on attractiveness and then asked the neural network to rate the attractiveness of 33 images.

The findings show that 85 per cent of the time, the neural network's ratings fell within one point of the human subjects' ratings.

"So what [the neural network is] doing is coming up with its own rating for those images based on some sort of understanding of what it thinks the population finds as attractive," Chauvin told CTV.ca in a telephone interview.

Chauvin was assisted in his research by Dr Marcello Guarini from the Department of Philosophy and Dr Chris Abeare from the Department of Psychology.

He will present his findings this fall at the International Conference for Neural Computation in Madeira, Portugal.

In his research paper, Chauvin points to myriad research that has found that rating facial beauty is consistent across the globe and that specific features, such as facial symmetry, are important for determining facial attractiveness.

when it comes to violating social rules. Eighty-three per cent of the pedestrians in one study followed a well-dressed jaywalker who violated a "wait" crossing signal, whereas only 48 per cent followed a citizen dressed in lower-status clothing.[90] Women who are wearing a suit jacket as part of their outfit are rated as being more powerful than those wearing only a dress or skirt and blouse.[91]

As we get to know others better, the importance of clothing shrinks.[92] This fact suggests that clothing is especially important in the early stages of a relationship, when making a positive first impression is necessary in order to encourage others to get to know us better. This advice is equally important in personal situations and in employment interviews. In both cases, your style of dress (and personal grooming) can make all the difference between the chance to progress further and outright rejection.

Distance

The study of the way people and animals use space has been termed **proxemics**. Preferred spaces are largely a matter of cultural norms. For example, people living in hyper-dense Hong Kong manage to live in crowded residential quarters that most North Americans would find intolerable.[93] Edward T. Hall has defined four types used in mainstream Anglo–North American culture.[94] He says that we choose a particular distance depending on how we feel toward the other person at a given time, the context of the conversation, and our personal goals.

Intimate distance begins with skin contact and ranges out to about 18 inches (45 centimetres). The most obvious context for intimate distance involves interaction with people to whom we're emotionally close—and then mostly in private situations. Intimate distance between individuals also occurs in less intimate circumstances: visiting a doctor, dentist, or

Cultural Idiom
jaywalker
A person who crosses the street without obeying traffic signals.

proxemics
The study of how people and animals use space.

intimate distance
One of Hall's four distance zones, ranging from skin contact to 18 inches (45 centimetres).

"One of the ideas is that there is some sort of objective basis for assessing facial attractiveness. Some sort of biological inclination to like those things and not like others," Chauvin said. "That a computer can recognize patterns in faces would further suggest that there are objective characteristics."

While computers are unlikely to replace humans as beauty-pageant judges, Chauvin said there are some practical implications for his research.

Marketing and advertising companies could use a neural network to assess how their target audience may respond to their casting choices.

"If you want a population's opinion about what attractiveness is, you can take a one-time poll and have them rate any given number of images on attractiveness features," Chauvin said. "And then if an advertising campaign has a model, they could input the model into the neural network and find out what the population thinks about that individual without having to poll the population over and over again for each advertisement."

Chauvin also said the research may one day lead to neural networks identifying telltale facial characteristics of some diseases.

While that research is in its infancy, the next step in Chauvin's study will be to determine if the neural network can also mimic how the subjects assessed the personality characteristics of the faces in the images.

Andrea Janus, www.CTV.ca, 18 July 2009

QUESTION: Some people might think of what this article is saying as a "chicken and egg" phenomenon. Do you think that once it is used extensively by professional communicators, the computer program might start influencing people's perception of what is beautiful, rather than simply reflecting popular taste?

personal distance
One of Hall's four distance zones, ranging from 18 inches (45 centimetres) to 4 feet (1.2 metres).

social distance
One of Hall's four distance zones, ranging from 4 to 12 feet (1.2 to 3.6 metres).

public distance
One of Hall's four distance zones, extending outward from 12 feet (3.5 metres).

hairdresser, and during some athletic contests. Allowing someone to move into the intimate zone usually is a sign of trust.

Personal distance ranges from 18 inches (45 centimetres) at its closest point to 4 feet (1.2 metres) at its farthest. Its closer range is the distance at which most relational partners stand in public. We are uncomfortable if someone else "moves into" this area without invitation. The far range of personal distance runs from about 2.5 to 4 feet (45 to 75 centimetres). This is the zone just beyond the other person's reach—the distance at which we can keep someone "at arm's length." This term suggests the type of communication that goes on at this range: interaction is still reasonably personal but less so than communication that occurs a foot (30 centimetres) or so closer.

Social distance ranges from 4 to about 12 feet (1.2 to 3.6 metres). Within it are the kinds of communication that usually occur in business situations. Its closer range, from 4 to 7 feet (1.2 to 2.1 metres), is the distance at which conversations usually occur between salespeople and customers and between people who work together. We use the far range of social distance—7 to 12 feet (2.1 to 3.6 metres)—for more formal and impersonal situations. This is the range at which we generally sit from the boss.

Public distance is Hall's term for the farthest zone, running outward from 12 feet (3.5 metres). The closer range of public distance is the one most instructors use in the classroom. In the farther range of public space—25 feet (7.5 metres) and beyond—two-way communication becomes difficult. In some cases it's necessary for speakers to use public distance

New Generation of Opera Singers Slimming Down before Belting Out

Move over firefighters. Opera singers are the new hunks in town.

Increased competition for scarce entertainment dollars, the introduction of HD videos and rising demands for action onstage are causing a sea of change in operatic circles.

Websites such as Barihunks and Hunkentenor are devoted to promoting both the physiques and singing talents of opera stars.

It's one of the reasons you'll find tenor Adam Fisher dripping with sweat four mornings a week at a west-end YMCA. He has run the 20 minutes from his home to work out with weights for an hour before running back home and slogging through a six-hour opera rehearsal. He also does yoga every other day for flexibility.

"People are used to the Broadway level of perfection, where singers are fit and good-looking," says Fisher, who appears in Toronto Operetta Theatre's *La Vie Parisienne*, opening May 2. "Opera is making every effort to catch up to that." This is partly because the modern audience refuses to suspend disbelief when a singer fails to physically suit the role.

In 2004, soprano Deborah Voigt lost a role with the Royal Opera House due to her weight. The incident sparked a debate about superficial values encroaching on the musical purity of opera. Voigt ultimately slimmed down and was recast with the opera company.

Guillermo Silva-Marin, artistic director of Toronto Operetta Theatre, insists this is not about being superficial or dumbing down opera in any way. "There is a demand for this. The general consensus is that theatrical truth must be paid attention," he says. "A consumptive Mimi doesn't make sense if the soprano looks a little too robust."

Silva-Marin calls the widespread belief that singers need heft for strength a fallacy and notes a need for performers to be healthy and agile. "I have just asked two of my soloists to do cartwheels, after performing a cancan," he says. He admits to having quietly taken singers aside and advising them to lose weight and get healthy. These are performers he'd love to cast, but singing chops alone won't win them a part.

Marshall Pynkoski, co-artistic director of Opera Atelier and a former ballet dancer, says the belief that you need to be hefty to succeed in opera has been debunked by medicine and science. "It is muscular control, not weight, that supports strong singing," he says. Pynkoski keeps free weights at the rehearsal

owing to the size of their audience, but we can assume that anyone who voluntarily chooses to use it when he or she could be closer is not interested in having a dialogue.

Choosing the optimal distance can have a powerful effect on how we regard others and how we respond to them. For example, students are more satisfied with teachers who reduce the distance between themselves and their classes. They also are more satisfied with the course itself, and they are more likely to follow the teacher's instructions.[95] Likewise, medical patients are more satisfied with physicians who are not standoffish.[96]

Time

Social scientists use the term **chronemics** for the study of how human beings use and structure time. The way we handle time can express both intentional and unintentional messages.[97] Social psychologist Robert Levine describes several ways that time can communicate.[98] For instance, in a culture like ours that values time highly, waiting can be an indicator of status. "Important" people (whose time is supposedly more valuable than that of others) may be seen by appointment only, whereas it is acceptable to intrude without notice on lesser beings. To see how this rule operates, consider how natural it would be for the CEO of a company to arrive, unannounced and uninvited, in a subordinate's office, whereas some employees would never go near the boss's office without an appointment. A related rule is that low-status people must never make more important people wait. It would be a serious mistake to show up late for a job interview, although the interviewer might keep you cooling your heels in the lobby. Important

chronemics
The study of how humans use and structure time.

Cultural Idiom
cool your heels
To wait impatiently.

hall so singers can work out at every opportunity and he acts as a personal trainer to many. He also practises what he preaches by working out three times a week at the YMCA.

"No one is at their best pulling 100 extra pounds," he says, "I want (singers) to be strong, to be their best." He adds that, "Most of the audience doesn't know if the voice is good or bad. But they know if they have an exciting time. "We have to make this rarefied art form into excellent storytelling for the audience. People are looking for something else, something more."

Although he wishes opera was all about singing, baritone Vasil Garvanliev noticed a huge change about five years ago. "A lot of people today are casting with their eyes," says Garvanliev, who lifts weights to improve his strength and endurance. He worried about taking his shirt off for Opera Atelier's *Der Freischütz*, but is so comfortable with his body now that he's preparing to be photographed nude for an art show. He is also one of the "it" guys on Barihunk.

Meanwhile, tattoos haven't hurt Aaron Ferguson's career. "Opera is casting more and more like film. You have to look the part physically," says Ferguson, who got to show off his abs in *Der Freischütz*. "It's a big advantage having the option of looking physically intimidating." Women are taking part in the opera fitness challenge, too.

Mezzo-soprano Wallis Giunta worked out with a trainer for two months before she appeared this winter in the Canadian Opera Company's *La clemenza di Tito* as a character who ran on the spot in athletic gear for most of the opera.

Singers know it's no longer enough to "park and bark," says mezzo-soprano Rihab Chaieb.

"You can't just sing anymore. Directors won't hire someone who is too fat for the part or who can't move." She remembers seeing *Romeo and Juliet* as a teenager when the two leads couldn't embrace because "their bellies were so big."

Now a member of the COC's Ensemble Studio, Chaieb runs five kilometres three times a week and also does yoga for flexibility. When people see her slim frame, Chaieb often hears, "You don't look like an opera singer."

Trish Crawford, *Toronto Star*, 26 April 2013

QUESTIONS: Although it's wonderful that these artists are staying fit, is it fair to demand physical attractiveness in a medium that has, traditionally, ignored looks in favour of talent? How does this example highlight a distinct bias in societal views of attractiveness?

people are often whisked to the head of a restaurant or airport line, whereas the presumably less exalted are forced to wait their turn.

The use of time depends greatly on culture.[99] In some cultures, punctuality is critically important, whereas in others it is barely considered. One psychologist discovered the difference between North and South American attitudes when teaching at a university in Brazil.[100] He found that some students arrived halfway through a two-hour class and that most of them stayed put and kept asking questions when the class was scheduled to end. A half-hour after the official end of the class, the professor finally closed the discussion because there was no indication that the students intended to leave. This flexibility of time is quite different from what is common in most Canadian universities and colleges!

Even within a country, rules of time vary. Sometimes the differences are geographic.[101] In Montreal, the party invitation may say "9 p.m.," but nobody would think of showing up before 9:30. In Calgary, though, guests are expected to show up on time, or perhaps even a bit early. Even within the same geographic area, different groups establish their own rules about the use of time. Consider your own experience. In school, some instructors begin and end class punctually, whereas others are more casual. With some people you feel comfortable talking for hours in person or on the phone, whereas with others time seems to be precious and not meant to be "wasted."

> **Cultural Idiom**
> **stay put**
> To remain where you are.

Understanding Diversity

Distinct Society: Discovering Montreal's Vibrant Deaf Culture

When you are a teenager, one party can change your entire life. The party that changed Daphnée Ménard from deaf to Deaf—a medical condition versus a cultural identity—happened one night when she was fifteen, and, as with any momentous social event, at first she was nervous about going. "My friend said, 'Come on, there'll be people signing. It's super-fun, you'll see.' I kind of hesitated, because I was really just in the hearing world at that point," she says, sitting cross legged on the brown leather couch in her parents' basement. When she walked into the party, she heard some kids speaking French—the oralist ones who, like her, had been coached to speak and read lips; some, like her, with implants. The others were using a language Ménard dimly remembered: the hand gestures, facial expressions, and sweeping arm movements of [*Langue des Signes Québécois*] *LSQ.* "When I talked to the people there," she says, "it was really something special, because they had all lived the same thing as me. It was at that moment that I first thought, I'm not alone." Her voice, usually brash and matter-of-fact, drops in wonder.

She started going to Deaf social events, hanging out every Friday night at a cultural centre in Montreal to play pool and sign *LSQ.* "Within a year and a half, I was signing perfectly," she says. That summer, she went to a camp for deaf youth at *Notre-Dame-de-l'Île-Perrot*, where she met a boy from Ottawa. They

Territoriality

Whereas personal space is the invisible bubble we carry around as an extension of our physical being, **territory** is fixed space. Any area, such as a room, house, neighbourhood, or country, to which we assume some kind of "rights" is our territory. Not all territory is permanent. We often stake out space for ourselves in the library, at the beach, and so on by using markers such as books, clothing, or other personal possessions.

The way people use space can communicate a good deal about power and status relationships. Generally, we grant people with higher status more personal territory and greater privacy.[102] We knock before entering the boss's office, whereas an employer can usually walk into a subordinate's work area without hesitating. In traditional colleges and universities, professors have offices, dining rooms, and even washrooms that are private, whereas students, who are presumably less important, have no such sanctuaries.

> **territory**
> A fixed space that an individual assumes some right to occupy.

Environment

The physical environment people create can both reflect and shape interaction. This principle is illustrated right at home. The impressions that household interior designs communicate can be remarkably accurate. Researchers showed 99 students images of the insides or outsides of

started dating, and he convinced her to try something: going out in public without her cochlear implant. Part of Ménard's implant is embedded in her skull, but there is also an external microphone that clips onto her ear, connected by a wire to a transmitter she must wear on a belt. It can be awkward to move around with, as well as a fashion liability, but she had never gone out without it.

"At first, I was like, if I'm going out in public I *have* to wear my implant. People don't sign, so I have no choice." But her boyfriend showed her how to get around. "If I'm in a restaurant, I'll ask for a paper and pencil, like this;" she draws a square in the air with her fingers and makes a writing motion. "I'll write down, I want a hamburger, I want this and that." Initially, she felt weird showing that she was deaf, and especially because she can speak it felt weird not to. But as she came to accept and feel proud of her Deaf identity, she began to think that maybe it was not all up to her to fit herself into a hearing world. Maybe others could also make an effort to accommodate her.

In September 2012, she recorded a video in *LSQ* and posted it on YouTube. It is called "My Opinion on Cochlear Implants," and in it she looks angry. She signs:

All day, I stayed patient. I listened to my teacher. When the day was done and I got back home, I cried almost every night. I was not happy. . . . The government is stupid to think that if an implanted child can talk and communicate, everything will be perfect and work out fine. . . . Being Deaf is like a religion. A Deaf needs to be with other Deaf, why? Because we are the same. We think alike and understand each other! . . . This is my message: if a child is born deaf, keep him deaf! This is this child's identity and reality. Later, when he is older, he may choose. . . .If I had to start my life over, for sure I would not have gotten the cochlear implant.

But what makes Deaf culture so distinctive? "Even for me," says Ménard, "I find it really hard to explain." Sometimes when she speaks French, her fingers give a lexical twitch, moving to half-form a sign. "I ask my friends sometimes, other Deaf, like, 'What is it?' I know there's a difference! But it's really rare to find someone who can give an answer."

Linda Besner, http://thewalrus.ca/distinct-society
(Photo by François Pesant)

12 upper-middle-class homes and then asked them to infer the personality of the owners from their impressions.[103] The students were especially accurate after glancing at interior images. The decorating schemes communicated accurate information about the homeowners' intellectualism, politeness, maturity, optimism, tenseness, willingness to take adventures, family orientations, and reservedness. The home exteriors also gave viewers accurate perceptions of the owners' artistic interests, graciousness, privacy, and quietness.

Besides communicating information about the designer, an environment can shape the kind of interaction that takes place in it. In one experiment, researchers found that the attractiveness of a room influenced the happiness and energy of the people working in it.[104] The experimenters set up three rooms: an "ugly" one, which resembled a maintenance worker's closet in the basement of a campus building; an "average" room, which was a professor's office; and a "beautiful" room, which was furnished with carpeting, drapes, and comfortable furniture. The subjects in the experiment were asked to rate a series of pictures as a way of measuring their energy and feelings of well-being while at work. Results of the experiment showed that, while in the ugly room, the subjects became tired and bored more quickly and took longer to complete their task. When they moved to the beautiful room, however, they rated the faces they were judging higher, showed a greater desire to work, and expressed feelings of importance, comfort, and enjoyment. The results teach a lesson that isn't surprising: workers generally feel better and do a better job when they're in an attractive environment.

In a more therapeutic and less commercial way, physicians have also shaped environments to improve communication. Psychologist Robert Sommer found that redesigning the convalescent ward of a hospital greatly increased the interaction among patients. In the old design, seats were placed shoulder to shoulder around the edges of the ward. When the chairs were grouped around small tables so that patients faced each other at a comfortable distance, the number of conversations doubled.[105]

The design of an entire building can shape communication among its users. Architects have learned that the way housing projects are designed controls to a great extent the contact neighbours have with each other. People who live in apartments near stairways and mailboxes have much more contact with neighbours than do those living in less heavily travelled parts of the building, and tenants generally have more contacts with immediate neighbours than with people even a few doors away.[106] Architects now use this information to design buildings that either encourage communication or increase privacy, and house hunters can use the same knowledge to choose a home that gives them the neighbourhood relationships they want.

So far we have talked about how designing an environment can shape communication, but there is another side to consider. Watching how people use an already existing environment can be a way of telling what kind of relationships they want. For example, Sommer watched students in a college library and found that there's a definite pattern for people who want to study alone. While the library was uncrowded, students almost always chose corner seats at one of the empty rectangular tables.[107] Finally, each table was occupied by one reader. New readers would then choose a seat on the opposite side and far end of an occupied table, thus keeping the maximum distance between themselves and the other readers. One of Sommer's associates tried violating these "rules" by sitting next to, and across from, other female readers when more distant seats were available. She found that the approached women reacted defensively, either by signalling their discomfort through shifts in posture, by gesturing, or by eventually moving away.

Social Media and Non-Verbal Communication

Social media have emerged as a major new medium for human communication. As Marshall McLuhan so famously said: "the medium is the message"—how is social media changing our non-verbal communication habits? Probably in many ways, since, according to a 2010 study by Statistics Canada, 94 per cent of those under the age of 45, 80 per cent of those aged 45–64, 51 per cent of those 65–74, and 27 per cent of those 75 and over used the internet.[108] This means that the vast majority of Canadians are living a part of their lives online. Just thinking about each of the most popular social media demonstrates these differences:

Facebook

On Facebook, users have a broad selection of ways to interact with others: status updates, comments, "likes," shared videos, amongst many others. This richness provides many different non-verbal gestures: sometimes sharing a funny video or a cat meme can be the most effective reply to lighten the tone with someone who is arguing with you, or using an emoticon or sharing an emotional music video is the best way to communicate your mood. Neither of these examples are verbal.

Twitter

Twitter offers different challenges than Facebook because of two factors: severe limitations on message length (140 characters) and the speed with which the tweet stream flows. These two factors mean that any language you use has to be extremely brief, evocative, and to the point. As anyone who has tried to express themselves in an emotional moment knows, it is hard to capture anything resembling a real feeling in 140 characters or less—especially when they are blipping by on your friends' screens so quickly. Many twitter users therefore make very effective use of acronyms (e.g., LOL), emoticons, and onomatopoeia (e.g., "argh!," "blech," etc.) to get their message across. As well, with the addition of Vine to Twitter, a whole new world of nonverbal communication has been opened to the user—now they can send six-second bursts of video to express a message. The possibilities of Vine are endless: while an emoticon can express a simple feeling, a vine can capture a whole range of facial expressions.

Tumblr

Tumblr is a blogging tool that relies largely on republishing the posts of others. This means that users can express themselves by sharing an animated gif, a photo, or a quote from the Tumblr blog of someone else. This is a form of non-verbal communication and it is a powerful indicator of your state of mind and what you have in your heart at any given moment.

Google+ and Google Glass

While Google+ has not acquired as many users as the other personal social networking environments, it offers two key features that make it a powerful medium for expressing yourself nonverbally: Google Hangouts and Google Glass. Google Hangouts enable quick, easy, and free video conferencing for users while using collaborative productivity tools such as Google Docs—this means that the feeling of working around a table in the office can be replicated virtually, with many of the nonverbal gestures one may use in face-to-face communication. Google Glass opens an entirely new set of nonverbal communication opportunities. The fact that users are wearing the internet and interacting with the physical world through a pair of social media lenses powered by a heads-up display (HUD), brings the world of social media gestures together with the more familiar "real world"—it will be fascinating to see how this impacts how we communicate nonverbally. Imagine the initial awkwardness when you realize that someone is not only talking to you in person, but checking out your online presence and making jokes about your status update of that morning. Our conversations may become truly hybridized between the real and virtual worlds!

Summary

Non-verbal communication consists of messages expressed by non-linguistic means. There are non-verbal dimensions to all spoken language, and there are sign languages that are not spoken.

Non-verbal behaviour is an integral part of virtually all communication, and non-verbal skill is a positive predictor of relational success. There are several important characteristics of non-verbal communication. First is the simple fact that it exists—that communication occurs even in the absence of language. This leads to the second characteristic: it is impossible *not* to communicate non-verbally. Humans constantly send messages about themselves that are available for others to receive. The third characteristic is that non-verbal communication is ambiguous; there are many possible interpretations for any behaviour. This ambiguity makes it important for the receiver to verify any interpretation before jumping to conclusions about the meaning of a non-verbal message. Finally, non-verbal communication is different from verbal communication in complexity, flow, clarity, impact, and intentionality.

Some non-verbal communication is influenced by culture and gender. While there are some universal expressions, even the manner in which these expressions are used reflects the communicator's culture and gender. And behaviours that have special meanings in one culture may express different messages in another. We stated that non-verbal communication serves many functions: repeating, substituting, complementing, accenting, regulating, and contradicting verbal behaviour, as well as deceiving.

F. The Rules of Touch

Like most types of non-verbal behaviour, touching is governed by cultural and social rules. Imagine you are writing a guidebook for visitors from another culture. Describe the rules that govern touching in the following relationships. In each case, describe how the gender of the participants affects the rules:

1. an adult and a 5-year-old;

2. an adult and a 12-year-old;

3. two good friends; and

4. an employer and employee.

G. Distance Violations

You can test the importance of distance for yourself by violating the cultural rules for use of the proxemic zones outlined on pages 153–5.

1. Join with a partner. Choose which one of you will be the experimenter and which will be the observer.

2. In three situations, the experimenter should deliberately use the "wrong" amount of space for the context. Make the violations as subtle as possible. You might, for instance, gradually move into another person's intimate zone when personal distance would be more appropriate. (Be careful not to make the violations too offensive!)

3. The observer should record the verbal and non-verbal reactions of others when the distance zones are violated. After each experiment, inform the people involved about your motives and ask whether they were consciously aware of the reason for any discomfort they experienced.

H. The Power of Non-Verbal Insight

Being aware of the communicative power of non-verbal behaviour can often give you an edge in understanding and influencing it. Suppose that your skill at controlling your own non-verbal behaviour became great enough that you were able to present yourself to others in precisely the way you desire (even if the image wasn't completely accurate), and your ability to analyze others' non-verbal behaviour gave you a high degree of accuracy in interpreting others' unexpressed feelings.

Go to the park or to some other public place and observe people around you. Ask yourself these questions:

1. Who is the person I am looking at?

2. What components of his or her identity can I determine by noting non-verbal behaviour?

3. What element of non-verbal behaviour is giving me the best clues?

Write down your observations with a brief description of the person you are looking at, including his or her appearance, age, gender, and clothing.

I. Clothing and Impression Management

Using clothing as a method of creating impressions is a fact of life. Discover for yourself how dressing can be a type of deception.

1. Identify three examples from your experience when someone dressed in a manner that disguised or misrepresented his or her true status or personal attributes. What were the consequences of this misrepresentation for you or others?

2. Now identify three occasions in which you successfully used clothing to create a favourable but inaccurate impression. What were the consequences of this deception for others?

3. Based on your conclusions, define any situations when clothing may be used as an unethical means of impression management. List both "misdemeanours," in which the consequences are not likely to cause serious harm, and "felonies," in which the deception has the potential to cause serious harm.

J. Social Media and Non-Verbal Communication

Social media provide an interesting hybrid communication environment. On the one hand, social media are largely print-based and completely mediated, which is to say that we use a machine (i.e., a computer, a tablet, a smartphone, or Google Glass) as the channel through which to communicate. However, since much of the content of our social media communication is audio and video, there is lots of room to express non-verbal communication. This is an exercise to see whether social media are changing non-verbal communication.

1. Keep a log of your conversations via social media for three days. That is to say, save your tweets, video chats, texts, and status updates using screen shots or the video record function on your favourite video chat software.

2. Make a list of the non-verbal communication cues you are using: body language, emoticons, acronyms (e.g., LOL) and any other forms you can think of.

3. Now, observe yourself for a day. Keep a log of your non-verbal communication in your face-to-face real world interactions (e.g., shrugs, funny faces you make, whether you raise your voice, or how close you stand to others).

4. Compare the two lists and ask yourself: are you a different person on social media than you are in face-to-face communication?

Further Reading

Bowden, Mark, *Winning Body Language: Control the Conversation, Command Attention, and Convey the Right Message without Saying a Word* (New York: McGraw-Hill, 2010).
How much does body language count over spoken words? Research reveals that people "count" nonverbal communication as much as 55 to 90 per cent over the words said. Bowden, a trainer of Fortune 50 CEOs and G8 world leaders, shares ways to "intelligently communicate" through nonverbal means.

Burgoon, Judee K. and Aaron E. Bacue, "Nonverbal Communication Skills," in John O. Greene and Brant R. Burleson, eds, *Handbook of Communication and Social Interaction Skills* (Mahwah, NJ: Erlbaum, 2003).
This chapter investigates how people can improve their non-verbal communication skills through the use of examples and a systematic method.

Hickson, Mark, Don W. Stacks, and Nina-Jo Moore, *Nonverbal Communication: Studies and Applications* (Los Angeles: Roxbury, 2004).
This book offers a sophisticated introduction to both the theory and the practice of non-verbal communication.

Waldron, Vincent, and Jeffrey Kassing, *Managing Risk in Communication Encounters: Strategies for the Workplace* (Thousand Oaks, CA: Sage, 2010).
This book focuses on the how some daily interactions can be very risky and threaten identities, relationships, and sometimes careers. The authors offer useful guidelines, based on real-life case studies on topics such as voicing dissent, repairing broken relationships, managing privacy, responding to harassment, offering criticism, and communicating emotion.

Study Questions

1. Describe a situation from your own experience in which your non-verbal communication sent a message that your language did not.

2. Recall examples of at least three times that your non-verbal behaviour was ambiguous and misinterpreted by another.

3. Give one example of each form of non-verbal communication functions that you have observed in other people's behaviour. For each example, comment on whether the non-verbal communication function was effective or not.

4. Describe three different situations in which physical attractiveness had an effect on a communication outcome. Describe what the communicator could have changed to make his or her form of attractiveness more appropriate to achieving a different outcome.

5. Give two examples of how choice of clothing affects how someone's communication was perceived by others. How would a different choice of apparel have modified the effect on perception of the person?

5

Listening

After studying the material in this chapter . . .

You should understand:

- ✔ the most common misconceptions about listening;
- ✔ the five components of the listening process;
- ✔ the most common types of ineffective listening;
- ✔ the challenges that make effective listening difficult; and
- ✔ the skills necessary to listen effectively in informational, critical, and empathic settings.

You should be able to:

- ✔ identify situations in which you listen ineffectively and explain the reasons for your lack of effectiveness;
- ✔ identify the consequences of your ineffective listening;
- ✔ follow the guidelines for informational listening;
- ✔ analyze an argument or claim by evaluating the credibility of its proponent, the soundness of its reasoning, and the quality of the evidence offered; and
- ✔ apply appropriate response styles in an empathic listening context.

Chapter Highlights

Most people need to think about listening in a new way:

» There's a difference between hearing and listening.

» Listening isn't a natural ability, and it takes effort and practice to listen well.

» It's probable that people will hear the same message in different ways.

Two approaches can help you become a better listener:

» Minimize faulty listening behaviours.

» Understand some of the reasons why you listen poorly.

Most people use one of four personal listening styles:

» content-oriented,

» people-oriented,

» action-oriented, or

» time-oriented.

There are three ways to listen and respond:

» for information;

» to critically evaluate a speaker's ideas; and

» to help others with their problems.

In a world where almost everyone acknowledges the importance of better communication, the need for good listening is obvious. On the most basic level, listening is just as important as speaking. After all, it's impossible for communication to occur without someone receiving a message. (Imagine how ridiculous it would be to speak to an empty room or talk into a cell-phone with no signal.)

If rate of occurrence is a measure of importance, then listening easily qualifies as the most important kind of communication. We spend more time listening to others than in any other type of communication. One study revealed that of their total communicating time, university students spent an average of 14 per cent writing, 16 per cent speaking, 17 per cent reading, and a whopping 53 per cent listening.[1] On the job, listening is by far the most common form of communication. On average, employees of major corporations in North America spend about 60 per cent of each working day listening to others.[2]

No matter how importance is measured, listening is arguably just as essential as speaking. When the Conference Board of Canada profiled the most important on-the-job communication skills in 2000, listening and understanding ranked at the top of the list; they are also implicit in the teamwork emphasized elsewhere in the report.[3] A study examining the link between listening and career success revealed that better listeners rose to higher levels in their organizations,[4] and a survey of personnel managers identified listening as the most critical skill for working effectively in teams.[5] In small groups, people who listen well tend to be seen by other members as leaders.[6]

Listening is just as important in personal relationships. In one survey, marriage counsellors identified "failing to take the other's perspective when listening" as one of the most common communication problems among the couples with whom they work.[7] When another group of adults was asked which communication skills were most important in family and social settings, listening was ranked first.[8] In committed relationships, listening to personal information in everyday conversations is considered an important factor in overall satisfaction.[9] In short, effective listening is essential to effective relational communication.[10]

Understanding Diversity

Nine Soft Skills No Immigrant Should Be Without!

Skilled immigrants often focus on improving technical skills after coming to Canada, and they are shocked when they are told they have "no Canadian experience." I've realized that this albatross around immigrants' necks is actually a vague way of saying: "You lack the soft skills I am looking for in an employee."

I believe there are nine soft skills that no immigrant should be without:

1. *Communication skills.* Communication skills—both spoken and written—are critical for immigrants. I can't stress enough how important it is for career success to be able to not only speak in English, but also write clearly and persuasively.

2. *Local language skills.* I still smile when I think back to my first job in Canada when I was asked to put my "John Hancock" on a courier document. As I looked at the courier, he said to me, "I mean your signature." In a corporate environment, your language skills have to evolve to understand local phrases and business jargon.

3. *Presentation skills.* In a recent survey, senior managers rated the ability to make presentations as a top qualification. Now this could mean a formal presentation to clients or a more casual way of presenting yourself in meetings and with colleagues.

4. *Small talk.* Do you sense a theme here? Most of the soft skills I've mentioned so far all relate back to communicating. Water cooler chitchat is a part of corporate life. But be careful not to cross the line of what's taboo.

Nevertheless, experience shows that much of the listening we do is not at all effective. We frequently misunderstand others and are misunderstood in return. We become bored and feign attention while our minds wander. We engage in a battle of interruptions where each person fights to speak without hearing the other's ideas.

Some of this poor listening is inevitable, perhaps even justified. But in other cases we can become better receivers by learning a few basic listening skills. This chapter will help you become a better listener by giving you some important information about the subject. We'll talk about some common misconceptions concerning listening and show you what really happens when listening takes place. We'll discuss some poor listening habits, explain why they occur, and suggest better alternatives.

Misconceptions about Listening

In spite of its importance, listening is misunderstood by most people. Because these misunderstandings so greatly affect our communication, we need to debunk four common misconceptions.

Listening and Hearing Are Not the Same Thing

Hearing is the process in which sound waves strike the eardrum and cause vibrations that are transmitted to the brain. **Listening** occurs when the brain reconstructs these electrochemical impulses into a representation of the original sound and then gives them meaning. Barring illness, injury, or earplugs, hearing can't be stopped: your ears will pick up sound waves and transmit them to your brain whether you want them to or not. Listening, however, isn't automatic. Many times we hear but do not listen. Sometimes we deliberately tune out unwanted signals—everything from a neighbour's lawnmower or the roar of nearby traffic to a friend's boring remarks or a colleague's unwanted criticism.

Cultural Idiom
tuned in
To be focused and paying attention.

tune out
To not listen.

---

hearing
The process wherein sound waves strike the eardrum and cause vibrations that are transmitted to the brain.

listening
The process wherein the brain reconstructs electrochemical impulses generated by hearing into representations of the original sound and gives them meaning.

---

5. *Leadership and initiative.* Staying invisible is why many immigrants are overlooked when it comes time for promotions. Take some initiative, share your ideas, ask questions, and encourage others to collaborate as well!

6. *Conflict resolution and negotiation.* It is important to learn how to disagree with a colleague or even your boss without getting emotional about it! And if things go too far, learn to apologize.

7. *Accepting constructive criticism.* Constructive criticism is part of any learning curve. To accept criticism, understand that we are not perfect and learning is a continuous process, at work and in life.

8. *Flexibility.* Show your employer that you're willing to learn and adapt. The labour market and economy are changing all the time, and we must change, too.

9. *Business etiquette.* Workplace customs and practices may be different in Canada than your homeland. Something as simple as calling your boss by his or her first name may seem odd to you, but it's normal practice here.

There are many more soft skills, of course, but these nine are the ones that tend to get lost in translation. So let's start reviewing these in more depth over the next few months and see where it takes us!

Nick Noorani, *Canadian Immigrant*, 24 May 2011

A closer look at listening—at least the successful variety—shows that it consists of several stages. After hearing, the next stage is **attending**—the act of paying attention to a signal. An individual's needs, wants, desires, and interests determine what is attended to, or *selected*, to use the term introduced in Chapter 2.

The next step in listening is **understanding**—the process of making sense of a message. Chapter 3 discussed many of the ingredients that combine to make understanding possible: a grasp of the syntax of the language being spoken, semantic decoding, and knowledge of the pragmatic rules that help us figure out a speaker's meaning from the context. In addition to these steps, understanding often depends on the ability to organize the information we hear into recognizable form. As early as 1948, Ralph Nichols showed how successful understanding is related to a large number of factors, notably verbal ability, intelligence, and motivation.[11]

Responding to a message consists of giving observable feedback to the speaker. Offering feedback serves two important functions: it helps you clarify your understanding of a speaker's message, and it shows that you care about what the speaker is saying.

Listeners don't always respond visibly to a speaker, but research suggests that they should. One study of 195 critical incidents in banking and medical settings showed that a major difference between effective and ineffective listening had to do with the kind of feedback offered.[12] Good listeners showed that they were attentive through non-verbal behaviours such as keeping eye contact and reacting with appropriate facial expressions. Their verbal behaviour—answering questions and exchanging ideas, for example—also demonstrated their attention. It's easy to imagine how other responses would signal less effective listening. A slumped posture, bored expression, and yawning send a clear message that you are not tuned in to the speaker.

Adding responsiveness to our listening model demonstrates the fact, discussed in Chapter 1, that communication is transactional in nature. Listening isn't just a passive activity. As listeners, we are active participants in a communication transaction. At the same time that we receive messages we also send them.

The final step in the listening process is **remembering**.[13] Research has revealed that people remember only about half of what they hear *immediately after hearing it*.[14] This is true even when people work hard at listening. This situation would probably not be too bad if the half remembered right afterwards were retained, but it isn't. Within two months, half of the half is forgotten, bringing what we remember down to about 25 per cent of the original message. This loss doesn't even take the full two months: people start forgetting *immediately* (within just eight hours the 50 per cent remembered drops to about 35 per cent). Given the amount of information we process every day—from instructors, friends, the internet, TV, and other sources—the **residual message** (what we remember) is a small fraction of what we hear.

Listening Is Not a Natural Process

Another common myth is that listening is a natural activity, like breathing. The truth is that listening is a skill much like speaking. Everybody does it, but few people do it well. One study in particular illustrates this point: 144 managers were asked to rate their listening skills. Astonishingly, not one described him or herself as a "poor" or "very poor" listener, whereas

attending
The process of focusing on certain stimuli from the environment.

understanding
The act of interpreting a message by following syntactic, semantic, and pragmatic rules.

responding
Providing observable feedback to another person's behaviour or speech.

remembering
The act of recalling previously introduced information. Recall drops off in two phases: short-term and long-term.

residual message
The part of a message that a receiver can recall after short- and long-term memory losses.

Table 5.1 Comparison of Communication Activities

	Listening	Speaking	Reading	Writing
Learned	First	Second	Third	Fourth
Used	Most	Next to most	Next to least	Least
Taught	Least	Next to least	Next to most	Most

94 per cent rated themselves as "good" or "very good."[15] The favourable self-ratings contrasted sharply with the perceptions of those who reported to the managers, many of whom said their boss's listening skills were weak.

As we have already discussed, some poor listening is inevitable. The good news is that listening can be improved through instruction and training.[16] Despite this fact, the amount of time devoted to teaching listening is far less than that devoted to other types of communication. Table 5.1 reflects this upside-down arrangement.

> *I can't help hearing, but I don't always listen.*
>
> **George Burns, actor and comedian**

Listening Requires Effort

Most people assume that listening is fundamentally a passive activity in which the receiver absorbs a speaker's ideas, rather like the way a sponge absorbs water. As we will show later in this chapter, every kind of listening requires mental effort by the receiver. And experience shows that passive listening almost guarantees that the respondent will fail to grasp at least some of the speaker's ideas and will misunderstand others.

All Listeners Do Not Receive the Same Message

We also tend to assume that when two or more people are listening to a speaker, they all are hearing and understanding the same message. In fact, this isn't the case at all. In Chapter 2 we

pointed out the many factors that cause each of us to perceive an event differently. Physiological factors, personal interests and needs, and our social roles and cultural backgrounds all shape and distort the raw data we hear into uniquely different messages.

Overcoming Challenges to Effective Listening

Despite the importance of good listening, people seem to get worse at the skill as they grow older.[17] In one experiment, teachers at various grade levels were asked to stop their lectures periodically and ask students what they had just been talking about. Ninety per cent of grade one children could repeat what the teacher had been saying, and 80 per cent of grade twos could do so. But when the test was repeated with teenagers, the results were much less impressive: only 44 per cent of junior high-school students and 28 per cent of high-school students could repeat their teachers' remarks.

Research suggests that adult listening skills are even poorer—at least in some important relationships. One experiment found that people listened more attentively and courteously to strangers than to their spouses. When faced with decision-making tasks, couples interrupted one another more frequently and were generally less polite than they were to strangers.[18]

In the following section we'll take a look at the kinds of poor listening habits that plague communication.

Faulty Listening Behaviours

Most people have one or more habits that keep them from understanding important messages.

Pseudo-listening

pseudo-listening
An imitation of true listening in which the receiver's mind is elsewhere.

Pseudo-listening is an imitation of the real thing. Pseudo-listeners give the appearance of being attentive: they look you in the eye, nod and smile at the right times, and may even answer you occasionally. Behind that appearance of interest, however, something entirely different is going on, because pseudo-listeners use a polite facade to mask thoughts that have nothing to do with what the speaker is saying.

Selective Listening

selective listening
A listening style in which the receiver responds only to messages that interest him or her.

Selective listeners respond only to the parts of a speaker's remarks that interest them, rejecting everything else. We are all selective listeners from time to time—for instance, when we screen out TV or radio ads while keeping an ear cocked for the program to resume. In other cases, selective listening occurs in conversations with people who expect a thorough hearing but get their partner's attention only when the conversation turns to the partner's favourite topic—perhaps money, sex, sports, shopping, or some particular person. Unless and until you bring up one of these pet topics, you might as well talk to a tree.

Cultural Idiom
keeping an ear cocked
To listen alertly.

pet
To be one's favourite.

Defensive Listening

defensive listening
A response style in which the receiver perceives a speaker's comments as an attack.

Defensive listeners take innocent comments as personal attacks. Teenagers who see a parent's questions about friends and activities as distrustful snooping are defensive listeners, as are touchy parents who view any questioning by their children as a threat to their parental authority. Many defensive listeners are insecure people who suffer from shaky public images and avoid admitting this by projecting their insecurities onto others.

Ambushing

Ambushers listen carefully, but only because they are collecting information to attack what you have to say. The criminal lawyer preparing to cross-examine a witness is a good example of an ambusher. People talking to an ambusher will often become justifiably defensive.

Insulated Listening

Insulated listeners are nearly the opposite of selective listeners. Instead of screening the conversation for topics they want to hear about, they screen for topics they want to avoid and then simply tune out. If you specifically draw their attention to a problem—perhaps an unfinished job, poor grades, or the like—they may seem to have heard you, but they'll promptly forget what you've just said.

Insensitive Listening

People often don't express their thoughts or feelings openly but instead communicate them subtly through choice of words or non-verbal clues or both. **Insensitive listeners** don't receive these messages clearly. They aren't able to look beyond the words and behaviour to understand their hidden meanings; instead, they take a speaker's remarks at face value.

Stage Hogging

Stage hogs differ somewhat from the other types of faulty listeners we've described. It's not just that they don't receive the other person's messages clearly. Instead, stage hogs (sometimes called "conversational narcissists") try to turn the topic of conversation to themselves rather than showing interest in the speaker.[19] Interruptions are a hallmark of stage hogging, and they are a common feature of Western speech: a study comparing Thai and Anglo-Canadian negotiators found that the Canadians were more likely than Thais to interrupt another person in conversation.[20] Besides preventing the listener from learning potentially valuable information, stage hogging can damage the relationship between the interrupter and the speaker. For example, applicants who interrupt the questions of a potential employer during a job interview are likely to be rated less favourably than job seekers who wait until the interviewer has finished speaking before they respond.[21]

When confronted with stage hogs, people respond in one of two ways. Sometimes the strategy is passive: talking less, tuning out the stage hog, showing boredom non-verbally, or leaving the conversation. Other strategies are more active: trying to recapture the floor, hinting about the stage hog's dominance, or confronting the speaker about his or her narcissism. Reactions like these give stage hogs a taste of their own medicine, turning the conversation into a verbal tug-of-war.

ambushing
A style in which the receiver listens carefully to gather information to use in an attack on the speaker.

insulated listening
A style in which the receiver ignores undesirable information.

insensitive listening
Failure to recognize the thoughts or feelings that are not directly expressed by a speaker, instead accepting the speaker's words at face value.

Cultural Idiom
at face value
To understand something literally.

stage hogging
A listening style in which the receiver is more concerned with making his or her own point than with understanding the speaker.

Cultural Idiom
a taste of their own medicine
To retaliate by responding in a similar manner.

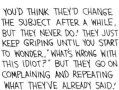

UNDERSTANDING COMMUNICATION TECHNOLOGY

Can Avatars Help Close the Doctor-Patient Communication Gap?

You've probably experienced the frustration of going to the doctor's office and coming out more confused or uncertain about your symptoms. Effective listening is a skill that both the patient and the doctor need to have in order to ensure that the best medical help is given. Technology might be the answer. In his article below, systems engineering expert Robert N. Charette explains the use of avatars and how it could improve the flow of information between doctor and patient.

Communication in a doctor's office is like a marriage gone bad: As you describe to your doctor what pain or symptoms you have, you realize that while the doctor may hear you, he or she isn't really listening. And in the other direction, you hear the doctor's words, but do you walk away with a full understanding of the diagnosis, what exactly you're being prescribed, why, and what the risks are?

In a recent article in the *London Telegraph*, fully 25 per cent of National Health Service patients complained that their doctors discuss their conditions as if they weren't there; 20 per cent reported that "they were not given enough information about their condition and treatment;" and 25 per cent confessed that "there was no one they could talk to about their worries and fears."

Another recent story about doctors' people-skills—and lack thereof—in the *Wall Street Journal* sums up the issue nicely: "Doctors are rude. Doctors don't listen. Doctors have no time. Doctors don't explain things in terms patients can understand." The introduction of electronic health records [EHR] has, ironically, often made things worse. A recent study noted that even as EHR systems have "allowed [doctors] to spend more face-to-face time with patients," they nonetheless often prove to be a "distraction" as doctor attention becomes focused on keyboards and not patients.

The *WSJ* article talks about how medical schools, malpractice insurers, and major hospitals are trying to improve patient-doctor communication, and for good reason: A break-down in patient-doctor communication is cited in at least 40 per cent of malpractice claims. Further, research confirms that poor communication often leads patients to not follow their prescribed treatments regimens, whereas the opposite also seems to be true. Doctor-patient communication can be improved by having doctors coached in practices like the Four Habits, which, the *WSJ* says, "teaches doctors how to create rapport with patients, elicit their views, demonstrate empathy, and assess their ability to follow a treatment regimen."

If new technology is partly to blame, it can also help. An article at *Health Management Technology* describes the use of speech-based "virtual assistants" to capture patient data and automatically enter it into a patient's EHR, for example, allowing the doctor to talk to the patient without the distraction of having to type what is being said.

Recently, I spoke to André Elisseeff, one of the founders of Nhumi ("new-me") Technologies about the use of avatars to improve patient-doctor communication. You may recall that Elisseeff and his team created (while working for IBM's Zurich Research Lab) a "Google Earth for the Body" as a means of visualizing a person's EHR using a 3-D image of the human-body. At Nhumi, he developed the idea further into an avatar system that could be used to depict adverse drug reactions. Elisseeff's team late last year created a new visual search engine to explore the human body using a detailed, interactive 3-D model to depict human anatomy. Calling it the "HealthCorpus,"

Reasons for Poor Listening

What causes people to listen poorly? There are several reasons, some of which can be avoided and others that are sad but inescapable facts of life.

Effort

Listening effectively is hard work. The physical changes that occur during careful listening show the effort it takes: heart rate quickens, respiration increases, and body temperature rises.[22] Notice that these changes are similar to the body's reaction to physical effort. This is no coincidence, because listening carefully to a speaker can be just as taxing as more obvious efforts. You can manage the effort that's required to listen well if you prepare yourself for the

they have put medical data, FDA data, and user-generated content into a single site that lets a person search this integrated content by clicks on a virtual body.

Elisseeff told me that the new site is meant "for the patient to help indicate to the doctor where it hurts," and correspondingly, allows the doctor "to explain to the patient why it hurts."

HealthCorpus is also designed at giving a patient something tangible to refer back to when they leave the doctor's.

"We asked some GPs about how they would use the system, the first thing they told us is that they would use it to educate the patients, and second, give patients [a visual record] so they don't go home with empty hands," Elisseeff said.

The latter use might be the most important. The research reported in *WSJ*, for instance, found that 80 per cent of patients forget what the doctor told them as soon as they leave the office and 50 per cent of what patients do remember is actually incorrect, especially in regard to the risks of the treatment prescribed. Other studies indicate that 50 per cent of patients don't take their prescribed medications, and that some 70 per cent of the non-adherence is intentional. The reasons for non-adherence include patients not believing their doctor's diagnosis, not sharing their doctor's belief about the severity of the condition, or a belief that the detrimental side-effects outweigh the benefits of the medications prescribed. Using HealthCorpus can help a doctor address each of these issues.

Elisseeff told me, for example, how one doctor used the avatar on HealthCorpus to show a patient what was going on with his ankle and foot, and how he needed to strengthen certain muscles in order to relieve the pain the patient felt. The patient could "see" (on the 3-D Model) exactly which muscles

the doctor was referring to, grasp how they were causing the problem, and understand that until the muscles were strengthened, whatever pain the patient felt was "normal." With greater understanding, a patient is more motivated to follow a doctor's treatment plan.

Elisseeff also believes that an avatar-based approach could also help overcome another patient complaint: scolding doctors. No one likes to be nagged by their doctor over something you are doing (or not doing), even (or especially) if you know your doctor is right—we disengage from listening or even rebel against the advice being given, in the face of what we perceive as a verbal "attack." The avatar as a personal "proxy" might alleviate these natural defensive mechanisms. By talking dispassionately instead about the state of the avatar, and what happens to it when a treatment isn't followed, a patient might be more willing to listen to what the doctor is saying.

The hope is that by using HealthCorpus, the patient and doctor can have a richer conversation and diminish the fears and misunderstandings that seem inevitable when visiting the doctor. Maybe then, Elisseeff says, the patient-doctor dialogue can focus on what needs to be done to get better instead of talking past one another.

Robert N. Charette, *IEEE Spectrum*, 4 May 2013

QUESTIONS: How does the use of a digital avatar in medical communications highlight more traditional issues presented in communicative listening and engagement? Do you think medical avatars are a feasible solution for problematic communications between patient and doctor?

task. If you know that passive listening won't be enough, you can invest the energy to understand others.

Message Overload

The amount of speech most of us encounter every day makes careful listening to everything we hear impossible. As we've already seen, many of us spend as much as one-third of the time we're awake listening to verbal messages—from instructors, co-workers, friends, family, salespeople, and total strangers. This means we often spend five hours or more a day listening to people talk. If you add this to the amount of time we spend listening to messages on the TV, radio, and internet, you can see that it's impossible for us to keep our attention totally focused for that amount of time. Therefore, we have to let our attention wander at times. If you can

consciously decide which messages are worth your attention, you can devote the time it takes to understand them.

Rapid Thought

Listening carefully is also difficult for a physiological reason. Although we are capable of understanding speech at rates up to 600 words per minute, the average person speaks between 100 and 140 words per minute.[23] Thus, we have a great deal of mental "spare time" to spend while someone is talking. And the temptation is to use this time in ways that don't relate to the speaker's ideas, such as thinking about personal interests, daydreaming, planning a rebuttal, and so on. The trick is to use this spare time to understand the speaker's ideas better rather than to let your attention wander. Try to rephrase the speaker's ideas in your own words. Ask yourself how the ideas might be useful to you. Consider other angles that the speaker might not have mentioned.

Psychological Noise

Another reason we don't always listen carefully is that we're often wrapped up in personal concerns that are of more immediate importance to us than the messages others are sending. It's hard to pay attention to someone else when you're anticipating an upcoming test or thinking about the wonderful time you had last night with good friends. Yet, we still feel we have to "listen" politely to others, so we continue with our charade. It usually takes a conscious effort to set aside your personal concerns if you expect to give others' messages the attention they deserve.

Figure 5.1 illustrates four ways in which preoccupied listeners lose focus when distracted by psychological noise. Everyone's mind wanders at one time or another, but excessive preoccupation is both a reason for and a sign of poor listening.

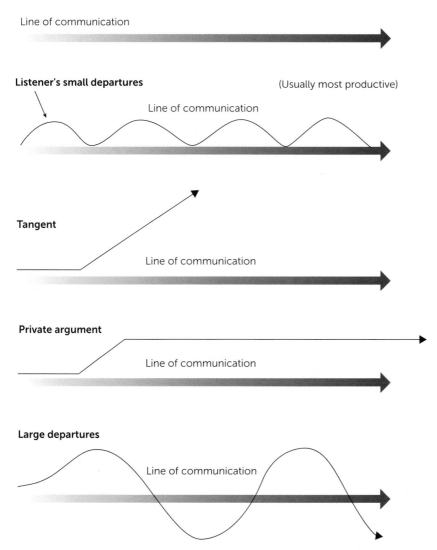

Line of communication

Listener's small departures   (Usually most productive)

Line of communication

Tangent

Line of communication

Private argument

Line of communication

Large departures

Line of communication

FIGURE 5.1 Four Thought Patterns

Source: A.D. Wolvin and C.G. Coakley, *Perspectives on Listening* (Norwood, NJ: Ablex, 1993), 115.

Physical Noise

The world in which we live often presents distractions that make it hard to pay attention to others. The sound of traffic, music, other people's talking, and so on interfere with our ability to hear well. Also, fatigue or other forms of discomfort can distract us from paying attention to a speaker's remarks. Consider, for example, how the efficiency of your listening decreases when you are seated in a crowded, hot, stuffy room that is surrounded by traffic and other noises. In such circumstances even the best intentions aren't enough to ensure clear under-standing. You can often listen better by insulating yourself from outside distractions. This may involve removing the sources of noise: turning off the television, shutting the book you were reading, closing the window, and so on. In some cases, you and the speaker may need to find a more hospitable place to speak in order to make listening work.

Hearing Problems

Sometimes a person's listening ability suffers because of a medical condition, specifically a hearing problem—the most obvious sort of physiological noise, as defined in Chapter 1. After a hearing problem has been diagnosed, it's often possible to treat. The real tragedy occurs when a hearing loss goes undetected. In such cases, both the person with the impairment and others can become frustrated and annoyed at the ineffective communication that results. If you suspect that you or someone you know suffers from hearing loss, it's wise to have a physician or audiologist perform an examination.

Faulty Assumptions

We often give others a mental brush-off because we assume their remarks don't have much value. When one business consultant asked some of her clients why they interrupted colleagues, she received the following responses:

- "My idea is better than theirs."
- "If I don't interrupt them, I'll never get to say my idea."
- "I know what they are about to say."
- "They don't need to finish their thoughts since mine are better."
- "Nothing about their idea will improve with further development."
- "It is more important for me to get recognized than it is to hear their idea."
- "I'm more important than they are."[24]

The egotism behind these comments is stunning. Dismissing others' ideas before considering them may be justified sometimes, but it's obviously a mistake to rule out so much of what others say—especially when you consider how you would feel if other people dismissed your comments without hearing you out.

Talking Has More Apparent Advantages

It often appears that we have more to gain by speaking than by listening. Whatever the goal—to win over a prospective employer, to convince others to support your candidate, or to describe the way you want your hair cut—the key to success seems to be the ability to speak well. Another apparent advantage of speaking is the chance it provides to gain the admiration, respect, or liking of others—or so you may think. Tell jokes, and everyone may think you're a real wit. Offer advice, and they might be grateful for your help. Tell them all you know, and they could be impressed by your wisdom.

Although speaking at the right time can lead people to appreciate you, talking too much can result in the kind of stage hogging we alluded to earlier. Not all interruptions are attempts at stage hogging. One study revealed a difference between male and female interrupters.[25] Men typically interrupted conversations far more than women. Their goal was usually to control the discussion. Women interrupted for very different reasons: to communicate agreement, to elaborate on the speaker's idea, or to participate in the topic of conversation. These sorts of responses are more likely to be welcomed as a contribution to the conversation and not as attempts to grab the stage.

If you find yourself hogging the conversation, try a simple experiment: limit the frequency and length of your responses to a fraction of their usual amount. If you were speaking 50 per cent of the time, cut back to 25 per cent—or even less. If you interrupt the speaker every 15 seconds, try to let him or her talk for closer to a minute. You are likely to discover that you're learning more—and probably gaining the appreciation of the other person.

Cultural Differences

The way members of different cultures communicate can affect listening.[26] For instance, one study of young adults from various countries showed marked differences in listening preferences. Young Germans favoured an action-oriented approach: they engaged speakers directly and were highly inquisitive. This style contrasts with the indirect approach of high-context Japanese listeners. Young Israelis were also less vocal than Germans and focused on careful analysis of others' statements. By contrast, young Americans emphasized the social dimension of a conversation and were more focused on how much time a conversation was taking.

Media Influences

A final challenge to serious listening is the influence of contemporary mass media, especially television, radio, and the internet. A growing amount of programming consists of short segments: news items, commercials, videos, and so on. (Think of YouTube, your Facebook feed, blogs, and MuchMusic.) In the same vein, news consists mainly of brief stories with a declining portion of text and a growing amount of graphical information. This is especially true with news aggregator sites such as www.Digg.com or www.reddit.com/r/canada, which feature catchy headlines on a bulletin board with links to the full story. Sites like these also place personal blogs, tabloid news, and articles from serious newspapers, such as *The Globe and Mail* or Halifax's *The Chronicle-Herald*, on an equal platform. And 24-hour news networks run headlines across the bottom of the screen (known as a "news ticker" or "crawler"), and sometimes weather forecasts across the top, while an announcer simultaneously reads news items. These trends discourage the kind of focused attention that is necessary for careful listening, especially to complicated ideas and feelings.

Social Media Influences

While the sound-bite culture of television and radio is often blamed for decreasing people's listening skills and attention spans, social media have introduced a new set of challenges. We have all been faced with someone who is constantly engrossed in their tablet or smartphone, even while they are walking, eating, or using the restroom! This constant distraction is impacting how we communicate and what is acceptable listening practice. Among many, the act of checking one's smartphone in the middle of a conversation with a furtive (or not so furtive) glance is considered an acceptable act. While this may not be the case inter-generationally, it will be interesting to see how the fast-paced world of online chat, Facebook status updates, and tweets merges with our physical world interactions, through such wearable computing devices such as Google Glass or smart watches. These emerging new social norms will have an important

Cultural Idiom
grab the stage
To gain attention.

While the right to talk may be the beginning of freedom, the necessity of listening is what makes that right important.

Walter Lippmann, political commentator

COMMUNICATING ONLINE

Twenty Business Texting Etiquette Tips

The increasing popularity of texting as a means of business communication is forcing us to rethink what is socially acceptable communication behaviour. Texting might be the norm for communicating with friends and even family, but is it appropriate to send a work-related text to a colleague? Or is using this social medium for "shop talk" an invasion of privacy? How do you know if your colleagues are even comfortable talking about work through texting? Study entrepreneur Todd Smith's 20 tips for keeping your business texting professional and efficient.

1. *Don't send a text unless it's urgent.* When you send people a text, in most cases you will be interrupting them. The default settings on most mobile phones ring or vibrate when it receives a text message. So if you are going to interrupt someone, make sure you have a good reason.

2. *Don't send a text message if you can send an e-mail.* Most business professionals check their e-mail at least twice a day and almost all of them prefer communication by e-mail rather than texting. People don't like being interrupted unless it's urgent and they are more productive if they respond to all their messages during scheduled blocks of time. For most people it's also more efficient to type messages on a computer rather than on a phone. E-mails are also stored on your computer's hard drive, while text messages can disappear into the ether.

3. *Don't send a text if you should make a call.* If you know that the subject of your message will require back and forth communication, either pick up the phone and call the person or if it's not time sensitive, send an e-mail requesting a specific time to talk. Business relationships are seldom built or strengthened through text messaging, so use it sparingly.

4. *Avoid texting people who don't text you.* According to a *Success Magazine* survey, only 4% of the business professionals surveyed prefer texting to other forms of communication. If you have never received a text message from someone, consider that they may not like to text.

5. *Don't text bad news.* If you have bad news to share with people, give them the courtesy of a call. E-mailing or texting bad news is a cop out.

6. *Don't type in CAPS.* Reading CAPS is harder and is generally referred to as YELLING!

7. *Don't assume people know what all the acronyms and text slang mean.* Not everyone knows that ttyl means "talk to you later" or jk means "just kidding." Say what you mean and make sure your messages present you as a business professional.

8. *Don't text during meetings.* If you send or read texts during a meeting, your actions convey that the meeting is not important to you. After all, how can you focus on the discussion that's taking place if you are texting? It would be

effect on what we consider acceptable or effective listening behaviour in the future. For now, we can focus on trying to be as respectful as possible of those with whom we communicate by gauging their comfort level with social media technologies. The answer here is: be attentive and listen carefully to how the person you are communicating with is responding to you. If that person is giving you non-verbal or verbal signals that checking your smartphone is a bad listening behaviour for them, then you should probably turn the phone over on the table and put it into "silent mode."

Personal Listening Styles

Not everyone listens the same way. Communication researchers have identified four styles, each of which has both strengths and weaknesses.[27]

just like having a verbal side conversation. Clearly inconsiderate and disrespectful.

9. *Use punctuation.* Type your texts using the same punctuation you would use in your e-mails. Since these are business texts, make sure they present you well.

10. *Don't text after business hours unless there's a good reason.* If you have something to share with someone after business hours, consider using e-mail. If you want people to respect your family and personal time, respect theirs. You also run the risk of losing your influence if you don't respect people's private time.

11. *Proof your messages.* Take a few seconds to make sure you don't have any misspellings or improper language. Be proud of the messages you send.

12. *Get to the point.* Since a text message is limited to a small number of words, get to the point in your message and keep it from spilling over into another message. If you have a lot to share, consider picking up the phone or sending an e-mail.

13. *Include your name.* Unless you are absolutely certain that the recipient of your text has your name plugged into their phone, add your name to the end of the message.

14. *Watch your tone.* Make sure you pay close attention to the tone of your message. If you are upset about something, pick up the phone and call the person.

15. *Return text messages.* If someone sends you a text, they expect a response in a reasonable period of time. Show that you are a responsible person by returning all messages in a timely manner.

16. *Don't send a text after leaving a message.* As a general rule, if you call someone, you should always leave a message. After leaving a message, don't follow up with a text message unless it is urgent. Consider that your call interrupted them once. You don't want your text to interrupt them a second time.

17. *Don't leave people hanging.* If you are done with a text conversation, let the person know.

18. *Don't waste people's time.* Don't send unnecessary text messages. As an example, when a text conversation is clearly over, don't send another message. Once again, every text you send is likely to interrupt someone's activity, meeting, or train of thought.

19. *Show respect and courtesy.* Whatever you do, consider how it affects those around you. Unless it's urgent, avoid sending texts when you are spending time with people.

20. *Not while you are driving.* While this seems like common sense, the number of people sending text messages in cars is shocking. Next to drunk drivers, distracted drivers are the second leading cause of fatal automobile accidents.

—Todd Smith, *Little Things Matter*, 2 March 2010.

Content-Oriented Listening

As the label that characterizes them suggests, **content-oriented listeners** are most interested in the quality of messages they hear. They look for details and are good at analyzing an issue from several perspectives. They give weight to the messages of experts and other credible sources of information. Content-oriented listeners often enjoy ideas for their own sake and are willing to spend time exploring them in thorough exchanges of ideas.

A content-oriented approach is valuable when the goal is to evaluate the quality of ideas and when there is value in looking at issues from a wide range of perspectives. It is especially useful when the topic is a complicated one. On the other hand, a content-oriented approach risks annoying people who don't have the same sort of analytical orientation. A content-oriented approach can take more time than others may be willing to give, and the content-oriented listener may challenge ideas in a way that can be perceived as overly critical or even hostile.

> **content-oriented listening**
> A listening style that focuses on the content of a message.

> **Cultural Idiom**
> **give weight to**
> To give priority to something.

Understanding Diversity

Raising a Canadian: Immigrant Children Develop Different Views

When Michelle emigrated from Hong Kong to Canada, she expected to face many challenges in adapting to a new culture and way of life. "What I didn't predict," she says, "was the strain it would have on the relationship between my daughter and me."

Rita was 11 when she became a Canadian. "Before moving to Canada, Rita had been responsible and respectful toward me, and we had a good relationship," Michelle says. "But within a few years of living in Canada, that all changed."

Rita began talking back to her mother and acting out. "She started breaking curfew and hanging out with a bad crowd," Michelle says. "She stopped listening to me completely."

According to Michelle, her daughter became "really Canadian," wearing Western-style clothes, listening to pop music, and speaking almost exclusively in English. "She was no longer interested in many Chinese traditions she used to love, like celebrating the Chinese New Year," she says. Michelle was worried that Rita would forget Chinese culture and felt alienated from her daughter's life. She struggled to maintain parental authority, and frequently felt overwhelmed.

"I wasn't sure what to do. I felt like I was failing as a parent," she says.

Clashing Cultures

According to Ontario-based social worker and counsellor Gary Direnfeld, the experiences Michelle faced are tremendously common. "These are tough situations," he says, "particularly for immigrants who speak another language, who come from war-torn countries or countries where there is conflict, or who have a distrust of governments and social services."

Refugees and immigrant families draw on culture, tradition, and family experience in parenting styles. Many immigrant groups have more traditional values, which can be different to the values of mainstream Canadian culture. Chinese parents, for example, are more likely to emphasize behavioural control, discipline, and obedience than Western Canadian parents.

So, when children adopt the language, culture, and value system of a new country quicker than parents, values can clash. Direnfeld believes that it's less a question of whether the children will be changed by the host culture, but rather how and to what degree. "Children frequently adapt sooner and quicker

[than their parents]," he says. They may have disagreements about appropriate gender roles and dress, expectations for academic performance or discipline styles.

He provides a scenario he frequently encounters in his counselling practice, that of an Asian Canadian family with teenage boys. The parents worked hard to provide a good education for their sons, but the teenagers began to resent the rules imposed on them, and began gravitating toward a counter-culture lifestyle and getting in trouble with the law. "They were not necessarily bad kids," Direnfeld explains, "but were having trouble adapting."

Direnfeld believes that to a certain extent, some boundary pushing from children is normal. "It doesn't matter if it's here, Bangladesh, Timbuktu, or Canada," he says, "children are born to push parental limits."

For the children of immigrant parents, however, this boundary pushing is generally more pronounced as children will naturally assimilate to the host culture to a greater extent than their parents. Parents can also experience personal conflict between their traditional and mainstream values, which can make it difficult to decide the best way to relate to their children.

Being Canadian

As well as being difficult for parents, adjusting to life in Canada can be a difficult process for the children, too.

"Living in Canada is so different from Hong Kong," says Michelle's daughter, Rita. "Everything is different—the people, the places, school."

Although she spoke English before moving to Canada, Rita struggled to adjust to the practices common among other Canadian teenagers, such as leisure time spent outside of the family, more relaxed academic standards, and relating to other family members. "When I was younger, I went over to friends' houses and saw how their parents treated them. I realized my mom was way stricter on me, and I didn't think it was fair."

Rita also struggled with feeling like she belonged in Canada, and was embarrassed by her mother's cultural traditions.

"To the child that wants desperately to fit in, [traditional customs and beliefs] can cause embarrassment or shame," explains Direnfeld. "They may not want to be seen with the parents."

Forming an Ethnic Identity

Vancouver-based psychologist Aneesa Shariff, who has researched ethnic identity and parenting stress in South Asian families, believes this can result in youth feeling torn between cultures. Forming an ethnic identity and negotiating between their heritage culture and the dominant culture is a normal and essential part of development. "The child wants to integrate more because it's important for them to get along with their peers and classmates," she says.

"If the process of forming an ethnic identity during adolescence isn't fully explored and resolved," she says, "it can result in a fragmented sense of self where they don't emerge from that stage having a clear sense of who they are."

Like Rita, Shariff believes that youth can then act out or lead a double life, "behaving one way in the home and another outside of the home." Others may hide their feelings to bend to the will of their parents, or gravitate toward counterculture groups or gangs. As well as causing conflict within the family, these actions can result in mental health problems such as depression, anxiety, substance abuse, eating disorders, types of delinquent behaviours, and academic failure.

Finding the Balance

According to Shariff, immigrant parents must decide how much they wish to adopt the values and practices of Canadian culture, and how much they want to retain their own. They must also support their children in forming an ethnic identity, while encouraging a healthy parent–child relationship. "It's not always an easy or smooth process to go through," she says.

She suggests parents reflect on what their expectations on themselves are, what their role is, and what's important to them.

"Talk about it with your children and come to compromises," she suggests. Use empathy and open dialogue, and engage in positive activities such as watching movies together and participating in heritage cultural activities.

"We as parents have to appreciate that as much as we want to keep some semblance of where we came from, over the years and decades and generations, our youngsters will change. They won't be as immersed in their country of origin as their parents," says Direnfeld.

While it's important to maintain a strong connection to ethnic heritage, it is also vital that children and young adults develop a positive identity as Canadians. "[Parents need to] recognize that behaviour in their children as a normal developmental part of adolescents," says Shariff.

Direnfeld suggests encouraging children to spend time in their own culture so they can experience pride and joy for who they really are. Direnfeld is Jewish, and after moving from a Jewish enclave in Toronto to a predominantly white neighbourhood, he felt "like a fish out of water." "I spoke English, I was white, and yet I was different," he says.

To encourage acculturation, his parents invited Direnfeld's neighbourhood friends to experience their religious traditions, and encouraged their son to experience theirs. "So rather than run from, we *invite* to," he says. "We celebrate our differences."

Four years after immigrating to Canada, Michelle and Rita still disagree about some things, but overall their relationship has improved. "Take the time to listen to your children," Michelle says. "Don't be afraid to speak your mind."

Adds Rita, "It can be tough to get used to a new culture and way of living. It gets better and it's easier if you have your family to talk to."

Ultimately, parents play a central role in all aspects of children's lives. The challenge for immigrant parents is to adapt and find reasonable strategies to support cultural expectations. Parents who successfully adapt to these strategies stand the best chance of developing a good relationship with their children, adjusting to Canadian culture, and raising healthy and happy Canadians.

Emily Rose, *Canadian Immigrant*, 4 February 2013, http://canadianimmigrant.ca/family/raising-a-canadian-immigrant-children-develop-different-views/attachment/kid

QUESTION: The author describes the richness of the Canadian experience that the mother profiled in the article and her children have encountered and how it caused some challenges for her as a parent. How might developing more powerful listening skills improve the relationships between immigrants and their "Canadianized" children?

People-Oriented Listening

**people-oriented
listening**
A listening style that is
primarily concerned with
creating and maintaining
positive relationships.

People-oriented listeners are especially concerned with creating and maintaining positive relationships. They tune into others' moods, and they respond to speakers' feelings as well as their ideas. People-oriented listeners are typically less judgmental about what others have to say than are content-oriented types. They are more interested in understanding and supporting people than in evaluating them.[28]

A people orientation comes with a strong concern for relationships that has obvious strengths but also some less obvious drawbacks. It is easy to become overly involved with others' feelings. People-oriented listeners, in an effort to be congenial and supportive, may lose their detachment and ability to assess the quality of information others are giving. Less personally oriented communicators can view these listeners as overly expressive and even intrusive.

Action-Oriented Listening

**action-oriented
listening**
A listening style that is
primarily concerned with
accomplishing the task
at hand.

Unlike people-oriented listeners, who focus on relationships, and content-oriented listeners, who are fascinated with ideas for their own sake, **action-oriented listeners** are most concerned with the task at hand. Their main concern is to figure out what sort of response is required by a message. They want to get to the heart of the matter quickly, and so they appreciate clear, concise messages and often translate others' remarks into well-organized mental outlines.

Action-oriented listening is most appropriate when the goal is taking care of business. These listeners keep a focus on the job at hand and encourage others to be organized and concise. But their no-nonsense approach isn't always appreciated by speakers who lack the skill or inclination to be clear and direct. Action-oriented listeners seem to minimize emotional issues and concerns, which may be an important part of business and personal transactions.

Time-Oriented Listening

**time-oriented
listening**
A listening style that is
primarily concerned
with minimizing the time
necessary to accomplish
the task at hand.

Time-oriented listeners are most concerned with efficiency. They view time as a scarce and valuable commodity, and they grow impatient when they view others as wasting it. A time orientation can be an asset when deadlines and other pressures demand fast action. On the other hand, a time orientation can put off others when it seems to disregard their feelings. Also, an excessive focus on time can hamper the kind of thoughtful deliberation that some jobs require.

Cultural Idiom
put off
To displease.

As you read the preceding descriptions, you may have found that you use more than one of these listening styles. If so, you aren't alone: 40 per cent of the people who used "The Listening Styles Profile" reported at least two strong listening preferences.[29] Whichever styles you use, it is important to recognize that you can control the way you listen and to use the styles that best suit the situation at hand. When your relationship with the speaker needs attention, adopt a people-oriented approach. When clarity is the issue, be an action-oriented listener. If analysis is called for, put on your content-oriented persona. And when the clock is what matters most, become a model of

COMMUNICATION ON-SCREEN

The King's Speech (2010)
Directed by Tom Hooper.

Academy Award winner—for Best Picture, Actor, Director, and Screenplay—*The King's Speech* charts the ascendance of King George VI (Colin Firth) to the throne and his friendship with an Australian speech therapist, Lionel Logue (Geoffrey Rush). Thrust upon the throne by the abdication of his irresponsible brother, King George VI must overcome a crippling stammer and fear of public speaking to declare war on Germany in 1939 and rally a nation in his first wartime radio broadcast. The film highlights a great number of communications topics from public speaking, to syntax, psychology, active listening, and a myriad of social contexts and their impact on effective communication.

time orientation. You can also boost your effectiveness by assessing the listening preferences of your conversational partners and adapting your style to them.

Informational Listening

Informational listening is the approach to take when you want to understand another person. When you are an informational listener, your goal is to make sure you are receiving the same thoughts the other person is trying to convey—not always an easy feat when you consider the forces that interfere with understanding (see pp. 103–7).

The situations that call for informational listening are endless and varied: following an instructor's comments in class, listening to a friend's account of a night out, absorbing the sales pitch for a new printer you're thinking of buying, learning about your family history from a relative's tales, swapping ideas in a discussion about politics or sports—the list goes on and on. You can become more effective as an informational listener by approaching others with a constructive attitude and by using some simple but effective skills.

Don't Argue or Judge Prematurely

Since the time of the ancient Greeks and Romans, Western civilization has admired the ability to persuade others.[30] This tradition has led us to measure the success of much communication in terms of whether it changes the way others think and act. Recall, for example, what often happens when people encounter someone with differing opinions. Rather than try to understand one another, their conversation often turns into an argument or debate (sometimes friendly, and sometimes not) in which the participants try to change one another's minds.

Persuasion is certainly one important goal of communication, but it isn't the only one. Most people would agree with the principle that it's essential to understand a speaker's ideas before judging them. Despite this common-sense fact, all of us are guilty of forming snap judgments, or evaluating others before hearing them out. This tendency is greatest when the speaker's ideas conflict with our own.

It's especially tempting to counterattack when others criticize you, even when those criticisms might contain valuable truths and when understanding them might lead to a change for the better. But even when there is no criticism or disagreement, we tend to evaluate others based on sketchy first impressions, forming snap judgments that aren't at all valid. And not all premature judgments are negative. It's also possible to jump to overly favourable conclusions about the quality of a speaker's remarks when we like that person or agree with the ideas being expressed. The lesson is clear: listen first, make sure you understand, and then evaluate or argue, if you choose.

Separate the Message from the Speaker

The first recorded cases of blaming the messenger for an unpleasant message occurred in ancient Greece. When messengers would arrive reporting losses in battles, their generals were known to respond to the bad news by having the

> **informational listening**
> Listening in which the goal is to receive accurately the same thoughts the speaker is trying to convey.

> *We can communicate an idea around the world in seventy seconds but it sometimes takes years for an idea to get through [a quarter] inch of human skull.*
>
> **Charles Kettering, American inventor and founder of Delco**

The Chinese characters that make up the verb "to listen" tell us something significant about this skill.

Ear

Eyes

Undivided Attention

Heart

聽

Calligraphy by Angie Au

Cultural Idiom
write off
To dismiss as worthless or unimportant.

messengers put to death. Irrational reaction is still common (though fortunately less violent) today. Consider a few situations in which there is a tendency to get angry with a communicator bearing unpleasant news: an instructor who tries to explain why you did poorly on a major paper; a friend who explains what you did to make a fool of yourself at the party last night; the boss who points out how you could do your job better. At times like this, becoming irritated with the bearer of unpleasant information can not only cause you to miss important information but also harm your relationships.

There's a second way that confusing the message and the messenger can prevent you from understanding important ideas. At times you may mistakenly discount the value of a message because of the person who is presenting it. Even the most boring instructors, the most irritatingly responsible friends, and the most demanding bosses occasionally make good points. If you write off everything a person says before you consider it, you may be cheating yourself out of some valuable information.

Be Opportunistic

Even if you listen with an open mind, sooner or later you will find yourself hearing information that is either so unimportant or so badly delivered that you're tempted to tune out. Although making a quick escape from such tedious situations is often the best thing to do, there are times when you can profit from paying close attention to apparently worthless communication. This is especially true when you're trapped in a situation where the only alternatives to attentiveness are pseudo-listening or downright rudeness.

An opportunistic listener who is willing to invest the effort can find some value in even the worst situations. Consider how you might listen opportunistically when you find yourself locked in a boring conversation with someone whose ideas are worthless. Rather than torture yourself until escape is possible, you could keep yourself amused—and perhaps learn something useful—by listening carefully until you can answer the following (unspoken) questions:

- Is there anything useful in what this person is saying?
- What led the speaker to come up with ideas like these?
- What lessons can I learn from this person that will keep me from sounding the same way in other situations?

Listening with a constructive attitude is important, but even the best intentions won't always help you understand others. The following skills can help you figure out messages that otherwise might be confusing, as well as help you see how those messages can make a difference in your life.

Look for Key Ideas

Cultural Idiom
long-winded
To speak for a long time.

It's easy to lose patience with long-winded speakers who never seem to get to the point—or have a point, for that matter. Nevertheless, most people do have a central idea, what we call a "thesis" in Chapter 12. By using your ability to think more quickly than the speaker can talk, you may be able to extract the thesis from the surrounding mass of words you're hearing. If you can't figure out what the speaker is driving at, you can always ask in a tactful way by using the skills of questioning and paraphrasing, which we'll examine next.

Ask Questions

Questioning is about asking for additional information to clarify your idea of the sender's message. If you ask directions to a friend's house, typical questions might be "Is your place an apartment?" or "How long does it take to get there from here?" In more serious situations, questions could include "What's bothering you?" or "Why are you so angry?" or "Why is that so important?" Notice that a key element of these questions is that they ask the speaker to elaborate on information already given.

Despite the many benefits, not all questions are equally helpful. Whereas **sincere questions** are aimed at understanding others, **counterfeit questions** are really disguised attempts to send a message, not receive one. Counterfeit questions come in several varieties:

- *Questions that make statements.* "Are you serious?" "You did what?" Comments like these are certainly not genuine requests for information. Emphasizing certain words can also turn a question into a statement: "You lent money to *Tony*?" We also use questions to offer advice. The person who responds with, "Are you going to stand up to him and give him what he deserves?" clearly has stated an opinion about what should be done.
- *Questions that carry hidden agendas.* "Are you busy Friday night?" is a dangerous question to answer. If you say, "No," thinking the person has something fun in mind, you won't like hearing, "Good, because I need some help moving my piano."
- *Questions that seek "correct" answers.* Most of us have been victims of question-askers who want to hear only a particular response. "Which shoes do you think I should wear?" can be a sincere question—unless the asker has a preference you're being asked to confirm. When this happens, the asker isn't interested in listening to contrary opinions, and "incorrect" responses get shot down. Some of these questions may venture into delicate territory. "Honey, do you think I look ugly?" can be a request for a "correct" answer.
- *Questions that are based on unchecked assumptions.* "Why aren't you listening to me?" assumes the other person isn't paying attention. "What's the matter?" assumes that something is wrong. "Why don't you respond to my texts?" assumes that the other person is ignoring you, when they may, instead, simply be busy. As we explained in Chapter 2, perception-checking is a much better way of checking out assumptions: "When you kept looking over at the TV, I thought you weren't listening to me, but maybe I was wrong. Were you paying attention?"

Unlike counterfeit questions, sincere questions are genuine requests for new information that clarifies a speaker's thoughts or feelings. Although the value of sincere questioning might seem obvious, people don't use this information-seeking approach enough. Communicators are often reluctant to show their ignorance by asking for an explanation of what seems like an obvious point. At times like this, it's a good idea to recall a quote attributed to Confucius: "He who asks a question is a fool for five minutes. He who does not ask is a fool for life."

sincere question
A question posed with the genuine desire to learn from another person.

counterfeit question
A question that disguises the speaker's true motive, which does not include a genuine desire to understand the other person.

Cultural Idiom
to stand up to
To confront courageously.

shot down
To be rejected or defeated.

Paraphrase

Questioning is often a valuable tool for increasing understanding. Sometimes, however, questions won't help you understand a speaker's ideas any better. In fact, as the humorous series of drawings in Figure 5.2 suggests, questions can even lead to greater misunderstandings. Now consider another type of feedback—one that would tell you whether you understood what was said before you begin asking additional questions. This sort of feedback, termed **paraphrasing**, involves restating in your own words the message you thought the speaker had just sent, without adding anything new.

paraphrasing
Feedback in which the receiver rewords the speaker's thoughts and feelings. Can be used to verify understanding, demonstrate empathy, and help others solve their problems.

- *"So I go through the lights, just past the high school, and I'll see the arena, is that right?"*
- *"So you need me to work both this Saturday and next Saturday—right?"*
- *"When you said, 'Don't worry about the low grade on the quiz,' did you mean it won't count against my grade?"*

In other cases, a paraphrase will reflect your understanding of the speaker's feelings:

- *"You said you understand, but you look confused. Are you?"*
- *"You seem to be in a hurry. I get the idea you don't want to talk now. Is that right?"*
- *"You said 'Forget it,' but it sounds like you're mad. Are you?"*

Whether your paraphrasing reflects a speaker's thoughts or feelings, and whether it focuses on a specific comment or a general theme, the key to success is to restate the other person's comments in your own words as a way of cross-checking the information. If you simply repeat the speaker's comments verbatim, you will sound foolish—and you still might be misunderstanding what has been said. Notice the difference between simply parroting a statement and really paraphrasing:

Cultural Idiom
parroting
To repeat without understanding.

bleeding-heart liberals
Persons motivated by sympathy rather than practicality.

boosts the odds
To increase the chances of success.

SPEAKER: I'd like to go, but I can't afford it.
PARROTING: You'd like to go, but you can't afford it.
PARAPHRASING: So if we could find a way to pay for you, you'd be willing to come. Is that right?

SPEAKER: Wow, you look terrific!
PARROTING: You think I look terrific.
PARAPHRASING: You think I've lost weight?

As these examples suggest, effective paraphrasing is a skill that takes time to develop. You can make your paraphrasing sound more natural by taking any of three approaches, depending on the situation:

1. Change the speaker's wording.

SPEAKER: The gun control registry is just another failed idea of bleeding-heart liberals.

PARAPHRASE: Let me see if I've got this right: You're mad because you think having a gun control registry sounds good, but it's costly and doesn't actually help to keep guns out of the hands of criminals. [Reflects both the speaker's feeling and the reason for it.]

2. Offer an example of what you think the speaker is talking about.

When the speaker makes an abstract statement, you may suggest a specific example or two to see if your understanding is accurate.

SPEAKER: Craig is such an idiot. I mean, what was he thinking?

PARAPHRASE: You think that joke about Daria's boyfriend was pretty offensive, huh? [Reflects the listener's guess about speaker's reason for objecting to the behaviour.]

3. Reflect the underlying theme of the speaker's remarks.

When you want to summarize the theme that seems to have run through another person's conversation, a complete or partial perception check is appropriate.

PARAPHRASE: You keep reminding me to be careful. Sounds like you're worried that something might happen to me. Am I right? [Reflects both the speaker's thoughts and feelings and explicitly seeks clarification.]

Learning to paraphrase isn't easy, but it can be worth the effort, because it offers two very real advantages. First, it boosts the odds that you'll accurately and fully understand what others are saying. We've already seen that using one-way listening or even asking questions may lead you to think that you've understood a speaker when, in fact, you haven't. Paraphrasing, on the other hand, serves as a way of double-checking your interpretation for accuracy. Second, paraphrasing guides you toward sincerely trying to understand another person instead of using non-listening styles such as stage hogging, selective listening, and so on. If you force yourself to reflect the other person's ideas in your own words, you'll spend your mental energy trying to understand that speaker instead of using less constructive listening styles. For this reason, some communication experts suggest that the ratio of questioning and paraphrasing to confronting should be at least 5:1, if not more.[31]

FIGURE 5.2 Asking Questions Doesn't Guarantee Understanding

COMMUNICATION ON-SCREEN

Who's on First? (1937)

Performed by Bud Abbott and Lou Costello.

This classic comedy routine made popular in the late 1930s by Abbott and Costello illustrates the importance—and the difficulty—of informational listening. In the sketch, Costello asks Abbott to identify some of the players on his baseball team. With names like "Who" (the first baseman), "What" (the second baseman), and "I Don't Know" (the third baseman), it's easy for Costello to believe that Abbott is being evasive. Much of the humour depends on the two characters' mistaking questioning for paraphrasing, exemplified in the following exchange:

> Costello: Well, then who's playing first?
> Abbott: Yes.
> Costello: I mean the fellow's name on first base.
> Abbott: Who.
> Costello: The fellow playin' first base.
> Abbott: Who.
> Costello: The guy on first base.
> Abbott: Who is on first.
> Costello: Well, what are you askin' me for?
> Abbott: I'm not asking you—I'm telling you. Who is on first.
> Costello: I'm asking you—who's on first?
> Abbott: That's the man's name.
> Costello: That's who's name?
> Abbott: Yes.

Cultural Idiom

scramble to catch up
To begin in a hurried fashion that which should have been started sooner.

pin down
To specifically identify.

critical listening
Listening in which the goal is to judge the quality or accuracy of the speaker's remarks.

Cultural Idiom
put you off
To cause one displeasure.

Take Notes

Understanding others is crucial, of course, but comprehending their ideas doesn't guarantee that you will remember them. As you read earlier in this chapter, listeners usually forget almost two-thirds of what they hear.

Sometimes recall isn't especially important. You don't need to retain many details of the vacation adventures recounted by a neighbour or the childhood stories told by a relative. At other times, though, remembering a message—even minute details—is very important. The lectures you hear in class are an obvious example. Likewise, it can be important to remember the details of plans that involve you: the time of a future appointment, directions to a spot where you're meeting friends, or instructions given to you by a manager at work.

At times like these it's smart to take notes instead of relying on your memory. Sometimes these notes may be simple and brief: a phone number jotted on a scrap of paper or a list of things to pick up at the market. In other cases—a lecture, for example—your notes need to be much longer. When detailed notes are necessary, a few simple points will help make them effective:

1. *Don't wait too long before beginning to jot down ideas.* If you don't realize that you need to take notes until five minutes into a conversation, you're likely to forget much of what has been said and miss out on other information as you scramble to catch up.

2. *Record only key ideas.* Don't try to capture every word of a long message. If you can pin down the most important points, your notes will be easier to follow and much more useful.

3. *Develop a note-taking format.* The exact form you choose isn't important. Some people use a formal outlining scheme with headings designated by Roman numerals, letters, and numbers; others use simple lists. You might come up with useful symbols: boxes around key names and numbers or asterisks next to especially important information. Once you have developed a consistent format, your notes will help you not just to remember information but also to mould others' ideas into a shape that's useful to you.

Critical Listening

Whereas the goal of informational listening is to understand a speaker, the goal of **critical listening** (also called "evaluative listening") is to judge the quality of a message in order to decide whether to accept or reject it. At first the words "critical" and "evaluative" may put you off, because both words carry the negative connotations of carping and fault-finding. But critical listeners don't have to be hostile. Critical listening—at least in the sense we're discussing

UNDERSTANDING COMMUNICATION TECHNOLOGY

Young Adults Damaging Hearing with Poor MP3 Player Listening Habits

iPods, MP3 Players, and Recreational Music Sony Walkmans first came to the attention of the public in the early 1980s and we have had portable music ever since. The 1990s saw the introduction of portable CD players, and more recently MP3 players such as the iPod have become available. It is tempting to wonder whether listening to music with earphones is dangerous, but this is actually not the problem. The listener will always adjust the volume of their music to a comfortable listening level, and the ear does not know whether the music came from a radio loudspeaker or an earphone. There are subtle differences between loudspeakers and earphones, but nothing significant.

The issue is one of "portability." Whenever there is background noise, we prefer sound (such as speech and music) to be louder. This is called the Lombard Effect, also known as the cocktail party effect. Because of technical advancements we can now take music with us onto the subway, in our cars, when jogging beside a noisy road, and to the gym. Once there is traffic noise or other background environmental sound, the volume is turned up. When we are in environments with background noise, we tend to turn up the volume to unsafe levels. It is these unsafe levels, combined with the duration (or how long we listen to the music) that will determine safe and unsafe levels.

Most young people will agree that music needs to be loud, but the trick is that this loud music does not need to be intense. Huh? Although related, loudness and intensity are actually two different things.

Intensity relates to the physical vibration in the air and can be measured with a sound level meter, usually in a unit called a decibel (DB). Loudness is merely our subjective feeling about the intensity. While we use loudness to set the volume control of the MP3 player, it is the intensity of the music that causes

hearing loss. There is no such thing as a "loudness meter"—loudness is a very individual thing.

We know from years of research that any sound over 85 decibels can eventually cause hearing loss. It is quite amazing how quiet 85 decibels really is—a dial tone on a phone is 85 decibels. A potentially damaging noise or music level actually does not sound loud. However, it is not only the intensity (in decibels) but also how long we listen to the music. It turns out that 85 decibels for 40 hours each week is the same as 88 decibels for only 20 hours; 91 decibels for 10 hours; 94 decibels for only 5 hours; and so on. While we don't listen to music for 40 hours a week, many of us do listen for 5 or 6 hours (while on the subway or gym, for example).

Here is a guideline derived from recent research by Dr Brian Fligor of Harvard University: It is safe to listen to 120 minutes of music at 60 per cent of the volume. This is called the 120/60 rule and will provide the listener with half of their daily dose of music—you can still mow the lawn, and do other noisy things throughout the day. Moderation is also important; if your favourite song comes on, turn up the volume; just turn it back down to 60 per cent or lower, when the song ends.

April 2014, www.canadianaudiology.ca/consumer/ipods-mp3-players-and-recreational-music.html

QUESTIONS: Do you find that you listen to your MP3 player longer than recommended in this article? How has having an MP3 player affected your lifestyle and daily routine? Has it made you a better listener or less attentive to the people and things around you? Do you think that MP3 players are changing our norms about what we think is polite or rude? Are we becoming more forgiving of people who are oblivious to others while paying attention to their MP3 player?

here—involves evaluating an idea to test its merit. In this sense, we could say that non-critical listeners are unquestioning, or even naive and gullible. Critical listening is appropriate whenever someone is trying to persuade you to buy a product, to act in a certain way, or to accept a belief—to cite just a few examples. You will be most effective as a critical listener if you follow the guidelines below.

Listen for Information before Evaluating

The importance of listening for information before evaluating it seems almost too obvious to mention, yet all of us are guilty of judging a speaker's ideas before we completely understand them. The tendency to make premature judgments is especially strong when the idea conflicts with our own beliefs.

You can avoid the tendency to judge before understanding by following the simple rule of paraphrasing a speaker's ideas before responding to them. The effort required to translate the other person's ideas into your own words will keep you from arguing, and if your interpretation is mistaken, you'll know immediately.

Evaluate the Speaker's Credibility

The acceptability of an idea often depends on its source. If a long-time family friend and self-made millionaire invited you to invest your life savings in jojoba fruit futures, you might be grateful for the tip. If your deadbeat brother-in-law made the same offer, you would probably laugh off the suggestion.

Chapter 12 examines credibility in detail, but two questions provide a quick guideline for deciding whether or not to accept a speaker as an authority:

1. *Is the speaker competent*? Does the speaker have the experience or the expertise to qualify as an authority on the subject? Note that someone who is knowledgeable in one area may not be as well qualified to comment in another. For instance, the friend who can answer any question about computer programming might be a terrible adviser when the subject turns to romance.
2. *Is the speaker impartial*? Knowledge alone isn't enough to certify a speaker's ideas as acceptable. People who have a personal stake in a topic are more likely to be biased. The unqualified praise lavished on a product by a sales representative working on commission may be more suspect than the mixed review you get from a user of the same product. This doesn't mean you should disregard any comments you hear from an involved party—only that you should consider the possibility of intentional or unintentional bias.

Examine the Speaker's Evidence and Reasoning

Speakers usually offer some kind of support to back up their statements. A dealer who argues that domestic cars are just as reliable as imports might cite frequency-of-repair statistics from consumer reports or refer you to satisfied customers. A professor arguing that students don't work as hard as they used to might offer test papers or essays from now and 20 years ago to back up the thesis.

Chapter 12 describes several types of supporting material that can be used to prove a point: definitions, descriptions, analogies, statistics, and so on. Whatever form the support takes, you can ask several questions to determine the quality of a speaker's evidence and reasoning:[32]

1. *Is the evidence recent enough*? In many cases, old evidence is worthless. If the honours were earned several years ago, the cuisine from an "award-winning" restaurant may be barely edible today. The claim "Tony's a terrible goalie" may have been true in the past, but people do change. Before you accept even the most credible evidence, be sure it isn't obsolete.
2. *Is enough evidence presented*? One or two pieces of support may be exceptions and not conclusive evidence. You might have heard this example of generalizing from limited evidence: "I never wear seat belts. I knew somebody who wasn't wearing his seatbelt in an accident, and his life was saved because he was thrown clear from the car." Although not wearing seat belts might have been safer in this instance, experts agree that when you consider all vehicle accidents, the chances of avoiding serious injury are much greater if you wear a seat belt.

3. *Is the evidence from a reliable source*? Even a large amount of recent evidence may be worthless if the source is weak. Your cousin the health-food fanatic might not have the qualifications to talk about the poisonous effects of commercially farmed vegetables; the opinion of an impartial physician, nutritionist, or toxologist would carry more weight. And if someone recommends a new cure for headaches that they read about on the Web, be sure to ask them for the specific source. There is no doubt that much useful information can be found from reputable sites on the internet; the trick is distinguishing it from the specious information disseminated on the greater number of sites of dubious credibility.

4. *Can the evidence be interpreted in more than one way*? A piece of evidence that supports one claim might also support others. For example, you might hear someone cite statistics showing women are underrepresented in the management of a company as evidence of a conspiracy to exclude them from positions of power. The same statistics, though, could have other explanations: perhaps fewer women have been with the company long enough to be promoted, or perhaps this is a field that has not attracted large numbers of women. Alternative explanations don't necessarily mean that the one being argued is wrong, but they do raise questions that need to be answered before you accept an argument.

Besides taking a close look at the evidence a speaker presents, a critical listener will look at how that evidence is put together to prove a point. Logicians have identified a number of *logical fallacies*—errors in reasoning that can lead to false conclusions. Logicians have identified over 100 fallacies;[33] some of the common ones are discussed in Chapter 11.

YOUNG COMMUNICATOR PROFILE

EMILY MORRICE

Blogger, *Our Nest in the City*; Christian Missionary & Church Planter

Studying human communication opened my eyes to the various media and styles of communication and how the transmitted message can be interpreted and understood in many diverse ways. My focus on mass communication and cultural studies enabled me to learn how a message communicated in one culture can be interpreted radically differently when communicated to someone from another culture. The same is true of mass communication versus communicating to a handful of people. This is monumentally beneficial in my career with an international faith-based NGO, in my work as a mommy blogger with 15,000 hits per month, and as an entrepreneur with a new Etsy store.

On a daily basis I engage with people from all over the world from very diverse cultural and religious backgrounds, and my training in human communication has helped me adapt to and understand the different elements of their perspectives. Whether it be cultural location, language, the power of a family or diaspora's influence, university students travel through many gatekeeping layers to experience and discover a personal faith. At the root of my job is being a good critical and empathic listener. Those are both skills that you can learn using, as long as you take communication seriously! My job educating and guiding these students depends on me being a great communicator and listening to really understand students with strong heritage ties to their roots in Quebec, North Africa, the Caribbean, Southeast Asia, and beyond.

CRITICAL THINKING PROBE

Understanding and Evaluating

Think of three recent incidents when trying to understand the other person would have been the most appropriate listening style. Then think of three *different* situations in which an evaluative approach would have been the most appropriate way to listen.

Based on your conclusions (and perhaps those of your classmates), develop a set of guidelines describing when it's best to listen purely for information, suspending judgment and attempting to uncritically understand another person's point of view. Next, describe the circumstances when it is more appropriate to listen and evaluate.

Examine Emotional Appeals

Sometimes emotion alone may be enough to persuade you. You might "lend" your friend $20 just for old time's sake, even though you don't expect to see the money again soon. In other cases, it's a mistake to let yourself be swayed by emotion when the logic of a point isn't sound. The excitement or fun in an ad or the lure of low monthly payments probably aren't good enough reasons to buy a product you can't afford. The fallacies described in Chapter 11 will help you recognize flaws in emotional appeals.

Empathic Listening

We listen both critically and for information out of self-interest. In **empathic listening**, however, the goal is to build a relationship or to help the speaker solve a problem.[34] Empathic listening is the approach to use when others seek help for personal dilemmas. Sometimes the problem is a big one: "I want to end the relationship, but I don't know the best way to do it." At other times the problem is more modest: "I can't decide whether to get her the earrings or a new iPod." Empathic listening is also a good approach to take when you simply want to become better acquainted with others and show them that their opinions and feelings matter to you.

The two goals of helping others and building a relationship aren't mutually exclusive. Empathic listening can accomplish both of them, because when listening helps another person, the relationship between that person and the listener improves.[35] For example, couples who communicate in ways that show they understand one another's feelings and ideas are more satisfied with their marriages than couples who express less understanding. The opposite is also true: in marriages where husbands do not give emotional responses to their wives, the stress level grows.

Whatever the relationship and topic, there are several styles by which you can respond empathically to another person's remarks.[36] Each of these styles has its advantages and disadvantages. As you read them, you can aim toward choosing the best style for the situation at hand.

Advising

When approached with another's problem, the most common tendency is to try to help by offering a solution—in other words, by **advising**.[37] Although such a response is sometimes valuable, often it isn't as helpful as you might think.[38] In fact, researchers have discovered that advice is actually unhelpful at least as often as it is helpful.[39]

There are several reasons why advice doesn't work especially well. First, it can be hard to tell when the person with the problem wants to hear the listener's idea of a solution.[40] Sometimes the request is clear: "What do you think I should do?" At other times, though, it isn't clear whether certain statements are requests for direct advice. Ambiguous statements include requests for opinions ("What do you think of Paolo?"), attempts to solicit information ("Would that be an invasion of privacy?"), and announcements of a problem ("I'm really confused about . . .").

empathic listening
Listening in which the goal is to help the speaker solve a problem.

advising
A helping response in which the receiver offers suggestions about how the speaker should deal with a problem.

Even when someone with a problem asks for advice, offering it may not be helpful. Your suggestion may not offer the best course to follow, in which case it can even be harmful. There's often a temptation to tell others how we would behave in their place, but it's important to realize that what's right for one person may not be right for another. A related consequence of advising is that it often allows others to avoid responsibility for their decisions. Someone who follows a suggestion of yours that doesn't work out can always pin the blame on you. Finally, in many cases people simply don't want advice: they may not be ready to accept it, and what they might really need is to talk out their thoughts and feelings.

Advice is most welcome under two conditions: when it has been requested and when the adviser seems concerned with respecting the face needs of the recipient.[41]

Before offering advice, you need to be sure that four conditions are present:

1. *Be confident that the advice is correct.* You may be certain about some matters of fact, such as the guidelines for completing a course assignment or the cost of a product you recently had to buy, but resist the temptation to act like an authority on matters you know little about. It is both unfair and unwise to make a suggestion when you aren't positive that it's the best choice. Realize that just because a course of action worked for you doesn't guarantee that it will work for everybody.
2. *Ask yourself whether the person seeking your advice seems willing to accept it.* In this way you can avoid the frustration of making good suggestions only to find that the person with the problem had another solution in mind all the time.
3. *Be certain that the receiver won't blame you if the advice doesn't work out.* You may be offering the suggestions, but the choice and responsibility for accepting them are up to the recipient of your advice.
4. *Deliver your advice supportively, in a face-saving manner.* Advice that is perceived as being offered constructively, in the context of a solid relationship, is much better than critical comments offered in a way that signals a lack of respect for the receiver.[42]

Judging

A **judging** response evaluates the sender's thoughts or behaviours in some way. The judgment may be favourable—"That's a good idea" or "You're on the right track now"—or unfavourable—"That kind of attitude won't get you anywhere." But in either case it implies that the person doing the judging is in some way qualified to pass judgment on the speaker's thoughts or behaviours.

Cultural Idiom
pin the blame on
To claim the fault lies elsewhere.

judging
A reaction in which the receiver evaluates the sender's message either favourably or unfavourably.

Sometimes negative judgments are purely critical. How many times have you heard a response like "Well, you asked for it!" or "I told you so!" or "You're just feeling sorry for yourself."? Although comments like these can sometimes serve as verbal slaps that bring problemholders to their senses, they usually make matters worse.

At other times negative judgments are less critical. These involve what we usually call *constructive criticism*, which is intended to help the problem-holder improve in the future. This is the sort of response given by friends about everything from the choice of clothing to the choice of friends. Another common setting for constructive criticism occurs in school, where instructors evaluate students' work to help them master concepts and skills. But whether it's justified or not, even constructive criticism runs the risk of arousing defensiveness because it may threaten the self-concept of the person at whom it is directed.

Judgments have the best chance of being received well when two conditions exist:

1. *The person with the problem should have requested an evaluation from you.* An unsolicited judgment is often likely to trigger a defensive response. But if the person is an employee receiving feedback from a superior or an athlete taking tips from a coach or trainer, the judgment is a natural part of improving one's performance and should be expected, even if it hasn't been asked for.

2. *Your judgment is genuinely constructive and not designed as a put-down.* If you are tempted to use judgments as a weapon, don't fool yourself into thinking that you are being helpful. Often the statement "I'm telling you this for your own good" simply isn't true.

If you can remember to follow these two guidelines, your judgments will probably be less frequent and better received.

Analyzing

In an **analyzing** statement, the listener offers an interpretation of a speaker's message. Analyses like these are probably familiar to you:

- "I think what's really bothering you is . . ."
- "She's only doing it because . . ."
- "I don't think you really meant . . ."
- "Maybe the problem started when he . . ."

Interpretations are effective when they help people with problems consider alternative meanings—meanings they would never have thought of without your help. Sometimes a clear analysis will make a confusing problem suddenly clear, either suggesting a solution or at least providing an understanding of what is occurring.

At other times, analysis can create more problems than it solves. There are two problems with analyzing. First, your interpretation may not be correct, in which case it will not help and may create new problems. Second, even if your interpretation is correct, expressing it may not be useful. There's a chance that it will arouse defensiveness (because an accurate assessment implies superiority and judgment); and even if it doesn't, the person may not be able to understand your view of the problem without working it out personally.

How can you know when it's helpful to offer an analysis? There are several guidelines to follow:

1. *Offer your interpretation in a tentative way, not as absolute fact.* There's a big difference between saying, "Maybe the reason is . . ." or "It seems to me that . . ." and insisting "Here's where your problem is. . . ."
2. *Your analysis ought to have a reasonable chance of being correct.* An inaccurate interpretation—especially one that sounds plausible—can leave a person more confused than before.
3. *Be sure that the other person will be receptive to your analysis.* Even if you're completely accurate, your thoughts won't help if the problem-holder isn't ready to consider them.
4. *Be sure that your real motive for offering an analysis is to help the other person.* It can be tempting to offer an analysis to show how brilliant you are or even to make the other person feel bad for not having thought of the right answer in the first place. Needless to say, an analysis offered under such conditions isn't helpful.

Questioning

Earlier on in this chapter we talked about **questioning** as one way to understand others better. A questioning response can also be a way to help others think about their problems and understand them more clearly.[43] For example, questioning can help a problem-holder define vague ideas more precisely. You might respond to a friend with a line of questioning: "You said Patrice has been acting 'differently' toward you lately. What has she been doing?" Here's another example of a question that helps clarify: "You told your roommates you wanted them to help out more around the apartment. What would you like them to do?"

Questions can also encourage a problem-holder to examine a situation in more detail by talking either about what happened or about personal feelings; for example, "How did you feel when they turned you down? What did you do then?" This type of questioning is particularly helpful when you are dealing with someone who is quiet or is unwilling under the circumstances to talk about the problem very much.

Although questions have the potential to be helpful, they also run the risk of confusing or distracting the person with the problem. The best questioning follows these principles:

1. *Don't ask questions just to satisfy your own curiosity.* You might become so interested in the other person's story that you want to hear more. "And then what did he say?" you might be tempted to ask. "What happened next?" Responding to questions like these might confuse the person with the problem, or even leave him or her more agitated than before.

questioning
Feedback that usually requests the speaker to supply additional information in order to clarify or expand the receiver's understanding. Also, a style of helping in which the receiver seeks additional information from the sender. Some questioning responses are really disguised advice.

Cultural Idiom
turned you down
Your request or offer was rejected.

2. *Be sure your questions won't confuse or distract the person you're trying to help.* For instance, asking someone, "When did the problem begin?" might provide some clue about how to solve it—but it could also lead to a long digression that would only confuse matters. As with advice, it's important to be sure you're on the right track before asking questions.

3. *Don't use questions to disguise your suggestions or criticism.* We've all been questioned by parents, teachers, or other figures who seemed to be trying to trap us or indirectly to guide us. In this way, questioning becomes a strategy used by a questioner who already has some idea of what direction the discussion should take but isn't willing to tell you directly.

Supporting

> **supporting**
> A response style in which the receiver reassures, comforts, or distracts the person seeking help.

A **supporting** response can take several forms:

AGREEMENT: "You're right—the landlord is being unfair."
"Yeah, I thought that class was never going to end."

UNDERSTANDING COMMUNICATION TECHNOLOGY

Digital Distraction

How many times have you gone to a lecture only to find you're watching the YouTube video the person sitting in front of you is watching instead of listening to the professor's lecture? Active listening is crucial for understanding and retaining lecture material, and most of us can agree that laptops can be a distraction in a classroom. At the same time, access to the internet can mean new ways of learning and participating. Professor Terence Day discusses the pros and cons of laptop use in the classroom. Read his article and see if you are for using laptops or for banning them.

Our students must be paying attention in class because they're busily using their laptops to type every word from our lectures. Or maybe not.

A quick look from the back of university and college lecture theatres shows that many students with wireless laptops are engaged in non-academic activities, including instant messaging, checking e-mails, playing games, and social networking on sites such as Facebook.

Some faculty members have dealt with this situation by imposing outright bans on laptops in classrooms. But Canadian universities and colleges have spent millions of dollars on wireless networks, so a total ban seems counterproductive or at least a waste of resources.

Perhaps surprisingly, the relative advantages and disadvantages of wireless laptops in the classroom are still being debated in the educational research literature. Anecdotally, stories of students misusing the technology are legion. Jean

Boivin, an economics professor at Montreal's *École des Hautes études Commerciales*, for example, was shocked when he read in a newspaper article that one of his students had lost thousands of dollars day-trading from a wireless laptop in his classroom.

Guy Plourde, a chemistry professor at the University of Northern British Columbia, is likely typical of many faculty members who'd like to see a complete ban on laptops. He says he's frustrated when students—heads raised briefly from their computers—want him to repeat what he said because they didn't pay attention the first time.

Concerns are also being voiced by students themselves. Dawn Lomas of the Learning Success Centre at Ryerson University and Michael Howard of the Economics Department at the University of Waterloo have both received complaints from students who say they couldn't concentrate in class because other students around them were using their laptops to play games or watch DVDs.

Despite this, most students don't appear to support a total laptop ban. Laurie Harrison, the ombudsperson at Simon Fraser University, has fielded several complaints from students after their professor banned laptops in the classroom.

So what are the alternatives? Margaret Wilson, coordinator of university teaching services at the University of Alberta, suggests that it is best to deal with distractive students individually. Request that they refrain from disturbing others during class and if their actions continue then the professor may appropriately ask them to leave.

OFFERS TO HELP:	"I'm here if you need me."
	"Let me try to explain it to him."
PRAISE:	"I don't care what the boss said: I think you did a great job!"
	"You're amazing, and if he doesn't recognize it, that's his problem."
REASSURANCE:	"The worst part is over. It will probably get easier from here."
	"I know you'll do a great job."
DIVERSION:	"Let's catch a movie and get your mind off this."
	"That reminds me of the time we . . ."
ACKNOWLEDGEMENT:	"I can see that really hurts."
	"I know how important that was to you."
	"It's no fun to feel unappreciated."

There's no question about the value of receiving support when faced with personal problems. "Comforting ability" and social support have been shown to be among the most important communication skills a friend—or a teacher or a parent—can have.[44] In other instances,

But the deeper issue, say most experts, is that students need to be actively engaged in their learning. Teresa Dawson, director of the Learning and Teaching Centre at the University of Victoria, suggests faculty employ such active-learning approaches as shared exercises, problem-based learning and the new clicker technologies that allow simultaneous class response to questions. "Kinesthetic learners, in particular, need to be active in class and so if we make them sit passively it is harder for them to learn," she says.

And faculty members can integrate laptops into that active learning. Gary Poole, director of the Centre for Teaching and Academic Growth at the University of British Columbia, believes that it is important for faculty members to "bring activities to class that invite the constructive use of internet connections and feature measures of accountability for that use."

For example, students can be asked to work in groups to either solve a problem requiring internet access or to find a resource on the Web that is relevant to a topic at hand. "Each group would then be responsible for reporting to the class and perhaps displaying their findings," he says. Others suggest that it may be appropriate to have laptop-free periods without necessarily having a complete ban.

Which leads to what I believe is the best suggestion, from Tracy Roberts, an instructional designer with the Centre for Teaching and Educational Technologies at Royal Roads University: have the students come up with the policy, and develop an agreement with them. This approach is consistent with the fact that universities and colleges across Canada increasingly encourage students to take responsibility for their own learning. Students are the ones most affected by both digital distractions and laptop bans. It makes sense to include them in the decision-making process.

So, at the beginning of the semester, I brought up the laptop issue in my first-year physical geography class. At first the students didn't see the point of having the discussion. But once we got beyond the idea of students having "the right" to bring laptops into the classroom, and whether that right was absolute even if it affected the people around them, the discussion became more productive.

We discussed, for example, whether it was better for people with laptops to sit in a special section of the room so that they wouldn't affect other people. Not only was it a useful discussion on laptops, it also helped to frame issues such as the importance of class attendance, respect for other students, and readiness to actively participate in class. Try it, and let me know how it goes.

Terence Day, universityaffairs.ca, 5 November 2007

QUESTIONS: Do you think that banning laptops will improve students' listening in lecture? Or are these students just employing a different technique of listening, more appropriate to their lifestyles and thinking processes? Do you find that having your laptop open during lecture or class is distracting to you? Try shutting it down and just using paper for a week to see if that makes a difference.

this kind of comment isn't helpful at all; in fact, it can even make things worse. Telling a person who is obviously upset that everything is all right or joking about a serious matter can trivialize the problem. People might see your comment as a put-down, leaving them feeling worse than before.

As with the other styles we'll discuss, supporting can be helpful, but only in certain circumstances.[45] For the occasions when supporting is an appropriate response, follow these guidelines:

1. *Make sure your expression of support is sincere.* Phony agreement or encouragement is probably worse than no support at all, because it adds the insult of your dishonesty to whatever pain the other person is already feeling.
2. *Be sure the other person can accept your support.* Sometimes we become so upset that we aren't ready or able to hear anything positive.

Even if your advice, judgments, and analysis are correct and your questions are sincere, and even if your support comes from the best motives, these responses often fail to help. One recent survey demonstrates how poorly such traditional responses work.[46] Mourners who had recently suffered the death of a loved one reported that 80 per cent of the statements made to them were unhelpful. Nearly half of the statements were advice: "You've got to get out more;" or "Don't question God's will." Despite their frequency, these responses were helpful only three per cent of the time. The next most frequent response was reassurance, such as "She's out of pain now." Like advice, this kind of support was helpful only three per cent of the time. Far more helpful were expressions that acknowledged the mourner's feelings.

One American Red Cross grief counsellor explained to survivors of the September 11 terrorist attacks in New York that simply being present can be more helpful than trying to reassure grief-stricken family members who had lost loved ones in the tragedy:

> Listen. Don't say anything. Saying "it'll be okay," or "I know how you feel" can backfire. Right now that's not what a victim wants to hear. They want to know people are there and care about them. Be there, be present, listen. The clergy refer to it as a "ministry of presence." You don't need to do anything, just be there or have them know you're available.[47]

Prompting

Advising, judging, analyzing, questioning, and supporting are all active approaches to helping that call for a great deal of input from the respondent. Another approach to problem-solving is more passive. **Prompting** involves using silences and brief statements of encouragement to draw others out as a way to help them solve their own problems. Consider this example:

IBRAHIM: Elena's dad is selling his laptop for only $1200, but if I want it I have to buy it now. He's got another interested buyer. It's a great deal, and he's only had it a year. But buying it would wipe out my savings. At the rate I spend money, it would take me a year to save up this much again.

VESNA: Uh huh.

IBRAHIM: I wouldn't be able to take that ski trip over reading week . . . but I sure could save time with a faster machine. That computer I'm using now is so out of date.

VESNA: That's for sure.

prompting
Using silence and brief statements of encouragement to draw out a speaker.

Understanding Diversity

School's Playground Planning Includes Hearing-Impaired Kids

When children from Saskatoon's St. Philip School choose equipment for their community playground, they'll give some extra consideration to their playmates with hearing impairment. Pupils at the school will get to vote next month on the climbing structures, swings, and slides community members will erect this fall in the spot where aging equipment now stands.

Even the pre-readers will get to vote by placing stickers on posters with their favourite equipment, a process dubbed "dot-mocracy," said Ryan Lacoursiere, a member of the parents' committee that has been working for two years to raise money and community participation.

"It's kind of a grassroots movement. The idea is to get the community involved. Get your neighbours out helping, inspire others to realize we all have the power, we all have a voice if we work together. Hopefully we can inspire our kids to see they can achieve great things too," he said. "It will develop a sense of ownership and pride in the project to maintain it and protect it for years to come."

The school community has a heightened awareness of hearing impairment because the division's itinerant teachers, who specialize in working with deaf and hard of hearing students, make their home base at St. Philip and nine children at the school have hearing loss, said Donella Hoffman, a spokesperson for the Greater Saskatoon Catholic Schools division. "It's a new playground for the community and they want to make sure they include all the children," Hoffman said.

Lacoursiere said dry-eraser boards could be posted on the site to help with communication and steel equipment could be chosen over plastic or wood because the metal vibrates, providing another sensation and mode of communication. The St. Philip's committee got together to fill out numerous lengthy funding applications.

They were thrilled to learn their project was chosen by Let Them Be Kids, a national charity that helps fund playground construction. That application included a telephone conference call with the committee and some children who will use the park. One hearing impaired student joined the call using the Skype computer program and a local interpreter.

Let Them Be Kids will match locally raised funds for the playground, which could have a six-figure price tag, Lacoursiere said. The committee has already raised almost $24,000 and is "reaching for the stars," with a goal of $75,000 to $80,000 to be raised locally, he said. Events include bingos, a casino night, a student art auction, and steak nights. "If we wanted to make this happen, we had to take it upon ourselves."

Betty Ann Adam, *The StarPhoenix*, 23 May 2013

QUESTIONS: How does this story reflect the diverse concepts of listening described in this chapter, as well as literal issues of hearing? How are "hearing" and "listening" different?

IBRAHIM: You think I should buy it?

VESNA: I don't know. What do you think?

IBRAHIM: I just can't decide.

VESNA: [silence]

IBRAHIM: I'm going to do it. I'll never get a deal like this again.

Prompting works especially well when you can't help others make a decision. At times like this your presence can act like a catalyst to help others find their own answers. Prompting will work best when it's done sincerely. Your non-verbal behaviours—eye contact, posture, facial expression, tone of voice—have to show that you are concerned with the other person's problem. Mechanical prompting is likely to irritate instead of help.

Paraphrasing

Earlier we discussed the value of paraphrasing to understand others. The same skill can be used as a helping tool. When you use this approach, be sure to reflect both the thoughts and the feelings you hear being expressed. This conversation between two friends shows how reflecting can offer support and help a person find the answer to her own problem:

ANNELISA: I've had the strangest feeling about my boss lately.

VISHAL: What's that? [A simple question invites Jen to go on.]

ANNELISA: I'm starting to think maybe he has this thing about women—or maybe it's just about me.

VISHAL: You mean he's coming on to you? [Vishal paraphrases what he thinks Annelisa has said.]

ANNELISA: Oh no, not at all! But it seems like he doesn't take women—or at least me—seriously. [Annelisa corrects Vishal's misunderstanding and explains herself.]

VISHAL: What do you mean? [Vishal asks another simple question to get more information.]

ANNELISA: Well, whenever we're in a meeting or just talking around the office and he asks for ideas, he always seems to pick men. He gives orders to women—men, too—but he never asks the women to say what they think.

VISHAL: So you think maybe he doesn't take women seriously, is that it? [Vishal paraphrases Annelisa's last statement.]

ANNELISA: Yeah. Well, he sure doesn't seem interested in their ideas. But that doesn't mean he's a total woman-hater or a male chauvinist pig. I know he counts on some women in the office. Our accountant Teresa has been there forever, and he's always saying he couldn't live without her. And when Brenda got the new computer system up and running last month, I know he appreciated that. He gave her a day off and told everybody how she saved our lives.

VISHAL: Now you sound confused. [Reflects her apparent feeling.]

ANNELISA: I am confused. I don't think it's just my imagination. I mean I'm a good producer, but he has never—not once—asked me for my ideas about how to improve sales or anything. And I can't remember a time when he's asked any other women. But maybe I'm overreacting.

VISHAL: You're not positive whether you're right, but I can tell that this has you concerned. [Vishal paraphrases both Annelisa's central theme and her feeling.]

ANNELISA: Yes. But I don't know what to do about it.

VISHAL: Maybe you should . . . [Starts to offer advice but catches himself and decides to ask a sincere question instead.] So what are your choices?

ANNELISA: Well, I could just ask him if he's aware that he never asks women's opinions. But that might sound too aggressive and angry.

VISHAL: And you're not angry? [Tries to clarify how Annelisa is feeling.]

ANNELISA: Not really. I don't know whether I should be angry because he's not taking ideas seriously, or whether he just doesn't take my ideas seriously, or whether it's nothing at all.

VISHAL: So you're mostly confused. [Reflects Annelisa's apparent feeling again.]

ANNELISA: Yes! I don't know where I stand with my boss, and not being sure is starting to get to me. I wish I knew what he thinks of me. Maybe I could just tell him I'm confused about what's going on here and ask him to clear it up. But what if it's nothing? Then I'll look insecure.

VISHAL: [Vishal thinks Annelisa should confront her boss, but he isn't positive that this is the best approach, so he paraphrases what Annelisa seems to be saying.] And that would make you look bad.

ANNELISA: I'm afraid maybe it would. I wonder if I could talk it over with anybody else in the office and get their ideas.

VISHAL: See what they think. . . .

ANNELISA: Yeah. Maybe I could ask Brenda. She's easy to talk to, and I do respect her judgment. Maybe she could give me some ideas about how to handle this.

VISHAL: Sounds like you're comfortable with talking to Brenda first.

ANNELISA: (warming to the idea.) Yes! Then if it's nothing, I can calm down. But if I do need to talk to the boss, I'll know I'm doing the right thing.

VISHAL: Great. Let me know how it goes.

Reflecting a speaker's ideas and feelings in this way can be surprisingly helpful.[48] First, paraphrasing helps the problem-holder sort out the problem. In the dialogue you just read, Vishal's paraphrasing helped Annelisa pin down the real source of her concern: what her boss thinks of her, not whether he doesn't take women seriously. The clarity that comes from this sort of perspective can make it possible to find solutions that weren't apparent before. Paraphrasing is also helpful because it helps the problem-holder unload more of the concerns he or she has been carrying around, often leading to the relief that comes from catharsis. Finally, listeners who reflect the speaker's thoughts and feelings (instead of judging or analyzing, for example) show their involvement and concern.

Paraphrasing can be helpful, but it is no panacea. A study by noted researcher John Gottman revealed that "active listening" (a term sometimes used to describe paraphrasing) by itself was not a trait that distinguished happily married couples from troubled ones.[49] Because empathy is the ingredient that makes paraphrasing thoughts and feelings helpful, it is a mistake to think of reflective listening as a technique that you can use mechanically. Carl Rogers, the psychologist generally considered the foremost advocate of active listening, made the case against mechanical paraphrasing strongly: "I am not trying to 'reflect feelings.' I am trying to determine whether my understanding of the client's inner world is correct—whether I am seeing it as he or she is experiencing it at this moment."[50] In other words, reflecting is not an end in itself; rather, it is one way to help others by understanding them better.

There are several factors to consider before you decide to paraphrase:

1. *Is the problem complex enough?* Sometimes people are simply looking for information and not trying to work out their feelings. At times like this, paraphrasing would be out of place. If someone asks you for the time of day, you'd do better simply to give her the information than to respond by saying, "You want to know what time it is." If you're fixing dinner, and someone wants to know when it will be ready, it would be exasperating to reply "You're interested in knowing when we'll be eating."

2. *Do you have the necessary time and concern?* The kind of paraphrasing we've been discussing here takes a good deal of time. If you're in a hurry to do something besides listen, it's wise to avoid starting a conversation you won't be able to finish. Even more

important than time is concern. It's not necessarily wrong to be too preoccupied to help or even to be unwilling to exert the considerable effort that active listening requires. You can't help everyone with every problem. It's far better to state honestly that you're unable or unwilling to help than to pretend to care when you really don't.

3. *Are you genuinely interested in helping the other person*? Sometimes as you listen to others, it's easy to relate their thoughts to your own life or to seek more information just to satisfy your own curiosity. Remember that paraphrasing is a way of helping someone else. The general obligation to reciprocate the other person's self-disclosure with information of your own isn't necessary when the goal is to solve a problem. Research shows that speakers who reveal highly intimate personal information don't expect, or even appreciate, the same kind of disclosure from a conversational partner.[51] Rather, the most competent and socially attractive response is one that sticks to the same topic but is lower in intimacy. In other words, when we are opening up to others, we don't appreciate their pulling a conversational take-away such as "*You're* worried? So am I! Let me tell you about how *I* feel. . . ."

4. *Can you withhold judgment*? You've already seen that paraphrasing allows other people to find their own answers. You should use this style only if you can comfortably paraphrase without injecting your own judgments. It's sometimes tempting to rephrase others' comments in a way that leads them toward the solution you think is best without ever clearly stating your intentions. As you will read in Chapter 7, this kind of strategy is likely to backfire by causing defensiveness if it's discovered. If you think the situation meets the criteria for advice described earlier in this chapter, you should offer your suggestions openly.

5. *Is your paraphrasing in proportion to other responses*? Although active listening can be a very helpful way of responding to others' problems, it can become artificial and annoying when it's overused. This is especially true if you suddenly begin to use it as a major response. Even if such responses are potentially helpful, this sudden switch in your behaviour will be so out of character that others might find it distracting. A far better way to use paraphrasing is to gradually introduce it into your repertoire of helpfulness, so that you can become comfortable with it without appearing too awkward. Another way to become more comfortable with this style is to start using it on real but relatively minor problems, so that you'll be more adept at knowing how and when to use it when a big crisis does occur.

When and How to Help

Before committing yourself to helping another person—even someone in obvious distress—make sure your help is welcome. There are many cases in which others prefer to keep their concerns to themselves. In these cases your efforts to get involved may not be useful and can even be harmful. In one survey, some people reported occasions when social support wasn't necessary because they felt capable of handling the problem by themselves.[52] Many regarded uninvited help as an intrusion, and some said it left them feeling more nervous than before. The majority of respondents expressed a preference for being in control of whether their distressing situation should be discussed with even the most helpful friend.

When help is welcome, there is no single best way to provide it. Research shows that all styles can help others accept their situation, feel better, and have a sense of control over their problems.[53] But there is enormous variability in which style will work with a given person.[54] This fact explains why communicators who are able to use a wide variety of helping styles are usually more effective than those who rely on just one or two styles.[55]

You can boost the odds of choosing the best helping style in each situation by considering three factors. First, think about the situation and match your response to the nature of the problem. Sometimes people need your advice. At other times they will find your encouragement and support most helpful, and at still other times they will benefit most from your analysis or judgment. And, as you have seen, there are times when others can find their own answer with help from your probes and paraphrasing.

Second, besides considering the situation, you should think about the other person when deciding which style to use. Some people are able to consider advice thoughtfully, whereas others use suggestions to avoid making their own decisions. Many communicators are extremely defensive and aren't capable of receiving analysis or judgments without lashing out. Still others aren't equipped to think through problems clearly enough to profit from paraphrasing and probing. Sophisticated helpers choose a style that fits the person.

Third, think about yourself when deciding how to respond. Most of us instinctively use one or two helping styles. You may be best at listening quietly, offering a prompt from time to time. Or perhaps you are especially insightful and can offer a truly useful analysis of the problem. Of course, it's also possible to rely on a response style that is unhelpful. You may be overly judgmental or too eager to advise, even when your suggestions aren't invited or productive. As you think about how to respond to another's problems, consider both your strengths and weaknesses.

Summary

Even the best message is useless if it goes unreceived or if it is misunderstood. For this reason, listening—the process of understanding the full meaning of an oral message—is a vitally important part of the communication process. We began our look at the subject by identifying and refuting several myths about listening. Our conclusion here was that effective listening is a skill that needs to be developed in order for us to be truly effective in understanding others.

We next took a close look at five steps in the process of listening: hearing, attending, understanding, responding, and remembering. We described some of the challenges that make effective listening so difficult. We described seven faulty listening behaviours and 10 more reasons why people often listen poorly. You can become a better listener by recognizing which of these tendencies characterize your communication.

This chapter also discussed several personal listening styles: content-oriented, people-oriented, action-oriented, and time-oriented. The chapter pointed out that most people favour one of these styles and that problems arise when different types of listeners interact. All of these styles have advantages and drawbacks, and effective listeners will use each one when it is most appropriate for the circumstances.

The chapter continued by examining three types of listening. Informational listening is the proper approach to take when the goal is to understand another person's ideas. Information can be best gained with an active approach to listening. This active approach can involve either questioning or paraphrasing—restating the speaker's message in your own words.

Critical listening is appropriate when the goal is to judge the quality of an idea. A critical analysis will be most successful when the listener ensures correct understanding of a message before passing judgment, when the speaker's credibility is taken into account, when the quality of supporting evidence is examined, and when the logic of the speaker's arguments is carefully assessed.

The aim of empathic listening is to help the speaker, not the receiver. Various helping responses include advising, judging, analyzing, questioning, supporting, prompting, and paraphrasing the speaker's thoughts and feelings. Listeners can be most helpful when they use a variety of styles, focus on the emotional dimensions of a message, and avoid being too judgmental.

Key Terms

action-oriented listening   184

advising   194

ambushing   173

analyzing   196

attending   170

content-oriented listening   183

counterfeit question   187

critical listening   190

defensive listening   172

empathic listening   172

hearing   169

informational listening   185

insensitive listening   173

insulated listening   173

judging   195

listening   169

paraphrasing   188

people-oriented listening   184

prompting   200

pseudo-listening   172

questioning   197

remembering   170

residual message   170

responding   170

selective listening   172

sincere question   187

stage hogging   173

supporting   198

time-oriented listening   184

understanding   170

Activities

A. Your LQ (Listening Quotient)

Explain the poor listening behaviours listed on pages 172–3 to someone who knows you well. Then ask him or her to describe which, if any of them, you use. Also explore the consequences of your listening behaviour.

B. Your Listening Style Preferences

You can analyze your effectiveness as a listener by answering the following questions:

1. Which of the listening styles described earlier do you use?

2. Does your listening style change in various situations, or do you use the same style most or all of the time?

3. What are the consequences (beneficial and harmful) of the listening styles you use?

4. How could you adapt your listening styles to improve your communication effectiveness?

C. Informational Listening Practice

Effective informational listening isn't easy. It takes hard work and concentration. You can improve your skill in this important area and convince yourself of the difference good informational listening makes by following these steps:

1. Find a partner with whom you have an important relationship. This may be a family member, lover, friend, fellow worker, or even an "enemy" with whom you interact frequently.

2. Invite your partner to explain his or her side of an issue that the two of you have difficulty discussing. Your job during this conversation is to understand your partner. You should not even attempt to explain your position. (If you find the prospect of trying to understand the other person distressing, consider how this attitude might interfere with your ability to listen carefully.)

3. As your partner explains his or her point of view, use the skills outlined on pages 185–200 to help you understand. You can discover how well you are grasping your partner's position by occasionally paraphrasing what you think he or she is saying. If your partner verifies your paraphrase as correct, go on with the conversation. If not, try to listen again and play back the message until your partner confirms your understanding.

4. After the conversation is over, ask yourself the following questions:
   a. As you listened, how accurate was your first understanding of the speaker's statements?
   b. How did your understanding of the speaker's position change after you used paraphrasing?
   c. Did you find that the gap between your position and that of your partner narrowed as a result of you both using paraphrasing?
   d. How did you feel at the end of your conversation? How does this feeling compare to your usual emotional state after discussing controversial issues with others?
   e. How might your life change if you used paraphrasing at home? At work? With friends?
   f. See how many pieces of information you can elicit from others by giving out the minimal pieces of information. See how many pieces of information you can elicit from a stranger whom you meet on campus.

Write down what you've learned immediately after having each conversation. See what patterns emerge in the types of people you are most capable of empathizing with and of getting to open up to you and which ones seem unreachable to you.

D. Empathic Response Styles

This exercise will help you improve your ability to listen empathically in the most successful manner. For each of the following statements:

1. Write separate responses, using each of the following styles:
   advising,
   judging,
   analyzing,
   questioning,
   supporting,
   prompting, and
   paraphrasing.

2. Discuss the pros and cons of using each response style.

3. Identify which response seems most effective, explaining your decision.
   a. At a party, a guest you have just met for the first time says, "Everybody seems like they've been friends for years. I don't know anybody here. How about you?"
   b. Your best friend has been quiet lately. When you ask if anything is wrong, she snaps "No!" in an irritated tone of voice.
   c. A co-worker says, "The boss keeps making sexual jokes around me. I think it's a come-on, and I don't know what to do."
   d. It's registration time at university. One of your friends asks if you think he or she should enroll in the communication class you've taken.
   e. Your roommate remarks, "It seems like this place is always a mess. We get it cleaned up, and then an hour later it's trashed."

Further Reading

Burleson, Brant R, "Emotional Support Skills," in John O. Greene and Brant R. Burleson, eds, *Handbook of Communication and Social Interaction Skills* (Mahwah, NJ: Erlbaum, 2002).
This review of research describes what types of communication provide emotional support.

Donoghue, Paul J, *Are You Really Listening? Keys to Successful Communication* (Notre Dame, IN: Sorin Books, 2005).
This is another communication book that was written by experts in the mental health field. The book is divided into three parts, with the first part looking at listening in a variety of relationships, the second part focusing on faulty listening behaviours, and the final section teaching the reader how to be a better listener.

Leeds, Dorothy, *The Seven Powers of Questions: Secrets to Successful Communication in Life and Work* **(New York: Penguin, 2001).**
This practical book shows the many ways questions can be useful beyond seeking information. They can encourage others to open up, and even enhance our control over a situation.

Steil, Lyman K., and Richard K. Bommelje, *Listening Leaders: The 10 Golden Rules to Listen, Lead & Succeed* **(Edina, MN: Beaver's Pond Press, 2005).**
A comprehensive look at how leaders can apply the subtle yet important skill of listening to make a difference in their organizations.

Study Questions

1. Describe situations from your own experience that illustrate the misconceptions about listening outlined on pages 169–172.

2. Recall examples of at least three of the faulty listening behaviours described on pages 172–3.

3. Describe how a situation at work or school might look and sound different, depending on which of the personal listening styles described on pages 180–5 was used.

4. Apply the guidelines in the second half of this chapter to three situations that require good listening: one informational, one critical, and one empathic.

PART II
Interpersonal Communication

PROFESSIONAL PROFILE

Heather Pullen, MCM, APR

A career is a journey you only take once. Mine has been interesting, fulfilling, and sometimes surprising. The most important thing is that I have no regrets.

The first surprise came as I graduated from Carleton University with a bachelor's degree in journalism and political science. After labouring as a student for four years, I was convinced I would change the world as an investigative journalist. Instead I found myself working as a sports reporter for daily newspapers. Like so many new grads, I set aside my dreams in order to pay the bills.

As it turned out, sports reporting was a great training ground. I learned how to tackle subjects I knew nothing about. I learned to write fast and well. And I learned the importance of earning the respect of the people you're writing about, and the people you're writing for.

That experience prepared me for the next stage in my journey: working as a producer and reporter for CBC Radio. The versatility I'd developed as a reporter enabled me to contribute successfully to a wide variety of programs in news, current affairs, entertainment, and, yes, sports.

The next surprise came when I decided to leave journalism to take a public relations job at a Toronto hospital. Although my CBC friends were appalled that I was going to "the dark side," I was excited to join a caring organization with a mission to improve the lives of others. The public relations role in healthcare draws heavily on our skills and instincts as storytellers, as the battle against disease is constantly intriguing and often dramatic. It has been a privilege to share the stories of patients and the remarkable people who care for them.

With young children and a husband whose work involves regular travel, I made the next surprising career decision seven years later. I left the security of a well-paying job to open my own healthcare PR agency. With significant experience and a good reputation, I was able to attract all the business I wanted. For nine years, I balanced my need for professional challenge with my children's needs for very involved parenting.

In 2002, I returned to corporate communications. The move surprised those who knew how successful my consultancy was, but joining Hamilton Health Sciences as manager of public relations and communications made perfect sense. My children were more independent, and I knew that I wanted to be part of something big, built on a shared vision aimed at improving the healthcare system. The work is tremendously challenging, and tremendously rewarding.

I don't know where my journey will take me next. However, my enthusiasm for the field of communication has been re-invigorated by my decision to complete a master's degree in communication management. I now appreciate the significant body of scholarship that informs our profession and am committed to contributing in any way to the advancement of that work.

My journey continues, and I can't wait to see what's around the corner!

6

Understanding Interpersonal Relationships

After studying the material in this chapter . . .

You should understand:

- ✔ the characteristics that distinguish interpersonal relationships from impersonal ones;
- ✔ the content and relational dimensions of every message;
- ✔ the role of metacommunication in conveying relational messages;
- ✔ the dimensions and influences of intimacy in relationships;
- ✔ Knapp's model of relational development and deterioration;
- ✔ tension in relationships;
- ✔ the reasons for self-disclosure and the Johari Window model of self-disclosure;
- ✔ the characteristics of and guidelines for effective and appropriate self-disclosure; and
- ✔ the functions served by lies, equivocation, and hints.

You should be able to:

- ✔ identify interpersonal and impersonal communication;
- ✔ identify the content and relational dimensions of a message;
- ✔ distinguish among types of intimacy and influences on intimacy;
- ✔ identify the stages of relationships and the dialectical tensions present in a relationship;
- ✔ identify the degree of self-disclosure in your relationships and the functions this serves;
- ✔ compose effective and appropriate disclosing messages; and
- ✔ identify the types of non-disclosing messages you use, the functions of these messages, and their ethical validity.

Chapter Highlights

Truly interpersonal communication has several characteristics that make it worth studying:

» It is qualitatively different from less personal relationships.

» It has, like all messages, both content and relational dimensions.

» It can address relational matters explicitly through metacommunication.

Intimacy is a special dimension of interpersonal relationships:

» It has several dimensions.

» Men and women sometimes value and express intimacy differently.

» Cultural background influences how we communicate intimacy.

Communication scholars have explored some forces that shape interpersonal relationships:

» Developmental models describe how communication in relationships changes over time.

» Dialectical models describe forces that always operate in relationships.

» No matter which model is used, relationships are constantly changing.

The subject of self-disclosure is an important one in the study of interpersonal relationships:

» People disclose (or withhold) personal information for a variety of reasons.

» Models can help us understand how self-disclosure operates.

» Regardless of the reason, self-disclosure in relationships possesses several characteristics.

» Several guidelines can help you decide whether or not to disclose personal information.

This chapter introduces the vitally important topic of interpersonal relationships. We will begin by exploring what kinds of communication make a relationship interpersonal. Next, we will discuss a number of ways—both subtle and obvious—used to show others how we regard them and what kind of relationship we are seeking with them. We will go on to explore two approaches that characterize how communication operates throughout the lifetime of relationships. Finally, we will look at the role of self-disclosure in interpersonal communication.

Characteristics of Interpersonal Relationships

What is interpersonal communication? How does it differ from other types of interaction? When and how are interpersonal messages communicated? In this section, we will address these important questions as a way of introducing the topic of interpersonal relationships.

What Makes Communication Interpersonal?

The most obvious way to define interpersonal communication is to look at the *context*—the number of people involved. In this sense we could say that all communication between two people, or dyadic communication, is interpersonal. In many ways, dyadic communication is different from the kind that goes on in other contexts (such as that of small groups which will be discussed in Chapters 8 and 9). For example, unlike groups involving more than two people, dyads are complete and cannot be subdivided. If one person withdraws from the other, the relationship is finished. This indivisibility means that, unlike the members who make up a group, the partners in a dyad can't form coalitions to get their needs met; instead they must work matters out with one another.

Although looking at communication by context is useful, this approach raises some problems. Consider, for example, a routine transaction between a sales clerk and customer or the rushed exchange when you ask a stranger on the street for directions. While in a purely *contextual* sense communication of this sort meets our definition of "interpersonal," it hardly seems personal in any sense of the word. In fact, after transactions like this we commonly remark, "I might as well have been talking to a machine."

The impersonal nature of many two-person exchanges has led some scholars to say that quality, not quantity, is what distinguishes interpersonal communication. **Qualitatively interpersonal communication** occurs when people treat one another as unique individuals, regardless of the context in which the interaction occurs or the number of people involved.[1] When quality of interaction is the criterion, the opposite of interpersonal communication is **impersonal communication**, not group, public, or mass communication.

The greater part of our communication, even in dyadic contexts, is relatively impersonal. We chat pleasantly with shopkeepers or fellow commuters on the subway or bus; we discuss the weather or current events with most classmates and neighbours; we deal with

qualitatively interpersonal communication Interaction in which people treat one another as unique individuals, regardless of the context in which the interaction occurs or the number of people involved.

impersonal communication Strategies used by communicators to influence the way others view them.

"Don't walk away from me while I'm not paying any attention to you."

co-workers in a polite way. But considering the number of people we communicate with, qualitatively interpersonal interaction is rather scarce. This scarcity isn't necessarily unfortunate. Most of us don't have the time or energy to create personal relationships with everyone we encounter—or even to act in a personal way all the time with the people we know and love best. In fact, the scarcity of qualitatively interpersonal communication contributes to its value. Like precious metals, qualitatively interpersonal relationships are special because of their scarcity. You can get a sense of how interpersonal your relationships are by trying Activity A at the end of the chapter.

Interpersonal Communication and the Internet

Before we begin our discussion of the impact of the internet on interpersonal communication it is important to note how pervasive internet use has become across Canada. Statistics Canada's 2012 Canadian Internet Use Survey demonstrated that 83 per cent of Canadians had home internet access (as opposed to 79 per cent in 2010), with a significant, and persistent, urban (85 per cent) versus rural (75 per cent) divide. When examined according to income, the divide between rich and poor was much more stark: 95 per cent of households with incomes in the highest-income quartile (incomes over $87,000) had home internet access versus 62 per cent among households in the lowest-income quartile (incomes below $30,000). It is interesting however to note that while access in the lowest quartile was up from 54 per cent in 2010, it was down from 97 per cent in the highest quartile. Another fascinating aspect to the digital divide is that in 2012, older, lower-income Canadians (people over 65 in the lower-income quartile) lagged with 28 per cent internet access versus 95 per cent access among individuals 16-24 in households in the lowest-income quartile. When it came to connected households, Figure 6.1 demonstrates that while desktop and laptop computers were the devices most commonly used to access the internet, wireless handheld devices (smartphones, tablets, and music players) and game consoles had a significant percentage of users.

An interesting point of note is that the percentage of the population which used internet technologies such as Skype or FaceTime to do voice or video calls rose from 24 per cent in 2010 to 43 per cent in 2012.

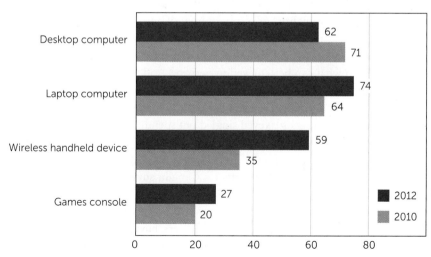

Percentage of Canadian households with internet access

FIGURE 6.1 Devices Used to Access the Internet

Source: Statistics Canada, "Individual internet use and e-commerce," *The Daily*, 28 October 2013. Reproduced and distributed on an "as is" basis with the permission of Statistics Canada.

Table 6.1 Households with Home Internet Access

	2010 %	2012 %
Canada	**79**	**83**
Newfoundland and Labrador	74	79
Prince Edward Island	73	78
Nova Scotia	77	80
New Brunswick	70	77
Quebec	73	78
Ontario	81	84
Manitoba	73	80
Saskatchewan	76	83
Alberta	83	86
British Columbia	84	86

Source: Statistics Canada, "Individual internet use and e-commerce," *The Daily*, 28 October 2013. Reproduced and distributed on an "as is" basis with the permission of Statistics Canada.

There's no question that mediated relationships conducted via e-mail, text messaging, and telephone pass the test of being contextually interpersonal. But what about their quality? Is online communication a poor substitute for face-to-face contact, or is it a rich medium for developing close personal relationships? In one survey, approximately 25 per cent of the respondents who used the internet regularly reported spending less time talking in person and on the phone with friends and family members.[2] Another survey revealed that people who relied heavily on the internet to meet their communication needs grew to rely less and less on their face-to-face networks. More significantly, they tended to feel more lonely and depressed as their online communication increased.[3] Finally, in 2010, people spent less time socializing face-to-face, talking on the telephone, and having meals in restaurants than ever before, with direct face-to-face interaction declining 7 per cent since 1998.

Despite findings like these, a growing body of research disputes the notion that mediated communication lacks quality.[4] Writing (online, of course) in *CMC Magazine*, Brittney G. Chenault summarized research concluding that e-mail, chat rooms, internet newsgroups, and computer conferences can and do allow electronic correspondents to develop a degree of closeness similar to what can be achieved in person.[5] And a 2005 Statistics Canada survey of internet use revealed that although users spent substantial time alone, they did not differ significantly in their desire to spend more time with family and friends. In fact, more than one-quarter of the internet users surveyed singled out spending time with family and friends as their number one priority for the hours when they were not online (see Table 6.2).

Although spending time with family and friends was important to internet users, Ben Veenhof and colleagues' report on the Statistics Canada survey found that, for every hour of internet use, people spent one hour less with family members living inside or outside the household (see Figure 6.2).[6] The same report shows that non-users spent more time than users in traditional social activities, like socializing with others, having meals with household members, and playing with children (see Table 6.3). Furthermore, people who spent more than one hour on the internet per day were less likely to know their neighbours (39.9 per cent) than non-users (45.8 per cent).[7] This point is exaggerated when one considers that the average computer use across all age groups in Canada in 2010 was 1 hour and 23 minutes. However, internet users spent as much time as non-users conversing in-person with other household members and spent more time on the phone than non-users. The study also found that the internet's heaviest users tend to be young persons, who have lived in their neighbourhoods for shorter periods of time than non-users.

Table 6.2 The Internet and the Way We Spend Our Time

The findings come from the 2005 General Social Survey on time use, which asked respondents to provide a detailed account of all of their activities over a 24-hour period.

Non-users

- Shared their time equally with household members and people from outside the household. Heavy users spent about one hour less with both sets of people.

Moderate users

- Spent about 26 more minutes by themselves than non-users during day. But heavy internet users were alone nearly two hours (119 minutes) longer than non-users, even when comparing people from similar-sized households.

Heavy users

- Lead a considerably different lifestyle than individuals who do not surf the Web, according to a new study examining its impact on Canadians.
- Devoted less time to socializing with their spouse or partner, as well as their children and friends. And they tended to stay at home, showing less interest in outdoor activities than non-users.
- Devoted significantly less time than non-users to paid work and chores around the home, as well as less time sleeping, relaxing, resting, or thinking.
- Spent a considerable amount of their time on the Web using e-mail or chat groups. They were also more likely to spend time conversing with others over the phone.
- Spent an average of 33 minutes less time each day than non-users on domestic work, such as child care and housekeeping.
- Less likely than non-users to say they knew "most" or "many" of the people in their neighbourhood. They were also more likely to describe their sense of belonging to their community as "somewhat" or "very" weak.
- Spent more time reading books than non-users, and moderate users were also likely to spend more time reading newspapers than non-users.
- Although internet users spent less time with others generally, they identified having about the same number of close relationships with people outside the household as non-users.
- Heavy internet users and non-users spent about the same amount of time, just over two hours, watching television during the day.

All three groups

- Although internet users spent substantial time alone, particularly heavy users, they did not differ significantly from non-users in their desire to spend more time with family and friends. In fact, this was the most popular choice for all three groups. More than one-quarter of individuals in each group singled out time with family and friends as their number-one priority for spending additional time.

Definitions

- **Internet use** covers personal use of the internet over a 24-hour period and does not include use of the internet for other reasons (e.g., work or school).
- **Non-users** are those who did not spend at least five minutes on the internet at any one time during the day (respondents in the survey were asked not to report activities that were less than five minutes in duration).
- **Moderate users** are those who spent between five minutes and one hour on the internet during the day.
- **Heavy users** are those who spent more than one hour on the internet during the day.

Source: Statistics Canada, "General Social Survey: The Internet and the Way We Spend Our Time (2005). Reproduced and distributed on an "as is" basis with the permission of Statistics Canada.

Along with examining the social effects of screen-based media, researchers have also investigated its health effects. A 2009 study compared Canadian and American participants' experiences with physical activity and screen-based media and how these experiences related to various health indicators. They found a generally good relationship between physical activity and positive health indicators (e.g., fitness, weight control, etc.), although they also found a link between physical activity and physical aggression. Screen-based media use was negatively linked to most positive health indicators and positively related to several of the negative health indicators. It is important to note one exception: screen-based media were linked to positive peer relationships. These patterns were very similar in both Canada and the United States.

In terms of quantity of internet use, Figure 6.3 and Table 6.4 demonstrate that Canadians are using electronic communication tools to maintain their personal relationships whereas a survey of Canadians conducted by Leger Marketing and McMaster University revealed that Figure 6.2b indicates that since then, the use of social media has mushroomed in 2014, with 89 per cent of Canadians using Facebook. Figure 6.2 shows that e-mail use is a large component of Canadians' internet patterns and grows when Canadians are using the internet for larger periods of time: those who use the internet for less than an hour per day spend an average of 22.9 minutes on e-mail, while those who use the internet for more than one hour spend 50 minutes on e-mail. Figure 6.4 indicates a growing percentage of Canadians are using social media for "keeping in touch with friends or family" (84 per cent in 2014), "sharing information and ideas" (49 per cent) and meeting new people (19 per cent). As well, the same McMaster–Leger study indicated that Canadians find social media to enhance their enjoyment of television

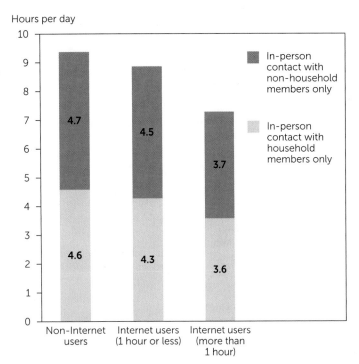

	2014	**2011**	**2009**
Facebook	89%	87%	77%
YouTube	70%	76%	65%
Skype	50%	44%	—
Wikipedia	49%	61%	—
Twitter	62%	32%	8%
LinkedIn	55%	25%	10%
Google	34%	—	—
Pinterest	29%	—	—

FIGURE 6.2a Average Time Spent per Day, In-Person Contact with Household Members and Non-Members, Canada, 2005[1]

[1] All figures are adjusted to control for age, sex, number of children aged 14 and under in respondent's household, day of week, education level and time spent at work. Adjusted figures for time spent with households members also control for number of persons living in the household.
Source: Statistics Canada, General Social Survey Cycle 19: Time Use (2005). Reproduced and distributed on an "as is" basis with the permission of Statistics Canada.

FIGURE 6.2b Overall Use of Social Media

Source: Sévigny, A. & Scholz, D., "Social Media Reality Check 3.0" (Social Media and Society Conference, Ryerson University, Toronto, ON, October, 2014).

Table 6.3 Average Time Spent per Day on Traditional Social Activities, Internet Users and Non-Users, Canada, 2005[1] (in minutes per day)

	Non-users		Internet Users (1 hour or less)				Internet Users (more than 1 hour)			
	Time	Adj. Time[1]	Time	Difference	Adj. Time[1]	Adj. Difference	Time	Difference	Adj. Time[1]	Adj. Difference
Socializing (without meals)	25.6	26.3	20.8	-4.8*	19.5	-6.8**	23.3	-2.3	16.6	-9.7**
Socializing (with meals, excluding restaurant meals)	30.2	30.6	25.1	-5.1*	24.9	-5.7*	22.0	-8.2**	16.6	-14.0**
Socializing at bars, clubs (without meals)	4.1	4.3	3.6	-0.5	2.9	-1.4	4.7	0.6	3.0	-1.3
Playing with children	5.8	5.9	4.6	-1.2	4.5	-1.4*	2.7	-3.1**	2.3	-3.6**
Face-to-face, conversation with household members[2]	5.7	5.7	6.5	0.8	7.0	1.3	5.0	-0.7	5.1	-0.6
Talking on the phone	4.4	4.4	6.7	2.3**	6.7	2.3**	7.3	2.9**	7.2	2.8**

* The difference from non-users is statistically significant at the 95% confidence level (p < .05).
** The difference from non-users is statistically significant at the 99% confidence level (p < .01).
[1] All figures are adjusted to control for age, sex, number of children aged 14 and under in respondent's household, day of week, education level, and time spent at work.
[2] Adjusted figures for face-to-face conversation with household members also control for number of persons living in the household.
Source: Statistics Canada, "General Social Survey, Cycle 19: Time Use" (2005). Reproduced and distributed on an "as is" basis with the permission of Statistics Canada.

(31 per cent) and that 33 per cent of Canadians upload pictures, video or status message while attending live sport or entertainment events. Figure 6.3b illustrates in compelling terms that 75 per cent of Canadians of all ages are using social media once a day or more. Furthermore, a 2010 survey found that e-mail is still, overwhelmingly, the primary activity online across all age groups, with Canadians 65 and older recording the *lowest* usage at 89.7 per cent and users 16–24 averaging 96.8 per cent. The statistics demonstrate a definite upward trend in line with educational achievement, with university-educated people using the internet to communicate with friends and relatives much more than those who have not had a university education. An interesting finding is that Canadians who are recent immigrants tend to use the internet to communicate with friends and relatives more than the Canadian-born.

Even more significant than the quantity of online communication is its quality: 55 per cent of internet users said that e-mail had improved communications with family, and 66 per cent said that their contact with friends had increased because of e-mail. Among women, the rate of satisfaction was even higher: 60 per cent reported better contact with family and 71 per cent with friends. Over three-quarters of the internet users polled said they never felt ignored by another household member's spending time online.[8] The majority of the internet users surveyed said that e-mail, websites, and chat rooms had a "modestly positive impact" on their ability to communicate more with family members and make new friends. Again, women had a higher satisfaction rate, with 60 per cent reporting better contact with family and 61 per cent with friends.

Content and Relational Messages

Virtually every verbal statement contains two kinds of messages. **Content messages**, which focus on the subject being discussed, are the most obvious. The content of such statements as "It's your turn to do the dishes" or "I'm busy Saturday night" is obvious.

content messages
Messages that communicate information about the subject being discussed.

UNDERSTANDING COMMUNICATION TECHNOLOGY

Internet Dangers Exposed

The internet has allowed us to communicate with friends and family instantaneously wherever they may be in the world. While there are many benefits to the increased communication offered by being connected online, we all know there are certain negative aspects. In the following article, Kathleen Harris discusses the potential dangers of the internet, especially for young people. As you read, think about how you use the internet and whether you are following safe practices or not.

Young Canadians should proceed with caution when putting their personal lives online, Canada's privacy czar warns.

In her annual report to Parliament, Privacy Commissioner Jennifer Stoddart said today's youth are playing out their lives in public in ways their parents and grandparents would find "unthinkable." While there are many benefits, surrendering too much personal information can also come with negative long-term consequences.

"Such openness can lead to greater creativity, literacy, networking, and social engagement," Stoddart said. "But putting so much of their personal information out into the open can also expose young people to cyberbullying or leave an enduring trail of embarrassing moments that could haunt them in future."

With increased texting, blogging, and online posting, unguarded personal information is "low-hanging fruit" for unscrupulous marketers, illegal data brokers, and identity thieves, Stoddart said. She found that while young people are most likely to embrace new technology, they're least likely to worry about the impact or consider risks associated with posting photos, videos, and personal opinions online.

Pointing to Stoddart's recent high-profile battle with Facebook over retention of personal information, University of Ottawa professor and internet privacy expert Michael Geist said Canadian privacy law is in a strong position to deal with evolving issues thanks to Stoddart's "aggressive" defence of privacy rights.

But he conceded most Canadians—especially youth—can use a reminder about long-term repercussions.

"Putting up photos of you and your friends in compromising situations—sometimes there are people who can trace that," he warned.

Candace Salmon, a 25-year-old Ottawa woman who has grown up in the digital age, isn't worried about using Facebook but uses caution.

"I don't post my phone number or photos which are vulgar or irresponsible," she said. "My benchmark is 'if I wouldn't want my parents to see it, I won't post it.'"

Stoddart's annual report also lists industries that drew the most complaints to her office, including financial institutions (banks, collection agencies, credit bureaus, financial advisers), insurance companies, sales (car dealerships, pharmacies, real estate, stores), and telecommunication and transportation sectors. An Ekos Research poll done for the commissioner's office in March found only 12 per cent of Canadians thought businesses took their obligation to protect consumers' personal information "very seriously."

The inquiries branch of the Personal Information Protection and Electronic Documents Act handled 6344 inquiries, down about 17 per cent from a year earlier.

Kathleen Harris, National Bureau Chief, 7 October 2009

QUESTIONS: The author describes how information and communication technologies make us susceptible to surveillance. Do you think that reduced privacy in the digital world is a bad thing for us personally, socially, or culturally? Why or why not?

---

relational messages
Messages that express the social relationship between two or more individuals.

affinity
The degree to which people like or appreciate one another. As with all relational messages, affinity is usually expressed non-verbally.

However, content messages aren't the only kind that are exchanged when two people interact. Virtually all communication—both verbal and non-verbal—contains **relational messages**, which make statements about how the parties feel toward one another.[9] These relational messages express communicators' feelings and attitudes involving one or more dimensions.

Affinity

One dimension of relational communication is **affinity**, or the degree to which people like or appreciate one another. Just looking at two people interacting, you can often get a good idea of how much each likes the other, even if you can't hear what's being discussed.

Minutes per day

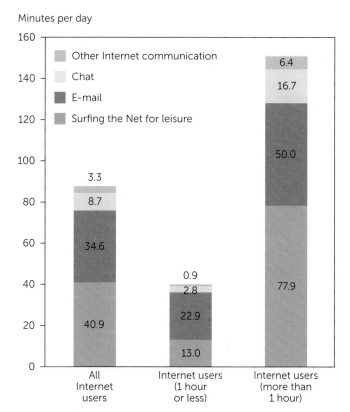

FIGURE 6.3a Average Time Spent per Day by Internet Users on E-mail, Chatting, and Other Internet Communication, Canada, 2005

Source: Statistics Canada, "General Social Survey Cycle 19: Time Use" (2005). Reproduced and distributed on an "as is" basis with the permission of Statistics Canada.

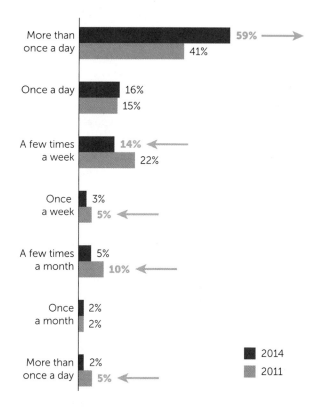

FIGURE 6.3b Frequency of Use

Source: Sévigny, A. & Scholz, D., "Social Media Reality Check 3.0" (Social Media and Society Conference, Ryerson University, Toronto, ON, October, 2014).

Respect

Respect is the degree to which we admire others and hold them in esteem. Respect and affinity might seem identical, but they are actually separate dimensions of a relationship.[10] For example, you might like a three-year-old child tremendously without respecting her. Likewise, you could respect a boss's or teacher's talents without liking him. Respect is a tremendously important and often overlooked ingredient in satisfying relationships. It is a better predictor of relational satisfaction than liking, or even loving.[11]

Immediacy

Communication scholars use the term **immediacy** to describe the degree of interest and attraction we feel toward and communicate to others. Immediacy is different from affinity. A situation of high immediacy would be the feeling of connection and excitement that students feel for a very popular professor. The students want to talk to her because they are interested in her subject matter and because they are attracted to her caring and magnetic personality. It's easy to imagine four combinations of these dimensions: high affinity and high immediacy; high affinity and low immediacy; low affinity and low immediacy; and low affinity and high immediacy.

respect
The degree to which we hold others in esteem.

immediacy
The degree of interest and attraction we feel toward and communicate to others. As with all relational messages, immediacy is usually expressed non-verbally.

Table 6.4 Online Activities From Any Location, 2012

Activity	Percentage of Internet Users
E-mail	93
Window shopping or browsing for information on goods or services	77
Electronic banking (e.g., paying bills, viewing statements, transferring funds between accounts)	72
Reading or watching the news	71
Using social networking sites	67
Searching for medical or health-related information	67
Travel information or making travel arrangements	66
Visiting or interacting with government websites	63
Researching community events	58
Downloading or watching movies or video clips online	54
Obtaining or saving music (free or paid downloads)	50
Making telephone calls online	43
Using an instant messenger	40
Downloading or watching TV online	39
Listening to the radio online	38
Obtaining or saving software (free or paid downloads)	38
Formal education, training or school work	37
Searching for employment	36
Playing online games	35
Researching investments	27
Contributing content or participating in discussion groups (e.g., blogging, message boards, posting images)	24
Selling goods or services (e.g., through auction sites)	23

Source: Statistics Canada, "Individual internet use and e-commerce," *The Daily*, 28 October 2013. Reproduced and distributed on an "as is" basis with the permission of Statistics Canada.

Control

In every conversation and every relationship there is some distribution of **control**: the amount of influence communicators seek. Relational partners can share control equally, or one person can have more and the other(s) less. An uneven distribution of control won't cause problems as long as everyone involved accepts that arrangement. Struggles arise, though, when people disagree on how control should be distributed in their relationship.

You can get a feeling for how relational messages operate in everyday life by recalling the examples at the beginning of this section. Imagine two ways of saying "It's your turn to do the dishes": one that is demanding and another

control
The social need to
influence others.

that is matter-of-fact. Notice how the different non-verbal messages make statements about how the sender views control in this part of the relationship. The demanding tone says, in effect, "I have a right to tell you what to do around the house," whereas the matter-of-fact one suggests, "I'm just reminding you of something you might have overlooked." Likewise, you can easily visualize two ways to deliver the statement "I'm busy Saturday night," one with little affection and the other with much liking.

Notice that in each of these examples the relational dimension of the message was never discussed. In fact, most of the time we aren't conscious of the relational messages that bombard us every day. Sometimes we are unaware of relational messages because they match our belief about the amount of affinity, respect, immediacy, and control that is appropriate. For example, you probably won't be offended if your employer tells you to do a certain job because you agree that managers have the right to direct employees. In other cases, however, conflicts arise over relational messages even though content is not disputed. If your manager delivers the order in a condescending, sarcastic, or abusive tone of voice, you probably will be offended. Your complaint wouldn't be with the order itself but rather with the way it was delivered. "I may work for this company," you might think, "but I'm not a slave or an idiot. I deserve to be treated like a human being."

How are relational messages communicated? As the employer–employee example suggests, they are usually expressed non-verbally. To test this for yourself, imagine how you could act while saying, "Can you help me for a minute?" in a way that communicates each of the following attitudes:

- superiority,
- aloofness,
- friendliness,
- helplessness,
- sexual desire, and
- irritation.

Although non-verbal behaviours are a good source of relational messages, remember that they are ambiguous. The sharp tone you take as a personal insult might stem from fatigue, and the interruption you perceive as an attempt to ignore your ideas might be a sign of pressure that has nothing to do with you. Before you jump to conclusions about relational clues, it's a

good idea to practise the skill of perception-checking that you learned in Chapter 2: "When you use that tone of voice to tell me it's my turn to do the dishes, I get the idea you're mad at me. Is that right?" If your interpretation was indeed correct, you can talk about the problem. On the other hand, if you were overreacting, perception-checking can prevent a needless fight.

Metacommunication

metacommunication
Messages (usually relational) that refer to other messages; communication about communication.

As the preceding example of perception-checking shows, not all relational messages are nonverbal. Social scientists use the term **metacommunication** to describe messages that refer to other messages.[12] In other words, metacommunication is communication about communication. Whenever we discuss a relationship with others, we are metacommunicating: "It sounds like you're angry at me," or "I appreciate how honest you've been." Metacommunication is an essential ingredient in successful relationships. Sooner or later there are times when it becomes necessary to talk about what is going on between you and the other person. The ability to focus on the kinds of issues described in this chapter and in Chapter 7 can help to keep the relationship on track.

Metacommunication is an important method of solving conflicts in a constructive manner. It provides a way to shift discussions from the content level to relational questions, where the problem often lies. For example, consider a couple bickering because one partner wants to watch television, whereas the other wants to talk. Imagine how much better the chances of a positive outcome would be if they used metacommunication to examine the relational problems that were behind their quarrel: "Look, it's not the TV watching itself that bothers me. It's that I imagine you watch so much because you're mad at me or bored. Are you feeling bad about us?"

Metacommunication isn't just a tool for handling problems. It is also a way to reinforce the good aspects of a relationship: "I really appreciate it when you compliment me about my work in front of the boss." Comments like this serve two functions: they let others know that you value their behaviour, and they boost the odds that the other people will continue the behaviour in the future.

Cultural Idiom
on the one hand
From one point of view.

on the other hand
From the other point of view.

Despite the benefits of metacommunication, bringing relational issues into the open does have risks. Discussing problems can be interpreted in two ways. On the one hand, the other person might see it in a positive light—"Our relationship is working because we can still talk things out." On the other hand, your desire to focus on the relationship might look like a bad omen—"Our relationship isn't working if we have to keep talking it over." Furthermore, metacommunication does involve a certain degree of analysis ("It seems like you're angry at me"), and some people resent being analyzed. These cautions don't mean verbal metacommunication is a bad idea. They do suggest, though, that it's a tool that needs to be used carefully.

Intimacy in Interpersonal Relationships

Even the closest relationships involve a mixture of personal and interpersonal communication. We alternate between a "we" and a "me" orientation, sometimes focusing on connecting with others and at other times focusing on our own needs and interests. In the next few pages we will examine how these apparently conflicting drives for intimacy and distance affect our communication.

Dimensions of Intimacy

The dictionary defines *intimacy* as arising from "close union, contact, association, or acquaintance." This definition suggests that the key element of intimacy is closeness, one element that "ordinary people" have reported as characterizing their intimate relationships.[13] However, it doesn't explain what *kinds* of closeness can create a state of intimacy.

In colloquial use, of course, intimacy is almost always used to mean a very particular form of closeness, so much so that the term "intimate relations" is used as a euphemism for any contact between people with decidedly sexual undertones. If an elementary school teacher refers to her close mentoring relationship with a particular student as "intimate" when speaking about it with a colleague, it is entirely plausible that the colleague might report the matter to a superior. The association of the word with these connotations extends so far that many department stores call the women's undergarments section "Intimates."

In sociological literature, **intimacy** is used somewhat more broadly and can have several qualities. The first is *physical*. Even before birth, the developing fetus experiences a kind of physical closeness with its mother that will never happen again, "floating in a warm fluid, curling inside a total embrace, swaying to the undulations of the moving body and hearing the beat of the pulsing heart."[14] As they grow up, fortunate children are continually nourished by physical intimacy: being rocked, fed, hugged, and held. As we grow older, the opportunities for physical intimacy are less regular but still possible and important. Some, but by no means all, physical intimacy is sexual. In one survey, only one-quarter of the respondents (who were university students) stated that intimacy necessarily contained a romantic or sexual dimension.[15] Other forms of physical intimacy include affectionate hugs, kisses, and even struggles. Companions who have endured physical challenges together—in athletics or emergencies, for example—form a bond that can last a lifetime.

In other cases, intimacy comes from *intellectual* sharing. Not every exchange of ideas counts as intimacy, of course. Talking about next week's mid-term with your instructor or classmates isn't likely to forge strong relational bonds. But when you engage another person in an exchange of important ideas, a kind of closeness develops that can be powerful and exciting.

A third quality of intimacy is *emotion*: exchanging important feelings. This chapter will offer several guidelines for disclosing your thoughts and feelings to others. If you follow those guidelines, you will probably recognize a qualitative change in your relationships.

If we define *intimacy* as being close to another person, then *shared activities* can be some of the ways to achieve this state. Shared activities can include everything from working side by side at a job to meeting regularly at the gym. Although shared activities are no guarantee of intimacy, people who spend time together can develop unique ways of relating that transform the relationship from an impersonal one that could be done with anybody to one with interpersonal qualities. For example, several forms of play often characterize both friendships and romantic relationships. Partners invent private codes, joke around by acting like other people, tease one another, and play games—everything from having punning contests to arm wrestling.[16]

Some intimate relationships exhibit all four qualities: physical intimacy, intellectual exchanges, emotional disclosure, and shared activities. Other intimate relationships exhibit only one or two. Some relationships, of course, aren't intimate in any way. Acquaintances, roommates, and co-workers may never become intimate. In some cases even family members develop smooth but relatively impersonal relationships.

> **intimacy**
> A state of closeness between two (or sometimes more) people. Intimacy can be manifested in several ways: physically, intellectually, emotionally, and through shared activities.

Not even the closest relationships always operate at the highest level of intimacy. At some times you might share all of your thoughts or feelings with a friend, family member, or romantic partner, and at other times you might withdraw. You might freely share your feelings about one topic and stay more aloof in another one. The same principle holds for physical intimacy, which waxes and wanes in most relationships. The dialectical view of relational maintenance described later in this chapter explains how intimacy can wax and wane, even in the closest relationships.

Male and Female Intimacy Styles

Until recently most social scientists believed that women were better at developing and maintaining intimate relationships than men.[17] This belief grew from the assumption that the disclosure of personal information is the most important ingredient of intimacy. Most research does show that women (taken as a group, of course) are more willing to share their thoughts and feelings than men are.[18] In terms of the amount and depth of information exchanged, female–female relationships are at the top of the disclosure list. Male–female relationships

Understanding Diversity

Dating and Intimacy in Multicultural Canada

Immigrant Parents Are Gradually Accepting Interracial Relationships

When Praga, of Tamil heritage, entered into a relationship with Ken, a Caucasian Canadian, she knew she would have a difficult time when it came time to tell her parents. Delaying that inevitability, they, at first, kept their relationship quiet. When she felt the time was right to tell them about Ken, she arranged to have her brother and brother-in-law present. Ken waited at a convenience store nearby.

"When I told my parents, my mom immediately started to cry and my dad just left the room. He just said, 'No way,'" says Praga. "They actually didn't speak to me for a month. We all lived together, but they still continued to ignore me. They went to all sorts of astrologers for guidance. It took them a really long time to accept Ken and to agree to meet him. They didn't tell my other family members because they were really ashamed of 'the situation.'"

After the initial shock wore off, the situation improved. "Things are OK now," continues Praga. "My relatives have all met him and I am sure they have their own opinions, but we try to look on the positive side." More and more immigrant families in Canada have been dealing with this situation over the last decade. Between 1996 and 2006, there has been a 33 per cent increase in interracial relationships and that trend shows no indication of slowing down. If four per cent of relationships were interracial in 2006, then that number can be estimated to

jump to 10 per cent by 2016. As Canada's population continues to become more diverse due to immigration, there is simply greater opportunity for individuals to fall in love with someone from a different ethnocultural background, especially among younger generations who have been born or mostly raised in Canada's diverse environment. The rate of mixed couples also increases in urban settings, with cities like Vancouver at the top.

Two Perspectives

According to Carl James, a professor of sociology at York University, immigrant parents usually fall into two camps when it comes to interracial relationships. Many, like Praga's parents, are strongly opposed to the idea, at least initially. Where they come from, interracial marriage is an unfamiliar concept, and even though they chose to immigrate to a multicultural country, it was certainly not something they had expected to have to deal with personally.

"Home is a sacred place and any invasion of that cannot be taken lightly," explains James. But James points out there are just as many parents who want their sons and daughters to marry outside their culture because of what it might symbolize or represent. "Immigrants expect their children to do better than them," he says. Such parents, says James, consider the effect the union will have on their son's or daughter's social mobility in the adopted country.

come in second, whereas relationships between men have less disclosure than any other type. At every age, women disclose more than men, and the information they disclose is more personal and more likely to involve feelings. Although both sexes are equally likely to reveal negative information, men are less likely to share positive feelings.[19]

Through the mid-1980s many social scientists interpreted the relative lack of male self-disclosure as a sign that men were unwilling, or even unable, to develop close relationships. Some argued that the female trait of disclosing personal information and feelings makes them more "emotionally mature" and "interpersonally competent" than men. Personal growth programs and self-help books urged men to achieve closeness by learning to open up and share their feelings.

Scholarship conducted over the past decade, however, has begun to show that male–female differences aren't as great as they seem,[20] and emotional expression isn't the *only* way to develop close relationships. Unlike women, who value personal talk, men grow close to one another by doing things. In one study more than 75 per cent of the men surveyed said that their most meaningful experiences with friends came from activities other than talking.[21] They reported

> **Cultural Idiom**
> **to open up**
> To talk about subjects that otherwise might be withheld.

When Phuong first told her Chinese family about her intention to marry Frank (names changed for privacy), an Italian Canadian, they were concerned only with the fact that Frank had no university education and worked in the trades. They saw this as Phuong marrying below her. Frank's family, on the other hand, appeared to have no issue about him marrying a Chinese woman.

Cultural Differences

Over the years, Frank and Phuong have had more than a few problems related to their cultural differences. But, these days, 12 years into their relationship, Phuong says most of what she and Frank disagree about have more to do with regular male/female conflicts, the kind that can exist in any relationship, interracial or not.

One cultural problem that has continued to persist has to do with religion. Phuong had been raised by Buddhist parents and is not particularly religious herself; Frank had been raised in a typical Italian Catholic household and he and his family are very religious. Phuong agreed to a Catholic wedding only because Frank's church did not require her to convert to Catholicism, which she was opposed to doing.

The church did have some requirements of the couple, however. Before going forward with the wedding, Frank and Phuong had to take marriage counselling sessions. "If you want to get married in a Catholic church, you have to take marriage classes to make sure you are compatible," says Phuong.

Three Main Challenges

James says that the main challenges specific to interracial relationships come down to three things—religious practices, cuisine, and language. The challenge is usually greater for the parents of the couple who, if they are immigrants, are likely to be raised in a culture where there was no interracial marriage at all and are more set in their ways. When Praga's parents chose to come to Canada, they did not envision their daughter marrying outside the culture. But Ken will soon be part of their family. They have to learn more about his culture, and he about theirs. It's a big change.

For Frank's family, although they did not oppose his decision to marry a Chinese woman, they remained rigid about their expectations for a Catholic wedding, and later a baptism for their grandson. On the positive side, men and women in an interracial marriage are much more prepared for the challenges they face as a couple, says James, because they are already willing to make compromises and are open to change.

Nirushan Sivagnanasuntharam, canadianimmigrant.ca,
16 July 2012

QUESTIONS: What does the growing prominence of interracial dating mean for the immigration and family relationships? Do you think that something is lost, culturally, when someone enters into a relationship with someone from another ethic or cultural group? Why or why not?

that through shared activities they "grew on one another," developed feelings of interdependence, showed appreciation for one another, and demonstrated mutual liking. Likewise, men regarded practical help from other men as a measure of caring. Research like this shows that, for many men, closeness grows from activities that don't depend heavily on disclosure; instead, a friend is a person who does things *for* you and *with* you.

The difference between male and female measures of intimacy helps explain some of the stresses and misunderstandings that can arise between the sexes. For example, a woman who looks for emotional disclosure as a measure of affection may overlook an "inexpressive" man's efforts to show he cares by doing favours or spending time together. Fixing a leaky faucet or taking a hike may look like ways to avoid getting close, but to the man who proposes them, they may be measures of affection and bids for intimacy. Likewise, differing ideas about the timing and meaning of sex can lead to misunderstandings. Whereas many women think of sex as a way to express intimacy that has already developed, men are more likely to see it as a way to *create* that intimacy.[22] In this sense, the man who encourages sex early in a relationship or after a fight may not just be driven by testosterone—he may view the shared activity as a way to build closeness. By contrast, the woman who views personal talk as the pathway to intimacy may resist the idea of physical closeness before the emotional side of the relationship has been discussed.

Intimacy can also have very negative consequences in cultures other than English-Canadian. Two studies published in 2009 examined how in some cultures that put a high value on female loyalty, honour-related relationship violence is indirectly permitted. Also, in such cultures, women who remain in abusive relationships are rewarded for their sacrifice. The first study compared Latinos and southern US Anglos with northern US Anglos, and the second compared Chileans and Anglo-Canadians. The Latino, Chilean, and southern US Anglo

cultures have strong honour traditions, whereas the northern US Anglo and Anglo-Canadian cultures do not. Both studies presented examples of abuse to the participants. Compared to non–honour-culture participants, those from honour cultures were relatively more favourable to the woman if she stayed in the relationship, despite being abused. If the conflict between male and female partners was jealousy-related, honour-culture participants excused the man's abusive language, whereas the man was not excused for his abusive language when the disagreement related to rational choices, such as spending too much money.[23] A woman in an honour-based culture is expected to bear a heavier burden when she enters a relationship with a man than a woman in a non–honour-based culture.

Cultural Influences on Intimacy

The notion of how much intimacy is desirable and how to express it varies from one culture to another.[24] In one study, researchers asked residents of Britain, Japan, Hong Kong, and Italy to describe their use of 33 rules that governed interaction in a wide range of communication behaviours: everything from the use of humour to handshaking to the management of money.[25] The results showed that the greatest differences between Asian and European cultures focused on the rules for dealing with intimacy: showing emotions, expressing affection in public, engaging in sexual activity, respecting privacy, and so on. Culture also plays a role in shaping how much intimacy we seek in different types of relationships. For instance, Japanese respondents seem to expect more intimacy in friendships, whereas Anglo-North Americans look for more intimacy in romantic relationships.[26]

A study conducted by researchers from Canada's Queen's and York universities and China's Xi'an University of Architecture and Technology compared the romantic involvements of Canadian and Chinese adolescents. The study also investigated how young people's romantic involvements related to their friendships and parental relationships. The study showed that the Chinese adolescents were less likely to be romantically involved and had generally lower levels of romantic experience, including fewer close romantic relationships. Of all the participants, Chinese girls reported being the least involved in romantic experiences. The link between romance and friendships was important in both cultures: while friendships were more intimate in Canada and parent relationships were closer in China, friendship relationships were positively related to romantic relationships in both cultures. Interestingly, the Chinese adolescents indicated that parents were negatively connected with romantic experiences.[27]

In some collectivist cultures, such as Taiwan and Japan, there is an especially large difference in the way members communicate with members of their "in-groups" (such as family and close friends) and with those they view as outsiders.[28] They generally do not reach out to strangers, often waiting until they are properly introduced before entering into a conversation. Once introduced, they address outsiders with a degree of formality. They go to extremes to hide unfavourable information about in-group members from outsiders, adhering to the principle that one doesn't wash dirty laundry in public. By contrast, members of more individualistic cultures, like those in Canada, Australia, and New Zealand, make less of a distinction between personal relationships and casual ones. They are more familiar with strangers and disclose a greater amount of personal information, making them excellent "cocktail party conversationalists." Social psychologist Kurt Lewin captured the difference nicely when he noted that Anglo-North Americans are easy to meet but difficult to get to know, whereas Germans are difficult to meet but then easy to know well.[29]

Cultural Idiom
wash dirty laundry in public
To disclose personal and private problems and concerns to those beyond one's family or group.

Relational Development and Maintenance

Qualitatively interpersonal relationships aren't stable; they are constantly changing. Communication scholars have explored the way relationships develop and shift from two perspectives: developmental and dialectical.

A Developmental Perspective

One of the best-known explanations of how communication operates in relationships was created by Mark Knapp, whose **developmental model** broke down the rise and fall of relationships into 10 stages, contained in the two broad phases of "coming together" and "coming apart."[30] Other researchers have suggested that any model of relational communication ought to contain a third part of relational maintenance—communication aimed at keeping relationships operating smoothly and satisfactorily.[31]

The following stages are especially descriptive of intimate, romantic relationships and close friendships. The pattern for other intimate relationships, such as families, would follow different paths. Some valuable relationships don't require a high level of intimacy. They are based on other, equally important foundations: career activities, shared political interests, and religion, to mention just a few.[32]

Initiating

The stage of initiation involves the initial contact made with another person. Knapp restricts this stage to conversation openers, both in initial contacts and in contacts with acquaintances: "Nice to meet you," "How's it going?" and so on.

Although an initial encounter is necessary to the succeeding interaction, its importance is overemphasized in books offering advice on how to pick someone up at a bar or a party. These books suggest fail-proof openers ranging from "Excuse me, I'm from out of town, and I was wondering what people do around here at night," to "How long do you cook a leg of lamb?" Whatever your preference for opening remarks, this stage is important because you are formulating your first impressions and presenting yourself as interested in the other person.

> **developmental model**
> A model claiming that the nature of communication is different in various stages of interpersonal relationships.

> **Cultural Idiom**
> **to pick someone up**
> To make an acquaintance with sexual purposes in mind.

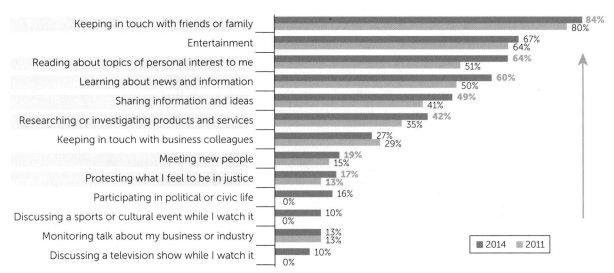

FIGURE 6.4 Uses for Social Media

Notes: 31 per cent find that interacting on social media enhances their enjoyment of TV shows or cultural/sporting events. 33 per cent upload pictures, video, or status messages while attending live sports or entertainment events.
Source: Sévigny, A. & Scholz, D., "Social Media Reality Check 3.0" (Social Media and Society Conference, Ryerson University, Toronto, ON, October, 2014).

Initiating relationships can be particularly hard for people who are shy. Making contact with others through the internet can be helpful for people who have a hard time conversing in person. One study of an online dating service found that participants who identified themselves as shy expressed a greater appreciation for the system's anonymous, non-threatening environment than did non-shy users.[33] The researchers found that many shy users employed the online service specifically to help overcome their inhibitions about initiating relationships in face-to-face settings.

Experimenting

In the stage of experimenting, the conversation develops as people use "small talk" to get acquainted. We ask: "Where are you from?" or "What do you do?" or "Do you know Jean-Louis Balthazar? He lives in Trois Rivières, too."

Though small talk might seem meaningless, Knapp points out that it serves four purposes:

1. It is a useful process for uncovering integrating topics and openings for more penetrating conversation.
2. It can be an audition for a future friendship or a way of increasing the scope of a current relationship.
3. It provides a safe procedure for indicating who we are and how another can come to know us better (reduction of uncertainty).
4. It allows us to maintain a sense of community with our fellow human beings.

The relationship during this stage is generally pleasant and uncritical, and the commitments are minimal. Experimenting may last 10 minutes or 10 years.

The willingness to pursue relationships with strangers is partly a matter of personal style. Some people are outgoing and others shy. But culture also plays a role in orientations to newcomers, especially ones from a different ethnic or cultural background. Research suggests that members of some cultures—Chinese and Japanese, for example—are more cautious in their first encounters with strangers and make more assumptions about them based on their backgrounds than do Anglo-North Americans and most Europeans.[34] This fact might explain why people from certain backgrounds appear unfriendly, when in fact they are simply operating by a different set of rules.

Intensifying

It is during the intensifying stage that the kind of truly interpersonal relationship defined earlier in this chapter begins to develop. Several changes in communication patterns occur. Expressions of feelings toward the other become more frequent. Dating couples, for example, use a wide range of communication strategies to describe their feelings of attraction.[35] About a quarter of the time they express their feelings directly, using metacommunication to discuss the state of the relationship. More

---

Cultural Idiom
small talk
An unimportant or trivial conversation.

One word frees us of all the weight and pain of life; That word is love.

**Sophocles,
ancient Greek
tragedian playwright**

📷 COMMUNICATION ON-SCREEN

Lars and the Real Girl (2007)
Directed by Craig Gillespie.

A wonderfully strange Academy Award–nominated Canadian-American film about a socially inept young man, Lars (Ryan Gosling), who develops a romantic relationship with an anatomically correct sex doll "named" Bianca. Due to their concern and care for Lars, his family and community treat Bianca as a real person, even giving her a "job" as a model in a storefront window. Through Lars's public relationship with Bianca, he begins to interact with more people, something he was strongly adverse to previously. This highly unconventional route helps Lars learn how to mediate professional, familial, and romantic interpersonal relationships and overcome his issues with intimacy. As Dr. Alan Ravitz, a child and adolescent psychiatrist, notes, "I know it sounds kinky, but it isn't—at all. Through his relationship with the doll, he learns how to relate to real people. The film is incredibly psychologically insightful" (www.childmind.org/en/press/brainstorm/ravitz-report-lars-and-real-girl).

often they use less-direct methods of communication, such as spending greater amounts of time together, asking for support from one another, doing favours for the partner, giving tokens of affection, hinting and flirting, expressing feelings non-verbally, getting to know the partner's friends and family, and trying to look more physically attractive. Touching is more common during this stage than in either earlier or later ones.[36] Several other changes mark the intensifying stage. Forms of address become more familiar. The parties begin to see themselves as "we" instead of as separate individuals. It is during the intensifying stage that people begin to express feelings of commitment directly to one another: "I'm really glad we met." "You're the best thing that's happened to me in a long time."

Integrating

As the relationship strengthens, the parties begin to take on an identity as a social unit. Invitations begin to be addressed to the couple. Social circles merge. The partners begin to take on each other's commitments: "Sure, we'll spend Thanksgiving with your family." Common property may begin to be designated—*our* apartment, *our* car, *our* song.[37] Partners develop their own rituals for everything from expressing intimacy to handling daily routines.[38] They even begin to speak alike, using common words and sentence patterns.[39] In this sense, the integration stage is a time when we give up some characteristics of our old selves and become different people.

As we become more integrated with others, our sense of obligation to them grows.[40] We feel obliged to provide a variety of resources such as class notes and money, whether or not the other person asks for them. When intimates do make requests of one another, they are relatively straightforward. Gone are the elaborate explanations, inducements, and apologies. In short, partners in an integrated relationship expect more from one another than they do in less-intimate associations.

Bonding

During the bonding stage, the parties make symbolic public gestures to show the world that their relationship exists. The most common form of bonding in romantic relationships is a wedding ceremony and the legal ties that come with it. Bonding generates social support for the relationship. Both custom and law impose certain obligations on partners who have officially bonded.

Bonding marks a turning point in a relationship. Up until this point, the relationship may have developed at a steady pace: experimenting has gradually moved into intensifying and then into integrating. Now, however, there is a spurt of commitment. The public display and declaration of exclusivity make this a critical period in the relationship.

Relationships don't have to be romantic to have a bonding stage. Business contracts form a bond between associates; initiation into a sorority or fraternity also creates a bond. These acts "officialize" a relationship and involve a measure of public commitment.

Differentiating

Once two people have formed a commonalty, they need to re-establish individual identities. This is the point where the "hold me tight" orientation that has existed shifts, and "put me down" messages begin to occur (see page 233). Partners use a variety of strategies to gain privacy from one another.[41] Sometimes they confront the other party directly, explaining that they don't want to continue a discussion. At other times they are less direct, offering non-verbal cues, changing the topic, or leaving the room.

Differentiation is likely to occur when a relationship begins to experience the first, inevitable stress. This need for autonomy doesn't have to be a negative experience, however. People need to be individuals as well as parts of a relationship, and differentiation is a necessary step toward autonomy. The key to successful differentiation is maintaining a commitment to the relationship while creating the space for being an individual as well.

Circumscribing

So far we have been looking at the growth of relationships. Although some relationships may reach a plateau of development, going on successfully for as long as a lifetime, others pass through several stages of decline and dissolution. In the circumscribing stage, communication between members decreases both in quantity and quality. Restrictions and restraints characterize this stage, and dynamic communication becomes static. Rather than discuss a disagreement (which requires some degree of energy on both parts), members opt for withdrawal: either mental (silence or daydreaming and fantasizing) or physical (where people spend less time together). Circumscribing doesn't involve total avoidance; that comes later. Rather, it entails a certain shrinking of interest and commitment.

Stagnating

If circumscribing continues, the relationship begins to stagnate. Members behave toward each other in old, familiar ways without much feeling. No growth occurs. The relationship is a shadow of its former self. We see stagnation in many workers who have lost enthusiasm for their job yet continue to go through the motions for years. The same occurs for some couples who unenthusiastically have the same conversations, see the same people, and follow the same routines without any sense of joy or novelty.

Understanding Diversity

The Love Poll

What do you think qualifies as cheating? More than 15,000 Canadians coast to coast participated in our online poll.

Percentage who would not be tempted to cheat even if they knew they wouldn't get caught:

Women	74%
Men	47%

Have you ever cheated on a partner?

No	60%
Yes	40%

What do you think qualifies as cheating?

	Yes	No
Flirting	10%	90%
Kissing	69%	31%
Oral sex	77%	23%
Intercourse	85%	15%
Emotional intimacy	51%	49%

Have you ever been cheated on?

No	50%
Yes	50%

Would you try to work it out with a partner if they cheated on you?

Yes	22%
No	32%

If it was a one-time mistake, and they begged for forgiveness.

	Men	Women
Yes	47%	37%
No	32%	31%

Note: May not add up to 100 due to rounding

Percentage of respondents who would not tell if they witnessed a good friend's partner cheating on them because they feel it is none of their business:

Alberta	26%
British Columbia	30%
Ontario	29%
Quebec	35%

Trish McAlaster, *The Globe and Mail*, 3 July 2009

QUESTIONS: What does this poll tell you about relationships in Canada? Do you think the results of this poll are realistic? Where does cheating fit in the relationship stages discussed in this chapter?

"Gloria, am I supposed to be mailing it in or just going through the motions today?"

Avoiding

When stagnation becomes too unpleasant, parties in a relationship begin to create distance between each other. Sometimes this is done under the guise of excuses ("I've been sick lately and can't see you"), and sometimes it is done directly ("Please don't call me; I don't want to see you now"). In either case, by this point the handwriting about the relationship's future is clearly on the wall.

Terminating

Characteristics of this final stage include summary dialogues about where the relationship has gone and the desire to dissociate. The relationship may end over dinner, with a note left on the kitchen table, with a phone call, or with a legal document stating the dissolution. Depending on each person's feelings, this stage can be quite short, or it may be drawn out over time, with bitter jabs at one another.

The deterioration of a relationship from bonding to circumscribing, stagnating, and avoiding isn't inevitable. One of the key differences between marriages that end in separation and those that are restored to their former intimacy is the communication that occurs when the partners are unsatisfied.[42] Unsuccessful couples deal with their problems by avoidance, indirectness, and less involvement with one another. By contrast, couples who "repair" their relationship communicate much more directly. They confront one another with their concerns and spend time and effort negotiating solutions to their problems.

Relationships don't always move toward termination in a straight line. Rather, they often move along a back-and-forth pattern, where the trend is toward dissolution.[43] Regardless of how long it takes, termination doesn't have to be totally negative. Understanding each other's investment in the relationship and need for personal growth may dilute the hard feelings. In fact, many relationships aren't so much terminated as redefined. A divorced couple, for example, may find new, less intimate ways to relate to each other.

A Dialectical Perspective

Developmental models, like the one just described, suggest that communication differs in important ways at various points in the life of a relationship. According to these stage-related models, the kinds of interaction that happen during initiating, experimenting, or intensifying are different from the kinds that occur during differentiating, circumscribing, or avoiding.

Not all theorists agree that a stage-related model is the best way to explain interaction in relationships. Some suggest that communicators wrestle with the same kinds of challenges whether a relationship is brand new or decades old. They argue that communicators seek important but inherently incompatible goals throughout virtually all of their relationships. This **dialectical model** suggests that struggling to achieve these goals creates **dialectical tensions:** conflicts that arise when two opposing or incompatible forces exist simultaneously. In recent years, communication scholars have identified the dialectical tensions that make successful communication challenging.[44] They suggest that the struggle to manage these dialectical tensions creates the most powerful dynamics in relational communication. Three of the most powerful dialectical tensions are connection versus autonomy, predictability versus novelty, and openness versus privacy.

Connection versus Autonomy

No one is an island. Recognizing this fact, we seek out involvement with others. But, at the same time, we are unwilling to sacrifice our entire identity to even the most satisfying relationship. The conflicting desires for connection and independence are embodied in the *connection–autonomy dialectic*. Research on relational breakups demonstrates the consequences for relational partners who can't find a way to manage these very different personal needs.[45] Some of the most common reasons for relational breakups involve failure of partners to satisfy one another's needs for connection: "We barely spent any time together;" "He wasn't committed to the relationship;" "We had different needs." But other relational complaints involve a partner's excessive demands for connection: "I was feeling trapped;" "I needed freedom."

The levels of connection and autonomy that we seek can change over time. In his book *Intimate Behavior,* Desmond Morris suggests that each of us repeatedly goes through three stages: "hold me tight," "put me down," and "leave me alone."[46] This cycle becomes apparent in the first years of life, when children move from the "hold me tight" stage that characterizes

dialectical model
A model claiming that, throughout their lifetime, people in virtually all interpersonal relationships must deal with equally important, simultaneous, and opposing forces such as connection and autonomy, predictability and novelty, and openness versus privacy.

dialectical tensions
Inherent conflicts that arise when two opposing or incompatible forces exist simultaneously.

COMMUNICATING ONLINE

One in Five Young Women Has Broken Up via Social Media

Surely the only thing more humiliating than being dumped is being dumped in public—especially if there is a record of it that will live online forever. That is an increasingly common fate, judging by a new survey of 4000 women around the world by AVG Technologies, which found that 19 per cent of women ages 18–25 said they have ended a relationship by posting on Facebook. Meanwhile 38 per cent of women in the same age-range said they have broken up via text message.

What's more, your social profile might keep you from getting a date in the first place, as 35 per cent of women surveyed worldwide said they use social media to check out their dates before meeting them in person (in February a Match.com survey of 5000 US singles found that 48 per cent of single American women said they research dates on Facebook, compared to 38 per cent of single American men). According to the AVG survey the most important material for pre-date evaluations and reviews was pictures, followed by common friends, interests, and comments, in that order. There was however considerable variation by nationality: fewer than a quarter of French women said they look at social media before a date, compared to 34 per cent of Canadians, while fully 61 per cent of Brazilian women ages 18–25 said they had canceled a date based on information obtained via social media. French women were also less likely to secretly read their partners' text or e-mail messages (18 per cent, compared to 40 per cent of Canadian women and 50 per cent of Brazilian women).

In a sign of widespread mobile addiction (or some other trend less flattering to the male ego), over half of women in France, Germany, and Canada said they would rather give up sex for a week than their mobile device, according to AVG. This echoes the results of a recent survey of 2000 US and Canadian women by Weber Shandwick and KRC Research, published in March, which found that intensive social media users are more likely to enjoy online socializing than dating or spending time with their partner.

Of course, social media also deserve credit for helping people meet each other. A survey of 2000 men and women in the US and the UK by Havas Worldwide, also published in March, found that 50 per cent of those polled know someone whose romantic relationship started online. On the down side, however, 25 per cent indicated that they know someone whose offline relationship ended because of their actions online. Another survey, publicized in February by the *New York Daily News*, found that 67 per cent of cheaters said they have a "fake" Facebook account for philandering, while half said they have a secret e-mail or Twitter account.

In addition to enabling romance, social media can be an erotic channel in its own right: according to the Match.com survey mentioned above, one-third of the singles surveyed (32 per cent) have sent a "sext," and over half (51 per cent) have received one. In addition, 42 per cent of single men surveyed said they wouldn't be offended if someone shared a revealing pic they sent, compared to 13 per cent of women.

Erik Sass, Mediapost.com, 25 May 2013

QUESTIONS: Does the increased blending of the public/private divide, as shown in the above article, highlight other issues for relationships in "the Facebook era?" How has the changing topography of relationships affected you?

infancy into a new "put me down" stage of exploring the world by crawling, walking, touching, and tasting. This move for independence isn't all in one direction. The same three-year-old who insists "I can do it myself" in August may cling to parents on the first day of junior kindergarten in September. As children grow into adolescents, the "leave me alone" orientation becomes apparent. Teenagers who used to happily spend time with their parents now may groan at the thought of a family vacation or even the notion of sitting down at the dinner table each evening. More time is spent with friends or alone. Although this time can be painful for parents, most developmental experts recognize it as a necessary stage in moving from childhood to adulthood.

As the need for independence from family grows, adolescents take care of their "hold me tight" needs by associating with their peers. Friendships during the teenage years are vital, and the level of closeness with contemporaries can be a barometer of happiness. This is the time when physical intimacy becomes an option, and sexual exploration may provide a new way of achieving closeness.

In adult relationships, the same cycle of intimacy and distance repeats itself. In marriages, for example, the "hold me tight" bonds of the first year are often followed by a desire for independence. This need for autonomy can manifest itself in a number of ways, such as the desire to make friends or engage in activities that don't include the spouse, or the need to make a career move that might disrupt the relationship. As we note later on in the discussion of relational stages, this movement from closeness to autonomy may lead to the breakup of relationships, but it can also be part of a cycle that redefines the relationship in a new form that can recapture or even surpass the intimacy that existed in the past.

Predictability versus Novelty

Stability is an important need in relationships, but too much of it can lead to feelings of staleness. The *predictability–novelty dialectic* reflects this tension. Humorist Dave Barry exaggerates only slightly when he talks about the boredom that can come when husbands and wives know each other too well:

> After a decade or so of marriage, you know everything about your spouse, every habit and opinion and twitch and tic and minor skin growth. You could write a seventeen-pound book solely about the way your spouse eats. This kind of intimate knowledge can be very handy in certain situations—such as when you're on a tv quiz show where the object is to identify your spouse from the sound of his or her chewing—but it tends to lower the passion level of a relationship.[47]

CRITICAL THINKING PROBE
Stages in Non-Romantic Relationships

Knapp's model of relational development and decline offers a good description of communication stages in traditional romantic relationships. Some critics have argued that it doesn't characterize other sorts of relationships so well. Identify your position in this debate by following these steps:

1. Explain how well (or how poorly) the model describes one other type of relationship: among co-workers, friends (either close or more distant), parent and child, or another relational context of your choosing.

2. Construct a model describing communication stages in the relationship type you just identified. How does this model differ from Knapp's?

"Look, you seem nice, and I don't want to hurt your feelings, but I was really drunk when we met, got married and bought this house."

COMMUNICATING ONLINE

Six Web Design Tips Based on Brain Science

Scientists continue to make discoveries about the human brain and how it works, and their findings can help us improve our communication, both in person and online. Andy Crestodina, the strategic director of a web design company, has put together a list of tips on how to design a website that will get your point across to your audience based on what we know about "brain science."

Some web design tips are supported by actual brain science. Research into the brain reveals tendencies. These tendencies translate into tips for designing websites. In fact, specific parts of the brain relate to specific marketing methods.

The Frontal Lobe (planning, logic, motivation)

The frontal lobe is associated with "executive functions" such as motivation, planning, attention, and short-term memory. It considers options and the consequences of actions.

1. List Order and "Serial Position Effect"
When ordering your navigation (or any lists within your copy), put the important stuff at the beginning and end. The readers' attention and retention are lowest in the middle. As visitors scan the page, the first and the last items are most likely to stay in short-term memory.

Also, don't include too many items. Short term memory can only hold around seven items. If your navigation includes more than seven links, break it up into smaller groups.

2. Marketing Copy and "Loss Aversion"
Humans are not efficient cost/benefit calculators. We tend to overvalue losses and undervalue gains. In other words, losses are more painful than gains are pleasurable.

This aversion to losses can be useful to web designers and copywriters. Here are some tips for writing copy with loss aversion in mind:

- Emphasize the costs of not using your product or service.
- Group costs together, list benefits separately.
- Emphasize immediate gains.
- Create urgency with limited time offers. If the product is scarce, say so.

3. Social Proof and Supportive Content: Herd Behavior
People tend to do what other people are doing. So giving evidence that others have selected you makes choosing your company seem like a good choice. The goal is to make any decision other than using your company seem outside the norm.

Add supportive messages:
- testimonials from clients or reviews from customers;
- social media widgets showing the size of your following;
- endorsements from relevant influencers;
- "As seen in . . ." logos of media where your company has been mentioned; and
- trust seals, including association memberships, security certificates, and awards.

These elements improve the initial value judgment of your website and your company.

Temporal Lobe (language)

Together with the frontal lobe, the temporal lobe plays a key role in language comprehension. This is where language and meaning is processed.

Although too much familiarity can lead to the risk of boredom and stagnation, nobody wants a completely unpredictable relational partner. Too many surprises can threaten the foundations upon which the relationship is based ("You're not the person I married!").

The challenge for communicators is to juggle the desire for predictability with the need for novelty that keeps the relationship fresh and interesting. People differ in their need and desire for stability and surprises, so there is no optimal mixture of the two. As you will read shortly, there are a number of strategies people can use to manage these contradictory drives.

4. Word Choice and Readability

Labels in navigation and copy in pages must be easy for visitors to understand. Use the common words that visitors expect. Avoid long sentences. Don't use jargon. Long sentences and fancy words force the temporal lobe to work harder. Not good.

Copy that works well for "low literacy" users works well for everyone. It's not about dumbing it down; it's about using simple language that everyone can understand. Even PhDs prefer to read at an 8th grade level.

A big word might make you sound smart, but it risks making the reader feel dumb. A reader who doubts themselves is unlikely to take action. And you want to inspire action, right? Be simple and accessible in your writing.

Occipital Lobe (vision)

This is the visual processor of the brain, handling spatial, color, and motion perception.

5. Colors and "Von Restorff Effect"

In the 1930s, German scientist Hedwig von Restorff discovered that when given a list of ten items, people remember items if they are a color different from the others. This is because the occipital lobe is sensitive to visual differences, or "pattern interrupters."

Web marketer, Paras Chopra, conducted experiments that showed how standout colors aren't just remembered more, they're clicked more: 60% more!

Pick an "action color" for all of your links, buttons, and rollover effects. Make it a color that's distinct from the brand colors used throughout the design (these are the "passive colors"). Use the action color nowhere else but in the clickable items.

Amygdala (basic emotions)

The amygdalae (there are two) are key in the formation and storage of emotional memories.

6. Headlines: Emotion and Virality

According to eye tracking studies, headlines aren't just the first thing seen on a page, they're looked at more than anything else. And not all headlines get shared equally.

Headlines and images can quickly spark emotions. Research shows that emotional headlines get shared more. A lot more. The three types of emotions that get shared the most: anxiety, anger, and inspiration.

Especially for blog posts, write headlines that trigger very positive (or very negative) emotions. In the words of Antonio Damasio, "We are not thinking machines that feel, we are feeling machines that think."

Results May Vary

Web marketing is a science, and science is about testing. Try these techniques in your web design and web marketing, and measure the results. You may find that some tips work better than others. But any technique that takes brain anatomy into account is likely to work well!

—Andy Crestodina, orbitmedia.com, 1 May 2013

Openness versus Privacy

As Chapter 1 explained, disclosure is one characteristic of interpersonal relationships. Yet, along with the need for intimacy, we have an equally important need to maintain some space between ourselves and others. These sometimes-conflicting drives create the *openness–privacy dialectic.*

Even the strongest interpersonal relationships require some distance. On a short-term basis, the desire for closeness waxes and wanes. Lovers may go through periods of much sharing and

Understanding Diversity

Mapping Her Musical Landscape

"I can't write by a fireplace," says Inuit singer Elisapie Isaac. "I need a window. I need to feel connected to something, to see the sky or whatever. I think it's because I'm from this small town where you can see far. No matter what building I'm in, my inspiration is the window."

Isaac spent almost three years sitting by her window, so to speak, and the songs she found there became the substance of her recent solo recording debut, *There Will Be Stars*. After several years as the singing half of the Quebec electro-folk duo Taima, the 32-year-old performer and filmmaker (who began a short Canadian tour on Thursday at Toronto's Drake Hotel) has mapped out her own musical landscape.

"I just wanted it to be sweet and warm, I wanted it to breathe," she says of the album, which was produced by Éloi Painchaud. She's talking mainly about the shape-shifting sounds on the record. The songs, by contrast, are often about hard, uncomfortable situations: the ragged end of a love affair; the intensity of a deep winter spent in a small northern settlement (Salluit, in

Nunavik); the dislocation many Inuit feel whether they stay in the North or head south, as Isaac did 10 years ago.

"Tears and emotions, that's what motivates me," she says.

Isaac moved from Montreal to study journalism, then quit school to take a job researching a circumpolar documentary about Inuit people, and made her own half-hour NFB documentary: *Si le temps le permet* (2003), about Aboriginal men in the North and their conflicted feelings about traditional and urban ways. With guitarist Alain Auger, she also started Taima and made a Juno-winning record that sold 25,000 copies.

A second disc was on their agenda, but the initial sessions felt "a bit forced," Isaac says. She bought a guitar and started writing, not at all sure she could assume the creative functions that, in Taima, had largely been Auger's.

One of the disc's strongest songs was also one of the first written. "Why Would I Cry?" is a calm and stately tune about reclaiming personal autonomy at the end of a punishing relationship. "It's a love song, of course, and also an affirmation,"

times of relative withdrawal. Likewise, they experience periods of passion and then periods of little physical contact. Friends have times of high disclosure where they share almost every feeling and idea and then disengage for days, months, or even longer. Figure 6.5 illustrates some patterns of variation in openness uncovered in a study of college students' communication patterns.[48] The students reported the degree of openness in one of their important relationships—a friendship, romantic relationship, or marriage—over a range of 30 conversations. The graphs show a definite pattern of fluctuation between disclosure and privacy in every stage of the relationships.

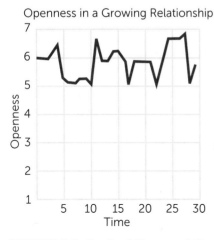

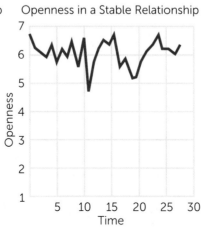

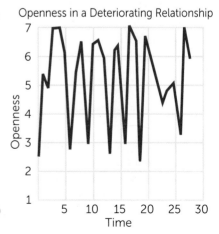

FIGURE 6.5 Cyclical Phases of Openness and Withdrawal in Relationships

she says. "I was at a point when I was tired of crying all the time, and this song was the turning point, when I decided that what I choose to do is really my choice."

"It was also a turning point musically, because the melody and the way it's written are so simple. I knew that was what I wanted to do." In a way, it was a return to the powerful simplicity of the English hymns and folk songs she sang as a little girl, often on local northern radio.

Isaac grew up in an adoptive family, after she and a brother were "given away" to a distant relative. The hard phrase sounds mild in her softly accented English.

"Up north, it's really common for people to be adopted, not taboo in any way," she says. "My mother wasn't married, and my grandmother said, 'The next baby you have, you should give it to my second cousin, because she's older and she can't have kids.' My grandmother passed away before I was born, but my mother respected her decision. She almost had no choice. But I never heard her crying over it, and I have a great relationship with her."

Her father is a Newfoundlander. Isaac is still getting to know that side of her family, even as she, now the mother of a four-year-old, thinks of making another film about Inuit women in the North, and about the disappearance of traditional rituals.

"There are so many energies, I sometimes wonder, where do I go?" she says. "I was named after four different women. I used to think that was such a cool thing. But when you're named after four different women, you sort of become those different women. I thought it was such a cool thing, but it kind of messed me up."

A fine mess, and a fine album too.

Robert Everett-Green, *The Globe and Mail*, 6 February 2010

QUESTIONS: How do you think that Elisapie Isaac's relationships have influenced her art? Do you think her blended cultural identity, half Inuit and half Newfoundlander, was a challenge for her? How does her story relate to your life experience and your identity?

Strategies for Managing Dialectical Tensions

Managing the dialectical tensions outlined in these pages presents communication challenges. There are a number of strategies by which these challenges can be managed.[49] One of the least functional is *denial* that tensions exist. People in denial insist that "everything is fine," that the inevitable tugs of dialectical tensions really aren't a problem. For example, co-workers who claim that they're *always* happy to be members of the team and *never* see conflicts between their personal goals and the organization's goals are probably operating in a state of denial.

Disorientation is another response to dialectical tensions. In this response, communicators feel so overwhelmed and helpless that they are unable to confront their problems. In the face of dialectical tensions they might fight, freeze, or even leave the relationship. A couple who discover soon after the honeymoon that living a "happily ever after" conflict-free life is impossible might become so terrified that they would come to view their marriage as a mistake.

In the strategy of *selection*, communicators respond to one end of the dialectical spectrum and ignore the other. For example, a couple caught between the conflicting desires for stability and novelty might find their struggle to change too difficult to manage and choose to stick with predictable, if unexciting, patterns of relating to one another.

Communicators choose the strategy of *alternation* to alternate between one end of the dialectical spectrum at some times and the other end at other times. Friends, for example, might manage the autonomy–connection dialectic by alternating between times when they spend a large amount of time together and other times when they live independent lives.

A fifth strategy is *segmentation*, a tactic in which partners compartmentalize different areas of their relationship. For example, a couple might manage the openness–closedness dialectic by sharing almost all their feelings about mutual friends with one another while keeping certain parts of their past romantic histories private.

Moderation is a sixth strategy. This strategy is characterized by compromises, in which communicators choose to back off from expressing either end of the dialectical spectrum. Adult children, for example, might manage the revelation–concealment dialectic with their inquisitive parents by answering some (though not all) unwelcome parental questions.

Communicators can also respond to dialectical challenges by reframing them in terms that redefine the situation so that the apparent contradiction disappears. Consider a couple who wince when their friends characterize them as a "perfect couple." On one hand, they want to escape from the "perfect couple" label that feels confining, but on the other hand, they enjoy the admiration that comes with this identity. By pointing out to their friends that "ideal couples" aren't always blissfully happy, they can both be themselves and keep the admiration of their friends.

A final strategy for handling dialectical tensions is *reaffirmation*—acknowledging that dialectical tensions will never disappear, accepting or even embracing the challenges they present. The metaphorical view of relational life as a kind of roller coaster reflects this orientation, and communicators who use reaffirmation view dialectical tensions as part of the ride.

> *One man all by himself is nothing. Two people who belong together make a world.*
>
> **Hans Margolius,
> German philosopher**

Characteristics of Relational Development and Maintenance

Whether you analyze a relationship in terms of stages or dialectical dynamics, two characteristics are true of every interpersonal relationship. As you read about each, consider how it applies to your own experience.

Relationships Are Constantly Changing

Relationships are certainly not doomed to deteriorate, but even the strongest ones are rarely stable for long periods of time. In fairy tales a couple may live "happily ever after," but in real life this sort of equilibrium is less common. Consider a husband and wife who have been married for some time. Although they have formally bonded, their relationship will probably shift from one dimension of a relational dialectic to another, and forward or backward along the spectrum of stages. Sometimes the partners will feel the need to differentiate from one another, and at other times they will seek intimacy. Sometimes they will feel secure in the predictable patterns they have established, and at other times one or both will be hungry for novelty. The relationship may become more circumscribed, or even stagnant. From this point the marriage may fail, but this fate isn't certain. With effort, the partners may move from the stage of stagnating to experimenting, or from circumscribing to intensifying.

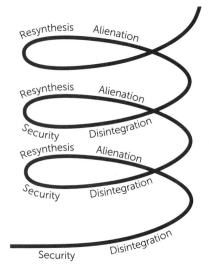

FIGURE 6.6 A Helical Model of Relational Cycles

Communication theorist Richard Conville describes the constantly evolving nature of relationships as a cycle in which partners move through a series of stages, returning to ones they previously encountered—although at a new level (see Figure 6.6).[50] In this cycle, partners move from security (integration, in Knapp's terminology) to disintegration (differentiating) to alienation (circumscribing) to resynthesis (intensifying, integrating) to a new level of security. This process repeats itself again and again.

Movement Is Always to a New Place

Even though a relationship may return to a stage it has previously experienced, it will never be the same. For example, most healthy long-term relationships will go through several phases of experimenting, when the partners try out new ways of behaving with one another. Though the same general features characterize each phase, the specifics will feel different each time. As you learned in Chapter 1, communication is irreversible. Partners can never go back to "the way things were." Sometimes this fact may lead to regrets: it's impossible to take back a cruel comment or forget a crisis. On the other hand, the irreversibility of communication can make relationships exciting, because it lessens the chance for boredom.

Self-Disclosure in Interpersonal Relationships

"We don't have any secrets," some people proudly claim. Opening up certainly is important. Earlier in this chapter you learned that one ingredient in qualitatively interpersonal relationships is disclosure. You've also learned that we find others more attractive when they share certain private information with us. Given the obvious importance of self-disclosure, we need to take a closer look at the subject. Just what is it? When is it desirable? How can it best be done?

The best place to begin is with a definition. **Self-disclosure** is the process of deliberately revealing information about oneself that is significant and that others would not normally know. Let's take a closer look at some parts of this definition. Self-disclosure must be *deliberate*. If you accidentally mentioned to a friend that you were thinking about quitting a job or proposing marriage, that information would not fit into the category we are examining here. Self-disclosure must also be *significant*. Revealing relatively trivial information—the fact that you like fudge, for example—does not qualify as self-disclosure. The third requirement is that *others would not know the information being revealed*. There's nothing noteworthy about telling others that you are depressed or elated if they already know how you're feeling.

> **self-disclosure**
> The process of deliberately revealing information about oneself that is significant and that would not normally be known by others.

As Table 6.5 shows, people self-disclose for a variety of reasons. Some involve developing and maintaining relationships, but other reasons often drive revealing personal information. The reasons for disclosing vary from one situation to another, depending on several factors. The first important factor in whether we disclose seems to be how well we know the other person.[51] When the target of disclosure is a friend, the most frequent reason people give for volunteering personal information is relationship maintenance and enhancement. In other words, we disclose to friends in order to strengthen the relationship. The second important reason is self-clarification—to sort out confusion to understand ourselves better.

With strangers, reciprocity becomes the most common reason for disclosing. We offer information about ourselves to strangers in hopes of learning more about them, so we can decide whether and how to continue the relationship. The second most common reason is impression formation. We often reveal information about ourselves to strangers to make ourselves look good. This information, of course, is usually positive—at least in the early stages of a friendship.

Table 6.5 Reasons for Self-Disclosure

Reason	Example/Explanation
Catharsis	"I need to get this off my chest. . . ."
Self-clarification	"I'm really confused about something I did last night. If I tell you, maybe I can figure out why I did it. . . ."
Self-validation	"I think I did the right thing. Let me tell you why I did it. . . ."
Reciprocity	"I really like you. . . ." (Hoping for a similar disclosure by the other person)
Impression management	Salesperson to customer: "My boss would kill me for giving you this discount. . . ." (Hoping disclosure will build on trust)
Relationship maintenance and enhancement	"I'm worried about the way things are going between us. Let's talk." or "I sure am glad we're together!"
Control	Employee to boss, hoping to get a raise: "I got a job offer yesterday from our biggest competitor."

Source: Adapted from V.J. Deriega and J. Grezlak, "Appropriateness of Self-Disclosure," in G.J. Chelune, ed., *Self-Disclosure* (San Francisco, CA: Jossey-Bass, 1979).

Models of Self-Disclosure

Over several decades, social scientists have created various models to represent and understand how self-disclosure operates in relationships. In the next few pages we will look at two of the best-known models.

Breadth and Depth: Social Penetration

Social psychologists Irwin Altman and Dalmas Taylor describe two ways in which communication can be more or less disclosing.[52] Their **social penetration model** is pictured in Figure 6.7. The first dimension of self-disclosure in this model involves the **breadth** of information volunteered—the range of subjects being discussed. For example, the breadth of disclosure in your relationship with a fellow worker will expand as you begin revealing information about your life away from the job, as well as on-the-job details. The second dimension of disclosure is the **depth** of the information being volunteered, the shift from relatively non-revealing messages to more personal ones.

Depending on the breadth and depth of information shared, a relationship can be defined as either casual or intimate. In a casual relationship, the breadth may be great, but not the depth. A more intimate relationship is likely to have high depth in at least one area. The most intimate relationships are those in which disclosure is great in both breadth and depth. Altman and Taylor see the development of a relationship as a progression from the periphery of their model to its centre, a process that typically occurs over time. Each of your personal relationships probably has a different combination of breadth of subjects and depth of disclosure. Figure 6.8 illustrates self-disclosure in one relationship.

What makes the disclosure in some messages deeper than others? One way to measure depth is by how far it goes in two of the dimensions that define self-disclosure. Some revelations are certainly more *significant* than others. Consider the difference between saying "I love my family"

social penetration model
A model describing how intimacy can be achieved through the breadth and depth of self-disclosure.

breadth
The range of topics about which an individual discloses.

depth
The level of personal information a person reveals on a particular topic.

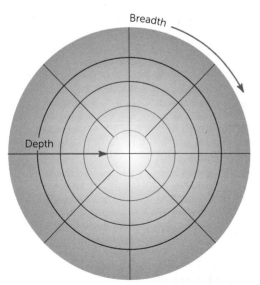

FIGURE 6.7 Social Penetration Model

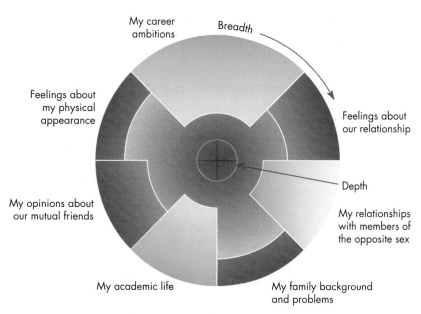

FIGURE 6.8 Sample Model of Social Penetration

and "I love you." Other statements qualify as deep disclosure because they are private. Sharing a secret you've told to only a few close friends is certainly an act of self-disclosure, but it's even more revealing to divulge information that you've never told anyone.

Self-Disclosure, Self-Awareness, and Relational Quality: The Johari Window

Another model that helps represent how self-disclosure operates is the **Johari Window**.[53] (The window takes its name from the first names of its creators, Joseph Luft and Harry Ingham.) Imagine a frame inside which is everything there is to know about you: your likes and dislikes, your goals, your secrets, your needs—everything (see Figure 6.9).

Of course, you aren't aware of everything about yourself. Like most people, you're probably discovering new things about yourself all the time. To represent this, we can divide the frame containing everything about you into two parts: the part you know about and the part you don't know about, as in Figure 6.10.

We can also divide this frame containing everything about you in another way. In this division the first part contains the things about you that others know, and the second part contains the things about you that you keep to yourself. Figure 6.11 represents this view.

When we impose these two divided frames one atop the other, we have a Johari Window. By looking at Figure 6.12 you can see the "*everything about you*" window divided into four parts.

Part 1 represents the information of which both you and the other person are aware. This part is your *open area*. Part 2 represents the *blind area:* information of which you are unaware but the other person knows. You learn about information in the blind area primarily through feedback. Part 3 represents your *hidden area:* information that you know but aren't willing to reveal to others. Items in this hidden area become public primarily through self-disclosure, which is the focus of this chapter. Part 4 represents information that is *unknown* to both you and others. At first, the unknown area seems impossible to verify. After all, if neither you nor others know what it contains, how can you be sure it exists? We can deduce its existence because we are constantly discovering new things about ourselves. It is not unusual to discover,

> **Johari Window**
> A model that describes the relationship between self-disclosure and self-awareness.

FIGURE 6.9 The Johari Window: Everything about You

FIGURE 6.10 The Johari Window: Known to Self; Not Known to Self

FIGURE 6.11 The Johari Window: Known to Others; Not Known to Others

for example, that you have an unrecognized talent, strength, or weakness. Items move from the unknown area into the open area either directly when you disclose your insight or through one of the other areas first.

Interpersonal relationships of any depth are virtually impossible if the individuals involved have little open area. Going a step further, you can see that the individual who is less open, that is, who possesses the smaller open area, limits a relationship. Figure 6.13 illustrates this situation with Johari Windows. A's window is set up in reverse so that A's and B's open areas are adjacent. Notice that the amount of communication (represented by the arrows connecting the two open areas) is dictated by the size of the smaller open area of A. The arrows originating from B's open area and being turned aside by A's hidden and blind areas represent unsuccessful attempts to communicate.

You have probably found yourself in situations that resemble Figure 6.13. Perhaps you have felt the frustration of not being able to get to know someone who was too reserved. Perhaps you have blocked another person's attempts to build a relationship with you in the same way. Whether you picture yourself more like Person A or Person B, the fact is that self-disclosure on both sides is necessary for the development of any interpersonal relationship. This chapter will describe just how much self-disclosure is optimal and of what type.

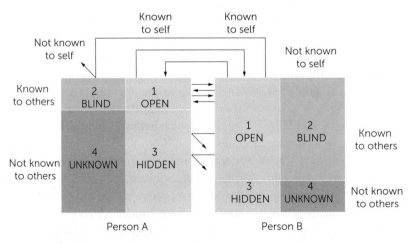

FIGURE 6.12 The Johari Window: Open; Blind; Hidden; Unknown

FIGURE 6.13 The Johari Window: Self-Disclosure Levels in Two-Way Communication

Characteristics of Effective Self-Disclosure

Self-disclosure can certainly be valuable, but using it effectively requires an understanding of how it operates. Here are some findings from researchers that will help you decide when and how disclosure works best.

Self-Disclosure Is Influenced by Culture

The level of self-disclosure that is appropriate in one culture may seem completely inappropriate in another one. Disclosure is especially high in mainstream Anglo-North American society. In fact, people born and bred in English Canada and the United States are more disclosing of themselves—not just to friends but to acquaintances and even strangers—than members of any other culture studied.[54] By contrast, Germans tend to disclose little about themselves except in intimate relationships with a select few, and Japanese people reveal very little about themselves in even their closest relationships.

Cultural differences like this mean that what counts as disclosing communication varies from one culture to another. If you were raised in English Canada, you might view people from certain other cultures as undisclosing or standoffish. But the amount of personal information that people from other traditions disclose might actually be quite revealing by the standards of their culture. The converse is also true: to people from some other cultures, English Canadians probably look like exhibitionists, ready to spew personal information to anyone within earshot.

When communicating with people from different cultures it's important to consider their standards for appropriate disclosure. Don't mistakenly judge them according to your own standards. Likewise, be sensitive about honouring their standards when talking about yourself. In this sense, choosing the proper level of self-disclosure isn't too different from choosing the appropriate way of dressing or eating when encountering members of a different culture: what seems familiar and correct at home may not be suitable with strangers. As you read on, realize that the characteristics and guidelines that suit mainstream English-Canadian culture may not apply in other contexts.

> **Cultural Idiom**
> **standoffish**
> To be unfriendly.
>
> **earshot**
> The distance at which one can hear something or someone.

Self-Disclosure Usually Occurs in Dyads

Although it is possible for people to disclose a great deal about themselves in groups, such communication usually occurs in one-to-one settings. Revealing significant information about yourself involves a certain amount of risk, and limiting the disclosure to one person at a time minimizes the chance that your disclosure will lead to unhappy consequences.

Effective Self-Disclosure Is Usually Symmetrical

Recall the small amount of successful two-way communication between A and B, as well as B's unsuccessful attempts to communicate in Figure 6.13. In situations such as this one, it's easy to imagine how B would soon limit the amount of disclosure to match that of A. On the other hand, if A were willing to match the degree of disclosure given by B, the relationship would move to a new level of intimacy. In either case, we can expect that the degree of disclosure between partners will often stabilize at a symmetrical level.

Effective Self-Disclosure Occurs Incrementally

Although instances occur in which partners start their relationship by telling everything about themselves to each other, such instances are rare. In most cases, the amount of disclosure increases over time. We begin relationships by revealing relatively little about ourselves; then if our first bits of self-disclosure are well-received and bring on similar responses from the other person, we're willing to reveal more. This principle is important to remember. It would usually be a mistake to assume that the way to build a strong relationship would be to reveal the most private details about yourself when first making contact with another person. Unless the circumstances are unique, such baring of your soul would be likely to scare potential partners away rather than bring them closer.

Self-Disclosure Is Relatively Rare

Most conversations—even among friends—focus on everyday mundane topics and disclose little or no personal information.[55] Even partners in intimate relationships rarely talk about personal information.[56] Whether or not we open up to others is based on several criteria, some of which are listed in Table 6.6.

What is the optimal amount of self-disclosure? You might suspect that the correct answer is "the more, the better," at least in personal relationships. Research has shown that the matter isn't this simple, however.[57] For example, there seems to be a curvilinear relationship between openness and satisfaction in marriage, so that a moderate amount of openness produces better results than either extreme disclosure or withholding. One good measure of happiness is how well the level of disclosure matches the expectations of communicators. If we get what we believe is a reasonable amount of candour from others, we are happy. If they tell us too little—or even too much—we become less satisfied.

Guidelines for Appropriate Self-Disclosure

One fear we've had while writing this chapter is that a few overenthusiastic readers may throw down their books and begin to share every personal detail of their lives with whomever they can find. As you can imagine, this kind of behaviour isn't an example of effective interpersonal communication.

No single style of self-disclosure is appropriate for every situation. Let's take a look at some guidelines that can help you recognize how to express yourself in a way that's rewarding for you and the others involved.[58]

Is the Other Person Important to You?

There are several ways in which someone might be important. Perhaps you have an ongoing relationship deep enough so that sharing significant parts of yourself justifies keeping your present level of togetherness intact. Or perhaps the person to whom you're considering disclosing is someone with whom you've previously related on a less personal level. If you now see a chance to grow closer, disclosure may be the path toward developing that personal relationship.

Is the Risk of Disclosing Reasonable?

> **Cultural Idiom**
> **opening yourself up**
> Letting yourself become vulnerable.

Take a realistic look at the potential risks of self-disclosure. Even if the probable benefits are great, opening yourself up to almost certain rejection may be asking for trouble. For instance, it might be foolhardy to share your important feelings with someone you know is likely to either betray or ridicule your confidences. On the other hand, knowing that your partner is trustworthy and supportive makes the prospect of speaking out more reasonable.

Table 6.6 Some Criteria Used to Reveal Family Secrets

Intimate Exchange
Does the other person have a similar problem?
Would knowing the secret help the other person feel better?
Would knowing the secret help the other person manage her problem?

Exposure
Will the other person find out this information, even if I don't tell her?
Is the other person asking me directly to reveal this information?

Urgency
Is it very important that the other person know this information?
Will revealing this information make matters better?

Acceptance
Will the other person still accept me if I reveal this information?

Conversational Appropriateness
Will my disclosure fit into the conversation?
Has the topic of my disclosure come up in this conversation?

Relational Security
Do I trust the other person with this information?
Do I feel close enough to this person to reveal the secret?

Important Reason
Is there a pressing reason to reveal this information?

Permission
Have other people involved in the secret given their permission for me to reveal it?
Would I feel okay telling the people involved that I have revealed the secret?

Membership
Is the person to whom I'm revealing the secret going to join this group (i.e., family)?

Source: Adapted from A.L. Vangelisti, J.P Cauglhin, and L. Timmerman, "Criteria for Revealing Family Secrets," *Communication Monographs* 68 (2001): 1–27.

Revealing personal thoughts and feelings can be especially risky on the job.[59] The politics of the workplace sometimes require communicators to keep feelings to themselves in order to accomplish both personal and organizational goals. You might, for example, find the opinions of a boss or customer personally offensive but decide to bite your tongue rather than risk your job or lose goodwill for the company.

> **Cultural Idiom**
> **to bite your tongue**
> To remain silent.
>
> **in the same vein**
> Related to an idea.

Are the Amount and Type of Disclosure Appropriate?

A third point to realize is that there are degrees of self-disclosure. Telling others about yourself isn't an all-or-nothing decision. It's possible to share some facts, opinions, or feelings with one person while reserving riskier ones for others. In the same vein, before sharing very important information with someone who does matter to you, you might consider testing reactions by disclosing less personal data.

Is the Disclosure Relevant to the Situation at Hand?

The kind of disclosure that is often characteristic of highly personal relationships usually isn't appropriate in less personal settings. For instance, a study of classroom communication revealed that sharing all feelings—both positive and negative—and being completely honest resulted in less cohesiveness than having a "relatively" honest climate in which pleasant but superficial relationships were the norm.[60]

Even in personal relationships—with close friends, family members, and so on—constant disclosure isn't a useful goal. The level of sharing in successful relationships rises and falls in cycles. You may go through a period of great disclosure and then spend another period of relative non-disclosure. Even during a phase of high disclosure, sharing everything isn't necessarily constructive. Usually the subject of appropriate self-disclosure involves the relationship rather than personal information. Furthermore, it is usually most constructive to focus your disclosure about the relationship on the "here and now" as opposed to "there and then." "How am I feeling now?" "How are we doing now?" These are appropriate topics for sharing personal thoughts and feelings. There are certainly times when it's relevant to bring up the past but only as it relates to what's going on in the present.

Is the Disclosure Reciprocated?

Cultural Idiom
talking your heart out
To reveal your innermost thoughts and feelings.

There's nothing quite as disconcerting as talking your heart out to someone only to discover that the other person has yet to say anything to you that is half as revealing as what you've been saying. And you think to yourself, "What am I doing?" Unequal self-disclosure creates an unbalanced relationship, one doomed to fall apart.

There are few times when one-way disclosure is acceptable. Most of them involve formal, therapeutic relationships in which a client approaches a trained professional with the goal of resolving a problem. For instance, you wouldn't necessarily expect to hear about a physician's personal ailments during a visit to a medical office. Nonetheless, it's interesting to note that one frequently noted characteristic of effective psychotherapists, counsellors, and teachers is a willingness to share their feelings about a relationship with their clients.

Will the Effect Be Constructive?

Self-disclosure can be a vicious tool if it's not used carefully. Psychologist George Bach suggests that every person has a psychological "belt line."[61] Below that belt line are areas about which the person is extremely sensitive. Bach says that jabbing at a "below-the-belt" area is a surefire way to disable another person, although usually at great cost to the relationship. It's important to consider the effects of your candour before opening up to others. Comments such as "I've always thought you were pretty unintelligent" or "Last year I made love to your best friend" *may* sometimes resolve old business and thus be constructive, but they also can be devastating—to the listener, to the relationship, and to your self-esteem.

Is the Self-Disclosure Clear and Understandable?

When you express yourself to others, it's important that you share yourself in a way that's intelligible. This means describing the *sources* of your message clearly. For instance, it's far better to describe another's behaviour by saying, "When you don't answer my phone calls or drop by to visit anymore . . ." than to complain vaguely, "When you avoid me. . . ."

It's also vital to express your *thoughts* and *feelings* explicitly. "I feel worried because I'm afraid you don't care about me" is more understandable than "I don't like the way things have been going."

Deception, Hinting, and Equivocation

Although honesty is desirable in principle, it often has risky, potentially unpleasant consequences. This explains why communicators—even those with the best intentions—aren't always completely honest when they find themselves in situations when honesty would be uncomfortable.[62] Three common alternatives to self-disclosure are lies, equivocation, and hinting.

YOUNG COMMUNICATOR PROFILE

JOEY COLEMAN

Independent Crowdsourced Journalist in Hamilton, Ontario

If you don't have an online presence, you're not going to succeed in communications. If you're not willing to take a risk online, you'll never achieve much of anything. If you don't take big risks, you'll never reach your full potential.

By the time you read this in the 3rd edition (they really do update textbooks), I will have succeeded or failed at my latest venture—but will be successfully advancing my career regardless.

Today, I run Canada's first crowdfunded independent local news website. I've raised over $23,000 dollars in the past six months to support my journalism, and am the most followed journalist in my community on Twitter. If the news happens in Hamilton, I'm there and I'm livestreaming.

I started with a blog in 2004 during my first year of university, built a strong following of loyal readers, and maintained strongly ethical standards in my communications.

In 2007, Canada's national newsweekly Maclean's hired me as the founding reporter/blogger of their online university news site. Why did Maclean's hire me, a student with no professional experience—who didn't even apply for the job? My blog had a large following; I knew how to communicate.

I knew how to effectively use Web 2.0 tools to collect information; and was widely respected among their target audience. In 2009, I moved my higher-education coverage to Canada's national newspaper *The Globe and Mail*'s website.

2010 saw me decided to leave national reporting to cover local affairs in my hometown where I took a lead role in founding an open data movement.

During the next two years, I built my brand covering local affairs and breaking news, while paying my bills working as a parking lot supervisor at a local hospital.

In 2012, after not getting hired by any local media outlet due, in large part, to my strong open source philosophies, I asked my readers if they would make a financial contribution to my journalism. I asked for, and raised, $10,000.

I license all my work under a Creative Commons open culture Attribution-ShareAlike license. For major public safety stories, I put my work and livestreams into the public domain.

My journalism is funded not only because of the content, but also by the relationships I've built with my community and the trust I'm privilege to have from readers.

Your reputation is the only thing you control. How do you build your career using the web? The key to successfully using the social web is authenticity and focus. Find your niche (Hint: communications is not a niche in and of itself), become an expert, write about it, and be human every once in a while.

Use the tools to connect to people, not to spread propaganda. The Web is not your dumping ground; don't use it as such. You must participate to succeed. Communicate your niche and connect with other people interested in that area.

Then, extend your network to related topics. Build relationships. When someone in your network tweets about cheese in Wisconsin—and you're interested in that cheese—respond back. It's off-topic, but that's how you build relationships.

Tweet off-topic yourself. I often tweet about my pinball obsession. Once you have a relationship, make it mutually beneficial. I've called my Twitter contacts many times for comments and they always take my calls—some of these people don't normally take media calls.

As a journalist, I'm always looking for stories and sources. To be effective professional communicators, you must learn my interests as a journalist, then suggest people and stories, and you'll succeed in securing the all-valuable "earned media," that is, placement of the message you are promoting in the media that I write for.

The Web is not the messiah some people make it out to be. It is a tool that needs to be used properly; misuse is worse than no use, and no use is failure. Most of all, don't spend your entire day talking about social media to other self-proclaimed "social media experts!"

Lies

To most people, lying appears to be a breach of ethics. Although lying to gain unfair advantage over an unknowing victim seems clearly wrong, another kind of untruth isn't so easy to dismiss as completely unethical. White lies, more appropriately called **altruistic lies,** are defined (at least by the people who tell them) as being harmless, or even helpful, to the person to whom they are told.[63] As Table 6.7 shows, at least some of the lies we tell are indeed intended to be helpful, or are at least relatively benign. Whether or not they are innocent, altruistic lies are certainly common. In one study, 130 subjects were asked to keep track of the truthfulness of their everyday conversational statements.[64] Only 38.5 per cent of these statements proved to be totally honest. In another experiment, 147 people between the ages of 18 and 71 kept a log of all the lies they told over a one-week period. Both men and women reported being untruthful in approximately one-fifth of their conversations that lasted over 10 minutes.[65] Over the course of the week, the subjects reported lying to about 30 per cent of the people with whom they had one-on-one conversations. The rate was much higher in some relationships. For example, dating couples lie to each other in about one-third of their interactions, and college students told at least one lie to their mothers in half of their conversations. In yet another study, subjects recorded their conversations over a two-day period and later counted their own deceptions. The average lie rate: 3 fibs for every 10 minutes of conversation.[66]

What are the consequences of discovering that you've been lied to? In an interpersonal relationship, the discovery can be traumatic. As we grow closer to others, our expectations about their honesty grow stronger. Discovering that you've been deceived requires you to redefine not only the lie you just uncovered but also many of the messages you previously took for granted. Was last week's compliment really sincere? Was your joke really funny, or was the other person's laughter a put-on? Does the other person care about you as much as he or she claimed?

Research has shown that deception does, in fact, threaten relationships; however, not all lies are equally devastating. Feelings of dismay and betrayal are greatest when the relationship is most intense, when the importance of the subject is high, and when there is pre-existing suspicion that the other person isn't being completely honest. Of these three factors, the importance of the information lied about proved to be the key factor in provoking a relational crisis. We may be able to cope with "misdemeanour" lying, but "felonies" are a grave threat. In fact, the discovery of major deception can lead to the end of the relationship. More than two-thirds

TABLE 6.7 Some Reasons for Lying

Reason	Example
Acquire resources	"Oh, please let me add this class. If I don't get in, I'll never graduate on time!"
Protect resources	"I'd like to lend you the money, but I'm short myself."
Initiate and continue interaction	"Excuse me, I'm lost. Do you live around here?"
Avoid conflict	"It's not a big deal. We can do it your way. Really."
Avoid interaction or take leave	"That sounds like fun, but I'm busy Saturday night." "Oh, look what time it is! I've got to run!"
Present a competent image	"Sure, I understand. No problem."
Increase social desirability	"Yeah, I've done a fair amount of skiing."

Source: Adapted from categories originally presented in C. Camden, M.T. Motley, and A. Wilson, "White Lies in Interpersonal Communication: A Taxonomy and Preliminary Investigation of Social Motivations," *Western Journal of Speech Communication* 48 (1984): 315.

of the subjects in one study reported that their relationship had ended since they discovered a lie. Furthermore, they attributed the breakup directly to the lie. If preserving a relationship is important, honesty—at least about important matters—really does appear to be the best policy. [67]

Equivocation

Lying isn't the only alternative to self-disclosure. When faced with the choice between lying and telling an unpleasant truth, communicators can—and often do—equivocate. As Chapter 3 explained, **equivocal language** has two or more equally plausible meanings. Sometimes people send equivocal messages without meaning to, resulting in confusion. "I'll meet you at the apartment," could refer to more than one place. But other times we are deliberately vague. For instance, when a friend asks what you think of an awful outfit, you could say, "It's really unusual—one of a kind!" Likewise, if you are too angry to accept a friend's apology but don't want to appear petty, you might say, "Don't mention it."

The value of equivocation becomes clear when you consider the alternatives. Consider the dilemma of what to say when you receive an unwanted present—an ugly painting, for example—and the giver asks what you think of it. How can you respond? On the one hand, you need to choose between telling the truth and lying. On the other hand, you have a choice of whether to make your response clear or vague. Figure 6.14 displays these choices. After considering the alternatives, it's clear that an equivocal but true response is far preferable to the other choices in several respects. First, it spares the receiver from embarrassment. For example, rather than flatly saying "no" to an unappealing invitation, it may be kinder to say "I have other plans"—even if those plans are to stay home and watch TV.

Besides saving face for the recipient, honest equivocation can be less stressful for the sender than either telling the truth bluntly or lying. Because equivocation is often easier to accept than the cold, hard truth, it spares the teller from feeling guilty. It's less taxing on the

---

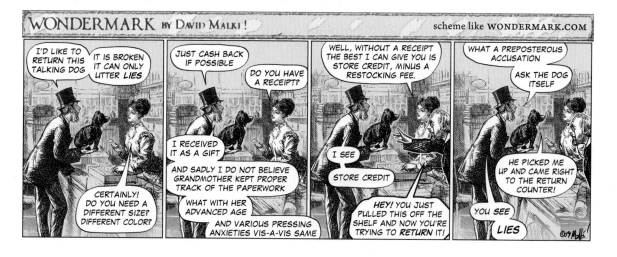

> **COMMUNICATION ON-SCREEN**
>
> ### *The Invention of Lying* (2009)
> **Directed by Ricky Gervais & Matthew Robinson.**
>
> This comedy is set in a universe very similar to our own but with one glaring difference: no one can tell a lie. To our eyes, the complete honesty that underscores all communication in this world appears both hilarious and deeply discomforting, but something approaching a normal human society nonetheless appears to operate relatively smoothly. That is, until Mark Bellison (Ricky Gervais) suddenly acquires the ability to lie. Gifted with a tremendous advantage over his hapless peers, Bellison inadvertently sparks a religious movement with himself as its leading prophet. As he comes to terms with the interpersonal implications of deception, Bellison is forced to confront what limits, if any, he must place on himself in order to live a happy life.

equivocal language
Language with more than one likely interpretation.

Cultural Idiom
less taxing on
Something that is less demanding.

WONDERMARK BY DAVID MALKI !   scheme like WONDERMARK.COM

University Of Toronto Study Shows That Toddlers Can Lie

What comes out of the mouths of babes isn't always the unvarnished truth. Indeed, toddlers can start lying before they're out of diapers, a new University of Toronto study shows.

"We were very surprised that so many kids lied and lied so early," says Kang Lee, a senior child psychologist at the school's Institute of Child Study. Lee's paper, published in the January edition of the American Psychological Association journal Developmental Psychology, pushes the onset of lying back some 18 months from the age previous research has suggested it would begin.

For the study, Lee enlisted 41 two-year-olds and 24 three-year-olds.

His team placed three toys behind the children's backs and asked them to guess what they were by the sounds they made. "Let's say the first was a car and it made an engine sound and the child said 'oh, it's a car'," he says. The second might be a toy dog, which barked and was also easy to guess. "Then we said there was a third toy and if you guess that right you get a prize," Lee says. "But the third toy, let's say it was a Barney, but we played music that had nothing to do with Barney so there was no way they could guess correctly what it was." The researchers would then leave the room, telling the children they could not turn to peek—which the majority of them were caught on hidden cameras doing within seconds.

And upon their return, Lee's team asked the kids if they'd looked while they'd been left alone.

"What we found was about 25 per cent of the two year olds would lie to us," Lees says. What his team found as well was that those puny prevaricators were also more cognitively advanced than their truthful peers. In particular, Lee says, the little liars had better developed "executive functioning"—the higher thinking skills that emerge as we learn.

They also had a more acute "theory of mind," which allows humans to reasonably guess what other people are thinking. "If I were to lie to you, the reason I lie to you is because I know you do not know what I know," he says. "So that requires me to read your mind."

This does not mean, however, that early lying is a sign that the kids who do it are innately smarter than their truthful counterparts, Lee says. "They're not going turn into (geniuses)," he says. "Nor are they liable to become chronic liars as they mature," Lee says. Indeed, by the time children reach the age of seven, almost 100 per cent of them will lie to cover mistakes or transgressions.

Lee's past research has helped to push the onset of lying back from school-aged children to three-year-olds. "Going back 30 years ago people thought that kids simply do not lie until they get to elementary school years or even later," Lee says. "But in the last 10 to 15 years we have been looking at kids from three and above and we found half of three-year-olds would tell lies." Lee's latest study may even indicate that children start equivocating at pre-verbal ages. "So far I don't have a scientific method (to test this) yet," he says. "But I suspect I can still find some (non-verbal) kids were capable of telling lies with actions or with other means of communications."

Joseph Hall, *Toronto Star*, 24 January 2013

QUESTIONS: This study shows that lying is a skill tied to understanding another's mind. How do you think lying can be seen as a developmental tool? Do you think that lies deserve the social stigma they are given? Explain.

conscience to say "I've never tasted anything like this" than to say "This meal tastes terrible," even though the latter comment is more precise. Few people want to lie, and equivocation provides an alternative to deceit.[68]

A study by communication researcher Sandra Metts and her colleagues shows how equivocation can save face in difficult situations.[69] Several hundred university students were asked how they would turn down unwanted sexual overtures from a person whose feelings were important to them: either a close friend, a prospective date, or a dating partner. The majority of students chose a diplomatic reaction ("I just don't think I'm ready for this right now") as being more face-saving and comfortable than a direct statement like "I just don't feel sexually attracted to you." The diplomatic reaction seemed sufficiently clear to get the message across but not so blunt as to embarrass or even humiliate the other person. (Interestingly, men said they would be able to handle a direct rejection more comfortably than women. The researchers

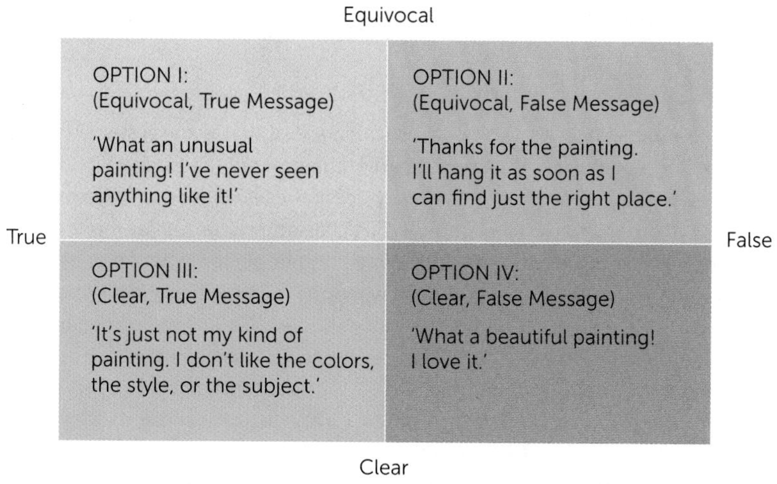

	Equivocal	
True	OPTION I: (Equivocal, True Message) 'What an unusual painting! I've never seen anything like it!'	OPTION II: (Equivocal, False Message) 'Thanks for the painting. I'll hang it as soon as I can find just the right place.'
	OPTION III: (Clear, True Message) 'It's just not my kind of painting. I don't like the colors, the style, or the subject.'	OPTION IV: (Clear, False Message) 'What a beautiful painting! I love it.'	**False**
	Clear	

FIGURE 6.14 Dimensions of Truthfulness and Equivocation

suggest that one reason for the difference is that men stereotypically initiate sexual offers and thus are more likely to expect rejection.)

Besides preventing embarrassment, equivocal language can also save the speaker from being caught lying. If a potential employer asks about your grades during a job interview, you would be safe saying, "I had a B average last semester," even though your overall grade average is closer to C. The statement isn't a complete answer, but it is honest as far as it goes. As one team of researchers put it, "Equivocation is neither a false message nor a clear truth, but rather an alternative used precisely when both of these are to be avoided."[70]

Given these advantages, it's not surprising that most people will usually choose to equivocate rather than tell a lie. In a series of experiments, subjects chose between telling a face-saving lie, telling the truth, and equivocating. Only 6 per cent chose the lie, and between 3 and 4 per cent chose the hurtful truth. By contrast, over 90 per cent chose the equivocal response.[71] People say they prefer truth-telling to equivocating,[72] but given the choice, they prefer to finesse the truth.

Hinting

Hints are more direct than equivocal statements. Whereas an equivocal message isn't necessarily aimed at changing others' behaviour, a hint seeks to get the desired response from others. Some hints are designed to save the receiver from embarrassment:[73]

Face-Saving Hint	**Direct Statement**
"These desserts are terribly overpriced."	"You're too overweight to be ordering dessert."
"I know you're busy; I'd better let you go."	"I'm bored. I want to get out of this conversation."

Other hints are strategies for saving the sender from embarrassment:

Face-Saving Hint	**Direct Statement**
"I'm pretty sure that smoking isn't permitted here."	"Your smoking bothers me."
"Gee, it's almost lunchtime. Have you ever eaten at that new Italian restaurant around the corner?"	"I'd like to invite you out for lunch, but I don't want to risk a 'no' answer to my invitation."

Is It Ever Right to Lie?

Is it ever right to lie? Suppose the Nazis come to your door asking if you are hiding a Jewish family. You are. Should you say "No?" Or, on a mundane level, your spouse or lover walks in with a silly new hairdo and asks, "Do you like it?" Does morality dictate that you ruin the evening? Or can you, in both cases, finesse the answer, not lying but not telling the truth either, perhaps by avoiding an answer to the question?

The demand for honesty is contextual. It depends on what the truth concerns. The Bible tells us not to bear false witness against our neighbor. Perjury, we can agree, is wrong: the consequences can be awful. But it seems to me absolutely crucial to distinguish here between public and private life. Perjury, by its very nature, is public, as is politics. Sex, with a few obvious exceptions, is part of our private life. And just about everyone is less than forthright about sex.

Not all untruths are malicious. Telling the truth can complicate or destroy social relationships. It can undermine precious collective myths. Honesty can be cruel. Sometimes, deception is not a vice but a social virtue, and systematic deception is an essential part of the order of the (social) world.

In many countries—Japan and Western Samoa, for example—social harmony is valued far more than truthfulness as such. To tell another person what he or she wants to hear, rather than what one might actually feel or believe, is not only permitted but expected. Could we not begin to see our own enlightened emphasis on "seeking the truth at all costs" as one more ethnocentric peculiarity, another curious product of our strong sense of individualism, and a dangerously unsociable conception?

The obvious truth is that our simplest social relationships could not exist without the opaque medium of the lie. The best answer to the question "What are you thinking?" is often "Oh, nothing." Perhaps deception, not truth, is the cement of civilization—cement that does not so much hold us together as safely separate us and our thoughts. Some things are better left in the dark.

The success of a hint depends on the other person's ability to pick up the unexpressed message. Your subtle remarks might go right over the head of an insensitive receiver—or one who chooses not to respond to them. If this does happen, you still have the choice to be more direct. If the costs of a straightforward message seem too high, you can withdraw without risk.

It's easy to see why people choose hints, equivocations, and white lies instead of complete self-disclosure. These strategies provide an easier way to manage difficult situations than the alternatives for both the speaker and the receiver. In this sense, successful liars, equivocators, and hinters can be said to possess a certain kind of communicative competence. On the other hand, there are certainly times when honesty is the right approach, even if it's painful. At times like these, evaders could be viewed as lacking the competence or the integrity to handle a situation most effectively.

Are hints, benign lies, and equivocations an ethical alternative to self-disclosure? Some of the examples in these pages suggest the answer is a qualified "yes." Many social scientists and philosophers agree. Some argue that the morality of a speaker's *motives* for lying ought to be judged, not the deceptive act itself.[74] Others ask whether the *effects* of a lie will be worth the deception. Ethicist Sissela Bok offers some circumstances where deception may be justified: doing good, avoiding harm, and protecting a larger truth.[75] Perhaps the right questions to ask, then, are (1) whether an indirect message is truly in the interests of the receiver, and (2) whether this sort of evasion is the only effective way to behave. Bok suggests another way to check the justifiability of a lie: imagine how others would respond if they knew what you were really thinking or feeling. Would they accept your reasons for not disclosing?

In contrast to Kant, for whom the rule against lying was a moral law, a "categorical imperative" never to be overridden, utilitarian philosophers insist that lying is wrong only because a lie does, in fact, cause more harm than good. There is no absolute prohibition here, rather perhaps a "rule of thumb," and there may well be many cases, such as the "white lies" described above, in which lying causes no harm and may even be commendable. The problem, as Nietzsche so wisely complains, is "not that you lied to me, but that I no longer believe you." It is not the breach of the principle against lying that is so troublesome, nor is it the consequences of the lie or the character of the liar. It is that lying compromises and corrupts our relationships.

In other words, the wrongness of lying does not have to do primarily with breaches of principle or miscalculations of harm and good. Lying is wrong because it constitutes a breach of trust, which is not a principle but a very particular and personal relationship between people.

What is wrong with lying, in other words, is not exactly what philosophers have often supposed. Lying undermines relationships by undermining trust. But trust may just as often be supported by mutual myths, by religious faith, by a clear understanding of what is private and personal and what is "the public's right to know." Trust is usually violated by lies, but trust can be more deeply damaged by a violation of personal boundaries, which in turn may invite lies and deception to protect what has been violated.

Robert C. Solomon

QUESTIONS: Do you feel that lying is ever justified? What are some instances when you have felt obliged to lie? Why did you lie? Can you relate to Robert Solomon's arguments? Do you think he's right that trust makes lying necessary to protect personal boundaries?

Summary

An interpersonal relationship is one in which two or more people meet one another's social needs to a greater or lesser degree. Communication can be considered interpersonal according to either the context or the quality of interaction. Regardless of which definition is used, communication in relationships consists of both content and relational messages. Explicit relational messages are termed *metacommunication*.

Intimacy is a powerful need for most people. Intimacy can be created and expressed in a variety of ways: physically, emotionally, intellectually, and through shared activities. The notion of levels of intimacy has varied according to historical period, culture, and gender. Along with the desire for closeness, a need for distance is equally important. These opposing drives lead to conflicting communication behaviour at different stages in people's lives and their relationships. The challenge is to communicate in a way that strikes a balance between intimacy and distance.

Some communication theorists suggest that intimate relationships pass through a series of stages, each of which is characterized by a unique mode of communication. These stages fall into three broad phases: coming together, relational maintenance, and coming apart. Although the movement within and between these stages does follow recognizable patterns, the amount and direction of movement are not predetermined. Some relationships move steadily toward termination, whereas others shift backward and forward as the partners redefine their desires for intimacy and distance.

Other theorists take a dialectal view, arguing that the same series of opposing desires operates throughout the entire span of relationships. These dialectical drives include autonomy versus connection, predictability versus novelty, and openness versus privacy. Since these opposing forces are inevitable, the challenge is to develop strategies for dealing with them that provide relational satisfaction.

Self-disclosure is the process of deliberately revealing significant information about oneself that would not normally be known. The social penetration model can describe the breadth and depth of self-disclosure. The Johari Window model reveals an individual's open, blind, hidden, and unknown areas. Complete self-disclosure is not common, nor is it always desirable. Several guidelines to help determine when it is and is not appropriate were discussed. The chapter concluded by describing three widely used alternatives to self-disclosure: lies, equivocation, and hints. It discussed the conditions under which these alternatives can be appropriate.

Key Terms

affinity   219
altruistic lies   250
breadth   242
content messages   218
control   221
depth   242
developmental model   228
dialectical model   233
dialectical tensions   233
equivocal language   251

immediacy   221
impersonal communication   212
intimacy   223
Johari Window   243
metacommunication   222
qualitative interpersonal communication   212
relational messages   219
respect   219
self-disclosure   241
social penetration model   242

Activities

A. Interpersonal Communication: Context and Quality

1. Examine your interpersonal relationships in a contextual sense by making two lists. The first should contain all of the two-person relationships in which you have participated during the past week. The second should contain all your relationships that have occurred in small-group and public contexts. Are there any important differences that distinguish dyadic interaction from communication with a larger number of people?

2. Now make a second set of two lists. The first one should describe all of your relationships that are interpersonal in a qualitative sense, and the second should describe all the two-person relationships that are more impersonal. Are you satisfied with the number of qualitatively interpersonal relationships you have identified?

3. Compare the lists you developed in Steps 1 and 2. See what useful information each one contains. What do your conclusions tell you about the difference between contextual and qualitative definitions of interpersonal communication?

B. Identifying Relational Messages

To complete this exercise, you will need the help of a partner with whom you communicate on an ongoing basis.

1. Pick three recent exchanges between you and your partner. Although any exchanges will do, the most interesting ones will be those in which you sense that something significant (positive or negative) was going on that wasn't expressed overtly.

2. For each exchange, identify both the content and relational messages that you were expressing. Identify relational messages in terms of dimensions such as affinity, respect, immediacy, and/or control.

3. Explain the concept of relational messages to your partner, and ask him or her to identify the relational messages received from you during the same exchanges. How closely does your partner's perception match your analysis of the relational messages?

4. Now identify the relational messages you interpreted your partner as sending during the three exchanges.

5. Ask your partner to describe the relational messages he or she believed were sent to you on these occasions. How closely did your interpretation match your partner's explanation?

Based on your analysis of these three exchanges, answer the following questions:

1. What significant kinds of relational messages are exchanged in your relationship?

2. How accurate are you in decoding your partner's relational messages? How accurate is your partner in decoding your relational messages?

3. What lessons have you learned from this exercise that can improve the quality of your relationship?

C. Your IQ (Intimacy Quotient)

Answer the following questions as you think about your relationship with a person important in your life:

1. What is the level of physical intimacy in your relationship?

2. What intellectual intimacy do you share?

3. How emotionally intimate are you? Is your emotional intimacy deeper in some ways than in others?

4. Has your intimacy level changed over time? If so, in what ways?

After answering these questions, ask yourself how satisfied you are with the amount of intimacy in this relationship. Identify any changes you would like to occur, and describe the steps you could take to make them happen.

D. Striking a Balance between Intimacy and Distance

Choose an important interpersonal relationship with someone you encounter on a frequent and regular basis. You might choose a friend, family member, or romantic partner.

For at least a week, chart how your communication with this relational partner reflects your desire for either intimacy or distance. Use a seven-point scale, in which behaviour seeking high intimacy receives a seven and behaviour seeking to avoid physical, intellectual, and/or emotional contact receives a one. Use ratings from two through six to reflect intermediate stages. Record at least one rating per day, making more detailed entries if your desire for intimacy or distance changes during that period.

After charting your communication, reflect on what the results tell you about your personal desire for intimacy and distance. Consider the following questions:

1. Which state—intimacy or distance—seemed most desirable for you?

2. To the degree that you seek intimacy, which variety or varieties are most important to you: intellectual, emotional, and/or physical?

3. Was the pattern you charted during this week typical of your communication in this relationship over a longer period of time?

4. Do you seek the same mixture of intimacy and distance in other relationships?

5. Most importantly, are you satisfied with the results you discovered in this exercise? If not, how would you like to change your communication behaviour?

E. Juggling Dialectical Tensions

Identify one situation in which you are trying to manage dialectical tensions in your life. (Describe which of the dialectical forces described in this chapter are in operation.) Then answer the following questions:

1. Which of the strategies for managing dialectical tensions listed on pages 239–40 do you use?

2. How effective is the strategy (or strategies) that you have chosen?

3. Would an alternative strategy be more effective for managing the tensions in this situation?

4. How might things go differently if you choose the alternative strategy?

F. Reasons for Disclosing

Recall recent personal examples of times when you have disclosed personal information for each of the reasons listed in Table 6.7. Explain your answer by describing:

- the target of your self-disclosure;
- the information you disclosed; and
- your reason(s) for disclosing.

Based on your findings, decide which of the reasons for self-disclosure are most characteristic of your communication. Note: In order to protect privacy, this exercise can be conducted in class by having each member submit anonymous entries.

G. Effective Self-Disclosure

Choose a self-disclosing message that is important enough for you to consider sharing. Use the guidelines on pages 246–8 to craft the message in a way that maximizes the chances of having it received successfully. Share your message strategy with classmates, and get their opinion of whether it needs refinement.

H. The Ethics of Lying and Equivocating

Research shows that virtually everyone lies, equivocates, and hints for a variety of reasons. Explore the ethical legitimacy of your lies and equivocations by following these directions:

1. For a two-day period, keep track of:
    a. your lies, equivocations, and hints;
    b. your reason for taking one of these approaches in each situation; and
    c. the positive and negative consequences (for you and the other person) of avoiding self-disclosure.

2. Based on your analysis of the information collected in Step 1, identify the ethical legitimacy of each type of non-disclosing communication. Are any sorts of deception justifiable? Which sorts are not? How would you feel if you discovered the other person had not been straightforward with you under similar circumstances?

Further Reading

Bugeja, Michael, *Interpersonal Divide: The Search for Community in a Technological Age* (New York: Oxford University Press, 2005).
The author argues that media and technology have eroded our sense of community. He analyzes the "interpersonal divide"—the void that he claims develops when we spend too much time in virtual rather than real communities—and makes the case for face-to-face communication in an increasingly mediated world.

Canary, Daniel J., and Marianne Dainton, *Maintaining Relationships through Communication* (Mahwah, NJ: Erlbaum, 2003).
As its name suggests, this volume explores the ways in which people communicate to maintain various types of relationships. Contexts include interaction among family members, romantic partners, friends, and colleagues. Other chapters address dimensions including culture, long-distance relationships, and computer-medical contexts.

Mashek, Debra, J., and Arthur Aron, *Handbook of Closeness and Intimacy* (Mahwah, NJ: Erlbaum, 2004).
This handbook brings together the latest thinking on the scientific study of closeness and intimacy. The chapters address questions including: What are closeness and intimacy? What individual differences and situations play a role in closeness and intimacy? Is there a dark side to closeness and intimacy?

Tannen, Deborah, *I Only Say This Because I Love You: How the Way We Talk Can Make or Break Family Relationships throughout Our Lives* (New York: Random House, 2001).

Tannen explains why talking about even the most innocuous subjects with family members can sometimes be so painful. She looks behind content issues and highlights relational themes that often trigger criticism, disapproval, and rejection on the one hand and pain on the other. Tannen also explains how some of the dialectical tensions described in this chapter operate, focusing especially on how family communication must balance the need for connection with the desire for control.

Turkle, Sherry, *Alone Together: Why We Expect More from Technology and Less from Each Other* (New York: Basic Books, 2011).

Turkle explains that our digital communication tools are making us less likely to actually engage in meaningful social activity, which in turn makes us feel lonely. She says that while technology has brought us closer together, we experience greater feelings of loneliness because we are each lost in the private universes of our smartphones and other digital devices.

Study Questions

1. Think of three relationships that you are currently in, and, for the next two days, list all of the messages you exchange with these three people. Categorize them under the types of relational messages outlined in this chapter: affinity, respect, immediacy, and control.

2. Think of three examples of different types of relationships you are engaged in right now (e.g., school, friendly, workplace, romantic). List examples of metacommunication that you engage in with these different sorts of relationship. Are you more likely to metacommunicate in certain types of relationships?

3. What are your experiences of intimacy in your relationships? Identify three relationships and then discuss how your intimacy functions within them. Do you have different comfort levels in different sorts of relationships (e.g., friendships versus workplace, parental versus romantic)? List how cultural differences play a role in the intimacy you experience in these relationships.

4. Reflect on three of your most important relationships, whether they are in your past or present. They can be friendships, work relationships, or romantic. Consider how these three relationships map onto the stages of relational development and maintenance. Are all your relationships where you want them to be on the relationship ladder described on pages 228–33?

5. List the three important relationships that you used as examples for the previous question. Now write down whether the dialectical method describes their development better than the stage-based model. Write down how the three most important dialectical tensions (connection versus autonomy, predictability versus novelty, and openness versus privacy) relate to your three important relationships.

6. How does self-disclosure play a role in the three relationships you have been examining? How does your self-disclosure, as well as that of the person you are in a relationship with, correspond to the Johari Window? Map out on a piece of paper the differences in your self-disclosure in all three relationships. Do you disclose more or differently in the three relationships? Why?

7. Using the same three relationships, ask yourself whether you have lied or used equivocation with the people you are in a relationship with. Why did you do it? Did it achieve a positive result for you? Was your lying or equivocation done to protect the relationship or to protect yourself?

8. Again, using the same three relationships, think about how technology has affected your interpersonal relationships. Has it brought you closer to your partners? How has it brought you closer? How has it made you feel more separate from them? Is it how you use technology that affects the quality of your relationships? Or is it the way that you communicate through different information communication technologies like smartphones or tablets?

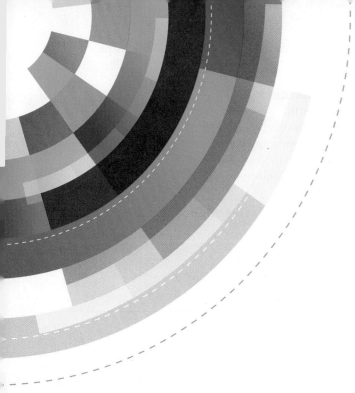

7

Improving Interpersonal Relationships

After studying the material in this chapter . . .

You should understand:

✔ the role of communication climate in interpersonal relationships;

✔ types of messages that contribute to confirming and disconfirming climates;

✔ the unavoidable but potentially problematic role of conflict in interpersonal relationships;

✔ characteristics of non-assertive, directly aggressive, passive-aggressive, indirect, and assertive communications;

✔ the influence of gender and culture on conflict styles; and

✔ the differences between win-lose, lose-lose, compromising, and win-win approaches to conflict resolution.

You should be able to:

✔ identify disconfirming messages and replace them with confirming ones, using the Gibb categories of supportive communication;

✔ describe the degree to which you use non-assertive, directly aggressive, passive-aggressive, indirect, and assertive messages and choose more satisfying responses as necessary;

✔ compose and deliver an assertive message, using the behaviour-interpretation-feeling-consequence-intention format; and

✔ apply the win-win approach to an interpersonal conflict.

Chapter Highlights

Communication climates are intangible but critical ingredients in relational satisfaction. In the first part of this chapter, you will learn:

» what makes some messages confirming and other messages disconfirming;

» how communication climates develop; and

» some tips for creating positive communication climates.

The second half of this chapter focuses on conflict in relationships, including:

» the nature of conflict;

» how people express conflict;

» the influence of gender and culture on conflict in relationships; and

» methods of conflict resolution, including the win-win approach.

No matter how satisfying your relationships, there are almost certainly ways they could be better. At times even best friends, close families, and productive co-workers become dissatisfied. Sometimes the people involved are unhappy with each other. At other times, one person's problem is unrelated to the relationship. In either case, there's a desire to communicate in a way that makes matters better.

The ideas in this chapter can help you improve the important relationships in your life. We'll begin by talking about the factors that make communication "climates" either positive or negative before moving on to methods for understanding and resolving interpersonal conflicts.

Communication Climates in Interpersonal Relationships

Personal relationships are a lot like the weather. Some are fair and warm, others are stormy and cold; some are permanently clouded by smog, others are healthy. Some relationships have stable climates, whereas others change dramatically—calm one moment and turbulent the next. You can't measure interpersonal climate by looking at a thermometer or glancing at the sky, but it's there nonetheless. Every relationship has a feeling, or a pervasive mood, that colours the interactions of the participants. The term **communication climate** refers to the emotional tone of a relationship. A climate doesn't involve specific activities, but instead focuses on the way people feel about each other as they carry out those activities. Consider two communication classes, for example. Both meet for the same length of time and follow the same syllabus. It's easy to imagine how one of these classes might be a friendly, comfortable place to learn, whereas the other might be cold and tense—even hostile. The same principle holds for families, among co-workers, and in other relationships: communication climates are a function more of the way people feel about one another than of the tasks they perform.

Confirming and Disconfirming Messages

What makes some climates positive and others negative? A short but accurate answer is that the *communication climate is determined by the degree to which people see themselves as valued.* When we believe others view us as important, we are likely to feel good about our relationship. On the other hand, the relational climate suffers when we think others don't appreciate or care about us.

Messages that show others that they're valued have been called **confirming responses**.[1] In one form or another, confirming responses say "you exist," "you matter," "you're important." In fact, it's an oversimplification to talk about one type of confirming message: confirming communication really occurs on three increasingly positive levels:[2]

- *Recognition.* The most fundamental act of confirmation is to recognize the other person. Recognition seems easy and obvious, and yet there are many times when we don't respond to others on this basic level. Failure to write or visit a friend is a common example. So is failure to return an e-mail or a phone call. Avoiding eye contact and not approaching someone you know on campus, at a party, or on the street all send negative messages. Of course, this lack of recognition may simply be an oversight. You might not notice your friend, or the pressures of work and school might prevent you from staying in touch. Nonetheless, if the other person *perceives* that you are avoiding contact, the message has the effect of being disconfirming.

communication climate
The emotional tone of a relationship as it is expressed in the messages that the partners send and receive.

confirming response
A response that conveys valuing, caring, and/or respecting another person.

The worst sin towards our fellow creatures is not to hate them, but to be indifferent to them; that's the essence of inhumanity.
George Bernard Shaw, Irish playwright and co-founder of the London School of Economics

- *Acknowledgement.* Acknowledging the ideas and feelings of others is a stronger form of confirmation. Listening is probably the most common form of acknowledgement. Of course, counterfeit listening—ambushing, stage hogging, pseudo-listening, and so on—has the opposite effect of acknowledgement. More active acknowledgement includes asking questions, paraphrasing, and reflecting. Not surprisingly, employees rate managers who solicit their suggestions highly—even when the managers don't accept every suggestion.[3] As you read in Chapter 5, reflecting the speaker's thoughts and feelings can be a powerful way to offer support when others have problems.

- *Endorsement.* Whereas acknowledgement signals that you're interested in another's ideas, endorsement means that you agree with them. It's easy to see why endorsement is the strongest type of confirming message, because it communicates the highest form of valuing. The most obvious form of endorsement is agreeing. Fortunately, it isn't necessary to agree completely with another person in order to endorse her or his message. You can probably find something in the message that you endorse. "I can see why you were so angry," you might reply to a friend, even if you don't approve of his outburst. Of course, outright praise is a strong form of endorsement and one you can use surprisingly often after you look for opportunities to compliment others. Non-verbal endorsement can also enhance the quality of a relational climate. For example, women rate men who agree with them as more physically attractive than those who fail to do so.[4]

> *We are here to add what we can to life, not to get what we can from life.*
>
> **William Osler, Canadian physician and co-founding professor of Johns Hopkins Hospital**

It's hard to overstate the importance of confirming messages. For instance, a positive climate is the best predictor of marital satisfaction.[5] Satisfied couples have a 5:1 ratio of positive to negative statements, whereas the ratio for dissatisfied partners is 1:1.[6] Positive, confirming messages are just as important in families. The satisfaction that siblings feel with one another, for example, drops sharply as aggressive, disconfirming messages increase.[7] Confirmation is just as important in the classroom, where motivation and learning increase when teachers demonstrate a genuine interest and concern for students.[8]

In contrast to confirming communication, messages that deny the value of others have been labelled **disconfirming responses**. These show a lack of regard for the other person either by disputing or by ignoring some important part of that person's message.[9] *Disagreement* can certainly be disconfirming, especially if it goes beyond disputing the other person's ideas and attacks the speaker personally. However, disagreement is not the most damaging kind of disconfirmation. It may be tough to hear someone say, "I don't think that's a good idea," but a personal attack like "You're crazy" is even tougher to hear. Far worse than disagreements are responses that *ignore* others' ideas—or even their existence.

> **disconfirming response**
> A message that expresses a lack of caring or respect for another person.

Not all disconfirming behaviour is unintentional. Table 7.1 lists a number of deliberate tactics that have been used to create distance in an undesired relationship. It's easy to see how each of them is inherently disconfirming.

As you read in Chapter 6, every message has a relational dimension along with its content. This means that, whether we know it or not, we send and receive confirming and disconfirming

Table 7.1 Distancing Tactics

Tactic	Description
Avoidance	Evading the other person.
Deception	Lying to or misleading the other person.
Degrading	Treating the other person with disrespect.
Detachment	Acting emotionally disinterested in the other person.
Discounting	Disregarding or minimizing importance of what the other person says.
Humouring	Not taking the other person seriously.
Impersonality	Treating the other person like a stranger; interacting with him or her as a role rather than a unique individual.
Inattention	Not paying attention to the other person.
Non-immediacy	Displaying verbal or non-verbal clues that minimize interest, closeness, or availability.
Reserve	Being unusually quiet and uncommunicative.
Restraint	Curtailing normal social behaviours.
Restrict topics	Limiting conversation to less personal topics.
Shorten interaction	Ending conversations as quickly as possible.

Source: Adapted from J.A. Hess, "Distance Regulation in Personal Relationships: The Development of a Conceptual Model and a Test of Representational Validity," *Journal of Social and Personal Relationships* 19 (2002): 663–83.

messages virtually whenever we communicate. Serious conversations about our relationships may not be common, but we convey our attitudes about one another even when we talk about everyday matters. In other words, it isn't *what* we communicate about that shapes a relational climate so much as *how* we speak and act toward one another.

It's important to note that disconfirming messages, like virtually every other kind of communication, are a matter of perception. Communicators are likely to downplay the significance of a potentially hurtful message that they consider to be unintentional.[10] On the other hand, even messages that aren't intended to devalue the other person can be interpreted as disconfirming. Your failure to return an e-mail or phone call might simply be the result of a busy schedule, but if the other person views the lack of contact as a sign that you don't value the relationship, the effect can be powerful.

How Communication Climates Develop

As soon as two people start to communicate, a relational climate begins to develop. If the messages

COMMUNICATION ON-SCREEN

Frost/Nixon (2008)

Directed by Ron Howard.

It has been five years since Richard Nixon's (Frank Langella) role was uncovered in the Watergate scandal of 1972, which forced his presidential retirement two years later. Reporters have been clamouring for an interview with the tarnished ex-leader, in large part reflecting the outraged American public's dissatisfaction with the lack of admission or guilt from Nixon. In Australia, a Ryan Seacrest-like talk show host, David Frost (Michael Sheen), decides to offer Nixon $500,000 out of pocket for the interview. Viewing Frost as a fluff television personality and an easy opponent, Nixon agrees. The Frost/Nixon interview is stuff of legend with Tricky Dick (Nixon) verbally sparring with the outclassed Frost, until the final round, when Frost lays down a stirring argumentative uppercut. A wonderful depiction of debate at its finest, the film fascinatingly charts the thrilling communicative chess match between these unlikely competitors and highlights the ways in which we often deceive others, as well as ourselves.

are confirming, the climate is likely to be a positive one. If they disconfirm one another, the climate is likely to be hostile, cold, or defensive.

Verbal messages certainly contribute to the tone of a relationship, but many climate-shaping messages are non-verbal. The very act of approaching others is confirming, whereas avoiding them can be disconfirming. Smiles or frowns, the presence or absence of eye contact, tone of voice, the use of personal space—all of these and other cues send messages about how the parties feel toward one another.

After a climate is formed, it can take on a life of its own and grow in a self-perpetuating **spiral**—a reciprocating communication pattern in which each person's message reinforces the other's.[11] In positive spirals, one partner's confirming message leads to a similar response from the other person. This positive reaction leads the first person to be even more reinforcing. Negative spirals are just as powerful, though they leave the partners feeling worse about themselves and each other. Research shows how spirals operate in relationships to reinforce the principle "what goes around, comes around." In one study of married couples, each spouse's response in conflict situations was similar to the other's statement.[12] Conciliatory statements (those that support, accept responsibility, agree, etc.) were likely to be followed by conciliatory responses. Confrontational acts (such as criticism, hostile questions, and fault-finding) were likely to trigger aggressive responses. The same pattern held for other kinds of messages: avoidance triggered avoidance, analysis triggered analysis, and so on.

Escalatory conflict spirals are the most visible way that disconfirming messages reinforce one another.[13] One attack leads to another until a skirmish escalates into a full-blown battle. Although they are less obvious, **de-escalatory conflict spirals** can also be destructive.[14] Rather than fighting, the parties slowly reduce their dependence on one another, withdraw, and become less invested in the relationship.

Spirals rarely go on indefinitely. Most relationships pass through cycles of progression and regression. If the spiral is negative, partners may find the exchange growing so unpleasant that they switch from negative to positive messages without discussing the matter. In other cases they may engage in metacommunication. "Hold on," one party might say, "this is getting us nowhere." In some cases, however, partners pass the point of no return, leading to the breakup of the relationship. Positive spirals, too, have their limits: even the best relationships go through periods of conflict and withdrawal, although a combination of time and communication skills can eventually bring the partners back into greater harmony.

Creating Positive Communication Climates

It's easy to see how disconfirming messages can pollute a communication climate. But what are some alternative ways of communicating that encourage positive relationships? The work of rhetorical ethicist Jack Gibb provides a picture of what kinds of messages lead to both positive and negative spirals.[15]

After observing groups for several years, Gibb was able to isolate six types of defence-arousing communication and six contrasting behaviours that seemed to reduce the level of threat and defensiveness. The **Gibb categories** are listed in Table 7.2. Using the supportive types of communication and avoiding the defensive ones will increase the odds of creating and maintaining positive communication climates in your relationships.

Evaluation versus Description

The first type of defence-provoking behaviour Gibb noted was **evaluative communication**. Most people become irritated at judgmental statements, which are likely to be interpreted as

---

spiral
A reciprocal communication pattern in which each person's message reinforces the other's.

escalatory conflict spiral
A reciprocal pattern of communication in which messages, either confirming or disconfirming, between two or more communicators reinforce one another.

de-escalatory conflict spiral
A communication spiral in which the parties slowly lessen their dependence on one another, withdraw, and become less invested in the relationship.

Cultural Idiom
what goes around, comes around
The belief that positive or negative actions done to others will ultimately result in positive or negative things happening to you.

hold on
To wait.

the point of no return
The stage in a process after which there is no possibility of stopping or reversing it.

Gibb categories
Six sets of contrasting styles of verbal and non-verbal behaviour. Each set describes a communication style that is likely to arouse defensiveness and a contrasting style that is likely to prevent or reduce it. Developed by Jack Gibb.

evaluative communication
Messages in which the sender judges the receiver in some way, usually resulting in a defensive response. Synonymous with *"you" language.*

"you" language
Language that judges another person, increasing the likelihood of a defensive reaction. Synonymous with *evaluative communication.*

descriptive communication
Messages that describe the speaker's position without evaluating others. Synonymous with *"I" language.*

"I" language
Language that describes the speaker's position without evaluating others. Synonymous with *descriptive communication.*

controlling message
Message in which the sender tries to impose some sort of outcome on the receiver, usually resulting in a defensive reaction.

problem orientation
A supportive style of communication in which the communicators focus on working together to solve their problems instead of trying to impose their own solutions on one another.

Table 7.2 The Gibb Categories of Defensive and Supportive Behaviours

Defensive Behaviours	Supportive Behaviours
1. Evaluation	1. Description
2. Control	2. Problem orientation
3. Strategy (Manipulation)	3. Spontaneity (Straightforwardness)
4. Neutrality (Indifference)	4. Empathy
5. Superiority	5. Equality
6. Certainty (Dogmatism)	6. Provisionalism

signalling a lack of respect. Evaluative language has often been described as **"you" language** because most of these statements contain an accusatory use of that word. For example:

- You don't know what you're talking about.
- You're not doing your best.
- You smoke too much.

Unlike evaluative "you" language, **descriptive communication** focuses on the speaker's thoughts and feelings instead of judging the listener. One form of descriptive communication is **"I" language**.[16] Instead of putting the emphasis on judging another's behaviour, the descriptive speaker explains the effect on him or her of the other's action. For instance, instead of saying, "You talk too much," a descriptive communicator would say, "When you don't give me a chance to say what's on my mind, I get frustrated." Notice that statements such as this include an account of the other person's behaviour in addition to an explanation of its effect on the speaker and a description of the speaker's feelings.

Control versus Problem Orientation

A second defence-provoking message involves some attempt to control the other person. A **controlling message** occurs when a sender seems to be imposing a solution on the receiver with little regard for the receiver's needs or interests. The control can range from relatively small matters (where to eat dinner or what show to watch) to large ones (whether to remain in a relationship or how to spend a large tax return).

Whatever the situation, people who act in controlling ways create a defensive climate. Researchers have found that the communication of abusive couples was characterized by opposition to one another's viewpoints.[17] The unspoken message this kind of behaviour communicates is "I know what's best for you, and if you do as I say, we'll get along."

By contrast, in **problem orientation**, communicators focus on finding a solution that satisfies both their needs and those of the others involved. The goal here isn't to "win" at the expense of your partner but rather to work out some arrangement in which everybody feels like a winner. The "Comparison of Dialogue and Debate" box above shows several important differences between controlling and problem-oriented communication. The last section of this chapter has a great deal to say about "win–win" problem-solving as a way to find problem-oriented solutions.

A Comparison of Dialogue and Debate

People will always have disagreements. The way they handle them both creates and reflects relational climates. The following list contrasts the very different types of communication that characterize dialogue and debate. As you review them, consider how dialogue confirms the other person, even in the face of disagreement, whereas debate is fundamentally disconfirming.

- Dialogue is collaborative: two or more sides work together toward common understanding.
- Debate is oppositional: two sides oppose each other and attempt to prove each other wrong.
- In dialogue, finding common ground is the goal.
- In debate, winning is the goal.
- Dialogue enlarges and possibly changes the participants' points of view.
- Debate affirms the participants' own points of view.
- Dialogue reveals assumptions for re-evaluation.
- Debate defends assumptions as truth.
- Dialogue causes introspection about one's own position.
- Debaters critique the others' positions.
- Dialogue opens the possibility of reaching a better solution than any of the original ones.
- Debate defends one's own positions as the best and excludes other positions.
- Dialogue involves a genuine concern for the other person and seeks not to alienate or offend.
- Debate involves countering the other position without focusing on feelings or relationships and often belittles or deprecates the other position.

Adapted from R. Poliner and J. Benson, *Dialogue: Turning Controversy into Community.*

Strategy versus Spontaneity

The third communication behaviour that Gibb identified as creating a poor communication climate is **strategy**. A more accurate term to describe this type of behaviour is *manipulation*. Manipulation is the source of irritation in the workplace when a colleague acts friendly to peers while striving to curry favour with the boss.[18] One of the surest ways to make people defensive is to get caught trying to manipulate them. Nobody likes to be a guinea pig or a sucker, and even well-meant manipulation can cause bad feelings.

Spontaneity is the label Gibb used as a contrast to strategy. A better term might be *straight-forwardness*. Despite the misleading label, spontaneous communication doesn't have to be blurted out as soon as an idea comes to you. You might want to plan the wording of your message carefully so that you can express yourself clearly. The important thing is to be honest. A straightforward message may not always get you what you want, but in the long run it's likely to pay dividends in a positive relational climate.

Neutrality versus Empathy

Gibb used the term **neutrality** to describe a fourth behaviour that arouses defensiveness, but a more descriptive term would be *indifference*. A neutral attitude is disconfirming because it

strategy
A defence-arousing style of communication in which the sender tries to manipulate or trick a receiver. Also, the general term for any type of plan, as in the plan for a persuasive speech.

spontaneity
Supportive communication behaviour in which the sender expresses a message without any attempt to manipulate the receiver.

neutrality
A defence-arousing behaviour in which the sender expresses indifference toward a receiver.

Cultural Idiom
in the long run
Over an extended period of time.

communicates a lack of concern for another's welfare. In short, it implies that the other person isn't very important to you.

The damaging effects of neutrality become apparent when you consider the hostility that most people feel towards the large, impersonal organizations they have to deal with: "They think of me as a number instead of a person;" "I felt as if I were being handled by computers and not people." These two common statements reflect reactions to being handled indifferently.

Empathy is an approach that confirms the other person. Having empathy means accepting another's feelings, or putting yourself in another's place. This doesn't mean you need to agree with that person. Gibb noted the importance of non-verbal messages in communicating empathy. He found that facial and bodily expressions of concern are often more important to the receiver than the words used.

Superiority versus Equality

Superiority is a fifth type of communication that creates a defensive climate. When people seem to believe they are better than we are, their attitude is likely to trigger a defensive response.

We often meet people who possess knowledge or talents greater than ours. But your own experiences will tell you that it isn't necessary for these people to project an attitude of superiority. Gibb found ample evidence that many who have superior skills and talents are capable of conveying an attitude of **equality**. These people are able to communicate the view that although they may have greater talent in certain areas, they see others as having just as much worth.

Certainty versus Provisionalism

Dogmatism is another term for the behaviour Gibb calls **certainty**. Messages that suggest the speaker's mind is already made up are likely to generate defensiveness.

superiority
A defence-arousing style of communication in which the sender states or implies that the receiver is inferior.

equality
A type of supportive communication suggesting that the sender regards the receiver as worthy of respect.

certainty
Messages that dogmatically imply that the speaker's position is correct and that the other person's ideas are not worth considering. Likely to generate a defensive response.

YOUNG COMMUNICATOR PROFILE

STEVE DOLSON

Social Media Consultant/
Founder, 2Social.ca, *LXRY
Magazine*

My dad, Gary Dolson, was in public relations in the automotive industry, using his communications background to make uninteresting things, interesting.

I started my career in a co-op position after convincing an automotive garage that social media were the next big thing. I used my love for making things distinctly interesting and engaging through social media platforms, and used this as a vehicle to broadcast the brand messages.

I worked in the real estate industry, managing social media accounts for large condo developments and big real estate associations and, after loving the use of social media to represent and adding personality to businesses, I decided to start my own company. 2Social is a social media and branding agency I created in 2011 to help Canadian businesses improve their online presence.

After starting 2Social, blogging became a vital and prevalent aspect. With my other love for writing, I saw another gap in the market when it came to Canadian luxury. Not satisfied with how luxury was being represented in Canada, I then founded and built *LXRY Magazine* (www.lxry.ca) from the ground up. *LXRY* is an online luxury magazine that showcases luxury products and services that are available in Canada.

I continue to use communications as a vehicle to promote Canadian businesses, improve messages that are broadcast by companies and, above all, continue to make seemingly uninteresting things, interesting.

In contrast to dogmatic communication is **provisionalism**, in which people may have strong opinions but are willing to acknowledge that they don't have a monopoly on the truth and will change their stand if another position seems more reasonable.

There is no guarantee that using Gibb's supportive, confirming approach to communication will build a positive climate. But the chances for a constructive relationship will be greatest when communication consists of the kind of constructive approach described here. Besides boosting the odds of getting a positive response from others, supportive communication can leave you feeling better in a variety of ways: more in control of your relationships, more comfortable, and more positive toward others.

> **provisionalism**
> A supportive style of communication in which the sender expresses a willingness to consider the other person's position.

> **Cultural Idiom**
> **boosting the odds of**
> To increase the likelihood of occurrence.

Managing Interpersonal Conflict

Even the most supportive communication climate won't guarantee complete harmony. Regardless of what we may wish for or dream about, a conflict-free world just doesn't exist. Even the best communicators, the luckiest people, are bound to wind up in situations where their needs don't match the needs of others. Money, time, power, sex, humour, and aesthetic taste, as well as a thousand other issues, arise and keep us from living in a state of perpetual agreement.

For many people the inevitability of conflict is a depressing fact. They think that the existence of ongoing conflict means that there's little chance for happy relationships with others. Effective communicators know differently, however. They realize that although it's impossible to *eliminate* conflict, there are ways to *manage* it effectively. And those effective communicators know the main theme of this chapter—that managing conflict skilfully can open the door to healthier, stronger, and more satisfying relationships.

A study led by Phillip Sullivan at the University of Windsor examined how hockey players actually benefit from the conflicts that arise naturally among teammates. The traditional

> **Cultural Idiom**
> **to wind up in**
> To end up being in.
>
> **open the door to**
> To remove barriers.

view of friction between players is that it is bad for team chemistry. However, if we take a more nuanced view of both conflict and cohesion, certain types of conflict can be seen to foster team unity. After interviewing 62 hockey players, the researchers found that constructive conflict led to greater cohesion among teammates, although negative conflict tended to destroy team morale. This suggests that perfect harmony is not always the best means of maintaining good chemistry.[19]

The Nature of Conflict

Whatever forms they may take, all interpersonal conflicts share certain similarities. Joyce Hocker and William Wilmot provide a thorough definition of "conflict." They state that **conflict** is an expressed struggle between at least two interdependent parties who perceive incompatible goals, scarce rewards, and interference from the other parties in achieving their goals.[20] A closer look at the various parts of this definition helps to develop a clearer idea of how conflicts operate.

> **conflict**
> An expressed struggle between at least two interdependent parties who perceive incompatible goals, scarce rewards, and interference from the other party in achieving their goals.

> **Cultural Idiom**
> **dirty look**
> A facial expression indicating displeasure.

Expressed Struggle

A conflict doesn't exist unless both parties know that some disagreement exists. You may be upset for months because a neighbour's barking dog keeps you from getting to sleep at night, but no conflict exists between the two of you until the neighbour learns about your problem. Of course, the expressed struggle doesn't have to be verbal. You can show your displeasure with somebody without saying a word. Giving a dirty look, using the silent treatment, and avoiding the other person are all ways of expressing yourself. But one way or another, both parties must know that a problem exists before they're in conflict.

Perceived Incompatible Goals

Conflicts often look as if one party's gain will be another's loss. For instance, consider the neighbour whose dog keeps you awake at night. Does somebody have to lose? A neighbour who brings a barking dog inside might have to deal with an anxious pet whining or scratching at the back door to go out; however, if he or she lets Fido out to bark at the raccoons, you're still awake and unhappy.

The goals in this situation really aren't completely incompatible—solutions do exist that allow both parties to get what they want. For instance, you could achieve peace and quiet by closing your windows or getting a pair of earplugs. Your neighbour could take the restless dog for a walk around the block instead of letting it out. If any of these solutions proves workable, then the conflict disappears.

Unfortunately, people often fail to see mutually satisfying answers to their problems. And as long as they perceive their goals to be mutually exclusive, they create a self-fulfilling prophecy in which the conflict is very real.

Perceived Scarce Rewards

In a conflict, people believe there isn't enough of a particular resource to go around. The most obvious example of a scarce resource is money—a cause of many conflicts. If an employee asks for a raise and the employer would rather keep the money or use it to expand the business, then the two parties are in conflict.

Time is another scarce commodity. As authors and professionals, we are constantly in the middle of struggles about how to use the limited time we have to spend. Should we work on this book? Spend time with our families? Devote our attention to other research projects? Enjoy the luxury of being alone? With only 24 hours in a day we're bound to end up in conflicts with our families, editors, students, and friends—all of whom want more of our time than we have available to give.

Interdependence

However antagonistic they might feel toward each other, the parties in a conflict are usually dependent on each other. The welfare and satisfaction of one party depend on the actions of the other. If this weren't true, then even in the face of scarce resources and incompatible goals there would be no need for conflict. Interdependence exists between conflicting nations, social groups, organizations, friends, and romantic partners. In each case, if the two parties didn't need each other to solve the problem, both would go their separate ways. In fact, many conflicts go unresolved because the parties fail to understand their interdependence. One of the first steps toward resolving a conflict is to adopt the attitude that "we're in this together."

Styles of Expressing Conflict

Communication scholars have identified a wide range of ways communicators handle conflicts.[21] Table 7.3 describes five ways people can act when their needs are not met. Each one has very different characteristics.

Non-Assertion

Non-assertion is the inability or unwillingness to express thoughts or feelings in a conflict. Sometimes non-assertion comes from a lack of confidence. At other times, people lack the awareness or skill to use a more direct means of expression.

> **non-assertion**
> The inability or unwillingness to express one's thoughts or feelings when necessary.

Table 7.3 Individual Styles of Conflict

	Non-assertive	**Directly Aggressive**	**Passive-Aggressive**	**Indirect**	**Assertive**
Approach to Others	I'm not okay; you're okay.	I'm okay; you're not okay.	I'm okay; you're not okay.	I'm okay; you're not okay. (But I'll let you think you are.)	I'm okay; you're okay.
Decision-Making	Lets others choose.	Chooses for others. They know it.	Chooses for others. They don't know it.	Chooses for others. They don't know it.	Chooses for self.
Self-Sufficiency	Low.	High or low.	Looks high, but usually low.	High or low.	Usually high.
Behaviour in Problem Situations	Flees; gives in.	Outright attack.	Concealed attack.	Strategic, oblique.	Direct confrontation.
Response of Others	Disrespect, guilt, anger, frustration.	Hurt, defensiveness, humiliation.	Confusion, frustration, feelings of manipulation.	Unknowing compliance or resistance.	Mutual respect.
Success Pattern	Succeeds by luck or charity of others.	Beats out others.	Wins by manipulation.	Gains unwitting compliance of others.	Attempts "win-win" solutions.

Source: Adapted from *The Assertive Woman* © 1970, 1987, 1997, and 2000, by Stanlee Phelps and Nancy Austin, San Luis Obispo, CA: Impact, 1975, p. 11; and Gerald Piaget, American Orthopsychiatric Association, 1975.

Understanding Diversity

Whether Attack Ads "Work" Is the Wrong Question

Q: Lately, much has been written against bullying. Rightly so. But when political parties focus on the personality of opponents through attack ads rather than discussing issues, isn't this just another form of bullying? And given that these ads are all over TV and seen by young people, don't they validate this behaviour?

A: The last hallelujah had barely faded from the Liberal coronation before the Conservatives fired the first salvo of their campaign to prove young Justin (good grief, he's 41!) isn't ready for prime time. In some respects these weren't attack ads at all. Given that Trudeau did say he'd consider making Quebec a separate country and that he thought Quebecers "are better than the rest of Canada," it's fair to serve up those quotes—even if they are from an earlier stage of life. Trudeau is hardly the first politician held accountable for past indiscretions: Stephen Harper's musings from his days with the National Citizens Coalition have, fairly, been used against him as well.

Other elements, however, cross the line. The circus music, the sneering shot about being "born with a famous name," and the footage of him taking off his shirt at a charity event (Oh. My. God.) all slip into the realm of character assassination. They don't descend to the assault on Chrétien and his crooked grin—but they are tentative first steps down the same rocky road. What's more distressing than the ads, however, is the tenor of discussion about them. Polls have been commissioned, academics with higher foreheads than mine interviewed, politicians questioned and cross-examined about what we all seem to agree is the central question: Do attack ads work?

Am I the only one who thinks this the wrong question? In fact, not just wrong, but frankly, a wicked question. What does it mean to say these ads "work?" It doesn't mean public discourse about issues is, in any sense, enhanced. It doesn't mean voter turnout is increased, or respect for the political process deepened, or the country strengthened. No, to say attack ads work means that the "attacker" benefits, gets more power, earns more money, has more control, while the "attacked" is weakened, diminished, left powerless.

"Works," in this sense, simply means "I win, you lose. I get to be the big man by making you look like a wimp." Lots of nasty things in our society work, in this sense, quite nicely. Yes, let's start with bullying. It often works rather well, in the tawdry way we've defined: Creepy little twerps with crummy self-esteem feel important when they humiliate others. Terrorism works, too, as we've been reminded again recently—a whole city was shut down, every major media outlet placed on monovision, by two losers who are now famous around the world. If that's not a victory, what would one would look like?

Hockey violence apparently works, as do the antics of North Korea's Kim Jong Un and Syrian leader Bashar Assad—judging by YouTube, all three create throngs of adoring worshippers. What sort of country, what kind of world do we become when we refuse to ask whether an action is right, just, decent, even (forgive me) kind—and instead settle for the sad, second-class question: "Do you think it will work?"

Ken Gallinger, "Ethically Speaking" columnist,
The Toronto Star, 26 April 2013

QUESTIONS: The author of this article makes some *very* strong claims about attack ads and the nature of political conflict. Are his critiques justified? Do you think politics would be improved if it were less aggressive? Finally, the author makes the distinction between what is right (as in a moral decision) and what is correct (as in a choice). Do you think this distinction is fair?

Sometimes people know how to communicate in a straightforward way but choose to behave non-assertively. For example, women on dates are less likely to clearly refuse unwanted sexual advances from people they would like to see again than from people they have no intention of meeting for another date.[22]

Non-assertion is a surprisingly common way of dealing with conflicts. One survey examined the conflict level of husbands and wives in normal "non-distressed" marriages. Over a five-day period, spouses reported that their partners engaged in an average of 13 behaviours that were "displeasurable" to them but that they had only *one* confrontation during the same period.[23]

Non-assertion can take a variety of forms. One is *avoidance*—either physical (steering clear of a friend after having an argument) or conversational (changing the topic, joking, or denying

> **Cultural Idiom**
> **steering clear of**
> To avoid something.

that a problem exists). People who avoid conflicts usually believe it's easier to put up with the status quo than to face the problem head-on and try to solve it. *Accommodation* is another type of non-assertive response. Accommodators deal with conflict by giving in and putting the needs of others ahead of their own.

Despite the obvious drawbacks of non-assertion, there are situations when accommodating or avoiding is a sensible approach. Avoidance may be the best course if a conflict is minor and short-lived. For example, you might let a friend's annoying moodiness pass without saying anything, knowing that she's just having one of her rare bad days. Likewise, you might not complain to a neighbour whose sprinkler occasionally hits your front walk. You may also reasonably choose to keep quiet if the conflict occurs in an unimportant relationship, as with an acquaintance whose language you find offensive but whom you don't see often. Finally, you might choose to keep quiet if the risk of speaking up is too great: getting fired from a job you can't afford to lose, being humiliated in public, or even risking physical harm.

Direct Aggression

Whereas non-assertors avoid conflicts, communicators who use **direct aggression** embrace them. A directly aggressive message strikes the receiver in a way that attacks his or her position and even dignity. Many directly aggressive responses are easy to spot: "You don't know what you're talking about." "That was a stupid thing to do." "What's the matter with you?" Other forms of direct aggression come more from non-verbal messages than from words. It's easy to imagine statements like "What is it now?" or "I need some peace and quiet" being expressed in a hostile way.

Verbal aggressiveness may get you what you want in the short run. Yelling "Shut up" might stop the other person from talking, and saying "Get it yourself" may save you from some exertion, but the relational damage of this approach probably isn't worth the cost. Direct aggression can be hurtful, and the consequences for the relationship can be long-lasting.[24]

Passive Aggression

Passive aggression, which occurs when a communicator expresses his or her hostility in an indirect way, is far more subtle than its directly aggressive cousin. Psychologist George Bach terms this behaviour **crazymaking**[25] and identifies several varieties. For example, "pseudo-accommodators" pretend to agree with you ("I'll be on time from now on") but don't comply with your request for change. "Guiltmakers" try to gain control by making you feel responsible for changing to suit them: "I really should be studying, but I'll give you a ride." "Jokers" use humour as a weapon and then hide behind the complaint ("Where's your sense of humour?") when you object. "Trivial tyrannizers" do small things to drive you crazy instead of confronting you with their complaints: "forgetting" to give you messages, playing music too loud, and so

direct aggression
An expression of the sender's thoughts or feelings, or both, that attacks the position and dignity of the receiver.

passive aggression
An indirect expression of aggression, delivered in a way that allows the sender to maintain a facade of kindness.

crazymaking
Passive-aggressive messages sent in indirect ways that frustrate and confuse the recipient.

▶ COMMUNICATION ON-SCREEN

"Coach's Corner" (1980–present)

On "Coach's Corner," a feature on CBC television's *Hockey Night in Canada*, we see two very different styles of handling conflict—and that is the basis of the public's interest in the segment. Former NHL coach Don Cherry is a very successful aggressive communicator. While his on-air behaviour is repellent to many, he manages to bully and dominate his mild-mannered counterpart, Ron MacLean, in a way that makes for engaging viewing. He raises his voice, expresses populist outrage, and uses facial expressions of disgust and disdain to support points, whether he is speaking or not. He reinforces his persona by defending the more brutish and grinding elements of hockey and promoting a nostalgic "return to basics" approach to issues around safety and violence. The basis of his popularity remains, despite the fact that he breaks Canadian social norms of "niceness" and is openly aggressive with his counterpart for the duration of his segment.

on. "Withholders" punish their partners by keeping back something valuable, such as courtesy, affection, or humour.

Indirect Communication

The clearest communication is not necessarily the best approach. **Indirect communication** conveys a message in a roundabout manner, in order to save face for the recipient.[26] Although indirect communication lacks the clarity of an aggressive or assertive message, it involves more initiative than non-assertion. It also has none of the hostility of passive-aggressive crazy-making. The goal is to get what you want without arousing the hostility of the other person. Consider the case of the neighbour's annoying dog. One indirect approach would be to strike up a friendly conversation with the owners and ask if anything you are doing is too noisy for them, hoping they would get the hint.

Because it saves face for the other party, indirect communication is often kinder than blunt honesty. If your guests are staying too long, it's probably kinder to yawn and hint about your big day tomorrow than to bluntly ask them to leave. Likewise, if you're not interested in going out with someone who has asked you out to a movie, it may be more compassionate to claim that you're busy than to say "I'm not interested in seeing you."

COMMUNICATING ONLINE

Blogging

While so much of today's online communication emphasizes brevity and immediacy, blogging—which allows communicators more time and space—continues to be enormously popular. A blog post can feel like a one-way conversation, but it's important to remember that people are reading your posts and reacting to them. You need to be wary of presenting any sort of conflict in your writing, especially if you are responding to reader's comments. Grad student and blogger Melonie Fullick presents tips for how to make your blog a success.

While many forms of online communication tend toward extreme brevity and away from print, blogging is a way of letting audiences deep into your or your organization's inner world. You can use blogs to talk about your ethics, processes, and philosophy. You can also tell anecdotes illustrated by photos or videos embedded in your blog that reveal your heart and soul or that of the organization you are blogging for. Here are some tips that will help you become a more effective blogger.

Purpose and audience are key. Understand why you're writing, and for whom. There are many different "genres" of blog—food blogs, travel blogs, science blogs, to name a few—and each type has different goals and audiences. Even if your blog doesn't fit neatly into a category, it helps to have some idea of what audience might find it relevant.

Give your blog, and each post, original titles that make sense. Run online searches of potential titles so that you don't end up duplicating a pun or catchy phrase that others have already used. The title for each post should indicate something about the content (and preferably it should contain key words or terms).

Update regularly, and keep posts concise. Frequent, shorter updates are more likely to keep people interested and encourage them to return to your blog. Focus in on something and explain it well. If an issue takes more than 750 words to discuss, you should either home in on a specific angle or split it into a series of posts, each dealing with a slice of the larger topic.

Be "social." Share your posts through other online tools like Twitter, LinkedIn, and Facebook. Make sure social share buttons are enabled on your posts so others can share them quickly and easily through their existing networks. Similarly, you should read and recommend other people's posts, and leave substantive comments on them (along with a link to your

At other times we communicate indirectly in order to protect ourselves. You might, for example, test the waters by hinting instead of directly asking the boss for a raise, or by letting your partner know indirectly that you could use some affection instead of asking outright. At times like these, an oblique approach may get the message across while softening the blow of a negative response.

The advantages of protecting oneself and saving face for others help explain why indirect communication is the most common way people make requests.[27] The risk of an indirect message, of course, is that the other party will misunderstand you or fail to get the message at all. There are also times when the importance of an idea is so great that hinting lacks the necessary punch. When clarity and directness are your goals, an assertive approach is in order.

Assertion

People who use **assertion** handle conflicts by expressing their needs, thoughts, and feelings clearly and directly but without judging others or dictating to them. They have the attitude that most of the time it is possible to resolve problems to everyone's satisfaction. Possessing this attitude and the skills to bring it about doesn't guarantee that assertive communicators will always get what they want, but it does give them the best chance of doing so. An additional

> **Cultural Idiom**
> **test the waters**
> To tentatively try something.
>
> **oblique**
> To be evasive or indirect
>
> **soften the blow**
> To ease the effect of something.
>
> **punch**
> Something that is done with emphasis.

> **assertion**
> Direct expression of the sender's needs, thoughts, or feelings, delivered in a way that does not attack the receiver's dignity.

---

blog). Write guest posts for other people's sites if you want to further increase your visibility.

Be generous. Link to other content that relates to what you're discussing, particularly if it's by other bloggers who've written well on something. There are often ongoing "threads" of conversation that happen among the many voices participating. Try to link to those posts to provide context and to offer kudos to others who've tackled an issue in a smart, interesting way, or who've presented a unique angle or argument.

Be yourself. Write about what you know and what interests you, from your perspective, with your own "voice. While you should read other blogs (and books, papers, and magazines) in the same area and have a sense of your position among them, don't let the number of blogs "out there" put you off. Just think about what *you* want to add to the discussion you're joining. For example, addressing a broad topic through the lens of a personal experience can help you to refine your perspective and contribute something original.

Give it time. Not only does it take time to write a good blog post, it also takes time to "find" your readers. The great thing about a blog is that older posts are still around when new readers arrive, so they can go back and read your earlier, less-viewed posts if they notice and enjoy the recent ones.

Don't let negative comments get you down. No matter what you write, someone will always be there to disagree, critique, or even wilfully misinterpret what you're saying. Depending on what you're writing about and how much exposure you get, there may also be "trolls" who comment merely to get a reaction. While you should bear this in mind as you write, don't let it put you off; you can't please everyone, and that shouldn't be your goal. Engage with the serious comments that further the discussion, and don't lose sleep over the petty ones.

Lastly, there's no getting around this: you need to write about *interesting things, and write well*. You need a subject, a style, and careful proofreading. It's much harder for people to take you seriously if your writing is full of errors that could have been avoided with more attention; and no-one will read what you're writing if you're not looking at topics they care about, or addressing them in a thoughtful and accessible way. No matter how good your page looks or how many times you share it, it's always the substance that counts.

Melonie Fullick, Blogger, *University Affairs* magazine

benefit of such an approach is that whether or not it satisfies a particular need, it maintains the self-respect of both the assertors and those with whom they interact. As a result, people who manage their conflicts assertively may experience feelings of discomfort while they are working through the problem. They usually feel better about themselves and each other afterward—quite a change from the outcomes of non-assertion or aggression.

Characteristics of an Assertive Message

Knowing *about* assertive messages isn't the same as being able to express them. Communicating assertively works for a variety of messages: those conveying your hopes, your problems, your complaints, and your appreciations. Besides giving you a way to express yourself directly, this format also makes it easier for others to understand you. A complete assertive message has five parts, which we will discuss below.

1. Behavioural Description

As we noted in Chapter 3, a behavioural description is an objective picture of the behaviour in question, without any judging or editorializing. Put in terms of Gibb's categories, it uses descriptive rather than evaluative language. Notice the difference between a behavioural description and an evaluative judgment:

> **Behavioural description:** "You asked me to tell you what I really thought about your idea, and then when I gave you my opinion, you told me I was too critical."

> **Evaluative judgment:** "Don't be so touchy! It's hypocritical to ask for my opinion and then get mad when I give it to you."

Judgmental words like "touchy" and "hypocritical" invite a defensive reaction. The target of your accusation can reply, "I'm not touchy *or* hypocritical!" It's harder to argue with the facts stated in an objective, behavioural description. Furthermore, the neutral language reduces the chances of a defensive reaction.

2. Your Interpretation of the Other Person's Behaviour

After describing the behaviour in question, an assertive message expresses the communicator's interpretation. This is where you can use the perception-checking skill outlined in Chapter 2 (pp. 53–4). Remember that a complete perception check includes two possible interpretations of the behaviour:

> **Interpretation A:** "Maybe you reacted defensively because my criticism sounded too detailed—because my standards seemed too high."

> **Interpretation B:** "Your reaction made me think that you really didn't want to know my opinion. You were just fishing for a compliment when you asked my opinion."

Whether you offer two interpretations (as in the previous list) or just one (as in the examples that follow), the key is to label your hunches as such instead of suggesting that you are positive about what the other person's behaviour means.

Not everything that is faced can be changed, but nothing can be changed until it is faced.

James Baldwin, American novelist and playwright

Cultural Idiom

touchy
Quickly offended with little provocation.

fishing for a compliment
Trying to get another to say what one wants to hear.

3. A Description of Your Feelings

Expressing your feelings adds a dimension to a message. For example, consider the difference between these two responses:

- "When you kiss me on the neck while I'm working [behaviour], I think you probably want to fool around [interpretation], and *I feel aroused* [feeling]."
- "When you kiss me on the neck while I'm working [behaviour], I think you probably want to fool around [interpretation], and *I feel anxious* [feeling]."

Adding feelings to the situation we presented earlier makes the assertive message clearer as well:

SURPRISE PARTY

- "When you said I was too critical after you asked me for my honest opinion [behaviour], it seemed to me that you really didn't want to hear a critical remark [interpretation], and *I felt stupid for being honest* [feeling]."

4. A Description of the Consequences

A consequence statement explains what happens as a result of the behaviour you have described, your interpretation, and the ensuing feeling. There are three kinds of consequences:

1. *What happens to you, the speaker*:
    - "When you forgot to give me the phone message yesterday [behaviour], *I didn't know that my doctor's appointment was delayed, and I wound up sitting in the office for an hour when I could have been studying or working* [consequences]. It seems to me that you don't care enough about how busy I am to even write a simple note [interpretation], and that's why I got so mad [feeling]."
    - "I appreciate [feeling] the help you've given me on my term paper [behaviour]. It tells me you think I'm on the right track [interpretation], and *this gives me a boost to keep working on the idea* [consequences]."

2. *What happens to the person you're addressing*:
    - "When you get drunk at a party after I've warned you to slow down [behaviour], you act like a fool: *you make crude jokes that offend everybody, and end up taking embarrassing photos which end up on Facebook, Instagram, even YouTube!* [consequences], and you know I hate excessive drinking and I don't think you realize how this makes you look [interpretation], and I'm worried [feeling] about how this reflects on me, on us, and how this affects your health and future."

3. *What happens to others*:
    - "You probably don't know because you couldn't hear her cry [interpretation], but when you rehearse your lines for the play without closing the doors [behaviour],

the baby can't sleep [consequence]. I'm especially concerned [feeling] about her because it looks like she's coming down with something."

- "I thought you'd want to know [interpretation] that when you kid Jamaal about his height [behaviour], he gets embarrassed [feeling] and *usually becomes sulky or leaves* [consequences]."

A consequence statement for our ongoing example might sound like this:

- "When you said I was too critical after you asked me for my honest opinion [behaviour], it seemed to me that you really didn't want to hear a critical remark [interpretation]. I felt stupid for being honest [feeling]. *Now I'm not sure whether I should tell you what I'm really thinking the next time you ask* [consequence]."

5. A Statement of Your Intentions

Intention statements are the final element in the assertive format. They can communicate three kinds of messages:

1. *Where you stand on an issue*:
   - "When you call us "girls" after I've told you we want to be called "women" [behaviour], I get the idea you don't appreciate how important the difference is to us [interpretation] and how demeaning it feels [feeling]. Now I'm in an awkward spot: either I have to keep bringing the subject up, or else drop it and feel bad [consequence]. *I want you to know how much this bothers me* [intention]."
   - "I'm really grateful [feeling] to you for speaking up for me in front of the boss yesterday [behaviour]. That must have taken a lot of courage [interpretation]. Knowing that you're behind me gives me a lot of confidence [consequence], and *I want you to know how much I appreciate your support* [intention]."

2. *Requests of others*:

   "When you didn't call last night [behaviour] I thought you were mad at me [interpretation]. I've been thinking about it ever since [consequence], and I'm still worried [feeling]. *I'd like to know if you are angry* [intention]."

   "I really enjoyed [feeling] your visit [behaviour], and I'm glad you had a good time, too [interpretation]. *I hope you'll come again* [intention]."

3. *Descriptions of how you plan to act in the future*:

   "I've asked you three times now to repay the $25 I lent you [behaviour]. I'm getting the idea that you've been avoiding me [interpretation], and I'm pretty angry about it [feeling]. I want you to know that unless we clear this up now, *you shouldn't expect me to lend you anything again* [intention]."

Why is it so important to make your intentions clear? Because failing to do so often makes it hard for others to know what you want from them or how to act. Consider how confusing the following statements are because they lack a clear statement of intention.

- "Thanks for the invitation, but I really should study Saturday night." [Does the speaker want to be asked out again, or is he or she indirectly suggesting that he or she doesn't ever want to go out with you?]

- "To tell you the truth, I was asleep when you came by, but I should have been up anyway." [Is the speaker saying that it's okay to come by in the future, or is he or she hinting that he or she doesn't appreciate unannounced visitors?]

You can see from these examples that it's often hard to make a clear interpretation of another person's ideas without a direct statement of intention. Notice in the following examples how much more direct the statements become when the speakers make their positions clear:

- "Thanks for the invitation, but I really should study Saturday night. *I hope you'll ask me again soon.*"
- "To tell you the truth, I was asleep when you came by, but I should have been up anyway. *Maybe next time you should phone before dropping in so I'll be sure to be awake.*"

In our ongoing example, adding an intention statement would complete the assertive message:

- "When you said I was too critical after you asked me for my honest opinion [behaviour], it seemed to me that you really didn't want to hear a critical remark [interpretation]. That made me feel stupid for being honest [feeling]. Now I'm not sure whether I should tell you what I'm really thinking the next time you ask [consequence]. *I'd like to get it clear right now: do you really want me to tell you what I think or not* [intention]?"

Before you try to deliver messages using the assertive format outlined here, there are a few points to remember. First, it isn't necessary or even wise to put the elements in the order described here in every case. As you can see from reviewing the examples, it's sometimes best to begin by stating your feelings. At other times, you can start by sharing your intentions or interpretations or by describing consequences.

You also should word your message in a way that suits your style of speaking. Instead of saying, "I interpret your behaviour to mean'" you might choose to say, "I think . . ." or "It seems to me . . ." or perhaps "I get the idea. . . ." In the same way, you can express your intentions by saying, "I hope you'll understand (or do) . . ." or perhaps "I wish you would. . . ." It's important that you get your message across, but you should do it in a way that sounds and feels genuine to you.

Realize that there are some cases in which you can combine two elements in a single phrase. For instance, the statement ". . . and ever since then I've been wanting to talk to you" expresses both a consequence and an intention. In the same way, saying, ". . . and after you said that, I felt confused" expresses a consequence and a feeling. Whether you combine elements or state them separately, the important point is to be sure that each one is present in your statement.

Finally, it is important to realize that it isn't always possible to deliver messages such as the ones here all at one time, wrapped up in neat paragraphs. It will often be necessary to repeat or restate one part many times before your receiver truly understands what you're saying. As you've already read, there are many types of psychological and physical noise that make it difficult for us to understand each other. Just remember: you haven't communicated successfully until the receiver of your message understands everything you've said. In communication, as in many other activities, patience and persistence are essential.

Gender and Conflict Style

While the *Men Are from Mars, Women Are from Venus* theory of gender, which states that men and women actually speak entirely different languages, doesn't hold up under scrutiny, men and women often approach conflicts differently. Even in childhood, males are more likely to be overtly aggressive, demanding, and competitive, whereas females are more co-operative, or at least less directly aggressive. Studies of children from preschool to early adolescence have shown that boys typically try to get their way by ordering one another around: "Lie down." "Get off my steps." "Gimme your arm." By contrast, girls are more likely to make proposals for action, beginning with the word "Let's," as in "Let's go find some." "Let's ask her if she has any markers." "Let's move *these* out *first*."[28] Whereas boys tell each other what role to take in pretend play ("You be the doctor; I'll be the patient"), girls more commonly ask each other what role they want ("Will you be the patient for a few minutes?") or make a joint proposal ("We can both be doctors"). Furthermore, boys often make demands without offering an explanation ("Look, I want the wire cutters right now"). By contrast, girls often give reasons for their suggestions ("We have to *clean* them first to get rid of the germs"). When girls do have conflicts and disagreements, they are more likely to handle them via indirect aggression such as excluding someone from peer groups and complaining to others.[29] However, gender isn't the only variable that determines how children will handle conflict. For example, girls are more likely to assert themselves with boys when their friends are also present.[30]

Differences like these often persist into adulthood. One survey of university students revealed that men and women viewed conflicts in contrasting ways.[31] Regardless of their cultural background, female students described men as being concerned with power and more interested in content than relational issues. Phrases used to describe male conflict styles included "The most important thing to males in conflict is their egos;" "Men don't worry about feelings;" and "Men are more direct." By contrast, women were described as being more concerned with maintaining the relationship during a conflict. Phrases used to describe female conflict styles included "Women are better listeners;" "Women try to solve problems without controlling the other person;" and "Females are more concerned with others' feelings."

Research confirms some of these reports.[32] Limited evidence suggests that women are more likely than men to use indirect strategies instead of confronting conflict head-on. They are also more likely to compromise and give in to maintain relational harmony. Men, by contrast, are more likely to use aggression to get their way.

After a relational conflict begins, men are often more likely than women to withdraw if they become uncomfortable or fail to get their way. The reason why men tend to avoid and

women assert may have little to do with gender stereotypes: women may demand more from their partners because historically they have had more to gain by complaining.[33] When men benefit from the status quo, they protect their situation by withdrawing. To understand this "demand–withdraw" dynamic, consider a stereotypical housekeeping situation in which the woman complains because the man doesn't do his share. Speaking up has the potential to change the woman's situation for the better, whereas avoiding the discussion enables the man to maintain his situation.

Differences like these don't mean that men are incapable of forming good relationships. Instead, the stereotypical male notion of what a good relationship is differs from the stereotypical female notion. For some men, friendship and aggression aren't mutually exclusive. In fact, many strong male relationships are built around competition—at work or in athletics, for example. Women can be competitive, too, but they also are more likely to use logical reasoning and bargaining than aggression.[34] When men communicate with women, they become less aggressive and more co-operative than they are in all-male groups.

Most theorists suggest that the primary reason for differences in conflict style is socialization.[35] Some social scientists have proposed that a "threshold of assertiveness" may exist for people, especially women, allowing them to behave in an assertive way up to a point, but no further. Because women have typically been perceived as more compliant and co-operative, they may have seen themselves as reaching this threshold sooner than men, at which time they would back off. Because men have been expected to be more assertive—or even aggressive— they find it more comfortable to persist in seeking to meet their needs. As sex-role stereotyping becomes less common, it is likely that the differences between male and female conflict styles may become smaller.

> **Cultural Idiom**
> **back off**
> To stop or quit.

Cultural Influences on Conflict

Communication style in situations of conflict varies widely from one culture to another. The English-Canadian preference for a rational, straight-talking, calm yet assertive approach is not the norm in other cultures.[36] In French-Canadian culture, for example, there is typically a greater tolerance for expressions of intense emotion. Similarly, French Canadians are the least likely to keep secrets from their spouses; the most likely are non–French-Canadian residents of Saskatchewan or Manitoba.[37] But ethnicity isn't the only factor that shapes individuals' preferred conflict style: their degree of assimilation also plays an important role. For example, Canadians of Hispanic descent with strong Hispanic cultural identities are more likely to seek accommodation and compromise than Hispanic-Canadians with weaker cultural ties.[38]

Not surprisingly, people from different regions often manage conflict quite differently. In individualistic cultures like that of English Canada, the goals, rights, and needs of each person are considered important, and most people would agree that it is an individual's right to stand up for himself or herself. By contrast, collectivist cultures (more common in Latin America and Asia) consider the concerns of the group to be more important than those of any individual. In these cultures, the kind of assertive behaviour that might seem perfectly appropriate to a North American would seem rude and insensitive.

Another factor that distinguishes the North American and northern European cultures from others is their low-context cultural style.[39] Low-context cultures place a premium on assertiveness, on being direct and literal. By contrast, high-context cultures like that of Japan value self-restraint and avoid confrontation. Preserving and honouring the dignity of the other person are prime goals, and communicators go to great lengths to avoid embarrassing a conversational partner. For this reason, people in these cultures prefer to rely on subtle hints and shared knowledge of social conventions. In Japan, for example, even a simple request like "Close the door" would be

◉◢◀ COMMUNICATION ON-SCREEN

Scott Pilgrim vs. the World (2010)
Directed by Edgar Wright.

Scott Pilgrim (Michael Cera) is in love with Ramona Flowers (Mary Elizabeth Winstead). But there is one problem—well, seven problems— namely, Ramona's seven evil ex-boyfriends whom Scott must defeat in battle to win her love. As Scott progresses through his battles with Ramona's dating history, he must also face his own personal history, even resulting in a literal faceoff with himself. Scott must literally, and figuratively "get a life" and accept responsibility in his end of the conflict as well. Featuring fantastic music, incredible effects, and action, *Scott Pilgrim vs. the World* is a love note to Toronto, video games, and the ups and downs of relationships, even if they usually don't involve nearly so many laser swords.

CRITICAL THINKING PROBE
Valuing Diversity in Conflict Styles

The preceding section made it clear that conflict styles are shaped by social and cultural influences. Choose a conflict style different from yours—by virtue of gender or culture—and identify the assumptions on which it is based. Next, suggest how people with different styles can adapt their assumptions and behaviours to communicate in a more satisfying manner.

too straightforward.[40] Instead, a remark such as "It's chilly today" would serve to convey the request in an indirect way. To take a more important example, Japanese people are reluctant to simply say "no" to a request. A more likely answer would be "Let me think about it for a while," which anyone familiar with Japanese culture would recognize as a refusal. When indirect communication is a cultural norm, it is unreasonable to expect more straightforward approaches to succeed.

It isn't necessary to look at Eastern cultures to encounter cultural differences in conflict. The style of some other cultures within the Western world differs in important ways from the northern European and North American norm. These cultures see verbal disputes as a form of intimacy and even a game. Canadians visiting Greece, for example, often think they are witnessing an argument when they are overhearing a friendly conversation.[41] A longitudinal study of child development, conducted by Statistics Canada and Human Resources Development Canada, demonstrated that there are many differences between immigrant children and Canadian-born children. For example, immigrant children tend to experience a period of poverty while their families adjust to living in Canada. Many Canadian children grow up in poverty too, but do so mostly because of family dysfunction. As a result, poverty has a smaller effect on immigrant children than their Canadian counterparts. Furthermore, immigrant children tend to experience less conflict in their homes, more family cohesion, and fewer mental health problems than Canadian children. These differences seem to disappear in one generation as immigrants and their children assimilate into English- or French-Canadian culture.[42]

Methods of Conflict Resolution

No matter what the relational style, gender, or culture of the participants, every conflict is a struggle to have one's goals met. Sometimes that struggle succeeds, and at other times it fails. In the remainder of this chapter we'll look at various approaches to resolving conflicts and see which ones are most promising.

Win–Lose

win–lose problem-solving
An approach to conflict resolution in which one party reaches its goal at the expense of the other.

In **win–lose problem-solving**, one party achieves its goal at the expense of the other. People resort to this method of resolving disputes when they perceive a situation as being an "either–or" one: either I get what I want, or you get your way. The most clear-cut examples of win–lose situations are certain games, such as baseball or poker, in which the rules require a winner and a loser. Some interpersonal issues seem to fit into this win–lose framework: two co-workers seeking a promotion to the same job, for instance, or a couple who disagrees on how to spend their limited money.

Power is the distinguishing characteristic in win–lose problem-solving because it is necessary to defeat an opponent to get what you want. The most obvious kind of power is physical. Some parents threaten their children with warnings such as "Stop misbehaving, or I'll send you to your room." Adults who use physical power to deal with each other usually aren't so blunt, but the legal system is the implied threat: "Follow the rules, or we'll lock you up."

Real or implied force isn't the only kind of power used in conflicts. People who rely on authority of many types engage in win–lose methods without ever threatening physical coercion. In most jobs, supervisors have the potential to use authority in the assignment of working hours, job promotions, desirable or undesirable tasks, and, of course, in the power to fire an unsatisfactory employee. Teachers can use the power of grades to coerce students to act in desired ways.

Even the usually admired democratic principle of majority rule is a win–lose method of resolving conflicts. However fair it may be, this system results in one group's getting its way and another group's being unsatisfied.

There are some circumstances when win–lose problem-solving may be necessary, such as when there are truly scarce resources and where only one party can achieve satisfaction. For

instance, if two suitors want to marry the same person, only one can succeed. And to return to an earlier example, it's often true that only one applicant can be hired for a job. But don't be too willing to assume that your conflicts are necessarily win–lose: as you'll soon read, many situations that seem to require a loser can be resolved to everyone's satisfaction.

There is a second kind of situation when win–lose is the best method. Even when co-operation is possible, if the other person insists on trying to defeat you, then the most logical response might be to defend yourself by fighting back. "It takes two to tango," as the old cliché goes, and it also often takes two to co-operate.

A final and much less frequent situation in which you might be justified in refusing to back down is one in which the other person is clearly harming others. Few people would deny the importance of restraining an aggressor even if that person's freedom is sacrificed in the process.

> **Cultural Idiom**
> **it takes two to tango**
> It takes two people to cause disagreement.

Lose–Lose

In **lose–lose problem-solving**, neither side is satisfied with the outcome. Although the name of this approach is so discouraging that it's hard to imagine how anyone could willingly use it, in truth lose–lose is a fairly common way to handle conflicts. In many instances the parties will both strive to be winners, but as a result of the struggle, both end up losers. On the international scene many wars illustrate this sad point. A nation that gains military victory at the cost of thousands of lives, large amounts of resources, and a damaged national consciousness hasn't truly won much. On an interpersonal level the same principle holds true. Most of us have seen battles of pride in which both parties strike out and both suffer.

> **lose–lose problem-solving**
> An approach to conflict resolution in which neither party achieves its goals.

Compromise

Unlike lose–lose outcomes, a **compromise** gives both parties at least some of what they wanted, though both sacrifice part of their goals. People usually settle for compromises when they see partial satisfaction as the best they can hope for. Although a compromise may be better than losing everything, this approach hardly seems to deserve the positive image it has with some people. In his valuable book on conflict resolution, management consultant Albert Filley makes an interesting observation about our attitudes toward this approach.[43] Why is it, he asks, that if someone says, "I will compromise my values," we view the action unfavourably, yet

> **compromise**
> An approach to conflict resolution in which both parties attain at least part of what they seek through self-sacrifice.

we talk admiringly about parties in a conflict who compromise to reach a solution? Although compromises may be the best obtainable result in some conflicts, it's important to realize that both people in a dispute can often work together to find much better solutions. In such cases *compromise* is a negative word.

Most of us are surrounded by the results of bad compromises. Consider a common example: the conflict between one person's desire to smoke cigarettes and another's need to breathe clean air. The win–lose outcomes of this conflict are obvious: either the smoker abstains or the non-smoker gets polluted lungs—neither result is very satisfying. But a compromise in which the smoker gets to enjoy only a rare cigarette or must retreat outdoors and in which the non-smoker still must inhale some fumes or feel like an ogre is hardly better. Both sides have lost a considerable amount of both comfort and goodwill. Of course, the costs involved in other compromises are even greater. For example, if a divorced couple compromises on child care by haggling over custody and then finally, grudgingly, agrees to split the time with their children, it's hard to say that anybody has won.

Win–Win

win–win problem-solving
An approach to conflict resolution in which the parties work together to satisfy all their goals.

In **win–win problem-solving**, the goal is to find a solution that satisfies the needs of everyone involved. Not only do the parties avoid trying to win at the other's expense, but they also believe that by working together it is possible to find a solution that allows both to reach their goals.

Some compromises approach this win–win ideal. You and the seller might settle on a price for a used car that is between what the seller was asking and what you wanted to pay. Although neither of you got everything you wanted, the outcome would still leave both of you satisfied. Likewise, you and your companion might agree to see a film that is the second choice for both of you in order to spend an evening together. As long as everyone is satisfied with an outcome, it's accurate to describe it as a win–win solution.

Table 7.4 Choosing the Most Appropriate Method of Conflict Resolution

1. Consider deferring to the other person:
   • when you discover you are wrong;
   • when the issue is more important to the other person than it is to you;
   • to let others learn by making their own mistakes; or
   • when the long-term cost of winning may not be worth the short-term gains.

2. Consider compromising:
   • when there is not enough time to seek a win-win outcome;
   • when the issue is not important enough to negotiate at length; or
   • when the other person is not willing to seek a win-win outcome.

3. Consider competing:
   • when the issue is important and the other person will take advantage of your non-competitive approach.

4. Consider co-operating:
   • when the issue is too important for a compromise;
   • when a long-term relationship between you and the other person is important; or
   • when the other person is willing to co-operate.

Although compromises can be a type of win–win outcome, the best solutions are ones in which all the parties get everything they want.

A win–win approach sounds ideal, but it is not always possible, or even appropriate. Table 7.4 suggests some factors to consider when deciding which approach to take when facing a conflict. There will certainly be times when compromising is the most sensible approach. You will even encounter instances when pushing for your own solution is reasonable. Even more surprisingly, you will probably discover that there are times when it makes sense to willingly accept the loser's role.

Steps in Win–Win Problem-Solving

Although win–win problem-solving is often the most desirable approach to managing conflicts, it is also one of the hardest to achieve. In spite of the challenge, it is definitely possible to become better at resolving conflicts. The following discussion outlines a method to increase your chances of being able to handle your conflicts in a win–win manner, so that both you and others have your needs met. As you learn to use this approach you should find that more and more of your conflicts end up with win–win solutions. And even when total satisfaction isn't possible, this approach can preserve a positive relational climate.

As it is presented here, win–win problem-solving is a highly structured activity. After you have practised the approach a number of times, this style of managing conflict will become almost second nature to you. You'll then be able to approach your conflicts without the need to follow the step-by-step approach. But for the time being, try to be patient and trust the value of the following pattern. As you read through the steps, imagine yourself applying them to a problem that's currently bothering you.

Cultural Idiom
second nature
Something that is easy and natural.

Identify Your Problem and Unmet Needs

Before you speak out, it's important to realize that the problem causing the conflict is yours. Whether you want to return an unsatisfactory piece of merchandise, complain to noisy neighbours because your sleep is being disturbed, or request a change in working conditions from your employer, the problem is yours. Why? Because in each case you are the person who is dissatisfied. You are the one who has paid for the defective article; the merchant who sold it to you has the use of your money. You are the one who is losing sleep as a result of your neighbours' activities; they are content to go on as before. You, not your boss, are the one who is unhappy with your working conditions.

Realizing that the problem is yours will make a big difference when the time comes to approach your partner. Instead of feeling and acting in an evaluative way, you'll be more likely to share your problem in a descriptive way, which will not only be more accurate but also will reduce the chance of a defensive reaction.

After you realize that the problem is yours, the next step is to identify the unmet needs that leave you feeling dissatisfied. Sometimes a relational need underlies the content of the issue at hand. Consider these cases:

- A friend hasn't returned some money you lent long ago. Your apparent need in this situation might be to get the cash back. But a little thought will probably show that this isn't the only, or even the main, thing you want. Even if you were rolling in money, you'd probably want the loan repaid because of your most important need: *to avoid feeling victimized by your friend's taking advantage of you.*
- Someone you care about who lives in a distant city has failed to respond to several e-mails. Your apparent need may be to get answers to the questions contained in the e-mails, but it's likely that there's another, more fundamental need: *the reassurance that you're still important enough to deserve a response.*
- You post a video of yourself playing guitar on YouTube only to receive negative comments. Where is the positive reinforcement and why is the internet just full of jerks? *Perhaps there is another option; perhaps those comments, although potentially harsh, have some validity to them, and the issues that you need to overcome in order to improve are being addressed, but you can't see the forest for the trees.*

As you'll soon see, the ability to identify your real needs plays a key role in solving interpersonal problems. For now, the point to remember is that before you voice your problem to your partner, you ought to be clear about which of your needs aren't being met.

Make a Date

Unconstructive fights often start because the initiator confronts a partner who isn't ready. There are many times when a person isn't in the right frame of mind to face a conflict: perhaps owing to fatigue, being in too much of a hurry to take the necessary time, upset over another problem, or not feeling well. At times like these, it's unfair to "jump" a person without notice and expect to get his or her full attention for your problem. If you persist, you'll probably have an ugly fight on your hands.

After you have a clear idea of the problem, approach your partner with a request to try to solve it. For example: "Something's been bothering me.

Cultural Idiom
rolling in
possessing large amounts of

Cultural Idiom
frame of mind
One's mood or mental state.

to jump
To attack.

Can we talk about it?" If the answer is "yes," then you're ready to go further. If it isn't the right time to confront your partner, find a time that's agreeable to both of you.

Describe Your Problem and Needs

Your partner can't possibly meet your needs without knowing why you're upset and what you want. Therefore, it's up to you to describe your problem as specifically as possible. When you do so, it's important to use terms that aren't overly vague or abstract. Recall our discussion of behavioural descriptions in Chapter 3 in order to clarify your problem and specific needs.

Partner Checks Back

After you've shared your problem and described what you need, it's important to make sure that your partner has understood what you've said. As you can remember from the discussion of listening in Chapter 5, there's a good chance—especially in a stressful conflict situation—of your words being misinterpreted.

It's usually unrealistic to insist that your partner paraphrase your problem statement, and fortunately there are more tactful and subtle ways to make sure you've been understood. For instance, you might try saying, "I'm not sure I expressed myself very well just now—maybe you should tell me what you heard me say so I can be sure I got it right." In any case, be absolutely sure that your partner understands your whole message before going any further. Legitimate agreements are tough enough, but there's no point in getting upset about a conflict that doesn't even exist.

Solicit Partner's Needs

After you've made your position clear, it's time to find out what your partner needs in order to feel satisfied about this issue. There are two reasons why it's important to discover your partner's needs. First, it's fair. After all, the other person has just as much right as you to feel satisfied, and if you expect help in meeting your needs, then it's reasonable that you behave in the same way. Second, just as an unhappy partner will make it hard for you to become satisfied, a happy partner will be more likely to co-operate in letting you reach your goals. Thus, it is in your own self-interest to discover and meet your partner's needs.

You can learn about your partner's needs simply by asking about them: "Now I've told you what I want and why. Tell me what you need to feel okay about this." After your partner begins to talk, your job is to use the listening skills discussed earlier in this book to make sure you understand.

Check Your Understanding of Your Partner's Needs

Paraphrase or ask questions about your partner's needs until you're certain you understand them. The surest way to accomplish this is to use the paraphrasing skills you learned in Chapter 5.

Negotiate a Solution

Now that you and your partner understand each other's needs, the goal becomes finding a way to

---

◄ COMMUNICATION ON-SCREEN

Goon (2011)

Directed by Michael Dowse.

Charting the career of a hockey "goon," Doug Glatt (Seann William Scott) and his brother Pat (Jay Baruchel) are attending a minor league hockey game when, after Pat taunts the visiting team, one of the players climbs into the stands and begins calling Pat homosexual slurs. In defense of his gay brother, Doug knocks the player out, prompting the crowd to cheer him on. Doug is soon called up to the Halifax Highlanders as an enforcer to protect a nervous prospect (Marc-Andre Grondin) from a violent veteran enforcer named Ross "the Boss" Rhea (Live Schreiber). Despite having no hockey ability, and equipped only with his brother's figure skates, Doug must come to terms with both his lion-hearted *and* his goon side to help a friend, get the girl, and prove that fists don't solve every problem, even in the coolest game on earth. Described by Steve Gravestock as "the Canadian comedy counterpart to Jimi Hendrix's version of the 'The Star Spangled Banner:' sacrilegious, twisted and, somehow, perversely patriotic."[44]

meet them. The best way to do this is to develop as many potential solutions as possible and then evaluate them to decide which one best meets the needs of both. The following steps can help communicators develop a mutually satisfying solution.

1. *Identify and define the conflict.* We've discussed this process in the preceding pages. It consists of discovering each person's problem and needs, setting the stage for meeting all of them.

2. *Generate a number of possible solutions.* In this step you and your partner work together to think of as many means as possible to reach their stated ends. The key word here is quantity: it's important to generate as many ideas as you can think of without worrying about which ones are good or bad. Write down every thought that comes up, no matter how unworkable; sometimes a far-fetched idea will lead to a more workable one.

3. *Evaluate the alternative solutions.* This is the time to talk about which solutions will work and which ones won't. It's important for you both to be honest about your willingness to accept an idea. If a solution is going to work, you both have to support it.

4. *Decide on the best solution.* Now that you've looked at all the alternatives, pick the one that looks best to you and your partner. It's important to be sure that you both understand the solution and are willing to try it out. Remember: your decision doesn't have to be final, but it should look potentially successful.

Follow Up on the Solution

Cultural Idiom
to keep on top of
To be in control
of something.

You can't be sure the solution will work until you try it out. After you've tested it for a while, it's a good idea to set aside some time to talk over how things are going. You may find that you need to make some changes or even rethink the whole problem. The idea is to keep on top of the problem and to keep using creativity to solve it.

Win–win solutions aren't always possible. There will be times when even the best-intentioned people simply won't be able to find a way of meeting all their needs. In cases like this, the process of negotiation has to include some compromising. But even then the preceding steps haven't been wasted. The genuine desire to learn what the other person wants and to try to satisfy those desires will build a climate of goodwill that can help you find the best solution to the present problem and also improve your relationship in the future.

One typical comment people have after trying the preceding method of handling conflicts is "This is a helpful thing sometimes, but it's so rational! Sometimes I'm so uptight I don't care about defensiveness or listening or anything . . . I just want to yell and get it off my chest!"

Cultural Idiom
uptight
To be anxious.

blowing off steam
To release excess energy
or anger.

tying in
To find a way to
relate something to
something else.

When you feel like this, it's almost impossible to be rational. At times like these, probably the most therapeutic thing to do is to express your feelings in what Bach calls a "Vesuvius"—an uncontrolled, spontaneous explosion. A Vesuvius can be a terrific way of blowing off steam, and after you do so, it's often much easier to figure out a rational solution to your problem.

So we encourage you to have a Vesuvius with the following qualifications: be sure your partner understands what you're doing and realizes that whatever you say doesn't call for a response. He or she should let you rant and rave for as long as you want without getting defensive or "tying in." Then, when your eruption subsides, you can take steps to work through whatever still troubles you.

Summary

This chapter explored several factors that help make interpersonal relationships satisfying or unsatisfying. We began by defining *communication climate* as the emotional tone of a relationship as it is expressed in the messages being sent and received. We examined factors that contribute to positive and negative climates, learning that the underlying factor is the degree to which a person feels valued by others. We examined types of confirming and disconfirming messages, and then looked in detail at Gibb's categories of defensiveness-arousing and supportive behaviours.

The second half of the chapter dealt with interpersonal conflict. We saw that conflict is a fact of life in every relationship and that the way conflicts are handled plays a major role in the quality of a relationship. There are five ways people can behave when faced with a conflict: non-assertive, directly aggressive, passive-aggressive, indirect, and assertive. Each of these approaches can be appropriate at times, but the chapter focused on assertive communication skills because of their value and novelty for most communicators. We saw that conflict styles are affected by both gender and culture.

There are four outcomes to conflicts: win–lose, lose–lose, compromise, and win–win. Win–win outcomes are often possible, if the parties possess the proper attitudes and skills. The final section of the chapter outlined the steps in win–win problem-solving.

Key Terms

assertion   275

certainty   268

communication climate   262

compromise   283

confirming response   262

conflict   270

controlling message   266

crazymaking   273

de-escalatory conflict spiral   265

descriptive communication   266

direct aggression   273

disconfirming response   263

equality   268

escalatory conflict spiral   265

evaluative communication   266

Gibb categories   266

"I" language   266

indirect communication   274

lose–lose problem-solving   283

neutrality   267

non-assertion   271

passive aggression   273

problem orientation   267

provisionalism   269

spiral   265

spontaneity   267

strategy   267

superiority   268

win–lose problem-solving   282

win–win problem-solving   284

"you" language   266

Activities

A. Your Confirming and Disconfirming Messages

You can gain an understanding of how confirming and disconfirming messages create communication spirals by trying the following exercise:

1. Identify the communication climate of an important personal relationship. Using weather metaphors (sunny, gloomy, calm) may help.

2. Describe several confirming or disconfirming messages that have helped create and maintain the climate. Be sure to identify both verbal and non-verbal messages.

3. Show how the messages you have identified have created either escalatory or de-escalatory conflict spirals. Describe how these spirals reach limits and what events cause them to stabilize or reverse.

4. Describe what you can do to either maintain the existing climate (if positive) or change it (if negative). Again, list both verbal and non-verbal behaviours.

B. Constructing Supportive Messages

This exercise will give you practice in sending confirming messages that reflect Gibb's categories of supportive behaviour. You will find that you can communicate in a constructive way—even in conflict situations.

1. Begin by recalling at least two situations in which you found yourself in an escalatory conflict spiral.

2. Using the Gibb categories, identify your defence-arousing messages, both verbal and non-verbal.

3. Now reconstruct the situations, writing a script in which you replace the defence-arousing behaviours with the supportive alternatives outlined by Gibb.

4. If it seems appropriate, you may choose to approach the other people in each of the situations you have described and attempt to replay the exchange. Otherwise, describe how you could use the supportive approach you developed in Step 3 in future exchanges.

C. Constructing Assertive Messages

Develop your skill at expressing assertive messages by composing responses for each of the following situations:

1. A neighbour's barking dog is keeping you awake at night.

2. A friend hasn't repaid the $20 she borrowed two weeks ago.

3. Your boss made what sounded like a sarcastic remark about the way you put school before work.

4. An out-of-town friend phones at the last minute to cancel the weekend you planned to spend together.

5. A friend keeps tagging you in embarrassing pictures on Facebook despite you repeatedly asking them not to.

Now develop two assertive messages you could send to a real person in your life. Discuss how you could express these messages in a way that is appropriate for the situation and that fits your personal style.

D. Problem-Solving in Your Life

1. Recall as many conflicts as possible that you have had in one relationship. Identify which approach best characterizes each one: win–lose, lose–lose, compromise, or win–win.

2. For each conflict, describe the consequences (for both you and the other person) of this approach.

3. Based on your analysis, decide for yourself how successful you and your partner are at managing conflicts. Describe any differences in approach that would result in more satisfying outcomes. Discuss what steps you and your partner could take to make these changes.

E. Choosing an Ethical Conflict Style

At first glance, assertiveness seems like the most ethical communication style to use when you are faced with a conflict. The matter might not be so clear, however. Find out for yourself by following these steps:

1. Decide for yourself whether it is ever justifiable to use each of the other conflict styles: non-assertion, direct aggression, passive aggression, and indirect communication. Support your position on each style with examples from your own experience.

2. Explain your answer to classmates who disagree, and listen to their arguments.

3. After hearing positions that differ from yours, work with your classmates to develop a code of ethics for expressing conflict messages.

Further Reading

Greene, John O., and Brant R. Burleson, *Handbook of Communication and Social Interaction Skills* (Mahwah, NJ: Erlbaum, 2003).
This book focuses specifically on the nature of skills that contribute to effective communication. Chapters address topics such as managing conversations, impression management, arguing, and persuasion. Selected chapters also focus on specific types of interpersonal relationships, including those between romantic partners, spouses, friends, parents and children, people from different cultures, and people in health care.

Nixon, Peter, *Dialogue Gap: Why Communication Isn't Enough and What We Can Do About It, Fast* (Hoboken, NJ: John Wiley and Sons, 2012).
This book discusses how communication is not always sufficient when it come to effective negotiations. He discusses how the ability to connect and engage is of crucial importance in our small networked world.

Segal, Jeanne, *The Language of Emotional Intelligence: The Five Essential Tools for Building Powerful and Effective Relationships* (New York: McGraw-Hill, 2008).
Emotional intelligence is the ability to analyze and manage one's own emotions, as well as how to strengthen relationships by effectively interpreting others' emotions. Segal, a psychologist and sociologist, believes that emotional intelligence is a necessary life skill. Her book gives people a step-by-step approach to reading other people, calming one's own emotions, and strengthening both the verbal and nonverbal tactics that influence our relationships.

Study Questions

1. What weather-related adjectives would you use to describe the communication climate in your relationship with your best friend? With your employer? With your parents? With your significant other? With an instructor? What kinds of supportive communication described by Gibb (pp. 266–9) might improve this climate?

2. How would you describe your friend/employer/parent/significant other/instructor's style of handling concerns about your partnership (pp. 270–6)? How would you describe the style you might choose for dealing with your concerns?

3. Describe how you might choose an assertive, win–win approach to addressing your concerns with one of the people you have described in questions 1 or 2. Might your approach be different if your partner had a different cultural or gender identity? What do you think might be different?

PART III
Communication in Groups

PROFESSIONAL PROFILE

Andrew Laing

Okay, close your eyes and imagine you are a first-year university student of mass communications effects in the early twentieth century. New technologies such as wireless, mass circulation dailies, telephone, film, and radio are having successive, percussive effects on the populace, and there is much misinformation and, consequently, great demand for research to better understand what these effects may be. In response, you are part of a new group of researchers developing innovative methods and theories to explain these effects. Over the years, you prosper.

Now open your eyes. It's the twenty-first century, but it's *plus ça change* for communications research. Nielsen ratings, agenda-setting effects and other methodological structures carefully built over the last 100 years are crumbling, victims to the fragmentation of media and audiences caused by our own current successive waves of new technologies: mobile wireless devices, Twitter, Facebook, digital mainstream news sites, audio/video streaming, piracy, and so much more. New technologies are once again creating both considerable misinformation about effects and, with it, a huge demand for research and measurement.

This time, it will be harder. New technologies today aren't *creating* mass audiences: they're breaking them apart. The internet defies the idea of an audience that exists within a defined time period and geographic space. Data are another problem. Social media produce staggering amounts of structured and unstructured data that can overwhelm researchers.

Since answering a small job ad in *The Globe and Mail* 25 years ago, I've watched this unfold as both a student and business person making a living understanding media effects. My clients, such as Royal Bank, Rogers, KPMG, the Ontario Ministry of Health, the Canadian Cancer Society, and many more, want to understand these trends, putting both commercial and research demands on me and my team of analysts. While I came into this profession with basic research skills taught at any university communications program, the field will demand a wider skill set in the years to come. Database mining, computer coding, textual analysis, will have to be added to a solid understanding of research methodologies and a firm grasp of statistics, on top of a brave, new thinking about the relationship of media, technology and people.

Yes, it is daunting to open your eyes. However, the academic and professional opportunities both professionally and academically in studying communications have never been greater. It is vitally important that communications students learn the basic methodologies and the new skills to understand these effects, and embrace the enormity of it all.

Andrew Laing, MBA, PhD, President, Cormex Research

8

Social Media and Communication Theory

After studying the material in this chapter . . .

You should understand:

✔ the characteristics of social media and how they differ from those of traditional mass media;

✔ the history of the development of social media;

✔ the features of the various types of social media;

✔ the effects of social media on our sense of self and our mobility, as well as in the realms of marketing and traditional mass media;

✔ the benefits and dangers of social media; and

✔ the major theories of mass media, including those of the two Canadian communication pioneers, Harold Innis and Marshall McLuhan.

You should be able to:

✔ select the right social media outlet for different sorts of messages;

✔ distinguish between the different varieties of social media and choose the one most appropriate to your task at hand;

✔ use social media effectively to build a personal digital brand;

✔ avoid the dangers of social media by policing your image;

✔ apply Harold Innis's time-binding and space-binding theory to different media; and

✔ apply Marshall McLuhan's theories of the medium is the message, the tetrad, and hot and cool media.

Chapter Highlights

Social media represent a radical re-thinking of how people and organizations broadcast messages to one another. Social media have several important characteristics:

» They are participatory, dynamic, and create community.

Social media can be categorized according to the following types:

» zines, blogs, microblogs;
» social networking websites, wikis;
» social news aggregators;
» social bookmarking websites; and
» social photo and video sharing websites.

Social media are having a major impact on different parts of our lives by

» changing our sense of self;
» affecting how we move, consume, and behave through geo-tagging;
» changing the way we market goods; and
» transforming traditional mass media.

Social media present both a huge opportunity and pose many risks:

» They provide the opportunity to build a permanent, profitable online brand that promotes your values, goals, and dreams, as long as you police your image.
» They provide a perfect venue for destroying your reputation if used incorrectly.

The communication theories discussed in this chapter are:

» concepts of Harold Innis and Marshall McLuhan;
» flow theories, such as bullet theory, two-step flow theory, and multi-step flow theory;
» social learning theory;
» individual differences theory;
» diffusion of innovation theory;
» cultivation theory;
» agenda-setting theory; and
» cumulative effects theory.

Our lives are all being affected in some way by media. Whether it is popular culture affecting our identities or public relations campaigns facilitating our relationships with one another and with organizations, we are awash in messages. Each of these messages makes us think about the world differently. Even if we reject a message, it still becomes part of our mental landscape. As soon as someone makes you consider something, they have found a way of entering your mindspace. That fact is at the centre of mediated communication.

Mediated communication differs from much of the communication we have studied so far in this text. It consists of messages transmitted through a channel, be it print (newspapers and magazines), broadcast (television, radio, and internet), entertainment (movies and music), or social media (microblogging, personal social networking, photo/video sharing, etc.). As discussed in Chapter 1, we use the term "mass communication," or "mass media," to refer collectively to these methods of communicating messages to large, widespread audiences. But there is another aspect of mediated communication which does not have to do with mass messages. An e-mail or text message to a friend or phone call to a relative is mediated, in that it depends on a device for its transmission, yet it is intended for one recipient, not for a mass audience. In this sense, mediated communication, though it does not involve face-to-face contact, can possess many of the qualities of interpersonal communication described in this text.

Most of us are inherently interested in the glamour and power of mass communication, and we enjoy learning about it. All of us have been touched by the excitement of feeling the connectivity and instant feeling of celebrity that social media can offer. Some want to explore the possibility of a career in media or public relations. Others just want to be informed users of media. This chapter is designed to help you start analyzing how mediated communication, both traditional and social media, affects your life—for better and for worse. We begin by discussing mediated communication from the perspective of social media. We then take a tour of the different sorts of social media that are popular and powerful (at the time of the printing of this book) and investigate how they can be effective for communicating messages in various aspects of our lives. We also take a moment to explore how social media may be affecting the mass media, such as newspapers, television, and radio.

In the second half of the chapter, we discuss several mass media theories that have been prevalent in the field of communication studies. Starting with Harold Innis and Marshall McLuhan, the two foundational Canadian communication theorists, we go on a flash tour of the other established communication theories to see how they explain the impact of mediated communication on our social and cultural lives.

Social Media

Social media, which have risen in prominence since 2008, are a form of mediated communication that permit people to develop and categorize networks of friends and acquaintances by various dimensions of affinity, such as likes and dislikes, profession, taste, and ethnic or religious group, among many others. In fact, social media amplify the various forms of interpersonal communication that we have discussed so far in this text. They force us to write more, communicate verbally more, and be much more aware of the impact that the medium we use to communicate has on a receiver's interpretation of our message.

In essence, social media force us into *dialogue* with the people and organizations (see the feedback model described in Chapter 1) with whom we are communicating, whereas before the best we could expect from traditional media would be *two-way symmetrical communication* (see the linear communication model described in Chapter 1). For example, someone reading your text message can't understand your emotional state in the same way that someone standing in front of you might, so you use emoticons and perhaps append an image or video using a tool like Snapchat or Instagram to drive home your emotional state. Social media have been at the forefront of a communication revolution. From Facebook and Twitter to LinkedIn, Instagram, and Pinterest, these sites, and many others, are changing the way we interact all over the world. More recent examples like the Arab Spring, Idle no More, the Occupy movement, and even the debunked Kony 2012 campaign show how our social lives and economy are being transformed by social media in both subtle and overwhelming ways. Were Harold Innis with us today, he might say that social media have brought us to the brink of a new form of civilization.

What makes a medium social? While many different answers have been proposed by business gurus, dating coaches, academics, public relations experts, and, of course, the creators of social media services themselves, there is a consensus that the main answer lies in *human interaction*.

A more elaborate definition might say that social media allow for the flow of content, particularly content generated by the users of social media themselves, to other people. Some social media, such as Facebook, Google+, or LinkedIn, demand that users validate membership in their friend lists, facilitating their sharing of posted content with people or organizations with which they have a pre-existing relationship. Other forms, such as blogs, Tumblr, Twitter, Instagram, Pinterest, or even wikis, permit users to share content with people they may or may not know, thereby supporting the creation of relationships. For example, a person living in Whitehorse can **tweet** messages, images, and links that he or she finds fascinating and accumulate **followers** whom he or she may or may not know, eventually creating a national or perhaps even global community. For the purposes of our discussion in this chapter, we define **social media** as social environments that are meant to be used at little or no cost to publish and share messages and information generated by participants.

Businesses sometimes use the term **user-generated content** when referring to social media, meaning that most of the valuable information available from social media isn't generated by a big organization, such as the CBC or Vidéotron, as is the content of mass media. Instead, social media content is generated by the users themselves. This means that social media are an incarnation of Marshall McLuhan's dictum "the medium is the message" (see page 328); it is the conversations, stories, photos, links, videos, and works of art that users post to social media sites like Facebook, Twitter, Instagram, or Reddit that make those sites useful. Without the content uploaded and commented on by users, social media would all look exactly the same: empty, meaningless, lifeless shells.

Comparing Social Media and Traditional Mass Media

Social media have two things in common with many other media, including books, letters, or even television shows: they contain messages and they use a channel. The messages can be any form of expression by a human or artificial intelligence: art, text, videos, music, and so on. The channel can be electronic, through a computer application—or app—available on a server (wikis, Facebook, Twitter, Instagram), through mobile computing devices (tablet or

tweet
A message sent through the microblogging service, Twitter.

follower
A twitter user who has subscribed to the tweets of another user.

social media
Social environments that are meant to be used at little or no cost to publish and share messages and information generated by participants.

user-generated content
Social media content that is generated by their users, not by large organizations.

laptop), or through a smartphone app (most sites have apps for the major smartphone platforms: BlackBerry, iPhone, Android, and Windows). Surprisingly, social media can also be distributed through physical channels such as zines, graffiti, or slogans that are distributed through viral campaigns or through simple word-of-mouth. For example, a grassroots or telephone-tree campaign can be an efficient way to raise awareness of an upcoming club or group event. There are also many creative people who are using physical messages to have a crossover impact into digital—think of the viral nature of British graffiti artist Banksy whose works of social commentary are painted on walls in the cityscape, but which are then often distributed via digital communication to millions and millions via the internet.

Where social media differ from traditional media are that the former must have a persistent social interface, that is, a software infrastructure that allow users to build and maintain their interpersonal relationships through the social medium. For example, a user's tweets persist on Twitter and are available for followers to read and respond to. A history of these conversations is also available, allowing the relationship to build over time. Facebook, Google+, and other **social networking sites** allow users to create virtual social communities that persist on their respective servers.

Another key difference between social media and traditional mass media is accessibility. In the past, individuals were not empowered to spread their messages globally because they had no access to the gatekeepers of traditional mass media. One of the defining qualities of traditional mass media is that their content is mostly produced at great cost by large corporations. Production also requires high levels of technical expertise and training in communication arts. The only way that most ordinary people could communicate through traditional mass media was to write a letter to the editor or to call a phone-in show. If you were very capable, you might find a way to be interviewed by a reporter or talk show host, but that possibility is beyond the reach of most.

Social media have given the public easy access to global communication, opening the floodgates to the multitude of messages that users can generate and spread. Social media have suddenly given users the ability to make their voices heard by and their stories known to others all over the world. As a result, social media have shrunk the world. Nowhere is this more evident than in the various revolutionary wave collectively named the Arab Spring, wherein people around the world, through social media, were exposed to sweeping protests, clashes, and civil wars that swept over countries such as Syria, Yemen, Egypt, and Libya. Rikia Saddy, a Canadian professional communicator, has described how the use of social media allowed the voice of the people to be heard, as opposed to those of the leaders and, in turn, was a force for destabilizing power.[1]

Social media also differ from traditional mass media in terms of immediacy. It not only takes a long time to create, edit, and produce content for mass media, but there can also be a long time between these stages and broadcast. By comparison, social media are instantaneous; users post information immediately from their smartphones, iPads, computers, or

social networking site
A social medium that allows users to create virtual social communities in which they share content, exchange messages, and build relationships.

even Google Glass. Furthermore, the expected level of production quality and "finish" is lower for social media content because everyone knows that the content is user-generated using amateur or **prosumer** equipment.

Finally, social media content is very changeable. When a newspaper is printed, its articles can no longer be edited. The best the newspaper can do is publish a retraction or a correction. Social media content, however, is constantly being edited and re-edited. Think of what happens when a developing story is posted to a newspaper website, such as globeandmail.com. Often the story will start as a stub, basically a headline and a "lead" (the first line of a news story), and be enhanced throughout the day by staff writers until it becomes a full article. How can traditional newsprint compete with this process? Especially when the electronic version of the paper is being beamed wirelessly to iPads, Kobos, or Kindles? Furthermore, sites like Twitter "discover" a story as a collective. An example of this is @DeLobarstool, who tweeted, "uhh explosions in Boston," which is credited as the first online record of the Boston Marathon bombings in 2013.[2] Over the course of the next few days a virtual manhunt took place and information was updated, retweeted, further updated, and retweeted again. Reddit in fact had to issue an apology for how the Reddit community "identified" the second bomber but was mistaken.[3] This brings issues of journalistic integrity and the changing role that the truth may play in traditional reporting, as well as the ethical burden to verify the truth or check the wild spread of rumours that user-driven sites such as Reddit bear in moments of crisis.

Although there are significant differences between these two types of media, they are not mutually exclusive. In fact, there exists a form, known as **community media,** that blends some of the qualities of both social and mass media to form a middle ground. Community media are often paid for by cable or large media companies as part of their license application to the Canadian Radio-television and Telecommunications Commission (CRTC). An excellent example of community media is a cable access channel (such as Hamilton's Cable 14 or CPAC, Canada's national Cable Public Affairs Channel)—a channel that is funded by the cable operators but staffed by a combination of professionally trained technicians and broadcasters and local amateur broadcasters, writers, and interviewers.

Community media are a fascinating compromise between industrial media and social media: they allow a significant amount of user-generated content to appear through talk shows, phone-in shows, and broadcasts of community events, but they also bring professional production quality, access to newswires, and other tools of the industrial media. These latter qualities are possible because of **media convergence,** the tendency of large corporations such as Rogers or Bell Canada Enterprises to own and integrate various types of media outlets (e.g., radio and TV stations, newspapers, book publishing companies, and the internet) so that content can be shared and rebroadcast. Although critics claim that media convergence reduces consumer choice for information, access to multiple resources allows companies to produce sophisticated community cable programming.

Another threat to equality on the internet comes from the threat to **net neutrality**. In the past, it was not legal for internet service providers such as Bell, Rogers, Vidéotron, or Telus to

---

prosumer
A person who is both a producer and a consumer (e.g., a blogger is a prosumer of journalism and opinion).

community media
A form of media that blends qualities of both social media and traditional mass media.

media convergence
The tendency for large corporations to own and integrate various types of media outlets so that content can be shared and rebroadcast. Some critics claim that this reduces consumer choice for information.

net neutrality
When a company providing internet service treats all clients equally.

offer differential speeds to different internet sites. An example of non-net neutrality is when Verizon demanded that Netflix pay a special fee for its video viewers to have faster internet access than other video service providers' clients. In Canada, internet service is regulated by the CRTC, which makes eliminating net neutrality very difficult, since the CRTC is mandated to operate in the public interest. Recently, however, this trend is changing and ISPs have discovered a lucrative new revenue source: charging websites for preferential information transmission speeds. Many net neutrality advocates, such as Michael Geist, professor of law at Carleton University, contend that Canada is less likely to face a challenge to net neutrality because internet service providers are regulated by the Canadian Radio-television and Telecommunications Commission, which treats net neutrality as telecom regulation.[4] Whereas in the United States, the Federal Communications Commission treats it as an issue of information provision. The Telecommunications Act states that no Canadian carrier can "unjustly discriminate or give an undue or unreasonable preference toward any person, including itself, or subject any person to an undue or unreasonable disadvantage."[5] This means that it would be very difficult for Canadian ISPs to challenge net neutrality by providing preferential access to information to certain sites over others.

Are Social Media Completely New?

The simple answer to this question is that, while the software programs that drive popular social media services have only been around since about 2003, the technological underpinnings of the internet which allow social media to connect people the way they do were actually

Understanding Diversity

This Ghost Pine Interview Is True

When Jeff Miller launched his *Ghost Pine: All Stories True* punk zine in 1996, he didn't realize he was about to embark on a 13-year journey that would lead him from Ottawa to Montreal, from a punk scene to a vegan kitchen and some odd places in between. Jeff recorded those true-life experiences in *Ghost Pine*, and though the zine folded in 2009 it now lives on in the best-of anthology, *Ghost Pine: All Stories True* (Invisible Publishing, April 2010).

Torontoist: Can you give us an overview of your book, *Ghost Pine: All Stories True*?

Jeff Miller: The book collects the best of my zine, *Ghost Pine*, which came out for 13 years between 1996 and 2009. [It's broken down] into sections that deal with recurring themes time and time again within the zine. This book is [a] collection of stories, and a coming of age. You can see my coming of age when you read through its pages. I thought it would be an interesting document of my progress as a writer and as a human, but also as a document for cultural change. During the time

the zine was active there were a lot of changes in the world. I never really wrote a lot about what's happening around me, I often focused on the smaller details of my life. But when I read it now, little details about how the world was a different place back then jumped out at me. I found this interesting and worthwhile exploring in a collection.

TO: What inspired you to start a zine, way back in 1996?

JM: *Ghost Pine* was inspired by the hard-core punk scene in Ottawa. When I was growing up, there was a vibrant music scene there. A bunch of great bands played every weekend. To me, it was [an] amazing participant-based scene, it didn't feel like there was an audience. Everyone was taking part in some way. I had this idea to keep the scene going, and in order to participate, I needed to do something. Since I was always writing, I thought a zine was the best way to contribute [to] it. The zine evolved from there. It went from being a ranty thing to a selection of autobiographical stories with a beginning, middle, and end, without the same antagonism. The big shift occurred when

developed in the mid-twentieth century. The internet's precursor, ARPANET, was developed in 1969, and the World Wide Web was developed by Tim Berners-Lee at CERN (European Organization for Nuclear Research/*Organisation Européenne pour la Recherche Nucléaire*). Berners-Lee also built the first website, which went live on 6 August 1991. The forerunners of the current forms of social media, which we will discuss in the following sections, were also developed during this time.

Zines: Counter-Cultural, Print-Based Social Media

While a **zine** can appear in various forms, including print or electronic magazine, newsletter, or broadsheet, it is generally defined as a self-published, non-commercial publication that often covers specialized or unconventional subject matter. An active zine culture has existed for many years, with independent artists distributing their publications through special channels which are based on familiarity and community. Because zines often focus on subjects not covered in the mainstream media, there is often a connection made between personal identity and these alternative issues.[6] This means that, through zines, people seek a form of representation that they don't find in mass media content. The connection to alternative communities like punk and Riot Grrrl is a good example. There are also many zines about trans- and homosexuality, race issues, and peace activism. The accessibility of the medium has meant that zine-makers are also a very diverse group, including many races, the young and old, and the transgender, homosexual, and cisgender. An excellent example of a zine was Jeff Miller's *Ghost Pine* (see page 300). Zine-makers often form communities of readers, authors, and distributors

> **zine**
> A self-published, non-commercial publication, in either print or electronic format, that often covers specialized or unconventional subject matter.

the fourth issue came out in 1998. I started trying to observe the world, write about my experiences in a way that people could relate to.

TO: Why was the zine called *Ghost Pine*?

JM: Originally it was called *Otaku*, the Japanese word for nerd. At the time thought it as [*sic*] a nice metaphor. The punk scene was about collecting rare records and being on top of that kind of thing. I eventually got tired of that name and wanted to concentrate on the details of everyday life. I wanted a name that would be welcoming, accessible, and reflect what the zine is about. I had this baseball cap since I was a kid, I didn't know where it came from or anything about it, but it featured a picture of a ghost hiding under a pine tree. Under this image, it said "Ghost Pine." I really liked this. It was a metaphor for what I wanted to do with the zine, when I explored the small details in life, details or moments that are rather mundane and meaningless, but when you expand upon them, they end up meaning so much in people's lives.

TO: Why did you decide to end the zine in 2009?

JM: I found it more difficult to write about myself. I thought maybe I was less interesting now that I've grown up. I'm a bit shyer now. My life is more stable and change occurs differently when you're older. Some of the things that I was going through didn't really fit in stories in the same way. When I was younger, everything seemed to happen in story form. The timeline was different too. In a period of a month, events would happen that I perceived as life-changing. Now I find the changes happening in my life are more long-term things that can't be summed up so succinctly.

Erin Balser, books.torontoist.com, 13 April 2010

QUESTION: Why do you think *Ghost Pine* could be viewed as similar to social media? How do the author's feelings of discomfort about writing about himself mirror many people's insecurity about revealing too much of themselves on social media?

COMMUNICATION ON-SCREEN

Catfish (2010)
Directed by Henry Joost and Ariel Schulman.

Yaniv "Nev" Schulman is a young photographer living in New York City. One day he receives a painting of one of his photos from a talented 8-year-old artist from Michigan named Abbie Pierce. Nev and Abbie quickly become friends on Facebook, which broadens into him befriending her whole family: mother (Angela), father (Vince), and attractive older sister Megan. The documentary follows the burgeoning online relationship between Megan and Nev, which begins to take strange turns when Nev discovers that the songs Megan has been sending Nev of her singing, are all MP3s of other people's YouTube performances. Moreover, many of the claims about Abbie's art career turn out to be lies, prompting suspicion from Nev and the filmmakers. Urged to continue the relationship, despite the unease, by his documentarian friends, Nev decides to travel to Michigan in order to make an impromptu appearance at the Pierce family home. What the filmmakers discover upon their arrival is truly shocking, sad and unnerving, and highlights so many of the issues, dangers, and lies of the computerized social media age we interact in today. Catfish has been criticized for being a "false-documentary," however, one of its central themes is the confusing nature of truth in the internet age, so maybe it's all part of the message that what exists online and what exists off, are often at odds.

that are almost identical in structure to Facebook and other social networking websites.

GeoCities

Another good example of a precursor to present-day social media is GeoCities, founded by David Bohnett and John Rezner in late 1994. The model was similar to social media inasmuch as users were encouraged to design their own web pages in "cities" that were modelled after existing urban areas, such as Paris or Capitol Hill (Washington, DC). This model matched the social media idea of building communities of content by geographic and ethno-cultural affinity.

However, GeoCities never became fully fledged social media and was unavailable in most parts of the world. The most serious problem with the model was that there were very limited opportunities for the audience to contribute feedback. Although "guestbooks" enabled users to leave comments and notes, this feature allowed only one-way communication between the site owner and the user. All a user could do was leave a message on the site owner's website, which was very similar to traditional mass media. Furthermore, GeoCities lacked the ability for users to send exclusive content to friends and family or to form any kind of conversational relationship between users outside of the guestbook. A lack of two-way interactivity made the GeoCities concept fall short of the third element of our definition of social media: relationship- and community-building.

Web 2.0

In 2004, following the initial dot-com boom and bust, communication and multimedia experts coined a new term to name a second wave of internet development: *Web 2.0*. Web 2.0 emphasized incorporating interactivity and community-building principles into commercial websites, marking a move away from websites as static repositories of information. A good analogy for this change is that websites pre-Web 2.0 were like filing cabinets and Web 2.0 websites were more like libraries. A filing cabinet is a static object that is about the files it contains: you can put a file in it or take a file out of it. A library is a dynamic object that is about you, the user: you can wander the stacks, interact with others, consult the librarian, or use the computer, however, it is still arguably only isolated pockets of knowledge.

Web 3.0, often called the *Semantic Web*, is less about linear access of knowledge (click on X and learn about X) and more about *how* knowledge is accessed, integrated, and contextualized. Regarding social media, Web 3.0 is less about how you show *things* on your Facebook wall, and more about how everything you experience online is connected, integrated, and part of a bigger world. In essence, Web 3.0 is about websites and machines communicating with one another *about you* rather than *with you*. For example, you can install sensors on your home's electrical and plumbing systems and have your smartphone post your electricity and water usage to your blog automatically. While much of Web 3.0 is still at the "hacking" and "maker" stage, some technologies such as thermostats, fire alarms, health monitors, and door keys have seen commercial internet-enabled solutions. For this reason, Web 3.0 has also been labeled the "internet of things" or "industrial internet" where devices do most of the communicating between each other, rather than with people.

Some technological philosophers argue that the struggle with Web 3.0 reflects one of the cornerstone philosophical questions: does the world make sense, or do we simply try to make sense of the world? The biggest development from both Web 2.0 and Web 3.0 is that we are changing the world with every tweet, post, and "like," as well as linking new household or automotive features to the internet. When *Time* named its 2006 Person of the Year "You," it was evident that the social media revolution had become truly widespread and was well on its way toward transforming world culture and communication practices. Web 3.0 is just the natural extension of the wired world into our everyday lives.

Types of Social Media

Social media are a big part of our lives, but most of us have probably experienced only one or two varieties. In this section we will discuss the different types of social media and a few examples of each.

Blogs

From a contraction of the words "web" and "log," a **blog** generally describes a website in which an individual or an organization enters, in reverse-chronological order, regular commentary on events, philosophical musings, and/or personal opinions about an area of expertise. Sometimes bloggers will enrich their commentary with multimedia content, such as images or

> **blog**
> A website that features, in reverse-chronological order, an individual's or organization's regular commentary on events, philosophical musings, and/or personal opinions about an area of expertise. Blogs may also include images, sound clips, and video clips.

sound and video clips. The word "blog" has also entered common English usage as a verb, as in "I blogged the concert I went to last night."

Blogs started in the mid-1990s. One of the earliest bloggers was Justin Hall, a student at Pennsylvania's Swarthmore College, who started his blog in 1994. Four years later, Bruce Abelson launched OpenDiary. In 1999, Brad Fitzpatrick launched LiveJournal and, with Meg Hourihan, Blogger, which was bought by Google in 2003. In May of that same year, Matt Mullenweg created WordPress, a set of website-design software tools, mostly used as a basis for blogging, although WordPress has since become one of the most popular general website design tools around the world.[7] Since then, other blogging engines have been developed, such as Tumblr, which combines the microblogging function of "re-tweeting" with a more traditional blog format. Tumblr has gained popularity very quickly because of its strongly visual presentation and the ability to easily start publishing your content as well as commenting on and republishing the content of others. While WordPress requires a significant investment of time to set up and master, Tumblr allows bloggers to get set up in minutes and start producing striking content quickly. Tumblr users sacrifice control over the structure and function of their blogs for the benefit of ease-of-use. WordPress allows the user an astonishing array of options, plugins, and tools to customize their blog to their specific needs. Blogs increasingly serve as general websites integrating various social media channels maintained by the person, such as their Instagram, Twitter, Pinterest, YouTube, and other feeds.

Varieties of Blogs

There are several different sorts of blogs. In this section we describe many of them.

Personal Blogs

Many people maintain their own blogs, sharing information with friends and family or expressing their most intimate thoughts about things they've found on the internet. Melonie Fullick, a former communications student at McMaster University, maintains a beautiful photoblog called Panoptikal (panoptikal.blogspot.com), wherein she posts her photography and adds her thoughts and comments.

Others will maintain a blog to build a personal public brand as an expert in a particular subject area. Joey Coleman, who is profiled in Chapter 6, started a blog (joeycoleman.ca) about higher education when he was a student at the University of Manitoba and was eventually hired by *Maclean's*. Using crowdfunding website Indiegogo.com to raise money from individuals, he has emerged as Canada's first and leading independent micro-local journalist, covering happenings in the city of Hamilton, Ontario, for his devoted audience of tens of thousands. Some professors blog to get messages pertaining to their research or political beliefs out to the larger public, beyond the wall of the university or college. Michael Geist, a professor of law at the University of Ottawa, uses his blog (michaelgeist.ca) to promote his perspectives on copyright legislation more widely than if he were to publish them exclusively in scholarly journals. Sidney Eve Matrix, a Queen's National Scholar in the Department of Film and Media at Queen's University, uses her blog (sidneyevematrix.net) to explore ideas "about trends in the digital production, distribution and consumption of social media including advertising, television, music, movies, gaming, and social networking."[8]

Professional Blogs

Professional blogs, such as Canadian journalist and conservative political commentator David Akin's On the Hill (http://blogs.canoe.ca/davidakin/) and the Canadian urban music and entertainment news and gossip blog (hiphossip.com), have significantly influenced the distribution of information by breaking stories before the traditional mass media. Political bloggers have made a huge impact by expanding discussions on topics that the traditional mass media have been rather conservative about. Another example of a very influential professional blog is ThreeHundredEight.com, which is maintained by statistician and political wonk, Éric Grenier. This site has become a must-read for hundreds of thousands of Canadians who want to make sense of the confusing world of political polls during and between elections. Grenier's blog has created many opportunities for him, one of which is his frequent contributions to *The Globe and Mail*, where he talks about statistical trends and the predictions he mentions in his blog. From the Israeli–Palestinian conflict to Canada's involvement in the Afghan War to various political scandals, bloggers have blown the conversations wide open, allowing every detail to be published and every opinion, no matter how passionate, to be expressed. Although some traditionalists try to dismiss bloggers as gossips, most members of the public and the traditional mass media recognize the powerful contribution that the blogosphere has made to our global dialogue.

COMMUNICATION ON-SCREEN

Gossip Girl (2007–2012)
Created by Josh Schwartz and Stephanie Savage.

"Hey Upper East-Siders, Gossip Girl here, your one and only source into the scandalous lives of Manhattan's elite." So began every episode of the popular series *Gossip Girl*. Revolving around the anonymous gossip of an unnamed blogger, the show used the format of a tell-all website to focus on the lives of its characters. The running mystery of the show—the true identity of "Gossip Girl"—was stoked in each episode's closing lines: "And who am I? That's one secret I'll never tell. You know you love me. XO XO Gossip Girl."

What made the show fascinating is not so much the content of its narrative but the reflections it provided to its viewers. The show used social media and connected technology more effectively than any other of the time. Websites, smartphones, live streaming, blog posts, the strategy of refreshing a page religiously to gain new notifications: these were all devices that *Gossip Girl* used with fervent regularity. Regularly featuring whatever new social media site was "in" at the time, such as Facebook, Foursquare, and Instagram, the show, as Zoe Fox of Mashable.com argues, contributed to creating a generation that "thrives on Facebook likes, receives validation from blog hits, and is turned on by retweets."[9] *Gossip Girl* underperformed on television; however, in an almost ironic twist, it flourished online, with the show gaining a ravenous cult following. Its stars became regular features on gossip websites. *Gossip Girl* was arguably the first show about the connected generation, the Millennials, who have been raised on the internet, are always online via phones or computers, and intimately understand a digital world where the private/public spheres are blurred.

Corporate and Organizational Blogs

As part of their internet strategy, most corporations and organizations maintain a blog documenting daily corporate life. Corporate blogs, such as that of real estate company Century 21 Canada (century21.ca/Blog) or Joe Thornley of Thornley Fallis (propr.ca), a Canadian marketing and public relations agency, are used for branding, marketing, and promotional purposes. Not-for-profit organizations, such as the British Columbia Cancer Foundation (bccancerfoundation.wordpress.com); lobbying organizations, such as the Canadian Taxpayers Federation (taxpayer.com/blog); and political offices, such as that of MP Carolyn Bennett (carolynbennett.liberal.ca/blog) also often maintain blogs. For organizations such as these, blogs are an easy, entertaining, and inexpensive means of disseminating key messages.

> **Cultural Idiom**
> **blogosphere**
> The collection of all blogs in the world; the universe of blogs.

Vlogs (Video Blogs)

A **vlog** is a blog in which a user produces and publishes video entries as part of the blog's content. The rise of video resources such as YouTube, Google Video, Vimeo, and others has facilitated the rise of internet television, of which vlogging is a variety. There has been a lot of growth in Canadian vloggers over the last couple of years with many popular new channels from every sector: beauty, fashion, sports, parenting, business, feminism, sexuality, and politics. A search for "Canadian vloggers" or "List of Canadian vloggers" will reveal a world of possibilities for you to explore.

> **vlog**
> A blog in which the creator produces and publishes video entries as part of the blog's content.

Former Leafs General Manager Brian Burke Files Defamation Suit

Former Toronto Maple Leafs general manager Brian Burke has filed a lawsuit with BC Supreme Court, saying he was defamed in online comments accusing him of having an extra-marital affair with a sports reporter. Burke alleges the online comments published by 18 people, whose identities are unknown to him, are untrue.

Burke's statement of claim says the online comments were widely circulated on social media. His statement says the online remarks claim that Burke was fired as the president and general manager of the Toronto Maple Leafs because [of] what the comments say was a sexual relationship with Rogers Sportsnet reporter Hazel Mae.

"Contrary to popular belief, the reason for Burke's firing was not his willingness to pull off the Roberto Luongo trade. . . ." says one of the comments noted in the court documents. "Well it didn't take long for Brian Burke and Hazel Mae to hook up. In the summer of 2012, Sportsnet removed her from the glass desk because she wouldn't fit, insisting that she stand while on air."

According to the statement of claim, the online postings went on to suggest that Mae was pregnant, and that the "lucky dad" is Burke. In a statement released on Friday, Burke's lawyer Peter Gall said the comments, allegedly made under pseudonyms such as "Slobberface" and "Mowerman," are false and defamatory, and that they have hurt both Burke's and Mae's

The Blogosphere Community

Several blog-specific search engines have been developed over the last several years. Bloglines, and Technorati are two very popular ones. As well, there are blog communities that have grown up in the blogosphere, including WordPress and MyBlogLog. In Canada, several groups have organized their blogosphere. Two good Canadian resource for blogs are: Canadian Blog Directory (blogscanada.ca) and Top Canadian Blogs (topblogs.ca).

Dangers of Blogging

While blogging is a great way to begin building a personal or organizational brand, it can also expose you to a lot of unwanted attention. Blogging about other people, posting photographs of others without their permission, or making unsubstantiated claims about the motivations, beliefs, activities, or behaviours of others can lead to lawsuits against you or your organization. Posting excessively personal details about yourself, your friends, or your family can be very hurtful. Even if people don't pursue legal action against you, they may no longer trust you.

families. "Brian has decided that it is time to stop people who post comments on the internet from thinking they can fabricate wild stories with impunity," Gall said. "Brian is determined to find the authors of the lie about him and those who have circulated the lie."

The court documents say Burke is suing for losses and damages to his reputation. His lawyer is also seeking to have each of the 18 defendants restrained from publishing the statements on the internet. None of the claims have been proven in court, and a statement of defence has not been filed. Burke, who is married to CTV News Channel anchor Jennifer Burke, was fired as the general manager of the Leafs in January. The former Vancouver Canucks general manager is now the part-time scout for the Anaheim Ducks.

Iain MacKinnon, who represents Mae, said in an e-mail Saturday that his client supports Burke's legal action. "Hazel Mae fully supports the lawsuit brought forth by Mr. Burke and feels strongly that people should be held accountable for writing and spreading malicious lies over the internet," MacKinnon said. "Ms. Mae is still considering all of her legal options. She will not be commenting further on the matter at this time."

The Canadian Press, 26 April 2013

QUESTIONS: Do you think people feel that spreading spurious rumours online is different than offline? Why? Do you think that people see their identities online as being different from their offline personas?

Finally, revealing too much personal information can lead to **cyberstalking** (the stalking or harassing of an individual or organization using the internet or other types of electronic communication), stalking, or even break-ins and assaults. Some dangerous people use the anonymity of the internet to post terrible comments, filled with threats of violence, sexual assault, or sick personal fantasies, on people's blogs.

Microblogs

Microblogs began around 2003 and were originally known as *tumblelogs,* a term coined in his blog by "why the lucky stiff" (his only known name). By 2008, however, the term **microblog** had become predominant. A microblog differs from a traditional blog in the length of its entries. Microblog entries will often consist of only a short, simple sentence, an image, a link, or an embedded video. The content of microblogs tends to be very "in the moment;" the microblogger will often report on what he or she is doing *on the spot.*

Microblogs often follow a subscriber or "follower" model. Twitter has emerged as the most prominent of all the microblogging services because of both clever marketing and an ever-expanding suite of services. Other leading services are Tumblr and some internationally

> **cyberstalking**
> The stalking or harassing of an individual or organization using the internet or other types of electronic communication.
>
> **microblog**
> A blog in which the entries are much shorter than traditional blogs and are "in the moment."

UNDERSTANDING COMMUNICATION TECHNOLOGY

Cyberstalking

We can all agree that the internet has opened up many outlets that allow us to find and express our voice, and even to find an audience that is willing to listen. With such open channels of communication comes a degree of vulnerability to unwanted followers, notable in the predatory behaviour known as cyberstalking.

Victims of Violence is a federally registered charity devoted to providing support to Canadian victims of violence. Its website includes an excellent research page on cyberstalking that all young people should read: http://bit.ly/ eKimNB.

oriented microblogging services such as Sina Weibo from China; Plurk, particularly popular in South-East Asia; and Identi.ca, a Canadian open-source alternative. Several microblogging services have already gone extinct, including emote.in from India, Jaiku from Finland, and Six Apart (6A) from Japan, demonstrating the power of large brands to dominate social media, given that people are generally attracted to microblogging services with many subscribers. Many social networking services such as Facebook, Myspace, xing, and LinkedIn offer **status updates**, which may be considered a form of microblogging.

If a user wants to aggregate all of his or her microblogging activities, services such as Hootsuite, FriendFeed, Cif2.net, and Tweetdeck are several sites that will bring together microblogs from many sites onto one web page.

It is also noteworthy that microblog entries are not exclusively published on the internet. Rather, they can be pushed straight to a cellphone or a smartphone. It is also possible to receive microblog entries through text messaging, instant messaging, short message service, e-mail, or even digital audio on your smartphone.

> **status update**
> A short sentence or sentence fragment posted to a social medium that contains a message describing what the communicator is thinking or doing at the time of writing.

Why Has Microblogging Taken Off?

Just as e-mail replaced the written note because it saved communicators time and effort, microblogging services offer a quicker and more efficient means of sending brief text, photo, audio, or video messages one-to-one, via direct message, or one-to-many, via broadcast to the microblog's subscribers. Microblogging has simplified the communication process through the brevity of its messages, further reducing the need for niceties and conventions.

Marshall McLuhan might have made the point that social media are returning our culture to an oral, tribal state, drawing it away from the written conventions demanded by handwritten letters toward the conversational style of e-mail and now to the bursts of messaging characterizing the microblog, which are similar to group or town-hall conversations.[10]

An excellent example of this occurrence is how people watching events on television, such as the Stanley Cup finals or the series finale of a popular television show, use Twitter. The event develops, either by suggestion of the organizers or by consensus, what is called a **hashtag,** a short, descriptive label preceded by a pound (#) sign that is included in tweets to make them easily searchable. For instance, during the NHL playoffs, #stanleycup is one of the most frequently used hashtags, making it a trending topic for weeks on Twitter's Canadian site. For an up-to-the-minute analysis of how the #stanleycup is doing, you can visit the online analytics website, hashtag.com, which tracks and evaluates hashtag use (www.hashtags.org/analytics/stanleycup/). Many people watch the televised proceedings while also participating in the ongoing Twitter conversation, turning what would have been an isolated experience into a communal one. Twitter has already developed its own mythology: during the airing of the *Lost* series finale on 23 May 2010, Twitter traffic was so overwhelming that the service nearly crashed. Hashtags can also be used to bring together followers of conferences or

> **hashtag**
> A short, descriptive label preceded by a pound (#) sign that is included in tweets to make them easily searchable.

conventions or journalistic coverage of a particular event, such as the popular demonstrations in Turkey in 2013.

An article published by Bill Heil and Mikolaj Piskorski in the *Harvard Business Review* offers some surprising insights into the world of Twitter. They collected a sample of 300,542 users in May 2009 and found that 80 per cent were followed by or followed at least one user. They also found that while men and women follow a similar number of Twitter users, men have 15 per cent more followers than women. Even more interesting was the fact that an average man is almost twice as likely to follow another man as a woman. The authors state that this is a stunning result, given that "on a typical online social network, most of the activity is focused around women—men follow content produced by women they do and do not know, and women follow content produced by women they know."[11] They also found that the median number of lifetime tweets for a Twitter user is one and that the top 10 per cent of Twitter users in the study contributed 90 per cent of the tweets. Their conclusion was that "Twitter resembles more of a one-way, one-to-many publishing service more than a two-way, peer-to-peer communication network."[12]

Instagram, Snapchat, BlackBerry Messenger, WhatsApp, and Vine

Microblogging is evolving quickly, moving away from simple text and toward audio, photo, and video communications. The incredible rise in popularity of visual microblogging services, such as Instagram and Snapchat, is a perfect example of that growth because it is a platform that relies very heavily on the maxim that "a picture is worth a thousand words." Within Twitter, for example, we have seen the rise of video usage through Vine, which allows users to post six frames of video in a repeating loop as their tweet.

Another category is the rise of social media networks from platforms that used to rely on text-based instant messaging solutions—the most popular of which are BlackBerry Messenger (BBM) and WhatsApp. These services used to offer functions very similar to classic text messaging, but are quickly emerging, allowing communities of users who have "accepted" connection to one another through a "friending" process. Users can then share images, audio, video, or even full duplex audio and video conversations. In essence, what we are witnessing is the convergence of all media: text, audio, video, and photo into a one fluid, conversational, and easy-to-use channel. This reinforces the fact that social media communication is interpersonal in nature and is moving away from mass communication broadcasting models. It will be interesting to see whether BBM and WhatsApp challenge Twitter and other microblogging sites for interpersonal communication supremacy in the near future.

Social Networking Websites

As we mentioned at the beginning of this chapter, social networking websites enable users, either individuals or organizations, to build networks of "friends," linked through a variety of potential affinities, with whom

they share content, exchange messages, and build relationships. Users build profiles on these sites, sharing pieces of information about themselves, personal photos, notes, and invitations to affinity groups, events, and special interest websites. They then invite others to become their "friends" and can choose, through privacy settings, how much of their content will be visible to different categories of friends.

There are a massive number of social networking sites that have been developed since 2004; however, we will focus on the four major ones: Facebook, MySpace, LinkedIn, and Google+. For a comprehensive list of social networking sites, see the Wikipedia page devoted to cataloguing them, which is updated regularly: en.wikipedia.org/wiki/List_of_social_networking_websites.

Facebook

Facebook was first developed in 2004 as thefacebook.com, a project that provided a very clean interface with a simple blue and white design. It also offered a feeling of exclusivity and prestige, given that it was originally open only to members of the Harvard University community and, later, to other Ivy League colleges. As time passed, thefacebook.com became facebook.com and opened its doors to networks from other universities, then to networks of affinity from workplaces, to high schools, and finally to geographic locations such as countries, cities, and towns. Currently Facebook has over a billion users, making it the world's most popular social networking site.

Canadians have adopted Facebook in droves. In August 2013, the number of Canadians active on Facebook monthly was 19 million, with 14 million active *daily* users, of whom 9.4 million access Facebook through their tablet or smartphone. Canadians lead the way with more regular users per capita than any other nation. We also have the most average number of friends per user. While Facebook has maintained its clean design, its target market has changed significantly—in 2008 it transformed its status update model to compete with Twitter's micro-blogging model. In 2013 Facebook introduced an algorithm-based "Timeline" feature and, boldly, back in 2010, Facebook introduced the Open Graph model, which allowed it to compete with search engine companies such as Google for the right to organize and structure the World Wide Web through their new "Facebook Like" button. Website and blog developers may include this button on their sites, enabling users to have a web page mentioned in their Facebook profile and broadcast on the **feeds** of their friends. While this intimately inserted Facebook into the tissue of the Web, it also raised serious privacy issues and caused many people to leave Facebook to join more secure, less profit-oriented social networking services.[13]

> **feed**
> The constantly updated, reverse-chronological list of tweets issued by the people that a twitter subscriber is following.

MySpace

Founded in 2003, as a mimic of once popular social networking site "Friendster," MySpace competed with Facebook, generating traffic that matched and surpassed that of its chief rival from its inception until early 2008. It wasn't until April 2008 that MySpace was overtaken by Facebook, based on data generated by web analytic company Alexa, and the social media site has experienced a continued decline in members ever since. However, the fact that its pages are easy to personalize and the addition of special features for musicians have made MySpace an excellent and popular tool for indie bands, models, actors, and escorts to advertise their services. Part-owned by musician Justin Timberlake and rebranded the "new MySpace" in 2012, the networking site today is almost entirely geared towards bands and independent artists, with mass message options, tablet designs, and even a record label used to seek out new talent within its digital crevices. In June 2013 MySpace discontinued "Classic MySpace" in a reset of the site.

Cultural factors may have once influenced people in choosing either Facebook or MySpace. In 2009, social media researcher danah boyd made the following observations on the relationship between Facebook and MySpace among teenaged Americans:

> Those who are drawn to Facebook are more likely to represent privileged, educated, stronger socioeconomic backgrounds. They are more likely to be respectful of adult society and more likely to connect with adults who hold power over them. Those drawn to MySpace are more likely to come from immigrant families and from poorer, urban communities. They are more likely to be resistant to normative value and affiliate with subcultures.[14]

While the rebranded MySpace, with its appeal to musicians and artists, seems to be cultivating an image as a hipper alternative to its more mainstream rival, Facebook today has emerged as the predominant social networking site, with a broad appeal that cuts across cultures and subcultures.

LinkedIn

LinkedIn is a social networking site aimed at a professional audience. It permits users to share information about their professional experience, education, training, and achievements. Users can post a photo, their résumé, samples of their work, and reference letters. Users can also utilize the "Business Services" tool to search for jobs, or use the "Talent Solutions" page to post jobs or watch webcasts and read tips and insights on job recruitment. Users also invite other users to be their "contacts" and then share information with them through the link, as well as request them to endorse the user's skills and experience. One distinguishing feature of LinkedIn is that the age of the average user is much higher than that of Facebook or MySpace. LinkedIn has also become a major publisher of business intelligence and opinion, generating a large amount of in-house reporting and commentary that make the site a must-have for business professionals.

Google+

On June 28, 2011, Google launched its own social networking site, Google+. This service has grown incredibly quickly, becoming the world's second largest personal social networking site after Facebook, passing Twitter in January 2013. Google+ has several unique features, among the most popular are "Hangouts," which enables video chat, and document sharing via "Google Docs." Many users prefer the "circles" method of classifying friends into categories, since they enable more obvious control than Facebook over what friends can see on your profile. Google+ can be thought of as a social hub that brings together all of Google's other services in a networked fashion allowing users to collaborate and share content seamlessly across the Google family of services. Google+ has become particularly popular in professional circles, allowing for the creation of online knowledge-sharing communities such as SundayScience, started at McMaster University, which now has more than 10,000 followers who are discovering new wonders of science every weekend.[15]

Wikis

Wikis are websites that enable collaboration and sharing of information through the creation and simple editing of a number of linked web pages via a web browser such as Firefox, Safari, or Chrome. Wikis are powered by special software tools installed on **intranets**, or personal

---

wikis
Websites that enable collaboration and sharing of information by creating and editing linked web pages via a web browser.

intranets
Networks that have been sealed off from the general internet for secure and private use.

servers, which have been sealed off from the general internet for secure and private use. They are often used for collaborative writing or for tracking the development of a complicated project by allowing individuals to add content and edit the content of others. All edits are catalogued by the wiki software—all previous versions can be viewed at any time.

The most famous and largest example of a wiki is Wikipedia, an open encyclopedia whose contents are created and managed entirely by registered users. It is a crowdsourced project; the content is not generated by experts but by the collective intelligence and collaborative efforts of people all around the world. Because any user can create or edit a Wikipedia entry, the site features certain social phenomena that don't exist on other sites. "Editing wars" can be waged, evidenced by the edit history on popular entries. And users sometimes prank an organization by editing its Wikipedia entry with humorous comments and "facts."

Social News Aggregators

> **social news aggregators**
> Websites that allow registered users to post news stories to electronic bulletin boards.

Social news aggregators are websites that allow registered users to post news stories to electronic bulletin boards. Some of the most popular sites of this kind are the Huffington Post, Fark, Buzzfeed, Reddit, and Slashdot. Of these, the most popular by far, and the only one to have a Canadian page at the time of printing are Reddit (reddit.com/r/canada) and Huffington Post (huffpo.ca), which has come to resemble a blog website which contains more curated content and follows more stringent editorial practices. Social news aggregators have spread across the World Wide Web via "share" buttons on blogs and newspaper and current affairs websites, which enable users to share articles of interest on the social news websites. These websites can be criticized because they can be "gamed" through the use of artificial intelligence-based "bots," small software programs who "like" articles many hundreds if not thousands of times and thus drive up their scores, although this is becoming more difficult as the sites increase the sophistication of their user verification processes. The prevalence of "power posters"—the users whose posted articles are read or liked the most—indicates that these users are employing systematic strategies to up the scores of their posts.

> **Cultural Idiom**
> **drive up**
> To increase.

Social Bookmarking Websites

> **social bookmarking websites**
> Websites that permit registered users to organize, share, and manage lists of bookmarks of internet content.

Social bookmarking websites permit registered users to organize, share, and manage their lists of bookmarks of internet content in a fashion similar to the bookmarks that users save in their web browsers. Users can add descriptions to their bookmarks and tag them with categories. The websites then share the bookmarks in a newsfeed, similar to that of Facebook or Twitter. Delicious, the pioneering social bookmarking website, has integrated a feature for ranking bookmarks. It has been surpassed in popularity by such sites as Pinterest, StumbleUpon, Newsvine, and Digg. Users find social bookmarking services useful for consolidating their lists of bookmarks from many computers. These sites also offer users the ability to create a commented library of things they have seen on the internet—a very valuable resource to a student or professional who needs to have knowledge at his or her finger tips in a pinch.

Social Photo and Video Sharing Websites

For internet users who wish to share content such as photos or videos, social media have sprung up to create communities around these formats. Although there are many examples of this sort of social media such as Vine, Picasa, Instagram, and Hulu, the most popular by far are YouTube and Flickr. YouTube allows users to register and post videos or even to start channels through which they can aggregate videos that they have posted. The site also has a friend function that helps create communities among its users and allows them to subscribe and leave comments on each other's blogs. Flickr enables users to post high-quality images to the internet that may be shared with authorized others. Vine allows Twitter users to post six-second bursts of video, bringing non-verbal communication into the microblogging mix. In fact, many communication researchers and futurists believe that social media are inexorably moving away from text toward photos and video, since these can convey richer information, more quickly and naturally than simple text.

Social Media, the Self, and Society

Social media are having a big impact on how we interact with one another, but are they changing our personalities and our sense of self? As a subject of academic study, social media is still relatively new, and it hasn't yet generated a body of research large enough to make definitive conclusions. Nevertheless, some early findings are interesting. For example, a study by Catalina L. Toma of Columbia University indicates that social networking tools have a strong self-affirming value. The participants were asked to spend time on their own or a stranger's Facebook profile and were then given negative feedback on a task. Participants who had spent time on their own Facebook profiles were more accepting of the negative feedback than those who had not, performing identically to those who had performed a self-affirmation exercise before receiving the negative feedback.[16]

Shanyang Zhao, Sherri Grasmuch, and Jason Martin from Temple University investigated how individuals construct their identity on Facebook. They conducted a content analysis of 63 Facebook accounts and found that users predominantly "show rather than tell and stress group and consumer identities over personally narrated ones."[17] These findings suggest a sense of self that is distributed across marketing narratives and narratives attached to specific group identities rather than one that is constructed from users reflecting on and processing their personal experiences and inner identity.

Finally, a team of researchers from Cornell University and the Palo Alto Research Centre explored the impact on impression management of users' status updates on Facebook.[18] They found that, while people are often successful at projecting a positive image through their status updates, it is also often the case that they go too far and are thus perceived as self-important. Adam N. Joinson, a researcher at the University of Bath, suggested that people who use Facebook for social connection gratifications use it more frequently, whereas those who use it for content gratifications tend to spend more time on the site.[19] These findings would indicate that there is not a significant loss of a sense of self among Facebook users.

These studies, while limited and preliminary in nature, give us clues that indicate that the "social media self-concept" will be quite different than the self-concept of the user in "meatspace"—researchers are just not sure how or why. And considering a 2013 study by ComScore of users' browsing habits, which revealed that, on average, 27 per cent of every hour is spent on social networking sites, these studies of social media and their effects on identity are even more important.[20] As sociologist Jean Baudrillard mentions in his seminal book, *Simulation and Simulacra,*[21] we are accelerating the virtual world of digital media so quickly that perhaps one day, the world of simulation may replace the world of physical reality simply because the simulated world is more exciting and we feel better within it than in the real world. One only needs look at the recent launch of interactive headset technology such as Google Glass to consider the increased interweaving of user and technology.

Social Media and Mobility

Parallel to the content revolution occurring in the social media discussed thus far, there is another mobility revolution that is about to wash over our culture and economy. The emergence of smartphones such as the BlackBerry, iPhone, and Android as mass-market consumer technologies has meant that many of us carry in our pockets remarkable portable media devices which include a powerful internet browser, crystal clear screen, high-quality video and still camera, and sound playback. These devices also have GPS (global positioning system) built in, which permits the device to establish the user's precise location almost anywhere on earth. This has made geo-tagging a major component of future social media platforms; some of them, such as Twitter, have already integrated it. **Geo-tagging** enables people to map out their tweets, texts, and photos, generating a giant, interconnected web of messages that are pinned down to earth because the map of messages matches the physical geography so perfectly.

> **geo-tagging**
> The act of tagging a piece of posted content with the GPS coordinates of its author at the moment of posting.

A first such "location-based social networking service," Foursquare, enables users to "check in" at locations via the GPS function of their smartphones. It also permits them to leave a comment about the location and form circles of friends, in a similar fashion to other social networking sites. Users then compete to unlock "badges" which reward them for frequenting different types of locations, such as Tim Hortons or Second Cup coffee shops. Users can even become the "mayor" of a location if they are the person who has frequented it most regularly. Marketers are quickly realizing the potential of Foursquare for location-based marketing. For example, imagine that you have checked in at your favourite diner—a nearby café can send you a discount for desserts and try to entice you to have dessert at the café instead of at the diner where you are currently seated!

In 2012, researchers reported that users are beginning to switch from traditional social media to more mobile friendly apps such as WhatsApp, Snapchat, and Kik Messenger. Some argue that these switches are due in part to the climbing average age of Facebook users (41), and continued parental monitoring of their children's feeds, pushing younger users to new corners of the web and, in turn, increased privacy.[22]

The same concerns that exist with social media's influence on our sense of self apply here. As the real world becomes more and more intertwined with the simulated world of social media, when locations blur with the pure information of our tweets and blogs and posts, which reality will we choose? This is an important issue and one of the most fascinating things to consider regarding social media. Perhaps one of you will come up with the theory that explains it.

Many other services have incorporated some form of geo-tagging, such as location on Twitter, Facebook Places, and, most importantly, Google Maps. Google has broadened the

power of its mapping service by enabling users to create map overlays for specific regions and then pin content to actual geographic locations. Pins can be enriched with content and links to other forms of content. This is a powerful tool for linking real-world events to social media since maps have always been extremely popular among people—everyone likes to find their house on a globe!

Social Media, Public Relations, and Marketing

Social media are also transforming the world of public relations and marketing. Organizations seek to build lasting relationships and a strong feeling of affinity among their existing clients, potential clients, and stakeholders. In fact, social media allow them to open conversations that members of the public want to participate in. Through blogs, they attempt to capture the interest of their publics and keep them coming back to the organization's website. Through Facebook, they try to build a feeling of "belonging to the community" for their brands. And through Twitter, they use clever tweets to keep people thinking about their brand. The emerging key in social media marketing is finding a way of reaching opinion leaders and influencers. What time are they online? Which tweets are they retweeting? Which of the organization's posts are they sharing with their circles of friends on Facebook?

Chris Farias, a successful young entrepreneur who co-founded KITESTRING creative marketing + design, a marketing and creative design agency which specializes in social media marketing, describes his model of success as

Strategy x Creative = Branding

As a social media marketer, Farias (who is profiled in this chapter) looks for *social currency,* ideas that will be popular enough that opinion leaders and influencers will want to redistribute it to their networks of Facebook friends and Twitter followers.[23]

However, obtaining such currency requires a lot of sustained effort. Social currency will only be as effective as the amount of time you put into it. You can't just tweet for a couple of days and pick it up a week later. You've lost everyone. You have to do it every day. You have to be persistent. You have to be topical. You have to be conversational and current. You have to let people in on portions of your private life. You can't set out to make an item go viral, but you can prepare your audience by knowing them, knowing when they're listening, and what they're listening to.

> **Cultural Idiom**
> **go viral**
> When an item shared on social media is spread by others across their networks and becomes a cultural phenomenon for a short period of time.

Social Media and Traditional Media

Social media are transforming the world of traditional media and media consumption. Dr Andrew Laing, president of Cormex Research (who is profiled in this book), once visited Professor Sévigny's class and asked the 15 students a few simple questions before he gave his lecture:

1. How many of you read the print version of the newspaper at least once a week? (One hand went up.)
2. How many of you have a cable TV subscription? (Seven or eight hands went up.)

3. How many of you read the electronic version of a newspaper at least three times a week? (Every hand shot up.)

4. How many of you are current with the most popular television programs? (Almost every hand was raised.)

5. Do you download those shows from the internet or PVR them? (Every hand shot up.)

While this survey is anecdotal and certainly not scientific, it does signal a massive shift in the way people experience and consume media. In 2014, we asked the same questions, plus two others, of the Intro to Communications class: Can you name prominent journalists in at

YOUNG COMMUNICATOR PROFILE

CHRIS FARIAS

Creative Director and Partner, KITESTRING, a branding agency that specializes in social media marketing

Chris Farias is the Creative Director at KITESTRING, a strategic branding consultancy who were the first in their region to creatively leverage the power of conversation on social media for their clients' brands. Together with a small team of strategic thinkers, creators and communicators, Chris and his business partner Jenn Hudder have led KITESTRING to become an industry leader with their philosophy on how brands should interact in the social sphere.

This is a really exciting time to be an early twentysomething with an intuitive ability to grasp the workings of media! You're a part of the first generation who will naturally grow up digital specialists, having had exposure to computers from wee stages. In fact, all that digital experience has added up like credits towards an unofficial prerequisite for some exciting emerging career options. If you can answer "yes" to at least one of these questions, chances are you qualify:

- Did you see the Double Rainbow all the way across the sky before your best friend?
- Hey Girl, have you spent hours re-Tumbling Ryan Gosling memes until the tips of your thumbs go numb against your smartphone?
- Have you described your life status with a single emoticon?
- Kitteh can haz cheeseburger?

Lucky for you, all these hours spent pouring over your blog, Tumblr, Pinterest, Twitter, or Facebook account can also count towards valuable experience in these new digital communication professions if you learn how to leverage them wisely. If your love of frittering away the hours on social networks is the prerequisite for what is quickly becoming the millennial dream job, then what are the real life requirements?

Wikipedia says that a Community Manager ". . . works to build, grow, and manage communities around a brand or cause." Sound simple? Before we all rush to highlight the number of crops we've plowed in Farmville on our CVs and drift off into a swirl of pins about the versatility of mason jars, pay attention to the potential knowledge and experience you'll be exposed to in courses like this and others like it:

1. *Become a smarty-pants!*
If you want to be a social media professional, you're not hereby exempt from communication research or statistical analysis. In fact, understanding reporting tools (Like Google Analytics or TweetReach) are a must when to calculate the return on investment for your future employer. Social Media are still a foreign animal for most companies and online community management is still a new profession, so part of your job will likely include having to justify your existence on the company roster. Understanding where to

least one of the following areas: business, sports, fashion, or politics? (almost every hand was raised); and Can you name the newspapers or media they work for? (fewer than 10 hands went up). This suggests that the lines between journalism and blogging are fading, that journalists are known as individuals, separate from the newspaper brands they write for.

Anecdotally again, Professor Sévigny asked many of the same questions of a group of senior citizens at a session on communication literacy. Fascinatingly, the answers were much the same! This suggests that everything that traditional media executives used to think about how to research, develop, and sell media content to the populations of younger and older people must be completely rethought.

consider quantitative versus qualitative data in this role is also important! Knowing that the sheer quantity of followers you're corporate account has on Twitter is not nearly as important as the quality of engaging conversations you're having on it with your brand's community is only the beginning of when communication research and statistical analysis should direct social media and communication strategy.

2. *Learn when to fly by the seat of your pants.* While managing online communities often requires going with the flow of relevant trends and adapting to breaking news and situations, it might surprise you to know that most of the activity conducted by a Community Manager are the tactics of a well-planned strategy. How can you learn about corporate social media strategy? Listen up when the topic turns to case studies about major corporate social media flubs and the best practices that built successful campaigns alike. Read books, follow industry blogs, and seek out opinions of professionals in the industry who develop digital communication and social media strategy.

This doesn't mean that social media engagement can't ever wear spontaneous outfits. You'll learn to strike the perfect balance by combining the consistency of your brand's message with whatever your community is buzzing about—from puppies to the popular vote; you'll need to roll with social media content punches.

3. *Actually wear pants!*
Surprised? Did you think you'd get to work from behind the safety of your screen where no one can see what you're wearing? Sorry, this is not a gig for the anti-social. In fact, a lot of the work you'll be doing is offline with other people. Apart from in person meetings with company stakeholders, you'll likely have to personally engage with industry partners and both traditional media, like journalists, and the newly anointed, like bloggers or social media topic influencers. You'll likely also represent the brand at industry events, capturing highlights and happenings in real time on social networks and sharing in the fun with your community online.

If you do decide to take the professional social media management career path, you'll also need to "wear the pants" when it comes to taking charge of keeping your digital skills sharp and staying up to the minute in the ever-evolving social media world.

Now that you know more about what the role of a professional online Community Manager entails, you can help take the profession to the new heights by understanding the value a strategic communicator can bring to it.

So go ahead, tell your Mom that all those hours spent posting, tagging, tweeting, geo-locating, and pinning will be worth it once you combine it with communication research, analysis, strategy, and a reciprocal relationship with a lucky brand's online community members.

UNDERSTANDING COMMUNICATION TECHNOLOGY

How to Use Social Media to Find a Job

Social media has been a game-changer in terms of how people look for jobs, but as Toronto Star's *Krystal Yee reminds us, creating a dynamic online profile is an important way for potential employers to find out about us. As you consider Krystal Yee's advice, think of the opportunities social media can provide for you.*

Most of us use some form of social media every day, but how many of us use their power to advance our careers? Many job-hunting tips talk about cleaning up social media profiles, making accounts private, or using a false name, but often our social media presence can work for us. Reppler—a social media monitoring service—conducted a survey of hiring professionals, and found that 68 per cent would hire a candidate because of what they saw about them on a social networking site.

Social media have helped me countless times. I found and hired my real estate agent and my blog web designer from Twitter. Recently, I inquired on a freelance job posting online. The employer contacted me about 20 minutes after I submitted my resume. He told me he already follows me on Twitter, and felt like he already knows me. Having an active Twitter account gave me an advantage over any other candidate, because of the connection I had already made with that employer. Having a social media presence can positively impact your face-to-face networking activities, and can also help you tap into the hidden job market of positions that are not advertised.

Here are a few tips to using social media effectively:

Understand how you are perceived. Creating a social media presence takes time. To ensure you are conveying the right message about yourself to other people, consider using a social media monitoring website like Reppler. It's a completely free service that scans through the biggest social media networks—like Facebook, Twitter, LinkedIn, Flickr, and YouTube—and comes up with an Image Score, shows you any inappropriate content, and advises you of any privacy of security risks.

Build your connections. Gone are the days where you have to show up at every face-to-face networking event in order to get business cards and build your professional network. This is arguably one of the biggest benefits of social media,

Newspapers

When, in 2001, Google News began using computers and artificial intelligence systems to edit a website that brought its reading public the news of the world, many experts began to worry that no one would ever pay for news content again. In fact, Google News has highlighted how inefficient and conformist the international news industry has become, and at the time of this printing, Google has begun a program called "Google Surveys" with the world's major news-gathering and news publishing organizations that make readers pay for content by answering survey questions related to the content of the articles they wish to read. For example, answering a survey about their automotive preferences will give them access to an article about the latest sports cars. These surveys cost market researchers much less than traditional polling and provide a revenue source for media websites without having to put up a paywall.

Newspapers are changing as we speak. They are migrating away from print and towards electronic distribution models. They are embracing Twitter and communicating directly with subscribers who want to follow breaking stories in real time. Twitter is pushing users to the newspaper website. In early May 2010, *The Hamilton Spectator* tweeted that a "crocodilian-type" creature had been spotted in Hamilton Harbour. The newspaper then tweeted updates about the creature throughout the day, finally announcing that the search for the creature had been called off. The experience drove many people, especially young people who appreciated the schlocky humour of the story, to the newspaper's website. The following day's print edition of the paper contained the full story; however, it is very debatable whether these same people picked up a copy. The fact is that young people—and increasingly everyone else—aren't paying

> **Cultural Idiom**
> **paywall**
> A barrier that stops users from accessing the body of a news article if they have not paid for a subscription to the website or, depending on the model, the individual article

so take advantage of how easy it is to make connections. A few ways to grow your network are to friend or follow those with common interests, participate in Twitter chats, engage in discussion on Facebook pages, and send personalized messages to people you would like to connect with on LinkedIn.

Position yourself as an influencer. As a job seeker, marketing yourself on social media is about crafting your personal brand. And a great way to impress potential employers is to have your own blog about the industry you are most interested in. Not only will you be able to establish yourself as an influencer and expert in your field, but good content will always get shared and spread throughout social media networks.

Find opportunities. Social media aren't about pushing out messages and waiting to attract followers and conversation. It's about pursuing and networking with people who are more influential than you. As a job seeker, it's not very often that we get the opportunity to directly communicate with high-ranking executives, CEOs, and industry

influencers. Use this to your advantage to connect and engage with the companies and people you want to eventually work for. You can also use the Twitter search function to look for jobs using industry hashtags, or recruiters posting job ads. You can also use LinkedIn or Facebook to look for jobs through company pages.

Take your networking offline. One of the main functions of social media is to build your connections. But you have to remember to take your networking offline and meet face-to-face. That's where the real magic happens. Attend Facebook, LinkedIn, and Twitter meet-ups. Check out industry-related conferences, or just invite someone out for coffee.

Krystal Yee, *Toronto Star*, 1 December 2011

QUESTIONS: How do you use social media? Have you ever thought of using it find work? How would you change your use of social media to make it more effective for your job search?

---

for news delivered in hard copy. Evidence of this comes from the decision to stop publishing Montréal's *La Presse* newspaper in hardcopy and focus research and development on a free-of-charge app for smartphones and tablets. Through the introduction of innovative new interactive advertising templates, in spring of 2013, the *La Presse* app was generating over 40 per cent of the newspaper's revenues, without making users pay a subscription fee.

Television

Television is undergoing a transformation toward a watch-on-demand model of content delivery. Although broadcasters recently began caving in to their audience's preference for watching TV shows online, they have had trouble generating revenue through these sites because they have only recently found ways to deliver advertising through the online broadcasting model. Some producers are counting on revenues generated by the stunning quality of Blu-ray discs or the "extra features" that can be included on them. Others are relying on 4D high definition television broadcasting which delivers several times the resolution and clarity of 1080p HD. In September 2010, Steve Jobs, CEO of Apple, Inc., announced a new version of AppleTV that rents television programs or movies, in the digital equivalent of how we used to borrow movies from Rogers Video. Over the last five years streaming TV and movies have become a huge business. For example, in 2014 Apple TV released AirPlay and Amazon released Amazon Fire. As well, many TV networks (like Bravo, CityTV, AMC, and Global) released apps that can be downloaded on someone's tablet, computer, or device for no charge. The follower can then watch current episodes of the network's most popular series.

UNDERSTANDING COMMUNICATION TECHNOLOGY

Royalties Deal Breaks Barrier to Entry in Canada's Digital Music Streaming Market

If you enjoy streaming music over the internet, get ready for a lot more choice—and higher costs. A spring 2014 decision by the federal government has opened the door to music-streaming services previously unavailable in Canada. Will song-writers and recording artists get a fair share of the subscription fees music lovers pay? The Globe and Mail technology reporter Omar El Akkad assesses the situation.

After years of deliberation, the Canadian government has finally determined how much digital music-streaming services must pay in royalties every time a user listens to a song—a decision that could open the door for some of the most popular digital music sites in the United States to come north of the border.

On Friday, the Copyright Board of Canada issued a decision on the royalty rate that music streaming services must pay for the use of recordings. The ruling covers the period between 2009 and 2012, but finally offers some clarity as to how much streaming services can expect to pay in royalties in Canada.

The lack of clarity on royalty rates has likely contributed to some streaming services thinking twice about expanding into Canada. "It takes a little bit of time to make decisions, and in this digital world we live in, things change every three months," said Vanessa Thomas, managing director of Songza Canada, a digital streaming service that has operated in the country since 2012. "I think that's been a barrier to entry."

The copyright board determined that services such as Songza, which offer users streaming music through custom web-based stations, must pay 10.2 cents in royalties for every 1000 plays. The rate represents a victory for the music services, which had argued for a similar number. In contrast, Re:Sound, the agency that collects royalties in Canada on behalf of musicians and performers, had asked for a much higher royalty rate—between $1 and $2.30 per 1000 plays.

On average, the board estimates, a Web streaming service with $130,000 in revenues will pay royalties of about $7000 a year.

The ruling brings to an end, at least temporarily, a dispute between Re:Sound and a host of streaming services over digital royalty rates. Some of those services, such as Pandora, aren't currently available in Canada, but joined in the copyright board hearing anyway—likely in an effort to create the most favourable financial conditions possible before bringing their services north of the border.

"We are encouraged by the ruling," a Pandora spokesperson said. "The [copyright board's] decision has potential to encourage investment in innovative technologies and increase consumer choice in Canada."

While royalty rates for commercial radio and retail outlets that play music are fairly well-defined in Canada, rates for digital streaming were not. For years, services such as Songza

Radio

Radio is a spectacular exception to the trend. Canadians spend an enormous amount of time commuting, which has led to an explosion in the market for satellite radio services like Sirius Canada and XM Canada (the companies have merged and now offer a single set of channels under the SiriusXM brand). As well, conventional radio has flourished in the vehicle culture, as well as in busy workplaces where the drone of talk radio or music programming provides a welcome backdrop to a long and sometimes tedious workday. Interestingly, alongside the success of conventional and satellite radio, we have seen a surge in the availability of internet radio stations. Starting such a station doesn't cost a lot of money, and you can broadcast easily to a world audience. Again, workplace listening as well as home listening through computers is driving this growing trend. The interesting problem with internet radio is that subscribers are not used to paying for online radio content; the business model has yet to be made profitable. It has been argued that internet music streaming services, such as Spotify and Pandora, diminish the royalties that musicians and other performers receive for their work. As well, internet radio streaming from Scandinavia or China where stations can stream unfettered amounts of music without paying royalties to the musicians

opted to sign interim royalty deals with Re:Sound, rather than wait on the copyright board to make up its mind. Other services have avoided the Canadian market altogether.

The copyright board decision is focused exclusively on one of the fastest-growing areas of digital music—non-interactive and semi-interactive streaming services.

Interactivity refers to a user's ability to select what music is played. Traditional radio stations are non-interactive, because the listener can't chose [sic] the songs. Fully interactive services, such as YouTube, allow users to pick specific songs and listen to them as many times as they like. To avoid being classified as fully interactive, streaming sites allow users to skip only a certain number of songs every hour, and put other limitations on the listening experience.

Streaming services make money by running ads on their web sites, by partnering with sponsors to create branded digital radio stations, or by selling subscriptions.

According to the International Federation of the Phonographic Industry, streaming music service revenue jumped 50 per cent last year, even as traditional music downloads through sites such as iTunes dropped 2 per cent—the first such decline in history.

But many streaming services have yet to see the financial fruits of that growth. Songza, for example, has some three million users in Canada, but has yet to turn a profit.

There are already myriad royalty schemes by which companies that play music pay musicians and licence owners. In Canada, for example, brick-and-mortar stores that play music are charged royalties based on their store capacity. Because it is difficult for clothing stores and gyms to keep a detailed log of which songs they play, Re:Sound assumes that the music selection is essentially in line with what commercial radio stations play.

Ian MacKay, president of Re:Sound, said on average a Canadian radio station will pay about 10 per cent of its revenues in royalties for the music that makes up about 80 per cent of the station's daily content, and most non-music businesses that play music in the background will pay an essentially insignificant amount.

"I think lots of other industries would be happy with that deal," he said. "The average corner store is paying about a hundred bucks or less a year in royalties."

Omar El Akkad, *The Globe and Mail*, 18 May 2014

QUESTIONS: How do you think this new Canadian royalties deal will affect musicians? Do you think this will spur more musicians to write music? Would you be willing to pay for music streamed to you? If so, what sorts of music would you pay for, when and how?

are leading Canadian radio such as CBC to drop content that it must pay for so that they can compete—leaving artists with fewer royalties.

Using Social Media Effectively

The main advantage that social media offer is, as we have stressed throughout this chapter, interactivity and community-building. They permit people who may otherwise not have had ready access to a variety of types of content to suddenly have a world of possibilities open to them.

A second major advantage that social media confer is that of trust. When your "friend" on Facebook or someone you follow on Twitter posts something, you can make a judgment call on the person's credibility based on what you know of them. Presumably, you have "friended" this person or accepted his or her friend request because you felt some affinity toward him or her.

A third major advantage that social media give is the possibility of learning more about your friends by having a privileged glimpse at their lives through the content that they post online: their bookmarks on Pinterest, Delicious, or Stumbleupon, their likes and dislikes as well as photos and notes on Facebook, and their news clippings and videos posted to Reddit, Instagram, or Vine.

> *As technology advances, it reverses the characteristics of every situation again and again. The age of automation is going to be the age of "do it yourself."*
>
> **Marshall McLuhan, Canadian philosopher and communications theorist**

All of these advantages allow you to build a profile of your friends in your mind. It is as if you are in a constant (although somewhat one-sided) ongoing conversation with them, and, through the passage of time, you can deepen relationships with people who live far away. Consider that you are in a large interactive community, built on trust through which you share very private photos, notes, news clippings, blog posts, microblog entries, music selections, or likes and dislikes.

In many ways the melding of space-binding technology with a new, emergent time-binding culture signals a massive transformation that our society, culture, and economy is undergoing. We are shifting from a culture of check-boxes, categories, and organized information to one where information flows through a constant, ongoing digital conversation. As Marshall McLuhan famously stated, the greatest skill in the digital age is *pattern recognition*.

When you use social media, you must remember that you are establishing a pattern of online digital behaviour. Every time you post something to Twitter, a photo or status update to Facebook, a video to YouTube, or a bookmark to Pinterest or Delicious, you create a pattern of information that others decode and interpret. You can use this knowledge to build a strong personal brand that lends you credibility and reinforces your professional, moral, or community status. If you are a savvy user of social media, you can craft a permanent personal brand that will be very hard for others to discredit. As a student, you can build a portfolio of your achievements, thoughts, and ideals using social media that others will encounter when they surf the internet. You can inspire them to respect you and consult you for an opinion. You can move them with beautiful images and thoughts that you post. You can prove to the world that you are an expert and a good communicator of that expertise. In fact, many prospective employers will "google you" to find out more about you before they interview you. Having a digital footprint that you are proud of will help you get jobs, make friends, and build credibility. However, having negative or unflattering content about you floating in cyberspace can be very dangerous to your reputation, your job, and your relationship prospects. In the next section, we explore some of those dangers.

Dangers of Social Media

Social media are an incredibly powerful way to connect with others and build your reputation and credibility. However, they pose very serious reputational dangers if you are not savvy about how you use them.

The main truth to remember is that everything that you post to social media is *permanent*. As soon as you post an image or a text, or when someone else posts one about you, it is stored on a series of computers at the social media service's headquarters. The moment that another user views the image or reads the text, a copy of it may be stored on the hard drive of his or her computer. This image or text will probably end up being stored on hundreds, thousands, or even tens of thousands of computers worldwide. Furthermore, *you have instantly lost control of that image or text*. Others can interpret it as they choose. They can add comments to it. They can string it together with other pieces of information that they have gathered about you to "build a story" about you and then disseminate it to millions of other users within minutes using content aggregation services such as Storify. You can probably think of cases where someone sent inappropriate e-mails to a few friends, only to have them forwarded around the world. Another example is how text messages revealed Tiger Woods's marital infidelities.

Some young people do impulsive things. Drunken excess, sexual experimentation, drug-taking, or minor criminal activity such as theft, assault, or vandalism—all of these things can happen. If such activities are done in private and not recorded, it is the word of any witnesses against yours. Any allegations others may make about you are hearsay and are not very credible.

Now, imagine that some of those behaviours had been photographed or video-taped and posted to Facebook or YouTube. These are circumstances that could have nightmarish consequences for your future career and relationships—just think of the myriad examples of people posting videos of themselves being cruel to animals or other people, which lead to hundreds or thousands of internet users hunting them down and posting their personal information all over the internet. The thing to remember is that many of the people who have access to your social media profile *are not your friends*. Many of them are quasi-strangers who could easily choose to profit from your momentary misstep. Google CEO Eric Schmidt has recently said that young people may have to change their names and identities to escape from the garish or embarrassing social media profiles they have built.[24]

Protecting Yourself on Social Media

How can you protect yourself in the world of social media? The answer is simple. You must *police your image*. Here are some tips that could help keep you safe:

- Always think twice before posting something risqué to social media. Count to a hundred before pressing "send."
- Be aware of people taking digital pictures or videos of you. Refuse to sign a release form and tell the photographer/videographer that you do not authorize publication of your image. Be assertive about this.
- Be careful of people who cajole you into compromising situations during Spring Break or at parties, casinos, vacation resorts, or nightclubs. Chances are you may be under the influence of alcohol, drugs, or simply just the pounding music. Your judgment is suspect and you are more prone to impulsive behaviour. Also, locations such as these have a much higher than average number of people whose hidden agenda is to take advantage of you. There is an entire amateur porn industry that proves that "What happens in Vegas, stays in Vegas" just no longer applies.

In the digital age, there is no privacy and no distance. If you are aware of these facts, you can protect yourself easily and enjoy all of the incredible connectivity and community-building opportunities that social media can offer you.

> **Cultural Idiom**
> **police**
> To regulate or protect.

UNDERSTANDING COMMUNICATION TECHNOLOGY

The Internet Dilemma: Do People Have a Right to Be Forgotten?

Have you ever Googled yourself to see what comes up? It's an important exercise in impression management, because it shows you what kind of information will appear if someone else—a new acquaintance, a potential employer, even a distant relative—decides to look you up on the internet. In the following column, Drew Nelles, senior editor at The Walrus *and contributor to* The Globe and Mail, *looks at the transience and permanence of our online presence, and what it's like to have your life and legacy defined by a Google search.*

One of the most heartbreaking overlooked moments in the case of Rehtaeh Parsons—the 17-year-old Nova Scotian who killed herself in April after allegedly being raped and bullied—came in a blog post written by her father three days after her death.

"I had to write something about this," one line read. "I don't want her life to be defined by a Google search about suicide or death or rape. I want it to be about the giving heart she had."

The sentiment is so moving because it is so fruitless. The Parsons tragedy is hypermodern—someone photographed her during the alleged rapes; the photo was disseminated around her school; her classmates sent her cruel, crude messages—and Rehtaeh will, of course, be defined by her Google search. As we all increasingly are.

At the heart of the Internet is a tension between ephemera and permanence. Every tweet, Facebook post, and Instagram photo is a vehicle for instant gratification, but that information sticks around, squirrelled away forever—forgotten, until it isn't.

Typically, this is cast as an issue of privacy: Does a job applicant, for example, deserve to lose an opportunity because Googling her name pulls up some long-ago indiscretion? But it's more. Rehtaeh Parsons's father was worried his daughter would be memorialized by forces outside human control, by the inscrutable, impersonal logic of algorithms.

The difference between how humans remember and how the Internet remembers is deep and fundamental. Humans forget, or remember selectively; the Internet remembers everything.

"For almost all of human history, collecting information and storing information was time-consuming and costly, and therefore we stored as little as possible," says Viktor Mayer-Schönberger, a professor at Oxford University and the author of *Delete: The Virtue of Forgetting in the New Digital Age.* "Even the stuff we stored we rarely made use of, because retrieval was so expensive."

But digital technology massively decreased the cost of data storage, and made accessing that information far easier. Now, we're steeped not just in knowledge but in memory: of our checkered pasts, our personal failures, the ruined lives of our loved ones.

"Human forgetting actually performs a very important function for us individually as well as for society," Prof. Mayer-Schönberger says. "It lets us act and think in the present rather than be tethered to an ever-more-comprehensive past. The beauty of the human mind and human forgetting is that, as we forget, we're able to generalize, to abstract, to see the forest rather than the individual tree. And if we cannot forget, then all we will have are the individual trees to go by."

In Rehtaeh Parsons's case, all we have are those trees: the awful circumstances of her death, the official bungling of the investigation. A more human kind of memory would recall her as a whole person, someone with agency and interiority.

We live in an era of endless archiving. For $279, you can pre-order a "lifelogging camera" called Memoto, which attaches to your clothes and takes two geotagged photos every minute, around the clock: "This means that you can revisit any moment of your past." the copy reads.

Google Glass, the tech giant's much-hyped wearable computer, will also come with a camera. More nobly, the United Nations' Memory of the World project aims to preserve the world's "documentary heritage"—from the archives of the Dutch East India Company to the woodblocks of Vietnam's Nguyen Dynasty.

Even Facebook's Timeline redesign is a memorial project, creating as it does a single continuous stream of your entire existence on the social network.

The advantages of the Internet's vast archive are obvious: Never before has our knowledge been so far-reaching or esoteric. Political projects such as WikiLeaks hold governments to account; online memorials to deceased loved ones create easily accessible places of mourning.

Indeed, there's an emotional side to all this. A Tumblr called Sad YouTube collects poignant comments left on music videos. In one entry, someone with the username "napolean moran" recalls how the song *Have You Seen Her?* by the Chi-Lites reminds him of an old girlfriend. "I made a mistake and lost contact with her, a war came by and eventually had to leave my country [El Salvador] on self-imposed exile," he writes. "Ever since I think of her and wish I had the chance to at least say that I was so sorry. I will never forget her."

Mark Slutsky, the Montreal-based filmmaker behind the site, says YouTube plays an "unintentional role of archiving a haphazard oral history" of modern life. "People really are telling their stories—a moment that they remember that resonates with them, which might be lost or never shared if not for YouTube," he says. "It's serving a really interesting function of coaxing memories out of people."

But too much digital memory can also do us a disservice.

In the European Union, policy-makers are debating the "right to be forgotten"—an idea that sounds woolly but could soon become enshrined in law. In true EU fashion, the proposed changes are knotty and complex. But the idea is to grant users greater control over any personal information held by a company or government agency—that is, to establish a clear legal right to obtain personal data, stop it from being processed, or delete it entirely. The legislation would also harmonize data-privacy rules across the EU's 27 member states.

If the "right to be forgotten" is an attractive name, it's also a slightly misleading one. "It's actually more a right to delete than a right to be forgotten," says Jim Killock, the executive director of the Open Rights Group, a consumer advocacy organization. "The idea is not really about the forgetfulness of companies. The idea is that a company, when asked to remove your data, should delete it in full."

So, for example, you should have the right not just to delete your Facebook account, but to ensure that all your personal information is permanently scoured from the site. Indeed, one of the more disconcerting elements of online memory is our lack of control over our digital trails. Nowhere is this clearer than in the question of what to do with our e-mail and social media when we die. A mini-industry has cropped up to deal with this problem.

For example, Google recently announced a tool called Inactive Account Manager, granting you the option to posthumously send your Google data—Gmail messages, YouTube videos, and so on—to a friend or loved one, or to delete it entirely, so that our digital slates, in death, may be wiped clean.

The changing face of online memory is also apparent, in a slightly more frivolous form, in Snapchat, a smartphone app that embraces impermanence. Like countless other apps, Snapchat allows you to take a photo or video, and send it to friends. The difference is that, after 10 seconds or less, the photo is deleted forever. Not even the company holds on to the data. Its mascot, fittingly, is a ghost.

Although Snapchat's primary function might seem pornographic—imagine the consequence-free possibilities—it has proved more popular than that: 150 million auto-destructing photos now pass through the app every day. The company recently raised $13.5-million, and Facebook has released a copycat service called Poke. Snapchat has struck a chord, perhaps, because we all long to be forgotten.

But just as not everything should be remembered, surely not everything should be deleted. So how do we strike a balance? Prof. Mayer-Schönberger has one pragmatic suggestion: assigning optional expiry dates to data. For example, every Facebook post might exist for some predetermined amount of time before it vanishes.

"You could still share a lot of information," he notes. "You could at the same time, though, control how long you want to share something for, and that is up to you. You basically condition the digital tools to be forgetful."

To further illustrate the value of forgetting, Prof. Mayer-Schönberger points to *Funes the Memorious*, a short story by the great Argentine writer Jorge Luis Borges. The title character, a boy who suffered a horse-riding accident, is incapable of forgetting and becomes lost in specificity: the creation of a new numeric system, the classification of his every childhood memory.

"To think is to forget differences, generalize, make abstractions," Borges writes. "In the teeming world of Funes, there were only details, almost immediate in their presence."

And what about Rehtaeh Parsons? Although most of the media attention surrounding her death focused on "cyberbullying," the word itself hardly does justice to the misogynist torture she faced. Now, in death, she faces a different kind of malice: posthumous victim-blaming.

After her death, anonymous online trolls set up a fake "The Real Rehtaeh Parsons" Facebook account, and, last week, *National Post* columnist Christie Blatchford even suggested that the girl had lied about being raped.

Online, Rehtaeh faces a sort of permanent libel—even more ugly, in some ways, than the kind she faced in life, because it is public and available by typing a few words into a search bar. And it exists in perpetuity. Perhaps that's what her father meant when he wrote that he did not want his daughter "defined by a Google search." Not just that he didn't want the horrific circumstances of her death to serve as a tombstone, but that granting primacy to those circumstances gives power to her tormentors: the boys who raped her, the kids who bullied her, the police who dismissed her case, the trolls who still savage her memory.

Turning away from endless online memory does not mean that we should forget someone like Rehtaeh Parsons. But it could mean considering how our digital lives might be reshaped to better reflect what is best about human memory: its selectivity, its fallibility, its sensibility.

Otherwise, we could end up like poor Funes, afloat on a sea of endless detail, the broader view obscured by our own eternal knowledge.

Drew Nelles, *The Globe and Mail*, 3 May 2013

QUESTIONS: Do you engage in reputation management? How alert have you been to what identity you are projecting on the internet? Do you think we have the right to demand our postings be erased? Have you told lies or exaggerated yourself online? If so, why?

Key Theories of Communication

It is interesting that the average person, when asked, will say that society in general is indeed affected by the media, but that he or she personally is not. In fact, most people remain extremely interested in media effects and equally confused about them. Do violent television shows and films cause violence in society? Do print media contribute to society's moral decline? Does spending hours with "friends" on social media sites actually disconnect people from their families or neighbours?

A quick look at some key theories will help explain the effects that media have both on societies and on the people who inhabit them. Although these theories were all originally posed as theories of mass communication, they have been increasingly applied to interpersonal and converging media in recent research.[25]

Harold Innis's Theory of Time-Binding and Space-Binding Media

Harold Innis thought of media in the same way that he thought of the Canadian railway system—a necessary infrastructure that transports goods from one part of the country to another. Railways carry material goods, such as livestock, automobiles, or grain. In the case of newspapers or broadcast media, the goods transported are not of a material nature but are symbolic. Just as we saw in Chapter 1, all communication is symbolic. Broadcast media transport communication symbols to the furthest reaches of Canada, bringing information, education, entertainment, and news to all of its citizens who are capable of interpreting the media's messages. This information is a major factor in empowering those citizens to engage successfully and knowledgably in commerce, politics, education, culture, and society.

For Innis, radical ideas develop in the hinterland and spread inwards toward the centre of power. As the ideas get closer to this centre, they are adopted by an ever-wider cross section of the population, and thus become more conventional themselves. Once a radical message has completed its voyage from the hinterland to the centre of power and has been accepted and adopted by those citizens at the centre, the message has become conventional. Then a new radical message arises to eventually replace the old one, which is now a social convention. Innis claimed that new media create struggles between ideas and systems of power. In his famous article "Minerva's Owl," he lists how different empires rose and fell because of their reliance on certain types of media, from the clay and stylus at the beginnings of civilization to the parchment and pen during the Dark Ages, to the printing press during the Renaissance, and to the growth of cinema and radio in the twentieth century.[26]

An excellent example of this process is found in the music industry. A new radical band will generally be perceived as "alternative" when it starts its career. It will be listened to by culturally savvy people, who scorn Top 40 music and commercial bands in favour of novelty and originality. However, this band may eventually become popular beyond the indy fringe and gain currency with the general public. It starts to see its singles being played on commercial radio, rather than campus or alternative internet stations. Soon, the alternative band is selling millions of albums on iTunes, and its music is being played on Top 40 countdowns all over Canada. The radical alternative new band has become mainstream. Its original fans will now reject the once radical band, calling it a sellout. They will look for a new alternative band to listen to, one that no one in the mainstream knows about.

Harold Innis was also unique as a theorist because he applied the concepts of time and space to media. He made a distinction between two sorts of media: time-binding media and space-binding media.

Time-binding media collapse time by figuratively bringing their audiences back to the *original moment of communication* (see Table 8.1). Thus, the time between, for example, the moment of the first telling of a story and the moment of your hearing or reading it is collapsed. You *re-experience* the same moment in time as the initial telling. For societies that rely on time-binding communication media, time is circular. The stories are written on papyrus, stone, or vellum, for example—all materials that are difficult to work with and not very portable, but very durable. To cap it off, most people in time-binding societies are illiterate. These societies tend to be oral and traditional, and the knowledge they preserve tends to be practical or religious in nature. Why? Because the major medium of storage of information in a time-binding society is the human mind—and we all know how limited its storage capacity can be.

Space-binding media are more portable but less permanent than time-binding media (see Table 8.1). They include modern broadcast media such as radio, television, and mass circulation newspapers. Space-binding media, in opposition to time-binding media, *collapse space*—they convey information that is meant to reach as many citizens as possible over long distances. Another difference is that space-binding media don't last very long. Think of the difference between a DVD and a stone tablet. An average quality DVD will be fortunate to maintain its integrity for 20 years, whereas the stone tablet may still be around a thousand years after it was made. Societies that depend on space-binding media are very different than those dependent on time-binding media. Space-binding societies are prone to rapid change

> **time-binding media**
> A term coined by Harold Innis to describe types of media, such as storytelling, that collapse time by figuratively bringing their audiences back to the original moment of communication.
>
> **space-binding media**
> A term coined by Harold Innis to describe types of media, such as television, that collapse space by conveying information that is meant to reach as many citizens as possible over long distances.

Table 8.1 Characteristics of Time-Binding and Space-Binding Media and Societies

Time-Binding Media:
- are very durable;
- are created by a small class of experts (e.g., scribes or monks);
- collapse time and eliminate it as a constraint of the flow of stories and experiences from one generation to the next;
- include scribe-copied manuscripts on parchment or vellum, oral stories and songs, and traditional dances; and
- carry messages that last for generations, but reach very limited audiences.

Space-Binding Media:
- are not long-lasting;
- are easy to work with and transport;
- collapse space and eliminate it as a constraint on the flow of information;
- include radio, television, mass circulation newspapers, e-books, CDs, DVDs, Blu-rays, and telephones; and
- carry messages that deteriorate in a short time, but reach vast audiences.

Time-Binding Societies:
- are stable and long-lasting;
- are traditional;
- favour the preservation of traditional, practical, and religious knowledge; and
- have a circular concept of time; time flows and is not as divisible as in space-binding societies: "Time is cycling through important rituals."

Space-Binding Societies:
- are unstable and prone to rapid change;
- are materialistic and secular;
- tend toward imperialism; and
- have a linear concept of time; time is divided into measurable bits and value is attached to the bits: "Time is money."

because of the easy flow of information from one end of the society to the other. They are also very materialistic and secular. Space-binding media push standardized information out to millions of receivers, laying the foundation for a common system of education, a powerful national system of news and information, and the storage capacity for all of the records and data generated by a very large and complicated economy. As a result, space-binding societies often tend to become empires.

Marshall McLuhan's Theories

Marshall McLuhan accepted Harold Innis's concept of communication, but he took it in a more psychological direction. We will discuss three of his theories in this section: "the medium is the message," the tetrad, and hot versus cool media.

McLuhan made the famous observation, quoted earlier in this chapter that "the medium is the message." That is, the medium of communication is actually far more important to the receiver's interpretation of the message than the message's actual content. He said that the media extend our senses—the television extends the eye, clothing extends the skin, radio extends the ear. In essence, McLuhan claimed that media make us cyborgs, biological creatures whose abilities are extended by technology.

For example, imagine that you want to invite a friend to the movies tonight, and you want to increase the probability that he or she will come. How will you do it?

- You could ask your friend face-to-face by saying, "Would you like to go to the movies tonight? I hear there's a good one playing downtown." This would feel personal and intimate. The medium of face-to-face oral communication creates a feeling of immediacy and psychological intimacy.
- You could write him or her a note using the same words. This is slightly less personal than speaking face-to-face, but it is still in your handwriting and quite intimate. Plus, the fact that your friend can look at it again by taking it out of his or her pocket makes it more impactful.
- You could write an e-mail with the same sentences. This may be perceived as less intimate and more of a spur-of-the-moment thought on your part. Your friend may take the invitation more lightly because e-mails are typed in a standardized font—they are not personal. As well, he or she will probably not print it out and carry it in a pocket, like your written note.
- You could telephone your friend and say the same sentences, which is personal but not intimate. There is not only a great physical distance between the two of you, but your voice will also lose a lot of its features because of the quality of the telephone signal. Your "telephone voice" may sound disinterested, even though you are very eager to go!
- Finally, you could send a text message. Your friend might think that you're being spontaneous and asking him or her to the movies on a whim.

So you see, it is obvious that the same message sent via different media carries a very different value and meaning to your receiver. An effective communicator will take McLuhan's dictum to heart.

Another of McLuhan's ideas that gained enormous currency in the world of communications theory was his **tetrad,** which was composed of his four laws of the media. These laws can be expressed as questions to help us understand the power of a new medium:

Cultural Idiom
spur-of-the-moment
To occur without warning.

tetrad
The collective term given to Marshall McLuhan's four laws of media.

1. What does a new medium improve or enhance, make possible or accelerate?
2. When pushed to its limits, the new form will reverse to its original positive characteristics. What is the reversal potential of the new form?
3. What earlier action, form, or service is brought back into play by the new form? What older, previously obsolete form is brought back and becomes an essential part of the new form?
4. What is pushed aside or made obsolete by the new media?

McLuhan insisted that, although it can take years to feel the full effects, all four of these questions are answered simultaneously when a new medium breaks into the culture and begins to change it. Because "the medium is the message," everything changes as soon as a new medium becomes available, even if people don't know it yet. For example, let's look at the automobile:

- The automobile enhances speed.
- It reverses into gridlock and traffic jams.
- It retrieves the age of knights in shining armour on powerful steeds.
- It throws the horse and buggy into obsolescence.

Let's also look at the cellphone:[27]

- The cellphone enhances the voice.
- It reverses into an "invisible leash."
- It retrieves the cries of childhood. "Mom, Dad—I want attention, NOW!"
- It throws the telephone booth into obsolescence.

McLuhan also understood about where the internet would take us—he thought that the world was becoming a **global village**, which he considered a place where everyone is heavily concerned with everyone else's business. He said that, although books were our original teaching machine and are still very important, the nature of their role is changing. We now have many different machines to process information which are all about simultaneity. McLuhan thought that this new connectedness would make us more involved in one another's lives and in the politics and cultures of other countries, that the awareness electronic media would bring us would be accompanied by a sense of responsibility. This term was so prophetic, that it is now used as a sort of shorthand for the social and political life of the World Wide Web.

Finally, McLuhan created the concept of hot and cool media. For McLuhan, **hot media** are high definition, or explicit; they leave very little to the user's imagination. For example, a black-and-white textbook which describes mathematical formulae step by step would be a very hot medium.

> **global village**
> A reference to an effect of social media, which makes people more connected with others and involved in their lives, as well as the politics and cultures of other countries.

> **hot media**
> According to Marshall McLuhan, media that are explicit and leave very little to users' imaginations.

◁ COMMUNICATION ON-SCREEN

McLuhan's Wake (2002)
Directed by Kevin McMahon.

McLuhan's Wake is a visually stunning film, full of poetic insight on McLuhan's life. The film is narrated by performance artist Laurie Anderson and features commentaries from Eric McLuhan (Marshall's son), Neil Postman, Lewis Lapham, and Patrick Watson. By appealing to the five senses and using all forms of media, the film captures how McLuhan viewed the world. McLuhan managed, 30 years before the internet revolution, to predict with astonishing accuracy how information technology would change our culture and society. While his ideas were dismissed by his contemporaries as outlandish, he is now completely vindicated. This film tells his story.

cool media
According to Marshall McLuhan, media that are allusive require users to use their imaginations to supply missing information.

flow theories
Theories that deal mainly with how effects travel, or "flow," from the mass media to their audiences.

bullet theory
A theory that posits that mass media have direct, powerful effects on their audiences.

two-step flow theory
The theory that mass media effects operate in a two-step process, mostly in interaction with interpersonal communication.

Cultural Idiom
fill in the blanks
To supply missing information from one's own knowledge or imagination.

multi-step flow theory
The theory that mass media effects are part of a complex interaction.

Cultural Idiom
hype
Sensational overstatement of the interest or importance of an event, product, or idea to generate excitement and emotional attachment.

Cool media have the opposite tendency. They are allusive, leaving an awful lot to the imagination of the user, who has to fill in the blanks him- or herself. An excellent example of cool media are comic books which suggest action and use few words. The reader must fill in the rest of the details.

Flow Theories

Some of the earliest theories of media effects, **flow theories**, deal mainly with how effects travel, or "flow," from the mass media to their audiences.

Bullet Theory

Early mass media researchers—those who worked between the two world wars—developed an approach based on the idea that the media had direct, powerful effects.[28] According to this theory, later termed **bullet theory**, people who watched, say, violent movies would become violent, and those who read "immoral" comic books would become immoral. The problem for the researchers was that these powerful, bullet-like effects were very difficult to prove, especially over the long term. Eventually, this theory gave way to a different theoretical model: two-step flow theory.

Two-Step Flow Theory

Research during and after World War II focused on the idea that media effects operate in a two-step process, occurring mostly in interaction with interpersonal communication. Researchers characterized **two-step flow theory** this way: people would hear a message over the radio, perhaps a speech by a political candidate or a commercial message for a new type of laundry soap. Then, rather than immediately pledging their support for the candidate or buying the soap, they would discuss it with opinion leaders—people they knew, such as friends or relatives, whom they viewed as credible sources of information on a particular topic. If the opinion leaders gave positive feedback, the people who had heard the original message might become supporters of the candidate or product.

Multi-Step Flow Theory

Many communication researchers today believe that the theorists who devised two-step flow theory were moving in the correct direction but didn't go far enough. **Multi-step flow theory** posits that media effects are part of a complex interaction.[29] In that interaction, opinion leaders have their own opinion leaders, who in turn have opinion leaders. Your friend might be your opinion leader about what sort of computer to buy, but your friend probably formed his or her own opinions on the basis of those developed by other people.

Besides demonstrating how theories become more sophisticated as they are explored over time, flow theories demonstrate the importance of interpersonal communication in the effects of mass communication. They show that mass media don't operate in a vacuum; their effects are filtered on their way to the recipient through the reactions of others. It's worth noting that even though the bullet theory is largely discredited today, we still have daily examples of some types of mediated messages having the direct, powerful effects that early researchers predicted. Many products become overnight successes through advertising, without enough time passing to give interpersonal communication much time to operate. A new blockbuster movie, for example, can earn tens of millions of dollars during its first weekend thanks largely to hype—advertising and positive reviews appearing in the mass media. But for the great majority of mediated messages, effects depend largely on how they interact with interpersonal communication. After a movie's opening weekend, its box office receipts are determined largely by word-of-mouth communication.

Social Learning Theory

Flow theories aren't the only approach to studying media effects. **Social learning theory** offers a different perspective, beginning with the assumption that people learn how to behave by observing others—especially others portrayed in the mass media. The theory gained prominence from the experiments of Canadian psychologist Albert Bandura in the 1960s.[30] In Bandura's most famous studies, preschool children watched films in which an adult encountered Bobo, a three-foot-tall pop-up clown. One group of preschoolers saw a version in which the adult beat up Bobo and was then rewarded for being a "strong champion." Another group saw a version in which the adult assailant was scolded for being a bully and spanked with a rolled-up magazine. After watching the films, the children had their own chance to "play" with Bobo. Bandura discovered that the children who saw the adult model's aggression being rewarded treated the Bobo doll with greater violence than did those who saw the adult model punished.

The implications of social modelling are obvious. It's easy to imagine how a 13-year-old who has just watched UFC or the movie *Watchmen* might be inspired to lash out at one of his or her friends the first time a disagreement arises. However, the theory also suggests that viewing pro-social models can teach constructive behaviour. The same 13-year-old, if he or she had just watched *Glee,* might be inspired to use one of those characters' non-violent, communicative approaches to problem-solving, rather than using his fists.

Social learning theory makes sense, and the original laboratory studies produced impressive results. But in everyday life the theory doesn't hold up quite so well.[31] After all, behaviour that is modelled from the media might not be successful in the real world. For example, 13-year-olds who try out their martial arts skills on the playground might be punched in the nose by tougher adversaries. The pain of that punch might do more to determine those children's attitudes toward violence than all the television viewing they will ever do. Also, it's worth remembering that all individuals are different, and this fact plays a role in determining how people are influenced by media. For example, boys seem to be influenced more by violent media than girls are, whereas girls seem to be swayed more by the body image of their media models—they often try to be as slim as high fashion models, showing their sensitivity to an influence that seldom has the same effect on boys. Observations such as these led to the development of the individual differences theory.

Individual Differences Theory

As its name suggests, **individual differences theory** looks at how media users with different characteristics are affected by the mass media.[32] Certain users are more susceptible to some types of media messages than are others. For example, a viewer with a high level of education might be more susceptible to a message that includes logical appeals. In addition to level of education, individual differences that help determine how the media affect individuals include age, sex, geographic region, intellectual level, socioeconomic class, level of violence in the home, and so on.

In addition to these demographic factors, there are psychological characteristics that more subtly distinguish media users. **Diffusion of innovations theory** identifies five types of people with different degrees of willingness to accept new ideas from the media.[33] These types also predict who will be first to use and become competent in new media.[34]

Cultural Idiom
word-of-mouth
The transmission of a message from person to person through relationships. The message is repeated because the listener trusts the speaker's credibility.

social learning theory
A theory based on the assumption that people learn how to behave by observing others, especially others portrayed in the mass media.

individual differences theory
A theory that examines how mass media users with different characteristics are affected by media.

diffusion of innovations theory
A theory that identifies five types of people with different degrees of willingness to accept new ideas from the media: innovators, early adopters, early majority, late majority, and laggards.

1. *Innovators:* These are venturesome people who are eager to try new ideas. They tend to be extroverts and politically liberal. They are the first to try out and become competent in new media, such as the internet and the iPhone.
2. *Early adopters:* Less venturesome than innovators, these people still make a relatively quick, but informed, choice. Their somewhat more cautious approach makes them important opinion leaders within their social groups.
3. *Early majority:* These people make careful, deliberate choices after frequent interaction with their peers and their opinion leaders. They seldom act as opinion leaders themselves.
4. *Late majority:* More skeptical than the first three groups, these people tend to accept innovations less often. When they do adopt an innovation, they often do so out of economic necessity or increasing peer pressure.
5. *Laggards:* These people tend to be conservative, traditional, and the most resistant to any type of change. Their point of reference tends to be the past, and they tend to be socially isolated. Today, these are the people who are mystified by the internet and might not even own a computer.

Cultivation Theory

According to **cultivation theory**, the media shape—and sometimes distort—our perceptions of the world.[35] Cultivation theory therefore works hand in hand with the facets of perception discussed in Chapter 2.

Advanced by George Gerbner and his associates at the University of Pennsylvania, cultivation theory predicts that media will teach a common worldview, common roles, and common values. Over time, they suggest, the media "cultivate" a particular view of the world among users. For example, Gerbner's research found that people who watch a lot of television had a markedly different view of reality than did those who don't. The latter group overestimated their chances of being involved in some type of violence, overestimated the percentage of Americans who have jobs in law enforcement, and found people, in general, to be less trustworthy.

Cultivation theory suggests that the primary effect of television, therefore, is to give habitual viewers a perception that the world is less safe and upright, and more violent, than it really is. Gerbner's findings help explain society's increasing tolerance of violence. Researchers suspect that this desensitization has a profound effect on interpersonal communication by making people less caring about the feelings and reactions of other people.

Agenda-Setting Theory

Another important approach to media effects was posited by researchers Donald Shaw and Maxwell McCombs in the 1970s. Studying the way political campaigns were covered in the media, they coined the term **agenda-setting theory** to describe the main role of the media. The media, they argued, tell people not what to think but rather what to think about. In other words, the amount of media attention given to an issue affects the level of importance assigned to that issue by consumers of mass media. Shaw and McCombs explained their findings as follows:

> Perhaps more than any other aspect of our environment, the political arena—all those issues and persons about whom we hold opinions and knowledge—is secondhand reality. Especially in national politics, we have little personal or direct contact. Our knowledge comes primarily from the mass media. For the most part, we know only those aspects of national politics considered newsworthy enough for transmission through the mass media.[36]

In other words, the media might not change your point of view about a particular issue, but they will change your perception of what's important.[37]

Although Shaw and McCombs concentrated on political issues and the news media, the idea of agenda setting can easily be applied more broadly to all issues and to all media. For many media users, a social problem, if it is not discussed on the Web, on television, or in newspapers, may not exist at all. Agenda setting has important implications, since the issues that tend to influence government policy are those that have received attention from the public.[38]

Cumulative Effects Theory

Not all communication researchers accept the validity of agenda-setting theory. Some point out that while the media do, indeed, tell us what to think about, they do so slowly. **Cumulative effects theory** states that media messages are driven home through redundancy and have profound effects over time. According to this theory, the media latch on to certain themes and messages, which they gradually build up. There is a bandwagon effect as various newspapers, magazines, television and radio networks, websites, and other media take up the themes. Because the media are omnipresent and occupy such a prominent place in most people's lives, the media view becomes the widely accepted one within society.

Cumulative effects theory also describes a "spiral of silence" that occurs when individuals with divergent views become reluctant to challenge the consensus offered by the media. People unconsciously form perceptions of the distribution of public opinion. If they feel themselves to be in the minority, they are less likely to express their opinions. People who hold majority viewpoints tend to speak out confidently. For example, in times of war, some people might become concerned about civilian casualties inflicted on the other side, but they don't speak out about this issue if they feel that most people disagree.

> **cumulative effects theory**
> A theory that states that media messages are understood through redundancy and have profound effects over time.

> **Cultural Idiom**
> **driven home**
> To be made clear.

Summary

Social media have changed the way in which individuals, groups, and organizations communicate. They have broken down boundaries to creativity and broadcasting for individuals that were insurmountable under the regime of the traditional mass media.

There are many different forms of social media, including blogs, microblogs, social networking, wikis, social news aggregators, social bookmarking sites, and social photo and video sharing sites. Each offers a different means of communicating messages, sharing content, and building persistent communities.

Social media are having a major impact on our lives by changing our sense of self; affecting how we travel, consume, and behave through geo-tagging; changing the way we market goods; and also transforming traditional mass media such as radio, television, and newsprint.

Social media present both a huge opportunity and pose many risks. They provide the opportunity to build a permanent personal online brand that promotes your values, goals, and dreams, but they also provide a perfect venue for destroying your reputation. However, if you police your image online, you can have a very profitable and beneficial experience using social media.

Communication theories provide different models for explaining how messages move from communicators to receivers. They also attempt to explain how media might influence social, cultural, political, and economic effects.

Key Terms

agenda-setting theory   332

blog   303

bullet theory   330

community media   299

cool media   330

cultivation theory   332

cumulative effects theory   333

cyberstalking   307

diffusion of innovations theory   331

early adopters   332

early majority   332

feed   310

flow theories   330

follower   297

geo-tagging   314

global village   329

hashtag   308

hot media   329

individual differences theory   331

innovators   332

intranets   311

laggards   332

late majority   332

media convergence   299

microblog   307

multi-step flow theory   330

net neutrality   299

prosumer   299

social bookmarking sites   312

social learning theory   331

social media   297

social networking site   298

social news aggregators   312

space-binding media   327

status update   308

tetrad   328

time-binding media   327

tweet   297

two-step flow theory   330

user-generated content   297

vlog   305

wikis   311

zine   301

Activities

A. Social Media Autobiography

Construct your social media autobiography by asking yourself the following questions about each type of social media discussed in this chapter:

1. Do I use it?

2. Do my friends use it?

3. Have I posted pictures to it?

4. Has anyone else posted pictures of me to it?

5. Have I posted notes or status updates to it?

6. Have others mentioned me in their notes or their status updates?

7. Have I been tagged in photos or on notes?

8. Have I been tagged on compromising photos? If so, how are they compromising?

9. Do I know everyone who has taken my photo?

10. Have I posted video online?

11. Have others posted video of me online?

12. Is any of this video compromising? If so, in what way?

Summarize your findings in a brief paragraph. You might be surprised at how your social media autobiography reads!

B. Three-Day Digital Media Fast

This activity is deceptively simple. Put away all of your digital media devices for three days. Every time you get an urge to use one of these devices, log it in a notepad. Write down how you feel when you get the urge. What have you been thinking about? Were you sad? Lonely? Bored? You will be very surprised at how much insight into yourself you can gain by doing this simple exercise. You will learn what place digital technology occupies in your life. This is valuable knowledge in our digital device-saturated world!

C. Social Media Log

Use the following chart to keep a log of all of your uses of social media during the next three days.

Time/Date	Type of Social Media	Activity

Now write a one-paragraph summary of your social media activity and see what it looks like. You'll probably be amazed at how much time you spend on social media websites and what you do while you're on them. This is an excellent exercise for establishing a baseline of self-knowledge concerning social media.

D. Building a Personal Online Brand

This exercise will help you to identify the type of personal brand that you want to create and remind you of the type of material that you should and shouldn't be posting. Answer the following questions as honestly as possible:

1. Do I feel more loved on the internet than in real life? Why?

2. Why do I want to use social media?

3. What do I want to do professionally?

4. Is my profession of choice one that is based on credibility and trust? How?

5. Am I interested in ever running for political office?

6. Do I envision myself becoming a leader in my industry? An executive? A school principal? A public servant?

7. How do I think having compromising pictures, notes, or videos of myself on social media may impact my future?

8. How do I think having compromising pictures, notes, or videos of myself on social media impacts my credibility as a serious, moral person?

9. Could my social posts ever be misinterpreted negatively?

10. Would I want what I have posted recently to be the basis of my being judged as credible or not credible after I have finished my studies?

This inventory of questions will enable you to get a handle on your perceptions of the effects and potential effects of social media on your life. Now, answer the following questions:

1. How do I want to be perceived by a potential employer?

2. How do I want to be perceived by a potential spouse?

3. How do I want to be perceived by my neighbours?

4. How do I want to be perceived by my friends?

5. How do I want to be perceived by my immediate and extended family?

Now look at the answers to the first set of questions and compare them to your answers to the second set. Do the answers match up? Now answer the following questions:

1. What pictures promote me as I want to be perceived?

2. What videos promote me as I want to be perceived?

3. What notes promote me as I want to be perceived?

4. What status updates promote me as I want to be perceived?

5. What links promote me as I want to be perceived?

Write one-paragraph summaries for your answers to the questions in each section.

E. Posting Content about Your Friends

Imagine that you have videotaped some of your friends doing vulgar, drunken, or lewd things at a party. You think that some of the videos would be very funny to share on social media. Do you decide to share them? What would stop you? What would motivate you to post them anyway?

F. Applying Innis's and McLuhan's Theories to a Medium

Categorize the following list of media according to Innis's theories of space-binding and time-binding media (pp. 326-8); McLuhan's tetrad (pp. 328–9); and McLuhan's concepts of hot and cool media (pp. 329–30).

1. papyrus,

2. stone tablet,

3. song,

4. dance,

5. DVD,

6. writing paper,

7. Moleskine notebook,

8. smartphone,

9. internet,

10. HD TV,

11. Facebook,

12. Twitter,

13. written letter,

14. math textbook with no pictures,

15. newspaper,

16. iPad, and

17. e-mail.

Further Reading

Anderson, Chris, *Makers* (New York: Random House, 2012).
Anderson provides many examples to support his point that the internet has spawned a new age of entrepreneurship and enterprise.

Banksy. *Exit through the Gift Shop*, Paranoid Pictures, 2010.
This wickedly funny film describes how Banksy, a British graffiti artist, uses his public works of art to drive home his critical commentary about social justice.

Helprin, Mark, *Digital Barbarism: A Writer's Manifesto* (New York: Harper, 2008).
In this work of protest, Mark Helprin decries how copyright has been eroded and the writer's craft has declined with the digital age.

Joel, Mitch, *Ctrl Alt Delete: Reboot Your Business, Reboot Your Life* **(New York: Business Plus, 2013).**

Canadian Mitch Joel, whom *Marketing Magazine* has called the "Rock Star of Digital Marketing" and "one of North America's leading digital visionaries," has written a superb book that explains how you can use the opportunity posed by the need to go digital in your professional life to completely reboot how you organize things.

Lanier, Jaron, *You Are Not a Gadget* **(New York: Knopf, 2010).**

Lanier is considered the father of virtual reality technology. In this book, he argues that the internet has gone terribly wrong and has led us into a world of conformism and collectivism that will be bad for creativity.

MacArthur, Amber, *Power Friending* **(New York, Penguin: 2010).**

This book, by @AmberMac—a Canadian super social networker—is a readable and fun guide to using the power of social media to increase the reach of your personal and professional brand. A must read for active social media users.

O'Reilly Radar, www.radar.oreilly.com

Tim O'Reilly is a leader in publishing about the digital world. His blog is insightful, intelligent, and sometimes funny. This blog is a great place to keep abreast of the latest developments in digital culture and social media.

Shirky, Clay, *Here Comes Everybody* **(New York: Penguin, 2009).**

This book describes how the cultural closeness and speed brought about by social media is transforming the way people do business, innovate, invent, and make art. This book is very positive about networked culture.

Study Questions

1. List the social media services that you have used. How do they fit into the categories that are explained on pages 303–13? Do you find that you use them equally? Break the time up from 2010 until now—how have your usage patterns changed or evolved?

2. How do you use your smartphone (e.g., BlackBerry, iPhone) in your everyday life? Do you use the GPS functions it has? Do you have social media service apps such as Facebook or Twitter or Foursquare installed on it? Do you use it more than your computer to interact with others through social media? Why or why not?

3. Where do you get your news and entertainment? From the television? From the radio? From the newspaper? What percentage comes from social media for each medium now? Do you think that our society is indeed undergoing a permanent shift toward the internet, or will there always be a place for traditional media?

4. McLuhan is hailed as a prophet by many. As we have seen on pages 328–30, he predicted that technology would change society and turn it into a global village. Do you feel that happening around you? He also said that the "medium is the message" and that hot and cool media extend or limit our senses. Do you think that McLuhan was exaggerating or just fanciful? How do you see your interactions with your friends, family, and co-workers confirming or contradicting McLuhan's vision of the impact of technology on culture and society?

5. In a media world driven more and more by social media, who do you think are the new agenda setters and the gatekeepers (as defined on pp. 332–4)? Are the same elites still in charge or have everyday people achieved more impact?

6. How do you think Innis's theory of innovation (pg. 326) starting at the periphery and then standardizing as it moves to the centre of power relates to the "diffusion of innovations" theory (pp. 331–2)?

9

The Nature of Groups

After studying the material in this chapter . . .

You should understand:

✔ the characteristics that distinguish groups from other collections of people;
✔ the types of goals that operate in groups;
✔ the various types of groups;
✔ the characteristics of groups described in this chapter;
✔ the advantages and disadvantages of the decision-making methods introduced in this chapter; and
✔ the cultural influences that shape communication in groups.

You should be able to:

✔ identify the groups you presently belong to and those you are likely to join in the future;
✔ list the personal and group goals in groups you observe or belong to;
✔ identify the rules, norms, roles, and interaction patterns in groups you observe or belong to; and
✔ choose the most effective decision-making methods for a group task.

Chapter Highlights

Group communication possesses several important characteristics:

» Groups exist for a variety of purposes, and each has its own operating style.

» A true group is distinguished from a collection of individuals by interaction, interdependence, duration over time, and size.

» The stated goals of groups and the personal goals of individual members interact in ways that can affect success.

» Different types of groups exist to fulfill a variety of goals: learning, problem-solving, social, and personal growth.

» A group's rules, norms, roles, patterns of interaction, and methods of making decisions can shape the way members interact as well as their productivity and satisfaction.

» Powerful but sometimes subtle cultural factors influence the way groups operate.

How important are groups? You can answer this question for yourself by trying a simple experiment. Start by thinking of all the groups you belong to currently and have belonged to in the past: the family you grew up with, the classes you have attended, the companies you have worked for, the teams you have played on, the many social groups you have been a member of—the list is long. Now, one by one, imagine that you had never belonged to each of these groups. Start with the less important ones, and the results aren't too dramatic. Very soon, however, you will begin to see that a great deal of the information you have learned, the benefits you have gained—even your very identity—have all come from group membership.

On the job, groups are the setting in which most work takes place. In one survey, 75 per cent of the professionals surveyed reported that they "always" or "often" worked in teams.[1] In the growing multimedia field, the ability to work effectively as part of a team has been identified as the top non-technical job skill.[2] When negotiating is conducted by teams instead of individuals, the results are better for everyone involved.[3]

This doesn't mean that every group experience is a good one. Some are vaguely unrewarding, rather like eating food that has no taste and gives no nourishment. And others are downright miserable. Sometimes it is easy to see why a group succeeds or fails, but in other cases matters aren't so clear.[4]

This chapter will help improve your understanding of the nature of group communication. It will start by explaining just what a group is—because not every collection of people qualifies. It will go on to examine the reasons why people form groups and then look at several types of groups. Finally, it will conclude by looking at some common characteristics that all groups share.

> *Most of the decisions that affect our lives are not made by individuals, but by small groups of people in executive boardrooms, faculty meetings, town councils, quality circles, dormitory rooms, kitchens, locker rooms, and a host of other meeting places. In a democracy, the small group is the most basic way to get work done.*
>
> **Arthur Jensen, professor of educational psychology**

What Is a Group?

Imagine that you are taking a test on group communication. Which of the following would you identify as groups:

- a crowd of onlookers gawking at a burning building;
- several passengers at an Air Canada ticket counter discussing their hopes of finding space on a crowded flight; and/or
- an army battalion.

Because all these situations seem to involve groups, your experience as a canny test-taker probably tells you that a commonsense answer will get you in trouble here—and you're right. When social scientists talk about *groups,* they use the word in a special way that excludes each of the preceding examples.

What are we talking about when we use the word *group?* For our purposes a **group** consists of a *small collection of people who interact with each other, usually face-to-face, over time in order to reach goals.* A closer examination of this definition will show why none of the collections of people described in the preceding quiz qualifies as a group.

group
A small collection of people whose members interact with each other, usually face-to-face, over time in order to reach goals.

Interaction

Without interaction, a collection of people isn't a group. Consider the first example in our test. Though the onlookers all occupy the same area at the same time, they have virtually nothing to do with each other. Of course, if they should begin interacting—working together to give first aid or to rescue victims, for example—the situation would change. This requirement of interaction highlights the difference between true groups and collections of individuals who merely co-act—simultaneously engaging in a similar activity without communicating with one another. For example, students who passively listen to a lecture don't technically constitute a group until they begin to exchange messages with each other and their instructor. (This explains why some students feel isolated even though they spend so much time on a crowded campus. Despite being surrounded by others, they really don't belong to any group.)

As you read in Chapters 3 and 4, there are two types of interaction that go on in any communication setting. The most obvious type is verbal, in which group members exchange words either orally or in writing. But people needn't talk to each other in order to communicate as a group: non-verbal channels can do the job, too. We can see how by thinking again about a hypothetical classroom. Imagine that the course is in its tenth week and that the instructor has been lecturing non-stop for the entire time. During the first few meetings there was very little interaction of any kind: students were too busy scribbling notes and wondering how they would survive the course with their grade point averages and sanity intact. But as they became more used to the class, the students began to share their feelings with each other. Now there's a great amount of eye rolling and groaning as the assignments are poured on, and the students exchange resigned sighs as they hear the same tired jokes for the second and third time. Thus, even though there's no verbal exchange of sentiments, the class has become a group—interestingly, one that doesn't include the professor.

The explosion of communication technologies has led to the growth of "virtual groups"—people who interact with one another without meeting face to face. For a small cost (at least compared with in-person meetings), people, whether within the same office or around the world, can swap ideas via computer networks, speak with one another via telephone conference calls, and even have visual contact thanks to teleconferencing.[5] Despite the lack of personal contact between members, virtual teams actually can be superior to face-to-face teams in at least two ways. First, getting together is fast and easy. A virtual team can meet whenever necessary, even if the members are widely separated. This ease of interaction isn't just useful in the business world. For most groups of students working on class projects, finding a convenient time to meet can be a major headache. Virtual groups don't face the same challenges.

A second advantage of virtual teams is the levelling of status differences. When groups connect via computer networks, rank is much less prominent than when they meet face to face.[6] Because fear of authority figures can squelch creative thinking, virtual teams are a good device for making sure groups find the best solutions to problems.

Interdependence

In groups, members don't just interact: their members are *interdependent*.[7] The behaviour of one person affects all the others in what can be called a "ripple effect."[8] Consider your own experience in family and work groups: when one member behaves poorly, his or her actions shape the way the entire group functions. The ripple effect can be positive as well as negative: beneficial actions by some members help everyone.

Time

A collection of people who interact for a short while doesn't qualify as a group. As you'll soon read, groups who work together for any length of time begin to take on characteristics that aren't present in temporary aggregations. For example, certain standards of acceptable behaviour begin to evolve, and the way individuals feel about each other begins to affect their behaviour toward the group's task and toward each other. Thus, onlookers at a fire would have trouble qualifying as a group even if they briefly co-operated with one another to help out in the emergency. The time element clearly excludes temporary gatherings such as the passengers gathered around the Air Canada ticket counter. Situations like this one simply don't reflect many of the principles you'll be reading about in the next two chapters.

Size

Our definition of the term *groups* included the word *small*. Most experts in the field set the lower limit of group size at three members. This decision isn't arbitrary—there are some significant differences between two- and three-person communications. For example, the only ways for two people to resolve a conflict are to change one another's minds, give in, or compromise; in a larger group, however, members can form alliances either to put increased pressure on dissenting members or to outvote them.

There is less agreement about when a group stops being small.[9] Though no expert would call a 500-member army battalion a group in our sense of the word (it would be labelled an organization), most experts are reluctant to set an arbitrary upper limit. As long as it is not too large for each member to be able to know and respond to every other member, a group may be considered small. Our focus in these pages will be on collections of people ranging in numbers from three to between seven and twenty.

In task-oriented groups, bigger usually isn't better. Research suggests that the optimal size for a group is the smallest number of people capable of performing the task at hand effectively.[10] This definition makes it clear that there is no magic formula for choosing the best group size. The optimal number will change according to the task, as well as contextual factors such as politics, legal requirements, and institutional norms.[11] But generally speaking, as a group becomes larger, it is harder to schedule meetings, the members have less access to important information, and they have fewer chances to participate—three ingredients in a recipe for dissatisfaction.

Goals

Group membership isn't always voluntary, as some family members and most prison inmates will testify. But whether or not people choose to join groups, they usually hope to achieve one or more goals. At first the goal-related nature of group membership seems simple and obvious. In truth, however, there are several types of goals, which we will examine in the following pages.

individual goals
The motives of individual members that influence their behaviour in groups.

group goals
Goals that a group collectively seeks to accomplish.

Goals of Groups and Their Members

We can talk about two types of goals when we examine groups. The first type involves **individual goals**—the motives of individual members—whereas the second involves **group goals**—the outcome the group seeks to accomplish.

Individual Goals

The most obvious reason why individuals join groups is to meet their personal needs. Task orientation—getting the job done—is the most obvious type of individual motive for belonging to a group. Some people join study groups, for example, in order to improve their knowledge. Sometimes a member's task-related goals will have little to do with the group's stated purpose. Many merchants, for example, join service clubs such as Kiwanis, Rotary, or Lions primarily because doing so is good for business. The fact that these groups help achieve worthy goals such as helping the blind or disabled is fine, of course, but for many people it is not the prime motive for belonging.[12]

What about groups with no specifically defined purpose? Consider, for instance, gatherings of regulars at the beach on sunny weekends or a group of friends whose members eat lunch together several times a week. Collections such as these meet the other criteria for being groups: they interact, meet over time, and have the right number of members. But what are the members' reasons for belonging? In our examples here, the goals can't be sunbathing or eating because these activities could be carried out alone. The answer to our question introduces social orientation. In many cases people join together in order to have a sense of belonging, to exercise influence over others, and to gain the liking of others. Notice that none of these factors necessarily has much to do with the task: it's possible to meet social needs without getting the job done. Likewise, a group can be efficient—at least for a short while—without meeting the social needs of its members.

We join many, if not most, groups in order to accomplish both task and social goals. School becomes a place both to learn important information and to meet desirable friends. Our work becomes a means both of putting food on the table and of gaining recognition for our skills. The value of distinguishing between task and social goals becomes clear when we understand that, despite their importance, social goals are often not stated or even recognized by group members. Thus, one way of identifying and overcoming blocks to group effectiveness is to ask yourself whether the group is in fact achieving its members' social goals.

> **task orientation**
> Individual goals that involve accomplishing a task.

> **social orientation**
> Individual goals that involve affiliation, influence, and esteem of others.

Group Goals

So far we have discussed the forces that motivate individual group members. In addition to these individual forces, there also exist group goals. For example, athletic teams exist to compete with each other, and academic classes strive to transmit knowledge.

Sometimes there is a close relationship between group and individual goals. In athletic teams the group goal is to win, whereas individual members' goals include helping the group succeed. If you think about it for a moment, however, you'll see that the individual members have other goals as well: improving their physical ability, having a good time, overcoming the personal challenges of competition, and often gaining the social benefits that come from being an athlete. The difference between individual and group goals is even more pronounced when the two are incompatible. Consider, for instance, the case of an athletic team that has one player more interested in being a "star" (satisfying personal needs for recognition) than in helping the

COMMUNICATING ONLINE

Search Engine Optimization (SEO)

Creating a website may seem like a lonely experience, but there are tools out there that, when used correctly, can help you create a better experience for your audience. One of these tools is search engine optimization, or SEO. You should always keep SEO in the forefront of your mind, and always follow best practices. Skipping the basics of SEO will only leave your site's foundation a mess and prevent you from fully maximizing revenue opportunities. Check out the following tips from Victoria Edwards of Search Engine Watch to see how you can make sure you're getting the most out of SEO.

What is SEO, Exactly?
The goal of foundational SEO isn't to cheat or "game" the search engines. The purpose of SEO is to:

- Create a great, seamless user experience.
- Communicate to the search engines your intentions so they can recommend your website for relevant searches.

1. *Your website is like a cake.*
Your links, paid search, and social media act as the icing, but your content, information architecture, content management system, and infrastructure act as the sugar and makes the cake. Without it, your cake is tasteless, boring, and gets thrown in the trash.

2. *What search engines are looking for.*
Search engines want to do their jobs as best as possible by referring users to websites and content that is the most relevant to what the user is looking for. So how is relevancy determined?

- *Content*: Is determined by the theme that is being given, the text on the page, and the titles and descriptions that are given.

- *Performance*: How fast is your site and does it work properly?
- *Authority*: Does your site have good enough content to link to or do other authoritative sites use your website as a reference or cite the information that's available?
- *User Experience*: How does the site look? Is it easy to navigate around? Does it look safe? Does it have a high bounce rate?

3. *What search engines are NOT looking for.*
Search engine spiders only have a certain amount of data storage, so if you're performing shady tactics or trying to trick them, chances are you're going to hurt yourself in the long run. Items the search engines don't want are:

- *Keyword stuffing*: Overuse of keywords on your pages.
- *Purchased links*: Buying links will get you nowhere when it comes to SEO, so be warned.
- *Poor user experience*: Make it easy for the user to get around. Too many ads and making it too difficult for people to find content they're looking for will only increase your bounce rate. If you know your bounce rate it will help determine other information about your site. For example, if it's 80 per cent or higher and you have content on your website, chances are something is wrong.

4. *Know your business model.*
While this is pretty obvious, so many people tend to not sit down and just focus on what their main goals are. Some questions you need to ask yourself are:

- What defines a conversion for you?
- Are you selling eyeballs (impressions) or what people click on?

---

hidden agenda
An individual goal that group members are unwilling to reveal.

team win. Or recall classes you have known in which the personal goal of some students—to get by with the smallest possible amount of work—was inconsistent with the group goals of gathering and sharing information. Sometimes the gap between individual and group goals is public, but when it is not, an individual's goal becomes a **hidden agenda**. In either case, the discrepancy can be dangerous for the well-being of the group and needs to be dealt with. We'll have more to say about this subject in Chapter 10.

As long as the members' individual goals match those of the group, no conflicts are likely to arise. But when there is a clash between what members seek for themselves and what the group

- What are your goals?
- Do you know your assets and liabilities?

5. *Don't forget to optimize for multi-channels.*
Keyword strategy is not only important to implement on-site, but should extend to other off-site platforms, which is why you should also be thinking about multi-channel optimization. These multi-channel platforms include:

- Facebook,
- Twitter,
- LinkedIn,
- E-mail, and
- Offline, such as radio and TV ads.

Being consistent with keyword phrases within these platforms will not only help your branding efforts, but also train users to use specific phrases you're optimizing for.

6. *Be consistent with domain names.*
Domain naming is so important to your overall foundation, so as a best practice you're better off using sub-directory root domains (example.com/awesome) versus sub-domains (awesome.example.com). Some other best practices with domain names are:

- *Consistent domains*: If you type in www.example.com, but then you type in just example.com and the "www" does not redirect to www.example.com, that means the search engines are seeing two different sites. This isn't effective for your overall SEO efforts as it will dilute your inbound links, as external sites will be linking to www.example.com and example.com.
- *Keep it old school*: Old domains are better than new ones, but if you're buying an old domain, make sure that the previous owner didn't do anything shady to cause the domain to get penalized.
- *Keywords in URL*: Having keywords you're trying to rank for in your domain will only help your overall efforts.

7. *Optimizing for different types of results.*
In addition to optimizing for the desktop experience, make sure to focus on mobile and tablet optimization as well as other media.

- Create rich media content like video, as it's easier to get a video to rank on the first page than it is to get a plain text page to rank.
- Optimize your non-text content so search engines can see it. If your site uses Flash or PDFs, make sure you read up on the latest best practices so search engines can crawl that content and give your site credit for it.

8. *Focus on your meta data too.*
Your content on your site should have title tags and meta descriptions.

- Meta keywords are pretty much ignored by search engines nowadays, but if you still use them, make sure it talks specifically to that page and that it is also formatted correctly.
- Your meta description should be unique and also speak to that specific page. Duplicate meta descriptions from page to page will not get you anywhere.

Title tags should also be unique! Think of your title as a 4–8 word ad, so do your best to entice the reader so they want to click and read more.

—Victoria Edwards, *Search Engine Watch*, 31 December 2013

seeks, the collective goal is likely to suffer. The risk that individuals may put their own interests ahead of the group's is especially great when interdependence is low—that is, when members do not have to rely on one another in order to succeed. Jon Krakauer captures this situation clearly in his account of a team of climbers seeking to reach the peak of Mount Everest:

> There were more than fifty people camped on the Col that night, huddled in shelters pitched side by side, yet an odd feeling of isolation hung in the air. We were a team in name only, I'd sadly come to realize. Although in a

few hours we would leave camp as a group, we would ascend as individuals, linked to one another by neither rope nor any deep sense of loyalty. Each client was in it for himself or herself, pretty much. And I was no different: I sincerely hoped Doug got to the top, for instance, yet I would do everything in my power to keep pushing on if he turned around.[13]

Types of Groups

So far we have seen that groups fulfill a variety of goals. Another way of examining groups is to look at some of the functions they serve.

Learning Groups

When the term **learning group** comes up, most people think first about school. Although academic classes certainly qualify as learning groups, they aren't the only ones. Members of a scuba-diving class, friends who form a Bible study group, and members of a League of Women Voters chapter all belong to learning groups. Whatever the setting or subject, the purpose of learning groups is to increase the knowledge or skill of each member.

> **learning group**
> A group whose goal is to expand its knowledge about some topic other than itself or its individual members.
>
> **problem-solving groups**
> Task-related groups whose goal is to resolve a mutual concern of its members.

Understanding Diversity

Memo to Abercrombie & Fitch: Anger Those Millennials at Your Peril

What its recent display of corporate arrogance reveals is that the company doesn't know that "exclusionary" has never been less cool.

Clothes are flags waved by our bodies, but their signals are open to interpretation. To some, cargo shorts and a denim shirt send the message "summer casual" or "comfy." To others, cargo shorts and a denim shirt speak of defeat and lack of invention, the sartorial equivalent of a statement like: "Oh, I don't know. I'll just have vanilla," or "I don't really read fiction." Only in the dystopia of high school would the cargo–denim flag, and its accompanying baseball cap and flip-flops, be interpreted as "cool."

But youth is the target market of Abercrombie & Fitch, a brand whose look is built around cargo shorts and features hairless boy-band-aspirants in madras button-downs and skinny girls in mini-skirts and tank tops; clothes so generic they make Wal-Mart [sic] look runway-ready. A&F found itself publicly scolded recently when a 2006 quote from CEO Michael Jeffries resurfaced and began pinballing across the internet: "We go after the cool kids. We go after the attractive all-American kid with a great attitude and a lot of friends. A lot of people don't belong in our clothes and they can't belong. Are we exclusionary? Absolutely." What Abercrombie & Fitch doesn't seem to know is that "exclusionary" has never been less cool.

Nonetheless, in keeping with Jeffries's clubhouse attitude, the company rarely makes clothing above size 10 for women, and doesn't do XL or XXL. Men, on the other hand, are allowed to be a little chunkier.

The idea that a size 12 woman is a blight upon fashion, and the way that Jeffries's comments made him sound like a grown-up giving a freshman a wedgie, triggered a media maelstrom and a swell of consumer activism. There have been protests outside stores and a blogging mom in Ohio sent back her daughter's clothes. An online petition started by an 18-year-old boy who struggled with an eating disorder has garnered more than 73,000 signatures so far, bidding A&F to "Stop telling teens they aren't beautiful and start making clothes for young people of all shapes and sizes!" Ellen DeGeneres and Kristie [sic] Alley publicly booed the company for its bullying ways, and a comic viral video—hashtag #Fitchthehomeless—encourages disgruntled patrons to give away their A&F clothes to homeless people.

Abercrombie backpedalled with an apology, but Millennials aren't impressed: An American brand index survey by YouGov found that since Jeffries's comments exploded, consumer perception of the brand by those between 18 and 34 has dropped to its lowest point since last October. This generation may be screwed in terms of job prospects, but they have social media superpowers that are translating into consumer power, too. A

Problem-Solving Groups

Problem-solving groups work to resolve a mutual concern of members. Sometimes the problem involves the group itself, as when a family decides how to handle household chores or when co-workers meet to coordinate vacation schedules. At other times, the problem is external to the group. For instance, neighbours who organize themselves to prevent burglaries or club members who plan a fundraising drive are focusing on external problems.

Problem-solving groups can take part in many activities. One type is gathering information, as when several students compile a report for a class assignment. At other times, a group makes policy—for example, when a club decides whether

---

COMMUNICATION ON-SCREEN

Good God (2012)

Directed by Ken Finkleman.

The most recent series starring Finkleman's lead character George Finday, *Good God* follows in the footsteps of previous outings *The Newsroom*, *More Tears*, and *Good Dog*. Supposedly inspired by the launch of the Sun News Network, a Canadian version of Fox News, the show features the greedy, selfish Findlay (Finkleman) at the head of the conservative news channel despite not really aligning with its ideological viewpoints. The show centres on Findlay trying to deal with his whacky co-workers while still producing a successful, albeit cartoonish, news show. For all its self-deprecation and *Curb Your Enthusiasm*-like deadpan humour, the show is essentially about how teamwork must function, regardless of ideological differences.

---

single Facebook page eventually led to demonstrations in 52 countries recently against Monsanto, the agribusiness giant that's become a stand-in for the debate over genetically modified foods. Ignoring the impact of a kid with a smartphone is corporate arrogance.

Of course, Abercrombie & Fitch is a private company that can sew and sell whatever it likes, but in Canada, according to StatsCan, 7.6 million Canadian men and 5.6 million of women are either obese or overweight. That's a lot of potential customers who need clothes.

Jeffries's comments were hateful but also woefully out of touch for someone in an industry that requires a close reading of the culture. Casual discrimination against the fat just doesn't fly like it used to. What if Abercrombie & Fitch had announced it didn't want Chinese or gay people to sully their clothes? XL doesn't mean ugly, or unstylish. While the A&F scandal was blowing up, H&M put plus-size model Jennie Runk on its homepage, starring in a new swimsuit collection. Her size 12 body wasn't flagged as "plus," but simply integrated into the collection—a new flag for normal.

Abercrombie & Fitch seems caught in a 1950s version of youth culture, where jocks battle nerds, and phrases like "All-American" are code for blond (the company has paid out $40 million [US] in a class-action law suit about discriminatory hiring

practices). But Jeffries is 68, and he may have some personal complexes about what's attractive: His own face appears heavily surgeried—he has that surprised cat look—and he allegedly fired his personal pilot for being too old.

So perhaps he's been too busy to notice that nerds are the new cool. In *The Social Network*, it's not the Abercrombie & Fitch-styled blond rower twins that walk away with Facebook billions. The spoils go to Mark Zuckerberg, a fashion-free programmer in a no-logo sweatshirt. The internet unites the obsessives, and when those obsessions translate into consumer activism, corporations are forced to take note. They may be a generation living in their parents' basements, but until mom and dad cut off their WiFi, the Millennials have a kind of power that any 68-year-old looking for their business would do well to respect.

Katrina Onstad, *The Globe and Mail*, 30 May 2013

QUESTIONS: Clearly Abercrombie & Fitch is trying to cultivate a specific notion of what makes a group "cool" by using exclusionary language and tactics. What, if anything, is wrong with this? Compare these group tactics with those of, for instance, the more than 3000 people who signed the petition against them. How do these two group efforts differ? How are they the same?

or not to admit the public to its meetings. In some cases group members may delegate their decision-making power to a smaller group: when hiring, for example, a committee may be formed to interview candidates and decide which one to hire.

Social Groups

We have already mentioned that some groups serve strictly to satisfy the social needs of their participants. Some **social groups** are organized and others are informal. In either case, the inclusion, control, and affection that such groups provide are reasons enough for belonging.

Groups don't always fall neatly into just one category. For example, learning groups often have other functions. Consider the class for which you are reading this book: besides becoming more knowledgeable about communication, many of the students in your class are probably satisfying social needs by making new friends. Some are probably growing personally by applying the principles they are learning to their own lives. Groups of students—fellow employees or teammates, for instance—may even take the class together in order to focus on solving collective problems. Despite the multiplicity of goals, it's usually possible to characterize a group as primarily focused on learning, problem-solving, social, or growth goals.

Growth Groups

Unlike learning groups, in which the subject matter is external to the members, **growth groups** focus on teaching the members more about themselves. Consciousness-raising groups, marriage encounter workshops, counselling, and group therapy are all types of growth groups. These are unlike most other types of groups in that there is no real collective goal: the entire purpose of the group is to help the members identify and deal with their personal concerns.

Characteristics of Groups

Whatever their function, all groups have certain characteristics in common. Understanding these characteristics is a first step to functioning more effectively in your own groups.

Rules and Norms

Many groups have formal **rules**—explicit, officially stated guidelines that govern what the group is supposed to do and how the members should behave. In a classroom, these rules include how absences will be treated, whether papers must be typed or may be handwritten, and so on. Alongside the official rules, an equally powerful set of standards also operates, often without ever being discussed. Sociologists call these unstated rules norms. **Norms** are shared values, beliefs, behaviours, and procedures that govern a group's operation. For instance, you probably won't find a description of what jokes are and aren't acceptable in the bylaws of any groups you belong to, yet you can almost certainly describe the unstated code if you think about it. Is sexual humour acceptable? How much, and what types? What about religious jokes? How much kidding of other members is proper? Matters such as these vary from one group to another, according to the norms of each one.[14]

There are three categories of group norms: social, procedural, and task. **Social norms** govern relationships between members. How honest and direct will members be with one another? What emotions will and won't be expressed, and in what ways? Matters such as these are handled by the establishment of social norms, which are usually implicit. **Procedural norms** outline how the group should operate. Will the group make decisions by accepting the vote of the

---

social groups
Groups in which the goal is to satisfy the social needs of its members.

Human relationships always help us to carry on because they always presuppose further developments, a future—and also because we live as if our only task was precisely to have relationships with other people.

Albert Camus, philosopher and Nobel Prize winner for literature

---

growth groups
Groups in which the goal is to help members learn more about themselves.

rules
Explicit, officially stated guidelines that govern group functions and member behaviour.

norms
Shared values, beliefs, behaviours, and procedures that govern a group's operation.

social norms
Group norms that govern the way members relate to one another.

procedural norms
Group norms that describe rules for the group's operation.

majority, or will the members keep talking until consensus is reached? Will one person run meetings, or will discussion be leaderless? **Task norms** focus on how the job itself should be handled. Will the group keep working on a problem until everyone agrees that its solution is the best one possible, or will members settle for an adequate, if imperfect, solution? The answer to this question becomes a task-related norm. All groups have social norms, and all except social groups also have procedural and task norms.

Table 9.1 lists some typical rules and norms. It is important to realize that the actual rules and norms that govern a group may fall short of cultural standards. Consider the matter of punctuality, for example. It is a cultural norm in our society that meetings should begin at the scheduled time, yet some groups operate on the (usually unstated) understanding that the real business won't commence until approximately 10 minutes later. On a more serious level, although it is a cultural norm that other people should be treated politely and with respect, some groups accept rude, uncivil behaviour—failure to listen, sarcasm, even outright hostility—between their members.

It is important to recognize a group's norms. Following them is one way to gain acceptance into the group, and identifying norms that cause problems can sometimes be a way to help the

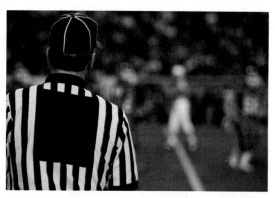

task norms
Group norms that govern the way members handle the job at hand.

Table 9.1 Typical Rules and Norms in Two Types of Groups

Family

Rules (Explicit)
- If you don't do the chores, you don't get your allowance.
- If you're going to be more than a half-hour late, phone home so the others don't worry about you.
- If the gas gauge reads "empty," fill up the tank before bringing the car home.
- Don't make plans for Sunday nights. That's time for the family to spend together.
- Daniel gets to watch *Sesame Street* from 5:00 to 6:00 p.m.

Norms (Unstated)
- When Dad is in a bad mood, don't bring up problems.
- Don't talk about Sheila's divorce.
- It's okay to tease Lupe about being short, but don't make comments about Shana's complexion.
- As long as the kids don't get in trouble, the parents won't ask detailed questions about what they do with their friends.
- At family gatherings, try to change the subject when Uncle Max brings up politics.

Business Meetings

Rules (Explicit)
- Regular meetings are held every Monday morning at 9:00 a.m.
- The job of keeping minutes rotates from person to person.
- Meetings last no more than an hour.
- Don't leave the meetings to take phone calls except in emergencies.

Norms (Unstated)
- Use first names.
- It's okay to question the boss's ideas, but if she doesn't concede after the first remark, don't continue to object.
- Tell jokes at the beginning of the meeting, but avoid sexual or ethnic topics.
- It's okay to talk about "gut feelings," but back them up with hard facts.
- Don't act upset when your ideas aren't accepted, even if you're unhappy.

group operate more effectively. For instance, some groups make a habit of responding to new ideas with criticism, sarcasm, or indifference. Pointing this norm out to members might be a way to change the unwritten rules and thereby improve the group's work.

If norms are rarely stated, how is it possible to identify them? There are two sets of clues that can help. First, look for behaviours that occur often.[15] For instance, notice what time meetings begin. Observe the amount of work that members are willing to contribute to the group. See what kinds of humour are and aren't used. Habitual behaviours like these point to the unspoken rules that the group lives by. Second, look for clues that members are being punished for violating norms. Most punishments are subtle, of course: pained expressions from other members when a speaker talks too much, no laughter following an inappropriate joke, and so on.

Roles

roles
The patterns of behaviour expected of group members.

formal roles
Roles assigned to a person by group members or an organization, usually to establish order.

informal roles
Roles usually not explicitly recognized by a group that describe functions of group members, rather than their positions. Sometimes called "functional roles."

Whereas norms may be defined as acceptable group standards, **roles** are the patterns of behaviour expected of members. As with norms, some roles are officially recognized. These **formal roles** are assigned by an organization or group partly to establish order. Formal roles usually come with a title, such as "assistant coach," "treasurer," or "customer service representative." By contrast, **informal roles** (sometimes called "functional roles") are rarely acknowledged with a label.[16] Table 9.2 lists some of the most common informal roles in task-oriented groups. As the list shows, the names given to informal roles describe the functions that the various members perform within the group rather than their formal positions. The easiest functional roles to identify are usually those of leaders and followers, but you can probably think of many other examples in groups you have known.

Informal roles are not formally assigned to members. In fact, they are rarely even recognized as existing. Many informal roles may be filled by more than one member, and some of them may be filled by different people at different times. The important fact is that, at crucial times, every informal role must be filled by someone.

"Rules Are the Only Thing We've Got"

"What are we? Humans? Or animals? Or savages? What's grownups going to think? Going off—hunting pigs—letting fires out—and now!"

A shadow fronted him tempestuously.

"You shut up, you fat slug!"

There was a moment's struggle and the glimmering conch jigged up and down. Ralph leapt to his feet.

"Jack! Jack! You haven't got the conch! Let him speak."

Jack's face swam near him.

"And you shut up! Who are you, anyway? Sitting there telling people what to do. You can't hunt, you can't sing . . ."

"I'm chief. I was chosen."

"Why should choosing make any difference? Just giving orders that don't make any sense . . ."

"Piggy's got the conch."

"That's right—favour Piggy as you always do . . ."

"Jack!"

Jack's voice sounded in bitter mimicry.

"Jack! Jack!"

"The rules!" shouted Ralph. "You're breaking the rules!"

"Who cares?"

Ralph summoned his wits.

"Because the rules are the only thing we've got!"

William Golding, *Lord of the Flies*

Table 9.2 Informal Roles of Group Members

	Typical Behaviours	Examples
Task Roles		
1. Initiator/Contributor	Contributes ideas and suggestions; proposes solutions and decisions; proposes new ideas or states old ones in a novel fashion.	"How about taking a different approach to this chore? Suppose we. . . ."
2. Information Seeker	Asks for clarification of comments in terms of their factual adequacy; asks for information or facts relevant to the problem; suggests information is needed before making decisions.	"Do you think the others will go for this?" "How much would the plan cost us?" "Does anybody know if those dates are available?"
3. Information Giver	Offers facts or generalizations that may relate to the group's task.	"I bet Chris would know the answer to that." "*Newsweek* ran an article on that a couple of months ago. It said. . . ."
4. Opinion Seeker	Asks for clarification of opinions made by other members of the group and asks how people in the group feel.	"Does anyone else have an idea about this?" "That's an interesting idea, Ruth. How long would it take to get started?"
5. Opinion Giver	States beliefs or opinions having to do with suggestions made; indicates what the group's attitude should be.	"I think we ought to go with the second plan. It fits the conditions we face in the Concord plant best. . . ."
6. Elaborator/Clarifier	Elaborates ideas and other contributions; offers rationales for suggestions; tries to deduce how an idea or suggestion would work if adopted by the group.	"If we followed Lee's suggestion, each of us would need to make three calls." "Let's see . . . at $0.35 per brochure, the total cost would be $525.00."
7. Coordinator	Clarifies the relationships among information, opinions, and ideas or suggests an integration of the information, opinions, and ideas of subgroups.	"John, you seem most concerned with potential problems. Mary sounds confident that they can all be solved. Why don't you list the problems one at a time, John, and Mary can respond to each one."
8. Diagnostician	Indicates what the problems are.	"But you're missing the main thing, I think. The problem is that we can't afford. . . ."
9. Orienter/Summarizer	Summarizes what has taken place; points out departures from agreed-on goals; tries to bring the group back to the central issues; raises questions about the direction in which the group is heading.	"Let's take stock of where we are. Helen and John take the position that we should act now. Bill says, 'Wait.' Rusty isn't sure. Can we set that aside for a moment and come back to it after we. . . ."
10. Energizer	Prods the group to action.	"Come on, guys. We've been wasting time. Let's get down to business."
11. Procedure Developer	Handles routine tasks such as seating arrangements, obtaining equipment, and handing out pertinent papers.	"I'll volunteer to see that the forms are printed and distributed." "I'd be happy to check on which of those dates are free."
12. Secretary	Keeps notes on the group's progress.	"Just for the record, I'll put these decisions in the memo and get copies to everyone in the group."
13. Evaluator/Critic	Constructively analyzes group's accomplishments according to some set of standards; checks to see that consensus has been reached.	"Look, we said we only had two weeks, and this proposal will take at least three. Does that mean that it's out of the running, or do we need to change our original guidelines?"

Continued

Table 9.2 (Continued)

	Typical Behaviours	Examples
Social/Maintenance Roles		
1. Supporter/Encourager	Praises, agrees with, and accepts the contributions of others; offers warmth, solidarity, and recognition.	"I really like that idea, John." "Priscilla's suggestion sounds good to me. Could we discuss it further?"
2. Harmonizer	Reconciles disagreements; mediates differences; reduces tensions by giving group members a chance to explore their differences.	"I don't think you two are as far apart as you think. Henry, are you saying _____? Benson, you seem to be saying _____. Is that what you mean?"
3. Tension Reliever	Jokes or in some other way reduces the formality of the situation; relaxes the group members.	"Let's take a break . . . maybe have a drink." "You're a tough cookie, Bob. I'm glad you're on our side!"
4. Conciliator	Offers new options when his or her own ideas are involved in a conflict; willing to admit errors so as to maintain group cohesion.	"Looks like our solution is halfway between you and me, John. Can we look at the middle ground?"
5. Gatekeeper	Keeps communication channels open; encourages and facilitates interaction from those members who are usually silent.	"Susan, you haven't said anything about this yet. I know you've been studying the problem. What do you think about _____?"
6. Feeling Expresser	Makes explicit the feelings, moods, and relationships in the group; shares own feelings with others.	"I'm really glad we cleared things up today." "I'm just about worn out. Could we call it a day and start fresh tomorrow?"
7. Follower	Goes along with the movement of the group passively, accepting the ideas of others, sometimes serving as an audience.	"I agree. Yes, I see what you mean. If that's what the group wants to do, I'll go along."

Source: Adapted from Gerald Wilson and Michael Hanna, *Groups in Context: Leadership and Participation in Decision-Making Groups* (New York: McGraw-Hill, 1986): 144–6.

task roles
Roles group members take on in order to help solve a problem.

social roles
Emotional roles concerned with maintaining smooth personal relationships among group members. Also termed "maintenance functions."

dysfunctional roles
Individual roles played by group members that inhibit the group's effective operation.

Notice that the informal roles listed in Table 9.2 fall into two categories: task and social. **Task roles** help the group accomplish its goals, while **social roles** (also called "maintenance roles") help the relationships among the members run smoothly. Not all roles are constructive. Table 9.3 lists several **dysfunctional roles** that prevent a group from working effectively. Research suggests that the presence of positive social roles and the absence of dysfunctional ones are key ingredients in the effectiveness of groups.[17]

What is the optimal balance between task and social functions? According to Robert Bales, one of the earliest and most influential researchers in the area, the ideal ratio is 2:1, with task-related behaviour dominating.[18] This ratio allows the group to get its work done while at the same time taking care of the personal needs and concerns of the members.

Role Emergence

We said earlier that most group members aren't aware of the existence of informal roles. You will rarely find members saying things like "You ask most of the questions, I'll give opinions, and she can be the summarizer." Yet it's fairly obvious that over time certain members do begin to fulfill specific roles. How does this role differentiation come about?

The personal characteristics of the various group members certainly help to determine the role that each will play. But personal skills and traits by themselves aren't enough to earn a member acceptance as possessor of a role, especially in newly formed groups without a formal

Table 9.3 Dysfunctional Roles of Group Members

	Typical Behaviours	**Examples**
Dysfunctional Roles		
1. Blocker	Interferes with progress by rejecting ideas or taking a negative stand on any and all issues; refuses to co-operate.	"Wait a minute! That's not right! That idea is absurd." "You can talk all day, but my mind is made up."
2. Aggressor	Struggles for status by deflating the status of others; boasts, criticizes.	"Wow, that's really swell! You turkeys have botched things again." "Your constant bickering is responsible for this mess. Let me tell you how you ought to do it."
3. Deserter	Withdraws in some way; remains indifferent, aloof, sometimes formal; daydreams; wanders from the subject, engages in irrelevant side conversations.	"I suppose that's right. . . .I really don't care."
4. Dominator	Interrupts and embarks on long monologues; is authoritative; tries to monopolize the group's time.	"Bill, you're just off base. What we should do is this. First. . . ."
5. Recognition Seeker	Attempts to gain attention in an exaggerated manner; usually boasts about past accomplishments; relates irrelevant personal experiences, usually in an attempt to gain sympathy.	"That reminds me of a guy I used to know. . . ." "Let me tell you how I handled old Marris. . . ."
6. Joker	Displays a lack of involvement in the group through inappropriate humour, horseplay, or cynicism.	"Why try to convince these guys? Let's just get the mob to snuff them out." "Hey, Carla, wanna be my roommate at the sales conference?"
7. Cynic	Discounts chances for group's success.	"Sure, we could try that idea, but it probably won't solve the problem. Nothing we've tried so far has worked."

Source: Adapted from "Functional Roles of Group Members" and "Dysfunctional Roles of Group Members" from *Groups in Context: Leadership and Participation in Decision-Making Groups* by Gerald Wilson and Michael Hanna, pp. 144–6.

leader. The process of role emergence has been studied extensively by communication scholar Ernest Bormann, who has identified a predictable series of stages that groups go through in role designation.[19] (Remember that this process is almost never discussed within groups and is rarely performed consciously.)

At first, members will make bids for certain roles. Someone with a particularly analytical mind, for example, might audition for the role of critic by pointing out flaws in a proposal. But in order for this role to "take," the group members must endorse the bid both verbally and non-verbally—by giving the would-be critic their attention and making positive comments about his or her observations. If the group does not support the first few bids, a sensitive candidate will likely decide to look for a different role.

Role-Related Problems and Solutions

Groups can suffer from at least three role-related problems. The first arises when one or more important informal roles—either task or social—go unfilled. For instance, there may be no information giver to provide vital knowledge or no harmonizer to smooth things over when members disagree.

In other cases the problem isn't an absence of candidates to fill certain roles but rather an overabundance of them. This situation can lead to unstated competition between members, which gets in the way of group effectiveness. You have probably seen groups in which two

YOUNG COMMUNICATOR PROFILE

CHRISTOPHER TUCKWOOD

Co-Founder, the Sentinel Project for Genocide Prevention

There is really no direct route to working in the genocide prevention field. I began as an undergraduate student studying medieval history at the University of Waterloo. While there, I became a campus leader in anti-genocide activism related to the crisis in Darfur, Sudan. Realizing that a more direct approach was needed to assist communities threatened by mass atrocities, my friend Taneem Talukdar and myself co-founded the Sentinel Project for Genocide Prevention, a Canadian NGO that uses innovative digital technologies to predict and prevent atrocities.

Technology plays an essential part in our mission because of the opportunity it provides for gathering early warning indicators and broadcasting warnings. In a world with rapidly growing rates of internet and mobile communications technology, people in even the least-developed regions can now be connected to a global early warning system.

I have continued to study the role that communication plays in crisis management and have continued to educate myself, earning a master's degree in disaster and emergency management from York University. Beyond my work with the Sentinel Project, Hatebase, and numerous human rights issues, I also write and speak on the role of technology in defending human rights.

Cultural Idiom
occupying their pet position
To play a favourite role.

people both want to be the tension-relieving comedian. In such cases, the problem arises when the members become more concerned with occupying their pet position than with getting the group's job done.

Even when there is no competition over roles, a group's effectiveness can be threatened when one or more members suffer from "role fixation"—performing a certain role even when the situation doesn't require it.[20] As you learned in Chapter 1, a key ingredient of communication competence is flexibility, the ability to choose the right behaviour for a given situation. Members who always take the same role—even a constructive one—lack competence, and they hinder the group. As in other areas of life, too much of a good thing can be a problem. You can avoid role-related trouble by following these guidelines:

- *Look for unfilled roles.* When a group seems to be experiencing problems, use the list in Table 9.2 as a kind of diagnostic checklist to determine which roles may need filling.
- *Make sure unfilled roles are filled.* After you have identified unfilled roles, you may be able to help the group by filling them yourself. If key facts are missing, take the role of information seeker and try to dig them out. If nobody is keeping track of the group's work, offer to play secretary and take notes. Even if you are not suited by skill or temperament to a job, you can often encourage others to fill it.
- *Avoid role fixation.* Don't fall into familiar roles if they aren't needed. You may be a world-class coordinator or critic, but these talents will only annoy others if you use them when they aren't needed. In most cases your natural inclination to be a supporter might be just the ticket to help a group succeed, but if you find yourself in a group where the members don't need or want this sort of support, your encouragement might become a nuisance.
- *Avoid dysfunctional roles.* Some of these roles can be personally gratifying, especially when you are frustrated with a group; however, they do nothing to help the group succeed, and they can damage your reputation as a team player. Nobody needs a blocker or a joker, for instance. Resist the temptation to indulge yourself by taking on any of the dysfunctional roles listed in Table 9.3.

Cultural Idiom
just the ticket
The right thing.

Patterns of Interaction

In Chapter 1 we said that communication involves the exchange of information between and among people. It almost goes without saying that this exchange needs to be complete and efficient for the communicators to reach their goals. In interpersonal and public speaking settings, information exchange is relatively uncomplicated, taking basically two routes: either between the two individuals in an interpersonal dyad or between the speaker and the audience in a public speaking situation. (Actually, this is a slight oversimplification. In public speaking situations, members of an audience also exchange messages with one another through their laughter, restless movements, and so on. Basically, though, it's still fair to say that the exchange of information is two-way.) In groups, however, things aren't so simple. The mathematical formula that identifies the number of possible interactions between individuals is:

$$N = \frac{(N - 1)}{2}$$

where N equals the number of members in a group. Thus, even in a relatively small five-member group, there are 10 possible combinations of two-person conversations and 75 possible multi-person interactions. The complex structure of groups affects both the quantity of information exchanged and the flow of information in other ways, too.

A look at Figure 9.1 (usually called a **sociogram**) will suggest the number and complexity of interactions that can occur in a group. Arrows connecting members indicate remarks shared between them. Two-headed arrows represent two-way conversations, whereas one-headed arrows represent remarks that did not arouse a response. Arrows directed to the centre of the circle indicate remarks made to the group as a whole. A network analysis of this sort can reveal both the amount of participation by each member and the recipients of every member's remarks. Thus, it provides a graphic look at who seems to be making the most significant contributions (at least in terms of quantity), as well as who is not contributing.

In the group pictured in Figure 9.1, person E appears to be connected to the group only through interaction with person A; E never addressed any other members, nor did any of them address E. Also notice that person A is both the most active and the most widely connected member. A addressed remarks to the group as a whole as well as to every other member and was the object of remarks from three individuals as well.

Sociograms don't tell the whole story because they do not indicate the quality of the messages being exchanged. Nonetheless, they are a useful tool in analyzing group communication. Communications theorists have identified several common network layouts, or **topologies,** which tend to have similar-looking sociograms. Each topology has its own strengths and weaknesses when it comes to facilitating effective group communication.

COMMUNICATION ON-SCREEN

Maurice Richard/The Rocket (2005)
Directed by Charles Binam.

A biopic of the legendary star of the NHL's Montreal Canadiens, this film traces the playing career of Maurice "The Rocket" Richard (Roy Dupuis), from his early days with the team. Of particular interest is the relationship between Richard and his coach, Dick Irvin (Stephen McHattie), whose role is to turn a 17-year-old budding superstar with tremendous raw skill, energy, and boundless love of the game into a team leader who would become a hero of Montreal Canadiens' fans everywhere.

---

sociogram
Graphic representation of the interaction patterns in a group.

topologies
Common network layouts, such as how the interactions between the participants in a seminar session are laid out, which tend to have similar-looking sociograms.

CRITICAL THINKING PROBE
Functional and Dysfunctional Roles

Identify the functional and dysfunctional roles in an established group. You might analyze a group that you belong to (e.g., an athletic team or class group), a group that you can observe in action (e.g., city council, faculty senate), or even a fictional group (e.g., those in the films featured in this chapter's "Communication On-Screen" boxes). How do the roles in the group you are analyzing contribute to the group's success (or lack of it)? How might members take on different roles to make the group more effective?

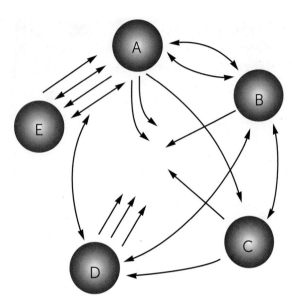

FIGURE 9.1 Patterns of Interaction in a Five-Person Group

all-channel network
A communication network in which all parties have equal access to one another.

chain network
A communication network in which information passes sequentially from one member to another.

If group members always stayed together and shared every piece of information with one another, their interaction would resemble the topology shown in Figure 9.2—what communication theorists have called an **all-channel network**. In such a group, the physical arrangement influences communication. It's obviously easier to interact with someone you can see well. Lack of visibility isn't a serious problem in dyadic settings, but it can be troublesome in groups. For example, group members seated in a circle are more likely to talk with the people across from them than with those on either side.[21] Different things happen when members are seated in rectangular arrangements. Research with 12-person juries showed that those sitting at either end of rectangular tables participated more in discussions and were viewed by other members as having more influence on the decision-making process.[22] Rectangular seating patterns have other consequences as well. Research conducted on six-person groups seated at rectangular tables showed that, as the distance between two persons increased, other members perceived them as being less friendly, less talkative, and less acquainted with each other.[23]

But not all groups meet face to face. The cooks, waiters, and dishwashers at a restaurant rarely sit down together to discuss their work, nor do the nurses, aides, and technicians who staff an 8- or 10-hour hospital shift. When group members aren't in immediate contact with one another, information can flow through a variety of other networks (see Figure 9.2). In a **chain network**, information moves sequentially from one member to another. A chain is an efficient way to deliver simple verbal messages or to circulate written information when it isn't possible for all team members to attend a meeting at one time. You might use this approach to route an important message to members of a team at work, asking each person to initial a memo and pass it along to the next person named on a routing slip. Chain networks are not very reliable for lengthy or complex verbal messages because the content of the message can change as it passes from one person to another.

Cultural Idiom
hashed out
Something that is discussed thoroughly.

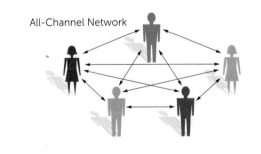

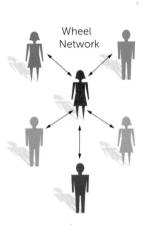

FIGURE 9.2 Small-Group Communication Networks

Another topology is the **wheel network**, in which one person acts as a clearinghouse, receiving and relaying messages to all other members. Like chains, wheel networks are sometimes a practical choice, especially if one member is available to communicate with others all or most of the time. This person can become the informational hub who keeps track of messages and people. Wheel networks can also be useful when relationships are strained between two or more members. In cases like this, the central member can serve as a mediator or facilitator, managing messages as they flow between others.

The success of a wheel network depends heavily on the skill of the **gatekeeper**—the person through whom information flows. If he or she is a skilled communicator, these mediated messages may help the group function effectively. But if the gatekeeper consciously or unconsciously distorts messages to suit personal goals or plays members off against one another, the group is likely to suffer.

Decision-Making Methods

Another way to classify groups is according to the way they make decisions. There are several approaches a group can use to make decisions. We'll look at each of them now, examining their advantages and disadvantages.[24]

Consensus

A decision arrived at by **consensus** is one that all group members support. Consensus decision-making requires that all members of the group have input into the process. The advantages of this approach are obvious: full participation tends to increase the quality of the decision as well as members' commitment to support it. Consensus is especially important in decisions on critical or complex matters. But consensus also has its disadvantages. It takes a great deal of time, which makes it unsuitable for emergencies. In addition, it can often be frustrating: emotions can run high on important matters, and patience in the face of such pressures is difficult. Because of the need to deal with these emotional pressures, consensus calls for more communication skill than do other decision-making approaches. As with many things in life, high rewards come at a proportionately high cost.

Majority Rule

Overzealous high-school civics teachers have encouraged many people to believe that the democratic method of majority decision-making is always superior, but this is not necessarily the case. Majority rule has its advantages in decisions that don't require the support of all group members. When a decision needs the backing of all members in order to be effective, however, majority rule is risky. Remember that even if 51 per cent of the members favour a decision, 49 per cent may still oppose it.

Besides producing unhappy members, decisions made under majority rule are often inferior in quality to decisions hashed out by group members until they reach consensus.[25] Under majority rule, members who recognize that they will be outvoted often participate less than those on the majority side, and the deliberations usually end after a majority opinion has formed—even though minority viewpoints might be worthwhile.

wheel network
A communication network in which a gatekeeper regulates the flow of information from all other members.

gatekeeper
Producers of mass messages, who determine what messages will be delivered to consumers, how those messages will be constructed, and when they will be delivered.

consensus
Agreement between group members about a decision.

During a [second-grade] science project . . . one of the seven-year-olds wondered out loud whether the baby squirrel they had in class was a boy or a girl. After pondering the issue for a few minutes, one budding scientist offered the suggestion that they have a class discussion about it and then take a vote.

Cal Downs, Wil Linkugel, and David M. Berg,
The Organizational Communicator

UNDERSTANDING COMMUNICATION TECHNOLOGY

U of T Assignment Raises Questions over the Collaborative Nature of Wikipedia

You may think that the dynamics of groups working exclusively online would be different to those of traditional groups working face-to-face. For example, in a virtual environment, you could suddenly find yourself in a working group that numbers in the thousands, which would be pretty difficult to manage in a small physical space! A closer look, however, shows that many of the topologies that work for traditional groups might work for online groups as well. Keep this in mind as you study Michelle Mcquigge's coverage of the conflict that arose between U of T and Wikipedia.

A recent dust-up between Wikipedia and Canada's largest university raises questions about how collaborative the popular website that bills itself as "the free encyclopedia that anyone can edit" truly is.

The online information portal recently took a professor from the University of Toronto to task for one of his classroom assignments. Steve Joordens urged the 1900 students in his introductory psychology class to start adding content to relevant Wikipedia pages. The assignment was voluntary, and Joordens hoped the process would both enhance Wikipedia's body of work on psychology while teaching students about the scientist's responsibility to share knowledge.

But Joordens's plan backfired when the relatively small contingent of volunteer editors that curate the website's content began sounding alarm bells. They raised concerns about the sheer number of contributions pouring in from people who were not necessarily well-versed in the topic or adept at citing their research.

Discussions in the Wikipedia community became very heated with allegations that articles were being updated with erroneous or plagiarized information. Some community members called for widespread bans on university IP addresses and decried the professor's assignment as a needless burden on the community. Joordens issued a statement defending his students, saying only 33 of the 910 articles edited were tagged for potential problems. But he also acknowledged that he did not understand the limited scope of the Wikipedia editorial community, which boasts a few thousand members compared to the more than 488 million people that visit the site every month.

"I assumed that the current core of editors was extremely large and that the introduction of up to 1000 new editors would be seen as a positive," Joordens said. "However, the current core of editors turns out NOT to be that large, and even if my students were bringing signal along with noise, the noise was just too much to deal with on the scale it was happening."

Joordens said the Wikipedia community became "annoyed and frustrated," adding that things became heated to a point he found "somewhat ridiculous." The animated discussion that's

Expert Opinion

Sometimes one group member will be defined as an expert and, as such, will be given the power to make decisions. This method can work well if that person's judgment is truly superior. For example, if a group is backpacking in the wilderness and one member is injured, it would probably be foolish to argue with the advice of a doctor in the group. In most cases, however, matters aren't so simple. Who is the expert? There is often disagreement on this question. Sometimes a member might think he or she is the best qualified to make a decision, but others will disagree. In a case like this, the group probably won't support that person's advice, even if it is sound.

Minority Control

Sometimes a few members of a group will form a committee to decide on a particular matter. This approach works well with non-critical questions, when it would be a waste of time for the whole group to study the issue in detail. When an issue is so important that it needs the support of everyone, it's best at least to have the committee report its findings for the approval of all members.

ensued from the incident highlights both the pros and cons of using social media in the classroom, experts said.

Sidneyeve Matrix, media professor at Queen's University, said crowdsourcing platforms like Wikipedia offer unparalleled opportunities for students to engage with their topics of study and to feel they're actively involved in the learning process. But collaborative projects can't survive without leadership, she said, adding the zealous editors at Wikipedia have an important role to play as gatekeepers. This case, she said, exposes the difficult balancing act at play. "I thought it was a lot more open than it is, but at the same time I'm seeing that more and more teachers are using it in their classrooms," she said. "The authenticity and verifiability of the information on the site has been improving, and that doesn't happen from the magic fairy. It happens from dedicated folks who are behind the scenes."

Jay Walsh, spokesman for the Wikimedia Foundation that operates Wikipedia, said the online encyclopedia is working to carve out its niche in the classroom. The website has established a pilot project that works closely with both teachers and students, he said, adding Joordens had some preliminary discussions with the company before carrying out his own plan. He described the professor's approach as "experimental," emphasizing that editors need to follow certain protocols when contributing to articles. The strong reactions and speedy response of the Wikipedia community, he said, is the very mechanism that makes the site attractive to educators.

"This response is pretty high-value within the Wikipedia community," he said. "It's conceivable for someone to interpret that response as being too fast or not giving us a chance, but in this case there seems to be an openness towards figuring out ways to make this kind of an initiative work."

Joordens agreed, saying he will limit the number of students who take on such voluntary assignments in the future and make sure they're up to speed with the site's editing practices. In turn, he called for Wikipedia members to back down from their hardline position on fledgling contributors. "Now that at least some members of the Wikipedia community are putting down their digital pitchforks, it is becoming more and more obvious to me that we all share the same goal of improving the quality and quantity of information on Wikipedia," he said. "If we could find ways of working together while also being respectful of one another, we could really do some great things."

Michelle Mcquigge, *The Canadian Press*, 2013, www.globalnews.ca

QUESTIONS: Can you identify the numerous "topologies" at play in this article? How do notions of authority and roles apply to the conflict between a professor and his class versus Wikipedia and its editors?

Authority Rule

Authority rule is the approach most often used by autocratic leaders (see Chapter 10). Though it sounds dictatorial, there are times when such an approach has its advantages. Because it is quick, it may be useful in cases where there simply isn't time for the group to decide what to do. Authority rule is also perfectly acceptable for routine matters that don't require discussion in order to gain approval. When overused, however, this approach causes problems. As Chapter 10 will show, group decisions are usually of higher quality and more likely to gain wide support than those made by an individual. Thus, failure to consult with members can reduce effectiveness even when the leader's decision is a reasonable one.

When the person in authority consults members before making a decision, it is possible to preserve some of the quality and commitment that come with group interaction, but this approach also has its disadvantages. In some cases other group members will be tempted to tell the leader what they think he or she wants to hear; in others they will compete to impress the decision-maker.

Selecting a Decision-Making Method

Which of these decision-making approaches is best? The answer can vary from one culture to another. Consensus is highly valued in Japan. British and Dutch business people also value the "all members on board" approach. By contrast, people in Germany, France, and Spain tend to prefer strong leaders and view a desire for consensus as somewhat wishy-washy.[26]

Culture notwithstanding, the most effective approach in a given situation depends on the circumstances:

- *The type of decision.* Some decisions are best made by an expert, whereas others will benefit from involving the entire group.
- *The importance of the decision.* If the decision is relatively unimportant, it's probably not worth involving all members of the group. By contrast, critical decisions probably require the participation, and ideally the buy-in, of all members.
- *Time available.* If time is short, it may not be possible to assemble the entire group for deliberations.[27]

When choosing a decision-making approach, weigh the pros and cons of each before you decide which one has the best chance of success in the situation your group is facing.

Cultural Idiom
wishy-washy
To lack decisiveness.

buy-in
To support.

Cultural Influences on Group Communication

In past generations, most groups in Canada were ethnically and culturally homogeneous. During the twentieth century, however, Canada became home to more than 13.4 million immigrants, and annual rates increased significantly in the 1990s. In 2010, the Canadian census found that 20.6 per cent of the population had been born outside Canada. More than 200 different ethnic origins—defined in the census as the ethnic or cultural group(s) to which an individual's ancestors belonged—were reported.

The proportion of visible minorities in Canada has also increased steadily over the past 20 years. Visible minorities are defined by the Employment Equity Act as "persons, other than Aboriginal peoples, who are non-Caucasian in race or non-white in colour." In 1981, visible minorities accounted for 5 per cent of the total population; by 2011, that figure had risen to 19 per cent.

The percentage of foreign-born residents in Canada has also become very significant. The distribution of foreign-born residents by census metropolitan area ranged from a low of 0.1 per cent in St John and New Brunswick to a high of 37 per cent in Toronto. Ninety-four per cent of

Canada's foreign-born population lives in four provinces: Ontario (3,611,400 immigrants or 53.3 per cent of Canada's total population), British Columbia (1,191,900/17.6 per cent), Quebec (974,900/14.4 per cent), and Alberta (644,100/9.5 per cent). In the Prairies, 5 per cent live in Manitoba and 2.3 per cent in Saskatchewan. The Maritimes had the smallest share of Canada's foreign born residents: with 0.9 per cent in Nova Scotia, 0.6 per cent in New Brunswick, 0.2 per cent in Prince Edward Island, and 0.2 per cent in Newfoundland and Labrador.[28]

Fortunately, the growing body of research about communicating across diversity offers encouraging news about what happens when people from different backgrounds get together. While homogeneous groups may be more cohesive,[29] diverse groups often develop better solutions to problems[30] and enjoy themselves more while working together.[31]

One ingredient in working effectively in diverse groups is understanding the often subtle cultural factors that shape communication. After surveying over 160,000 members of organizations in 60 countries, Geert Hofstede identified five cultural forces that shape the attitudes and behaviours of groups and individuals.[32] We will examine each of them in the following pages.

Individualism versus Collectivism

Some cultures value the individual, whereas others value the group. As Table 9.4 shows, the United States is one of the world's more individualistic societies, along with Canada, Australia, and Britain. By contrast, Latin American and Asian societies are generally more collectivistic.

In individualistic cultures people tend to feel that their primary responsibility is to themselves, whereas members of collectivistic societies feel loyalties and obligations to the groups of which they are members: the family, the community, the organization they work for, and their working teams. Members of individualistic societies gain most of their identity and self-esteem from their own accomplishments, whereas members of collectivistic societies are identified with the groups to which they belong. Individualistic cultures are also characterized by self-reliance and competition, whereas collectivistic cultures are more attentive to and concerned with the opinions of significant others.[33] Individualistic and collectivistic cultures have very different approaches to communication. For example, individualistic cultures are relatively tolerant of conflicts, state their opinions openly, and use direct, solution-oriented approaches. Members of collectivistic cultures, by contrast, prefer to avoid conflict and often seek less direct ways to express their message.[34]

It's easy to see how a culture's **individualistic** or **collectivistic orientation** can affect group communication. Members of collectivistic cultures are more likely to be team players, whereas members of individualistic cultures are far more likely to produce and reward stars. As members of highly

> **individualistic orientation**
> A cultural orientation focusing on the value and welfare of individual members, as opposed to a concern for the group as a whole.
>
> **collectivistic orientation**
> A cultural orientation focusing on the welfare of the group as a whole, rather than a concern by individuals for their own success.

COMMUNICATION ON-SCREEN

The Wizard of Oz (1939)
Directed by Victor Fleming.

This much-loved story illustrates how group members can achieve their personal goals by working together toward a common purpose. The Tin Man wants a heart; the Cowardly Lion wants courage; the Scarecrow wants a brain; and Dorothy wants to go home to Kansas. All the adventurers realize that helping one another is the best way to get what each wants. The characters embody the motto of another famous band of adventurers: "All for one and one for all."

Table 9.4 Cultural Values in Selected Countries

(Countries ranked lower on each list are closer to the mean)

Individualistic	Collectivistic
United States	Venezuela
Australia	Taiwan
Great Britain	Mexico
Canada	Philippines
Low Power Distance	**High Power Distance**
Israel	Philippines
New Zealand	Mexico
Germany	India
United States	France
Low Uncertainty Avoidance	**High Uncertainty Avoidance**
Singapore	Greece
India	Japan
Philippines	Peru
United States	Mexico
High Task Orientation	**High Social Orientation**
Japan	Sweden
Austria	Norway
Italy	Chile
Mexico	Portugal
Long-Term Focus	**Short-Term Focus**
China (includes Hong Kong and Taiwan)	Pakistan
Japan	Canada
South Korea	Great Britain
Brazil	United States
India	Australia

Source: Based on research summarized in G. Hofstede, *Culture and Organizations: Software of the Mind* (New York: McGraw-Hill, 1997).

individualistic cultures, North Americans often need to control their desire to dominate group discussions and to "win" in problem-solving situations. Consensus may be a desirable outcome, but it doesn't always come easily to individualists. By contrast, members of collectivistic cultures may be reluctant to speak out—especially if it means disagreeing—even when it would be in the best interests of the group.

> **Cultural Idiom**
> **speak out**
> To boldly say what one thinks.

Power Distance

> **power distance**
> The degree to which members are willing to accept a difference in power and status between members of a group.

Some cultures readily accept differences in power and status, whereas others accept them grudgingly, if at all. Most people in Canada and the United States believe in the principle of equality and reject the notion that some people are entitled to greater power or privilege than others. In other cultures, inequality is accepted as a fact of life.[35] **Power distance** refers to the degree to which members are willing to accept a difference in power and status between members of a group. In a culture with a high power distance, group members may willingly

Understanding Diversity

Baseball in Japan and the USA

The concept and practice of group harmony, or "wa," is what most dramatically differentiates Japanese baseball from the American game. It is the connecting thread running through all Japanese life and sports. While "Let It All Hang Out" and "Do Your Own Thing" are mottoes of contemporary American society, the Japanese have their own credo in the well-worn proverb "The Nail That Sticks up Shall Be Hammered Down." It is practically a national slogan.

Holdouts, for example, are rare in Japan. A player usually takes what the club deigns to give him and that's that. Demanding more money is evidence that a player is putting his own interests before those of the team.

In the pressure-cooker world of US pro sports, temper outbursts are considered acceptable, and at times even regarded as a salutary show of spirit. In Japan, however, a player's behaviour is often considered as important as his batting average. Batting slumps are usually accompanied by embarrassed smiles. Temper tantrums—along with practical joking, bickering, complaining, and other norms of American clubhouse life—are viewed in Japan as unwelcome incursions into the team's collective peace of mind.

When [Tokyo] Giants top pitcher Takashi Nishimoto ignored the instructions of a coach in practice one summer day in 1985, the coach punched him between the eyes. Nishimoto was also forced to apologize and pay a 100,000 yen fine for insubordination.

Moreover, untoward behaviour is also seen as a sign of character weakness and a "small heart," as well as being detrimental to the team's image overall. In Japan, a "real man" is one who keeps his emotions to himself and thinks of others' feelings.

Robert Whiting, *You Gotta Have Wa*

QUESTIONS: Do you think that the different cultural setting in Japan makes for a better sports environment? Do you think that gender norms could lead to workplace clashes between English Canadians and Japanese people? What are the similarities and differences that you see between English Canadians and Japanese people?

subordinate themselves to a leader—especially one whose leadership position is the product of socially accepted factors such as age, experience, training, or status. Members of cultures where low power distance is the norm may be less likely to feel that a particular group needs a leader, or to accept that the person who occupies that role automatically deserves unquestioning obedience. Supervisors, bosses, teachers, and so on certainly have the respect of the groups they lead in cultures where low power distance is the norm—but mostly because they earn it. In low power distance cultures, group members expect leaders to be more considerate of their interests and needs. "After all," they assume, "we're basically equal."

> **Cultural Idiom**
> **holdouts**
> Those who refuse to participate until they receive a satisfactory contract offer.

Uncertainty Avoidance

Some cultures accept—even welcome—risk, uncertainty, and change.[36] Others, characterized by **uncertainty avoidance**, prefer stability and tradition. Geography offers no clue to a culture's tolerance of uncertainty. Among the countries whose people tend to dislike surprises are Greece, Portugal, Turkey, Mexico, and Israel. Among those whose people are more comfortable with change are Denmark, Hong Kong, Ireland, and India.

It should come as no surprise that different attitudes towards uncertainty affect the way members of groups communicate. People who dislike uncertainty are uncomfortable with ambiguous tasks and reluctant to take risks. They tend to worry about the future, be loyal to their employers, and accept seniority as the basis for leadership. They view conflict as undesirable and are often willing to compromise when disagreements arise. By contrast, people from cultures with a higher tolerance for uncertainty are more willing to take risks, more accepting

> **uncertainty avoidance**
> The cultural tendency to seek stability and honour tradition instead of welcoming risk, uncertainty, and change.

of change, and more willing to break rules for pragmatic reasons. They accept conflict as natural and may be less willing to compromise when disagreements occur.

Task versus Social Orientation

The categories of task and social orientation, discussed earlier in this chapter, were originally labelled "masculine" and "feminine," based on the traditional notion that men are assertive and results oriented, whereas women are nurturing. In an era of increasingly flexible gender roles these labels are considered sexist and misleading, so we have substituted different labels. Groups in societies with a strong task orientation (Japan, Austria, Switzerland, and Mexico are examples) focus heavily on getting the job done. By contrast, groups in societies with a high degree of social orientation (including all the Scandinavian countries, as well as Chile, Portugal, and Thailand) are more likely to be concerned about members' feelings and ability to function smoothly as a team. When compared with other countries, Canada is almost exactly in the middle, balanced between task and social concerns.[37]

Task-oriented societies tend to focus on finding ways to improve team performance and ensure individual success through better training and so on. By contrast, groups in socially oriented societies focus more on collective concerns: co-operative problem-solving, maintaining a friendly atmosphere, and good physical working conditions. Problem-solving is still important in these cultures, but group members may be reluctant to take action if the personal costs to members—in stress and hard feelings—are likely to be high.

Short- versus Long-Term Orientation

Some cultures look for quick payoffs, whereas others are willing to defer gratification in pursuit of long-range goals. The willingness to work hard today for a payoff sometime in the future is especially common in East Asian cultures, including China, Japan, and South Korea. Western industrialized cultures are much more focused on short-term results.

As long as all group members share the same orientation toward payoffs, the chances for harmony are good. When some people push for a quick fix while others urge patience, conflicts are likely to arise.

It's easy to see how a society's cultural norms—its attitudes toward individuality, power distance, and uncertainty; its task or social orientation; and its emphasis on short- or long-term goals—can affect group behaviour. Whether the group is an athletic team, a military unit, a working group, or a family, the principle is the same. Cultural values shape what groups communicate about and how their members interact. Cultural factors don't account for every difference in group functioning, of course, but common assumptions do exert a subtle yet powerful effect on communication.

> **Cultural Idiom**
> **payoffs**
> Rewards or benefits that are gained from doing something.

Summary

Groups play an important role in many areas of our lives—families, education, employment, and friendships, to name just a few. Groups possess several characteristics that distinguish them from other communication contexts. They involve interaction and interdependence over time among a small number of participants with the purpose of achieving one or more goals. Groups have their own goals, as do individual members. Member goals fall into two categories: task-related and socially related. Sometimes individual and group goals are compatible, and sometimes they are in conflict.

Groups can be classified according to their functions. We have identified four types: learning, problem-solving, social, and growth groups. Whatever the type, every group has certain rules and norms, roles for individual members, patterns of interaction that are shaped by the group's structure, and approaches to decision-making.

Groups don't operate in a vacuum. The culture around them influences the way group members communicate with one another. This chapter has examined five ways in which culture influences interaction: individualism versus collectivism, power distance, uncertainty avoidance, task versus social orientation, and short- versus long-term goals.

Key Terms

all-channel network   356

chain network   356

collectivistic orientation   361

consensus   357

dysfunctional roles   352

formal roles   350

gatekeeper   357

group   340

group goals   342

growth groups   348

hidden agenda   344

individual goals   342

individualistic orientation   361

informal roles   350

learning group   346

norms   348

power distance   362

problem-solving groups   347

procedural norms   348

roles   350

rules   348

social groups   348

social norms   348

social orientation   343

social roles   352

sociogram   355

task norms   349

task orientation   343

task roles   352

topologies   355

uncertainty avoidance   363

wheel network   357

Activities

A. Your Membership in Groups

To find out what roles groups play in your life, complete the following steps:

1. Use the criteria of interaction, interdependence, time, size, and goals to identify the small groups to which you belong.

2. Describe the importance of each group to you, and evaluate how satisfying the communication is in each one.

3. Based on what you have read in this chapter, describe how communication operates in your groups and how it could be improved.

4. Describe how social media are changing the way you join groups and interact with people. Do you find yourself engaged in more virtual groups than others? Do you derive more or less satisfaction from virtual groups?

5. Discuss whether you think there are specific types of groups that you think are better served as virtual groups.

B. Group and Individual Goals

Think about two groups to which you belong.

1. What are your task-related goals in each?

2. What are your social goals in each?

3. Are your personal goals compatible or incompatible with those of other members?

4. Are they compatible or incompatible with the group goals?

5. What effect does the compatibility or incompatibility of goals have on the effectiveness of the group?

C. Norms and Rules in Action

Describe the explicit rules and desirable norms that you would like to see established in the following new groups, and describe the steps you could take to see that they are established:

1. A group of classmates formed to develop and present a class research project.

2. A group of neighbours meeting for the first time to persuade the city to install a stop sign at a dangerous intersection.

3. A group of eight-year-olds you will be coaching in a team sport.

4. A group of fellow employees who will be sharing new office space.

D. Choosing the Best Decision-Making Approach

Which of the decision-making approaches listed on pages 357–60 would be most appropriate in each of the following situations? Explain why your recommended approach is the best one for each situation.

1. Four apartment mates must decide how to handle household chores.

2. A group of hikers and their experienced guide become lost in a snowstorm and debate whether to try to find their way to safety or to pitch camp and wait for the weather to clear.

3. After trying unsuccessfully to reach consensus, the partners in a new business venture cannot agree on the best name for their enterprise.

4. A 25-member ski club is looking for the cheapest airfare and lodging for its winter trip.

5. A passenger falls overboard during an afternoon sail on your friend's 20-foot sailboat. The wind is carrying the boat away from the passenger.

E. Motives for Group Membership

Members often join a group for reasons unrelated to the group's stated purpose for existing. For example, some people belong to growth groups to fulfill social needs, and others speak out in task-oriented groups to satisfy their egos more than to help solve the stated problem. Develop a set of guidelines that describes when you believe it is and is not ethical to participate in groups without stating any hidden agendas.

Further Reading

Keyton, Joann, and Lawrence R. Frey, "The State of Traits: Predispositions and Group Communication," in Lawrence R. Frey, ed., *New Directions in Group Communication* (Thousand Oaks, CA: Sage, 2002).

This research-based chapter details the influence of individual personality styles on a group's effectiveness.

Levi, Daniel J., *Group Dynamics for Teams,* 4th edn (Thousand Oaks, CA: Sage, 2013).

The author opens with team basics and then moves to the all-important beginnings of working as a team while building on the processes a team experiences. A major section of the book (more than one hundred pages) deals with issues that face teams, including conflict, decision making, and diversity. Especially helpful to students is the appendix, "Guide to Student Team Projects."

Rothwell, J. Dan, *In Mixed Company,* 7th edn (Belmont, CA: Wadsworth, 2009).

This book is an easy-to-read, comprehensive look at the process of communication in small groups. Ideal for readers looking for more information on group communication, it does an excellent job of summarizing literally hundreds of research studies in a manner that makes their value in everyday interaction clear.

Zorn, Theodore E., Jr, and George H. Tompson, "Communication in Top Management Teams," in Lawrence R. Frey, ed., *New Directions in Group Communication* (Thousand Oaks, CA: Sage, 2002).

For career-minded readers, this essay offers insights into the communication skills of high-level managers.

Study Questions

Think back to a group that you participated in recently that was either successful or unsuccessful in meeting its goals. Write a brief description of the group's goals, its setting (physical, virtual) and its members. Then write a line or two about the group's success or failure. Now answer the following questions about your group:

1. What can you speculate are the individual goals of group members? Which of these goals did you find members shared, and which were using hidden agendas? How did those individual goals help or hinder the group in its pursuit of its goal? What could you have done to increase the chances that individual goals didn't interfere with the group's goal?

2. What procedural and task norms would have helped this group be successful? What social norms would have interfered with the group's success?

3. Given the group's task, which of the functional roles described on pages 350–2 do you think were most important to the success of your group? What role-related problems might arise if the roles you listed remain unfilled?

4. Did the group members' cultural backgrounds affect the functioning of the group? How and why? How might you have fixed cultural problems?

5. Would the group have benefited from using social media? How might a social media approach have affected the group's performance?

10

Solving Problems in Groups

After studying the material in this chapter . . .

You should understand:

- ✔ the advantages of solving problems in groups (and the situations where groups are not so effective);
- ✔ the characteristics of several common discussion formats;
- ✔ the advantages and drawbacks of computer-mediated groups;
- ✔ the steps in the rational problem-solving method;
- ✔ the developmental stages in a problem-solving group;
- ✔ the factors that contribute to group cohesiveness; and
- ✔ the various approaches to studying leadership.

You should be able to:

- ✔ decide when to use groups to solve problems and whether a face-to-face group meeting or computer-mediated meeting would be more practical;
- ✔ use the problem-solving steps outlined in this chapter to help complete a group task;
- ✔ suggest ways to build cohesiveness and participation in a group;
- ✔ analyze the sources of leadership and power in a group;
- ✔ suggest the most effective leadership approach for a specific task; and
- ✔ identify the obstacles to effective functioning of a specific group and suggest more effective ways of communicating.

Chapter Highlights

In this chapter we will discuss solving problems in groups, including:

» when (and when not) to use groups for solving problems;

» what formats are best for different problem-solving situations; and

» the pros and cons of computer-mediated groups.

While groups can solve problems in many different ways, the most successful groups tend to:

» follow a structured, six-step approach;

» understand the stages that groups go through while working on a problem; and

» maintain positive relationships and an optimal level of cohesiveness.

You will see that leadership and team-member influence come in many forms:

» Group members can use six types of power.

» The effectiveness of leaders can be defined in different ways.

» There are many different leadership styles, which are effective in different circumstances.

Finally, we'll look at the following pitfalls that can come with group problem-solving and how to avoid them:

» information underload and overload;

» unequal participation; and

» pressure to conform.

In Chapter 9 we described various types of groups—learning, problem-solving, social, and growth groups. Of all these, problem-solving groups have been studied most intensively by social scientists. Once we understand the nature of problem-solving, the reason becomes clear. Solving problems, as we define it here, doesn't refer only to situations where something is wrong. Perhaps *meeting challenges* and *performing tasks* are better terms. After you recognize this fact, you can see that problem-solving occupies a major part of working life. The figures from just one company illustrate the scope of group problem-solving: at 3M Corporation, managers spend a total of 4.4 million hours per year in meetings, at a cost to the company of $78.8 million in salaries.[1] Away from work, groups also meet to solve problems: non-profit organizations plan fundraisers, sports teams work to improve their collective performance, neighbours meet to improve the quality of life where they live, educators and parents work together to improve schools—the list is almost endless.

This chapter will focus on both the task and the relational aspects of problem-solving groups. In addition, it will explore the nature of leadership, defining that important term and suggesting how groups can be led most effectively. Finally, it will list several common problems that task-oriented groups can encounter and describe how to overcome them.

> **Cultural Idiom**
> **Muzak**
> Bland instrumental arrangements of popular songs which are often played in elevators, stores, and restaurants.
>
> **a ditty**
> A short, simple poem.

Problem-Solving in Groups: When and Why

For many people, groups are to problem-solving what Muzak is to music or Twinkies are to food—a joke. The snide remark "A camel is a horse designed by a committee" reflects this attitude, as does this ditty:

Search all your parks in all your cities . . .
You'll find no statues to committees![2]

Consensus-Building and the Canadian Constitution

For the first 115 years of its life as an independent nation, Canada did not have the right to amend its own Constitution without requesting the formal approval of the British Parliament. The main reason this colonial arrangement had dragged on for so long was that the federal and provincial governments had never been able to agree on a new set of rules for constitutional change. Should all 10 provinces have to agree to a change before it could become law? If not, how many would be enough? What proportion of the population should they represent? Should one province (Quebec in particular) have the power to veto a change that the others were prepared to accept? A means of amending Canada's Constitution in Canada instead of through the British Parliament could not be put in place until questions like these had been answered.

What triggered the final effort to resolve the matter was the May 1980 Quebec referendum on sovereignty-association, for Prime Minister Pierre Trudeau had promised to redefine Quebec's position in Canada if voters rejected the sovereignty option—which they did. Talks with the provinces accordingly resumed in the summer of 1980. By the next fall, however, only two provinces (Ontario and New Brunswick) had agreed to support Trudeau's plan, which centred on the incorporation within the Constitution of a Charter of Rights and Freedoms. The holdouts were hardly united in their objections—each had its own—but together they formed a united front that soon became known as the Gang of Eight.

When the First Ministers' Conference in Ottawa in early November 1981 appeared to be going nowhere on the issue, Trudeau proposed a compromise: agree to removing Constitutional amendment from the hands of the British Parliament now and leave the details of the Charter and amending formula to be worked out later; then, if no agreement was reached within two years, submit the outstanding issues to the public in a national referendum. Seven of the Gang of Eight refused, but—to their shock—Quebec Premier René Lévesque broke ranks and agreed. Accounts of Lévesque's motivation

This unflattering reputation is at least partly justified. Most of us would wind up with a handsome sum if we had a dollar for every hour we've wasted in groups. On the other hand, it's unfair to view all groups as bad, especially when this accusation implies that other types of communication are by nature superior. After all, we've also wasted time listening to boring lectures, reading worthless books, and making trivial conversation.

So what's the truth? Is group problem-solving a waste of effort, or is it the best way to manage a task? As with most matters, the truth falls somewhere between these two extremes. Groups do have their shortcomings, which we will discuss a little later. But problems can be avoided when these shortcomings are recognized. Extensive research has shown that the group approach is the most effective way to handle many tasks.

> **Cultural Idiom**
> **wind up**
> To end up with something; the final part of something.

Advantages of Group Problem-Solving

For more than 50 years, research comparing problem-solving by groups and individuals has shown that, in most cases, groups can produce more solutions to a problem than individuals working alone and that the solutions are of higher quality.[3] Groups have proved superior at a wide range of tasks—everything from assembling jigsaw puzzles to solving complex reasoning problems. There are several reasons why groups are so effective.[4]

Resources

For many tasks, groups possess a greater collection of resources than do most individuals. Sometimes the resources are physical. Three or four people can put up a tent or dig a ditch much faster than one person can. In other cases, though, pooling resources can actually lead to qualitatively better solutions. Think, for instance, of times when you have studied with other students for a test, and you will remember how much better the group was at preparing for all

---

vary: some say he was reluctant but agreed because a referendum appeared to be the most democratic solution; others that he welcomed the prospect of a showdown with Trudeau that he was sure to win.

In any event, at the end of the meeting Lévesque left to spend the night in Hull, Quebec (across the river from Ottawa), after asking the other premiers to let him know if anything came up before he rejoined them the next morning.

In fact something did come up: late in the night, the other premiers agreed to a compromise negotiated by Justice Minister Jean Chrétien and Saskatchewan Attorney General Roy Romanow. But Lévesque was not informed, let alone consulted. It was only when he arrived for breakfast the next morning that he learned an agreement had been reached during what has come to be known in Quebec as the "night of the long knives."

The new compromise was signed by Trudeau and nine premiers, but Lévesque refused to sign. Three weeks later the Quebec government announced that it would invoke its

traditional right, as representative of one of Canada's founding peoples, to veto the plan; however, the Supreme Court of Canada ruled that the province had never possessed such a right, either legally or by convention.

Today, more than a quarter of a century after the Constitution Act, 1982, became law—governing both the nine provinces that agreed to it and Quebec—the Quebec provincial government still has not signed it. The decision to throw consensus to the wayside and proceed without Quebec only deepened Quebecers' profound sense of alienation and fanned the flames of separatism.

QUESTIONS: A series of communication breakdowns led Quebec Premier René Lévesque to feel that he had been excluded from the constitutional negotiations. Where do you think things went wrong? How could Trudeau, Lévesque, and the other premiers have functioned better as a problem-solving group?

the questions that might be asked and at developing answers to them. (Of course, we have to assume that your fellow members cared enough about the exam to have studied for it before the meeting.) Furthermore, interaction among the group's members makes it easier to mobilize their resources. Talking about an upcoming test with others can jog your memory and remind you of things you might not have thought of if you had been working alone.

Accuracy

Another benefit of group work is the increased likelihood of catching errors. At one time or another, we all make stupid mistakes—like the man who built a boat in his basement and then wasn't able to get it out the door. Working in a group increases the chance that foolish errors like this won't slip by. Sometimes, of course, errors aren't so obvious, which makes it even more valuable to have more than one person checking for them. On the other hand, there is always some risk that group members will support each other in a bad idea. We'll discuss this problem later on, when we look at the pressure to conform that can develop in groups.

Commitment

Besides coming up with superior solutions, groups also generate a higher commitment to carrying them out. The idea that people are most likely to accept solutions they have helped create and will work harder to implement them is the principle behind **participative decision-making**, in which the people who will live with a plan help to develop it. This is an especially important principle for those in authority, such as supervisors, teachers, and parents. As professors, we have seen the difference between the sullen compliance of students who have been forced to accept a policy they disagree with and the much more willing co-operation of students who have helped develop it. Though the benefits of participative decision-making are great, we need to insert a qualification here: there are times when an autocratic approach—imposing a decision without discussion—is the most effective. We will discuss this question of when to be democratic and when to be directive in the leadership section of this chapter.

participative decision-making
Development of solutions with input by the people who will be affected.

When to Use Groups for Problem-Solving

Working in a group is not always the best way to solve a problem. Many jobs can be tackled more quickly and easily—even more efficiently—by one or more people working independently. Answering the following questions will help you decide when to solve a problem using a group and when to undertake it alone.[5]

Is the Job Beyond the Capacity of One Person?

Some jobs are simply too big for one person to manage. They may call for more information than a single person possesses or can gather. For example, a group of friends planning a large New Year's Eve party will probably have a better event if they pool their ideas than if one person tries to think of everything. Some jobs also require more time and energy than one person can spare. Planning the party could involve a variety of tasks: inviting the

guests, hiring a band, finding a suitable venue, buying food and drinks, and so on. It's both unrealistic and unfair to expect one or two people to do all this work.

Are Individuals' Tasks Interdependent?

Remember that a group is more than a collection of individuals working side by side. The best tasks for groups are ones where the individuals can help one another in some way. Think of a group of disgruntled tenants considering how to protest unfair rent hikes. In order to get anywhere, they realize that they have to assign areas of responsibility to each member: researching the law, recruiting new members, publicizing their complaints, and so on. It's easy to see that these jobs are all interdependent: recruiting new members, for example, will require publicity; and publicizing complaints will involve showing how the tenants' legal rights are being violated.

One manager let employees know how valuable they were with the following memo:

> YOU ARX A KXY PXRSON
>
> Xvxn though my typxwritxr is an old modxl, it works vxry wxll—xxcxpt for onx kxy. You would think that with all thx othxr kxys functioning propxrly, onx kxy not working would hardly bx noticxd; but just onx kxy out of whack sxxms to ruin thx wholx xffort.
>
> You may say to yoursxlf—Wxll I'm only onx pxrson. No onx will noticx if I don't do my bxst. But it doxs makx a diffxrxncx bxcausx to bx xffxctivx an organization nxxds activx participation by xvxry onx to thx bxst of his or hxr ability.
>
> So thx nxxt timx you think you arx not important, rxmxmbxr my old typxwritxr. You arx a kxy pxrson.

Even when everyone is working on the same job, there can be interdependence if different members fill the various functional roles described in Chapter 9. Some people might be better at task-related roles like information giving, diagnosing, and summarizing. Others might contribute by filling social roles such as harmonizing, supporting, or relieving tension. People working independently simply don't have the breadth of resources to fill all these functions.

Is There More than One Decision or Solution?

Groups are best suited to tackling problems that have no single, cut-and-dried answer: What's the best way to boost membership in a campus organization? How can funds be raised for a charity? What topic should the group choose for a class project? Gaining the perspectives of every member boosts the odds of finding high-quality answers to questions like these.

By contrast, a problem with only one solution won't take full advantage of a group's talents. For example, phoning merchants to get price quotes or looking up a series of books in the library doesn't require much creative thinking. Jobs like these can

Cultural Idiom

cut-and-dried
Something that is unambiguous.

boosts the odds of
To increase the chances of success.

COMMUNICATION ON-SCREEN

Cube (1997)

Directed by Vincenzo Natali.

In this brilliant Canadian horror cult classic, six people wake up in a brightly coloured cube with hatches on all four walls, ceiling, and floor. No one knows where they are, how they got there or why. One of the members, Quinn (Maurice Dean Wint), a police officer, discovers almost fatally that some of the rooms contain hidden traps like acid or razor blades. Reasoning that each person has distinct skills and a reason they were put together, they begin trying to unravel the clues of why they're there and how to get out. Using problem-solving, skills management, and teamwork, the team discovers, are the only ways they will survive the hellish cube.

YOUNG COMMUNICATOR PROFILE

JESSICA MARTIN

Reporter/Communications
Advisor, Toronto Transit
Commission

Social media have brought a new edge to the communications landscape—one that gives customers a significant level of influence in the branding of a company. Where industry and advertisers used to control the message, customers can now go public with unfiltered depictions of their experiences, good and bad. In response, companies are revising their approach to customer service.

When I started at the TTC over four years ago, there was a lack of customer outreach. It left users guessing when there was a delay, both what the issue was and how long the delay would last. As a communications team, we developed a plan to communicate these delays to external users through Twitter, Facebook, e-mail, text message and our website, and system users through the Public Address System, Platform Video Screens and Station Information Screens. The issues we faced were twofold; transparency and education. Since the majority of delays are caused by parades, police road closures, Passenger Assistance Alarms, and other occurrences that are out of our control, how then, do we educate customers with minimal backlash? In the end, we decided to send out notifications for any significant bus, streetcar or subway delay, explain the reason, and distribute an "all clear" once service has resumed. Here, in our view, transparency trumpeted potential negative feedback, as users could decide whether to wait out the delay or choose another method of travel.

The service has been highly received, with over 60,000 followers on Twitter, approximately 100,000 receiving e-mail updates and over 1.7 million daily riders receiving updates on the system, as they happen. What's more, Calgary and New York Transit has followed our lead in reaching out to its users.

As a young communicator with an honours degree in Multimedia and Mass Communications, I have played a significant role in the new way the TTC does business. My experience has given our communications team the ability to utilize all mediums to communicate information and adapt our approach as new technology comes online. A perspective, you too, can bring to your future work place.

be handled by one or two people working alone. Of course, it may take a group meeting to decide how to divide the work to get the job done most efficiently.

Is There Potential For Disagreement?

Tackling a problem as a group is essential if you need the support of everyone involved. Consider a group of friends planning a vacation. Letting one or two people choose the destination, schedule, and budget would be asking for trouble because their decisions would almost certainly disappoint at least some of the people who weren't consulted. It would be far smarter to involve everyone in the most important decisions, even if doing so took more time. After the key decisions have been settled, it might be fine to delegate relatively minor issues to one or two people.

Group Problem-Solving Formats

Groups meet to solve problems in a variety of settings and for a wide range of reasons. The formats they use are also varied. For example, a group may meet before an audience of people involved in or affected by the topic under discussion, like the citizens who attend a typical city council meeting or the members of the public who attend the CBC's town hall meetings. Audience members participate in a direct fashion, asking questions, responding to questions, and sometimes voicing their dissent.

Types of Problem-Solving Groups

This list of problem-solving formats and approaches is not exhaustive, but it provides a sense of how a group's structure can shape its ability to come up with high-quality solutions.

Breakout Groups

When a group is too large for all members to take part in discussions, **breakout groups**, also referred to as "buzz groups," can be used to maximize effective participation. In this approach, a number of subgroups (usually consisting of five to seven members) simultaneously discuss an issue and then report back to the group at large. The best ideas of each breakout group are then assembled to form a high-quality decision.

Problem Census

This approach is useful when groups want to identify important issues or problems. **Problem census** works especially well when some members are more vocal than others because it equalizes participation. Members use a separate card to list each of their ideas. The leader collects all the cards and reads them to the group one by one, posting each on a board visible to everyone. Because the name of the person who contributed each item isn't listed, issues are separated from personalities. As similar items are read, the leader posts and arranges them in clusters. After all items have been read and posted, the leader and members consolidate similar items into a number of ideas that the group needs to address.

Focus Groups

Focus groups are used as a market research tool to enable sponsoring organizations to learn how potential users or the public at large regards a new product or idea. Unlike other groups discussed here, focus groups don't include decision-makers or other members who claim any expertise on a subject. Instead, their comments are used by decision-makers to figure out how people in the wider world might react to ideas.

Parliamentary Procedure

Problem-solving meetings can follow a variety of formats. A session that uses **parliamentary procedure** observes specific rules about how topics may be discussed and decisions made. The standard reference book for parliamentary procedure is the revised edition of *Robert's Rules of Order*. Although the parliamentary rules may seem stilted and cumbersome, when well used they do keep a discussion on track and protect the rights of the minority against domination by the majority.

Panel Discussion

Another common problem-solving format is the **panel discussion**, in which the participants talk over the topic informally, much as they would in an ordinary conversation. A leader (called a "moderator" in public discussions) may help the discussion along by encouraging some members to comment, cutting off overly talkative ones, and seeking consensus when the time comes for making a decision.

Symposium

In a **symposium** the participants divide the topic in a manner that allows each member to deliver in-depth information without interruption. Although this format lends itself to good explanations of each person's decision, the one-person-at-a-time nature of a symposium won't

---

breakout groups
A group discussion strategy used when the number of members is too large for effective discussion. Subgroups simultaneously address an issue and then report back to the group at large. Also called "buzz groups."

problem census
Used to equalize participation in groups when the goal is to identify important issues or problems. Members first put ideas on cards, which are then compiled by a leader to generate a comprehensive statement of the issue or problem.

focus groups
Used in market research by sponsoring organizations to survey potential users or the public at large regarding a new product or idea.

parliamentary procedure
A problem-solving method in which specific rules govern the way issues may be discussed and decisions made.

panel discussion
A discussion format in which participants consider a topic more or less conversationally, without formal procedural rules. Panel discussions may be facilitated by a moderator.

symposium
A discussion format in which participants divide the topic in a manner that allows each member to deliver in-depth information without interruption.

COMMUNICATION ON-SCREEN

The Merchants of Cool: Where Does Cool Come From (2001)

Directed by Barak Goodman.

In this documentary, which aired on the PBS program *Frontline*, journalist Douglas Rushkoff investigates how young people are targeted by marketing experts. Rushkoff shows how "cool hunters" spend hours and days conducting surveys, focus groups, and participant research with tweens and teens to find out what young people find attractive, stimulating, terrifying, and beautiful. The merchants of cool want to find out what makes young people get excited about products, how they interact in groups, and why they socialize the way they do. Sombrely serious at times and absolutely hilarious at others, the program is required watching for students who want to understand how young people are targeted by marketing communicators.

forum
A discussion format in which audience members are invited to add their comments to those of the official discussants.

asynchronous discussion
A discussion that happens in a format where the participants don't have to reply to each other immediately, e.g., an internet discussion board.

Cultural Idiom

tweens
People who are in pre-adolescence, generally between the ages of 10 and 12.

lead to a group decision. The contributions of the members must be followed by the give-and-take of an open discussion.

Forum

A **forum** allows non-members to add their opinions to the group's deliberations before the group makes a decision. This approach is commonly used by public agencies to encourage the participation of citizens in the decisions that affect them.

Computer-Mediated Groups

Face-to-face meetings can be difficult. Just scheduling a session can be maddening: almost every date or time that one person suggests doesn't work for someone else. If the participants come from different locations, the time and cost of a meeting can be significant. Challenges don't end after a meeting time is finally arranged. Some members may be late. Others may have to leave early. And during the meeting interruptions are common: members may be sidetracked by off-the-topic digressions and other distractions. One or more people may dominate the conversation, whereas others rarely speak.

Given the drawbacks of meeting in person, the idea of using technology to create other ways of working together has strong appeal. As we mentioned in Chapter 9, conference calls and teleconferences allow group members to communicate in real time via telephone or computer, as if they were meeting in person. Another approach is an **asynchronous discussion**, which resembles e-mail: group members don't have to be online at the same time. They can log on to the network at their convenience, check messages others have sent, and contribute their own ideas for other team members to read later.

In the 1990s, communication researchers began to sort out the advantages and disadvantages of computer-mediated meetings as compared to face-to-face interactions.[6] Studies suggest that computer conferencing has several advantages. Most obviously, it is much easier to schedule and "meet" online because members don't need to leave their desks. Asynchronous meetings are especially convenient because group members can log on at their convenience, independent of other participants. Computer-mediated sessions also encourage more balanced participation: members who might have kept quiet in face-to-face sessions are more comfortable "speaking out" online. Furthermore, online meetings generate a permanent record of the proceedings, which can be convenient.

Despite their advantages, computer-mediated groups aren't a panacea. The lack of non-verbal cues makes it difficult to convey emotions and attitudes. Meeting in virtual space often means that it takes the group longer to reach a decision than it would if they met face to face. Because typing takes more time and effort than speaking, messages conveyed via computer can lack the detail of spoken ones. In some cases, members may not even bother to type out a message online that they would have shared in person. Finally, the string of separate messages that is generated in a computerized medium can be hard to track, sort out, and synthesize in a meaningful way.

Research comparing the quality of decisions made by face-to-face and online groups is mixed. Some studies have found no significant differences. Others have found that computer-mediated groups generate more ideas than people meeting in person, although they take longer to reach agreement on which ideas are best. The growing body of research suggests that certain types of computer-mediated communication work better than others. For example, asynchronous groups seem to make better decisions than those functioning in a real-time "chat" mode. Groups using special decision-support software perform better than ones operating without this advantage. Having a moderator also improves the effectiveness of online groups.

What use does this information have for groups who want to decide how to meet? Perhaps the most valuable lesson is that online meetings should not replace face-to-face ones but can be a supplement to in-person sessions. Combining the two forms of interaction can help groups operate both efficiently and effectively. After all, no matter where or how a group meets, the same factors influence its productivity, some of which are listed in Table 10.1.

> ## 🎥◀ COMMUNICATION ON-SCREEN
>
> ### *The Persuaders* (2003)
> **Directed by Barak Goodman and Rachel Dretzin.**
>
> In this *Frontline* documentary, Douglas Rushkoff leads us on a journey to discover how marketers research what consumers want and how they want to be persuaded. This film is full of group communication—from board meetings of advertising executives to focus groups, we are treated to an insider's view of how marketing works. In particular, there is an excellent 10-minute segment featuring Dr Clothaire Rapaille, the famous French market researcher who claims to have uncovered "culture codes" that unlock the secrets of desire and belief for consumers. Rapaille's research led to the relaunch of the Jeep Wrangler with round headlights and had significant input on the design of the new Boeing Dreamliner mega passenger plane.

Approaches and Stages in Problem-Solving

Groups may have the potential to solve problems effectively, but they don't always live up to this potential. What makes some groups succeed and others fail? Researchers spent much of the twentieth century asking this question. Two useful answers emerged from their work.

Table 10.1 Some Communication Factors Associated with Group Productivity

The group contains the smallest number of members necessary to accomplish its goals.

Members care about and agree with the group's goals.

Members are clear about and accept their roles, which match the abilities of each member.

Group norms encourage high performance, quality, success, and innovation.

The group members have sufficient time together to develop a mature working unit and accomplish its goals.

The group is highly cohesive and co-operative.

The group spends time defining and discussing problems it must solve and decisions it must make.

Periods of conflict are frequent but brief, and the group has effective strategies for dealing with conflict.

The group has an open communication structure in which all members may participate.

The group gets, gives, and uses feedback about its effectiveness.

Source: Adapted from research summarized in S.A. Wheelan, D. Murphy, E. Tsumaura, and S.F. Kline, "Member Perceptions of Internal Group Dynamics and Productivity," *Small Group Research* 29 (1998): 371–93.

UNDERSTANDING COMMUNICATION TECHNOLOGY

Health Conference Aims to Fill App Gap

It may seem like there's an app for everything, but a Hamilton conference organizer says the possibilities for apps in the health field is "huge and growing." Mohawk College instructor Christy Taberner is one of the organizers of a two-day technology and health conference, called Apps for Health, being held at the school this Thursday and Friday. "Individuals can input personal information . . . so they can become empowered and take control and responsibility for their own health," said Taberner on the power of apps.

Mohawk College expects 180 visitors including researchers, developers in the health and technology industries and students from across Ontario. The conference will focus on mobile solutions for the health care industry.

Taberner said mobile health can make health care more efficient and help with decision-making on an international level. Despite the benefits, the industry has a challenge. "The great challenge with e-health and [mobile] health is to engage in the next generation in this field and bring all these folks together to understand the challenges," said Mark Casselman, conference organizer and senior project manager of the Centre for eHealth Global Innovation.

On day two, student teams will tackle this challenge. Local non-profit and community organizations will present challenges they face in their domain, where they believe a mobile solution might exist. For example, the local Community Care Access Centre, a public health agency that provides care option information, is looking for a mobile solution for seniors and families to explore long-term care and alternate living options. International Child Care Canada, a health development organization, wants an app to provide health decision support to reduce infant mortality rates in rural Haiti.

For Taberner, the opportunity to link students, organizations, and developers is key. "A lot of the work is being done in the basements of peoples homes, I joke. We're all working on solutions but we're not really communicating with each other," said Taberner. "If we're really going to try to be innovative we need a place where innovators can connect. That's what we're really hoping will happen—coming up with some solutions together."

Julia Chapman, CBC News, 9 May 2012

QUESTIONS: By working collectively, this conference aims to achieve innovative mobile solutions to broad health-related issues. What are the advantages to this style of organizational problem-solving? What are the potential drawbacks?

A Structured Problem-Solving Approach

Although we often pride ourselves on facing problems rationally, social scientists have discovered that logic and reason usually play little part in the way we make decisions.[7] The tendency to use non-rational approaches is unfortunate because research shows that, to a great degree, a group's effectiveness is determined by whether or not it approaches a problem rationally and systematically.[8] Just as a poor blueprint or a shaky foundation can weaken a house, groups can fail by skipping one or more of the necessary steps in solving a problem.

As early as 1910, philosopher and psychologist John Dewey introduced his famous "reflective thinking" method as a systematic method for solving problems.[9] Since then, other experts have suggested modifications of Dewey's approach. Some emphasize answering key questions, whereas others seek "ideal solutions" that meet the needs of all members. Research comparing various methods has clearly shown that, although no single approach is best for all situations, a structured procedure produces better results than "no pattern" discussions.[10]

The following problem-solving model contains the elements common to most structured approaches developed in the last 80 years:

1. Identify the problem.
   a. What are the group's goals?
   b. What are individual members' goals?

2. Analyze the problem.
   a. Word the problem as a probative question.
   b. Gather relevant information.
   c. Identify impelling and restraining forces.
3. Develop creative solutions through brainstorming or the nominal group technique.
   a. Avoid criticism at this stage.
   b. Encourage "freewheeling" ideas.
   c. Develop a large number of ideas.
   d. Combine two or more individual ideas.
4. Evaluate the solutions.
   a. Which solution will best produce the desired changes?
   b. Which is most achievable?
   c. Which contains the fewest serious disadvantages?
5. Implement the plan.
   a. Identify specific tasks.
   b. Determine necessary resources.
   c. Define individual responsibilities.
   d. Provide for emergencies.
6. Follow up on the solution.
   a. Meet to evaluate progress.
   b. Revise approach as necessary.

> **Cultural Idiom**
> **freewheeling**
> Thinking that is
> unrestricted.

Identify the Problem

Sometimes a group's problem is easy to identify. The crew of a sinking ship, for example, doesn't need to conduct a discussion to understand that its goal is to avoid drowning or being eaten by a large fish.

There are many times, however, when the problems facing a group aren't so clear. As an example, think of an athletic team stuck deep in last place well into the season. At first the problem seems obvious: an inability to win any games. But a closer look at the situation might show that there are unmet goals—and thus other problems. For instance, individual members may have goals that aren't tied directly to winning: making friends and receiving acknow-ledgment as good athletes, not to mention the simple goal of having fun—of playing in the recreational sense of the word. You can probably see that, if the coach or team members took a simplistic view of the situation by looking only at the team's win–lose record, analyzing player errors, training methods, and so on, some important problems would probably go overlooked. In this situation, the team's performance could probably be best improved by working on the basic problems—the frustration of the players about having their personal needs unmet. What's the moral here? That the way to start understanding a group's problem is to identify the concerns of each member.

Cultural Idiom
dire straits
An extremely difficult
situation.

What about groups that don't have problems? Several friends planning a surprise birthday party and a family deciding where to go for its vacation doesn't seem to be in the dire straits of a losing athletic team: they simply want to have fun. In cases like these, it may be helpful to substitute the word *challenge* for the more gloomy word *problem*. However we express it, the same principle applies to all task-oriented groups: the best place to start work is to identify what each member seeks as a result of belonging to the group.

Analyze the Problem

After you have identified the general nature of the problem facing the group, you are ready to look at the problem in more detail. There are several steps you can follow to accomplish this important job.

Word the Problem as a Probative Question

If you have ever seen a formal debate, you know that the issue under discussion is worded as a proposition: "Canada should increase its spending on higher education," for example. Many problem-solving groups define their task in much the same way: "We ought to spend our vacation in the mountains," suggests one family member. The problem with phrasing problems as propositions is that such wording invites people to take sides. Though this approach is fine for formal debates (which are contests rather like football or card games), premature side-taking creates unnecessary conflict in most problem-solving groups.

A far better approach is to state the problem as a question. Note that this should be a **probative question**—an open one that encourages exploratory thinking. Asking, "Should we vacation in the mountains or at the beach?" still forces members to choose sides. A far better approach involves asking a question to help define the general goals that came out during the problem-identification stage: "What do we want our vacation to accomplish?" (i.e., "relaxation," "adventure," "low cost," and so on).

Notice that this question is truly exploratory. It encourages the family members to work co-operatively instead of forcing them to make a choice and then defend it. The absence of an either–or situation boosts the odds that members will listen openly to one another rather than listening selectively in defence of their own positions. There is even a chance that the co-operative, exploratory climate that comes from wording the question probatively will help the family arrive at consensus about where to vacation, eliminating the need to discuss the matter any further.

probative question
An open question used
to analyze a problem by
encouraging exploratory
thinking.

Gather Relevant Information

Groups often need to know important facts before they can make decisions or even understand the problem. We remember one group of students who was determined to do well on a class presentation. One of their goals was "to get an A grade." They knew that to do so, they would have to present a topic that interested both the instructor and the students in the audience. Their first job was to do a bit of background research to find out what subjects would be well received. They interviewed the instructor, asking what topics had been successes and failures in previous semesters. They tested some possible subjects on a few classmates and noted their reactions. As a result of this research they were able to modify their original probative question—"How can we choose and develop a topic that will earn us an A grade?"—into a more specific one—"How can we choose and develop a topic that contains humour, action, and lots of information (to demonstrate our research skills to the instructor), and that contains practical information that will improve either the audience's social life, academic standing, or financial condition?"

*A problem well stated
is a problem half
solved.*

**Charles Kettering,
inventor and social
philosopher**

Identify Impelling and Restraining Forces

Once members understand what they are seeking, the next step is to see what forces stand between the group and its goals. One useful tool for this task is **force field analysis**: listing the forces that help and hinder the group.[11] By returning to our earlier example of the troubled athletic team, we can see how the force field operates. Suppose the team defined its problem-question as "How can we (1) have more fun and (2) grow closer as friends?"

One restraining force in the first area was clearly the team's losing record. But, more interestingly, discussion revealed two other dampers on enjoyment: the coach's obsession with winning and his infectiously gloomy behaviour when the team failed. The main restraining force in the second area proved to be the lack of socializing among team members in non-game situations. The helping forces in the first area included the sense of humour possessed by several members and the confession by most players that winning wasn't nearly as important to them as everyone had suspected. The helping force in the second area was the *desire* of all team members to become better friends. In addition, the fact that members shared many interests was a significant plus.

It's important to realize that most problems have many impelling and restraining forces, all of which need to be identified during this stage. This may call for another round of research. After the force field is laid out, the group is ready to move on to the next step—namely, deciding how to strengthen the impelling forces and weaken the restraining ones.

Develop Creative Solutions

After the group has set up a list of criteria for success, the next job is to develop a number of ways to reach its goal. Considering more than one solution is important, because the first solution may not be the best one. During this development stage, creativity is essential.[12] The biggest danger is the tendency of members to defend their own idea and criticize others' ideas. This kind of behaviour leads to two problems. First, evaluative criticism almost guarantees a defensive reaction from members whose ideas have been attacked. Second, evaluative criticism stifles creativity. People who have just heard an idea rebuked—however politely—will find it hard even to think of more alternatives, let alone share them openly and risk possible criticism. The following strategies can help groups to be creative and maintain a positive climate.

force field analysis
A method of problem analysis that identifies the forces contributing to resolution of the problem and the forces that inhibit its resolution.

Cultural Idiom
damper
Something that reduces or restricts.

Creativity Killers in Group Discussion

Nothing squelches creativity like criticism. Although evaluating ideas is an important part of problem-solving, judging suggestions too early can discourage members from sharing potentially valuable ideas. Here is a list of creativity-stopping statements that people should avoid making in the development phase of group work.

"That's ridiculous."
"It'll never work."
"You're wrong."

"What a crazy idea!"
"We tried it before, and it didn't work."
"It's too expensive."
"There's no point in talking about it."
"It's never been done like that."
"We could look like fools."
"It's too big a job."
"We could never do that."
"It's too risky."
"You don't know what you're talking about."

Brainstorm

Probably the best-known strategy for encouraging creativity and avoiding the dangers just described is **brainstorming**.[13] There are four important rules connected with this strategy:

1. *Criticism is discouraged.* As we have already said, nothing will stop the flow of ideas more quickly than negative evaluation.
2. *"Freewheeling" is encouraged.* Sometimes even the most outlandish ideas prove workable, and even an impractical suggestion might trigger a workable idea.
3. *Quantity is sought.* The more ideas that are generated, the better the chances of coming up with a good one.
4. *Combination and improvement are desirable.* Members are encouraged to "piggyback" by modifying ideas already suggested and to combine previous suggestions.

Although brainstorming is a popular creativity booster, it isn't a guaranteed strategy for developing novel and high-quality ideas. In some experiments, individuals working alone were able to come up with a greater number of high-quality ideas than were small groups.[14]

Use the Nominal Group Technique

Because people in groups often can't resist the tendency to criticize one another's ideas, the **nominal group technique** was developed. It retains the key elements of brainstorming but lets members present their ideas without being attacked. As the following steps show, cycles of individual work alternate with group discussion:

1. Each member works alone to develop a list of possible solutions.
2. In round-robin fashion, each member in turn offers one item from his or her list. The item is listed on a chart visible to everyone. Other members may ask questions to clarify an idea, but no evaluation is allowed during this step.
3. Each member privately ranks his or her choice of the ideas in order, from most preferable (five points) to least preferable (one point). The rankings are collected, and the top ideas are retained as the most promising solutions.
4. A free discussion of the top ideas is held. At this point critical thinking (though not personal criticism) is encouraged. The group continues the discussion until a decision is reached, either by majority vote or by consensus.

Evaluate Possible Solutions

After it has listed possible solutions, the group can evaluate the usefulness of each. One good way of identifying the most workable solutions is to ask three questions:

1. *Will this proposal produce the desired changes?* One way to find out is to see whether it successfully overcomes the restraining forces in your force field analysis.
2. *Can the proposal be implemented?* Can the members strengthen impelling forces and weaken restraining ones? Can they influence others to do so? If not, the plan isn't a good one.
3. *Does the proposal contain any serious disadvantages?* Sometimes the cost of achieving a goal is too great. For example, one way to raise money for a group is to rob a bank. Although this plan might be workable, it creates more problems than it solves.

---

brainstorming
A method for creatively generating ideas in groups by minimizing criticism and encouraging a large quantity of ideas without regard to their workability or ownership by individual members.

Cultural Idiom
piggyback
To add onto something.

nominal group technique
Method for including the ideas of all group members in a problem-solving session.

Cultural Idiom
round-robin fashion
To go around in a circle, one after another.

Implement the Plan

Everyone who makes New Year's resolutions knows the difference between making a decision and carrying it out. There are several important steps in developing and implementing a plan of action:

1. *Identify specific tasks to be accomplished.* What needs to be done? Even a relatively simple job usually involves several steps. Now is the time to anticipate all the tasks facing the group. Remember everything now, and you'll avoid a last-minute rush later.
2. *Determine necessary resources.* Identify the equipment, material, and other resources the group will need in order to get the job done.
3. *Define individual responsibilities.* Who will do what? Do all the members know their jobs? The safest plan here is to put everyone's duties in writing, including the due date. This might sound compulsive, but experience shows that it increases the chance of having jobs done on time.
4. *Provide for emergencies.* Murphy's Law states, "Whatever can go wrong, will." Anyone experienced in group work knows the truth of this law. People forget or welsh on their obligations, get sick, or quit. Machinery breaks down. (One corollary of Murphy's Law is "The copying machine will be out of order whenever it's most needed.'") Whenever possible, you ought to develop contingency plans to cover foreseeable problems. Probably the single best suggestion we can give here is to plan on having all work done well ahead of the deadline, knowing that, even with last-minute problems, your time cushion will allow you to finish on time.

Follow Up on the Solution

Even the best plans usually require some modifications after they're put into practice. You can improve the group's effectiveness and minimize disappointment by following two steps:

1. *Meet periodically to evaluate progress.* Follow-up meetings should be part of virtually every good plan. The best time to schedule these meetings is as you put the group's plan to work. At that time, a good leader or member will suggest: "Let's get together in a week (or a few days or a month, depending on the nature of the task). We can see how things are going and take care of any problems."
2. *Revise the group's approach as necessary.* These follow-up meetings will often go beyond simply congratulating everyone for coming up with a good solution. Problems are bound to arise, and these periodic meetings, at which the key players are present, are the place to solve them.

Although these steps provide a useful outline for solving problems, they are most valuable as a general set of guidelines and not as a precise formula that every group should follow. As

Table 10.2 suggests, certain parts of the model may need emphasis depending on the nature of the specific problem; the general approach will give virtually any group a useful way to consider and solve a problem.

Despite its advantages, the rational, systematic problem-solving approach isn't perfect. The old computer saying "garbage in, garbage out" applies here: if the group doesn't possess creative talent, a rational and systematic approach to solving problems won't do much good. Despite its drawbacks, the rational approach does increase the odds that a group can solve problems successfully. Following the guidelines—even imperfectly—will help members analyze the problem, come up with solutions, and carry them out better than they could probably do without a plan.

Developmental Stages in Problem-Solving Groups

When it comes to solving problems in groups, research shows that the shortest distance to a solution isn't always a straight line. Communication scholar Aubrey Fisher analyzed tape recordings of problem-solving groups and discovered that many successful groups seem to follow a four-stage process when arriving at a decision.[15] As you read about his findings, visualize how they have applied to problem-solving groups in your experience.

In the **orientation stage**, members approach the problem and one another tentatively. In some groups people may not know one another well, and even in ones where they are well acquainted they may not know one another's positions on the issue at hand. For these reasons, people are reluctant to take a stand during the orientation stage. Rather than state their own positions clearly and unambiguously, they test out possible ideas cautiously and rather politely. There is little disagreement. This cautiousness doesn't mean that members agree with one another; rather, they are sizing up the situation before asserting themselves. The orientation stage can be viewed as a calm before the storm.

After members understand the problem and become acquainted, a successful group enters the **conflict stage**. During this stage, members take strong positions and defend them against those who oppose their viewpoint. Coalitions are likely to form, and the discussion may become polarized. The conflict needn't be personal: it can focus on the issues at hand while preserving

---

orientation stage
A stage in problem-solving groups when members become familiar with one another's position and tentatively volunteer their own.

conflict stage
A stage in problem-solving groups when members openly defend their positions and question those of others.

Cultural Idiom
sizing up
To assess something or someone.

TABLE 10.2 Adapting Problem-Solving Methods to Special Circumstances

Circumstances	Method
Members have strong feelings about the problem.	Consider allowing a period of emotional ventilation before systematic problem-solving.
Task difficulty is high.	Follow the structure of the problem-solving method carefully.
Many possible solutions.	Emphasize brainstorming.
High level of member acceptance required.	Carefully define needs of all members, and seek solutions that satisfy all needs.
High level of technical quality required.	Emphasize evaluation of ideas; consider inviting outside experts.

Source: Adapted from "Adapting Problem-Solving Methods", *Effective Group Discussion*, 10th ed., John Brilhart and Gloria Galanes, p. 291. Copyright © 2001.

the members' respect for one another. Even when the climate does grow contentious, conflict seems to be a necessary stage in group development. The give-and-take of discussion tests the quality of ideas, and weaker ones may suffer a well-deserved death here.[16]

After a period of conflict, effective groups move to an **emergence stage**. One idea might emerge as the best one, or the group might combine the best parts of several plans into a new solution. As they approach consensus, members back off from their dogmatic positions. Statements become more tentative again: "I guess that's a pretty good idea;" "I can see why you think that way."

Finally, an effective group reaches the **reinforcement stage**. At this point not only do members accept the group's decision, but they also endorse it. Whereas members used evidence to back up differing positions in the conflict stage, now they find evidence that will support the decision. Even if members disagree with the outcome, they do not voice their concerns. There is an unspoken drive toward consensus and harmony.

Ongoing groups can expect to move through this four-stage process with each new issue, so that their interaction takes on a cyclic pattern (see Figure 10.1). In fact, a group that deals with several issues at once might find itself in a different stage for each problem. In one series of studies, slightly less than 50 per cent of the problem-solving groups examined followed this pattern.[17] The same research showed that a smaller percentage of groups (about 30 per cent) didn't follow a cyclical pattern. Instead, they skipped the preliminary phases and focused on the solution.

What is the significance of the findings? They tell us that, like children growing toward adulthood, many groups can expect to pass through phases. Knowing that these phases are natural and predictable can be reassuring. It can help curb your impatience when the group

> (3) **emergence stage**
> A stage in problem-solving when the group moves from conflict toward a single solution.
>
> (4) **reinforcement stage**
> A stage in problem-solving groups when members endorse the decision they have made.

> *Who decides when the applause should die down? It seems like it's a group decision; everyone begins to say to themselves at the same time, "Well, okay, that's enough of that."*
>
> **George Carlin, comedian**

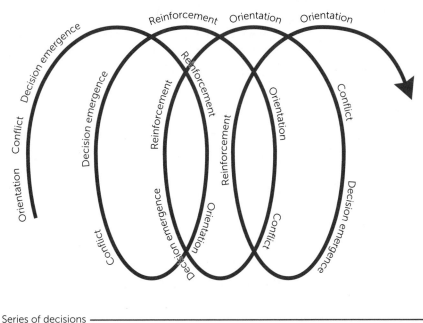

FIGURE 10.1 Cyclical Stages in an Ongoing Problem-Solving Group

Source: From John K. Brilhart, Gloria J. Galanes, and Katherine Adams, *Effective Group Discussion*, 10th ed. (New York: McGraw-Hill, 2001), p. 335. Reproduced with permission of The McGraw-Hill Companies.

COMMUNICATING ONLINE

Ten Tips for Running a Successful Crowdfunding Campaign

Crowdfunding platforms can open doors for entrepreneurs because they offer access to capital without having to navigate through the complicated traditional channels such as venture capital and angel investors. In addition, crowdfunding provides entrepreneurs with a way to engage their customer base and involve them in the exciting start-up phase of their company, all the while getting their product out into the market.

So for all of the budding entrepreneurs out there with big ideas and dreams of making them a reality, here are ten tips I have learned from my experience running a crowdfunding campaign:

1. *Create a prototype of your idea*. Crowdfunding campaigns are most successful when you have built the foundation of the project and are now asking for support to help take it to the next level. It also shows your belief in the project as you have invested time and personal money in the venture, which will support the all around credibility of your campaign.

2. *Pick your platform*. As the popularity of crowdfunding increases, so do the number of platforms available. Kickstarter and Indiegogo are the two largest. Other platforms to look into are: Crowdfunder, RocketHub, and Quirky.

3. *Build your project page*. Research similar projects that have been successful and make note of the type of detail they included on their page. Your project page is your opportunity to sell your idea and engage potential supporters to become involved in what you are doing and contribute to your campaign, so make sure it is well written with a clear objective—and includes pictures!

4. *Include video*. Campaigns with short videos (less than three minutes) are 50 per cent more successful than those without. A digital camera or smartphone will do just fine if you don't have access to more sophisticated equipment. It is also useful to watch the videos of similar campaigns to yours to see how they made them.

5. *Decide on your perks*. Perks are what people get for contributing to your campaign—they're the incentive to get involved. If you're launching a product with a tangible good, you should offer this as your perk. If you are raising money for an artistic endeavor then offer some way for the contributors to get involved, like a visit on set of a documentary, or previews to chapters of the book you are looking to publish. Be sure to include a $25-level perk, as statistically this is the most contributed dollar amount to crowdfunding campaigns.

6. *Set up your payment structure*. Different sites use different methods of payment, so make sure you look into what is required to set it up on your chosen site seven to ten days before you plan to go live. Indiegogo uses PayPal, but you need to upgrade to a premium account and verify your bank information, which can take up to seven days. You don't want to be all ready to go live and have no avenue to accept funding!

is feeling its way through an orientation stage. It can also help you feel less threatened when the inevitable and necessary conflicts take place. Understanding the nature of emergence and reinforcement can help you know when it is time to stop arguing and seek consensus.

Maintaining Positive Relationships

The task-related advice in the preceding pages will be little help if the members of a group don't get along. We therefore need to look at some ways to maintain good relationships among members. Many of the principles described earlier in this book apply here. Because these principles are so important, we will review them.

7. *Build a media list*. Research relevant media outlets to your project—include online magazines, newspapers, blogs, and YouTube channels. Make an Excel sheet with the name of the media outlet, the type of content they write on, as well as contact information. If you know anyone (friends of friends) who is an influencer, reach out to them to engage and involve them in your campaign. Your media list is never complete, so keep adding to it as you come across new blogs and journalists who you think would be interested in your story.

8. *Start pitching the media*. Write a skeleton of a pitch that describes who you are, what your project is, and why you are crowdfunding to get it off the ground. Beyond this core information, each e-mail should be tailored to the specific person/publication you are addressing. Include something you like about their site, or reasons you find their content engaging and informative. Keep these e-mails short and to the point, as bloggers and journalists receive hundreds of pitches a day. Start reaching out a few weeks before you plan to launch your campaign and then follow up once it is live. Only a small percentage will respond, which is why it is important to be persistent and continue to build your list and follow up.

9. *Reach out to family and friends*. Friends and family are going to be the backbone of your campaign, so be sure to get them involved early. A few weeks before you plan to go live send an e-mail to your extended network of family and friends telling them about your upcoming project, explaining what crowdfunding is, and preparing them for launch day.

Two days before you launch pre-write personalized e-mails that you will then set up to send out the morning of your launch. Yes, this is a lot of work, but you are asking for their money and support—people are more likely to respond to a personalized e-mail than to a mass distribution list. You should depend on friends and family for the first 20 to 30 per cent (and ideally get them to contribute in the first few days of going live). Statistically, strangers start getting involved in campaigns beyond the 20 to 30 per cent funded mark.

10. *Keep the energy going*: After the initial burst of activity that will come with your launch, the next phase is keeping up the momentum. That means focusing on getting more press and spreading the word about your exciting new project. Staying engaged and involved is key. And make sure you send frequent updates to your supporters. Updates are notifications that are sent to your contributors, or anyone who has elected to "follow" your campaign to keep them up to date on your progress. They can be anything from pictures, to recent press coverage, to what work you did on your project that day. Campaigns with more than 30 updates raise 400 per cent more funding than those with zero to five updates.

—Michelle Shemilt, *The Globe and Mail*, Friday 5 July 2013

Basic Skills

Groups are most effective when members feel good about one another.[18] Probably the most important ingredient in good personal relationships is mutual respect, and the best way to demonstrate respect for the other person is to listen carefully. A more natural tendency, of course, is to assume you understand the other members' positions and to interrupt or ignore them. Even if you are right, however, this tendency can create a residue of ill feelings. On the other hand, careful listening can at least improve the communication climate—and it may even teach you something.

Groups are bound to disagree sooner or later. When they do, the win–win problem-solving methods outlined in Chapter 7 boost the odds of solving the immediate issue in the most

> *Never doubt that a small group of thoughtful, committed citizens can change the world; indeed, it's the only thing that ever does.*
>
> **Margaret Mead, author and cultural anthropologist**

constructive way.[19] As you read in Chapter 9, taking votes and letting the majority rule can often leave a sizable minority whose unhappiness may haunt the group's future work. Consensus is harder to reach in the short term but far more beneficial in the long term.

Building Cohesiveness

Cohesiveness can be defined as the totality of forces that causes members to feel themselves part of a group and makes them want to remain in that group. You might think of cohesiveness as the glue that bonds individuals together, giving them a collective sense of identity.

Highly cohesive groups communicate differently than less cohesive ones. Members spend more time interacting, and there are more expressions of positive feelings for one another. They report more satisfaction with the group and its work. In addition, cohesive groups have greater control over the behaviour of their members.[20] With characteristics like these, it's no surprise that highly cohesive groups have the potential to be productive. In fact, one study revealed that cohesiveness proved to be the best predictor of a group's performance, both initially and over time.[21]

Despite its advantages, cohesiveness is no guarantee of success: if the group is united in supporting unproductive norms, members will feel close but won't get the job done. For example, consider a group of employees who have a boss they think is incompetent and unfair. They might grow quite cohesive in their opposition to the perceived tyranny, spending hours after (or during) work swapping complaints. They might even organize protests, work slowdowns, grievances to their union, or mass resignations. All these responses would boost cohesiveness, but they would not necessarily make the company more successful or help the employees.

Research has disclosed a curvilinear relationship between cohesiveness and productivity: up to a certain point, productivity increases as group members become a unified team. Beyond this point, however, the attraction that members feel for one another begins to interfere with the group's efficient functioning. Members may enjoy one another's company, but this enjoyment can keep them from focusing on the job at hand.

The goal, then, is to boost cohesiveness in a way that also gets the job done. There are eight factors that can contribute to both these objectives.

1. Shared or Compatible Goals

People draw closer when they share a similar aim or one solution will satisfy all of them, even if their specific goals are not the same. For example, members of a conservation group might have little in common until a part of the countryside they all value is threatened by development. Some members might value the land because of its beauty; others because it provides a place to hunt or fish; and still others because the nearby scenery increases the value of their property. As long as their goals are compatible, this collection of individuals will find a bond that draws them together.

2. Progress toward These Goals

While a group is making progress, members feel highly cohesive; when progress stops, cohesiveness decreases. All other things being equal, players on an athletic team feel closest when the team is winning. During extended losing streaks, players are likely to feel less positive about the team and less willing to identify themselves as members of the group.

3. Shared Norms and Values

Although successful groups will tolerate and even thrive on some differences in members' attitudes and behaviour, wide variation in definitions of what actions or beliefs are proper will reduce cohesiveness. If enough members hold different ideas of what behaviour is acceptable, the group is likely to break up. Disagreements over values or norms can arise in many areas, from the kind of humour or degree of candour regarded as acceptable to finances or the proportions of time allotted to work and play.

4. Lack of Perceived Threat between Members

Members of cohesive groups do not see one another as posing any threat to their status, dignity, or well-being (material or emotional). By contrast, the perception that such interpersonal threats do exist can be very destructive. Often competition arises within groups, and as a result members feel threatened. There may be a struggle over whom will be the nominal leader. Some members may perceive others as seeking to take over a functional role (problem solver, information giver, and so on), through either competition or criticism. Sometimes the threat is real, and sometimes it's only imagined, but in either case the group must neutralize it or face the consequences of reduced cohesiveness.

5. Interdependence of Members

Groups become cohesive when individual members' needs can be satisfied only with the help of other members. When a job can be done just as well by one person alone, the need for group membership decreases. Food co-operatives, neighbourhood yard sales, and community political campaigns are all examples of group efforts in which working together allows participants to achieve goals that they could not achieve if they acted alone.

Cultural Idiom
bickering
To quarrel.

6. Threat from Outside the Group

When members perceive a threat to the group's existence or image (groups have self-concepts, just as individuals do), they grow closer together. Almost everyone knows of a family whose members seem to fight constantly among themselves—until an outsider criticizes one of them. At this point the internal bickering stops, and for the moment the group unites against its common enemy. The same principle also works on a national scale when conflicting groups put aside their differences and join forces in the face of external aggression.

7. Mutual Perceived Attractiveness and Friendship

The factor of mutual attraction and friendship is somewhat circular because friendship and mutual attraction often are a result of the points just listed. Nevertheless, groups often do become close simply

---

CRITICAL THINKING PROBE
The Pros and Cons of Cohesiveness

1. Based on the information on pages 388–90 of this chapter and your own experiences, give examples of groups that meet each of the following descriptions:
   a. a level of cohesiveness so low that it interferes with productivity;
   b. an optimal level of cohesiveness; and
   c. a level of cohesiveness so high that it interferes with productivity.

2. For your answers to (a) and (c), offer advice on how the level of cohesiveness could be adjusted to improve productivity.

3. Are there ever situations where maximizing cohesiveness is more important than maximizing productivity? Explain your answer, supporting it with examples.

because the members like each other. A social group is a good example of a group that stays together because its members enjoy one another's company.

8. Shared Group Experiences

When members have been through some unusual or trying experience, they draw together. This explains why soldiers who have been in combat together often feel close and stay in touch for years after; it also accounts for initiation rituals such as the ordeal of fraternity pledging. Many societies have rituals in which all members take part, thus increasing the group's cohesiveness.

It's important to realize that the eight factors just described interact with one another, often in contradictory ways. For instance, group members who have been through thick and thin together may begin to lose their cohesion once that experience is over. Relationships can be strained when friends become less dependent on one another, especially if they begin to feel that the roles they played in the past are no longer appropriate. In cases like this, cohesiveness can be figured as the net sum of all attracting and dividing forces.

> **Cultural Idiom**
> **through thick and thin**
> To get through the good times and the bad.

Leadership and Power in Groups

Leadership . . . power . . . influence. For most of us, being in control of events ranks not far below parenthood in the hierarchy of values. We're asked, "What are you, a leader or a follower?" and we know which position is the better one. Even in groups without designated leaders, some members are more influential than others, and those who aren't out front at least some of the time are likely to feel frustrated.

The following pages will focus on how communication operates to establish influence. We will begin by looking at sources of power in groups, showing that not all influence rests with the person who is nominally in charge. We will then take a look at the communication behaviours that work best when one communicator is designated as the leader—or wants to acquire that role.

Power in Groups

> **power**
> The ability to influence others' thoughts and/or actions.

We can begin by defining **power** as the ability to influence others. A few examples show that influence can appear in many forms:[22]

- In a tense meeting, apartment dwellers are arguing over crowded parking and late-night noise. One tenant cracks a joke and lightens up the tense atmosphere.
- A project team at work is trying to come up with a new way to attract customers. The youngest member, fresh from a college advertising class, suggests a winning idea.
- Workers are upset after the boss passes over a popular colleague and hires a newcomer for a management position. Despite their anger, they accept the decision after the colleague persuades them that she is not interested in a career move anyhow.
- A teacher motivates students to meet a deadline by awarding bonus points for projects that are turned in early and deducting points for ones turned in late.

These examples suggest that power comes in a variety of forms. We will examine each of them now.

Legitimate Power

> **legitimate power**
> The ability to influence a group owing to one's position within it.

Sometimes the ability to influence others comes from **legitimate power** (also known as "position power"). Legitimate power originates in the holder's title—supervisor, parent, or professor, for example. In many cases we follow the directions of others without knowing much about their qualifications, simply because we respect the role they occupy. In church we honour the request of the minister to stand up or to sit down, and in courts we rise at judges' approach primarily because their positions confer authority on them.

Social scientists use the term **nominal leader** to label the person who is officially designated as being in charge of a group. But nominal leaders are not the only people with legitimate power. Traffic directors at road repair sites are unlikely to be in charge of the project, yet they possess legitimate power in the eyes of motorists, who stop and start at their command.

The easiest way to acquire legitimate power is to have it conferred upon you by an outside authority. But appointment isn't the only path to legitimate power: even in groups that start out with no official leader, members can acquire legitimate power by the acknowledgment of others. Juries elect forepersons, committees elect chairpersons, teams choose captains, and negotiating groups elect spokespeople. The subject of leadership emergence has been studied extensively.[23] Researchers have discovered several communicator characteristics that members who emerge as leaders possess: they speak up in group discussions without dominating others, they demonstrate their competence on the subject being discussed, they observe group norms, and they have the support of other influential members.

> **nominal leader**
> The person who is identified by title as the leader of a group.
>
> **coercive power**
> The power to influence others by the threat or imposition of unpleasant consequences.

Coercive Power

Coercive power may be wielded when influence comes from the threat or actual imposition of some unpleasant consequences. In school, at home, on the job, and in many other settings, we sometimes do what others tell us, not because of any respect for the wisdom of their decisions but rather because the results of not obeying would be unpleasant. Economic hardship, social disapproval, undesirable work, even physical punishment—all are coercive forces that can shape behaviour.

There are three reasons why coercion often isn't the most effective type of power. First, it's likely to create a negative communication climate because nobody likes to be threatened. Second, it can produce a "boomerang effect," leading some people to defy instructions and do exactly the opposite of what they've been told. Third, coercion may be used to tell others what not to do instead of establishing a clear idea of what you *do* want them to do. Telling an unproductive member, "If you can't contribute useful information, we'll kick you out of the group" doesn't offer much advice about what would count as "useful information."

> ### 🎥 COMMUNICATION ON-SCREEN
>
> #### *Star Trek* (2009)
>
> **Directed by J.J. Abrams.**
>
> In this "re-boot" of the classic 1960s television series, a rewriting of history by villainous Romulans results in a brash and undisciplined James T. Kirk (Chris Pine) growing up fatherless and joining Starfleet Academy late as a jaded 22-year-old. Called away on his first mission as an untested third-year cadet of dubious professionalism, a much more familiar Kirk begins to emerge in a crisis situation. Kirk steps into a leadership vacuum and earns the respect of his crewmates, including his greatest skeptic, Spock (Zachary Quinto).
>
> Kirk's leadership emergence is built around several of his personal attributes: not only does he bring savvy and courage to a brewing galactic confrontation, but he also leverages the talents of his crewmates, who feed off his confidence.

Social scientists say that coercion has the best chance of success when it involves denial of an expected reward rather than the imposition of a negative consequence.[24] For example, cancelling a promised bonus for members of a working group that doesn't meet its deadline is better than reducing their salaries. Even under circumstances like this, however, coercion alone is not as effective as the next kind of power: rewards.

Reward Power

Reward power involves the grant or promise of desirable consequences. Rewards come in a variety of forms. The most obvious are material reinforcers: money, awards, and so on. Other rewards can be social in nature. The praise of someone you respect can be a powerful motivator. Even spending time with people you like can be reinforcing.

Rewards don't come only from the official leader of a group. The goodwill of other members can sometimes be even more valuable. In a class group, for example, having your fellow students think highly of you might be a more powerful reward than the grade you could receive from the instructor. In fact, subordinates sometimes can reward nominal leaders just as much as the other way around. A boss might work hard to accommodate employees in order to keep them happy, for example.

Expert Power

Expert power exists when we are influenced by people because of what we believe they know or can do. For example, when a medical emergency occurs, most group members would gladly let a doctor, nurse, or paramedic make the decisions because of that person's obvious knowledge. In groups it isn't sufficient to *be* an expert: the other members have to view you as one. This means that it is important to make your qualifications known if you want others to give your opinions extra weight.

---

reward power
The ability to influence others by the granting or promising of desirable consequences.

expert power
The ability to influence others by virtue of one's perceived expertise on the subject in question.

We only need to look at what we are really doing in the world and at home and we'll know what it is to be Canadian.

Adrienne Clarkson, former Governor General of Canada

Information Power ⑤

As its name implies, **information power** comes from a member's knowledge that he or she can help the group reach its goal. Not all useful information comes from experts with special credentials. For instance, a fundraising group seeking donations from local businesses might profit from the knowledge that one member has about which merchants are hospitable to the group's cause. Likewise, a class group working on a term project might benefit from the knowledge of one student who has taken other classes from the instructor who will be grading their work.

Referent Power ⑥

Referent power flows from the respect, liking, and trust that others have for a member. If you have high referent power, you may be able to persuade others to follow your lead simply because they believe in you or because they are willing to do you a favour. Members acquire referent power by behaving in ways that others in the group admire and by being genuinely likable. The kinds of confirming communication behaviours described in Chapter 7 can go a long way toward boosting referent power. Listening to others' ideas, honouring their contributions, and taking a win–win approach to meeting their needs all lead to liking and respect.

After our look at various ways group members can influence one another, three important characteristics of power in groups become clearer:[25]

1. *Power is group-centred.* Power isn't something that an individual possesses. Instead, it is conferred by the group. You may be an expert on a particular subject, but if the other members don't think you are qualified to talk, you won't have expert power. You might try to reward other people by praising their contributions, but if they don't value your compliments, then all the praise in the world won't influence them.

2. *Power is distributed among group members.* Power rarely belongs to just one person. Even when a group has an official leader, other members usually have the power to affect what happens. This influence can be positive, coming from information, expertise, or social reinforcement. It can also be negative, coming from punishing behaviours such as criticizing or withholding the contributions that the group needs to succeed. You can appreciate how power is distributed among members by considering the effect that just one member can have by not showing up for meetings or failing to carry out his or her part of the job.

3. *Power isn't an either–or concept.* It's incorrect to assume that power is an either–or concept that members either possess or lack. Rather, it is a matter of degree. Instead of talking about someone as "powerful" or "powerless," it's more accurate to talk about how much influence he or she exerts.

By now you can see that power is available to every member of a group. Table 10.3 outlines ways of acquiring the various types of power we have just examined.

What Makes Leaders Effective?

Even though power is distributed among members of a group, it is still important to explore the special role played by the nominal leader. In the next few pages we will describe the communication-related factors that contribute to leader effectiveness.

> **information power**
> The ability to influence others by virtue of the otherwise obscure information one possesses.
>
> **referent power**
> The ability to influence others by virtue of the degree to which one is liked or respected.

Table 10.3 Methods for Acquiring Power in Small Groups

Power isn't the only goal to seek in a group. Sometimes being a follower is a comfortable and legitimate role to play. But when you do seek power, the following methods outline specific ways to shape the way others behave and the decisions they make.

Legitimate Authority

1. Become an authority figure. If possible, get yourself appointed or elected to a position of leadership. Do so by following Steps 2–5.

2. Speak up without dominating others. Power comes from visibility, but don't antagonize others by shutting them out.

3. Demonstrate competence on the subject. Enhance legitimate authority by demonstrating information and expertise power.

4. Follow group norms. Show that you respect the group's customs.

5. Gain support of other members. Don't try to carve out authority on your own. Gain the visible support of other influential members.

Information Power

1. Provide useful but scarce or restricted information. Show others that you possess information that isn't available elsewhere.

2. Be certain the information is accurate. One piece of mistaken information can waste the group's time, lead to bad decisions, and destroy your credibility. Check your facts before speaking up.

Expert Power

1. Make sure members are aware of your qualifications. Let others know that you have expertise in the area being discussed.

2. Don't act superior. You will squander your authority if you imply your expertise makes you superior to others. Use your knowledge for the good of the group, not ego building.

Reward and Coercive Power

1. Try to use rewards as a first resort and punishment as a last resort. People respond better to pleasant consequences than unpleasant ones, so take a positive approach first.

2. Make rewards and punishments clear in advance. Let people know your expectations and their consequences. Don't surprise them.

3. Be generous with praise. Let others know that you recognize their desirable behaviour.

Referent Power

1. Enhance your attractiveness to group members. Do whatever you can to gain the liking and respect of other members without compromising your principles.

2. Learn effective presentation skills. Present your ideas clearly and effectively in order to boost your credibility.

Source: Adapted from J. Dan Rothwell, *In Mixed Company: Small Group Communication*, 3rd edn (Fort Worth, TX: Harcourt Brace, 1998), 252–72.

trait theories of leadership
The belief that it is possible to identify leaders by personal traits, such as intelligence, appearance, or sociability.

Trait Analysis

Over 2000 years ago, Aristotle proclaimed, "From the hour of their birth some are marked out for subjugation, and others for command."[26] This is a radical expression of **trait theories of leadership**, sometimes labelled the "great man" (or "great woman") approach. Social scientists began their studies of leader effectiveness by conducting literally hundreds of studies that

Table 10.4 Some Traits Associated with Leaders

Factor No.	Factors Appearing in Three or More Studies	Frequency
1	Social and interpersonal skills	16
2	Technical skills	18
3	Administrative skills	12
4	Leadership effectiveness and achievement	15
5	Social nearness, friendliness	18
6	Intellectual skills	11
7	Maintaining a cohesive work group	9
8	Maintaining coordination and teamwork	7
9	Task motivation and application	17
10	General impression	12
11	Group task supportiveness	17
12	Maintaining standards of performance	5
13	Willingness to assume responsibility	10
14	Emotional balance and control	15
15	Informal group control	4
16	Nurturant behaviour	4
17	Ethical conduct, personal integrity	10
18	Communication, verbality	6
19	Ascendance, dominance, decisiveness	11
20	Physical energy	6
21	Experience and activity	4
22	Mature, cultured	3
23	Courage, daring	4
24	Aloof, distant	3
25	Creative, independent	5
26	Conforming	5

Source: Reprinted with the permission of The Free Press, a Division of Simon & Schuster Adult Publishing Group, from BASS & STOGDILL'S HANDBOOK OF LEADERSHIP by Bernard M. Bass. Copyright © 1974, 1981, 1990 by The Free Press. All rights reserved.

compared leaders to non-leaders. The results of all this research were mixed. Yet, as Table 10.4 shows, a number of distinguishing characteristics did emerge in several categories.

The majority of these categories involved social skills. For example, leaders talk more often and more fluently and are regarded as more popular, co-operative, and socially skilful.[27] Leaders also possess goal-related skills that help groups perform their tasks. They are somewhat more intelligent, possess more task-relevant information, and are more dependable than other members. Just as important, leaders want the role and act in ways that will help them achieve it. Finally, physical appearance seems to play a role in leadership. As a rule, leaders tend to be slightly taller, heavier, and physically more attractive than other members. They also seem to possess greater athletic ability and stamina.

Canadian researchers from the Royal Military College and the University of Western Ontario studied 174 officers in the Canadian Forces to see if they could demonstrate a link between personality traits and leadership success. They found that energy level, internal control, and, especially, dominance were associated with leadership.

On the other hand, trait theories have limited practical value. More recent studies have found that many other factors are important as well, and that not everyone who possesses "leadership traits" becomes a leader. In the 1980s two organizational researchers, Warren Bennis and Burt Nanus, interviewed 90 American leaders, including Ray Kroc, the founder of McDonald's; John Robinson, a professional football coach; and John H. Johnson, publisher of *Ebony* magazine. Their analysis led to the conclusion that the principle "leaders must be charismatic" is a myth.

> Some are, most aren't. Among the ninety there were a few—but damned few—who probably correspond to our fantasies of some "divine inspiration," that "grace under stress" we associated with JFK or the beguiling capacity to spellbind for which we remember Churchill. Our leaders were all "too human;" they were short and tall, articulate and inarticulate, dressed for success and dressed for failure, and there was virtually nothing in terms of physical appearance, personality, or style that set them apart from their followers. Our guess is that it operates in the other direction; that is, charisma is the result of effective leadership, not the other way around, and that those who are good at it are granted a certain amount of respect and even awe by their followers, which increases the bond of attraction between them.[28]

Leadership Style

As researchers began to realize that personality traits aren't the key to effective leadership, they began to look in other areas. Some scholars theorized that good leadership is a matter of communication style—the way leaders deal with members. Three basic approaches were identified: authoritarian, democratic, and *laissez-faire.*

The first approach was an **authoritarian leadership style** that relied on legitimate, coercive, and reward power to influence others. The second approach was a **democratic leadership style**, which invited other members to share in decision-making. The third approach was the *laissez-faire* **leadership style,** in which the leader gave up the power to dictate, transforming the group into a leaderless collection of equals. Early research suggested that the democratic style produced the highest-quality results,[29] but later studies found that matters weren't so simple.[30] For instance, groups with autocratic leaders proved more productive under stressful conditions, but democratically led groups did better when the situation was non-stressful.[31]

Research shows that there is some merit to the styles approach. One extensive study of more than 12,000 managers showed that a democratic approach to leadership correlated highly with success. Effective managers usually sought the advice and opinions of their subordinates, whereas average or unsuccessful ones were more authoritarian and less concerned with the welfare or ideas of the people who reported to them.[32] Despite this fact, a democratic approach isn't always the best one. For example, an autocratic approach gets the job done much more quickly, which can be essential in situations where time is of the essence.

Some researchers have focused on leadership style from a different perspective. Robert R. Blake and Anne A. McCanse developed an approach based on the relationship between the designated leader's concern with the task and with the relationships among members.[33] Their **Leadership Grid** consists of a two-dimensional model, pictured in Figure 10.2. The horizontal axis measures the leader's "concern for production." This involves a focus on accomplishing the organizational task, with efficiency being the main concern. The vertical axis

---

authoritarian leadership style
A leadership style in which the designated leader uses legitimate, coercive, and reward power to dictate the group's actions.

democratic leadership style
A style in which the nominal leader invites the group's participation in decision-making.

laissez-faire **leadership style**
A style in which the designated leader gives up his or her formal role, transforming the group into a loose collection of individuals.

Leadership Grid
A two-dimensional model that identifies leadership styles as a combination of a concern for people and the task at hand.

measures the leader's concern for people's feelings and ideas. Blake and Mouton suggest that the most effective leader is the one who adopts a 9,9 style—showing high concern for both task and relationships.

Situational Approaches

Most contemporary scholars are convinced that the best style of leadership varies from one set of circumstances to another.[34] In the 1960s, in an effort to pin down which approach works best in a given type of situation, psychologist Fred Fiedler attempted to find out when a task-oriented approach was most effective and when more relationship-oriented approaches were most effective.[35] From his research, Fiedler developed a situational theory of leadership. Although the complete theory is too complex to describe here, the general conclusion of situational leadership is that a leader's style should change with the circumstances. A task-oriented approach works best when conditions are either highly favourable (good leader–member relations, strong leader power, and a clear task structure) or highly unfavourable (poor leader–member relations, weak leader power, and an ambiguous task), whereas a more relationship-oriented approach is appropriate in moderately favourable or moderately unfavourable conditions.

situational leadership
A theory that argues that the most effective leadership style varies according to leader–member relations, the nominal leader's power, and the task structure.

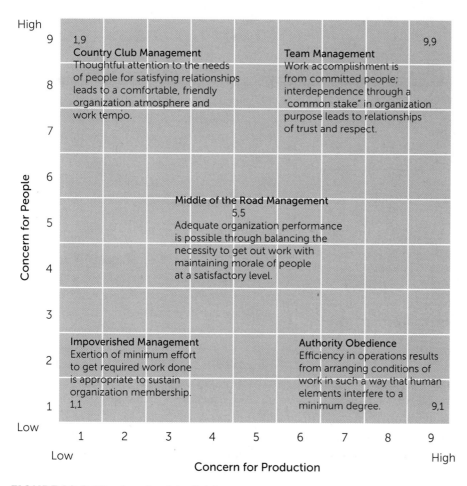

FIGURE 10.2 The Leadership Grid

Source: The Leadership Grid® figure from *Leadership Dilemmas–Grid Solutions*, by Robert R. Blake and Anne Adams McCanse (Houston: Gulf Publishing Co.), p. 29. Copyright © 1991 by Scientific Methods, Inc.

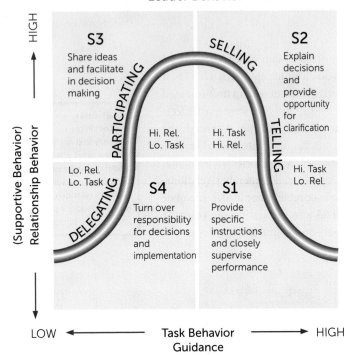

Situational Leadership® Leader Behavior

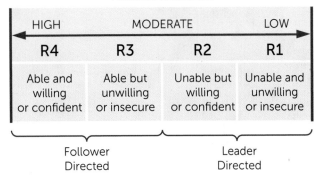

FIGURE 10.3 Hersey's Situational Leadership® Model

Source: © Copyright 2006. Reprinted with permission of the Center for Leadership Studies, Escondido, CA 92025. www.situational.com. All Rights Reserved.

More recently, Paul Hersey has suggested that a leader's focus on task or relational issues should vary according to the "readiness" of the group being led (see Figure 10.3).[36] "Readiness" involves the members' level of motivation, willingness to take responsibility, and the amount of knowledge and experience they have in a given situation. For example, a new, inexperienced group would need more task-related direction, whereas a more experienced group might require more social support and less instruction about how to do the job. A well-seasoned group could probably handle the job well without much supervision at all. Because an employee's readiness changes from one job to another, Hersey suggests that the best way to lead should vary as well.

Overcoming Dangers in Group Discussion

Even groups with the best of intentions often find themselves unable to reach satisfying decisions. At other times, they make decisions that later prove to be wrong. Though there's no foolproof method of guaranteeing high-quality group work, there are several dangers to avoid.

Information Underload and Overload

Information underload occurs when a group lacks information it needs to operate effectively. Sometimes the underload results from overlooking parts of a problem. We know of one group that scheduled a fundraising auction without considering whether there were any other events scheduled for the same time that might attract potential donors. They later found that their event was scheduled opposite an important football game, resulting in a loss of sorely needed funds. In other cases, groups suffer from underload because they simply don't conduct enough research. For example, a group of partners starting a new business has to be aware of all the start-up costs to avoid going bankrupt in the first months of operation. Overlooking one or two important items can make the difference between success and failure.

Sometimes groups can suffer from too much information. **Information overload** occurs when the flow or complexity of material is too great to manage. Having an abundance of information might seem like a blessing, but anyone who has tried to do conscientious library research has become aware of the paralysis that can result from being overwhelmed by an avalanche of books, magazine and newspaper articles, reviews, films, and research studies.

When too much information exists, it is hard to sort out the essential from the unessential. Group expert J. Dan Rothwell offers several tips for coping with information overload.[37] First, specialize whenever possible. Try to parcel out areas of responsibility to each member instead of expecting each member to explore every angle of the topic. Second, be selective. Take a quick look at each piece of information to see whether it has real value for your task. If it doesn't, move on to examine more promising material. Third, limit your search. Information specialists have discovered that there is often a curvilinear relationship between the amount of information a group possesses and the quality of its decision. After a certain point, gathering more material can slow you down without contributing to the quality of your group's decisions.

Unequal Participation

The value of involving group members in making decisions—especially decisions that affect them—is great.[38] When people participate, their loyalty to the group increases. (Your own experience will probably show that most group dropouts were quiet and withdrawn.) Broad-based participation has a second advantage: it increases the amount of resources focused on the problem. As a result, the quality of the group's decisions goes up. Finally, participation increases members' loyalty to the decisions that they played a part in making.

The key to effective participation is balance. Domination by a few vocal members can reduce a group's ability to solve a problem effectively. Research shows that the proposal receiving the largest number of favourable comments is usually the one chosen, even if it isn't the best one.[39] Furthermore, ideas of high-status members (who aren't always talkers) are given more consideration than those of lower-status members.[40] The moral to this story? Don't assume that quantity of speech or the status of the speaker automatically defines the quality of an idea. Instead, seek out and seriously consider the ideas of quieter members.

Not all participation is helpful, of course. It's better to remain quiet than to act out the kind of dysfunctional roles described in Chapter 9—cynic, aggressor, dominator, and so on. Likewise, the comments of a member who is uninformed can waste time. Finally, downright ignorant or mistaken input can distract a group.

You can encourage the useful contributions of quiet members in a variety of ways. First, keep the group small. In groups with three or four members, participation is roughly equal, but after size increases to between five and eight, there is a dramatic gap between the contributions of members.[41] Even in a large group you can increase the contributions of quiet members by soliciting their opinions. This approach may seem obvious, but in their enthusiasm to speak out, more verbal communicators can overlook the people who don't speak up. When normally reticent members do offer information, reinforce their contributions. It isn't necessary to go overboard by gushing about a quiet person's brilliant remark, but a word of thanks and an acknowledgment of the value of an idea increases the odds that the contributor will speak up again in the future. A third strategy is to assign specific tasks to normally quiet members. The need to report on these tasks guarantees that they will speak up. A fourth strategy is to use the nominal group technique (pg. 382), to guarantee that the ideas of all members are heard.

> **information overload**
> Decline in efficiency that occurs when the rate of complexity of material is too great to manage.
>
> **information underload**
> Decline in efficiency that occurs when there is a shortage of the information that is necessary to operate effectively.

> **Cultural Idiom**
> **go overboard**
> To do so much as to be excessive.
>
> **gushing about**
> To be overly enthusiastic.

LOOK, IF YOU'RE GOING TO HANG OUT WITH US, FIRST THING YOU GOTTA' DO IS LOSE THE BELL.

Different strategies can help when the problem is one or more members talking too much—especially when their remarks aren't helpful. If the talkative member is at all sensitive, withholding reinforcement can deliver a diplomatic hint that it may be time to listen more and speak less. A lack of response to an idea or suggestion can work as a hint to cut back on speaking. Don't confuse lack of reinforcement with punishment, however: attacking a member for dominating the group is likely to trigger a defensive reaction and cause more harm than good. If the talkative member doesn't respond to subtle hints, politely expressing a desire to hear from other members can be effective. The next stage in this series of escalating strategies for dealing with dominating members is to question the relevancy of remarks that are apparently off the wall: "I'm confused about what last Saturday's party has to do with the job we have to do today. Am I missing something?"

Pressure to Conform

There's a strong tendency for group members to go along with the crowd, which often results in bad decisions. A classic study by Solomon Asch illustrated this point.[42] College students were shown three lines of different lengths and asked to identify which of them matched with a fourth line. Although the correct answer was obvious, the experiment was a set-up: Asch had instructed all but one member of the experimental groups to vote for the wrong line. As a result, one-third of the uninformed subjects ignored their own good judgment and voted

> **Cultural Idiom**
> **off the wall**
> Something that is unconventional, ridiculous.
>
> **go along with the crowd**
> To agree with the majority.

Justin Trudeau's Feminine Mystique

The new Liberal leader is being portrayed as not manly enough—which won't hurt his polling numbers at all. Those early Conservative attack ads against Justin Trudeau are being widely interpreted as not-so-subtly casting doubt on the new Liberal leader's manliness. Among other telltale elements, they end with Trudeau's name unscrolling across TV screens—with a fairy-tale spray of animated sparkles—in a rather feminine, cursive script. As well, the ads were aired heavily during sports shows, suggesting the target viewer was the hockey-loving male.

But how susceptible is he to being portrayed as not man enough? To make that case, Conservative strategists must overcome the image of Trudeau pummelling then-Tory Sen. Patrick Brazeau (since kicked out of the party's caucus after being charged with assault and sexual assault) in a charity boxing brawl last year. And then there's the factor documented by the photos. . . . The throngs of women Trudeau often attracts, despite his being a married man with two young children, do not appear to be pressing close to him in order to demand that he flesh out his economic policy.

Might male voters be impressed, or will they resent his effect on their wives and girlfriends? The sexes do seem to perceive him differently. An EKOS poll found that 20 per cent of men who'd seen one of the Tory attack ads found it fair, compared to just 10 per cent of women. (Most of both sexes, however, about 70 per cent, thought the ad was unfair, with the rest not sure.)

It's possible the ads, particularly in light of their tactical placement in sports programs, represent a bid to counter a threat Trudeau already poses to the Conservative edge among male voters in recent elections. A Harris/Decima poll, conducted April 18–21, found that Stephen Harper was seen favourably by 44 per cent of men and 37 per cent of women. Trudeau beat him among women, perhaps unsurprisingly, with a 61 per cent favourable score—but was also rated favourably by 53 per cent of men.

John Geddes, *Maclean's*, 2 May 2013

QUESTIONS: These ads are attempting to portray a potential leader in a divisive light. How can bias undermine group cohesion and unity? Who benefits the most from this stereotype that is being constructed for Trudeau?

with the majority. If simple tasks like this one generate such conformity, it is easy to see that following the (sometimes mistaken) crowd is even more likely in the much more complex and ambiguous tasks that most groups face.

What Can We Learn About Leadership From Mark Carney?

Not many managers, when they change jobs, glean the kind of universal praise that greeted Mark Carney when it was announced this week that he will leave the top job at the Bank of Canada to become governor of the Bank of England.

Mr Carney has become the poster boy for the charming, sharp-dressing, get-to-the-point executive that many bosses would like to be, but aren't. So what is it about Mr Carney that makes him the quintessential leader, and an example to others who aspire to leadership?

"What impresses me about him is his steady hand and his calming voice," said Louis Gagnon, a professor of finance at Queen's University in Kingston, Ont., and a former bank executive. "He is an excellent communicator [who] goes straight to the point and makes himself heard."

Mr Carney is also remarkably good at explaining complex policy actions in a simple manner, Prof. Gagnon said, essentially "bringing transparency to a process that is inherently opaque." That ability to get the message across, along with the sense Mr Carney gives that he is in control of the situation, "are the hallmarks of a good leader," Prof. Gagnon said.

Executives who want to emulate Mr Carney should concentrate on communicating "frequently, and with precision," he said.

Mr Carney's ability to speak bluntly without offending was underlined in August, when he admonished Canadian business leaders for sitting on "dead money" instead of investing it or returning it to shareholders. Even those executives who disagreed with him avoided personal attacks, instead countering the central bank chief's polite tone with a reasoned counter-punch.

Mr Carney also drew in many Canadians who would not normally identify with his views, when he declared a year ago that the "Occupy" movement had legitimate complaints and that their protests were "entirely constructive."

Charles St-Arnaud, a former Bank of Canada economist who now works for Nomura Securities in New York, said it was clear what made Mr Carney a good manager when the two worked together briefly at the central bank about eight years ago. Mr Carney was deputy governor at the time, and Mr St-Arnaud was a relatively junior economist in the international section. Mr St-Arnaud said Mr Carney would come directly to his office to ask questions about reports he had written, bypassing the bank's formal chain of command. "I felt that he had read the report, and he knew who I was. He had very good interpersonal skills that made me feel confident."

As a manager, Mr Carney worked hard to know everyone in the organization, and that made each staff member feel they had a valuable role, Mr St-Arnaud said. "He is a very charismatic figure." Business executives who have watched Mr Carney's public persona say his strong leadership skills are apparent even to those outside the central bank. "[Mr Carney] is decisive, and has the courage and conviction to implement what he believes is the right thing, when he could have taken the easy or popular way out," said Daryl Ritchie, chief executive officer of accounting firm MNP LLP in Calgary. That makes people respect and trust him, even if they disagree, Mr Ritchie said. Matt Campbell, CEO of Rocky Mountain Dealerships Inc., a Calgary-based chain of construction and agriculture equipment dealers, said Mr Carney not only has an "aura that displays confidence," but he has surrounded himself with a strong support team.

But Mr Carney also has another advantage, which was not his own doing, Mr Campbell said. He presided over an economy that was in far better shape than others around the world during and after the recession. Much of the credit for that should go to the current government and Prime Minister Stephen Harper, Mr Campbell said. Mr Carney not only had a strong team, "but had strong support from his masters," Mr Campbell said. "Mark Carney is a star quarterback [but] the team was built and coached by Harper."

Richard Blackwell, *The Globe and Mail*, 29 November 2012

QUESTIONS: What aspects of leadership attributed to Mr Carney are mirrored in the previous chapter? The final paragraph notes that effective leadership is as much a product of teamwork and context as it is effort on the part of the leader. What other examples do you have that prove or disprove this statement?

groupthink
A group's collective striving for unanimity that discourages realistic appraisals of alternatives to its chosen decision.

Even when there's no overt pressure to follow the majority, more subtle influences motivate members—especially in highly cohesive groups—to keep quiet rather than voice any thoughts that deviate from what appears to be the consensus. Members think, "Why rock the boat if I'm the only dissenter?" "And if everybody else feels the same way, they're probably right."

With no dissent, the group begins to take on a feeling of invulnerability: an unquestioning belief that its ideas are correct and even morally right. As its position solidifies, outsiders who disagree can be viewed as the enemy, disloyal to what is obviously the only legitimate viewpoint. Social scientists use the term **groupthink** to describe the collective striving for unanimity that discourages realistic appraisals of alternatives to a group's chosen decision.[43] Several group practices can discourage this troublesome force.[44] A first step is to recognize the problem of groupthink as it begins to manifest itself. If agreement comes quickly and easily, the group may be avoiding the tough but necessary search for alternatives. Beyond vigilance, a second step to discourage groupthink is to minimize status differences. If the group has a nominal leader, he or she must be careful not to use various types of power that come with the position to intimidate members. A third step involves developing a group norm that legitimizes disagreement. After members recognize that questioning one another's positions doesn't signal personal animosity or disloyalty, a constructive exchange of ideas can lead to top-quality solutions. Sometimes it can be helpful to designate a person or subgroup as the "devil's advocate" who reminds the others about the dangers of groupthink and challenges the trend toward consensus.

Summary

Despite the bad reputation of groups in some quarters, research shows that they are often the most effective settings for problem-solving. They command greater resources, both quantitatively and qualitatively, than do either individuals or collections of people working in isolation; their work can result in greater accuracy; and the participative nature of the solutions they produce generates greater commitment from members.

However, groups aren't always the best forum for solving problems. They should be used when the problem is beyond the capacity of one person to solve, when tasks are interdependent, when there is more than one desired solution or decision, and when the agreement of all members is essential.

Groups use a wide variety of discussion formats when solving problems. Some use parliamentary procedure to govern decision-making procedures. Others use moderated panel discussions, symposia, or forums. The best format depends on the nature of the problem and the characteristics of the group.

Since face-to-face meetings can be time-consuming and difficult to arrange, computer-mediated communication can be a good alternative for some group tasks. Some group work can be handled via computer or teleconferencing, where members communicate in real time over digital networks. Other tasks can be handled via asynchronous discussions, in which members exchange messages at their convenience. Mediated meetings provide a record of discussion and may make it easier for normally quiet members to participate, but these meetings can take more time, and they lack the non-verbal richness of face-to-face conversation. Given these pros and cons, smart communicators will give thoughtful consideration to the circumstances before deciding to use the mediated approach.

Groups stand the best chance of developing effective solutions to problems if they begin their work by identifying the problem, avoiding the mistake of failing to recognize the hidden needs of individual members. The next step is analysis of the problem, including identification of forces both favouring and blocking progress. Only at this point should the group begin to develop possible solutions, taking care not to stifle creativity by evaluating any of them prematurely. During the implementation phase of the solution, the group should monitor the situation carefully and make any necessary changes in its plan.

Most groups can expect to move through several stages as they solve a problem. The first of these stages is orientation, during which the members sound each other out. The conflict stage is characterized by partisanship and open debate over the merits of contending ideas. In the emergence stage, the group begins to move toward choosing a single solution. In the reinforcement stage, members endorse the group's decision.

Groups that pay attention only to the task dimension of their interaction risk strains in the relationships among members. Many of these interpersonal problems can be avoided by using the skills described in Chapter 7 as well as by following the guidelines in this chapter for building group cohesiveness and encouraging participation.

Many naive observers of groups confuse the concepts of leader and leadership. We defined leadership as the ability to influence the behaviour of other members through the use of one or more types of power—legitimate, coercive, reward, expert, information, or referent. We saw that many nominal leaders share their power with other members. Leadership has been examined from many perspectives—trait analysis, leadership style, and situational variables.

Smart members will avoid some common dangers that threaten a group's effectiveness. They will make sure to get the information they need, without succumbing to overload. They will make sure that participation is equal by encouraging the contributions of quiet members and keeping more talkative people on track. They will guard against groupthink by minimizing the pressure on members to conform for the sake of harmony or approval.

Key Terms

asynchronous discussion   376
authoritarian leadership style   396
brainstorming   382
breakout groups   375
coercive power   391
cohesiveness   388
conflict stage   384
democratic leadership style   396
emergence stage   385
expert power   392
focus groups   375
force field analysis   381
forum   376
groupthink   402
information overload   398
information power   393
information underload   398
laissez-faire leadership style   396

Leadership Grid   396
legitimate power   390
nominal group technique   382
nominal leader   391
orientation stage   384
panel discussion   375
parliamentary procedure   375
participative decision-making   372
power   390
probative question   380
problem census   375
referent power   393
reinforcement stage   385
reward power   392
situational leadership   397
symposium   375
trait theories of leadership   394

Activities

A. When to Use Group Problem-Solving

Explain which of the following tasks would be best managed by a group:

1. collecting and editing a list of films illustrating communication principles;

2. deciding what the group will eat for lunch at a one-day meeting;

3. choosing the topic for a class project;

4. finding which of six companies had the lowest auto insurance rates; and/or

5. designing a survey to measure community attitudes toward a subsidy for local artists.

B. Increasing Group Creativity

You can improve your skill at increasing creativity in group discussions by trying the approaches described in this book. Your group should begin by choosing one of the following problems:

1. How can out-of-pocket student expenses (e.g., books, transportation) be decreased?

2. How can the textbook you are using in this (or any other) class be improved?

3. How could your class group (legally) earn the greatest amount of money between now and the end of the term?

4. What strategies can be used effectively when confronted with employer discrimination or harassment? (Assume you want to keep the job.)

5. Imagine that your group has been hired to develop a way of improving the course registration system at your institution. What three recommendations will be most effective?

Choose either brainstorming or the nominal group technique to develop possible solutions to your chosen problem. Explain why you chose the method. Under what conditions would the other method be more appropriate?

C. Stages in Group Development

Identify a problem-solving group, either from your personal experience or from a book or film. Analyze the group's approach to problem-solving. Does it follow the cyclical model pictured in Figure 10.1? Does it follow a more linear approach or no recognizable pattern at all?

D. Power in Groups

Think of examples from groups you have belonged to or observed in which members had and used each type of power discussed on pages 390–3. Describe the types of power you have possessed in groups. Evaluate whether your use of that power has helped or hindered the group's effectiveness.

E. Choosing the Most Effective Leadership Style

Think of two effective leaders you have known. How would you describe the style of each one: autocratic, democratic, or *laissez-faire*? Task- or relationship-oriented? Imagine that the two leaders were transferred, so that each one was directing the other's group. Would the same style work equally well in each situation? Why or why not?

F. Dealing with Overly Talkative and Quiet Group Members

Balancing participation in group discussions can involve stifling some members and urging others to speak up when they would prefer to be silent. Explore the ethical justification for these actions by answering the following questions:

1. Are there any circumstances when it is legitimate to place quiet group members in the position of speaking up when they would rather remain quiet? When does it become unreasonable to urge quiet members to participate?

2. Does discouraging talkative members ever violate the principles of free speech and tolerance for others' opinions? Describe when it is and is not appropriate to limit a member's contributions.

After developing your ethical guidelines, consider how you would feel if they were applied to you.

Further Reading

Cochran, Alice, *Roberta's Rules of Order* (San Francisco: Josey-Bass, 2004).
Robert's Rules of Order has served for over 125 years as a guide for using parliamentary procedure to bring order out of meetings that might otherwise be disorganized and even chaotic. Cochran has created a less formal approach that strives for consensus instead of majority rule. For groups that find the traditional approach too confining, this book may be a useful guide.

Engleberg, Isa N., and Wynn, Dianna R., *Working in Groups* (Boston: Allyn & Bacon, 2009).
Theoretical underpinnings of group communication are covered, as well as practical skills to strengthen problem-solving abilities, group motivation, and cohesion. Readers will learn how to enhance "team talk," but individual attributes are also discussed, such as communication anxiety and listening ability.

Wheelan, Susan A., "Group Size, Group Development, and Group Productivity," *Small Group Research* 40 (2) (2009): 247–62.
What is the "right size" of group members that can affect a group's productivity? This article reveals a study in which work groups from 329 nonprofit and for-profit organizations were analyzed, based on group productivity and developmental processes. The study revealed that groups containing as few as three to four members, but up to eight members, were more productive than their counterparts with more than nine members. Not surprisingly, this study underscores that more people and personalities in a group can have a profound effect on how much the group accomplishes.

Study Questions

Imagine you are organizing a fundraising plan for a not-for-profit group focused on environmental cleanup of a creek in your area. You announce that you are forming the group on Facebook and Twitter, and a very diverse group of people sign up. At your first meeting, you find that your call out has attracted the following people:

- a gay lawyer who is known as an active community volunteer;
- two teenage girls who are fashionably dressed and currently listening to their iPods;
- two neo-hippies who are sitting quietly, holding their hemp bags;
- two stay-at-home moms, who are primly dressed and constantly texting their children;
- a retired husband and wife who have lived in the neighbourhood for more than 30 years and are sad at how soiled it has become;
- two college or university students who want to complete their internship requirements for a communications course;

- a conservative immigrant construction worker from Brazil who has been working in a filthy environment and has had enough; and
- an immigrant from Vietnam who is good at fixing computers but doesn't speak English very well.

Your group has a solid deadline of one month to effectively fundraise for the campaign to have an environmental assessment done of the creek area. You face a town council that doesn't want to spend any money on the environment, and wants to ignore the polluted creek problem.

1. How can you use the structured problem-solving approach (outlined on pp. 378–84) to develop an effective fundraising plan?

2. What developmental stages in problem-solving groups (described on pp. 384–6) can you expect the group to experience as it develops its options? How can awareness of these steps make working together less troublesome and more rewarding?

3. What types of power (described on pp. 390–3) can you expect group members to have and use? How could those types of power affect the success of the group, for better or worse?

4. How can you use the advice on pp. 388–90 to build cohesiveness as you work on the list of options?

5. Choose either the styles or the situational approach to leadership on pp. 396–8 and describe how you would use your chosen style to be an effective leader.

PART IV
Persuasion and Public Communication

PROFESSIONAL PROFILE

Donald Smith

My title is Director of Operations in the Public Affairs Branch at the Canada Revenue Agency (CRA). I am responsible for national media relations, including the development of media relations policy and strategy, media monitoring, special event planning and speechwriting. In addition, I have liaison responsibilities for CRA's 32 communications specialists located across the country, I publish the quarterly employee magazine and I oversee the CRA's social media activities. A team of 14 talented people helps me accomplish all this.

The variety of challenges is what makes my job so enjoyable. It's a wonderful mix of scheduled deliverables and issues-oriented challenges that often arise without warning. On any given day I have a pretty good idea of what I'm going to be doing, but there are frequently surprises, and that is what keeps the job fresh.

The path I followed to reach the world of communications/public relations was somewhat circuitous, and started in journalism. I studied broadcasting and journalism and then spent the first 10 years of my career as a radio journalist. That led to a job as press secretary to a federal cabinet minister for five years. Next, I moved to a federal government department and worked in strategic communications, spent four years in the Communications and Consultation Secretariat at the Privy Council Office, then to my present position. It wasn't a typical entry into communications, but it wasn't atypical, either, for the time. Fortunately, my journalism background served me well, as I didn't formally study public relations until I enrolled in the Master of Communications Management Program at McMaster University at the age of 52. (Note to young communicators: learning is a lifelong endeavor.)

I believe that versatile communicators are the ones who will be the most employable in the coming years. Communicators will need the traditional skills such as writing, editing, analytical ability, media relations, still and video photography, etc. but will also need the knowledge required to take advantage of social media opportunities. It's not an either/or situation when it comes to traditional media and social media—they will need expertise to work with both.

Finally, if I had to name one skill set at which a young communicator preparing to enter the field should strive to excel, it would be writing. Without question, the development of superior writing skills should be the goal of all aspiring communicators. Senior executives in the public and private sector look to their communications team to provide polished material, be it a news release, speech, letter to the editor, or anything else. Young communicators should seek out opportunities to write in order to hone their skills and to start to build a portfolio. Technologies may change and evolve, but they are simply platforms for content.

11

Persuasion

After studying the material in this chapter . . .

You should understand:

- ✔ the characteristics of persuasion and the ethical questions involved;
- ✔ the differences between propositions of fact, value, and policy;
- ✔ the difference between the goals of convincing and activating;
- ✔ the difference between direct and indirect persuasion;
- ✔ the importance of setting a clear persuasive purpose;
- ✔ the various types of fallacies to avoid; and
- ✔ the characteristics of interpersonal persuasion strategies.

You should be able to:

- ✔ formulate an effective persuasive strategy to convince and to activate an audience;
- ✔ formulate a persuasive strategy based on ethical guidelines; and
- ✔ identify and use different interpersonal persuasion strategies.

Chapter Highlights

Persuasion has several important characteristics:

»   It is not coercive.

»   It is usually incremental.

»   It is interactive.

»   It can be ethical.

Persuasion can be categorized according to the following types:

»   type of proposition,

»   desired outcome, and

»   directness of approach.

Types of interpersonal persuasion include:

»   foot-in-the-door, door-in-the-face;

»   social exchange, low-balling;

»   that's-not-all; and

»   fear-then-relief.

Jennifer Morrow, a student at Lakehead University in Thunder Bay, Ontario, sums up her understanding of persuasive communication as follows:

> Persuasion is a central part of being human. We must persuade others that we are competent, intelligent, trustworthy, and open-minded. Persuasion can also be used to help people who cannot represent themselves—homeless people, abused women, the mentally ill. What could be more important or more fulfilling than that?

Not every student would agree with Jennifer on the joys of persuasive communication, but many college and university students across Canada and around the world are speaking out. They are becoming increasingly engaged in a variety of issues, including global ones such as the growing gap between rich and poor and the need for citizens and their governments to reduce greenhouse gas emissions. Students have staged anti-sweatshop protests at the University of Toronto. A few years ago, University of Ottawa students also protested a proposed speech by right-wing commentator Ann Coulter. In 2012, Quebec students staged massive demonstrations protesting Jean Charest's proposed significant tuition increases—they were demanding free tuition and brought Montreal to a standstill. These students are all engaged in the age-old activity of persuasion. How persuasion works and how to accomplish it successfully are complex topics. Our understanding of persuasion begins with classical wisdom and extends to the latest psychological research. We begin by looking at what we really mean by the term.

Characteristics of Persuasion

persuasion
The process of motivating someone, through communication and relationship-building, to change a particular attitude, belief, value, or behaviour.

Persuasion is the process of motivating someone, through communication and relationship-building, to change a particular attitude, belief, value, or behaviour. Implicit in this definition are several characteristics, which we'll discuss in the sections that follow.

Persuasion Is Not Coercive

Persuasion is not the same thing as coercion. If you held a gun to someone's head and said, "Do this, or I'll shoot," you would be acting coercively. Besides being illegal, this approach would be ineffective. As soon as the authorities had led you away in handcuffs, the person would stop following your demands.

This example is a bit far-fetched, but the failure of coercion to achieve lasting results is also apparent in less dramatic circumstances. Children whose parents are coercive often rebel as soon as they can; students who perform out of fear of an instructor's threats rarely appreciate the subject matter; and employees who work for abusive and demanding employers are often unproductive and eager to switch jobs as soon as possible. Persuasion, on the other hand, makes a listener *want* to think or act differently.

Persuasion Is Usually Incremental

Attitudes do not normally change instantly or dramatically. Persuasion is a process. When it is successful, it generally succeeds over time, in increments, and usually small increments at that. The realistic speaker, therefore, establishes goals and expectations that reflect this characteristic of persuasion.

Communication theorists explain this characteristic of persuasion through **social judgment theory**.[1] This theory tells us that when members of an audience hear a persuasive appeal, they compare it to opinions they already hold. The pre-existing opinion is called an **anchor**, but around this anchor there exist what are called **latitudes of acceptance**, **latitudes of rejection**, and **latitudes of non-commitment**. A diagram of any opinion, therefore, might look something like Figure 11.1.

People who care very strongly about a particular point of view (they are called "highly ego-involved" by communication researchers) will have a very narrow latitude of non-commitment. People who care less strongly will have a wider latitude of non-commitment. Research suggests that audience members simply will not respond to appeals that fall within their latitude of rejection. This means that persuasion in the real world occurs in a series of small movements. One persuasive speech may be but a single step in a larger campaign of persuasion. Consider, for instance, the various political communications disseminated in the months and weeks leading up to an election. Candidates watch the opinion polls carefully and adjust their appeals to the latitudes of acceptance and non-commitment of the undecided voters. With such information, a Liberal Party candidate may make pamphlets or information sheets targeted at Green Party voters because she feels that they may be susceptible to vote for her party, given the similarity of many Liberal and Green political positions.

Communicators who heed the principle of social judgment theory tend to seek realistic, if modest, goals in their communications. For example, if you were hoping to change audience

social judgment theory
Explanation of attitude change that posits that opinions will change only in small increments and only when the target opinions lie within the receiver's latitudes of acceptance and non-commitment.

anchor
The position supported by audience members before a persuasion attempt.

latitudes of acceptance
In social judgment theory, statements that a receiver would not reject.

latitudes of rejection
In social judgment theory, statements that a receiver could not possibly accept.

latitudes of non-commitment
In social judgment theory, statements that a receiver would not care strongly about one way or another.

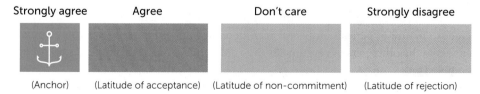

Strongly agree	Agree	Don't care	Strongly disagree
(Anchor)	(Latitude of acceptance)	(Latitude of non-commitment)	(Latitude of rejection)

FIGURE 11.1 Latitudes of Acceptance, Rejection, and Non-Commitment

views on the issue of abortion, social judgment theory suggests that the first step would be to consider a range of arguments, such as:

- Abortion is a sin.
- Abortion should be absolutely illegal.
- Abortion should be allowed only in cases of rape and incest.
- A woman should be required to have her husband's permission to have an abortion.
- A girl under the age of 18 should be required to have a parent's permission to have an abortion.
- Abortion should be allowed during the first three months of pregnancy only.
- A girl under the age of 18 should not be required to have a parent's permission before she has an abortion.
- A woman should not be required to have her husband's permission to have an abortion.
- Abortion should be a woman's personal decision.
- Abortion should be discouraged but legal.
- Abortion should be available anytime to anyone.
- Abortion should be considered simply a form of birth control.

You could then arrange these positions on a continuum and estimate how listeners would react to each one. The statement that best represents the listeners' point of view would be the anchor of your messaging. Other items that might also seem reasonable to them would make up their latitude of acceptance. Opinions that they would reject would make up their latitude of rejection. Those statements that are left would be the listeners' latitude of non-commitment.

Usually, an organization or an individual will shape a public relations or an advertising campaign around a most important **message**. For example, if you were part of a parents' organization trying to get a bylaw passed requiring dogs to be leashed when outside, your message could be "Dogs should be leashed so that our children can play outdoors safely." Once you have a message, you can structure any advertising, informative literature, **news releases**, **op-eds**, or other forms of persuasive communication around it. (See Appendix I for more on op-eds.) You can also evaluate the success or failure of your "messaging" by tracking how many citizens' attitudes, beliefs, values, or behaviours you aligned with your campaign's message because of your persuasive communication.

Social judgment theory suggests that you will have the best chance of changing audience attitudes if you begin by presenting an argument based on a position that falls somewhere within the listeners' latitude of non-commitment—even if this isn't the position that you want them to hold ultimately. If you push too hard by arguing a position in your audience's latitude of rejection, your appeals will probably backfire, making your audience more opposed to you than they were to begin with.

Persuasion Is Interactive

The transactional model of communication described in Chapter 1 makes it clear that persuasion is not something you do *to* other people but rather something you do *with* them. The interactive nature of persuasion is best seen in an argument between two people, in which openness to the other person's arguments is essential to settling the dispute. As one observer has pointed out:

> Arguments are not won by shouting down opponents. They are won by changing opponents' minds—something that can happen only if we give

message
A central theme, idea, or value that is transmitted to receivers through persuasive communication.

news release
A document that provides a reporter or editor with a newsworthy description of a particular person, event, service, or product.

op-ed
A mini-essay that appears as a stand-alone feature opposite the editorial page of a newspaper.

Cultural Idiom
backfire
To produce a result opposite of the one intended.

opposing arguments a respectful hearing and still persuade their advocates that there is something wrong with those arguments. In the course of this activity, we may well decide that there is something wrong with our own.[2]

In any sort of communication, both the communicator and the audience are active. The communicator can ensure this interactivity by taking an audience survey before communicating, by showing sensitivity to audience reactions during conversation or in writing, or by making him- or herself available for questions and feedback.

Persuasion Can Be Ethical

Even when they understand the difference between persuasion and coercion, some people are still uncomfortable with the idea of persuasive communication. They associate it with high-pressure hucksters: salespeople with their feet stuck in the door, telemarketers who won't take "no" for an answer, unscrupulous politicians taking advantage of beleaguered taxpayers, and so on. Indeed, many of the principles presented in this chapter have been used by unethical speakers for unethical purposes, but that is not what all—or even most—persuasion is about. Ethical persuasion plays a necessary and worthwhile role in everyone's life.

> **Cultural Idiom**
> **high-pressure hucksters**
> Aggressive and persistent salespeople.

Through ethical persuasion we influence the lives of others in many worthwhile ways. The person who says, "I do not want to influence other people" is really saying, "I don't want to get involved with other people," and that is an abandonment of one's responsibilities as a human being. Look at the good you can accomplish through ethical persuasion: you can convince a loved one to give up smoking or to exercise more regularly; you can get members of your community to conserve energy or to join together to refurbish a park; you can persuade an employer to hire you for a job where your own talents, interests, and abilities will be put to their best use.

Persuasion is considered ethical if it conforms to accepted standards. But what are the standards today? What if your plan is selfish and not in the best interest of your audience members, but you are honest about your motives—is that ethical? What if your plan is in the best interest of your audience members, but you lie to them to gain their consent? Philosophers and rhetoricians have argued for centuries over questions like these.

> **ethical persuasion**
> Persuasion in an audience's best interest that does not depend on false or misleading information to induce change.

There are many ways to define **ethical persuasion**.[3] For our purpose, we will define it as communication in the best interest of the audience that does not depend on false or misleading information to change an audience's attitude or behaviour. The best way to appreciate the value of this simple definition is to consider the many strategies, listed in Table 11.1, that do *not* fit it. For example, plagiarizing material from another source, inventing statistics to support your case, and faking enthusiasm about communicating with someone about something are clearly unethical. Lying may seem an effective alternative to get you out of a bind now and again, but you must remember that every lie you tell must be maintained, which can become very complicated.

Table 11.1 Unethical Communication Behaviours

1. Committing plagiarism.
   a. Claiming someone else's ideas as your own.
   b. Quoting without citing the source.

2. Relaying false information.
   a. Deliberate lying.
   b. Ignorant misstatement.
   c. Deliberate distortion and suppression of material.
   d. Fallacious reasoning to misrepresent truth.

3. Withholding information; suppression.
   a. About self (speaker); not disclosing private motives or special interests.
   b. About communication purpose.
   c. About sources (not revealing sources; plagiarism).
   d. About evidence; omission of certain evidence (card stacking).
   e. About opposing arguments; presenting only one side.

4. Appearing to be what one is not; insincerity.
   a. In words, saying what one does not mean or believe.
   b. In delivery (for example, feigning enthusiasm).

5. Using emotional appeals to hinder truth.
   a. Using emotional appeals as a substitute or cover-up for lack of sound reasoning and valid evidence.
   b. Failing to use balanced appeals.

Source: Adapted from Mary Klaaren Andersen, "An Analysis of the Treatment of Ethos in Selected Speech Communication Textbooks" (unpublished dissertation, University of Michigan, 1979), 244–7.

Cultural Idiom
lifting material
To use another's words or ideas as one's own.

propositions of fact
Claims bearing on issues in which there are two or more sides of conflicting factual evidence.

propositions of value
Claims bearing on issues involving the worth of some idea, person, or object.

propositions of policy
Claims bearing on issues that involve adopting or rejecting a specific course of action.

Besides being wrong on moral grounds, unethical attempts at persuasion have a major practical disadvantage: if your deception is uncovered, your credibility will suffer. If, for example, prospective buyers uncover your attempt to withhold a structural flaw in the condominium you are trying to sell, they will probably suspect that the property has other hidden problems. Likewise, if your communications professor suspects that you are lifting material from other sources without giving credit, your entire project will be suspect. One unethical act can cast doubt on truthful statements you make in the future. Thus, for pragmatic as well as moral reasons, honesty really is the best policy.

Categorizing Types of Persuasion

There are several ways to categorize the types of persuasive attempts you will make as a speaker. What kinds of subjects will you focus on? What results will you be looking for? How will you go about getting those results? In the following pages we will look at how each of these questions may be used to categorize persuasive attempts.

By Types of Proposition

Persuasive topics may be sorted in terms of the type of thesis statement (referred to as a "proposition" in persuasion) that you are advancing. There are three categories of proposition: **propositions of fact**, **propositions of value**, and **propositions of policy**.

Propositions of Fact

Some persuasive messages focus on propositions of fact, issues in which there are two or more sides with conflicting evidence. When presented with a proposition of fact, listeners are required to choose the truth for themselves. The following are some examples:

- Canada does [or does *not*] provide more peacekeeping services than other developed countries.
- Canada's national health care system is more [or is *less*] efficient than the US system of health care.

As these examples show, many propositions of fact can't be settled with a simple "yes" or "no," or with an objective piece of information. Rather, they are open to debate, and answering them requires careful examination and interpretation of evidence, usually collected from a variety of sources. That's why it is possible to debate questions of fact and why these propositions form the basis of persuasive speeches and not informative ones.

Propositions of Value

Propositions of value go beyond issues of truth or falsity and explore the worth of some idea, person, or object. Examples of propositions of value include the following:

- An arena full of enthusiastic fans gives [or does *not* give] the home team a decided advantage.
- The average Canadian's quality of life is [or is *not*] better than that of the average citizen of the United Kingdom.
- Secretly watching pornography is [or is *not*] a form of cheating on your partner.

In order to deal with most propositions of value, you will have to explore certain propositions of fact. For example, you won't be able to debate whether watching pornography behind your partner's back is immoral—a proposition of value—until you have dealt with propositions of fact such as whether your value system considers only physical infidelity to be cheating and whether experts believe that this will create distance in your relationship.

Propositions of Policy

Propositions of policy go one step beyond questions of fact or value; they recommend a specific course of action (a "policy"). Some questions of policy are the following:

- The Canadian government should [or should *not*] financially support NHL teams to keep them in Canadian cities.
- Genetic engineering of plants and livestock is [or is *not*] an appropriate way to increase the food supply.

Looking at persuasion according to the type of proposition is a convenient way to generate topics for a persuasive speech because each type of proposition suggests different topics. Selected topics could also be handled differently depending on how they are approached. For example, the central message of a political campaign op-ed could be crafted as a proposition

How to Sell a Pickle.

In my hand I have a pickle. It's a dill pickle by the way, if you were curious. Not only that, but I'm going to do my best to sell you this pickle.

To start, I think this pickle needs a name, especially since a brand name, paired with brand recognition is just about the easiest way to distinguish *this* pickle from the myriad pickles we encounter in our day to day. Branding allocates an identity upon an inanimate object, how you spin or project the "mood" or "attitude" of that brand gives it a unique identity. Pairing a product with a name or logo that inspires an emotional response is the best way to get a brand association started. Research has shown that even the briefest exposure to distinct logos (Nike/Adidas, Lays/Pringles, McDonald's/KFC, etc.) has the power to alter viewer responses toward the implied characteristic. For instance, a Mac image and PC image were shown to viewers before they were asked to do problem-solving exercises. The subtle exposure to these logos produced more practical thinking in one group, and more creative thinking in the other. Can you guess which logo each group viewed? Exactly. The fact that you know the answer illustrates this point precisely.

We ought to make this pickle into a fun, counter cultural, and distinctly individualistic pickle. *This* is a pickle for the forward thinking, counter cultural hipster. The best way to convey complex emotions or identities is to utilize a technique known as associative conditioning. Essentially this means pairing your product with another identity to reflect and convey that mood or persona more effectively. Examples of this would be when popular athletes advertise shoes; laundry detergent ads are filled with images of "freshness" such as rain, grass, and flowers; or even the subtle use of colour theory. In fact, 84.7 per cent of consumers cite colour as their primary purchasing reason. How about we start there?

In terms of colour, green is pretty solidly pickle territory, and green is well known to advertisers to be associated with health, confidence, and sexual prowess. Don't believe me about that last point? Well, studies have shown that, of all things, the green M&M has been found to send the most consistent sexual messages, and if it's good for M&Ms it's good for us. So, let's go with our sexy green, and call this pickle "Dill Murray." Named after beloved 80s comedy star, and eternally cool fella, Bill Murray. By associating our pickle with Mr Murray's brand, we reflect and adopt, subconsciously, the attributes of him, upon our product. Sound good?

Great! Half way there. We've got an image, a brand and a colour scheme. But how do you *sell* "Dill Murray" brand pickles? Your best bet is to go with buzz words. Although somewhat outdated, these classic terms consistently trigger lapses in a prospective buyer's associative reasoning and make consumers more likely to make impulse purchases. Furthermore, they can build a psychological bond with the product or retailer. Think of your favorite soda product. Are you a Coke or Pepsi fan? People tend to align themselves with specific products over another, regardless of rational analysis. Does it matter to your preference that

of fact ("Candidate X has done more for this community than Candidate Y"), a proposition of value ("Candidate X is a better person than Candidate Y"), or a proposition of policy ("We should get out and vote for Candidate X"). Remember, however, that a fully developed persuasive op-ed is likely to contain all three types of propositions. If you were preparing an op-ed advocating mandatory drug testing for university athletes (a proposition of policy), you might want to first prove that the use of performance-enhancing drugs among athletes is already widespread (a proposition of fact), that there are considerable health risks associated with this kind of drug use (another proposition of fact), and that the use of performance-enhancing drugs gives some athletes an unfair advantage over others (a proposition of value).

By Desired Outcome

We can also categorize persuasion according to two major outcomes: convincing and activating.

Convincing

convince
A speech goal that aims at changing audience members' attitudes, beliefs, or values.

When you set about to **convince** an audience, you want to change the way its members think. This doesn't mean that you have to swing them from one belief or attitude to a completely different one. Sometimes your audience members will already think the way you want them to,

numerous studies have shown that in a blind taste test, almost no one can tell the difference between Pepsi and Coke? If not, then you've developed a psychological bond with that product. These buzz terms, are used to build that exact bond between you and a product's "persona," convey notions of urgency for sales, and give false empowerment to purchaser and product. I think you can absolutely use this to sell Dill Murray.

Not only are these linguistic techniques used by advertisers, but police officers also use them in interrogations to convey either confidentiality, safety, or fear, powerlessness and intimidation; politicians use them constantly to convey trust, resilience and leadership; even parents use psychological triggers to calm or reassure their children or assert their dominance.

Terms like "limited time offer" give the consumer a fixed deadline, making a rational consideration period impossible. If you ever find yourself in the middle east in a bartering situation, you will find a thousand takes on this: "someone *just* came in looking for the same thing," or "it's our very last one," or "I can make you a special offer, but just this once," etc.

Buzz words like "No risk, free trial offer, money back guarantee . . . etc." assure the consumer that their fears of risky purchases are mitigated, while the word "free" is like candy for the fiscally calculating consumer mind.

"You don't want to miss this great offer!" is a fantastic one, but maybe not why you'd think. Studies have shown that people are more likely to purchase, agree with, and even enjoy a product more if they think it is targeted to them specifically, and if it encourages the purchaser via its advertising. Heck, reread this whole essay and notice how I've slowly and subtly shifted away from me trying to promote this pickle to getting *us* to promote it to, finally, *you* selling Dill Murray. Furthermore, there's been plenty of encouragement in order to get you invested in the Dill Murray brand. I have also consistently used the brand name, forming the building blocks of a brand relationship through saturation.

And that's the most important part about persuasion: the person being persuaded has to think that they are in control. Persuasion is a relationship, with every party thinking they are in control, but no one realizing that they are the one being swayed. So, the next time you see a brilliant ad with a famous 80s star promoting a limited time offer on fresh, crisp green pickles, custom-made *just for you*, consider how that pickle may end up in your hand. I sure did.

David Schokking, Instructor, Mohawk College,
Hamilton, Ontario, 23 May 2013

QUESTIONS: How does the article highlight both verbal and non-verbal techniques used in persuasion? Can you think of any examples of marketed persuasion that have worked on you, or someone you know? What brands do you have a "relationship" with?

but they will not be firmly enough committed to that way of thinking. When this is the case, your goal is to reinforce, or strengthen, their opinions. Strengthening an idea or opinion is still a type of change because you are causing an audience to adhere more strongly to a belief or attitude. In other cases, a communication designed to convince will begin to shift attitudes without bringing about a total change of thinking.

Activating

When you set about to **activate** an audience, you want to move its members to a specific behaviour. Whereas a speech, conversation, or op-ed designed to convince might spur listeners to action based on the ideas you've convinced them of, it won't be any specific action that you have recommended. In a speech to activate, you do recommend that specific action.

There are two types of action you can ask for—adoption or discontinuance. The former asks an audience to engage in a new behaviour; the latter asks an audience to stop behaving in an established way. If you were communicating for a political candidate and then asked for contributions to that candidate's campaign, you would be asking your audience to adopt a new behaviour. If you communicated against smoking and then asked your audience members to sign a pledge to quit, you would be asking them to discontinue an established behaviour.

> **activate**
> To move members of an audience toward a specific behaviour.

> **Cultural Idiom**
> **spur**
> To goad or give incentive in order to get a desired action or response.

By Directness of Approach

We can also categorize persuasion according to the directness of approach used by the speaker.

Direct Persuasion

direct persuasion
Persuasion that does not try to disguise the speaker's persuasive purpose.

Direct persuasion does not try to disguise the speaker's persuasive purpose in any way. In direct persuasion the speaker will make his or her purpose clear, usually by stating it outright early in the communication. This is the best strategy to use with a friendly audience, especially when you are asking for a response that the audience is likely to give you. Direct persuasion is the kind we hear in most academic situations. Justine Zaleschuk, a winner of the Canadian Association of Former Parliamentarians essay competition for undergraduate students at Canadian colleges and universities, used direct persuasion in a speech on "How to Improve Canada's Health Care System." In her introduction, she announced her intention to persuade in this way:

> It seems ironic that the very system created to care for our health and well-being has, itself, been reduced to such a pitiful and sickly state. Medicare has stumbled into the twenty-first century coughing up bills for the increasingly obscene costs of technology and pharmaceuticals. The system is exhausted by the constant headaches of waiting lists and hospital closures. It finds itself hobbling along on its insufficient crutches of underpaid, over-worked staff. With all of this misery the debate has jumped right to the point of whether or not to "pull the plug" on Medicare in order to pursue the tantalizing alternative of private health care. Yet few have stopped to consider if, possibly, the system merely needs a little bit of work—some modifications in conjunction with some basic upkeep—to survive. Medicare is not due for termination, but rather, consistent maintenance through a commitment to the financial, administrative, and human resource aspects of this system of health services.[4]

Indirect Persuasion

indirect persuasion
Persuasion that disguises or de-emphasizes the speaker's persuasive goal.

Indirect persuasion disguises or de-emphasizes the speaker's persuasive purpose in some way. If you were to open a conversation with the question, "Is a season ticket to the symphony worth

the money?"—when you intended to prove that it was—you would be using indirect persuasion. Any strategy that does not express the speaker's purpose at the outset is based on indirect persuasion.

Although it is meant to operate subtly, indirect persuasion is sometimes easy to spot. A television commercial that shows attractive young people romping on the ski hill on a beautiful day and then flashes the name of a brand of beer, cereal, or soft drink is indisputably using indirect persuasion. Political oratory sometimes relies on methods of indirect persuasion that are more difficult to spot. A political hopeful might be speaking ostensibly on some great social issue when the real persuasive message is "Please remember my name—and vote for me in the next election."

Creating the Persuasive Message

Preparing effective persuasive communication isn't easy, but it can be made easier by observing a few simple rules. These include setting a clear, persuasive purpose and avoiding fallacies.

Set a Clear, Persuasive Purpose

Remember that your objective in persuasive communication is to move the audience to a specific, attainable attitude or behaviour. When communicating to convince, the purpose statement will probably stress an attitude:

- *After reading my blog post, my audience will agree that steps should be taken to save whales from extinction.*

In communication meant to activate, the purpose statement will stress behaviour:

- *After listening to my presentation, my audience members will sign my petition.*

Your purpose statement should always be specific, realistic, and worded from the audience's point of view. "The purpose of this blog post is to save the whales" is not a purpose statement that has been carefully thought out. Your readers wouldn't be able to jump up and save the whales, even if they were motivated into a frenzy. They might, however, be able to support a specific piece of legislation.

A clear, specific purpose statement will help you stay on track as you go through all the stages of preparation for your persuasive communication. Because the main purpose of your communication is to have an effect on your audience, use this test regularly for every idea, every piece of evidence, and every organizational structure that you think of using. Ask yourself, "Will this help me to get my audience and co-communicators to think/feel/behave in the manner I have described in my purpose statement?" If the answer is "yes," you forge ahead.

Avoid Fallacies

A **fallacy** (from the Latin word meaning "false") is a mistaken or misleading argument. Although originally the term implied purposeful deception, most logical fallacies are not recognized as such by those who use them. Scholars have devoted lives and volumes to the description of various types

COMMUNICATION ON-SCREEN

Thank You for Smoking (2005)
Directed by Jason Reitman.

Based on a novel by Christopher Buckley, the film centres on Nick Naylor (Aaron Eckhart), the chief spokesperson for Big Tobacco, who uses spin tactics to lobby on behalf of cigarette use. Nick and his friends, a firearm lobbyist and an alcohol lobbyist, meet regularly, calling themselves "the Merchants of Death." On a trip to Hollywood to promote cigarette use in movies, Naylor brings his son Joey along, in hopes of teaching him the beauty of argument and persuasion. This film is notable for not following a traditional Hollywood formula. The lead is by no means a "good" man, but his use of argumentation often highlights the flaws in his opponent's claims, no matter how moral they may seem. As the film progresses, so too does the lead character's necessity to balance his argumentative and rhetorical skill with moral and ethical reflection.

> **fallacy**
> A mistaken or misleading argument.

"I've hired this musician to play a sad melody while I give you a sob story why I didn't do my homework. It's actually quite effective."

of logical fallacies. In the following sections we take a look at some of the most common ones to keep in mind when building your persuasive argument.[5]

Attack on the Person Instead of the Argument (*ad Hominem*)

ad hominem fallacy
A fallacious argument that attacks the integrity of a person to weaken his or her position.

reductio ad absurdum fallacy
Fallacious reasoning that unfairly attacks an argument by extending it to such extreme lengths that it looks ridiculous.

either–or fallacy
Fallacious reasoning that sets up false alternatives, suggesting that if the inferior one must be rejected, then the other must be accepted.

post hoc fallacy
Fallacious reasoning that mistakenly assumes that one event causes another because they occur sequentially.

In an *ad hominem* **fallacy** the speaker attacks the integrity of the person making an argument instead of the argument itself. At its crudest an *ad hominem* argument is easy to detect. Attacking someone's point of view by exclaiming, "How could anyone believe that fat-headed, ignorant slob?" is hardly persuasive. However, it takes critical thinking to catch more subtle *ad hominem* arguments. Consider this one: "All this talk about 'family values' is hypocritical. Take the example of a politician, a minister for family services, who makes a speech about the 'sanctity of marriage.' Then it comes out he was having an affair with his secretary, and his wife is suing him for divorce." The minister may well be a hypocrite, but his behaviour doesn't prove anything about the merits of family values.

Reduction to the Absurd (*Reductio ad Absurdum*)

A *reductio ad absurdum* **fallacy** unfairly attacks an argument by extending it to such extreme lengths that it looks ridiculous. For example, "If we allow developers to build homes on this parcel of land in the Shady Acres ravine, soon we will have no open spaces left. Fresh air and wildlife will be things of the past;" or "If we allow the administration to raise tuition this year, soon they will be raising it every year, and before we know it, only the wealthiest students will be able to go to school here." This extension of reasoning doesn't make any sense: developing one area doesn't necessarily mean that other areas have to be developed, and one tuition increase doesn't mean that others will follow. These policies might be unwise or unfair, but the *reductio ad absurdum* reasoning doesn't prove it.

Either–Or

An **either–or fallacy** sets up false alternatives, suggesting that if the inferior option must be rejected, then the other must be accepted. An angry citizen used either–or thinking to support a proposed city ordinance: "Either we outlaw alcohol in city parks, or there will be no way to get rid of drunks." This reasoning overlooks the possibility that there may be other ways to control public drunkenness besides banning all alcoholic beverages. The old saying "Canada—love it or leave it" is another example of either–or reasoning. Along the same lines is the either–or argument used by Quebec separatists, who claim that Quebec must achieve sovereignty and establish its own government or else lose its culture.

False Cause (*Post Hoc*)

A *post hoc* **fallacy** mistakenly assumes that one event causes another because they occur sequentially. An old joke is a useful illustration: Mac approaches Jack and asks, "Hey, why are you snapping your fingers?" Jack replies, "To keep the elephants away." Mac is incredulous, "What are you

---

🎥 COMMUNICATION ON-SCREEN

Man on Wire (2008)

Directed by James Marsh.

This beautiful British documentary chronicles Philippe Petit's legendary high-wire walk between the former Twin Towers of the World Trade Center. His walk lasted over an hour and, even in an age of CG special effects, it still captivates. The film is structured almost like a heist film, and features moving interviews with Petit himself, a strange reflective figure, and the many captivated people over a thousand feet below. For many, his walk was deemed "the artful crime of the century" and yet, despite knowing how it ends, this film is stunningly suspenseful. The beauty of the film is that, much like those people almost 40 years ago, and thousands of feet below, we are utterly engaged. The criminal nature of the crime is a distinct focal point, leading us to question: "What is art and what is crime?"

YOUNG COMMUNICATOR PROFILE

GURDEEP AHLUWALIA

Co-Host, CP24 Breakfast Weekend. Reporter/Anchor, CP24 and TSN SportsCentre

I've always been fascinated by the media. As a kid, getting ready for school, I'd be watching sports highlights or the morning news. Then, during breakfast, I'd read the newspaper—usually the sports section. It became apparent pretty early that I wasn't going to be an NHL superstar, so I figured the next best thing would be reporting on it for a living.

I went to McMaster and took a double major with mass media communications and sociology. I also spent a sizable chunk of time every week working for the campus newspaper as Sports Editor, as well as hosting and producing a weekly show on campus radio.

After my time at Mac, I immediately began internships behind the scenes at two television stations and a magazine. I was able to turn those opportunities into jobs within six months. After putting together a rough demo reel, I landed a job hosting a morning television show on a small, local cable channel. That lead [sic] to a hosting, producing, and reporting gig with another local station, which ultimately led me to my current job with CP24.

After two and a half years at CP24, I was able to add TSN to the mix—they're both Bell Media properties.

Currently, I am the co-host of CP24 Breakfast and a reporter/anchor with TSN SportsCentre.

While the television industry is very fluid and "hands on," studying communications gave me a firm theoretical understanding of underlying issues like gatekeeping, agenda setting, and ownership concentration. In a very transitional industry, this grounding helps me stay a step ahead of the game.

talking about? There aren't any elephants within a thousand miles of here." Jack smiles and keeps on snapping: "I know. Works pretty well, doesn't it?"

In real life, *post hoc* fallacies aren't always so easy to detect. For example, imagine an education critic pointing out that sexual promiscuity among adolescents began to increase about the same time that prayer in public schools was prohibited by the courts. A causal link may exist in this case: decreased emphasis on spirituality *could* contribute to promiscuity. But you would need evidence to establish a definite connection between the two events.

Appeal to Authority (*Argumentum ad Verecundiam*)

An **argumentum ad verecundiam fallacy** involves relying on the testimony of someone who is not an authority in the area under discussion. Relying on an expert is not necessarily a fallacy, of course. A Toronto starlet might be just the right person to offer advice on how to appear more glamorous, and a member of the Vancouver Canucks hockey team could be the best person to comment on what it takes to succeed in organized sports. But an *argumentum ad verecundiam* fallacy occurs when the celeb promotes a political candidate or the hockey player tells us why we should buy a certain kind of automobile. When considering endorsements and claims, it's smart to ask yourself whether the source is qualified to make them.

Bandwagon Appeal (*Argumentum ad Populum*)

An **argumentum ad populum fallacy** is based on the often dubious notion that because many people favour an idea, you should, too. Sometimes, of course, the mass appeal of an idea can be a sign of its merit. If most of your friends have enjoyed a film or a book, there is a good chance that you will as well. But in other cases, widespread acceptance of an idea is no guarantee of its

> **argumentum ad verecundiam fallacy**
> Fallacious reasoning that tries to support a belief by relying on the testimony of someone who is not an authority on the issue being argued.
>
> **argumentum ad populum fallacy**
> Fallacious reasoning based on the dubious notion that because many people favour an idea, you should, too.

COMMUNICATING ONLINE

Ten Ways to Use LinkedIn

Creating a persuasive message extends to establishing your online presence as a professional. You want to present an image of yourself as someone others will like and want to work with. Essentially, you want to persuade someone to hire you. LinkedIn is a social media website that provides a popular way of having an up-to-date resume online at all times, while also expanding your network of professional contacts. The following tips by Guy Kawasaki provide a great base for creating an image that will persuade anyone to hire you.

1. *Fully complete your profile*: Ensuring that this contains all relevant career history and interests. LinkedIn makes this easy by displaying a percentage score to show how complete your profile is. A LinkedIn profile basically acts as an online CV, so make sure you're being honest and describing yourself and career clearly.

2. *Edit profile to claim vanity URL*: This should be set to use your name (or closest match if unavailable) within the URL, for example: www.linkedin.com/in/kevingibbons—this will help you to optimise your own name in the search engines and also makes the URL easier to remember if promoted on business cards or e-mail signatures.

3. *Make your profile publicly available*: You can set the information which is publicly available to non-members/contacts, be careful with blocking too much information as this will also be unavailable to the search engines. As a minimum, I would recommend providing enough information for the search engines to index your profile and cache the external links you have listed! In terms of optimising your profile, the main goals are normally to rank for your own name, company name and possibly industry keywords related to this.

4. *Make connections*: Increase the reach of your profile by connecting with current and former work colleagues, clients, friends, and family. I'd also recommend adding any industry contacts, perhaps from people you have met at conferences/events or are connected with on other social media sites and share a similar interest.

5. *Request recommendations*: Obviously don't ask everyone, especially if you don't know them that well. But having recommendations will help your profile to stand out and will help to build trust in your reputation to visiting users. This will help improve the visibility of your own profile within internal LinkedIn searches too.

6. *Register a company profile*: If your company doesn't already have a company listing, you should create one! If your company does have a profile, you should encourage employees to create their own individual LinkedIn profiles and ensure the current employer entry is completed. This will automatically update all employees listed on the company profile, providing the company name is exactly matched.

7. *Make use of the three website hyperlinks*: For SEO value, LinkedIn is very good—they give you the opportunity to add three hyperlinks to websites of your choice. If you're not trying to optimise your site for "My Website," "My Portfolio," and "My Blog" it might be an idea to select "Other" and choose your own anchor text instead!

8. *Join related groups*: Find groups where other industry professionals have joined and look to participate in (or at least join) these groups. Adding value to your own profile and helping you to get found by other industry contacts.

9. *Use LinkedIn Answers*: This can help to build up your reputation within a field. For SEO it also builds the number of internal links pointing to your profile from within LinkedIn, therefore helping to strengthen your profile in the search engines!

10. *Optimise your job title*: LinkedIn now includes your job title within profile title tags. I'm not saying you should lie about your job, but within reason you could include descriptive keywords which may help to attract relevant search engine traffic. For example, using "SEO Account Manager" as a job title instead of "Account Manager," if appropriate.

—Guy Kawasaki, http://blog.guykawasaki.com/2007/01/ten_ways_to_use.html, 4 January 2007

validity. In the face of almost universal belief to the contrary, Galileo reasoned accurately that the earth is not the centre of the universe, and he suffered for his convictions. The lesson here is simple to comprehend but often difficult to follow: when faced with an idea, don't just follow the crowd. Consider the facts carefully, and make up your own mind.

Interpersonal Persuasion

Interpersonal persuasion is an area of research concerned with how people gain compliance from other people. That is to say, it is the study of the technique that people use in marketing, sales, or social psychology to persuade others to accept a product or an idea or to change their behaviours. In this section, we will examine several basic compliance-gaining techniques.

Foot-in-the-Door

This is a classic persuasion technique that has been practised since the dawn of time. It is based on the belief that if a persuader can just overcome initial resistance, that is, "get a **foot-in-the-door**," he or she can also overcome any impediments to the sale or persuasive proposition they are offering. Studies have shown that this approach is effective—if a persuader can convince someone to comply with a small request, then it is much easier to get that person to comply with another, much larger request.[6]

Door-in-the-Face

This technique is the inverse of the foot-in-the-door. With the **door-in-the-face** method, the persuader starts by making a large, outrageous first request which is almost certainly to be denied and then follows it up with a second, smaller request which seems more "reasonable" in the context of the first one. Robert B. Cialdini, and colleagues, designed an experiment where participants were asked to counsel juvenile delinquents for two years. All refused. However, 50 per cent of them agreed to a second request to chaperone juvenile delinquents on a trip to the zoo.[7]

interpersonal persuasion
An area of research concerned with how people gain compliance from other people.

foot-in-the-door
A persuasion technique based on the idea that if a persuader can overcome initial resistance, he or she can also overcome any other impediments to persuading his or her audience.

door-in-the-face
A persuasion technique in which a persuader makes a large, outrageous first request which is almost certainly to be denied followed by a smaller request which seems more "reasonable" in the context of the first request.

social exchange
A persuasion technique in which the persuader presents the target person with a material or psychological gift and, in exchange, is granted a request.

low-balling
A persuasion technique in which the persuader makes a first, reasonable request and, once it has been accepted, increases the cost of the transaction.

cognitive dissonance
The tension caused by holding two conflicting thoughts simultaneously.

Social Exchange

In **social exchange** compliance-gaining the persuader presents the target person with a material or psychological gift. When the persuader later approaches the target person with a request, he or she complies.

Low-Balling

In **low-balling**, the persuader makes a first, reasonable request that the target person accepts. The persuader then increases the cost of the transaction. Psychologically, once a person has complied to an earlier request, he or she experiences **cognitive dissonance** (see the box on pg. 426) when faced with the possibility of having to walk away from a commitment; therefore, the target person is likely to accept the second, more costly request. The challenge in this compliance-gaining technique is for the persuader to avoid making the second request seem outrageous. For example, when a person buys a car, he or she is initially offered a low price. However, when the person goes to sign the deal, he or she is offered additional packages such as extra warranties, undercoating, rust-proofing, etc. Many people, feeling that they have already got a "great deal" on the car, will make these impulsive purchases, which are highly profitable and significantly raise the dealership's margins on the auto purchase.

How to Persuade Anyone: Four Timeless Strategies

Author Dan Pink's latest book, *To Sell Is Human* argues that everyone is a salesperson. And it's true. Whether you're negotiating an acquisition, recruiting new talent, trying to ink an elusive client, or even just asking for a raise, you need to be well versed in the powers of persuasion.

So no matter your industry, no matter your title, no matter your years of experience, learning to persuade others through the spoken word is crucial to success. But how can you actually do that? Naturally, it all starts with language. By shaping your speech with a few rhetorical devices, you can capture your audience's attention and wedge your ideas in their memory.

Keep in mind that all of these strategies are useless if you don't understand your audience and what it values, or what your ultimate goal is. But once those details are hammered out, you can use the following strategies to better accomplish your purpose and win over your audience. Here are some of the most common rhetorical devices and how to use them to your advantage:

1. *Similes and metaphors.* Similes and metaphors are the bread and butter of persuasion. Simply enough, comparing a new concept to a familiar one quickly illuminates the new concept. Look at Abraham Lincoln's Gettysburg Address, which uses a metaphor of birth to describe both

the formation of the US ("conceived in liberty") and the road of reconstruction following the Civil War ("that this nation . . . shall have a new birth of freedom"). The comparison underscores the fragility of the nation and the time and effort required to care for freedom more so than if Lincoln just explained the logistics of rebuilding. When you're looking for buy-in to an unfamiliar, disruptive idea, try to package it with familiar concepts, especially ones that have seen success in the past.

2. *Parallelism.* Parallel structure arranges words or phrases on equal footing, often while creating a rhythm and a repetition to which the brain clings. Consider, for example, the final words of the Gettysburg Address: ". . . government of the people, by the people, for the people, shall not perish from the earth." Or for a more recent example, consider Steve Jobs introducing the world to the iPhone, coyly suggesting he's introducing three new products: "So, three things: a widescreen iPod with touch controls, a revolutionary mobile phone, and a breakthrough internet communications device. An iPod, a phone, and an internet communicator. An iPod, a phone . . . are you getting it? These are not three separate devices; this is one device, and we are calling it iPhone." By grouping together several different forms

That's-Not-All

The **that's-not-all** technique involves the persuader presenting a proposition and a cost without allowing the buyer to respond immediately. After a few seconds of mulling the cost over, the target person is presented with a gift to "sweeten the deal." This technique works because of the reciprocity principle—if someone does you a favour, you feel obliged to do one for them.

Fear-Then-Relief

The **fear-then-relief** technique occurs when the persuader causes the target person to feel fear and, after a short period of time, replaces the fear-causing threat with a gesture of kindness. In the momentary relief felt at the sudden change in emotions, the target person is more likely to comply. This technique is used by teachers when they tell a student "You know you are in danger of failing this course." And, after the fear of failure sinks in, "But if you stay for study group after school, you will pass." Chances are the student will agree to stay for the study period. Fear-then-relief is also used in the interrogation of suspects by police or military officers, who put the subject in a state of extreme anxiety and fear in the interrogation room and then relieve that fear. This is the origin of the good cop–bad cop routine that the police often use.

> **that's-not-all**
> A persuasion technique in which the persuader presents a proposition and a cost, followed by a gift.
>
> **fear-then-relief**
> A persuasion technique in which the persuader causes the target person to feel fear and then, after a short period of time, replaces the fear-causing threat with a gesture of kindness.

---

of government, three different products, or whatever else you might list together, you can paint a picture of a broader whole based on several representative parts.

3. *Repetition.* The more an idea is repeated, the more it's accepted as fact. Look, for example, at the Weather Channel's controversial decision to begin naming winter storms. While a number of meteorologists balked at the idea, The Weather Channel went full steam ahead in the buildup to the massive blizzard that slammed the Northeast earlier this year, peppering the name "Nemo" across its website and TV broadcast until the name was trending on Twitter and working its way into headlines. Look also at the number of times Steve Jobs uses the words revolutionary (12), and breakthrough (6), and variations of the phrase "reinvent the phone" (5) throughout his iPhone keynote. Through the power of repetition, he's reminding us what to think about the product he's revealing. So whether you're building a brand or selling a product, repeat your key messages and watch them take hold.

4. *Antithesis.* This rhetorical device pulls together two opposing forces or concepts to emphasize a particular contrast. One of the more powerful examples is from Martin Luther King, Jr's "I Have a Dream" speech. His line "I have a dream that my four little children will one day live in a nation where they will not be judged by the color of their skin but by the content of their character" sets "the color of their skin" in opposition to "the content of their character." This antithesis drives home the breadth of the gap between the current reality and the realization of King's dream, as well as emphasizes the contrast between the two ways of looking at a person, stressing how trivial "the color of their skin" ends up being. These types of comparisons can highlight differences between the past and the present, the present and the future, or two different ways of interpreting a situation.

Bottom line, your words matter, but how you arrange them matters even more. So next time you're preparing a presentation, a sales call, or even just a pep talk for a weekly meeting, try planting some of these rhetorical seeds and watch them take root. You don't have to be a salesperson to sell. All you need is language.

Dan Roitman, *Huffington Post Canada Business*, 20 May 2013

QUESTIONS: Can you think of specific real-world examples for each of these four strategies? Can you come up with more? Is there anything wrong with the premise that "everyone is a salesperson?"

Cognitive Dissonance

Description

This is the feeling of uncomfortable tension which comes from holding two conflicting thoughts in the mind at the same time.

Dissonance increases with:

- the importance of the subject to us;
- how strongly the dissonant thoughts conflict; and
- our inability to rationalize and explain away the conflict.

Dissonance is often strong when we believe something about ourselves and then do something against that belief. If I believe I am good but do something bad, then the discomfort I feel as a result is cognitive dissonance.

Cognitive dissonance is a very powerful motivator which will often lead us to change one or other of the conflicting belief or action. The discomfort often feels like a tension between the two opposing thoughts. To release the tension we can take one of three actions:

- change our behaviour;
- justify our behaviour by changing the conflicting cognition; or
- justify our behaviour by adding new cognitions.

Dissonance is most powerful when it is about our self-image. Feelings of foolishness, immorality, and so on (including internal projections during decision-making) are dissonance in action.

If an action has been completed and cannot be undone, then the after-the-fact dissonance compels us to change our beliefs. If beliefs are moved, then the dissonance appears during decision-making, forcing us to take actions we would not have taken before.

Cognitive dissonance appears in virtually all evaluations and decisions and is the central mechanism by which we experience new differences in the world. When we see other people behave differently to our images of them, when we hold any conflicting thoughts, we experience dissonance.

Dissonance increases with the importance and impact of the decision, along with the difficulty of reversing it. Discomfort about making the wrong choice of car is bigger than when choosing a lamp.

Research

[Leon] Festinger first developed this theory in the 1950s to explain how members of a cult who were persuaded by their leader, a certain Mrs Keech, that the earth was going to be destroyed on 21 December and that they alone were going to be rescued by aliens, actually *increased* their commitment to the cult when this did not happen (Festinger himself had infiltrated the cult, and would have been very surprised to meet little green men). The dissonance of the thought of being so stupid was so great that instead they revised their beliefs to meet with obvious facts: that the aliens had, through their concern for the cult, saved the world instead.

In a more mundane experiment, Festinger and [James M.] Carlsmith got students to lie about a boring task. Those who were paid $1 for the task felt uncomfortable lying.

Example: Smokers find all kinds of reasons to explain away their unhealthy habit. The alternative is to feel a great deal of dissonance. So what?

Using it: Cognitive dissonance is central to many forms of persuasion to change beliefs, values, attitudes, and behaviours. The tension can be injected suddenly or allowed to build up over time. People can be moved in many small jumps or one large one.

Defending: When you start feeling uncomfortable, stop and see if you can find the inner conflict. Then notice how that came about. If it was somebody else who put that conflict there, you can decide not to play any more with them.

Run by David Straker, ChangingMinds.org is one of the leading international websites for cataloguing and describing the techniques and theories of persuasion. Checking it regularly or signing up to David Straker's Twitter feed (twitter.com/changingminds) is a good idea for students interested in keeping abreast of the latest international developments in persuasion theory and practice.

David Straker, changingminds.org/explanations/ theories/cognitive_dissonance.htm, June 2014

Summary

Persuasion is central to our lives and is something that we practise almost every day. This chapter began by explaining that persuasion is the process of motivating someone, through communication and relationship-building, to change attitudes, beliefs, values, or behaviours. We then discussed the four characteristics of persuasion—non-coercive, usually incremental, interactive, and possibly ethical—and three persuasion categories—type of proposition, desired outcome, and directness of approach.

When creating a persuasive message, it is important to set a clear purpose and to avoid logical fallacies. This chapter describes several fallacies to keep in mind: *ad hominem*, *reductio ad absurdum*, either–or, *post hoc*, *argumentum ad verecundiam*, and *argumentum ad populum*.

One particular form of persuasive communication is found in marketing, sales, and social psychology. Interpersonal persuasion uses a set of techniques to gain compliance from people. This chapter discussed several methods of this type, including foot-in-the-door, door-in-the-face, social exchange, low-balling, that's-not-all, and fear-then-relief.

Key Terms

activate   417

ad hominem fallacy   420

anchor   411

argumentum ad populum fallacy   421

argumentum ad verecundiam fallacy   421

cognitive dissonance   424

convince   416

direct persuasion   418

door-in-the-face   423

either–or fallacy   420

ethical persuasion   413

fallacy   419

fear-then-relief   425

foot-in-the-door   423

indirect persuasion   418

interpersonal persuasion   423

latitudes of acceptance   411

latitudes of non-commitment   411

latitudes of rejection   411

low-balling   424

message   412

news release   412

op-ed   412

persuasion   410

post hoc fallacy   420

propositions of fact   414

propositions of policy   414

propositions of value   414

reductio ad absurdum fallacy   420

social exchange   424

social judgment theory   411

that's-not-all   425

Activities

A. Personal Persuasion

Think about a time when you changed your attitude about something. Was it after a discussion? Reading an online article or tweet? Was the persuasion interactive? Coercive? Incremental? Ethical? Explain your answer.

B. Propositions of Fact, Value, and Policy

Which of the following statements are propositions of fact, propositions of value, and propositions of policy?

1. "Three Strikes" laws that put criminals away for life after their third conviction are [*or* are *not*] fair.

2. Daycare for toddlers should [*or* should *not*] be the responsibility of government.

3. The mercury in dental fillings is [*or is not*] healthy for the dental patient.

4. Pay raises for MPs should [*or should not*] be delayed until an election has intervened.

5. The democratic process is compromised when an elected Member of Parliament crosses the floor to join another party.

6. Private clinics should [*or should not*] be allowed to perform MRIs and other procedures when hospital wait times are unacceptable.

7. A nutritionist and chef should [*or should not*] be on staff at every elementary school.

8. All forms of tobacco advertising should [*or should not*] be banned.

9. More breastfeeding support should [*or should not*] be provided to new mothers.

10. Cellphones are [*or are not*] dangerous to your health.

C. Find the Fallacy

Test your ability to detect shaky reasoning by identifying which fallacy discussed on pages 419-23 is exhibited in each of the following statements.

1. Some companies claim to be in favour of protecting the environment, but you can't trust them. Businesses exist to make a profit, and the cost of saving the earth is just another expense to be cut.

2. Take it from me, Google phones are much better than BlackBerrys. I used to only ever use a BlackBerry, but now they're all junk.

3. You should never use margarine. After all, the number of people with heart problems went up right after margarine became popular.

4. Carpooling to cut down on the parking problem is a stupid idea. Look around—nobody carpools!

5. I know that staying in the sun can cause cancer, but if I start worrying about every environmental risk I'll have to stay inside a bomb shelter breathing filtered air, never drive a car or ride my bike, and I won't be able to eat anything.

6. Theories of Intelligent Design are just a way for Bible-thumping, know-nothing fundamentalists to pass off creationism as science.

D. Interpersonal Persuasion

Identify several people who have tried to persuade you via interpersonal persuasion. They might be salespeople, politicians, teachers, members of the clergy, coaches, bosses, or anyone else. Identify which interpersonal persuasive technique each used with you. How did the scenarios play out? Did each person follow the technique to the letter? Do you think that he or she had been trained in persuasion?

E. The Credibility of Persuaders

Identify a person who has attempted to persuade you via interpersonal persuasion or mass communication. This person could be a celebrity, an authority figure, an expert, a teacher, a politician, or anyone else. Analyze this person's credibility in terms of the three dimensions discussed in the chapter. Which dimension is most important in terms of this person's effectiveness?

F. Analyzing Communication Behaviours

Read Table 11.1 carefully. The behaviours listed there are presented in an order that some communication experts would describe as most serious to least serious. Do you agree or disagree with the order of these ethical faults? State whether you would change the order of any of these behaviours and explain your answer. What other behaviours would you add to this list?

Further Reading

Perloff, Richard, M, *The Dynamics of Persuasion: Communication and Attitudes in the 21st Century* (New York: Routledge, 2010).
Perloff provides an up-to-date textbook looking at persuasion from social psychological and sociological perspectives. The book puts a special focus on the study of attitudes, beliefs, and values, combining theoretical and applied perspectives.

Rybacki, Donald, and Karyn Rybacki, *Advocacy and Opposition: An Introduction to Argumentation,* 7th edn (Boston: Allyn and Bacon, 2011).
The authors provide a practical approach to argumentation and critical thinking for the beginning student who needs to construct and present arguments on questions of fact, value, and policy—both in oral and written form. Their work offers a theoretical view of the nature of argument, a discussion of ethical principles of arguing as a form of communication, and a focus on how arguments are created.

Study Questions

1. Watch your Facebook or Twitter feed closely for three days. Note the types of persuasion techniques (pp. 413–18) the people and groups you follow use to try to persuade you to change (or reinforce) your attitudes, beliefs, values, or behaviours. Identify whether they are using indirect or direct persuasion.

2. Tune in to the national news broadcast on one of the major Canadian television channels. Write down the fallacies (pp. 420–23) that you hear in the reasoning of the people being interviewed. How many fallacies can you count in one news broadcast?

3. Imagine you are given the task of creating a campaign to motivate office workers to exercise more often. How could you use each of the types of interpersonal persuasion to convince people to be more active? Which types of persuasion are most effective?

12

Writing and Delivering Speeches

After studying the material in this chapter . . .

You should understand:

- ✔ the importance of defining a clear speech purpose;
- ✔ the differences among a general purpose, a specific purpose, and a thesis;
- ✔ the steps involved in organizing the body of a speech;
- ✔ the importance of effective introductions, conclusions, and transitions;
- ✔ the functions and types of supporting material and visual aids;
- ✔ the elements of a speech that help maintain an audience's attention;
- ✔ the necessity of analyzing a speaking situation;
- ✔ the differences among the various types of delivery; and
- ✔ the differences between facilitative and debilitative stage fright.

You should be able to:

- ✔ choose an effective speaking topic;
- ✔ formulate a purpose statement and thesis statement that will help you develop that topic;
- ✔ construct an effective speech outline using the organizing principles described in this chapter;
- ✔ develop an effective introduction, conclusion, and transitions;
- ✔ choose supporting material for a speech to make your points clear, interesting, memorable, and convincing;
- ✔ build persuasive arguments through audience analysis;
- ✔ follow the guidelines for effective extemporaneous, impromptu, manuscript, and memorized speeches; and
- ✔ overcome debilitative stage fright.

Chapter Highlights

Developing your topic begins with defining your purpose. You should understand and be able to state the following simply and clearly:

» your general purpose (to entertain, to inform, or to persuade);

» your specific purpose (expressed in the form of a purpose statement); and

» your central idea (expressed in the form of a thesis statement).

There are several tools that are designed to make the important job of structuring your speech easier and more effective. In this chapter we will look at:

» working outlines,

» formal outlines, and

» speaking notes.

Following a few simple principles will enable you to build an effective outline. These principles deal with:

» standard symbols,

» standard format,

» the rule of division, and

» the rule of parallel wording.

The effective use of supporting material is one of the most important aspects of speech preparation. In this chapter we will explore:

» functions of supporting material,

» types of supporting material, and

» styles of support, including narration and citation.

One of the first things to consider when preparing a speech is the style of delivery. In this chapter we will look at four types:

» extemporaneous,

» impromptu,

» manuscript, and

» memorized.

Visual aids are a unique type of supporting material. In this chapter we will examine:

» types of visual aids;

» media for the presentation of visual aids; and

» rules for using visual aids.

Stage fright is one of the most formidable barriers to effective public speaking. In this chapter, we will look at:

» the differences between facilitative and debilitative stage fright;

» the sources of debilitative stage fright; and

» ways to overcome debilitative stage fright.

Cultural Idiom
the toast
The speech given before a drink to honour someone.

Public speaking can be a horror for the shy person, but it can also be the ultimate act of liberation. . . .I hadn't realized the transformative effect it could have on the speaker herself.

Susan Faludi, journalist and author

A surprising number of people will give speeches that will change their lives. Some of these will be job related speeches, like the presentation that gets your new company funded or wins you a promotion. Some will be personal, such as the toast at your best friend's wedding or a eulogy for a lost relative.

You probably realize that the ability to speak well in public can benefit both your personal and professional life. You may also recognize that successful public speaking can be a liberating, transformative experience that boosts your self-confidence and helps you make a difference in the world. Yet most of us view the prospect of standing before an audience with the same enthusiasm we have for a trip to the dentist or the tax auditor. In fact, giving a speech seems to be one of the most anxiety-producing things we can do.

Despite the discomfort that speech giving causes, sooner or later you will need to talk to an audience of some kind, as part of a class project, as part of a job, or as part of a community action group. And even in less "speech-like" situations, you will often need the same skills that are important in speech giving: the ability to talk with confidence, to organize ideas in a clear way, and to make those ideas interesting and persuasive.

Attaining a mastery of public speaking is at least partially a matter of practice. But practice doesn't always make perfect; without a careful analysis of what you are doing, practice has a tendency to make old public speaking habits permanent rather than perfect. This chapter will provide you with tools to analyze and improve your performance as a public speaker.

Choosing a Topic

Often the difference between a successful and an unsuccessful speech is the choice of topic. Your topic should be familiar enough for your audience to understand yet be innovative enough to hold its attention. Two main guidelines will help you pick a topic that is right for you, your audience, and your assignment.

Cultural Idiom
stick with
To continue with something.

First, look for a topic early. The best student speakers usually choose a topic as soon as possible after a speech is assigned by their instructor, and then they stick with it. Picking a topic early is important to allow you to have adequate practice time, as well as time for ideas to "baste" in your mind. The longer you keep a topic in your mind, the more you will inspired by everyday observations and feelings and the better your speech will be.

Second, choose a topic that interests you. Your topic must be interesting to your audience, and the best way to accomplish that is to find a topic that is interesting to you. Your interest in a topic will also improve your ability to create the speech, and it will increase your confidence when it comes time to present it. You could use the following checklist as a guide to pick a topic.

Review:	Discuss current events:	Think about
newspapers,	international,	activities,
magazines,	national,	hobbies,
books,	local,	special interests,
various multimedia sources, and	family, and	personal experience, and
social media, such as Digg	friends over Facebook	different perspectives on
or Reddit Canada.	and Twitter.	the same idea.

Once you have chosen your topic you can begin developing it. Your first step in that task is defining your purpose.

Defining Purpose

No one gives a speech—or expresses *any* kind of message—without having a reason to do so. Even in subtler messages, the speaker always has a purpose: to evoke a response from the listener.

The first step in understanding the purpose is to formulate a clear and precise statement of that purpose. This requires an understanding of both *general purpose* and *specific purpose*.

General Purpose

Most students, when asked why they are giving a speech in a college or university class, will quickly cite course requirements. But you have to analyze your motives more deeply than that to develop a speech purpose that will influence your audience.

When we say you have to influence your audience, we mean you have to change it in some way. If you think about all the possible ways you could change an audience, you'll realize that they all boil down to three options, which happen to be the three **general purposes** for speaking:

1. *To entertain.* To relax your audience by providing it with a pleasant listening experience.
2. *To inform.* To enlighten your audience by teaching it something.
3. *To persuade.* To move your audience toward a new attitude or behaviour.

No speech could ever have just one purpose. A speech designed for one purpose will almost always accomplish a little of the other purposes. That said, two basic characteristics differentiate an informative topic from a persuasive topic.

First, an informative speech generally does not present information that an audience is likely to disagree with. Second, the informative speaker's intent, unlike that of the persuasive speaker, is not to change attitudes or to make the audience members feel differently about the topic. However, the informative speaker does try to make the topic important to the audience and certainly seeks a response—typically attention and interest—from listeners.

general purpose
A basic way to affect an audience. There are three options: to entertain, to inform, or to persuade.

Cultural Idiom
boil down to
To reduce to the basic elements.

Thus, we say that any speech is primarily designed for one of these purposes. A clear understanding of your general purpose gets you on the right track for choosing and developing a topic. Understanding your specific purpose will keep you on that track.

Specific Purpose

Whereas your general purpose is only a one-word label, your **specific purpose** is expressed in the form of a **purpose statement**—a complete sentence that describes exactly what you want your speech to accomplish. The purpose statement usually isn't used word for word in the actual speech; its purpose is to keep you focused as you plan.

If your speech's general purpose is to be informative, you might begin to frame your specific purpose by asking: "Do I seek to *describe, explain,* or *instruct?*"

A speech of **description** is the most straightforward type of informative speech. You generally divide this type of speech into the components of the thing you are describing. Whatever its topic, the speech of description creates a "word picture" of the essential details that make that thing what it is.

Explanations clarify ideas and concepts that are already known but not understood by an audience. Explanations often deal with the question of why. Why does the stock market rise or fall? Why do we have to wait until the age of 18 to vote?

Instructions teach something to the audience in a logical, step-by-step manner. The basis of training programs and orientations, they often deal with the question of "how to." Speeches of instruction might deal with *how to* prepare for a test or a job interview. This type of speech often features a demonstration or visual aid.

Criteria for a Good Purpose Statement

The types of informative speeches described above aren't mutually exclusive. There is considerable overlap, as when you give a speech about objects with the purpose of explaining them. Regardless of your speech's general purpose, however, there are three criteria for a good purpose statement:

1. **A Purpose Statement Should Be Receiver-Oriented.**
   Having a *receiver orientation* means that your purpose is focused on how your speech will affect your audience members. For example, if you were giving an informative talk on how to sue someone in small claims court, this would be an inadequate purpose statement:

   My purpose is to tell my audience about small claims court.

   Your purpose statement should refer to the response you want from your audience, not just what you want to tell them. It should tell what the audience members will know or be able to do after listening to your speech. Thus, the preceding purpose statement could be improved in this way:

   After listening to my speech, my audience will know more about small claims court procedures.

COMMUNICATION ON-SCREEN

Clone High (2002–2003)

In this criminally underrated Canadian comedy cartoon series, clones of famous historical figures such as Cleopatra, Gandhi, and Joan of Arc grow up in a high school, featuring a mad scientist as their principal. In one episode, titled *Election Blu-Galoo* (3 November 2002), Abraham Lincoln (Will Forte) and John F. Kennedy (Christopher Miller) compete for Student Body President. As the election race heats up, both contenders utilize increasingly corrupt electoral campaign schemes, climaxing in Lincoln performing extreme stunts with his sponsor "X-Stream Blu." When Abraham Lincoln realizes that his once idealistic campaign has been hijacked by an energy drink company he gives a rousing speech about the importance of integrity and purpose.

That's an improvement, because you have stated what you expect from your audience. But this purpose statement could be improved even more through the judicious application of a second criterion.

2. **A Purpose Statement Should Be Specific.**
   To be effective, a purpose statement should be worded specifically, with enough details so that, after your speech, you would be able to measure or test your audience to see if you had achieved your purpose. In the example given earlier, simply "knowing about small claims court" is too vague; you need something more specific, such as:

After listening to my speech, my audience will know how to win a case in small claims court.

This is an improvement, but it can be made still better by applying a third criterion.

3. **A Purpose Statement Should Be Realistic.**
   You must be able to accomplish your purpose as stated. You must aim for an achievable audience response. So a better purpose statement for this speech might sound something like:

After listening to my speech, my audience will be able to list the five steps for preparing a small claims case.

This purpose statement is receiver-oriented, specific, and realistic. It also suggests an organizational pattern for the speech ("the five steps"), which can be a bonus in a carefully worded purpose statement.

The Thesis Statement

Your next step in the focusing process is to formulate your **thesis statement**, which declares the central idea of your speech. The thesis statement for your small claims speech might be worded like this:

> *Arguing a case on your own in small claims court is a simple, five-step process that can give you the same results you would achieve with a lawyer.*

Unlike your purpose statement, your thesis statement is usually delivered directly to your audience. The thesis statement is usually formulated later in the speech-making process, after you have done some research on your topic.

thesis statement
A complete sentence describing the central idea of a speech.

Structuring the Speech

Knowing what you are talking about and *communicating* that knowledge are not the same thing. It's frustrating to realize you aren't expressing your thoughts clearly, and it's equally unpleasant to know that a speaker has something worth saying yet be unable to figure out just

basic speech structure
The division of a speech into introduction, body, and conclusion.

working outline
A constantly changing organizational aid used in planning a speech.

formal outline
A consistent format and set of symbols used to identify the structure of ideas.

what it is because the material is too jumbled to understand. Virtually every speech outline ought to follow the basic structure outlined in Figure 12.1.

This **basic speech structure** demonstrates the old aphorism for speakers: "Tell what you're going to say, say it, and then tell what you said." The clear, repetitive nature of the basic speech structure reduces the potential for memory loss because audiences have a tendency to listen more carefully during the beginning and ending of a speech.[1] Your outline will reflect this basic speech structure. Outlines come in all shapes and sizes, but the three types that are most important to us here are working outlines, formal outlines, and speaking notes.

Working Outlines, Formal Outlines, and Speaking Notes

A **working outline** is a construction tool used to map out your speech. The working outline will probably follow the basic speech structure but only in rough form. It is for your eyes only, so you can use whatever symbols and personal shorthand you find functional. Actually, you will probably create several drafts as you refine your ideas. As your ideas solidify, your outline will change accordingly, becoming more polished as you go along.

A **formal outline** serves several purposes. In simplified form, it can be used as a visual aid, displayed while you speak or distributed as a handout. It can serve as a record of a speech that was delivered. And in speech classes, instructors often use speech outlines to analyze student speeches. When one is used for that purpose, it is usually a full-sentence outline and includes the purpose, the thesis and topic, and/or title. Most instructors also require a bibliography of sources at the end of the outline. The bibliography should include full research citations, the correct form for which can be found in a style guide, such as *Fit to Print* by Joanne Buckley.[2]

Like your working outline, your speaking notes are for your use only, so the format is up to you. Many instructors also suggest that you fit your notes on one side of a set of note cards. Some recommend that you also have your introduction and conclusion on note cards, and still others advise that your longer quotations be written out on note cards.

Standard Symbols

A speech outline generally uses the following symbols:

> I.   Main point (Roman numeral)
>   A. Subpoint (capital letter)
>   1. Sub-subpoint (standard number)
>   a.   Sub–sub-subpoint (lowercase letter)

In the examples in this chapter, the major divisions of the speech—introduction, body, and conclusion—are not given symbols. They are listed by name, and the Roman numerals for their main points begin anew in each division. An alternative format is to list these major divisions with Roman numerals, main points with capital letters, and so on.

Standard Format

In the sample outlines in this chapter, notice that each symbol is indented a number of spaces from the symbol above it. Besides keeping the outline neat, the indentation of different-order ideas is actually the key to the technique of outlining; it enables you to coordinate and order ideas in the form in which they are most comprehensible to the human mind.

Proper outline form is based on a few rules and guidelines, which are discussed in the next sections. The first of these is the rule of division.

Introduction
I. Attention-getter
II. Preview

Body
I.
II.
III. } Three to five
IV.   main points
V.

Conclusion
I. Review
II. Final remarks

FIGURE 12.1 Basic Speech Structure

UNDERSTANDING COMMUNICATION TECHNOLOGY

Citing Web Sources

The internet is becoming an increasingly important source for speech research. When you list a Web source, you should provide the URL and the date you found it. You should also include, if possible, the author of the page, the organization that supports it, and the last date it was updated. A complete citation might look something like this:

T. Flynn and A. Sévigny, "The Paradox of Public Relations/Communications Management Education in Canada: Taught but Not Studied," *McMaster Journal of Communication* 6, updated 1 June 2010. Accessed 3 June 2010 at digitalcommons.mcmaster.ca/mjc

Note: The first five entries in the bibliography of the "Sample Speech Outline" box provide other examples of Web citations.

The Rule of Division

In formal outlines main points and subpoints always represent a division of a whole. Because it is impossible to divide something into fewer than two parts, you always have at least two main points for every topic. Then, if your main points are divided, you will always have at least two subpoints, and so on. Thus, the rule for formal outlines is "Never a 'I' without a 'II,' never an 'A' without a 'B,'" and so on.

Three to five is considered to be the ideal number of main points. It is also considered best to divide those main points into three to five subpoints, when necessary and possible. This practice is followed in the sample outline.

The Rule of Parallel Wording

Your main points should be worded in a similar or "parallel" manner. Whenever possible, subpoints should also be worded in a parallel manner. For your points to be parallel, they should each contain one, and only one, idea. This will enable you to completely develop one idea before moving on to another one in your speech. If you were discussing cures for indigestion, your topic might be divided incorrectly if your main points looked like this:

I.　"Preventive cures" help you before eating.
II.　"Participation cures" help you during and after eating.

You might actually have three ideas there and thus three main points:

I.　Prevention cures (before eating).
II.　Participation cures (during eating).
III.　Post-participation cures (after eating).

Organizing Your Points in a Logical Order

An outline should reflect a logical order for your points. You might arrange them from newest to oldest, largest to smallest, best to worst, or in one of the six ways that follow. The organizing pattern you choose ought to be the one that best develops your thesis.

Sample Speech Outline

Title: "Quebec Separatism: Three Different Points of View"

General purpose: To inform

Specific purpose: After listening to my speech, audience members will have a better understanding of what Quebec separatism represents for Aboriginal peoples in Quebec, French Canadians outside Quebec, and the Québécois themselves.

Thesis: Three communities—Aboriginal, French Canadians outside Quebec, and the Québécois—believe they would be affected in very different ways in the event of Quebec's separation from Canada.

Introduction

I. Attention-getter: In 1995, Canadians came very close to needing a passport to go shopping in Montreal!

II. Thesis statement

III. Preview of main points

Body

I. Why are Aboriginal people living in Quebec concerned about the idea of separation?

    A. They worry their interests would not be safeguarded in an independent Quebec.

        1. They have outstanding land claims for much of the territory of the current province of Quebec.

        2. They worry that an independent Quebec would not honour the financial commitments made to them by the Government of Canada.

    B. They worry that they might lose their cultures.

        1. They worry that they would not be encouraged to speak their languages and live their cultures.

        2. They worry that an independent Quebec might not provide schooling in Aboriginal languages and culture.

II. Why are French Canadians outside Quebec concerned about the idea of separation?

    A. They worry about preserving their cultural identity.

        1. They currently feel largely ignored by Quebec and fear that they would be abandoned entirely by an independent Quebec.

        2. They worry that the rest of Canada would no longer provide services or education in French.

    B. They worry about prejudice and retaliation.

        1. The rest of Canada might exclude French Canadians from social and economic opportunities.

        2. English-speaking Canadians who resent Quebec's separation might take out their resentment on francophones in the rest of Canada.

Time Patterns

> **time pattern**
> An organizing plan for a speech based on chronology.

Arrangement according to **time patterns**, or chronology, is one of the most common patterns of organization. The period of time could be anything from centuries to seconds. In a speech on airline food on Air Canada, a time pattern might look like this:

    I.   Early Air Canada food: a gourmet treat.

    II. The middle period: institutional food at 30,000 feet.

    III. Today's Air Canada food (unless you're in business class): the passenger with no spare money starves.

Arranging points according to the steps that make up a process is another form of time patterning. The topic "Recording a Hit Song" might use this type of patterning:

    I.   Find an agent.

    II. Record the demo tracks.

    III. Upload to YouTube.

    IV. Promote the song.

III. Why are many Québécois comfortable with the idea of separation?
   A. They believe that an independent Quebec would be fairer and more socially progressive than Canada is now.
      1. Historically, Québécois have had better relations with Aboriginal communities than English Canadians have.
      2. Quebec has done more than other provinces to support Aboriginal education.
   B. They believe that an independent Quebec would ensure a permanent francophone state in North America.
      1. An independent Quebec could be more forceful in arguing for French language rights outside its borders.
      2. An independent Quebec could negotiate French language rights for French Canadians outside Quebec as part of the separation agreement.
   C. They believe that an independent Quebec, without responsibilities to the rest of Canada, could provide better governance and make better use of its citizens' tax dollars.

Conclusion

I. Review of main points
II. Final remarks: Return to opening example, restate thesis: "Three communities—Aboriginal peoples, French Canadians outside Quebec, and the Québécois themselves—believe they would be affected in very different ways in the event of Quebec's separation from Canada."

Bibliography

Canadian Broadcasting Corporation, "Quebec Elections 1960–2003," available at archives.cbc.ca/IDD-1-73-651/politics_economy/quebec_elections/ (Accessed 1 April 2007.)

Canadian Broadcasting Corporation, "Separation Anxiety: The 1995 Québec Referendum," available at archives.cbc.ca/IDD-1-73-1891/politics_economy/1995_referendum/ (Accessed 1 April 2007.)

Clarke, George Elliott, "'Building bridges: Cultural pluralism is at the heart of Canadian identity, professor says," News@UofT, 5 May 2003. Accessed 1 April 2007.

Encyclopedia Britannica, "Canada: Québec Separatism," available at britannica.com/eb/article-43022/Canada (Accessed 1 April 2007.)

Global Security. "Quebec Separatism," available at globalsecurity.org/military/world/war/quebec.htm (Accessed 1 April 2007.)

McRoberts, Kenneth, *Beyond Quebec: Taking Stock of Canada* (Montreal: McGill-Queen's University Press, 2004).

ibid, Misconceiving Canada: The Struggle for National Unity (Toronto: Oxford University Press Canada, 1997).

Young, Robert A., *Secession of Quebec and the Future of Canada* (Montréal: McGill-Queen's University Press, 1997).

Time patterns are also the basis of **climax patterns**, which are used to create suspense. For example, if you wanted to create suspense in a speech about Canadian support for American military interventions, you could chronologically trace the steps that eventually led us into Vietnam, Bosnia, or Afghanistan in such a way that you build your audience's curiosity.

The climax pattern can also be reversed. When it is, it is called *anticlimactic organization*. If you started your speech by telling the audience that you were going to explain why a specific soldier was killed in a specific war, and then you went on to explain the things that caused that soldier to become involved in that war, you would be using anticlimactic organization.

> **climax pattern**
> An organizing plan for a speech that builds ideas to the point of maximum interest or tension.
>
> **space pattern**
> An organizing plan in a speech that arranges points according to their physical location.

Space Patterns

Space patterns are organized according to area. The area could be stated in terms of continents, centimetres, or anything in between. If you were discussing the Canadian North, for example, you could arrange the territories and provinces from west to east:

I. Yukon.
II. Northwest Territories.
III. Nunavut.
IV. Quebec.
V. Newfoundland and Labrador.

Topic Patterns

A topical arrangement or **topic pattern** is based on types or categories. These categories could be either well known or original; both have their advantages. Acronyms or words are often used to form a memorable topic pattern for your audience. Acronyms or words formed in this way are known as mnemonics. Carol Koehler, a professor of communication and medicine, uses the mnemonic "CARE" to describe the characteristics of a caring doctor:

C stands for **concentrate.** Physicians should hear with their eyes and ears. . . .
A stands for **acknowledge.** Show them that you are listening. . . .

R stands for **response.** Clarify issues by asking questions, providing periodic recaps. . . .
E stands for **exercise emotional control.** When your "hot buttons" are pushed. . . .[3]

Problem-Solution Patterns

The **problem–solution pattern**, as you might guess from its no-nonsense name, describes what's wrong and proposes a way to make things better. It is usually (but not always) divisible into two distinct parts, as in this example:

I.   The Problem: Homelessness (which could then be broken down into urban homelessness, suburban homelessness, and rural homelessness).
II. The Solution: A national homelessness institute (which would study the root causes of homelessness in the same way that the Canadian Mental Health Association studies the links between lifestyle and mental illness).

Cause-Effect Patterns

Cause–effect patterns are similar to problem–solution patterns in that they are basically two-part patterns: first you discuss something that happened, then you discuss its effects.

A variation of this pattern reverses the order. Persuasive speeches often have cause–effect or effect–cause as the first two main points. Leo Johnson, a former student at McMaster University, organized the first two points of a speech on "Poverty in Liberia"[4] like this:

I.   The effects of the problem.
   A. A lost generation of children.
   B. A large brain drain towards North America.
II. The causes of the problem.
   A. Tribal conflict and corrupt government.
   B. A lack of support from rich nations like Canada and the United States.

The third main point in this type of persuasive speech is often "solutions," and the fourth "the desired audience behaviour." Leo's final points were:

---

topic pattern
An organizing plan for a speech that arranges points according to logical types or categories.

problem–solution pattern
An organizing plan for a speech that describes an unsatisfactory state of affairs and then proposes a plan to remedy the problem.

cause–effect pattern
An organizing plan for a speech that demonstrates how one or more events result in another event or events.

 III. Solutions: Convince Canadian politicians and diplomats to help Liberia financially and morally.
 IV. Desired Audience Response: Contact local politicians and talk to them about the plight of Liberia.

Motivated Sequence

A variation of the problem–solution pattern, developed in the 1930s by Alan H. Monroe, contains five steps and has come to be known as the **motivated sequence:**[5]

 I. *The attention step draws attention to your subject.* ("Cheers for the urban guerillas of Vancouver, the dauntless men and women who let their dogs loose in the parks!"[6])
 II. *The need step establishes the problem.* ("In Canada, we tend to think that freedom for dogs encourages bad behaviour. Nothing could be further from the truth. Freedom actually improves a dog's conduct.")
 III. *The satisfaction step proposes a solution.* ("The time has come for Vancouver and other Canadian cities to unleash their dogs.")
 IV. *The visualization step describes the results of the solution.* ("In the splendid cities of Latin America, well-mannered dogs are accepted almost everywhere as a normal part of life. In Buenos Aires, dogs are welcome in the best hotels, enjoy large play groups in the parks, and are seldom seen on leashes.")
 V. *The action step is a direct appeal for the audience to do something.* ("Demand that parts of Stanley Park become leash-free. Dog lovers of Vancouver, unite!")

> **motivated sequence**
> A five-step plan used in persuasive speaking; also known as "Monroe's Motivated Sequence."

The Body of the Speech

The **introduction** and **conclusion** of a speech are vitally important, although they usually occupy less than 20 per cent of your speaking time. Listeners form their impression of a speaker early, and they remember what they hear last; it is, therefore, crucial to make those few moments at the beginning and end of your speech work to your advantage.

The Introduction

There are four functions of the speech introduction. It serves to capture the audience's attention, preview the main points, set the mood and tone of the speech, and demonstrate the importance of the topic.

Capturing Attention

There are several ways to capture an audience's attention. The following discussion shows how some of these ways might be used in a speech entitled "Communication between Plants and Humans."

Refer to the Audience
The technique of referring to the audience is especially effective if it is complimentary: "Julio's speech last week about how animals communicate was so interesting that I decided to explore a related topic: whether people can communicate with plants!"

Refer to the Occasion
A reference to the occasion could allude to the event of your speech, as in "Even though the focus of this course is human communication, it seems appropriate to talk about whether humans can communicate with plants."

> **introduction**
> The first structural unit of a speech, in which the speaker captures the audience's attention and previews the main points to be covered.
>
> **conclusion**
> The final structural unit of a speech, in which the main points are reviewed and final remarks are made to motivate the audiences to act or help listeners remember key ideas.

Refer to the Relationship between the Audience and the Subject

A reference to the relationship that the audience has to the subject will create a feeling of immediacy, as in "My topic, 'Communicating with Plants,' ties right in with our study of human communication. We can gain several insights into our communication with one another by examining our interactions with our little green friends."

Refer to Something Familiar to the Audience

The technique of referring to something familiar to the audience is especially effective if you are discussing a topic that might seem new or strange to that audience. Attention will be attracted to the familiar among the new in much the same way that we are able to pick out a friend's face in a crowd of strangers. For example, "See that lilac bush outside the window? At this very moment it might be reacting to the joys and anxieties that you are experiencing in this classroom."

Cultural Idiom
old hat
Something that is not new or different.

Cite a Startling Fact or Opinion

A statement that surprises audience members is bound to make them sit up and listen. This is true even for a topic that the audience considers old hat; if the audience members think

COMMUNICATING ONLINE

Ten Tips for Podcasting

YouTube and podcasts have brought the art of public speaking to the internet. The same rules for planning and delivering an effective speech to a group apply to making great podcasts or video blogs, even if you can't see your audience. Below, Sharon Housley, a marketing manager for podcasts and audio recordings, shares her top ten tips for making the most out of your own podcasts.

1. *Plan Accordingly*. When making the decision and commitment to podcast, it is important to think beyond the moment. Before starting, think about the time the podcast production will take. How will podcasting fit into a current schedule? How frequently will you podcast? How will hosting of podcasting files be handled? If the podcast is excessively popular, how will fees be generated to pay for hosting? What is the common theme that threads all podcasts in a series together? Think not only of a broad theme, but also various episodic themes that fit into a broader theme. What will make you distinct or different from others podcasting about similar content? By approaching podcasting with a little forethought, you will set yourself up for success.

2. *Original Content*. Just like any media company, in order to attract and maintain an audience, you will need to provide original content, or at the very least, present the content in an original way. Think about a long term strategy that will help your show distinguish itself from others.

3. *Get to The Point*. Jibber Jabber is fun, but not to the point of excluding quality content. Listeners in today's society don't have time for incessant rambling. If you have a point to make, make it in a reasonable amount of time. Minimize the fluff and focus on quality content.

4. *Do Your Homework*. Not only is faulty information a liability, but incorrect information will hurt a broadcasters long term reputation—just like a journalist's credibility is paramount to their success. It is important that the information that you provide is accurate. While being a shock jock might have short-term appeal to listeners, most will remain loyal to a source that has properly vetted all of their information.

5. *Consistency*. The best content is consistent content. Podcasts should contain compelling content with episodic titles that are united in common broad theme. The format of the podcast should be consistent, persistent, and stable. Each show should be about the same length and contain a common format.

they've heard everything about plant–human communication before, you might mention, "There is now actual scientific evidence that plants appreciate human company, kind words, and classical music."

Ask a Question

A rhetorical question causes your audience to think rather than to answer out loud. "Have you ever wondered why some people seem able to grow beautiful, healthy plants effortlessly, whereas others couldn't make a weed grow in the best soil?" This question is designed to make the audience respond mentally, "Yeah, why is that?"

Tell an Anecdote

A personal story perks up audience interest because it shows the human side of what might otherwise be dry, boring information. "The other night, while taking a walk in the country, I happened on a small garden that was rich with lush vegetation. But it wasn't the lushness of the vegetation that caught my eye at first. There, in the middle of the garden, was a man who was talking quite animatedly to a giant sunflower."

6. *Timeless Content*. Content that is timeless has a long shelf life. Broadcasters will benefit more from content that is timeless and can be effectively archived. "How to" content that solves problems will often have long term appeal and listening life. When choosing topics, consider the long term effects of a specific piece and determine whether it will fit with the broad theme of the show.

7. *Articulate Words*. The quality of the audio content does matter. Think of the last time you heard a good song, on a poorly tuned radio station; regardless of how much you like the song, most of us would move the dial along. Listeners will not want to strain to hear a podcast; pay particular attention to articulation. Another important item worth noting is that Podcasts have global reach and often global appeal. Minimizing an accent will often extend the podcast's listening audience.

8. *Optimize Podcasts*. Podcast titles should be optimized to incorporate data that relates to the contents of the podcast. Think about the themes when selecting a podcast channel title and description. Use critical and related keywords and phrases that relate to a common theme. The text in the feed is important for both feed optimization and for attracting listeners. Many of the podcast directories index the contents of podcasts using the information contained in the channel and item's titles and descriptions. Use these text fields to effectively capture the interest of listeners.

9. *Listener Expectations*. Invariably listeners will come to expect certain things from broadcasters. In order to maintain a listening audience, it is important that broadcasts are consistent and satisfy the expectations of listeners. While it is okay to experiment, straying too far from what a listener expects will often disappoint.

10. *Archive*. Many new listeners will want to review previous broadcasts. Consider ways to make older shows available through archives. Archives allow broadcasters another channel to benefit from the content. Maintaining archives of older podcasts might bring in new listeners and satisfy listeners who just can't get enough. Podcasts require effort, but by following basic guidelines and thinking things through, podcasts can be instrumental in increasing web traffic and communications within a community.

Sharon Housley, 2012, www.podcasting-tools.com/ 10-tips-podcasting.htm

Use a Quotation

Quotable quotes sometimes have a precise, memorable wording that would be difficult for you to equal. Also, they allow you to borrow from the credibility of the quoted source. For example, "Thorne Bacon, the naturalist, recently said about the possibility of plants and humans communicating, 'Personally, I cannot imagine a world so dull, so satiated, that it should reject out of hand arresting new ideas which may be as old as the first amino acid in the chain of life on earth.'"

Tell a Joke

If you happen to know (or can find) a joke that suits your subject and occasion, it can help you build audience interest: "We once worried about people who talked to plants, but that's no longer the case. Now we only worry if the plants talk back." Be sure, though, that the joke is appropriate to the audience, as well as to the occasion and to you as a speaker.

Previewing Main Points

After you capture the attention of the audience, an effective introduction will almost always state your thesis and give your listeners an idea of the upcoming main points. At a ceremony presenting the Community Award for Graduating Students, Hilary Weston, then Lieutenant Governor of Ontario, addressed the students of Toronto's Emory Collegiate Institute this way:

> If I remember my own schooldays correctly, the students attending today's assembly are torn between dreading a series of long-winded, boring speeches and hoping for a good, lengthy break from classes. I'm afraid I can try to address only one of these issues, because my remarks will be short—but I will try very hard not to be too boring!
>
> I always enjoy visiting schools—although, quite often, there is confusion among the students—and even the teachers—as to who is coming to visit. On one occasion, I rolled up to a school, full of beans, only to discover they were rather miffed that I wasn't the other Hillary—Mrs Clinton! They had prepared themselves with lots of questions about Bill and Monica—even from some of the more serious students—with questions about American politics and the role of a modern First Lady.
>
> So, just to set the record straight this time around: I'm not that Hillary, nor am I the Hilary Swank of Oscar fame—although you might think I have a very "swanky" job! This Hilary was appointed Lieutenant Governor of Ontario by the Prime Minister of Canada just over three years ago.
>
> I'm not here to give you a history lecture, but I would like to tell you a little about my role, so that you can impress your friends and families with your amazing knowledge of the Canadian constitutional process![7]

In this way, Ms Weston previewed her main points:

1. To explain to whom the lieutenant governor is responsible.
2. To explain for what the lieutenant governor is responsible.
3. To explain how the lieutenant governor is appointed.

Sometimes your preview of main points will be even more straightforward:

"I have three points to discuss: They are _____, _____, and _____."

Sometimes your plan will call for you *not* to refer directly to your main points in your introduction. Perhaps you want to build suspense, create a humorous effect, or stall for time to win over a hostile audience. Whatever the reason, you might preview only your thesis:

> "I am going to say a few words about _____."
> "Did you ever wonder about _____?"
> "_____ is one of the most important issues facing us today."

Setting the Mood and Tone of Your Speech

Notice, in the example just given, how Ms Weston immediately connects with her audience by relating how she felt about guest speakers when she was a student. She also uses an anecdote to keep the tone light and assures the group that she will not be delivering a lecture. This allows her to connect with the students, even though she is considerably older than them and probably also enjoys a higher standard of living than most of them. She shows them that she is going to approach her topic with wit and intelligence. Thus, she sets the mood and tone for her entire speech.

Demonstrating the Importance of Your Topic to Your Audience

Your audience members will listen to you more carefully if your speech relates to them as individuals. Based on your audience analysis, you should state directly *why* your topic is of importance to your audience members. This importance should be related as closely as possible to their specific needs at that specific time. In 1970, when then Prime Minister Pierre Elliott Trudeau addressed the people of Canada on the subject of the October Crisis, he established the importance of his topic in this way:

> I am speaking to you at a moment of grave crisis, when violent and fanatical men are attempting to destroy the unity and the freedom of Canada. One aspect of that crisis is the threat which has been made on the lives of two innocent men. These are matters of the utmost gravity and I want to tell you what the Government is doing to deal with them.
>
> What has taken place in Montreal in the past two weeks is not unprecedented. It has happened elsewhere in the world on several recent occasions; it could happen elsewhere within Canada. But Canadians have always assumed that it could not happen here and as a result we are doubly shocked that it has.
>
> Our assumption may have been naive, but it was understandable; understandable because democracy flourishes in Canada; understandable because individual liberty is cherished in Canada.
>
> Notwithstanding these conditions—partly because of them—it has now been demonstrated to us by a few misguided persons just how fragile a democratic society can be, if democracy is not prepared to defend itself, and just how vulnerable to blackmail are tolerant, compassionate people.[8]

Demonstrating the Importance of Your Topic to Others

In certain circumstances, a speaker might want to establish the importance of the topic not only to the audience but also to a wider group of people. In 2009, Boyd Neil, senior vice-president of corporate communications at Hill & Knowlton Canada, delivered a speech to the

Empire Club of Canada outlining the importance of corporate social responsibility in an age dominated by omnipresent social media. Much of Neil's introduction is devoted to establishing the importance of social media not only to young people but also to organizations.

> It's self-evident I think that trust in companies has declined significantly over the past few years although if you want to argue the point I can direct you to quite a number of studies that say so including H&K's own corporate reputation surveys that make the case. It has also become manifest that what can be called social tools—YouTube, Flickr, Facebook, Twitter, and blogging among others—have been catalysts for impugning corporate behaviour. Just ask Domino's Pizza or McNeil Consumer Healthcare, TASER International, Continental Airlines, or Dalhousie University.
>
> What is less obvious, I think, is how these tools can be used by organizations and companies to build trust. There are a number of hypotheses about social media and trust, which I hope we can test in our short panel discussion. By doing so, I think we will get a better understanding of what those of us who manage reputation both inside and outside organizations have to do differently. I'd like to get things going by posing a few axiomatic beliefs of my own about social media. My point of view comes from four or five years of blogging, engaging in social networks such as Facebook and Twitter, providing counsel to clients on transforming crisis reputation, and issue management strategies through the analysis and application of new social tools, teaching new directions in communications for two Canadian universities, and discussion online and in person with people much smarter than me, some of whom are here today.[9]

Such an extended preamble might be too long and too general for most speech occasions, but in the context of the fact that social media were probably a relatively new topic to many senior executives in the audience makes it highly appropriate. Only now does Neil introduce the main subject of his talk: social media tools have changed the media and information landscape and organization must adapt. Neil's introduction emphasizes three themes that he will discuss at length in the body of the speech:

1.   Large organizations are vulnerable ("It's self-evident I think that trust in companies has declined significantly over the past few years").
2.   Social media tools have served to reduce corporate reputation ("It has also become manifest that what can be called social tools—YouTube, Flickr, Facebook, Twitter, and blogging among others—have been catalysts for impugning corporate behaviour").
3.   Understanding and mastering social media tools will help companies not only avoid reputational crises but improve their reputations ("What is less obvious, I think, is how these tools can be used by organizations and companies to build trust").

The Conclusion

The conclusion, like the introduction, is an especially important part of your speech. Your audience members will tend to be listening carefully, expecting you to provide a convenient summary and a concluding statement that will be easy to remember. The conclusion has three essential functions: to restate your thesis, review your main points, and provide a memorable final remark.

You can restate your thesis by either repeating or paraphrasing it. Either way, your conclusion should include a short summary statement:

> "And so, after listening to what I had to say this afternoon, I hope you agree with me that the city cannot afford to lose the services of the Edmonton Humane Society."

You will probably also want to review your main points. This can be done directly:

> "I made three main points about the Humane Society today. They are. . . ."

But a less direct approach can be even more effective. For an example, first look back at the introduction to Trudeau's October Crisis speech, above, and then read his conclusion to that speech:

> Canada remains one of the most wholesome and humane lands on this earth. If we stand firm, this current situation will soon pass. We will be able to say proudly, as we have for decades, that within Canada there is ample room for opposition and dissent, but none for intimidation and terror.
>
> There are very few times in the history of any country when all persons must take a stand on critical issues. This is one of those times; this is one of those issues. I am confident that those persons who unleashed this tragic sequence of events with the aim of destroying our society and dividing our country will find that the opposite will occur. The result of their acts will be a stronger society in a unified country. Those who would have divided us will have united us.
>
> I sense the unease which grips many Canadians today. Some of you are upset, and this is understandable. I want to reassure you that the authorities have the situation well in hand. Everything that needs to be done is being done; every level of government in this country is well prepared to act in your interests.[10]

Let's take a closer look at how and why this conclusion was effective. In his introduction Trudeau raised three main points and established an atmosphere of uncertainty and alarm, which he highlighted with words like "crisis," "violent," "fanatical," "fragile," and "vulnerable." Now, in his conclusion, he returns to those themes, but this time the atmosphere is one of calm resolve and reassurance. A different emphasis in the language—"wholesome," "humane," "ample room," "stronger society," "unified country," "well in hand"—reinforces the message that the situation is under control.

Preview (from conclusion)	Review (from introduction)
1. Canada is facing a moment of grave crisis.	1. If we stand firm, this crisis will pass.
2. Fanatical men are attempting to destroy Canada's unity and freedom.	2. In the end, their actions will have the opposite effect.
3. A democratic society is fragile and must be prepared to defend itself.	3. Government authorities are doing what is necessary to defend our society.

You can ensure that your audience will remember your thesis if you conclude with a striking summary statement. Finally, your closing remarks will be most effective if you remember these four simple guidelines:

- *Don't end abruptly*: Make sure that your conclusion accomplishes everything it is supposed to accomplish. Develop it fully and use signposts such as "finally," "in conclusion," or "to sum up what I've been talking about."
- *But don't ramble either*: Prepare a definite conclusion, and never, never end by mumbling something like, "Well, I guess that's about all I wanted to say."
- *Don't introduce new points*: The worst kind of rambling is "Oh, yes, and something I forgot to mention."
- *Don't apologize*: End on a strong note. You can use any of the attention-getters suggested for the introduction to make the conclusion memorable. In fact, one kind of effective closing is to refer to the attention-getter you used in your introduction and remind your audience how it applies to the points you made in your speech.

Using Transitions

transition
A phrase that connects ideas in a speech by showing how one relates to the other.

Between the introduction and conclusion of your speech, **transitions** keep your message moving forward. They perform the following functions:

- They tell how the introduction relates to the body of the speech.
- They tell how one main point relates to the next main point.
- They tell how your subpoints relate to the points they are part of.
- They tell how your supporting points relate to the points they support.

Transitions, to be effective, should refer to the previous point and to the upcoming point, showing how they relate to one another and to the thesis. They usually sound something like this:

> "Like [previous point], another important consideration in [topic] is [upcoming point]."

> "But [previous point] isn't the only thing we have to worry about. [Upcoming point] is even more potentially dangerous."

> "Yes, the problem is obvious. But what are the solutions? Well, one possible solution is. . . ."

Sometimes a transition includes an internal review (a restatement of preceding points), an internal preview (a look ahead to upcoming points), or both:

> "So far we've discussed [previous points]. Our next points are [upcoming points]."

You can find several examples of transitions in the sample speech at the end of this chapter.

Supporting Material

It is important to organize ideas clearly and logically. But clarity and logic by themselves won't guarantee that you'll interest, enlighten, or persuade others; these results call for the use of supporting materials. These materials—the facts and information that back up and prove your ideas and opinions—are the flesh that fills out the skeleton of your speech. There are four functions of supporting material.

1. *To clarify*: As we explained in Chapter 3, people of different backgrounds tend to attach different meanings to words. Supporting material can help you avoid confusion by clarifying key terms and ideas.

2. *To make interesting*: A second function of support is to make an idea interesting or to catch your audience's attention. Find supports that are current and relevant, and that will capture their imagination.

3. *To make memorable*: A third function of supporting materials, related to the preceding one, is to make a point memorable. We have already mentioned the value of including "memorable" statements in a speech conclusion; but it is equally important to make sure that your audience retains important information throughout your speech. Using supporting material is another way to emphasize key points.

4. *To prove*: Finally, supporting material can be used as evidence, to prove the truth of what you are saying.

Types of Supporting Material

As you may have noted, each of the support functions outlined above could be fulfilled by several different types of material. Let's take a look at the main categories of supporting material.

Definitions

It's a good idea to define your key terms, especially if they may be unfamiliar to your audience or if you're using them in an unusual way. A good definition is simple and concise. If you were giving a speech on binge drinking, you might define that term as follows:

> *Researchers consider a person who has had five drinks on one occasion during the previous two weeks to be a binge drinker.*

Examples

An **example** is a specific case that is used to demonstrate a general idea. Examples can be either factual or hypothetical, personal or borrowed. Rick Hansen, the Canadian wheelchair athlete who travelled around the world to generate awareness of and support for people with disabilities, drew on his own experience for an example of how our lives can be changed for the good. If he had been injured a century earlier, he said, he likely would not have survived.[11]

Hypothetical examples can often be more powerful than factual examples, because hypothetical examples ask audience members to imagine something—thus causing them to become active participants in the thought. The late Alberta Premier Ralph Klein used a series of hypothetical examples to convince Albertans to "Imagine Alberta:"

example
A specific case that is used to demonstrate a general idea.

hypothetical example
An example that asks an audience to imagine an object or event.

Now is the perfect time for everyone [sic] of us to "Imagine Alberta" and all it can be: home to the most highly educated and skilled workforce in the world; pioneers in transforming an abundance of resources into new products and opportunities, while protecting our environment; innovators in the development of clean energy; a leader in the war on cancer. Imagine Alberta front and centre on the international stage, creating a quality of life second to none, and sharing our good fortune with people across the country, and around the world. . . .[12]

Statistics

Statistics are numbers that are arranged or organized to show that a fact or principle is true for a large percentage of cases. Statistics are actually collections of examples, which is why they are often more effective as proof than are isolated examples.

Because statistics can be powerful proof, there are certain rules to follow when using them. You should make sure that they make sense and that they come from a credible source. You should also cite the source of the statistic when you use it. Finally, you should reduce the statistic to a concrete image if possible.

Comparison and Contrast

We use comparisons all the time, often in the form of figures of speech such as similes and metaphors. A simile uses *like* or *as* to equate one thing with another: "Snow covered the town like a blanket." A metaphor, by contrast, makes the connection directly, without using *like* or *as*: "A blanket of snow covered the town;" "Snow blanketed the town;" "The town lay under a blanket of snow," and so on. An **analogy** is an extended comparison.

Analogies can be used to compare or contrast an unknown concept with a known one. For example, one Halifax doctor explained the importance of regular medical check-ups for an audience of men by comparing men to the cars they tend to love. He said that good car care means regular visits to the mechanic for tune ups to keep the car running at peak efficiency.

Anecdotes

An **anecdote** is a brief story with a point, often (but not always) based on personal experience. (The word anecdote comes from the Greek, meaning "unpublished item.") Politician and Canadian "father of medicare" Tommy Douglas was famous for his use of anecdotes. In an address to New Democratic supporters, he used the following anecdote to make the point that fighting the good fight for workers' rights is very rewarding:

About two weeks ago I was very tired and a bit low. We got word that the Canadian Pacific Railway (CPR) had been granted a 17% freight rate increase by the Transport Commission, in spite of appeals to the cabinet. . . . I had the battle of my life with

statistics
Numbers arranged or organized to show how a fact or principle is true for a large percentage of cases.

analogy
An extended comparison that can be used as supporting material in a speech.

anecdote
A brief personal story used to illustrate or support a point in a speech.

"Now, keep in mind that these numbers are only as accurate as the fictitious data, ludicrous assumptions and wishful thinking they're based upon!"

CPR lawyers and officials, and suddenly I felt ten years younger. I've been going on the momentum of that fight with the CPR ever since. I don't know whether it increases the adrenaline in my system, but a fight always makes me feel better.[13]

Quotation/Testimony

A well-chosen quotation allows you to take advantage of someone else's memorable wording. The benefits may be even greater if the quotation and its author are well known.

You can also use quotations as **testimony**, supporting a point by appealing to the authority of someone with particular knowledge of your subject. When former Prime Minister Jean Chrétien gave a speech in tribute to the recently deceased Pierre Trudeau, he used a combination of direct quotes and paraphrases of Trudeau's own words to evoke his feelings for Canada:

> Pierre Elliott Trudeau was a man like no other.
>
> A man of brilliance and learning. A man of action. A man of grace and style. A man of wit and playfulness. A man of extraordinary courage. A complex man, whose love of Canada was pure and simple.
>
> Pierre wrote about "a man who never learned patriotism in school, but who acquired that virtue when he felt in his bones the vastness of his land and the greatness of its founders." Pierre, too, came to love this land as he climbed its mountain peaks, conquered the rapids of its rivers and wandered the streets of its cities.[14]

Styles of Support: Narration and Citation

Most of the forms of support discussed in the preceding section could be presented in either of two ways: through narration or through citation. **Narration** means storytelling: you present your information in the form of a small drama, with a beginning, middle, and end. In the following example, Canadian Armed Forces General Rick Hillier used narrative in a speech on "The Men and Women of Canada's Armed Forces":

> The Prime Minister as you know went to Afghanistan about a month ago. I had the opportunity to meet him. We had about 25 or 30 men and women in uniform waiting to greet him and welcome him to Kandahar and to Afghanistan on the tarmac. He was a little bit late so I had a chance to talk to all those folks. A dust storm made the plane 45 minutes late. I was sitting there chatting to them about a variety of things, laughing and talking to about 15 men and [8] to 10 female soldiers. Out of those 15 men, nine of them had similar haircuts to Master Corporal Perry and Master Seaman Miller and I am trying to figure out whether my wife would like it if I did that. None of those folks knew who was arriving. We had a tight security

COMMUNICATION ON-SCREEN

Trudeau (2002)
Director, Jerry Ciccoritti

This documentary, starring Canadian film star Colm Feore as Pierre Elliott Trudeau documents the life and ascent of this most iconic of Canadian prime ministers. Starting with his first election in 1968, the film tells the story of this most unusual prime minister, focusing on his ability to handle very serious crises such as the October Crisis in Québec in 1970 during which he had to declare martial law and the repatriation of the constitution in 1982. The charm, personality, and persuasive powers of Mr Trudeau are brilliantly played by Colm Feore, who captures the power that Trudeau had over people—young and old, weak and powerful. A must-see for Canadian students of communication and persuasion.

testimony
Supporting material that proves or illustrates a point by citing an authoritative source.

Cultural Idiom
Trudeaumania
A widespread fascination with Pierre Elliott Trudeau among the Canadian public, especially during the election campaign of 1968.

narration
Presentation of supporting material as a story with a beginning, middle, and end within a speech.

blanket on and none of them knew who was arriving. They knew somebody was coming who we wanted them to greet. As the Prime Minister got off the aircraft one of our female master corporals said, "Sir, I'm really excited to welcome the Prime Minister, to meet the Prime Minister, I thought it was going to be Don Cherry."[15]

> **citation**
> A brief statement of supporting material within a speech.

By contrast, **citation** is a simple statement of the facts. Citation is usually more concise than narration, and it is always more precise in that it includes specific details about the source of the information. A citation will always include a phrase such as "According to the 25 July 2006 edition of *The Walrus* magazine" or "As Mr Knight made clear in an interview on 24 April of this year." General Hillier cited some statistics later in his speech:

> The last thing I have to tell you is we need recruits. We need Canadians. Now there have been a lot of naysayers out there who don't believe that we can actually recruit the number of men and women that we need. This past year, the fiscal year from April 1 of last year to March 31 just past, we had set a goal of 5,627 new recruits. That allowed us to meet attrition and to grow by 500 soldiers, which is all the money that we had for increased growth. As of the end of March 31 we were at 106 per cent of target. In fact, we succeeded even with our dinosaur methods of recruiting, even with our slow and ponderous and painful process, because I believe that most young Canadians can see and feel the excitement that I and these men and women who are here with me today feel and believe and see in what we do.[16]

Some types of support, such as anecdotes, naturally lend themselves to narration. Statistics, on the other hand, are nearly always presented in citation form. With the other types of support—examples, quotation/testimony, definitions, and analogies—you will often be able to use either narration or citation.

Using Visual Aids

Visual aids are graphic devices used in a speech to illustrate or support ideas. They can show how things look (photos of your trek to Nepal or the effects of malnutrition). They can show how things work (a demonstration of a new ski binding, a diagram of how seawater is made drinkable through desalination).

> **visual aids**
> Graphic devices used in a speech to illustrate or support ideas.
>
> **model**
> A replica of the object being discussed, usually used when it would be difficult or impossible to use the actual object.

Types of Visual Aids

There is a wide variety of types of visual aids. The most common types are discussed in the following sections.

Objects and Models

Sometimes the most effective visual aid is the actual thing you are talking about. This will be the case when that thing is portable and simple enough to use for a demonstration during your speech, such as a new hockey helmet designed to prevent concussion. A **model** is a scaled representation, used when the thing you are discussing is too large (the solar system), too small (a DNA molecule), or simply doesn't exist anymore (a Tyrannosaurus rex).

Diagrams

A **diagram** is any kind of line drawing that shows the most important properties of an object. Diagrams do not try to show everything about an item, just those parts that the audience most needs to be aware of and understand. A diagram is most appropriate when you need to simplify a complex object or event and make it more understandable to the audience.

Word and Number Charts

Word charts and **number charts** are visual depictions of key facts or statistics. Presenting facts and numbers in visual form reinforces what you say about them and makes them easier for your audience to understand and retain. Many speakers will also list the main points of their speech, or some key statistics, as a word chart, often in outline form.

Pie Charts

Pie charts are circle shapes divided into wedges. They can be used to show divisions of any whole: where your tax dollars go, the percentage of the population involved in various occupations, and so on. The wedges of the pie are organized from largest to smallest.

Bar and Column Charts

Bar charts compare two or more values by stretching them out in the form of horizontal rectangles. **Column charts** perform the same function as bar charts but use vertical rectangles.

Line Charts

A **line chart** maps out the direction of a moving point; it is ideally suited for showing changes over time. The time element is usually placed on the horizontal axis so that the line visually represents the trend over time.

Media for the Presentation of Visual Aids

Visual aids can be presented in several ways. For example, chalkboards or whiteboards can be found in most classrooms. The main advantage of these write-as-you-go media is that they allow you to be spontaneous and create your visual aids as you speak; for instance, you can use them to show responses from your audience.

Flip Pads and Poster Board

Flip pads are like oversized writing tablets attached to a portable easel. Flip pads combine the spontaneity of the chalkboard with portability, which means that you can prepare them in advance.

Handouts

The main advantage of handouts is that audience members can keep them for future reference. It's best, therefore, to pass them out at the end of the speech so that your audience is not distracted by them while you speak.

Projectors

Projectors are useful when your audience is too large to view handheld images. If the room has an ethernet or wireless internet connection, you could use an online presentation management

---

diagram
A line drawing that shows the most important components of an object.

word chart
A visual aid that lists words or terms in tabular form in order to clarify information.

number chart
A visual aid that lists numbers in tabular form in order to clarify information.

pie chart
A visual aid that divides a circle into wedges, representing percentages of the whole.

bar chart
A visual aid that compares two or more values by showing them as elongated horizontal rectangles.

column chart
A visual aid that compares two or more values by showing them as elongated vertical rectangles.

line chart
A visual aid consisting of a grid that maps out the direction of a trend by plotting a series of points.

tool such as Prezi. You can also use the internet to display short films from YouTube or Google Videos. A digital projector allows you to use a screen image directly from a computer screen, making it the most direct way to use computer software in presentations.

Other Electronic Media

Many other electronic media are available as presentation aids. Audio aids such as CDs can supply information that could not be presented any other way but in most cases you should use them sparingly to avoid overwhelming your audience.

Holding the Audience's Attention

No matter how supporting material is used, a speech will not be successful if it does not hold the audience's attention. We have all been in situations where we attended a speech and, regardless of how passionate we were about the topic or maybe even the speaker, found ourselves nodding off, or losing our concentration. That's why speeches have to be written with keeping people captivated as the main goal.

Make It Easy to Listen

Remember the complex nature of listening discussed in Chapter 5. For your speech to be well received, you must make it easy for your audience members to hear, pay attention, understand, and remember. This means that you should speak clearly and with enough volume to be heard by all your listeners. It also means that as you put your speech together, you should be mindful of those techniques, including the three given here, which recognize the way human beings process information.

UNDERSTANDING COMMUNICATION TECHNOLOGY

Some Great Alternatives to PowerPoint

Although PowerPoint is still an industry standard for presentations, some people find creating and viewing PowerPoint presentations to be boring, dry, and lacking in visual stimuli. Luckily, in the past few years, a number of alternatives have popped up, ranging in price from absolutely nothing, to a bit pricey.

1. *Prezi*: Prezi is a fantastic presentation alternative that takes your presentation and creates a movable, zooming, interactive metaphor. It begins with a template image like a tree, a cityscape, or stones on a pond. From there, you define your slides by choosing the sections of the image you wish to fill with text, images, and videos. When you present a Prezi show, you don't move from left to right. Instead, each click triggers a camera zoom, or scroll, to any of your sections. Cynthia Boris from Entrepreneur .com notes "Prezi can be useful for presenting interconnected ideas or nonlinear information such as a portfolio of past projects. It can also work well for presenting interconnected ideas."[17]

2. *Keynote*: Before you commit entirely to using PowerPoint, however, make sure you take a moment to check out Keynote, the Macintosh presentation software. Many people prefer Keynote because it is more flexible and allows more beautiful transitions from slide to slide.

3. *Open Source*. Another option is to "open source" which means using non-commercial software programs such as, PreZentit, OpenOffice Impress, or KPresenter. These programs are designed by groups of software programmers working in a completely open and egalitarian environment. They are a viable alternative to corporate software packages from Microsoft and Apple.

4. *PowToon or GoAnimate*: Animated infographics and visual aids can give your presentation a great pop and increase

Limit the Amount of Information You Present

Remember that you have become an expert on this topic and that you won't be able to transmit everything you know to your audience at one sitting. It's better to make careful choices about the three to five main ideas you want to get across and then develop those ideas fully.

Use Familiar Information to Increase Understanding of the Unfamiliar

Move your audience members from information that you can assume they know about, based on your audience analysis, to your newer information. For example, if you are giving a speech about how the stock market works, you could compare the daily activity of a broker with that of a salesperson in a retail store.

Use Simple Information to Build Understanding of Complex Information

Just as you move your audience members from the familiar to the unfamiliar, you can move them from the simple to the complex. An average college or university audience, for example, can understand the complexities of genetic modification if you begin with the concept of inherited characteristics.

engagement too. Both options involve a library of animated characters and scenarios to help you construct a narrative for your presentation. Combine the characters with cartoon props, basic shapes, and text effects using simple drag and drop options for a unique presentation indeed. Often cartoons work best for simple, bold concepts so keep it light and skip the small details.

5. *Cloud-based presentation software.* SlideRocket, Google Docs, and Zoho Docs are three examples of presentations that utilize cloud computing in order to share, edit, and instantly update presentations in any location. Although not as powerful as a PowerPoint presentation, Google Docs is free and allows for collaborative editing. Zoho Docs' main draw is its universality, with cloud-based interface supporting the import of nearly any file type. Beyond this, Zoho is highly intuitive and simple to navigate, allowing

for collaborative, selective, and interactive design elements along with near full web integration—such as being able to integrate Picasa, Flickr, or custom embeds to your website. SlideRocket is an example of a high-end presentation software package. Imagine everything PowerPoint offers, but with version control and privacy control, animation libraries and theme libraries, and image embeds, videos, chart, and special effect transitions. It also allows for real-time online feeds and even metrics to show who is viewing what, when, and for how long.

QUESTIONS: After reviewing the information on PowerPoint and the many other options, would you say that presentation software is a benefit or a detriment to effective public speaking? What would you like to see more of or less of in this type of technology?

Emphasize Important Points

Along with making it easy to listen to your speech, you should stress its important points through repetition and the use of signposts.

Repetition

Repetition is one of the age-old rules of learning. People are simply more likely to absorb and understand information that is stated more than once. This is especially true in a speaking situation, where your audience members cannot go back to pick up something they have missed the way they could with a piece of writing. If their minds have wandered the first time you said something, they just might pick it up the second time.

Redundancy can be effective when you use it to emphasize important points.[18] It can be ineffective, however, when you are redundant with obvious, trivial, or boring points, and you run an important point into the ground.

Signposts

Another way to emphasize important material is by using **signposts**, words or phrases that emphasize the importance of what you are about to say. You can state, simply enough, "What I'm about to say is important," or you can substitute some variation of that idea: "You should understand that . . . ," "The most important thing to remember is . . . ," "The three keys to this situation are . . . ," and so on.

Use Clear, Simple Language

Another technique for effective informative speaking is to use clear language—which means using precise, simple wording and avoiding jargon. Dictionaries and thesauri are handy tools for picking precise vocabulary. The online dictionary and the "thesaurus" function that can be found under the "tools/language" tab of most word processing programs can be consulted easily as you plan your speech. You should remember, though, that picking the right word—the most precise word—seldom means using a word that is unfamiliar to your audience. In fact, just the opposite is true. Important ideas should sound natural, not complicated to your audience.

Generate Audience Involvement

The final technique for effective speaking is to get your audience involved in your speech. **Audience involvement** is the level of commitment and attention that listeners devote to a speech. Educational psychologists have long known that the best way to teach people something is to have them do it; social psychologists have added to this rule by proving, through many studies, that involving an audience in a message increases the audience members' comprehension of, and agreement with, that message.

There are many ways to encourage audience involvement in your speech. One way is to follow the rules for good delivery by maintaining enthusiasm, energy, eye contact, and so on. Other ways include personalizing your speech, using audience participation, using volunteers, and having a question-and-answer period.

Personalize Your Speech

One way to encourage audience involvement is to give audience members a human being to connect with. In other words, don't be afraid to be yourself and to inject a little of your own personality into the speech. If you happen to be good at storytelling, make a narration part

---

**Cultural Idiom
run a point into the ground**
To over-elaborate an idea to the point where the audience is tired of hearing about it.

signpost
A word or phrase that emphasizes the importance of upcoming material in a speech.

audience involvement
Level of commitment and attention that listeners devote to a speech.

of your speech. If humour is one of your strengths, be funny. If you feel passionate about your topic, show it. Certainly, if you have any personal experience that relates to your topic, use it.

Use Audience Participation

Audience participation—having your listeners actually take part during your speech—is another way to increase their involvement in your message. For example, if you were giving a demonstration of isometric exercises (which don't require too much room for movement), you could have the entire audience stand up and do one or two sample exercises. (Exercise not only involves audience members psychologically, but also keeps them more alert physically.) If you were explaining how to fill out a federal income-tax form, you could give each audience member a sample form to fill out as you explain it. Outlines and checklists can be used in a similar manner for just about any speech.

> **audience participation**
> Listener activity during a speech; a technique to increase audience involvement.

Use Volunteers

If the action you are demonstrating is too expensive or intricate to allow all audience members to take part, you can select one or two volunteers to help you out. By doing this you will increase the psychological involvement of all the members because they will tend to identify with the volunteers.

Have a Question-and-Answer Period

A way to increase audience involvement that is nearly always appropriate, if time allows, is to encourage your audience to ask you questions at the end of your speech. Solicit questions, and be patient waiting for the first one. When the questions do start coming, the following suggestions might help you make your answers more effective:

1. *Listen to the substance of the question.* Don't zero in on irrelevant details; listen for the big picture—the basic, overall question that is being asked. If you are not really sure what the substance of a question is, ask the questioner to paraphrase it. Don't be afraid to let the questioners do their share of the work.
2. *Paraphrase confusing questions.* Use the active listening skills described in Chapter 5. You can paraphrase the question in just a few words: "If I understand your question, you are asking _____. Is that right?"
3. *Avoid defensive reactions to questions.* Even if the questioner seems to be calling you a liar, biased, or ill-informed, try to listen to the substance of the question and not to the possible attack on your personality.
4. *Answer the question as briefly as possible.* Then check the questioner's comprehension of your answer. Sometimes you can simply check his or her non-verbal response—if he or she seems at all confused, you can ask, "Does that answer your question?"

Analyzing the Audience

You need to analyze your audience and examine certain pertinent characteristics of your listeners when planning a speech. **Audience analysis** is the purest form of receiver orientation. It allows you to adapt to your listeners.

> **audience analysis**
> A consideration of characteristics including the type, goals, demographics, beliefs, attitudes, and values of listeners.

Audience Type

There are at least three types of audience you are likely to encounter. We could call these types "passersby," "captives," and "volunteers." Each type suggests different audience interests. *Passersby,* as the name implies, are people who aren't much interested—at least not in advance—in what you have to say. *Captives* are audience members who have gathered for some reason besides the joy of hearing you speak. Students in a required class often begin as a type of captive audience. *Volunteers* are audience members who have gathered together because of a common interest. Students in elective courses, especially those with long waiting lists, would fit into this type. Most university and persuasive communication classes are made up of a mixture of captives and volunteers, which means that you don't have to sensationalize your messages or use gimmicks, but you do have to maintain interest and provide depth.

Audience Purpose

Just as you have a purpose for communicating, the people you are communicating with have a purpose for gathering. Sometimes virtually all the members of your audience will have the same ostensible goal. The audience at a pre-natal class are probably all there for the same reason.

There are other times, however, when audience purpose can't be so easily defined. In some instances, different listeners will have different goals, some of which might not be apparent to the communicator. The audience at a political speech may be there for many different reasons: belief in the candidate and the cause, or because they are hostile and want to catcall. Becoming aware of as many of these motives as possible will help you predict what will interest people.

Demographics

Demographics are characteristics of your audience that can be labelled, such as number of people, gender, age, group membership, and so on. Demographic characteristics, such as the ones discussed here, might affect your message communication planning in a number of ways.[19]

Number of People

Message appropriateness varies with the size of an audience. With a small audience you can be less formal and more intimate—you can, for example, talk more about your own inner feelings and personal experiences. The larger your audience, the broader its range of interests and knowledge; with a small audience you can choose a more specific message.

Gender

Traditionally, men and women tend to be interested in different topics. Although these differences are becoming less pronounced, you might still find that more men than women are interested in hockey or lacrosse and that more women than men are interested in figure skating or modern dance. The guideline here might be: *Do not exclude or offend any portion of your audience on the basis of gender.*

Age

In many areas, younger people and older people have different interests. Your messaging concerning universal health care, child rearing, and school success should therefore reflect the age of your audience. Age-related differences can run deep; Aristotle observed long ago that

---

young people "have strong passions," that "their lives are spent not in memory but in expectation," and that they have high ideals because "they have not been humbled by life or learned its necessary limitations."[20]

Group Membership

The organizations to which the audience members belong provide more clues to their interests. Group membership is often an important consideration in post-secondary classes. Consider the difference between a typical university day class and a typical university night class. At many colleges and universities the evening students are generally older and tend to belong to civic groups, church clubs, and the local chamber of commerce. Daytime students tend to belong to sororities and fraternities, sports clubs, and social action groups.

These demographic characteristics are important examples, but the list goes on and on. Other important demographic characteristics that might be important include ethnic background, educational level, economic status, and hometown.

> **attitude**
> A predisposition to respond to an idea, person, or thing favourably or unfavourably.

Attitudes, Beliefs, and Values

Audience members' feelings about you, your message, and your intentions for them are central issues in audience analysis. One way to approach these matters is through a consideration of attitudes, beliefs, and values.[21] These characteristics are structured in human consciousness like the layers of an onion. They are all closely interrelated, but attitudes lie closer to the surface, whereas beliefs and values underlie them. An **attitude** is a predisposition to

> ### CRITICAL THINKING PROBE
> **Attitudes, Beliefs, and Values**
>
> Find a persuasive appeal in an advertisement, newspaper editorial, or another source. Identify an attitude, belief, or value that the source of the message is appealing to. Explain why you have identified the appeal the way you have (i.e., why it is an attitude or belief rather than a value, etc.). Explain why, in your opinion, this appeal is or is not effective.

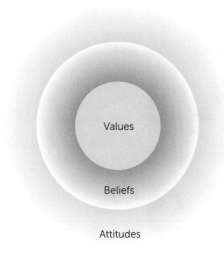

FIGURE 12.2 Structure of Attitudes, Beliefs, and Values

belief
An underlying conviction about the truth of an idea, often based on cultural training.

value
A deeply rooted belief about a concept's inherent worth.

The simplest way to customize a speech is to call members of the audience in advance and ask them what they expect from your session and why they expect it. Then use their quotes throughout your presentation.

Allan Pease, Australian author and body-language expert

respond to something in a favourable or unfavourable way. A **belief** is an underlying conviction about the truth of something, which is often based on cultural training. A **value** is a deeply rooted belief about a concept's inherent worth. An audience might, for example, hold the value that "freedom is a good thing." This value might be expressed in a belief such as "people should be free to choose their political leaders," which in turn could lead to the attitude that "voting is an important right and responsibility for all citizens." Finally, this could lead to a predisposition to vote—in other words, a positive attitude toward voting.

Figure 12.2 shows the relationship among attitudes, beliefs, and values. Experts in audience analysis, such as professional speechwriters or public relations practitioners, often try to concentrate on values. As one team of researchers pointed out, "Values have the advantage of being comparatively small in number, and owing to their abstract nature, are more likely to be shared by large numbers of people."[22]

You can often make an inference about audience members' attitudes by recognizing the beliefs and values they are likely to hold. For example, a group of Muslim Canadians might hold the value of "submitting to Allah's will." This might lead to the belief, based on their religious training, that women are not meant to perform the same functions in society as men. This, in turn, might lead to the attitude that women ought not to pursue careers as firefighters, police officers, or construction workers.

You may also be able to guess how audience members are likely to feel about some issues based on your knowledge of their attitudes on other issues. If your audience is made up of undergraduates who have a positive attitude toward liberation movements, for instance, it's a good bet they will also have positive attitudes toward civil rights and the environment. If they have a negative attitude toward collegiate sports, they probably also have a negative attitude toward fraternities and sororities.

Analyzing the Occasion

While analyzing the audience is necessary in speech writing, there is another element that must be analyzed: the *occasion*. To be successful, every choice you make in putting together your speech—your choice of purpose, topic, and all the developing material you use—must be appropriate to both of these components. The occasion of a speech is determined by the circumstances surrounding it. Three of these circumstances are *time, place,* and *audience expectations.*

Time

The time available for your speech is also an essential consideration. You should choose a topic that is broad enough to say something worthwhile but brief enough to fit your limits. "Wealth," for example, might be an inherently interesting topic to some students, but it would be difficult to cover such a broad topic in a 10-minute speech and still say anything significant. However, a topic like "How to Make Extra Money in Your Spare Time" could conceivably be covered in 10 minutes in enough depth to make it worthwhile.

YOUNG COMMUNICATOR PROFILE

DAVID SCHOKKING

Not-for-Profit Brand Manager, Branding Consultant

I spent the majority of my youth in the "squinty" category of life. Looking out at the horizon, nothing was ever really very clear. So it only makes sense that my inclusion in the communications world took a less than clear path as well. When I was young, I wanted to be two things: a stunt pilot or Batman. It occurred to me far too recently that I have neither the muscle tone, nor the necessary insurance money, for either of those options. In lieu of that, I went to university and studied film, anthropology, psychology, quantum physics, visual art, gender studies, and even got [a] certificate in professional ethics and a master's degree in Communications (which might be the only useful one of the bunch). But two fields have always steered me in the direction I currently find myself heading: acting and philosophy.

Acting is a strange world. The more you do it, the less you find it's about impersonating a character, and far more about reading an audience. You can't do Hamlet the same way twice or you'll be buried. Audiences have such divergent relationships with theatre, characters, and imagination that if you don't understand how to communicate, convey, and convince an audience effectively, you might as well be doing shadow puppets in a blanket fort alone in your bathroom, instead of a packed house at Stratford.

Philosophy was a game changer. It helped me organize everything I was trying to say and think and made me realize I hadn't even scratched the surface of the questions I was pondering. A good philosophy program can challenge the way you look at the world, question what you know and how/why you think you know it, and, most importantly, teach you how to argue and debate brilliantly. *Philossophis*, incidentally, means "love of wisdom." Not love of correctness, truth, or snobby Plato quotes. Philosophy took everything I learned in acting about *how* to say something and made sure I was, in fact, *saying something*.

Once I realized that what I've loved throughout has been conveying and presenting complex ideas clearly, excitingly, spectacularly, creatively, thoughtfully, fairly, *and* persuasively, I found that my squintiness [sic] had become a much clearer outlook. I stumbled upon a charity that grabbed my attention and helped them brand and market themselves. I love the challenge of ethically selling an idea, a moral obligation, or a crisis so that everyone involved is respected, from the audience to the victims to the charity itself, all while being able to still show the urgency of a given issue.

I may have gotten here squinting hopefully and awkwardly at a potential Batman filled future, stumbling around on the stage and on the page, but I wouldn't want it any other way.

Place

Your speech also occupies a physical space. The beauty or squalor of your surroundings and the noise or stuffiness of the room should all be taken into consideration. These physical surroundings can be referred to in your speech if appropriate.

Audience Expectations

Finally, your speech is surrounded by audience expectations. When you are considering the occasion of your speech, it pays to remember that every occasion is unique. Although there are obvious differences between a university seminar, a church sermon, and the roast at a stagette, there are also many subtle differences that will apply only to the circumstances of each unique event.

> **Cultural Idiom**
> **stagette**
> A celebration in honour of a woman about to marry.

Building Credibility as a Communicator

Credibility refers to the believability of a communicator. It is the important aspect of a communicator's ability to persuade. Credibility isn't an objective quality; it is a perception in the minds of the audience. It's important to earn a good reputation *before* you communicate, through your class comments and the general attitude you've shown.

It is also possible for credibility to change during a speaking event. In fact, researchers speak in terms of *initial credibility* (your credibility when you first prepare to write or speak), *derived credibility* (the credibility you acquire while writing and speaking), and *terminal credibility* (the credibility you still possess once you have finished speaking or have your writing read). It is not uncommon for a student with low initial credibility to increase his or her credibility while communicating and to finish with much higher terminal credibility.

Members of an audience form judgments about the credibility of a speaker or writer based on their perception of many characteristics, the most important of which might be called the "Three C's" of credibility: *competence, character,* and *charisma.*[23]

Competence refers to your expertise on your topic. Sometimes this competence can come from personal experience that will lead your audience or co-communicators to regard you as an authority on your subject.

The second component of credibility, *character,* reflects the importance of gaining the audience's trust in your honesty and impartiality. You should try to find ways to talk about yourself that demonstrate your integrity.

The term *charisma* as it is used in the popular press often suggests an almost mystical quality. In the context of public communication, charisma refers to the audience's perception of the communicator's enthusiasm and likeability. Whatever the definition, history and research have shown that audiences are more likely to be persuaded by a charismatic speaker or writer than by a less charismatic one who delivers the same information.

You can boost your likeability by showing that you like and respect your audience. Insincere flattery will probably backfire, but if you can find a way to give your listeners a genuine compliment, they'll be more receptive to your ideas.

> **credibility**
> The believability of a speaker or other source of information.

Delivery

In the following sections we'll look at types of speech delivery, guidelines for delivering a speech, and how to practise your speech.

Types of Delivery

There are four basic types of delivery—*extemporaneous, impromptu, manuscript,* and *memorized.* Each type creates a different impression and is appropriate under different conditions. Any speech may incorporate more than one of these types of delivery.

Extemporaneous

An **extemporaneous speech** is planned in advance but presented in a direct, spontaneous manner. Extemporaneous speeches are conversational in tone, which means that they give the audience members the impression that you are talking to them, directly and honestly. Extemporaneous speeches *are* carefully prepared, but they are prepared in such a way that they create what actors call "the illusion of the first time." In other words, the audience hears

> **extemporaneous speech**
> A speech that is planned in advance but presented in a direct, conversational manner.

your remarks as though they were brand new. This style of speaking is generally accepted to be the most effective, especially for a college or university class.

A speech presented extemporaneously will be researched, organized, and practised in advance, but the exact wording of the entire speech will not be memorized or otherwise predetermined. Because you speak from only brief, unobtrusive notes, you are able to move and maintain eye contact with your audience. In fact, one of the keys to successful extemporaneous speaking is to avoid your notes as much as possible. The extemporaneous speech does have some disadvantages. It's difficult to stay within exact time limits, to be exact in wording, or to be grammatically perfect.

Impromptu

An **impromptu speech** is a speech you give off the top of your head, without preparation. It is the kind you may have to give in an emergency, such as when a scheduled speaker becomes ill and you are suddenly called upon. It is, by definition, spontaneous—the delivery style necessary for informal talks, group discussions, and comments on others' speeches. It also can be an effective training aid; it can teach you to think on your feet and organize your thoughts quickly. To take full advantage of an impromptu speaking opportunity, remember the following points:

1. Use the time you have to prepare wisely.
2. Don't be afraid to be original.
3. Observe what is going on around you, and respond to it.
4. Keep a positive attitude.
5. Keep your comments brief.

Manuscript

Manuscript speeches are read word-for-word from a prepared text. Manuscript speeches are difficult and cumbersome, but they are sometimes necessary. Here are some guidelines:

1. While writing, keep in mind that a speech is not the same as a term paper: speeches are usually less formal, more repetitive, and more personal.[24]
2. Use short paragraphs. They make it easier to find your place in the script after you've looked up to make eye contact with your audience.
3. Print out the manuscript triple-spaced, in capital letters, and in 14-point font or larger. Underline the words you want to emphasize. This makes reading the text while you are at the podium much easier.
4. Use stiff paper so that it won't fold up or fly away during the speech. Print on only one side, and make sure the page numbers are visible.
5. Use the "numbered lines" feature that most word processors offer. This makes referring to parts of the speech a lot easier both when practising and when giving the speech.
6. Rehearse the speech until you can speak whole lines without looking at the manuscript.
7. Take your time, vary your speed, and try to concentrate on ideas rather than words.

Memorized

Memorized speeches—those learned by heart and performed without any aids—are the most difficult and often the least effective. They often seem excessively formal. However, like manuscript speeches, they may be necessary on certain occasions. They are used both in oratory contests and as memory-training devices.

Cultural Idiom
off the top of one's head
To do or say something with little time to plan or think about it.

wrap it up
To finish.

---

impromptu speech
A speech given off the top of one's head, without preparation.

---

manuscript speech
A speech that is read word-for-word from a prepared text.

---

memorized speech
A speech learned and delivered by rote without a written text.

There is only one guideline for a memorized speech: practise. The speech won't be effective unless you have practised it until you can present it with that "illusion of the first time" that we mentioned earlier.

Guidelines for Delivery — Non-Verbal auditory *behaviour*

The best way to consider guidelines for delivery is through examination of the non-verbal aspects of presenting a speech. As you read in Chapter 4, non-verbal behaviour can change, or even contradict, the meaning of the words a speaker utters. If audience members want to interpret how you feel about something, they are likely to trust your non-verbal communication more than your words. If you tell them, "It's great to be here today," but you stand before them slouched over with your hands in your pockets, looking like you wish you were *anywhere else,* they are likely to discount what you say. You should show enthusiasm through both the visual and auditory aspects of your delivery.

Visual Aspects of Delivery

Visual aspects of delivery include appearance, movement, posture, facial expression, and eye contact.

Appearance

Appearance is not a presentation variable as much as a preparation variable. Some communication consultants suggest new clothes, new glasses, and new hairstyles for their clients. In case you consider any of these, be forewarned that you should be attractive to your audience but not flashy. Research suggests that audiences like speakers who are similar to them, but they prefer the similarity to be shown conservatively.[25] Speakers are perceived to be more credible when they look businesslike.

> **Cultural Idiom**
> **flashy**
> To be showy or gaudy.

Movement

Movement is an important visual aspect of delivery. The way you walk to the front of your audience, for example, will express your confidence and enthusiasm. Nervous energy can cause your body to shake and twitch, which can be distressing both to you and to your audience as you are speaking. One way to control involuntary movement is to move voluntarily when you feel the need to move. Don't feel that you have to stand in one spot or that all your gestures need to be carefully planned in advance. Simply get involved in your message, and let your involvement create the motivation for your movement.

Remember: move with the understanding that it will add to the meaning of the words you use. It is difficult to bang your fist on a podium or take a step without conveying emphasis. Make the emphasis natural by allowing your message to create your motivation to move.

Posture

> **Cultural Idiom**
> **squared off**
> To be evenly aligned.

Generally speaking, good posture does not mean standing at military attention. It simply means standing with your spine relatively straight, your shoulders relatively squared off, and your feet set comfortably.

Good posture can help you control nervousness by allowing your breathing apparatus to work properly; when your brain receives enough oxygen, it becomes easier for you to think clearly. Good posture will also help you get a positive audience reaction because standing up straight makes you more visible. It also increases your audience contact because the audience members will feel that you are interested enough in them to stand formally, yet relaxed enough to be at ease with them.

Facial Expression

The expression on your face can be more meaningful to your audience than the words you say. Try it yourself with a mirror. Say, "You're a terrific audience," for example, with a smirk, with a warm smile, with a deadpan expression, and then with a scowl. It just doesn't mean the same thing. Remember also that it is nearly impossible to control facial expressions from the outside.

Eye Contact

Eye contact is perhaps the most important non-verbal facet of delivery because it increases your direct contact with your audience. It can also help you control your nervousness. For many people, the most frightening aspect of public speaking is not knowing how audience members will react. Direct eye contact is a form of reality testing that allows you to check audience responses as you speak. Usually, especially when you're addressing your classmates, you will find that your audience is more "with" you than you think.

Auditory Aspects of Delivery

As we noted in Chapter 4, your paralanguage—the way you use your voice—says a good deal about you, especially about your sincerity and enthusiasm. In addition, using your voice well can help you control your nervousness. It's another cycle: controlling your vocal characteristics will decrease your nervousness, which in turn will enable you to control your voice even more. Controlling your voice is mostly a matter of recognizing and using appropriate *volume, rate, pitch,* and *articulation.*

Volume

The **volume** or loudness of your voice is determined by the amount of air you push past the vocal folds in your throat. The key to controlling volume, then, is controlling the amount of air you use. The key to determining the *right* volume is audience contact. Your delivery should be loud enough so that your audience members can hear everything you say but not so loud that they feel you are talking to someone in the next room.

volume
The loudness of one's voice.

rate
The speed at which a speaker utters words.

Rate

Your speed in speaking is called your **rate**. There is a range of personal differences in speaking rate. Former Prime Minister Brian Mulroney is said to speak at around 90 words per minute, whereas one actor who is known for his fast-talking commercials speaks at about 250. Normal speaking speed, however, is between 120 and 150 words per minute. If you talk much more slowly than that, you may lull your audience to sleep. Faster speaking rates are stereotypically associated with speaker competence,[26] but if you speak too rapidly, you will tend to be unintelligible. Once again, your involvement in your message is the key to achieving an effective rate.

Pitch

The highness or lowness of your voice—**pitch**—is controlled by the frequency at which your vocal folds vibrate as you push air through them. Because taut vocal folds vibrate at a greater frequency, pitch is influenced by muscular tension. This explains why nervous speakers have a tendency occasionally to "squeak," whereas relaxed speakers seem to be more in control. Pitch will tend to follow rate and volume. As you speed up or become louder, your pitch will have a tendency to rise. If your range in pitch is too narrow, your voice will have a singsong quality. If it is too wide, you may sound overly dramatic. You should control your pitch so that your listeners believe you are talking *with* them rather than performing in front of them. Once again, your involvement in your message should take care of this naturally for you.

Articulation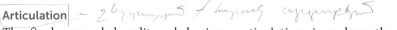

The final non-verbal auditory behaviour, **articulation**, is perhaps the most important. Articulation has a number of meanings, but in this context it means pronouncing all the parts of every word—and nothing else.

It is not our purpose here to condemn regional or ethnic dialects (though a considerable amount of research suggests regional dialects can create negative impressions).[27] What we suggest is not standardized but rather *careful* articulation. Incorrect articulation is usually nothing more than careless articulation. It is caused by:

- leaving off parts of words (deletion);
- replacing parts of words (substitution);
- adding parts to words (addition); or
- overlapping two or more words (slurring).

Many a pair of curious ears had been lured by that well-timed pause.

Li Ang, Taiwanese feminist writer

pitch
The highness or lowness of one's voice.

articulation
The process of pronouncing all the necessary parts of a word.

UNDERSTANDING COMMUNICATION TECHNOLOGY

Historic Canadian Speeches on the Web, in Libraries, and in Books

"Streaming technology" enables you to listen to audio programming and watch video programming over the internet. This means that you can hear how speeches from history—at least those made since recording technology was invented—actually sounded. You can hear how speakers handled auditory non-verbal characteristics such as volume, rate, pitch, and articulation. When video clips are available, you can even observe how they handled the visual aspects of delivery discussed in this chapter.

Many great Canadians have made speeches before the Empire Club. You can search the full text of all speeches on the organization's website (speeches.empireclub.org/).

The CBC has a very extensive site with many audio and video clips of great recorded speeches. For example, you can find archived speeches by American presidents who visited Canada, including Truman, Nixon, Reagan, and Obama (archives.cbc.ca/IDD-1-73-676/politics_economy/presidents/).

The website of the Prime Minister's Office (PMO) of the Government of Canada lists all the most significant speeches given by the Prime Minister (pm.gc.ca/eng/media.asp?category=2). This is often a good source of contemporary speeches. Library and Archives Canada also has an excellent website listing great speeches by Canadian prime ministers (collectionscanada.gc.ca/2/4/index-e.html).

Most Canadian universities and colleges subscribe to a resource called *Canadian Speeches*, which is available in both print and electronic formats. To find this resource, go to your library's catalogue and search for "Canadian speeches" in the "journal title" field.

Books such as *Great Canadian Speeches* are other useful resources for locating speeches. To find more books of Canadian speeches, try searching your library's catalogue using keywords like "Canadian" and "speeches."

Practising the Speech

In most cases, a delivery that sounds smooth and natural is the result of extensive practice. Once you've chosen the appropriate delivery type for the speech you will be giving, the best way to make sure that you are on your way to an effective delivery is to practise your speech repeatedly and systematically. One way to do that is to go through some or all of the following steps:

1. First, present the speech to yourself. "Talk through" the entire speech, including your examples and forms of support.
2. Record your speech and then watch or listen to it. Because we hear our own voices partially through our cranial bone structure, we are sometimes surprised at what we sound like to others. Videotaping is an especially effective tool for rehearsals because it lets you know what the audience will see as well as hear.[28]
3. Present the speech in front of a small group of friends or relatives.
4. Present the speech to at least one listener in the room in which you will present the final speech (or, if that room is not available, a similar room). Have your listener(s) critique your speech according to the guidelines for delivery discussed in the next section.

Dealing with Stage Fright

Communication scholars call the terror that strikes the hearts of so many novice speakers *communication apprehension* or *speech anxiety,* but those who experience it know it more commonly as *stage fright.*

Facilitative and Debilitative Stage Fright

Interestingly, the first step toward feeling less apprehensive about speaking is to realize that a certain amount of nervousness is natural and can be a good thing. **Facilitative stage fright** can help to improve your performance by causing you to think more rapidly and express yourself more energetically than you would if you were totally relaxed.

It is only when the level of anxiety is intense that it becomes **debilitative stage fright**, inhibiting effective self-expression. Intense fear causes trouble in two ways. First, the strong emotion keeps you from thinking clearly.[29] This has been shown to be a problem even in the preparation process: students who are highly anxious about giving a speech will find the preliminary steps, including research and organization, to be more difficult.[30] Second, intense fear leads to an urge to do something, anything, to make the problem go away. This urge to escape often causes a speaker to speed up his or her delivery, which results in a rapid, almost machine-gun speaking style. As you can imagine, this boost in speaking rate leads to even more mistakes, which only add to the speaker's anxiety. Thus, a relatively small amount of nervousness can begin to feed on itself until it grows into a serious problem.

Sources of Debilitative Stage Fright

Before we describe how to manage debilitative stage fright, it might be helpful to look at why people are afflicted with the problem.[31]

Previous Negative Experience

People often feel apprehensive about giving a speech because of unpleasant past experiences. Most of us are uncomfortable doing *anything* in public, especially if it is a form of performance

facilitative stage fright
A moderate level of anxiety about speaking before an audience that helps improve the speaker's performance.

debilitative stage fright
An intense level of anxiety about speaking before an audience, resulting in poor performance.

in which our talents and abilities are being evaluated. An unpleasant experience in one type of performance can cause you to expect a similar outcome to similar situations in the future.[32]

Irrational Thinking

irrational thinking
Beliefs that have no basis in reality or logic; one source of debilitative stage fright.

fallacy of catastrophic failure
The irrational belief that the worst possible outcome will probably occur.

fallacy of perfection
The irrational belief that a worthwhile communicator should be able to handle every situation with complete confidence and skill.

fallacy of approval
The irrational belief that it is vital to win the approval of virtually every person a communicator deals with.

Cognitive psychologists argue that it is the beliefs people have about events that cause them to feel nervous, not the events themselves. Certain irrational beliefs leave people feeling unnecessarily apprehensive. Psychologist Albert Ellis lists several such beliefs, or examples of **irrational thinking**, which we will call "fallacies" because of their illogical nature.[33]

Catastrophic Failure

People who succumb to the **fallacy of catastrophic failure** operate on the assumption that if something bad can happen, it probably will. Their thoughts before a speech resemble these:

"As soon as I stand up to speak, I'll forget everything I wanted to say."
"Everyone will think my ideas are stupid."
"Somebody will probably laugh at me."

Although it is naive to imagine that all your speeches will be totally successful, it is equally naive to assume they will all fail miserably. It helps to remember that nervousness is more apparent to the speaker than to the audience.[34] Beginning public speakers, when congratulated for their poise during a speech, are apt to make such remarks as "Are you kidding? I was dying up there."

Perfection

Cultural Idiom
a hole-in-one
To hit a golf ball into the hole with one swing of the club—a perfect shot.

Speakers who succumb to the **fallacy of perfection** expect themselves to behave flawlessly. Whereas such a standard of perfection might serve as a target and a source of inspiration (like the desire to make a hole-in-one while golfing), it is totally unrealistic to expect that you will write and deliver a perfect speech—especially as a beginner. It helps to remember that audiences don't expect you to be perfect.

Approval

The mistaken belief called the **fallacy of approval** is based on the idea that it is vital—not just desirable—to gain the approval of everyone in the audience. It is rare that even the best speakers please everyone, especially on topics that are at all controversial. You can't please all the people all the time—and it is irrational to expect you will.

Overgeneralization

The **fallacy of overgeneralization** might also be labelled the fallacy of exaggeration because it occurs when a person blows one poor experience out of proportion. Consider these examples:

"I'm so stupid! I mispronounced that word."

"I completely blew it—I forgot one of my supporting points."

"My hands were shaking. The audience must have thought I was a complete idiot."

A second type of exaggeration occurs when a speaker treats occasional lapses as if they were the rule instead of the exception. This sort of mistake usually involves extreme labels, such as "always" or "never." Consider these examples:

"I *always* forget what I want to say."

"I can *never* come up with a good topic."

"I can't do *anything* right."

fallacy of overgeneralization
Irrational beliefs in which conclusions (usually negative) are based on limited evidence or communicators exaggerate their shortcomings.

Overcoming Debilitative Stage Fright

There are five strategies that can help you manage debilitative stage fright:

1. *Use nervousness to your advantage.* Paralyzing fear is obviously a problem, but a little nervousness can actually help you deliver a successful speech. Use the strategies mentioned in this chapter to *control* your anxiety, but don't try to completely eliminate it.

2. *Be rational about your fears.* Some fears about speaking are rational. For example, if you haven't researched or practised your speech then you should be worried. It's also reasonable to be afraid of a hostile audience. But other fears are based on the fallacies you read about on the previous pages. It's not rational to indulge in catastrophic fantasies about what might go wrong.

3. *Maintain a receiver orientation.* Paying too much attention to your own feelings—even when you're feeling good about yourself—will take energy away from communicating with your listeners. Concentrate on your audience members rather than on yourself. Focus your energy on keeping them interested and on making sure they understand you.

4. *Keep a positive attitude.* Build and maintain a positive attitude toward your audience, your speech, and yourself as a speaker. Some communication consultants suggest that public speakers should concentrate on the following three statements immediately before speaking:

   "*I'm glad I have the chance to talk about this topic.*"

   "*I know what I'm talking about.*"

   "*I care about my audience.*"

   Another technique for building a positive attitude is known as **visualization**.[35] It requires you to use your imagination to visualize the successful completion of your speech. This technique has been used successfully with many athletes. Visualization can help make the self-fulfilling prophecy discussed in Chapter 2 work in your favour.

5. *Most important, be prepared*! Preparation is the most important key to controlling speech anxiety. You can feel confident if you know from practice that your remarks are well organized and supported and that your delivery is smooth. Researchers have determined that the highest level of speech anxiety occurs just before speaking, the second-highest level at the time the assignment is announced and explained, and the lowest level during the time you spend preparing your speech.[36] You should take

visualization
A technique for behaviour rehearsal (e.g., for a speech) that involves imagining the successful completion of the task.

advantage of this relatively low-stress time to think through the problems that might make you nervous during the actual speech.

Sample Speech

The following speech was presented by former Prime Minister Jean Chrétien in 1997 to mark the signing of the Ottawa Treaty, an agreement aimed at the elimination of anti-personnel landmines around the world.

This speech uses an impressive array of supporting material: quotations, testimony, examples, definitions, emotional appeals, analogies, personal reflections, and anecdotes. Emphasizing Canada's pre-eminence in the international anti-landmine campaign, Chrétien draws attention to the leading roles played by two members of his government, former foreign minister André Ouellet and in particular his successor, Lloyd Axworthy, in achieving the breakthrough that made this treaty possible. He also includes several references to the personal experiences behind his own commitment to the cause. Allusions to the many Canadian soldiers killed or maimed in war since 1914, including a peacekeeper who was killed by a landmine, and the awarding of the Nobel Peace Prize to Lester Pearson reinforce the message that Canada is well positioned to lead this international effort. At the same time he never lets his audience forget the urgency of taking immediate practical action for real people. This is an exemplary speech, delivered by one of Canada's most experienced and canny politicians.

The outline for this speech might look like this (the numbers in parentheses represent the corresponding paragraphs in the speech):

Introduction
    I.   Attention-getter. (1)
        The landmine epidemic: death remains after war is finished.
    II. Statement of thesis. (2)
        This conference marks a shift in the movement by highlighting the voices of those most affected by the issue, which are more eloquent than the voices of dignitaries and politicians.
    III. Preview of main points. (3)

Body
    I.   Individuals and organizations have worked hard to make the treaty possible. (3–7)
        Transition: "I welcome you to an historic occasion." (3)
        A. Goals and accomplishments of the conference. (3)
           1.   The majority of the world's nations will agree to the anti-landmine treaty.
           2.   A global partnership of governments, international institutions, and non-governmental groups will spearhead the movement.
           3.   Citizens in countries affected by landmines can begin to hope.
        B. Several powerful international organizations, celebrities, and dignitaries have lent and will lend support to the cause, including: (5)
           1.   The Red Cross and the International Campaign to Ban Landmines;
           2.   Diana, Princess of Wales, who was a supporter of the anti-landmine movement; and
           3.   UN Secretary-General Kofi Annan, who has made a pledge to engage the United Nations in the anti-landmine cause.

   II. Chrétien and Canada have long been committed to the anti-landmine cause. (6–11)
      Transition: Preview of main theme, the urgency to act. (6)
      A. Canada has a history of commitment to the cause. (6–8)
         1. In 1994, Chrétien raised the issue at the G-7 Summit.
         2. In 1996, Lloyd Axworthy organized a conference in Ottawa. (6–7)
         3. Within 14 months, Canada persuaded 100 countries to ban landmines. (8)
      B. Chrétien outlines his personal feelings and pledges to uphold Canada's commitment. (9–11)
         1. Chrétien's personal recognition of how many Canadians have been killed or maimed by landmines. (9).
         2. His delight at the widespread support for the treaty. (10)
         3. His promise of Canada's commitment to continue working to persuade those countries that have not agreed to the treaty. (11)
  III. The world and Canada are committed to the cause. (12)
      Transition: "Canada, my country, has never had landmine killing fields." (12)
      A. The consequences of landmines.
         1. Many peacekeepers have been killed, among them a Canadian. (12–13)
         2. Humans living in the affected regions have suffered devastating losses. (14)
      B. A call to the world to make a promise.
         1. To Admir. (15)
         2. To the dead. (16)
         3. To convince other nations. (17)
      C. Canada leads the way. (18–21)
         1. Canada is the first country to ratify the landmine treaty into law. (18)
         2. Canada pledges $100 million. (19)
         3. Canada calls on others to follow its lead. (20–1)

Conclusion

    I.   Final remarks. (22)
    II.   Review of main points. (22)
   III.   Restatement of thesis. (23)

Speech at the Conference for the Global Ban on Anti-Personnel Landmines (Jean Chrétien, Ottawa, 3 December 1997)

Distinguished Guests, Ladies and Gentlemen,

1 We have come together today to bring an end to the landmine epidemic. The sting of death remains long after the guns grow quiet, long after the battles are over.

2   At international conferences, there is always a great deal of talk and debate. But the most powerful voices here in Ottawa will not be the ones inside this conference site. They will be the cries of the victims of landmines—from the rice fields of Cambodia, to the suburbs of Kabul; from the mountainsides of Sarajevo to the plains of Mozambique. A chorus of millions of voices, pleading with the world, demanding the elimination of anti-personnel landmines.

3   I welcome you to an historic occasion. For the first time, the majority of the nations of the world will agree to ban a weapon which has been in military use by almost every country in the world. For the first time, a global partnership of governments, international institutions, and non-governmental groups has come together—with remarkable speed and spirit—to draft the treaty we will sign today. For the first time, those who fear to walk in their fields, those who cannot till their lands, those who cannot return to their own homes—all because of landmines—once again can begin to hope.

4   For all of them, for all of us, this is a day we will never forget.

5   The work of many nations, groups, and individuals has brought us to this moment. The International Committee of the Red Cross, whose surgeons have seen too many bodies shattered by landmines, offered early leadership. The International Campaign to Ban Landmines drove the cause with their enthusiasm and commitment. The late Princess of Wales seized the attention of the world when she exposed the human cost of landmines. And Secretary-General Kofi Annan showed courageous leadership. He recognized that the Ottawa process embodied a solemn commitment made by 156 UN members in 1996. A pledge to "pursue vigorously an effective, legally binding international agreement to ban the use, stockpiling, production, and transfer of anti-personnel landmines."

6   At the first G-7 Summit I attended as prime minister, in Naples in 1994, I raised the Canadian concern over the landmine epidemic. In 1995, our foreign minister, André Ouellet, committed Canada to the cause of banning landmines. And in 1996, Lloyd Axworthy brought new energy, commitment, and new urgency to world action. He convened a conference in Ottawa because we were not satisfied with what had been done to end the extermination in slow motion caused by landmines.

7   We knew that it was not good enough to end the landmine epidemic at some distant future date. Not with a hundred million mines planted all over the world. Not with thousands of innocent civilians—men, women, and children—dying every year. We knew we had to act. And we did.

8   At the end of that October conference, on behalf of Canada, Lloyd Axworthy challenged the world to return here just fourteen months later to sign a treaty banning the use, transfer, production, and stockpiling of anti-personnel landmines. His challenge marked a breakthrough. A breakthrough that has led directly to this historic moment. Back then, we believed if only a handful of countries came to sign, it would be an achievement. Today and tomorrow, more than 100 countries will sign this treaty. I want to say to Lloyd—your government is proud of you and your country is proud of you.

9   Like all of you here today, I have so many memories of the landmine campaign. Just last month—as every year—we honoured our war dead at the Cenotaph, just metres from this building. Standing there, I realized that, within weeks, we would be banning a weapon that has killed and maimed Canadian soldiers since the First World War.

10   I will never forget my discussions with prime ministers and presidents as they grappled with the consequences of signing this treaty, and my delight when they said that their governments would be in Ottawa in December. Of course, not all will be here, but even in the case of many who are absent, there is a new commitment to ban exports and end production. A commitment that would not be there if this conference were not taking place.

11   I give you my commitment that Canada will continue to work to persuade those who are not here to sign. We must always recognize that this treaty is open to all but can be hostage to none.

12　Canada, my country, has never had landmine killing fields. But in this century Canadian soldiers and peacekeepers have walked and died in those fields. As Secretary-General Annan knows so well, over 200 UN peacekeepers have died as landmine victims.

13　In June 1994, Master Corporal Mark Ifield, a Canadian peacekeeper in Croatia, was killed by a landmine. We honour those peacekeepers today as we remember all who have fallen victims of this horrible weapon.

14　And we listen to those who still fear like Admir Mujkic, a Grade 12 student, in East Tuzla in Bosnia. In an essay, he told us his dream and his fear:

> "I want to run through fields with my girlfriend. I want to pick the first violet for her, and to climb the trees in the forest . . . Should all my life be permanently marked with the word 'mine'?"

15　No Admir, it should not. Let us say to all the children of the world that you will walk again through the fields, and climb the trees in the forests, in a world free from mines.

16　And let us swear to those hundreds of thousands who have been murdered by landmines that we will not turn back. To the children whose very futures were stolen from them; to the families that were destroyed; to those who have lost limbs, who have lost lives: this slaughter must end. It will end. And that ending begins here—in Ottawa.

17　We will leave Ottawa proud of what we have done but very conscious of what is left to do. There are still many nations which must join us. There are still hundreds of thousands of victims to help. There are still tens of millions of mines to clear.

18　Certainly the commitment of the Government of Canada does not end with hosting this conference. I am proud to say that, by unanimous consent, both houses of our Parliament have ratified the treaty, and it has been proclaimed as law, making Canada the first nation in the world to ratify this historic convention.

19　On behalf of our government, I am also proud to announce today the establishment of a $100 million fund to implement this treaty. This means bringing it to life; making it truly global; clearing the mines; helping the victims. Both with immediate medical care and long-term help rebuilding their lives.

20　I know other countries are making similar contributions. I call on all countries to put forward the resources needed to rid the world of these buried killing machines—once and for all.

21　Jody Williams soon will go to Oslo to receive the Nobel Peace Prize. Forty years ago, a Canadian made the same journey. In bestowing the prize on Lester Pearson, the Nobel Academy said: "No matter how dark the outcome for the world may be, Lester Pearson is no pessimist. His efforts would not have been possible unless he had been supported by a strong faith in the final victory of the good forces of life."

22　Distinguished guests, ladies and gentlemen, we still have much work to do, but I am no pessimist. And obviously, neither are any of you. Today is a triumph for Jody Williams; for Lloyd Axworthy; for Secretary-General Annan; for all the many others who deserve our thanks. But to borrow those words of forty years ago in Oslo, it is the triumph of something else, something even bigger: it is the triumph of the forces of good in life.

23　Today, in Ottawa, let us celebrate that triumph. And let us commit here and now to even greater triumphs ahead.[37]

Summary

This chapter dealt with preparing a speech. Speech organization is a process that begins with choosing a topic, followed by developing a general and a specific purpose, and creating a thesis statement to express the central idea of a speech. The thesis is established in the introduction, developed in the body, and reviewed in the conclusion of a structured speech. The introduction will also gain the audience's attention, preview the main points, set the mood and tone of the speech, and demonstrate the importance of the topic to the audience. The conclusion will review your thesis and/or main points and supply the audience with a memory aid.

The process of organizing the body of a speech begins with listing the points you might want to make. These points are then arranged according to the principles of outlining. They are divided, coordinated, and placed in a logical order. Transitions from point to point help make this order apparent to your audience. Organization should follow the pattern that best suits your argument. The most common patterns are based on time (including building to a climax or anticlimax), space, topic, problem–solution, cause–effect, and motivated sequence.

Supporting materials are the facts and information you use to back up what you say. Supporting material has four purposes: to clarify, to make interesting, to make memorable, and to prove. Types of supporting materials include definitions, examples, statistics, analogies, anecdotes, quotations, and testimony. Any piece of support might combine two or more of these types. Support may be narrated (told in story form) or cited (stated briefly).

Visual aids help clarify complicated points and keep an audience informed about where you are in the general scheme of things. This chapter examined several types of visual aids: objects and models, diagrams, word and number charts, pie charts, bar and column charts, and line charts. These visual aids can be presented via flip pads and poster board, handouts, and projectors or other forms of electronic media. Whatever visual aids you use in your public speaking, it is important to ensure that they adhere to the rules regarding simplicity, size, attractiveness, appropriateness, and reliability.

A key objective in speech writing is to hold the audience's attention. This goal can be achieved by making the speech easy to listen to, emphasizing important points, using clear and simple language, and generating audience involvement.

Analyzing and adapting to your audience is a crucial part of your persuasive strategy. A persuasive communicator considers factors such as audience type; audience purpose; demographics; and attitudes, beliefs, and values to understand his or her audience. Furthermore, he or she uses this information to adapt to the audience by establishing common ground with its members, organizing the message according to the response that he or she expects to receive, and structuring the message to neutralize potential hostility.

There are four types of speech delivery: extemporaneous, impromptu, manuscript, and memorized. In each type, the speaker must be concerned with both visual and auditory aspects of the presentation. Visual aspects include appearance, movement, posture, facial expression, and eye contact. Auditory aspects include volume, rate, pitch, and articulation. The four most common articulation problems are deletion, substitution, addition, and slurring of word sounds.

One of the most serious problems in public speaking is debilitative (as opposed to facilitative) stage fright. Sources of debilitative stage fright include irrational thinking, which might consist of a belief in one or more of the fallacies mentioned in this chapter. There are several methods of overcoming speech anxiety. The first is to remember that nervousness is natural and should be used to your advantage. The others include being rational, receiver-oriented, positive, and prepared.

Key Terms

analogy   450

anecdote   450

articulation   466

attitude   459

audience analysis   457

audience involvement   456

audience participation   457

bar chart   453

basic speech structure   436

belief   460

cause—effect patterns   440

citation   452

climax pattern   439

column chart   453

conclusion   441

credibility   462

debilitative stage fright   467

demographics   458

description   434

diagram   453

example   449

explanation   434

extemporaneous speech   462

facilitative stage fright   467

fallacy of approval   468

fallacy of catastrophic failure   468

fallacy of overgeneralization   468

fallacy of perfection   468

formal outline   436

general purpose   433

hypothetical example   449

impromptu speech   463

instruction   434

introduction   441

irrational thinking   468

line chart   453

manuscript speech   463

memorized speech   463

model   452

motivated sequence   441

narration   451

number chart   453

pie chart   453

pitch   466

problem—solution pattern   440

purpose statement   434

rate   465

signpost   456

space pattern   439

specific purpose   434

statistics   450

testimony   451

thesis statement   435

time pattern   438

topic pattern   440

transition   448

value   460

visual aids   452

visualization   469

volume   465

word chart   453

working outline   436

Activities

A. Dividing Ideas

For practice in the principle of division, divide each of the following topics into three to five subcategories:

1. clothing,

2. academic studies,

3. popular internet sites,

4. television shows, and

5. exercise.

B. Building Outlines

Indicate which items would be main points and which would be sub-points in a speech entitled "World War II" by fitting them into the following outline form:

Japan desires an eastern empire	I.
Shortage of rubber tires	A.
Events of the war	B.
Nazi policy of expansion	II.
Japan seizes the Philippines	A.
Sugar rationing	B.
Effects of the war on America	C.
Germany attacks France	III.
Causes of the war	A.
Germany attacks Soviet Union	B.

C. Organizational Effectiveness

Take any written statement (of at least three paragraphs) that you consider effective. This statement might be an editorial in a newspaper, a short magazine article, or even a section of a textbook. Outline this statement according to the rules discussed in this chapter. Was the statement well organized? Did its organization contribute to its effectiveness?

D. The Functions of Support

For practice in recognizing the functions of support, identify three instances of support in Jean Chrétien's speech at the end of this chapter. Explain the function of each instance of support. (Keep in mind that any instance of support could perform more than one function.)

E. Your Attitudes, Beliefs, and Values

Being aware of your own attitudes is a big step toward becoming a good persuader. List 10 attitudes you think are the most important to you. Then list the beliefs and values that contribute to and support these attitudes. Do this for different areas of your life, such as politics, morals, cultural prejudices, etc.

Further Reading

McDermott, Martin, *Speak with Courage: 50 Insider Strategies for Presenting with Ease and Confidence* (CreateSpace Independent Publishing, a division of Amazon, 2010).
Martin McDermott, a 25-year professor of public speaking, presents 50 practical and emotional strategies to combat speech anxiety. The book is broken down into five sections: dealing with anxiety before presentations; practical strategies to ease anxiety while preparing a speech; dealing with emotional barriers to speaking; dealing with anxiety while speaking; and, finally, examining public speaking anxiety as it relates to the big picture of a person's life.

Empire Club of Canada, *Empire Club Speeches*, All Volumes (Toronto: Nabu Press).
Some of the most impressive Canadian speeches have been delivered by the nation's "who's who" at the venerable Empire Club. This series captures all the speeches ever delivered to the club.

Knowles, Elizabeth, ed., *The Oxford Dictionary of Quotations*, 7th edn (New York: Oxford University Press, 2009).
A valuable reference for quotations and testimony, this volume contains more than 20,000 quotations from over 3000 people, from Woody Allen to Émile Zola. The quotations are arranged alphabetically by author with comprehensive topical and keyword indexes.

Heath, Chip, and Dan Heath, *Made to Stick: Why Some Ideas Survive and Others Die* **(New York: Random House, 2007).**

In this immensely readable book, two brothers give the reader a recipe for success, literally! Chip and Dan Heath take their idea of stickiness, borrowed from another book, and pose the question: "Why do some ideas (like urban legends) live forever, while other, better ideas don't ever stay in the minds of the public?"

Morgan, N., "How to Become an Authentic Speaker," *Harvard Business Review* **86 (11) (2008): 115–19.**

As a speaker you can do everything right and still come across as insincere. The four aims presented in this article can connect you to the audience and allow you to become an authentic speaker.

Study Questions

Imagine you are making the case for a new, more advanced "reuse, reduce, recycle" campaign on campus. Complete the following steps:

1. Create an outline for a speech to kick off your campaign.

2. Describe one piece of supporting material you can use for each main point in the speech. Explain how it will make the speech more interesting, memorable, clear, and persuasive.

3. Make a list of your sources for citations, narratives, and statistics.

4. Write a brief point-form characterization of your audience. How will you connect with them? Will you use audience participation?

5. What are two different techniques you could use to capture attention?

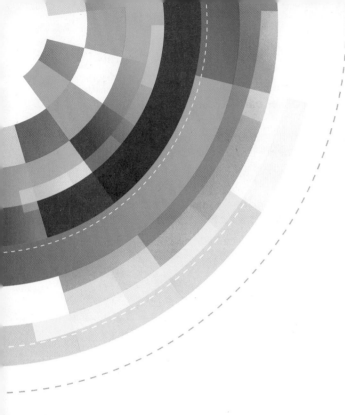

Appendix I

Persuasive Professional Writing

Persuasive Professional Writing

Dr Philip Savage

There is no getting around it: writing is both essential and, as American journalist Gene Fowler knew, "bloody" hard. However, good writing is key to success as a professional communicator—even in a multimedia era that many say is no longer dependent upon the written word. Many of the third- and fourth-year students I supervise in professional communication internships each year say the same thing in their first weeks of placement. Whether doing web design, writing speeches for politicians, or doing publicity, the basic professional writing skills they learned at university are the most challenging and yet useful parts of their professional training.

Good writing is a cornerstone of being a good communicator. As Heather Pullen, manager of public relations for Hamilton Health Sciences has said, "The most essential skill for a professional communicator is to be a good, clear, quick writer." Also, understanding the mechanics of professional writing will enable you to be a more critical participant in our message-saturated culture. By describing practical approaches to getting started in your own writing, this section will give you the basic tools you need to be an effective written communicator in most corporate, not-for-profit, government, or community settings.

The ability to write an effective news release, op-ed, blog, or briefing note can be the difference between success and failure for a campaign or a cause that you are involved with. Whether it is a community pool in your neighbourhood that you want kept open or a campaign for equal pay for woman employees in your workplace, knowing the professional writing skills in this section will be an ace in your pocket. Before describing these four forms of professional writing, we discuss two considerations about the practicality of planning writing: purpose and process.

The Purpose of Writing

Writing, whether creative, journalistic, or professional, is a rhetorical act that aims to motivate audiences to change beliefs, attitudes, or behaviour. Rhetoric as commonly understood "gets bad press"—people associate rhetoric, and professional communication, with manipulation. But we are not talking about improving your "empty rhetoric" here. Rhetoric in that sense is both unethical and because of that, ineffective over the long term.

I like to quote early broadcast journalist Edward R. Murrow, whose work at CBS exposed the anti-communist fear mongering of Senator Joseph McCarthy in the 1950s. That period and Murrow's integrity are captured in the 2005 George Clooney film *Good Night and Good Luck* and especially in Murrow's quote:

> To be persuasive, we must be believable; to be believable we must be credible;
> to be credible, we must be truthful.

There can be no real change if truth is not at your writing's core. If nothing else this section and indeed this entire book speaks to the need for relationships of trust in your communication.

To be clear about ethical and effective communication you should have two things foremost in your mind as you write: *purpose* and *audience*. Increasingly in an information-overloaded world we require a third dimension, which also is ethically important: *efficiency*. With that in mind, I suggest three questions to ask as you start to write:[1]

P	Purpose: What is the purpose of what I write?	
A	Audience: Who is the audience for what I write?	
E	Efficiency: How can I write it without wasting time?	

I suggest you "PAE-up" early. If you don't, you will pay later—with unclear goals you will write many drafts as you try to figure out the answers to what you want to say, to whom and in what form. And if the confusion on any of the three dimensions carries through into the writing, you not only waste the intended audience's time but also add "noise" to the communication. For example, during my professional career (especially at the CBC) I have written applications to the CRTC for new radio station licences.[2] When I wrote these applications I established my PAE goals:

1. *Purpose*: Our goal is to inform the CRTC about listener service problems and persuade them that the new CBC FM or digital satellite station would best provide the programming the public wanted.

2. *Audience*: We did not, as you might think, talk primarily to actual radio and TV audiences about our plans. In the report writing we addressed the six to eight individual CRTC commissioners who would sit in judgment at the regulatory hearing and make the decision.

3. *Efficiency*: We know that CRTC commissioners have a lot of applications and other hearings. So we made our writing as factual and as concise as possible, giving them the information they needed to justify their decision.

The Process of Writing

Being clear about purpose, audience, and efficiency is great, but you still have to write something. After clarifying goals, it is tempting to go right to the final written piece. However, it is important to both outline (see Chapter 12) and then draft your work before "polishing the gem" in a final revision or edit. The process includes four steps (see Table AI.1).

Pre-writing includes the PAE sections we discussed with a couple of additions: thinking about the best channel for the writing (perhaps a news release versus a report); and some level of research, that is, collecting new information you need to "'tell the story."

Outlining is the process of arranging your information, often by using point form or sub-phrases, just before the actual drafting in order to achieve clarity and impact. There are a number of ways to do this. For instance, you might outline the ideas sequentially or chronologically. You might also use a cause-and-effect approach—organizing the various situations and how they led to certain outcomes. Another way is the problem/options/solutions (POS) approach, where you identify a problem facing the group, describe the options for dealing with it (as well as the benefits and costs of each option), and then recommend a preferred solution. Finally, one can always use the journalistic practice of identifying the five Ws (Who, What, When, Where, and Why). This method works well for journalist-type writing, such as news releases. Alternatively, you can mix some of these approaches. For example, when I use the POS approach in my outlines, I tend to make sure that I cover the five Ws as well.[3]

Drafting is when you first begin to write out your sentences. In a way it is "wrapping sentences around" the outline or framework of your list of ideas and concepts. However, there is a temptation as you start writing full sentences and paragraphs to fine-tune the wording as you go. Don't strive for perfection at this point; keep writing without second-guessing yourself. An extreme form of this practice is known as "free-writing." In a quiet and undisturbed setting, write without stopping for 5 to 20 minutes on the subject. Do not worry about grammar, punctuation, fact checking, correct quotes, etc., but try to empty your mind on the subject—almost as a stream of consciousness.[4]

Whether you use free-writing or other drafting approaches, here are a few tips just to keep you writing in the drafting stage (Fowler's bloodletting proper):

1. *Start early.* If you can, start tough writing assignments early in the day (or even days before) the piece is due, avoiding the stress of immediate deadlines.
2. *Turn off the computer (or at least the WiFi connection).* Write about what you know without distractions. Don't stop to check Wikipedia or Google (or worse, friend updates on Facebook!).
3. *Talk it out.* If writing fails you, talk with a friend or colleague ("What do you think about this?" or "What if I put it like this?"). Or, talk to yourself out loud. Some writers talk into a tape/laptop recorder and then listen back.

TABLE AI.1 Writing in Four Stages

1. Pre-writing	Doing PAE, plus channel-selection and research.
2. Outlining	Arranging ideas for clarity and impact (e.g., five Ws).
3. Drafting	Writing meaningful words and sentences (e.g., "free-writing").
4. Editing	Polishing words and sentences (revising then proofreading).

4. *Skip around*. If you get a mental block dealing with one section, move to another idea or concept.
5. *Close the door*. Find a time and place to write without distractions.
6. *Take a break*. When it all gets too much, get a breath of fresh air. But be disciplined (e.g., one five-minute break after each hour of writing).

Editing actually has two equally important stages: revising and the final edit. Revising means reviewing your draft to determine if things are missing, repeated, illogical, or lacking in evidence or explanation. Go back to your originally stated goals and audience needs and see if what you drafted actually says what you intended to say to that particular person or group. Often the most productive revising is eliminating unnecessary words and phrases (keeping the goal of efficiency uppermost). A CBC journalist once told me that he always goes over his drafts and removes every adjective and adverb in his first revision. It forces him to look closely at the main construction of his story without "filler" words and creates a more direct style. He then reads the stripped-down draft and reinserts only the adjectives and adverbs required for comprehension. This trick of the trade also forces you to re-read your work with fresh eyes. Or better yet, have another person read what you have written (new, fresher eyes).[5]

The end stage of the editing is the proofread (or final edit) to ensure that your writing not only conforms to standards of good English—proper spelling, punctuation, and grammar— but also that it is stylistically appropriate.[6]

Four Major Professional Writing Forms

News Releases

The **news release** (historically, press release) is a "pseudo" news story written in the third-person that provides a reporter or editor with a newsworthy description of a particular person, event, service, or product, often on one single-spaced page of print. News releases are usually time-dependent; they are produced mindful of the various media news cycles (i.e., "old news is no news").

A common mistake is to think that the audience for the news release is the general public. In fact, the rhetorical purpose is to provide reporters with a professionally and efficiently written package of information with a sharp story angle so that they can write a story in their newspaper or broadcast program or on their website. This means "getting into the head" of a journalist and realizing that they have a radar for "puffery, flackery, and hyperbole."

News releases can be distributed to media outlets via e-mail or social media (usually with a link to the host organization's website) and, depending upon your market, additionally faxed or couriered (the latter if they are part of a full "press kit" with backgrounders, video, or other physical material, such as product samples).

My colleague, Jane Christmas, manager of public and media relations at McMaster University, refers to the "humble yet dynamic news release." She points out that the basic form of the news release has existed for over 100 years—since the days of circus showman and promoter P.T. Barnham in the late nineteenth century and the father of public relations, Edward T. Bernays, in the early twentieth century. But as Jane says, the news release remains the "workhorse for the PR industry." At the base of each—regardless of the multimedia complexity now possible—is writing that uses the key components listed in Table AI.2. An example of a real news release is on page 483.

news release
A document that provides a reporter or editor with a newsworthy description of a particular person, event, service, or product.

Cultural Idiom
puffery
Exaggerated praise that is often used in promotional material.

flackery
Publicity or promotional material.

hyperbole
An exaggerated statement or figure of speech that is not meant to be taken seriously.

getting into the head
Be able to empathize with the person you are communicating with.

TABLE AI.2 News Release Components: A Checklist for Inclusion

- Letterhead, name, address, phone number, web address.
- NEWS RELEASE in all caps.
- Contact person's name (at top or bottom).
- "Immediate Release" or release date.
- HEADLINE or TITLE in **boldface** or ALL CAPS.
- First paragraph: Date/city, then the five Ws.
- Additional paragraphs: Interesting text and quotes as appropriate.
- Final paragraph: Summary.
- Boilerplate.
- Information on further contacts, people to talk to.
- Basic font, page numbers, and ### or -30- (to indicate end of text).
- Action plan, calendar, photos, videos, and/or samples (if necessary).

> **op-ed**
> A mini-essay that appears as a stand-alone feature opposite the editorial page of a newspaper.

In this example there is a clear headline about a specific event that a reporter or editor could use. In the opening paragraph the five Ws are covered factually in terms of the "who" (Professors Sammon and Bontis), "what" (two of six OCUFA awards for teaching), "when" (announced 3 September 2009), "where" (in Ontario, with award presentation in Toronto discussed in later paragraphs), and why (for outstanding university teaching, again with more specifics in later paragraphs). Additional paragraphs make good use of quotes from the awarding body and the two professors, which give background and colour on the professors' commitment to teaching. The penultimate paragraph enlarges on the other recipients and gives specifics about the upcoming award presentation, whereas the final paragraph is a "boilerplate" or generic description of the organization providing the news release, in this case McMaster University.

Op-eds

An **op-ed** is a mini-essay that appears opposite the editorial page in newspapers as a stand-alone feature—historically in print editions but now also on media websites. Originally serving as a kind of extended letter to the editor, op-eds share some characteristics of journalistic columns (e.g., those written by Jeffrey Simpson in *The Globe and Mail* or by Rex Murphy on CBC's *The National*). An expert or a person engaged directly in specific issues or circumstances usually writes them. If timely and cogent, op-eds can stand out from the rest of the media content in a publication, broadcast, or web page, and may have a significant impact.[7]

Most op-eds run 500 to 750 words long. Like any article, they need to be factual and contain the five Ws. But they do not have to provide an impartial and fully balanced perspective, although they tend to be more persuasive if they acknowledge other points of view. For university students they seem, more than other professional writing formats, quite similar to a traditional short essay. Table A1.3 on page 484 lists the main features of op-eds. Keep in mind when reading the "Best Author" entry that organizations will sometimes submit unsolicited op-eds and sometimes—especially if the organization or its leader is well-known by media—they will be invited to comment on a topical issue. In each case the author and those helping to craft the piece need to study the submission criteria of the newspaper, website, or other media outlet.

1280 Main Street West, Hamilton, Ontario L8S 4L8, 905-525-9140, mcmaster.ca
NEWS RELEASE
McMaster Celebrates Gift from Iconic Ojibway Author, Marks 20 Years of Indigenous Studies

Hamilton, Ont. September 25, 2013—A program that began with Aboriginal students, leaders and scholars seeking to increase awareness of First Nations culture and issues through education is now celebrating 20 years of success.

This week, McMaster celebrates two decades since the formal establishment of its Indigenous Studies Program with events that include the announcement that Ojibway author Basil Johnston is donating his archives to the University's library.

Dawn Martin-Hill, now a professor of Anthropology, was still a student when she and others began advocating for an Indigenous Studies Program. She says the main challenge then was to develop trust among leaders at Six Nations and at McMaster that each was interested in the other.

While the program continues to grow and develop, when she looks back, she says she is proud of what its proponents have achieved, both at Six Nations and at McMaster.

"We were both frustrated and hopeful," she remembers. "In a way, it seems like it hasn't even been 20 years, and in a way it seems like it's been 100."

Anniversary celebrations begin on campus today (25 September) with the announcement that Basil Johnston has donated his papers to the university. (The event takes place at 7:30 p.m. in the University's Council Chambers, Gilmour Hall, Room 111.)

Johnston is the author of such books as *Moose Meat and Wild Rice*, *Ojibway Heritage*, *Indian School Days*, and *Crazy Dave*. His work is recognized for its authority in describing the richness and complexity of Anishinaabe life, including its humour.

His collection includes manuscripts, correspondence, and research materials in languages that include English, French, Ojibway/Chippewa, Cree, and Latin.

Johnston, 84, said it was simply time to gather up his archives and get them into the hands of people who might use and preserve them. He said he respects McMaster's Indigenous Studies Program and knows that the university's central location will make the collection accessible to as many users as possible.

"It's important that young people—university students—begin to study their backgrounds from our language and from our stories themselves," Johnston says. "We have our own valid way of looking at life and trying to live it out. I would hope that McMaster would carry that vision on."

Martin-Hill said Johnston's decision is a rewarding affirmation.

"For him to choose McMaster for this kind of valuable collection, I think it's a demonstration of the impact Indigenous Studies has had on the McMaster community becoming identified as a place that values Indigenous knowledge," she says.

Anishinaabe scholar and writer Hayden King, a PhD candidate at McMaster and an instructor at McMaster and Ryerson universities, is to discuss Johnston's significance at the event.

"His work has helped preserve and promote Anishinaabemowin (the language of Anishinaabe peoples) as well as ceremony and history," King says. "When Basil started writing, much of this knowledge was being threatened by policies designed to erode Indigenous cultures. So in many ways, Basil has been leading Anishinaabe peoples through the Seventh Fire Prophecy to pick up what Anishinaabe peoples left behind. There are very few accomplishments more worthy of celebration than this one."

-30-

For more information, please contact:
Andrew Baulcomb
Public Relations Coordinator McMaster University 905-525-9140 ext. 23585
baulcoad@mcmaster.ca

TABLE AI.3 Distinguishing Features of Op-Eds

Timely	Write about a current issue and event. No one wants to hear about how Neanderthals could make better decisions in an ice age past. But if you can argue that current government planning follows the same poor Neanderthal process and will lead to global warming, do so.
Lively and Strong	New and provocative arguments are good, and even better if strongly and passionately argued. You want this kind of reaction from editors and readers: "Wow! Did you see that unusual perspective on global warming?"
Not Promotional	While you may want to use an op-ed to further your organization (or one of its products or services), this is not the place for it. Build credibility about the range of insights and solutions you have to share.
Right Medium and Right Audience	Choose the media or website that fits the specific policy or decision-making venue you are interested in. For an argument against sewage waste flowing into Halifax Harbour, an op-ed in Halifax's *The Chronicle Herald* may be most appropriate. However, if you are trying to influence waste-treatment standards set by the federal government, aim for policy-makers and politicians at the federal level by writing in *The Globe and Mail*.
Best Author	As a professional communicator—rather than a subject expert—you probably will not write your own op-eds but would identify the best person in the organization to be the spokesperson for that point of view. However, you may help the appropriate person write the piece. If your local environmental organization is against the sewage dumping in Halifax Harbour, but your director has been clearly associated with only one political party, choose a more independent board member who can express similar views.

In July 2005 David Shipley, editor of the op-ed page in *The New York Times,* published some useful tips for authors and explained the process by which he would help edit contributors' articles. A McGill university site published to help its faculty experts gives this advice:

> The style of an op-ed should be lively and provocative, with a clear message and a transparent structure. Reading an op-ed should not be hard work for the general public. Both boilerplate jargon and hyperbolic, righteous indignation should be avoided; strong, colorful language and a memorable phrase or two will catch the editor's attention and lend support to the argument presented. The person in charge of the op-ed page looks for clarity, brevity and newsworthiness, as well as controversy. Intelligent, contrarian views expressed in a unique voice tend to receive a positive response.[8]

Blogs

In a sense, a blog is a series of personal mini-essays (usually about 250 words per entry). Unlike op-eds, blogs are not professionally edited and are not predominantly found in traditional media outlets or their websites. However, media outlets will house or link to blogs by their own reporters or outside experts. In addition, a number of companies, public agencies, and not-for profit organizations have their own blogs. In fact, many young professional communicators actually find that writing, managing, or even starting from scratch the organizational blog is a key entry point into professional writing.

The writing of blogs shares some of the basic aspects of writing the op-ed (see Table AI.4), but it is even more concise and is subject to the multimedia audiences' desire for an easy, quicker read. Yet like an op-ed, a good blog is valued for having a unique, passionate, and individual perspective.

Bloggers themselves are often keen to provide tips on how to blog better. The 10 tips in Table AI.5 are adapted from advice that fellow bloggers posted on Problogger.net several years ago, which is still one of the most viewed and valued blogs on blogging.

Briefing Notes

A **briefing note** is typically a 500- to 750-word document written in a strictly formatted structure designed to inform leaders within an organization about issues that require decisions. They developed—particularly in Canada—in the political and public service where Crown ministers at the federal or provincial level were required to make policy decisions or respond to questions on a specific topic. Often a leader is faced with dozens or even hundreds of issues to confront and decide upon daily, thus requiring professional written documents with an emphasis on efficiency and clarity.

> **briefing note**
> A document written in a strictly formatted structure designed to inform leaders about issues that require decisions.

TABLE AI.4 Blog Characteristics

Personal Commentary	Providing ongoing perspective and views by a single author on a particular topic. Originally some were simply online diaries but were elevated to experts covering politics, economics, or social issues.
Multimedia	A strength of the Web placement is the ability to combine text, images, video, audio, and most important, links to other online media that support or enlarge the insight provided.
Interactive	Most blogs provide a space for readers to leave comments or further the range of discussion with their own links to related content.

TABLE AI.5 Problogger Top 10 Tips

1. Make your opinion known.
2. Link like crazy.
3. Write less—250 words is enough.
4. Make headlines snappy.
5. Write with passion.
6. Include bullet point lists.
7. Edit your post.
8. Make your posts easy to scan.
9. Be consistent with your style.
10. Litter the post with keywords.

Source: Adapted from problogger.net/archives/2005/12/30/tens-tips-for-writing-a-blog-post/ (Accessed 17 May 2010).

TABLE AI.6 Briefing Note Structure

Header	Identify the recipient, author, date, and subject (similar to the header in an interoffice memo).
Issue	One to two sentences with concise statement of the issue or problem. No more than one paragraph.
Background	Two to four paragraphs with relevant information to understand the current situation. Usually includes some history, and in policy environments, the current legislation and policies.
Considerations	Two to four paragraphs showing the key facts, considerations, and developments that are relevant to the decision to be made.
Options	One to two paragraphs (often bulleted) with observations about the key two to three possible courses of action (often with a summary of cost and benefits included).
Recommendation	One to two paragraphs with a clear recommendation flowing from the background and options (similar to a report's executive summary).

Outside government, briefing notes have spread as a particularly useful professional writing tool to help decision-makers in companies and not-for-profit organizations. These leaders also welcome tightly written communication which distills complex information into short, clear, and well-structured documents and provides recommendations on how to act.

Table AI.6 shows the structure of the briefing note. I use this particular format extensively in the Media Law and Policy course that I teach at McMaster University. My experience is that even students who do not continue in law add it to their portfolio of key writing instruments because of its action-oriented style. A number of public policy courses at Canadian universities, particularly at the graduate level, provide details on the background and value of briefing notes on their websites. I find the University of Victoria's (web.uvic.ca/~sdoyle/E302/Notes/WritingBriefingNotes.html) particularly useful.

The briefing note example on page 487 was prepared by Erin Baxter (who completed my class in 2009 and finished her Master's degree in the McMaster University Communication and New Media graduate program).

Skill with briefing notes marks the professional communicator as particularly strategic in their thinking and communication and as analytic "big thinkers" within an organization. It also allows professional communicators to be integral in the communication of other experts—financial, engineering, policy—who interact with various decision-makers both within and outside the organization. That was my experience writing briefing notes at the CBC through the 1990s and 2000s, in areas as diverse as CRTC licence applications, engineering environmental assessments, network branding, and new programming strategies.

Minister of Canadian Heritage and Official Languages
Ministry of Canadian Heritage

FOR ACTION
Erin Baxter, Student Liason
N06-54317
McMaster University
16 March 2009

Proposal for a two-year pilot internship program for accepted upper-year Canadian university students studying within accredited journalism or communication programs.

ISSUE
The current recession is challenging broadcasters to work within lower budgets, thus, limiting opportunities for Canadian university students to couple theory with practicum through internships. Potential new CRTC initiatives to increase Canadian Content quotas and the secure future of broadcasting suggest that Canadian journalistic talent must be cultivated.

BACKGROUND
The Canadian Broadcasting Act sets that the mandate of the Canadian Broadcasting system is to strengthen the holistic fabric of Canada, promote the ongoing development of Canadian expression, and serve the Canadian public through programming and employment initiatives. In order to provide this Canadian programming, Canadian broadcasters must have educated Canadian voices to present viewers with culturally relevant information. Many of these voices can be found in accredited Canadian universities, learning the theoretical side of broadcast production. These students moving towards careers in Canadian journalism are of great value to the future of broadcasting and, therefore, governmental funding is needed to fulfill the Broadcasting Act mandate to serve these Canadian students with employment initiatives and provide a selection of eligible students with the practicum experience needed to prepare them for a career in Canadian journalism.

The CRTC is currently revisiting their decision to exempt new media from Canadian content regulations outlined in the Broadcasting Act. While a 1999 CRTC Public Notice stated that the Commission would not regulate new media under the Broadcasting Act, Canada's cultural sector is concerned about the lack of Canadian material on the World Wide Web and is calling the CRTC to intervene and establish regulations to ensure Canadian voices are available to Canadians. And as a 2006 report on "The Future Environment Facing the Canadian Broadcasting System" discovered, the amount of available Canadian content on the internet is also a concern for the new "broadband generation." Their concern is understandable as 60 per cent of these up-and-coming 12- to 29-year-olds describe the internet as their medium of choice, and while it is predicted that upcoming generations will not do away with traditional video content, they will demand this material be available online on a "time-and-place shifted basis." Thus, the need for astute Canadian journalists able to produce such online Canadian content, atop the 60 per cent Canadian content regulations for private and public television broadcasters, is bound to grow consistently in years to come.

Continued

Major broadcasters have recently had to adjust budgets due to a decline in advertising revenues. The CBC, having received $1.1 billion from the Canadian government is struggling to spread their budget for this year and discovering that jobs and programs cannot be sustained with estimated advertising revenue losses of up to $100 million. As a result, the broadcaster is challenged to operate with fewer employees. These budget cuts, which are being felt by other broadcasters including CTVglobemedia and CanWest Global, leave little opportunity for mentorship training as required by productive internships. Consequently, university journalism and communications students seeking to enter into Canadian journalism are left with an uneven balance of theory over practicum and may seek further training outside Canada.

CONSIDERATIONS

In the past, the Ministry of Canadian Heritage and the Canadian Heritage Portfolio have aided Canadian talent and content across the nation through the Canadian Content Development (CCD) as defined in CRTC Public Notice 2006–158, Commercial Radio Policy. The Ministry of Heritage has also been attentive to students seeking employment opportunities through the initiative Young Canada Works (YCW). YCW offers summer employment and internships to students and recent graduates to "put their skills to the test, build career equity." Thus, with this precedent of concern for post-secondary graduates, along with the need for Canadian journalists, a government-supplemented internship program will (1) provide opportunities for Canadian students to nurture their journalistic skills, (2) help to facilitate a smooth transition from university to the workplace for Canadian journalism and communication graduates, thereby keeping Canadian talent in Canada, (3) contribute to increasing quality Canadian content available to broadcasters, and, finally, (4) secure a future of informed journalism for future generations.

The federal government already funds an apprenticeship program similar to this internship initiative entitled the Apprenticeship Incentive Grant, which allocates $100 million per year to encourage students aiming for a career in the trades. While the federal government is a large supporter of post-secondary education, providing $9.7 billion in support during the 2008–09 year, a program similar to the Apprenticeship Incentive Grant for university students desiring to contribute to the valuable Canadian journalistic landscape is equally necessary.

RECOMMENDATION

In response to the need for additional Canadian content and the need to cultivate and nurture Canadian university students the Ministry of Heritage has multiple options:

— Take no action in the development of university students pursuing careers in Canadian journalism and leave the development of this field to post-graduate and college programs that will provide students with the practicum experience this internship initiative is designed to facilitate.
— Reallocate CDD funding to develop journalism students through an alternative bursary program without addressing the need for practicum.
— Implement a two-year pilot program to provide aid to Canadian universities training potential Canadian journalists by funding an enhanced system of internships.

This $1.5 million per year proposal would supplement the cost of 100 Canadian journalism and communication internships. The program would require $15,000 per student for each year of enrolment in the internship, which would be given to the university to cover the administrative costs and provide a minimum $10,000 honorarium to the host broadcaster.

While all of the above suggestions are viable, the third recommendation is most constructive and thus, most strongly suggested as it seeks long-term benefits for a range of parties, including students, universities, as well as current and future broadcasters for a comparably low economic cost. Furthermore, while this proposal is addressed to the Ministry of Heritage, the issue of journalism internships conveniently falls under the jurisdiction of several departments and agencies and, therefore, the weight of the proposed $1.5 million annual budget could be lightened through the co-operative assistance of Human Resources and Skills Development Canada, the CTF, and the CRTC, among others.

Erin E. Baxter

Contacts:
Erin Baxter, 905-525-9140
Department of Communication Studies and Multimedia
Philip Savage, 905-525-9140
Department of Communication Studies and Multimedia

Appendix II

Communicating for Career Success

The Selection Interview

For many people the short time spent facing a potential employer is the most important interview of a lifetime. A **selection interview** may occur when you are being considered for employment, but it may also occur when you are being evaluated for promotion or reassignment. In an academic setting, selection interviews are often part of the process of being chosen for an award, a scholarship, or admission to a graduate program. Being chosen for the position you seek depends on making a good impression on the person or people who can hire you, and your interviewing skills can make the difference between receiving a job offer and being an also-ran.

Preparing for the Interview

A good interview begins long before you sit down to face the other person. There are several steps you can take to boost your chances for success.

Background Research

Displaying your knowledge of an organization in an interview is a terrific way to show potential employers that you are a motivated and savvy person. Along with what you've learned from informational interviews, diligent Web browsing can reveal a wealth of information about a prospective employer and the field in which you want to work.

Most business firms, government agencies, and nonprofit agencies have websites that will help you understand their mission. If you're lucky, those websites will also contain the names of people you'll want to know about and possibly refer to during an interview.

Beyond an organization's own website, you can almost certainly find what others have published about the places where you might want to work. In your search engine, type the name of the organization and/or key people who work there. You are likely to be pleased and surprised at what you learn.

Create a Resume

No matter how extensive and supportive your network, sooner or later you will need a resume to provide a snapshot of your professional strengths and interests. For guidelines on the various types of resumes, type "create resume" into your favorite search engine. Figure AII.1 illustrates a common format for this document.

Along with a print version of your resume, it's smart to have a digital version posted on a Web-based job bank, sometimes called an online job board. Some popular sites include TalentEgg (talentegg.com) and Service Canada (www.servicecanada.gc.ca). These sites are great for people entering the job market and are filled with useful information and tips. Monster.ca, Eluta.ca, and Jobs.ca are search engines for new jobs in Canada.

When posting your resume online, there are several important steps to take to ensure that it displays correctly. A flawed resume can do more harm than good.

- Create your document in a word processing program, but save the final version as a PDF file.
- If you are e-mailing a resume, include it as an attachment. Do not paste the resume in the body of your e-mail, because the formatting may not transfer properly.
- Be aware that once you post or e-mail your resume, there is no guarantee of where it may be sent or copied. You may want to protect your privacy by including your e-mail address but not your home address or phone number.

Prepare for Likely Questions

Regardless of the organization and job, most interviewers have similar concerns, which they explore with similar questions. Here are some of the most common ones, with commentary on how you can prepare to answer them.

1. **Tell me something about yourself**.
   This broad, opening question gives you a chance to describe what qualities you possess that can help the employer (e.g., enthusiastic, motivated, entrepreneurial). Be sure to keep your answer focused on the job for which you're applying—this isn't a time to talk about your hobbies, family, or pet peeves.
2. **What makes you think you're qualified to work for this company**?
   This question may sound like an attack, but it really is another way of asking "How can you help us?" It gives you another chance to show how your skills and interests fit with the company's goals.
3. **What accomplishments have given you the most satisfaction**?
   The accomplishments you choose needn't be directly related to former employment, but they should demonstrate qualities that would help you be successful in the job for which you're interviewing. Your accomplishments might demonstrate creativity, perseverance in the face of obstacles, self-control, or dependability.
4. **Why do you want to work for us?**
   As the research cited in Table AII.1 shows, employers are impressed by candidates who have done their homework about the organization. This question offers you the chance to demonstrate your knowledge of the employer's organization and to show how your talents fit with its goals.

5.   **What college subjects did you like most and least?**

Whatever your answer, show how your preferences about schoolwork relate to the job for which you are applying. Sometimes the connection between college courses and a job is obvious. At other times, though, you can show how apparently unrelated subjects do illustrate your readiness for a job. For example, you might say, "I really enjoyed

---

JASON COLARUSSO
E-mail: jason.colarusso@connectmail.net   Phone: 587-242-3554

SUMMARY OF QUALIFICATIONS
– Academic background in political and economic dimensions of environmental policy
– Experience working in commercial and nonprofit organizations related to sustainability
– Strong work ethic and ability to work independently as necessary

EDUCATION
Current: University of Calgary
      Graduating (Bachelor of Science degree) in May 2013
      Major in Political Science, Political Economy Emphasis

Fall 2010: Lomonsov Moscow State University (Year Abroad Scholarship)
      Russian language program, ethnographic study of contemporary Russian culture

RELATED EXPERIENCE
December 2010–February 2011: Undergraduate Research Fellow, University of Calgary
      In Russia, analyzed the effectiveness of committees designed to create international environmental policy. Interviewed officials from municipal government, business, and nonprofit sectors in Russia, Ukraine, and Kazakhstan.

January 2010–present: Energy Blogger, Calgary Herald
(http://blogs.calgaryherald.com)
      Published dispatches on insights gained from travels in Russia and Central Asia for the award-winning website.

September 2009–October 2009: Assistant Communications Coordinator, Canadian Association of Petroleum Producers (CAPP)
      Assisted in coordinating media and fundraising events to educate public and recruited volunteers for an online campaign to promote Canada's oil and gas sector around the world.

March 2009–May 2009: Marketing and Communications Intern, Canadian Association of Oilwell Drilling Contractors
      Conducted individualized, in-depth sales and marketing research for the Association's members.

January 2009–March 2009: Intern, Canadian Energy Pipeline Association (CEPA)
      Conducted research to identify immediate environmental threats across California; helped develop funding proposals for major donors.

LANGUAGES
      Fluency in English, French, Italian
      Competence in Russian, Arabic, Mandarin Chinese

FIGURE AII.1 A Sample Resume Format

cultural anthropology courses because they showed me the importance of understanding different cultures. I think that those courses would help me a lot in relating to your overseas customers and suppliers."

6. **Where do you see yourself in five years**?

    This familiar question is really asking "How ambitious are you?" "How well do your plans fit with this company's goals?" "How realistic are you?" If you have studied the industry and the company, your answer will reflect an understanding of the workplace realities and a sense of personal planning that should impress an employer.

7. **What major problems have you faced, and how have you dealt with them**?

    The specific problems aren't as important as the way you responded to them. What (admirable) qualities did you demonstrate as you grappled with the problems you have chosen to describe? Perseverance? Calmness? Creativity? You may even choose to describe a problem you didn't handle well, to show what you learned from the experience that can help you in the future.

8. **What are your greatest strengths and weaknesses**?

    The "strength" question offers another chance to sell yourself. As you choose an answer, identify qualities that apply to employment. "I'm a pretty good athlete" isn't a persuasive answer, unless you can show how your athletic skill is job related. For instance, you might talk about being a team player, having competitive drive, or having the ability to work hard and not quit in the face of adversity. Whatever answer you give to the "weakness" question, try to show how your awareness of your flaws makes you a desirable person to hire. There are four ways to respond to this question:

    - *Discuss a weakness that can also be viewed as a strength.*

        "When I'm involved in a big project I tend to work too hard, and I can wear myself out."

    - *Discuss a weakness that is not related to the job at hand, and end your answer with a strength that is related to the job.*

        (for a job in sales) "I'm not very interested in accounting. I'd much rather work with people selling a product I believe in."

        (for a job in accounting) "I'm not great at sales and marketing. I'm at my best working with numbers and talking to people about them."

    - *Discuss a weakness the interviewer already knows about from your resume, application, or the interview.*

        "I don't have a lot of experience in multimedia design at this early stage of my career. But my experience in other kinds of computer programming and my internship in graphic arts have convinced me that I can learn quickly."

    - *Discuss a weakness you have been working to remedy.*

        "I know being bilingual is important for this job. That's why I've enrolled in a Spanish course."

TABLE AII.1 Communication Behaviours of Successful and Unsuccessful Interviewees

	Unsuccessful Interviewees	Successful Interviewees
Statements about the position	Had only vague ideas of what they wanted to do; changed "ideal job" up to six times during the interview.	Specific and consistent about the position they wanted; were able to tell why they wanted the position.
Use of company name	Rarely used the company name.	Referred to the company by name four times as often as unsuccessful interviewees.
Knowledge about company and position	Made it clear that they were using the interview to learn about the company and what it offered.	Made it clear that they had researched the company; referred to specific brochures, journals, or people who had given them information.
Level of interest, enthusiasm	Responded neutrally to interviewer's statements: "Okay," "I see." Indicated reservations about company or location.	Expressed approval of information provided by the interviewer nonverbally and verbally: "That's great!" Explicitly indicated desire to work for this particular company.
Picking up on interviewer's clues	Gave vague or negative answers even when a positive answer was clearly desired ("How are your math skills?")	Answered positively and confidently—and backed up the claim with a specific example of "problem solving" or "toughness."
Use of industry terms and technical jargon	Used almost no technical jargon.	Used technical jargon: "point of purchase display," "NCR charge," "two-column approach," "direct mail."
Use of specifics in answers	Gave short answers—ten words or fewer, sometimes only one word; did not elaborate. Gave general responses: "Fairly well."	Supported claims with specific personal experiences, comparisons, statistics, statements of teachers and employers.
Questions asked by interviewee	Asked a small number of general questions.	Asked specific questions based on knowledge of the industry and the company. Personalized questions: "What would my duties be?"
Control of time and topics	Interviewee talked 37 per cent of the interview time, initiated 36 per cent of the comments.	Interviewee talked 55 per cent of the total time, initiated subjects 56 per cent of the time.

Based on research reported by Lois J. Einhorn, "An Inner View of the Job Interview: An Investigation of Successful Communicative Behaviors," *Communication Education* (30 July 1981): 217–28.

9. **What are your salary requirements?**

Your answer should be based on knowledge of the prevailing compensation rates in the industry and geography in question. Shooting too high can knock you out of consideration, whereas shooting too low can cost you dearly. Give your answer naming a salary range and backing up your numbers: "Based on the research I've done about compensation in this area, I'd expect to start somewhere between $35,000 and $38,500." As you give your answer, watch the interviewer. If he or she seems to respond favorably, you're in good shape. If you notice signs of disapproval, follow up: ". . . depending, of course, on fringe benefits and how quickly I could expect to be promoted. However, salary isn't the most important criterion for me in choosing a job, and I won't necessarily accept the highest offer I get. I'm interested in going somewhere where I can get good experience and use my talents to make a real contribution." It's important to know your "bottom line" for compensation in advance so you don't end up accepting an offer at a salary you can't afford to take.

> **Cultural Idiom**
> **bottom line**
> One's minimum requirements.

Dress for Success

First impressions can make or break an interview. Research shows that many interviewers form their opinions about applicants within the first four minutes of conversation.[1] Physical attractiveness is a major influence on how applicants are rated, so it makes sense to do everything possible to look your best. The basic rules apply, no matter what the job or company: Be well groomed and neatly dressed.

The proper style of clothing can vary from one type of job or organization to another. A good rule of thumb is to come dressed as you would for the first day of work. When in doubt it's best to dress formally and conservatively. It's unlikely that an employer will think less of you for being overdressed, but looking too casual can be taken as a sign that you don't take the job or the interview seriously.

> **Cultural Idiom**
> **rule of thumb**
> A practical plan of action.

Come Prepared

Come to the interview with materials that will help the employer learn more about why you are ready, willing, and able to do the job. Bring extra copies of your resume. Come prepared to take notes—you'll need something to write on and a pen or pencil. If appropriate, bring copies of your past work: reports you've helped prepare, performance reviews by former employers, drawings or designs you have created in work or school, letters of commendation, and so on. Besides demonstrating your qualifications, items like these demonstrate that you know how to sell yourself. Bring along the names, addresses, and phone numbers of any references you haven't listed in your resume.

Know When and Where to Go

Don't risk sabotaging the interview before it begins by showing up late. Be sure you're clear about the time and location of the meeting. Research parking or public transportation to be sure you aren't held up by delays. There's virtually no good excuse for showing up late. Even if the interviewer is forgiving, a bad start is likely to shake your confidence and impair your performance.

Managing Your Anxiety

Feeling anxious about an employment interview is understandable. After all, the stakes are high—especially if you really want the job.

Realize that a certain amount of anxiety is understandable. If you can reframe those feelings as *excitement* about the prospect of holding a great job, the feelings can even work to your advantage.

If feelings of anxiety get out of hand, consider whether you are indulging yourself with any of the fallacies of catastrophic failure or perfection. Following the stage-fright guidelines in Chapter 12 (see pp. 467–70) can help shrink your concerns and give you ways of managing them.

During the Interview

There are several things you can do as an interviewee to make the interview a success.

Follow the Interviewer's Lead

Let the interviewer set the emotional tone of the session. Along with topics and verbal style, pay attention to the kinds of nonverbal cues described in Chapter 4: the interviewer's posture, gestures, vocal qualities, and so on. If he or she is informal, you can loosen up and be yourself, but if he or she is formal and proper, you should act the same way. A great deal depends on the personal chemistry between interviewer and applicant, so try to match the interviewer's style without becoming phony. If the tone of the interview doesn't fit well with you, this may be a signal that you won't feel comfortable with this company. It may be smart to see whether the interviewer's approach represents the whole company, either by asking for a tour or speaking with other employees on your own. This desire to learn about the company shows that you are a thinking person who takes the job seriously, so your curiosity isn't likely to offend the interviewer.

Keep Your Answers Brief

It's easy to rattle on in an interview, either out of enthusiasm, a desire to show off your knowledge, or nervousness, but in most cases long answers are not a good idea. The interviewer probably has lots of ground to cover, and long-winded answers won't help this task. A good rule of thumb is to keep your responses under two minutes.

Keep on the Subject

It is sometimes tempting to go overboard with your answers, sidetracking the discussion into areas that won't help the interviewer. It's often a good idea to ask the interviewer whether your answers are being helpful and then to adjust them accordingly.

Be Ready for Behavioural Interviews

Most sophisticated employers realize that past performance can be the best predictor of future behaviour. For that reason, there is an increasing trend toward **behavioural interviews**—sessions that explore specifics of the applicant's past performance as it relates to the job at hand. Typical behavioural questions include the following:

- Describe a time you needed to work as part of a team.
- Tell me about a time when you had to think on your feet to handle a challenging situation.
- Describe a time when you were faced with an ethical dilemma, and discuss how you handled it.

Your challenge, when faced with behavioural questions, is to answer in a way that shows the prospective employer how your past performance demonstrates your ability to handle the job you are now seeking. One format for constructing such answers has three parts:

1. Offer specific examples of a situation, and how you handled it.
2. Show the result of your behaviour.
3. Draw a connection between the incident you've described and the job you are seeking.

Here are some examples of good answers to behavioural questions:

Q: Give an example of a time when you were faced with an overwhelming amount of work.
A: Last year I was chairperson of the committee that organized a triathlon to raise money for a friend who had enormous medical bills after being in a car accident. When I took on the job, I had no idea how big it was: logistics, publicity, fund-raising, legal—it was huge. And some of the people who originally offered to help backed out halfway through the planning. At first I tried to do everything myself, but after a while I realized that this was not going to work. So I wound up recruiting more people, and my job turned out to be supporting

and encouraging them rather than doing it all. If I'm lucky enough to get this job, that's the approach I'd take as a manager.

Q: Tell me about a time when you had to work with someone you didn't like, or someone who didn't like you.

A: A very talented teammate in my marketing class term project kept making somewhat sexist jokes, even after I told him they made me uncomfortable. Changing teams wasn't possible, and I figured complaining to the professor would jeopardize our success on the project. So I did my best to act professionally, even in the face of those jokes. We got the job done, and received an outstanding evaluation, so I guess my discomfort was worth it. What I learned from this experience is that we don't always get to choose the people we work with, and that sometimes you have to put the job ahead of personal feelings.

Be Prepared to Ask Questions of Your Own

Besides answering the employer's questions, the selection interview is also a chance for you to learn whether the job and organization are right for you. In this sense, both the potential boss and the prospective employee are interviewing one another. Near the end of the interview, you'll probably be asked if you have any questions. It might seem as if you know all the important facts about the job, but a look at the following list suggests that a question or two can produce some useful information, as well as show the interviewer that you are also realistically assessing the fit between yourself and the organization:

1. Why is this position open now? How often has it been filled in the past five years? What have been the primary reasons for people leaving it in the past?
2. What is the biggest problem facing your staff now? How have past and current employees had trouble solving this problem?
3. What are the primary results you would like to see me produce?
4. How would you describe the management style I could expect from my supervisors?
5. Where could a person go who is successful in this position? Within what time frame?

Follow Up After the Interview

Follow up your interview with a note of thanks to the interviewer. (Many candidates don't take this step, which will make your response especially impressive.) Express your appreciation for the chance to get acquainted with the company, and let the interviewer know that the interview left you excited about the chance of becoming associated with it.

Most employment advisors agree that this is one situation where a handwritten message can be appropriate. Whether your thank-you message is handwritten or computer-generated, be sure to have a literate proofreader review it, as a mistake here can damage your prospects. One job seeker ruined her chances of employment by mentioning the "report" (instead of "rapport") that she felt with the interviewer.

Interviewing and the Law

Most laws governing what topics can and can't be covered in job interviews boil down to two simple principles: First, questions may not be aimed at discriminating on the basis of race, colour, religion, gender, sexual orientation, disabilities, national origin, or age. Second, questions must be in compliance with the Government of Canada's Employment Equity Act (www.hrsdc.gc.ca/eng/labour/employment_standards/). In other words, prospective employers may only ask about topics that are related to the job at hand. Another basic principle is that employers should ask the same job-related questions of all candidates. For example, if an interviewer asks whether one candidate has international experience, he or she should ask all others the same question.

These principles help distinguish between legal and illegal questions:

Illegal	Legal
Were you born in China?	Fluency in Mandarin Chinese is an important part of this job. Are you fluent in that language?
If you don't mind my asking, how did you get that limp?	Being on your feet for several hours per day is part of this job. Do you have any physical conditions that would make it hard to do that?
Do you have any children at home?	Are you able to work occasional nights and weekends?
Please tell me about any political clubs or organizations to which you belong.	Tell me about any job-related organizations you belong to that you think will enhance your ability to do this job.

Despite the law, there is a good chance that interviewers will ask illegal questions. This will probably have more to do with being uninformed than malicious. Still, when faced with a question that's not legal you will need to know how to respond. There are several options:

1. *Answer without objecting.* Answer the question, even though you know it is probably unlawful: "No, I'm not married. But I'm engaged." Recognize, though, that this could open the door for other illegal questions—and perhaps even discrimination in hiring decisions.
2. *Seek explanation.* Ask the interviewer firmly and respectfully to explain why this question is related to the job: "I'm having a hard time seeing how my marital status relates to my ability to do this job. Can you explain?"
3. *Redirect.* Shift the focus of the interview away from a question that isn't job related and toward the requirements of the position itself: "What you've said so far suggests that age is not as important for this position as knowledge of accounting. Can you tell me more about the kinds of accounting that are part of this job?"
4. *Refuse.* Explain politely but firmly that you will not provide the information requested: "I'd rather not talk about my religion. That's a very private and personal matter for me."
5. *Withdrawal.* End the interview immediately and leave, stating your reasons firmly but professionally: "I'm very uncomfortable with these questions about my personal life, and I don't see a good fit between me and this organization. Thank you for your time."

Cultural Idiom
gut level
One's instinctual level of feelings.

There's no absolutely correct way to handle illegal questions. The option you choose will depend on several factors: the likely intent of the interviewer, the nature of the questions, and, of course, your desire for the job—and finally, your gut level of comfort with the whole situation.

Notes

Chapter 1

1. For a discussion of the unique character of animal communication, see J. Liska, "Bee Dances, Bird Songs, Monkey Calls, and Cetacean Sonar: Is Speech Unique?" *Western Journal of Communication* 57 (1993): 1–26.

2. For an in-depth look at this topic, see S.B. Cunningham, "Intrapersonal Communication: A Review and Critique," in S. Deetz, ed., *Communication Yearbook* 15 (Newbury Park, CA: Sage, 1992).

3. L. Wheeler and J. Nelek, "Sex Differences in Social Participation," *Journal of Personality and Social Psychology* 35 (1977): 742–54.

4. J. John, "The Distribution of Free-Forming Small Group Size," *American Sociological Review* 18 (1953): 569–70.

5. D. Smith, "Are we getting through? Content Analysis of Canada Revenue Agency Media Clippings," (MCM Thesis, DeGroote School of Business, McMaster University, 2010).

6. K. Morris, "Crisis Communications: Challenges faced by Remote and Rural Communities in North Eastern Ontario," *McMaster Journal of Communication* 6 (2009).

7. J. Vecsi, "CNW Group and Leger Marketing Release 'Social Media Reality Check,'" CNW: A PR Newswire Co. (6 April 2009). Accessed 25 June 2014 at www.newswire .ca/en/story/466247/cnw-group-and-leger -marketing-release-social-media-reality -check

8. For a summary of the link between social support and health, see S. Duck, "Staying Healthy . . . with a Little Help from Our Friends?" *Human Relationships*, 2nd edn (Newbury Park, CA: Sage, 1992).

9. S. Cohen, W.J. Doyle, D.P. Skoner, B.S. Rabin, and J.M. Gwaltney, "Social Ties and Susceptibility to the Common Cold," *Journal of the American Medical Association* 277 (1997): 1940–4.

10. Three articles in *Journal of the American Medical Association* 267 (22/29 January 1992) focus on the link between psychosocial influences and coronary heart disease: R.B. Case, A.J. Moss, N. Case, M. McDermott, and S. Eberly, "Living Alone after Myocardial Infarction" (515–19); R.B. Williams, J.C. Barefoot, R.M. Calif, T.L. Haney, W.B. Saunders, D.B. Pryon, M.A. Hlatky, I.C. Siegler, and D.B. Mark, "Prognostic Importance of Social and Economic Resources among Medically Treated Patients with Angiographically Documented Coronary Artery Disease" (520–4); and R. Ruberman, "Psychosocial Influences on Mortality of Patients with Coronary Heart Disease" (559–60).

11. S. Cohen and T. Wills, "Stress, Social Support, and the Buffering Hypothesis," *Psychological Bulletin* 98 (1985): 310–57.

12. J. Caron, R. Tempier, C. Mercier, and P. Leouffre, "Components of Social Support and Quality of Life in Severely Mentally Ill, Low-Income Individuals in a General Population Group," *Community Mental Health Journal* 34 (1998): 459–76.

13. K.S. Courneya, R.C. Plotnikoff, S.B. Hotz, and N.J. Birkett, "Social Support and the Theory of Planned Behavior in the Exercise Domain," *American Journal of Health Behavior* 24, 4 (2000): 300–8.

14. J. Ali, "Mental Health of Canada's Immigrants," *Health Reports* (Ottawa: Statistics Canada, 2002): Catalogue 82-003-XIE: 13 (sup.): 101–11.

15. S. Jafari, S. Baharlou, R. Mathias, "Knowledge of Determinants of Mental Health among Iranian Immigrants of BC, Canada: A Qualitative Study," *Journal of Immigrant and Minority Health* 12, 1 (February 2010): 100–06.

16. R. Martin, "Is Laughter the Best Medicine? Humor, Laughter, and Physical Health," *Current Directions in Psychological Science* 11, 6 (2002): 216–20.

17. H.M. Lefcourt and S. Thomas, "Humor and Stress Revisited" in W. Ruch, ed., *The Sense of Humor: Explorations of a Personality Characteristic* (Berlin: Walter de Gruyter, 1998): 179–202.

18. J. Stewart, *Bridges, Not Walls: A Book about Interpersonal Communication*, 9th edn (New York: McGraw-Hill, 2004): 11.

19. R. Shattuck, *The Forbidden Experiment: The Story of the Wild Boy of Aveyron* (New York: Farrar, Straus & Giroux, 1980): 37.

20. For a fascinating account of Genie's story, see R. Rymer, *Genie: An Abused Child's Flight from Silence* (New York: HarperCollins, 1993). Linguist Susan Curtiss provides a more specialized account of the case in her book *Genie: A Psycholinguistic Study of a Modern-Day "Wild Child"* (San Diego: Academic Press, 1977).

21. C. Blatchford, "Custody Granted to Child Abusers," *National Post* (22 February 2003).

22. A.M. Nicotera, "Where Have We Been, Where Are We, and Where Do We Go?" in A.M. Nicotera and associates, eds, *Interpersonal Communication in Friend and Mate Relationships* (Albany: suny Press, 1993).

23. R.B. Rubin, E.M. Perse, and C.A. Barbato, "Conceptualization and Measurement of Interpersonal Communication Motives," *Human Communication Research* 14 (1988): 602–28.

24. R.A. Martin, P. Puhlik-Doris, G. Larsen, J. Gray, and K. Weir, "Individual Divergences in Uses of Humor and Their Relation to Psychological Well-Being: Development of the Humor Styles Questionnaire," *Journal of Research in Personality* 37 (2003): 48–75.

25. W. Goldschmidt, *The Human Career: The Self in the Symbolic World* (Cambridge, MA: Basil Blackman, 1990).

26. "Job Outlook 2004," National Association of Colleges and Employers (2004).

27. M.S. Peterson, "Personnel Interviewers' Perceptions of the Importance and Adequacy of Applicants' Communication Skills," *Communication Education* 46 (1997): 287–91.

28. M.W. Martin and C.M. Anderson, "Roommate Similarity: Are Roommates Who Are Similar in Their Communication Traits More Satisfied?" *Communication Research Reports* 12 (1995): 46–52.

29. R.B. Rubin and E.E. Graham, "Communication Correlates of College Success: An Exploratory Investigation," *Communication Education* 37 (1988): 14–27.

30. E. Kirchler, "Marital Happiness and Interaction in Everyday Surroundings: A Time-Sample Diary Approach for Couples," *Journal of Social and Personal Relationships* 5 (1988): 375–82.

31. R.L. Duran and L. Kelly, "The Influence of Communicative Competence on Perceived Task, Social and Physical Attraction," *Communication Quarterly* 36 (1988): 41–9.

32. C.E. Shannon and W. Weaver, *The Mathematical Theory of Communication* (Urbana: University of Illinois Press, 1949).

33. M. McLuhan, *Understanding Media: The Extensions of Man.* (Cambridge, MA: MIT Press, 1994).

34. K.R. Colbert, "The Effects of Debate Participation on Argumentativeness and Verbal Aggression," *Communication Education* 42 (1993): 206–14.

35. See, for example, M. Dunne and S.H. Ng, "Simultaneous Speech in Small Group Conversation: All-Together-Now and One-at-a-Time?" *Journal of Language and Social Psychology* 13 (1994): 45–71.

36. The issue of intentionality has been a matter of debate by communication theorists. For a sample of the arguments on both sides, see J.O. Greene, ed., *Message Production: Advances in Communication Theory* (New York: Erlbaum, 1997); M.T. Motley, "On Whether One Can(not) Communicate: An Examination via Traditional Communication Postulates," *Western Journal of Speech Communication* 54 (1990): 1–20; J.B. Bavelas, "Behaving and Communicating: A Reply to Motley," *Western Journal of Speech Communication* 54 (1990): 593–602; and J. Stewart, "A Postmodern Look at Traditional Communication Postulates," *Western Journal of Speech Communication* 55 (1991): 354–79.

37. S. Duck, "Relationships as Unfinished Business: Out of the Frying Pan and into the 1990s," *Journal of Social and Personal Relationships* 7 (1990): 5. For another example of the contextual base of communication, see V. Manusov, "Reacting to Changes in Nonverbal Behaviors: Relational Satisfaction and Adaptation Patterns in Romantic Dyads," *Human Communication Research* 21 (1995): 456–77.

38. K.J. Gergen, *The Saturated Self: Dilemmas of Identity in Contemporary Life* (New York: Basic Books, 1991): 158.

39. T.P. Mottet and V.P. Richmond, "Student Nonverbal Communication and Its Influence on Teachers and Teaching: A Review of Literature," in J.L. Chesebro and J.C. McCroskey, eds, *Communication for Teachers* (Needham Heights, MA: Allyn & Bacon, 2001).

40. M. Dainton and L. Stafford, "The Dark Side of 'Normal' Family Interaction," in B.H. Spitzberg and W.R. Cupach, eds, *The Dark Side of Interpersonal Communication* (Hillsdale, NJ: Erlbaum, 1993).

41. For a thorough review of this topic, see B.H. Spitzberg and W.R. Cupach, *Handbook of Interpersonal Competence Research* (New York: Springer-Verlag, 1989).

42. See J.M. Wiemann, J. Takai, H. Ota, and M. Wiemann, "A Relational Model of Communication Competence," in B. Kovacic, ed., *Emerging Theories of Human Communication* (Albany: SUNY Press, 1997).

43. For a review of the research citing the importance of flexibility, see M.M. Martin and C.M. Anderson, "The Cognitive Flexibility Scale: Three Validity Studies," *Communication Reports* 11 (1998): 1–9.

44. See G.M. Chen and W.J. Sarosta, "Intercultural Communication Competence: A Synthesis," in B.R. Burleson and A.W. Kunkel, eds, *Communication Yearbook* 19 (Thousand Oaks, CA: Sage, 1996).

45. See, for example, M.S. Kim, H.C. Shin, and D. Cai, "Cultural Influences on the Preferred Forms of Requesting and Re-Requesting," *Communication Monographs* 65 (1998): 47–66.

46. M.J. Collier, "Communication Competence Problematics in Ethnic Relationships," *Communication Monographs* 63 (1996): 314–36.

47. M. Bowman, "The Diversity of Diversity: Canadian–American Differences and Their Implications for Clinical Training and APA Accreditation," *Canadian Psychology* 41, 4 (2000): 230–43.

48. For an example of the advantages of cultural flexibility, see L. Chen, "Verbal Adaptive Strategies in US American Dyadic Interactions with US American or East-Asian Partners," *Communication Monographs* 64 (1997): 302–23.

49. For a discussion of the trait versus state assessments of communication, see D.A. Infante, A.S. Rancer, and D.F. Womack, *Building Communication Theory*, 3rd edn (Prospect Heights, IL: Waveland Press, 1996): 159–60. For a specific discussion of trait versus state definitions of communication competence, see W.R. Cupach and B.H. Spitzberg, "Trait versus State: A Comparison of Dispositional and Situational Measures of Interpersonal Communication Competence," *Western Journal of Speech Communication* 47 (1983): 364–79.

50. B.R. Burleson and W. Samter, "A Social Skills Approach to Relationship Maintenance," in D. Canary and L. Stafford, eds, *Communication and Relationship Maintenance* (San Diego: Academic Press, 1994): 12.

51. L.K. Guerrero, P.A. Andersen, P.F. Jorgensen, B.H. Spitzberg, and S.V. Eloy, "Coping with the Green-Eyed Monster: Conceptualizing and Measuring Communicative Responses to Romantic Jealousy," *Western Journal of Communication* 59 (1995): 270–304.

52. See B.J. O'Keefe, "The Logic of Message Design: Individual Differences in Reasoning about Communication," *Communication Monographs* 55 (1988): 80–103.

53. See, for example, A.D. Heisel, J.C. McCroskey, and V.P. Richmond, "Testing Theoretical Relationships and Non-Relationships of Genetically-Based Predictors: Getting Started with Communibiology," *Communication Research Reports* 16 (1999): 1–9; and J.C. McCroskey and K.J. Beatty, "The Communibiological Perspective: Implications for Communication in Instruction," *Communication Education* 49 (2000): 1–6.

54. S.L. Kline and B.L. Clinton, "Developments in Children's Persuasive Message Practices," *Communication Education* 47 (1998): 120–36.

55. M.A. de Turck and G.R. Miller, "Training Observers to Detect Deception: Effects of Self-Monitoring and Rehearsal," *Human Communication Research* 16 (1990): 603–20.

56. R.B. Rubin, E.E. Graham, and J.T. Mignerey, "A Longitudinal Study of College Students' Communication Competence," *Communication Education* 39 (1990): 1–14.

57. See, for example, R. Martin, "Relational Cognition Complexity and Relational Communication in Personal Relationships," *Communication Monographs* 59 (1992): 150–63; D.W. Stacks and M.A. Murphy,

"Conversational Sensitivity: Further Validation and Extension," *Communication Reports* 6 (1993): 18–24; and A.L. Vangelisti and S.M. Draughton, "The Nature and Correlates of Conversational Sensitivity," *Human Communication Research* 14 (1987): 167–202.

58. Research summarized in D.E. Hamachek, *Encounters with the Self*, 2nd edn (Fort Worth, TX: Holt, Rinehart and Winston, 1987): 8. See also J.A. Daly, A.L. Vangelisti, and S.M. Daughton, "The Nature and Correlates of Conversational Sensitivity," in M.V. Redmond, ed., *Interpersonal Communication: Readings in Theory and Research* (Fort Worth, TX: Harcourt Brace, 1995).

59. J. Kruger and D.A. Dunning, "Unskilled and Unaware of It: How Difficulties in Recognizing One's Own Incompetence Lead to Inflated Self-Assessments," *Journal of Personality and Social Psychology* 77, 6 (December 1999): 1121–34.

60. Adapted from the work of R.P. Hart as reported by M.L. Knapp in *Interpersonal Communication and Human Relationships* (Boston: Allyn & Bacon, 1984): 342–4. See also R.P. Hart and D.M. Burks, "Rhetorical Sensitivity and Social Interaction," *Speech Monographs* 39 (1972): 75–91; and R.P. Hart, R.E. Carlson, and W.F. Eadie, "Attitudes toward Communication and the Assessment of Rhetorical Sensitivity," *Communication Monographs* 47 (1980): 1–22.

61. Adapted from J.C. McCroskey and L.R. Wheeless, *Introduction to Human Communication* (Boston: Allyn & Bacon, 1976): 3–10.

62. R.K. Aune, "A Theory of Attribution of Responsibility for Creating Understanding." Paper delivered to the Interpersonal Communication Division of the 1998 International Communication Association Conference, Jerusalem, Israel.

63. W.B. Pearce and K.A. Pearce, "Extending the Theory of the Coordinated Management of Meaning (CMM) through a Community Dialogue Process," *Communication Theory* 10 (2000): 405–23. See also E.M. Griffin, *A First Look at Communication Theory*, 5th edn (New York: McGraw-Hill, 2003): 66–81.

64. J.A.M. Meerloo, *Conversation and Communication* (Madison, CT: International Universities Press, 1952): 91.

65. E. Eisenberg, "Jamming: Transcendence through Organizing," *Communication Research* 17 (1990): 139–64.

66. Adapted from D.D. Thornburg, "Jamming, Technology and Learning," *PBS Teacher Source Online*.

67. For a detailed rationale of the position argued in this section, see G.H. Stamp and M.L. Knapp, "The Construct of Intent in Interpersonal Communication," *Quarterly Journal of Speech* 76 (1990): 282–99. See also J. Stewart, "A Postmodern Look at Traditional Communication Postulates," *Western Journal of Speech Communication* 55 (1991): 354–79.

68. For a thorough discussion of communication difficulties, see N. Coupland, H. Giles, and J.M. Wiemann, eds, *Miscommunication and Problematic Talk* (Newbury Park, CA: Sage, 1991).

69. McCroskey and Wheeless, op. cit., 5.

Chapter 2

1. C.L.M. Shaw, "Personal Narrative: Revealing Self and Reflecting Other," *Human Communication Research* 24 (1997): 302–19.

2. P.M. Sias, "Constructing Perceptions of Differential Treatment: An Analysis of Coworkers' Discourse," *Communication Monographs* 63 (1996): 171–87.

3. A. Wilson and B.R. Slugoski, "Contribution of Conversational Skills to the Production of Judgmental Errors," *European Journal of Social Psychology* 28 (1998): 575–601.

4. J.M. Martz, J. Verette, X.B. Arriaga, L.F. Slovik, C.L. Cox, and C.E. Rusbult, "Positive Illusion in Close Relationships," *Personal Relationships* 5 (1998): 159–81.

5. J.C. Pearson, "Positive Distortion: The Most Beautiful Woman in the World," in K.M. Galvin and P.J. Cooper, eds, *Making Connections: Readings in Relational Communication*, 2nd edn (Los Angeles: Roxbury, 2000): 186.

6. Summarized in D.E. Hamachek, *Encounters with Others* (New York: Holt, Rinehart and Winston, 1982): 23–30.

7. For a review of these perceptual biases, see D.E. Hamachek, *Encounters with the Self*, 3rd edn (Fort Worth, TX: Harcourt Brace Jovanovich, 1992). See also T.N. Bradbury and F.D. Fincham, "Attributions in Marriage: Review and Critique," *Psychological Bulletin* 107 (1990): 3–33. For an example of the self-serving bias in action, see R. Buttny, "Reported Speech in Talking Race on Campus," *Human Communication Research* 23 (1997): 477–506.

8. D. Dunning and A.F. Hayes, "Evidence for Egocentric Comparison in Social Judgment," *Journal of Personality & Social Psychology* 71 (1996): 213–29.

9. B. Sypher and H.E. Sypher, "Seeing Ourselves as Others See Us," *Communication Research* 11 (January 1984): 97–115.

10. Reported by D. Myers, "The Inflated Self," *Psychology Today* 14 (May 1980): 16.

11. C. Symons and B. Johnston, "Self-Reference Affect in Memory: A Meta-Analysis," *Psychological Bulletin* 121 (1997): 371–94.

12. For more information see Louis Rosenfeld, "Insulin: Discover and Controversy," *Clinical Chemistry* (2002). Accessed 25 June 2014 at www.clinchem.org/content/48/12/2270.full

13. P. Lewicki, "Self Image Bias in Person Perception," *Journal of Personality and Social Psychology* 45 (1983): 384–93.

14. See, for example, P. Baron, "Self-Esteem, Ingratiation, and Evaluation of Unknown Others," *Journal of Personality and Social Psychology* 30 (1974): 104–9; and E. Walster, "The Effect of Self-Esteem on Romantic Liking," *Journal of Experimental and Social Psychology* 1 (1965): 184–97.

15. B. Mullen and G.R. Goethals, "Social Projection, Actual Consensus and Valence," *British Journal of Social Psychology* 29 (1990): 279–82.

16. P.A. Mongeau and C.M. Carey, "Who's Wooing Whom II? An Experimental Investigation of Date-Initiation and Expectancy Violation," *Western Journal of Communication* 60 (1996): 195–213.

17. See, for example, D.E. Kanouse and L.R. Hanson, "Negativity in Evaluations," in E.E. Jones, D.E. Kanouse, H.H. Kelley, R.E. Nisbett, S. Valins, and B. Weiner, eds, *Attribution: Perceiving the Causes of Behavior* (Morristown, NJ: General Learning Press, 1972).

18. V. Manusov, "It Depends on Your Perspective: Effects of Stance and Beliefs about Intent on Person Perception," *Western Journal of Communication* 57 (1993): 27–41.

19. T. Adler, "Enter Romance, Exit Objectivity," *APA Monitor* (June 1992): 18.

20. N. Villegas, "Assessing Reputation Management, Internal Communications and Perceptions in Oakville, Ontario," *McMaster Journal of Communication* 6 (1) (2009).

21. S.B. Algoe, B.N. Buswell, and J.D. DeLamater, "Gender and Job Status as Contextual Cues for the Interpretation of Facial Expression of Emotion," *Sex Roles* 3 (2000): 183–97.

22. See D.H. Solomon and M.L.M. Williams, "Perceptions of Social-Sexual Communication at Work: The Effects of Message, Situation, and Observer Characteristics on Judgments of Sexual Harassment," *Journal of Applied Communication Research* 25 (1997): 196–216.

23. J.K. Alberts, U. Kellar-Guenther, and S.R. Corman, "That's Not Funny: Understanding Recipients' Responses to Teasing,"

Western Journal of Communication 60 (1996): 337–57.

24. M.W. Baldwin and S.D.M. Dandeneau, "The Inhibition of Socially Rejecting Information Among People with High versus Low Self Esteem: The Role of Attentional Bias and the Effects of Bias Reduction Training," *Journal of Social and Clinical Psychology* 23 (2004): 584–602.

25. M.W. Baldwin, J.R. Baccus, and G.M. Fitzsimons, "Self-Esteem and The Dual Processing of Interpersonal Contingencies," *Self and Identity* 3 (2004): 81–93.

26. S.J. Unsworth, C.R. Sears, and P.M. Pexman, "Cultural Influences on Categorization Processes," *Journal of Cross-Cultural Psychology* 36 (2005): 662–88.

27. H. Giles, N. Coupland, and J.M. Wiemann, "Talk Is Cheap . . . But My Word Is My Bond: Beliefs about Talk," in K. Bolton and H. Kwok, eds, *Sociolinguistics Today: International Perspectives* (London: Routledge & Kegan Paul, 1992).

28. L.A. Samovar and R.E. Porter, *Communication between Cultures*, 2nd edn (Belmont, CA: Wadsworth, 1995): 199.

29. W. Lambert, "A Social Psychology of Bilingualism," in C. Bratt Paulston and G.R. Tucker, eds, *Sociolinguistics: The Essential Readings* (Oxford: Blackwell, 2003).

30. P. Andersen, M. Lustig, and J. Andersen, "Changes in Latitude, Changes in Attitude: The Relationship between Climate, Latitude, and Interpersonal Communication Predispositions." Paper presented at the annual convention of the Speech Communication Association, Boston (1987); P. Andersen, M. Lustig, and J. Andersen, "Regional Patterns of Communication in the United States: Empirical Tests." Paper presented at the annual convention of the Speech Communication Association, New Orleans (1988).

31. J.B. Stiff, J.P. Dillard, L. Somera, H. Kim, and C. Sleight, "Empathy, Communication, and Prosocial Behavior," *Communication Monographs* 55 (1988): 198–213.

32. D. Goleman, *Emotional Intelligence: Why It Can Matter More Than IQ* (New York: Bantam, 1995).

33. D.T. Regan and J. Totten, "Empathy and Attribution: Turning Observers into Actors," *Journal of Personality and Social Psychology* 35 (1975): 850–6.

34. F. Fincham, G. Paleari, and C. Regalia, "Forgiveness in Marriage: The Role of Relationship Quality, Attributions and Empathy," *Personal Relationships* 9 (2002): 27–37.

35. Don E. Hamachek, *Encounters with Others* (Los Angeles: Holt, Rinehart and Winston: 1982): 23–4.

36. J. Vorauer. "The Other Side of the Story: Transparency Estimation in Social Interaction," in G.B. Moskowitz, ed., *Cognitive and Social Psychology: The Princeton Symposium on the Legacy and Future of Social Cognition* (Hillsdale, NJ: Erlbaum, 2001): 261–76.

37. J. Vorauer and M. Ross, "Self-Awareness and Feeling Transparent: Failure to Express One's Self," *Journal of Experimental Psychology* 35 (1999): 415–40.

38. M. Conway and A. Howell, "Ego-Involvement Leads to Positive Self-Schema Activation and to a Positivity Bias in Information Processing," *Journal of Motivation and Emotion* 13, 3 (2005): 159–77.

39. M. Das, "The Identity Development of Mixed Race Individuals in Canada," Master's thesis written at University of Alberta (28 January 2010). Accessed 25 June 2014 at https://era.library.ualberta .ca/public/view/item/uuid:a661e5d0-d65d -4fe7-bb53-99616b645a02 Also available at http://hdl.handle.net/10402/era.27790.

40. Don E. Hamachek, *Encounters with the Self* (Los Angeles: Holt, Rinehart and Winston: 1982): 5–8. See also J.D. Campbell and L.F. Lavallee, "Who Am I? The Role of Self-Concept Confusion in Understanding the Behavior of People with Low Self-Esteem," in R. Baumeister, ed., *Self-Esteem: The Puzzle of Low Self-Regard* (New York: Plenum Press, 1993): 3–20.

41. A.W. Combs and D. Snygg, *Individual Behavior*, rev. edn (New York: Harper & Row, 1959): 134.

42. H.S. Sullivan, *The Interpersonal Theory of Psychiatry* (New York: Norton, 1953).

43. C.H. Cooley, *Human Nature and the Social Order* (New York: Scribner's, 1902). Contemporary research supports the power of reflected appraisal. See, for example, R. Edwards, "Sensitivity to Feedback and the Development of the Self," *Communication Quarterly* 38 (1990): 101–11.

44. J. Bartz and J.E. Lydon, "Close Relationships and the Working Self Concept: Implicit and Explicit Effects of Priming Attachment on Agency and Communion," *Personality and Social Psychology Bulletin* 30 (2004): 1389–1401.

45. C. McFarland, R. Buehler, and L. MacKay, "Affective Responses to Social Comparison with Extremely Close Others," *Social Cognition* 19 (2001): 547–86.

46. See also J. Keltikangas, "The Stability of Self-Concept during Adolescence and Early Childhood: A Six-Year Follow-Up Study," *Journal of General Psychology* 117 (1990): 361–9.

47. P.N. Myers and F.A. Biocca, "The Elastic Body Image: The Effect of Television Advertising and Programming on Body Image Distortions in Young Women," *Journal of Communication* 42 (1992): 108–34.

48. H. Giles and P. Johnson, "Ethnolinguistic Identity Theory: A Social Psychological Approach to Language Maintenance," *International Journal of Sociology of Language* 68 (1987): 69–99.

49. S.P. Banks, "Achieving 'Unmarkedness' in Organizational Discourse: A Praxis Perspective on Ethnolinguistic Identity," *Journal of Language and Social Psychology* 6 (1982): 171–90.

50. T.M. Singelis and W.J. Brown, "Culture, Self, and Collectivist Communication," *Human Communication Research* 21 (1995): 354–89. See also H.R. Markus and S. Kitayama, "A Collective Fear of the Collective: Implications for Selves and Theories of Selves," *Personality and Social Psychology* 20 (1994): 568–79.

51. J. Servaes, "Cultural Identity and Modes of Communication," in J.A. Anderson, ed., *Communication Yearbook* 12 (Newbury Park, CA: Sage, 1989): 396.

52. S. Heine, "Self as a Cultural Product: An Examination of East Asian and North American Selves," *Journal of Personality* 69 (2001): 881–906.

53. A. Bharti, "The Self in Hindu Thought and Action," in A.J. Marsella, G. DeVos, and F.L.K. Hsu, eds, *Culture and Self: Asian and Western Perspectives* (New York: Tavistock, 1985).

54. W.B. Gudykunst and S. Ting-Toomey, *Culture and Interpersonal Communication* (Newbury Park, CA: Sage, 1988).

55. L.A. Samovar and R.E. Porter, *Communication between Cultures*, 2nd edn (Belmont, CA: Wadsworth, 1995): 91.

56. D. Klopf, "Cross-Cultural Apprehension Research: A Summary of Pacific Basin Studies," in J. Daly and J. McCroskey, eds, *Avoiding Communication: Shyness, Reticence, and Communication Apprehension* (Beverly Hills, CA: Sage, 1984).

57. T.M. Steinfatt, "Personality and Communication: Classical Approaches," in J.C. McCroskey and J.A. Daly, eds, *Personality and Interpersonal Communication* (Newbury Park, CA: Sage, 1987): 42.

58. G.W. Allport and H.W. Odbert, "Trait Names, a Psychological Study," *Psychological Monographs* 47 (1936).

59. J. Kagan, *Unstable Ideas: Temperament, Cognition, and Self* (Cambridge, MA: Harvard University Press, 1989).

60. J.C. McCroskey and V. Richmond, *The Quiet Ones: Communication Apprehension*

and *Shyness* (Dubuque, IA: Gorsuch Scarisbrick, 1980). See also T.J. Bouchard, D.T. Lykken, M. McGue, and N.L. Segal, "Sources of Human Psychological Differences—The Minnesota Study of Twins Reared Apart," *Science* 250 (12 October 1990): 223–8.

61. K. Schwartz and G. Fouts, "Music Preferences, Personality Style and Developmental Issues of Adolescents," *Journal of Youth and Adolescence* 32 (3) (2004): 205–13.

62. P.D. MacIntyre and K.A. Thivierge, "The Effects of Speaker Personality on Anticipated Reactions to Public Speaking," *Communication Research Reports* 12 (1995): 125–33.

63. M. Stein and Y. Kean, "Disability and Quality of Life in Social Phobia: Epidemiological Findings," *American Journal of Psychiatry* 157 (2000): 1606–13.

64. J. Kolligan, Jr, "Perceived Fraudulence as a Dimension of Perceived Incompetence," in R.J. Sternberg and J. Kolligen, Jr, eds, *Competence Considered* (New Haven, CT: Yale University Press, 1990).

65. B.J. Zimmerman, A. Bandura, and M. Martinez-Pons, "Self-Motivation for Academic Attainment: The Role of Self-Efficacy Beliefs and Personal Goal Setting," *American Educational Research Journal* 29 (1992): 663–76.

66. R. Lockwood and Z. Kunda, "Superstars and Me: Predicting the Impact of Role Models on the Self," *Journal of Personality and Social Psychology* 73, 1 (1997): 91–103.

67. G. Downey and S.I. Feldman, "Implications of Rejection Sensitivity for Intimate Relationships," *Journal of Personality and Social Psychology* 70 (1996): 1327–43.

68. C.L. Kleinke, T.R. Peterson, and T.R. Rutledge, "Effects of Self-Generated Facial Expressions on Mood," *Journal of Personality and Social Psychology* 74 (1998): 272–9.

69. R. Rosenthal and L. Jacobson, *Pygmalion in the Classroom* (New York: Holt, Rinehart and Winston, 1968).

70. For a detailed discussion of how self-fulfilling prophecies operate in relationships, see P. Watzlawick, "Self-Fulfilling Prophecies," in J. O'Brien and P. Kollock, eds, *The Production of Reality*, 3rd edn (Thousand Oaks, CA: Pine Forge Press, 2001): 411–23.

71. C.M. Shaw and R. Edwards, "Self-Concepts and Self-Presentation of Males and Females: Similarities and Differences," *Communication Reports* 10 (1997): 56–62.

72. E. Goffman, *The Presentation of Self in Everyday Life* (Garden City, NY: Doubleday, 1959) and *Relations in Public* (New York: Basic Books, 1971).

73. W.R. Cupach and S. Metts, *Facework* (Thousand Oaks, CA: Sage, 1994). See also P. Brown and S.C. Levinson, *Politeness: Some Universals in Language Usage* (Cambridge, England: Cambridge University Press, 1987).

74. W.F. Sharkey, H.S. Park, and R.K. Kim, "Intentional Self Embarrassment," *Communication Studies* 55 (2004): 379–99.

75. M. Ross, E. Xun, and A. Wilson, "Language and Bicultural Self," *Personality and Social Psychology Bulletin*, 28 (2002): 1051–62.

76. J. Stewart and C. Logan, *Together: Communicating Interpersonally*, 5th edn (New York: McGraw-Hill, 1998): 120.

77. M.R. Leary and R.M. Kowalski, "Impression Management: A Literature Review and Two-Component Model," *Psychological Bulletin* 107 (1990): 34–47.

78. V. Brightman, A. Segal, P. Werther, and J. Steiner, "Ethological Study of Facial Expression in Response to Taste Stimuli," *Journal of Dental Research* 54 (1975): 141.

79. N. Chovil, "Social Determinants of Facial Displays," *Journal of Nonverbal Behavior* 15 (1991): 141–54.

80. M.R. Leary and R.M. Kowalski, "Impression Management: A Literature Review and Two-Component Model," *Psychological Bulletin* 107: 34–47.

81. M. Snyder, "Self-Monitoring Processes," in L. Berkowitz, ed., *Advances in Experimental Social Psychology* (New York: Academic Press, 1979) and "The Many Me's of the Self-Monitor," *Psychology Today* (March 1983): 341.

82. The following discussion is based on material in Hamachek, *Encounters with the Self*, 24–6.

83. L.M. Coleman and B.M. DePaulo, "Uncovering the Human Spirit: Moving beyond Disability and "Missed" Communications," in N. Coupland, H. Giles, and J.M. Wiemann, eds, *Miscommunication and Problematic Talk* (Newbury Park, CA: Sage, 1991): 61–84.

84. J.W. Vander Zanden, *Social Psychology*, 3rd edn (New York: Random House, 1984): 235–7.

85. J. Brown, C.R. Dykers, J.R. Steele, and A.B. White, "Teenage Room Culture: Where Media and Identities Intersect," *Communication Research* 21 (1994): 813–27.

86. J.B. Walther, "Computer-Mediated Communication: Impersonal, Interpersonal, and Hyperpersonal Interaction," *Communication Research* 23 (1996): 3–43.

87. J.T. Hancock and P.J. Durham, "Impression Formation in Computer-Mediated Communication Revisited: An Analysis of the Breadth and Intensity of Impressions," *Communication Research* 28 (2001): 325–47.

88. "People More Likely to lie on Twitter than in Real Life, Survey Reveals," *The Telegraph* (25 October 2010) Accessed 25 June 2014 at www.telegraph.co.uk/technology/social-media/8085772/People-more-likely-to-lie-on-Twitter-than-in-real-life-survey-reveals.html

89. *Street Cents*, 2001–2, Episode 7. CBC Television. 26 November 2001. For more on this episode, see www.cbc.ca/streetcents/guide/2001/07/s04-01.html

90. A. Lenhart, L. Rainie, and O. Lewis, "Teenage Life Online" (Washington, DC: Pew Internet and American Life Project, 2001).

91. P.B. O'Sullivan, "What You Don't Know Won't Hurt Me: Impression Management Functions of Communication Channels in Relationships," *Human Communication Research* 26 (2000): 403–31.

92. From Curiosity.com a division of Discovery.com. See Bambi Turner and Science Channel's "Do People Often Lie on Social Networks." Accessed 25 June 2014 at http://curiosity.discovery.com/question/do-people-lie-social-networks

Chapter 3

1. W.S.Y. Wang, "Language and Derivative Systems," in W.S.Y. Wang, ed., *Human Communication: Language and Its Psychobiological Basis* (San Francisco: Freeman, 1982): 36.

2. O. Sacks, *Seeing Voices: A Journey into the World of the Deaf* (Berkeley: University of California Press, 1989): 17.

3. Adapted from J. O'Brien and P. Kollock, *The Production of Reality*, 3rd edn (Thousand Oaks, CA: Pine Forge Press, 2001): 66.

4. M. Henneberger, "Misunderstanding of Word Embarrasses Washington's New Mayor," *New York Times* (29 January 1999).

5. C.K. Ogden and I.A. Richards, *The Meaning of Meaning* (New York: Harcourt Brace, 1923): 11.

6. S. Duck, "Maintenance as a Shared Meaning System," in D.J. Caharg and L. Stafford, eds, *Communication and Relational Maintenance* (San Diego: Academic Press, 1993).

7. D. Crystal, *Language and the Internet* (Cambridge, England: Cambridge University Press, 2001).

8. For definition examples see UrbanDictionary.com. Accessed 25 June 2014 at urbandictionary.com/define.php

?term=leet;urbandictionary.com/define
.php?term=geekspeak.

9. S. Tagliamonte and D. Denis, "OMG, It's So PC! Instant Messaging and Teen Language." Paper presented at NWAVE 34, New York City (20–3 October 2005).

10. W.B. Pearce and V. Cronen, *Communication, Action, and Meaning* (New York: Praeger, 1980). See also E.M. Griffin, *A First Look at Communication Theory*, 5th edn (New York: McGraw-Hill, 2003).

11. Genesis 2:19: This biblical reference was noted by D.C. Mader in "The Politically Correct Textbook: Trends in Publishers' Guidelines for the Representation of Marginalized Groups." Paper presented at the annual convention of the Eastern Communication Association, Portland, ME (May 1992).

12. G.W. Smith, "The Political Impact of Name Sounds," *Communication Monographs* 65 (1998): 154–72.

13. Research on the following pages is cited in M.G. Marcus, "The Power of a Name," *Psychology Today* 9 (October 1976): 75–7, 108.

14. D.H. Naftulin, J.E. Ware, Jr, and F.A. Donnelly, "The Doctor Fox Lecture: A Paradigm of Educational Seduction," *Journal of Medical Education* 48 (July 1973): 630–5. See also C.T. Cory, ed., "Bafflegab Pays," *Psychology Today* 13 (May 1980): 12; and H.W. Marsh and J.E. Ware, Jr, "Effects of Expressiveness, Content Coverage, and Incentive on Multidimensional Student Rating Scales: New Interpretations of the Dr. Fox Effect," *Journal of Educational Psychology* 74 (1982): 126–34.

15. J.S. Armstrong, "Unintelligible Management Research and Academic Prestige," *Interfaces* 10 (1980): 80–6.

16. S. Pinker, *The Language Instinct* (New York: Harper, 1995): 19.

17. For a summary of research on this subject, see J.J. Bradac, "Language Attitudes and Impression Formation," in H. Giles and W.P. Robinson, eds, *The Handbook of Language and Social Psychology* (Chichester, England: Wiley, 1990): 387–412.

18. H. Giles and P.F. Poseland, *Speech Style and Social Evaluation* (New York: Academic Press, 1975).

19. A.J. Browne and J. Fisk, "First Nations Women's Encounters with Mainstream Health Care Services," *Western Journal of Nursing Research* 23, 2 (2001): 126–47.

20. S. Romaine, *Language in Society: An Introduction to Sociolinguistics* (New York: Oxford University Press, 2002): 212.

21. C. Miller and K. Swift, *Words and Women* (New York: HarperCollins, 1991): 27.

22. F. Baider, "Sexism and Language: What can the Web teach us?" *TEXT Technology* 9 (1999): 2.

23. For a discussion of racist language, see H.A. Bosmajian, *The Language of Oppression* (Lanham, MD: University Press of America, 1983).

24. Ontario Human Rights Commission, "Paying the Price: The Human Cost of Racial Profiling," Inquiry Report. Approved by the commission 21 October 2003. Accessed 25 June 2014 at www.ohrc.on.ca/en/resources/discussion_consultation/RacialProfileReportEN/pdf

25. S.L. Kirkland, J. Greenberg, and T. Pyszynski, "Further Evidence of the Deleterious Effects of Overheard Derogatory Ethnic Labels: Derogation beyond the Target," *Personality and Social Psychology Bulletin* 12 (1987): 216–27.

26. For a review of the relationship between power and language, see J. Liska, "Dominance-Seeking Language Strategies: Please Eat the Floor, Dogbreath, or I'll Rip Your Lungs Out, O.K.?" in S.A. Deetz, ed., *Communication Yearbook* 15 (Newbury Park, CA: Sage, 1992). See also N.A. Burrell and R.J. Koper, "The Efficacy of Powerful/Powerless Language on Persuasiveness/Credibility: A Meta-Analytic Review," in R.W. Preiss and M. Allen, eds, *Prospects and Precautions in the Use of Meta-Analysis* (Dubuque, IA: Brown & Benchmark, 1994).

27. D. Tannen, *Talking from 9 to 5* (New York: Morrow, 1994): 101.

28. Geddes, "Sex Roles in Management: The Impact of Varying Power of Speech Style on Union Members' Perception of Satisfaction and Effectiveness," *Journal of Psychology* 126 (1992): 589–607.

29. L.A. Samovar and R.E. Porter, *Communication between Cultures*, 3rd edn (Belmont, CA: Wadsworth ITP, 1998): 58–9.

30. D. Cyr and A. Sèvigny, "*Traduire pour transmettre: le cas des langues amèrindiennes*," *Linguistica Antverpiensia* N.S. 2 (2004): 167–83.

31. H. Giles, J. Coupland, and N. Coupland, eds, *Contexts of Accommodation: Developments in Applied Sociolinguistics* (Cambridge, England: Cambridge University Press, 1991).

32. See, for example, R.A. Bell and J.G. Healey, "Idiomatic Communication and Interpersonal Solidarity in Friends' Relational Cultures," *Human Communication Research* 18 (1992): 307–35; and R.A. Bell, N. Buerkel-Rothfuss, and K.E. Gore, "Did You Bring the Yarmulke for the Cabbage Patch Kid?: The Idiomatic Communication

of Young Lovers," *Human Communication Research* 14 (1987): 47–67.

33. Romaine, op. cit., 78.

34. M. Wiener and A. Mehrabian, *A Language within Language* (New York: Appleton-Century-Crofts, 1968).

35. E.S. Kubanyu, D.C. Richard, G.B. Bower, and M.Y. Muraoka, "Impact of Assertive and Accusatory Communication of Distress and Anger: A Verbal Component Analysis," *Aggressive Behavior* 18 (1992): 337–47.

36. T.L. Scott, "Teens before Their Time," *Time* (27 November 2000): 22.

37. M.T. Motley and H.M. Reeder, "Unwanted Escalation of Sexual Intimacy: Male and Female Perceptions of Connotations and Relational Consequences of Resistance Messages," *Communication Monographs* 62 (1995).

38. T. Wallstein, "Measuring the Vague Meanings of Probability Terms," *Journal of Experimental Psychology* General 115 (1986): 348–65.

39. T. Labov, "Social and Language Boundaries among Adolescents," *American Speech* 4 (1992): 339–66.

40. K. Barber, *Six Words You Never Knew Had Something to Do with Pigs: And Other Fascinating Facts about the English Language* (Toronto: Oxford University Press, 2006): 36–8.

41. M. Kakutani, "Computer Slang Scoffs at Wetware," *Santa Barbara News-Press* (2 July 2000): D1.

42. M. Myer and C. Fleming, "Silicon Screenings," *Newsweek* (15 August 1994): 63.

43. S.I. Hayakawa, *Language in Thought and Action* (New York: Harcourt Brace, 1964).

44. E.M. Eisenberg, "Ambiguity as Strategy in Organizational Communication," *Communication Monographs* 51 (1984): 227–42; and E.M. Eisenberg and M.G. Witten, "Reconsidering Openness in Organizational Communication," *Academy of Management Review* 12 (1987): 418–26.

45. J.K. Alberts, "An Analysis of Couples' Conversational Complaints," *Communication Monographs* 55 (1988): 184–97.

46. B. Streisand, Crystal Awards Speech, delivered at the Women in Film luncheon (1992).

47. B. Morrison, "What You Won't Hear the Pilot Say," *USA Today* (26 September 2000): A1.

48. R.J. Sales and D. Brehm, "Vest Welcomes Frosh; Prof. Pinker Derides 'Euphemism Treadmill,'" Massachusetts Institute of Technology News Office (29 August 2001).

49. For detailed discussions of the relationship between gender and communication, see D.J. Canary and T.M. Emmers-Sommer,

Sex and Gender Differences in Personal Relationships (New York: Guilford, 1997); J. Wood, *Gendered Lives: Communication, Gender, and Culture* (Belmont, CA: Wadsworth, 1994); and J.C. Pearson, *Gender and Communication*, 2nd edn (Madison, WI: Brown & Benchmark, 1994).

50. See, for example, A. Haas and M.A. Sherman, "Reported Topics of Conversation among Same-Sex Adults," *Communication Quarterly* 30 (1982): 332–42.

51. R.A. Clark, "A Comparison of Topics and Objectives in a Cross Section of Young Men's and Women's Everyday Conversations," in D.J. Canary and K. Dindia, eds, *Sex Differences and Similarities in Communication: Critical Essays and Empirical Investigations of Sex and Gender in Interaction* (Mahwah, NJ: Erlbaum, 1998).

52. J.T. Wood, *Gendered Lives: Communication, Gender, and Culture*, 4th edn (Belmont, CA: Wadsworth, 2001): 141.

53. M.A. Sherman and A. Haas, "Man to Man, Woman to Woman," *Psychology Today* 17 (June 1984): 72–3.

54. S. Sherwood, "10 Ways Men and Women Communicate Differently" Accessed 25 June 2014 at http://dsc.discovery.com/tv-shows/curiosity/topics/10-ways-men-women-comminucate-differently.htm

55. A. Haas and M.A. Sherman, "Conversational Topic as a Function of Role and Gender," *Psychological Reports* 51 (1982): 453–4.

56. For a summary of research on the difference between male and female conversational behaviour, see H. Giles and R.L. Street, Jr, "Communication Characteristics and Behavior," in M.L. Knapp and G.R. Miller, eds, *Handbook of Interpersonal Communication* (Beverly Hills, CA: Sage, 1985): 205–61; and A. Kohn, "Girl Talk, Guy Talk," *Psychology Today* 22 (February 1988): 65–6.

57. A.J. Mulac, J.M. Wiemann, S.J. Widenmann, and T.W. Gibson, "Male/Female Language Differences and Effects in Same-Sex and Mixed-Sex Dyads: The Gender-Linked Language Effect," *Communication Monographs* 55 (1988): 315–35.

58. L.L. Carli, "Gender, Language, and Influence," *Journal of Personality and Social Psychology* 59 (1990): 941–51.

59. S. Marinelli, "Gender Imbalance in Canadian Op-Eds," Honours BA Thesis, Department of Communication Studies & Multimedia, McMaster University.

60. D.J. Canary and K.S. Hause, "Is There Any Reason to Research Sex Differences in Communication?" *Communication Quarterly* 41 (1993): 129–44.

61. C.J. Zahn, "The Bases for Differing Evaluations of Male and Female Speech: Evidence from Ratings of Transcribed Conversation," *Communication Monographs* 56 (1989): 59–74. See also L.M. Grob, R.A. Meyers, and R. Schuh, "Powerful? Powerless Language Use in Group Interactions: Sex Differences or Similarities?" *Communication Quarterly* 45 (1997): 282–303.

62. J.T. Wood and K. Dindia, "What's the Difference? A Dialogue about Differences and Similarities between Women and Men," in Canary and Dindia, op. cit.

63. D.L. Rubin, K. Greene, and D. Schneider, "Adopting Gender-Inclusive Language Reforms: Diachronic and Synchronic Variation," *Journal of Language and Social Psychology* 13 (1994): 91–114.

64. D.S. Geddes, "Sex Roles in Management: The Impact of Varying Power of Speech Style on Union Members' Perception of Satisfaction and Effectiveness," *Journal of Psychology* 126 (1992): 589–607.

65. For a thorough discussion of the challenges involved in translation from one language to another, see L.A. Samovar and R.E. Porter, *Communication between Cultures*, 4th edn (Belmont, CA: Wadsworth, 2001): 149–54.

66. The examples in this paragraph are taken from D. Ricks, *Big Business Blunders: Mistakes in International Marketing* (Homewood, IL: Dow Jones-Irwin, 1983): 41.

67. N. Sugimoto, "'Excuse Me' and 'I'm Sorry': Apologetic Behaviors of Americans and Japanese." Paper presented at the Conference on Communication in Japan and the United States, California State University, Fullerton, CA (March 1991).

68. A summary of how verbal style varies across cultures can be found in W.B. Gudykunst and S. Ting-Toomey, *Culture and Interpersonal Communication* (Newbury Park, CA: Sage, 1988): Ch. 5.

69. E.T. Hall, *Beyond Culture* (New York: Doubleday, 1959).

70. P. Clancy, "The Acquisition of Communicative Style in Japanese," in B.B. Schieffelin and E. Ochs, eds, *Language Acquisition and Socialization across Cultures* (Cambridge, England: Cambridge University Press, 1986).

71. Tannen, op. cit., 98–9.

72. *ibid.*, 99.

73. M.B. Levan, "'Creating a Framework for the Wisdom of the Community': Review of Victim Services in Nunavut, Northwest and Yukon Territories" (September 2003): sec. 4.2. Accessed 25 June 2014 at www.justice.gc.ca/en/ps/rs/rep/2003/rr03vic-3/rr03vic-3_04_02.html, sec. 4.2.

74. L. Leets and H. Giles, "Words as Weapons—When Do They Wound?" *Human Communication Research* 24 (1997): 260–301; and L. Leets, "When Words Wound: Another Look at Racist Speech." Paper presented at the annual conference of the International Communication Association, San Francisco (May 1999).

75. Almaney and A. Alwan, *Communicating with the Arabs* (Prospect Heights, IL: Waveland, 1982).

76. K. Basso, "To Give Up on Words: Silence in Western Apache Culture," *Southern Journal of Anthropology* 26 (1970): 213–30.

77. J. Yum, "The Practice of Uye-ri in Interpersonal Relationships in Korea," in D. Kincaid, ed., *Communication Theory from Eastern and Western Perspectives* (New York: Academic Press, 1987).

78. H. Giles and A. Franklyn-Stokes, "Communicator Characteristics," in M.K. Asante and W.B. Gudykunst, eds, *Handbook of International and Intercultural Communication* (Newbury Park, CA: Sage, 1989).

79. L. Sinclair, "A Word in Your Ear," in *Ways of Mankind* (Boston: Beacon Press, 1954).

80. J. Harris, *The Nurture Assumption: Why Children Turn Out the Way They Do* (New York: Free Press, 1999).

81. B. Whorf, "The Relation of Habitual Thought and Behavior to Language," in J.B. Carrol, ed., *Language, Thought, and Reality* (Cambridge, MA: MIT Press, 1956). See also Harry Hoijer, "The Sapir–Whorf Hypothesis," in Larry A. Samovar and Richard E. Porter, eds, *Intercultural Communication: A Reader*, 7th edn (Belmont, CA: Wadsworth, 1994): 194–200.

82. R. Ross, *Returning to the Teachings: Exploring Aboriginal Justice* (Toronto: Penguin Books, 1996) and Aboriginal Justice Implementation Commission, *Final Report* (Aboriginal Justice Inquiry of Manitoba, 2001). Accessed 25 June 2014 at www.ajic.mb.ca/reports/final_toc.html

83. H. Hoijer, quoted in T. Seinfaft, "Linguistic Relativity: Toward a Broader View," in S. Ting-Toomey and F. Korzenny, eds, *Language, Communication, and Culture: Current Directions* (Newbury Park, CA: Sage, 1989).

84. H. Rheingold, *They Have a Word for It* (Los Angeles: J.P. Tarcher, 1988).

85. K.A. Foss and B.A. Edson, "What's in a Name? Accounts of Married Women's Name Choices," *Western Journal of Speech Communication* 53 (1989): 356–73.

86. See J.N. Martin, R.L. Krizek, T.K. Nakayama, and L. Bradford, "Exploring Whiteness: A Study of Self-Labels for White

Americans," *Communication Quarterly* 44 (1996): 125–44.

87. T. Brown, "Predictors of Racial Label Preference in Detroit: Examining Trends from 1971 to 1992," *Sociological Spectrum* 19 (1999): 421–42. See also L. Harris, "On Our Own Terms: AJC Southern Focus Poll," *Atlanta Journal and Constitution* (25 July 1999): 1F.

88. S.J. Boatswain and R.N. Lalond, "Social Identity and Preferred Ethnic/Racial Labels for Blacks in Canada," *Journal of Black Psychology*, 26 (2000): 216–34.

89. M. Hecht, M.J. Collier, and S.A. Ribeau, *African American Communication: Ethnic Identity and Cultural Interpretation* (Newbury Park, CA: Sage, 1993). See also L.K. Larkey, K.L. Hecht, and J. Martin, "What's in a Name? African American Ethnic Identity Terms and Self-Determination," *Journal of Language and Social Psychology* 12 (1993): 302–17.

90. D. Niven and J. Zilber, "Preference for African American or Black," *Howard Journal of Communications* 11 (2000): 267–77.

91. R. King and S. Clarke, "Contesting Meaning: Newfie and The Politics of Ethnic Labelling," *Journal of Sociolinguistics* 6, 4 (2002): 537–56.

Chapter 4

1. For a survey of the issues surrounding the definition of nonverbal communication, see M. Knapp and J.A. Hall, *Nonverbal Communication in Human Interaction*, 5th edn (Belmont, CA: Wadsworth, 2002): Ch. 1.

2. L. Kelly, B. Kinkewich, H. Cromarty, N. St Pierre-Hansen, I. Antone, and C. Giles, "Palliative Care of First Nations People: A Qualitative Study of Bereaved Family Members," *Canadian Family Physician* 55, 4 (April 2009): 394–5.

3. F. Manusov, "Perceiving Nonverbal Messages: Effects of Immediacy and Encoded Intent on Receiver Judgments," *Western Journal of Speech Communication* 55 (Summer 1991): 235–53.

4. For a discussion of intentionality, see Knapp and Hall, op. cit., 9–12.

5. A.R. Dennis, S.T. Kinney, and Y.T. Hung, "Gender Differences in the Effects of Media Richness," *Small Group Research* 30 (1999): 405–37.

6. R.A. Schwier and S. Balbar, "The Interplay of Content and Community in Synchronous and Asynchronous Communication: Virtual Communication in a Graduate Seminar," *Canadian Journal of Learning and Technology*/La revue canadienne de l'apprentissage et de la technologie 28, 2 (Spring 2002).

7. See S.W. Smith, "Perceptual Processing of Nonverbal Relational Messages," in D.E. Hewes, ed., *The Cognitive Bases of Interpersonal Communication* (Hillsdale, NJ: Erlbaum, 1994).

8. J. Burgeon, D. Buller, J. Hale, and M. de Turck, "Relational Messages Associated with Nonverbal Behaviors," *Human Communication Research* 10 (Spring 1984): 351–78.

9. J.K. Burgoon, T.B. Birk, and M. Pfau, "The Association of Socio-Communicative Style and Relational Type of Perceptions of Nonverbal Intimacy," *Communication Research Reports* 14 (1997): 339–49.

10. G.Y. Lim and M.E. Roloff, "Attributing Sexual Consent," *Journal of Applied Communication Research* 27 (1999): 1–23.

11. "Safeway Clerks Object to 'Service with a Smile,'" *San Francisco Chronicle* (2 September 1998).

12. D. Druckmann, R.M. Rozelle, and J.C. Baxter, *Nonverbal Communication: Survey, Theory, and Research* (Newbury Park, CA: Sage, 1982).

13. M.T. Motley and C.T. Camden, "Facial Expression of Emotion: A Comparison of Posed Expressions versus Spontaneous Expressions in an Interpersonal Communication Setting," *Western Journal of Speech Communication* 52 (Winter 1988): 1–22.

14. See, for example, R. Rosenthal, J.A. Hall, M.R.D. Matteg, P.L. Rogers, and R. Archer, *Sensitivity to Nonverbal Communication: The PONS Test* (Baltimore, MD: Johns Hopkins University Press, 1979).

15. J.A. Hall, "Gender, Gender Roles, and Nonverbal Communication Skills," in R. Rosenthal, ed., *Skill in Nonverbal Communication: Individual Differences* (Cambridge, MA: Oelgeschlager, Gunn, and Hain, 1979): 32–67.

16. Research supporting these claims is cited in J.K. Burgoon and G.D. Hoobler, "Nonverbal Signals," in M.L. Knapp and J.A. Daly, eds, *Handbook of Interpersonal Communication*, 3rd edn (Thousand Oaks, CA: Sage, 2002).

17. S.E. Jones and C.D. LeBaron, "Research on the Relationship between Verbal and Nonverbal Communication: Emerging Interactions," *Journal of Communication* 52 (2002): 499–521.

18. P. Ekman and W.V. Friesen, *Unmasking the Face* (New York: Prentice Hall, 1975).

19. P. Ekman, W.V. Friesen, and J. Baer, "The International Language of Gestures," *Psychology Today* 18 (May 1984): 64–9.

20. McCarthy, K. Lee, S. Itakura, and D.W. Muir, "Gaze Display When Thinking Depends on Culture and Context," *Journal of Cross-Cultural Psychology* 39, 6 (2008): 716–29.

21. E. Hall, *The Hidden Dimension* (Garden City, NY: Anchor Books, 1969).

22. D.L. Rubin, "'Nobody Play by the Rule He Know': Ethnic Interference in Classroom Questioning Events," in Y.Y. Kim, ed., *Interethnic Communication: Recent Research* (Newbury Park, CA: Sage, 1986).

23. A.M. Warnecke, R.D. Masters, and G. Kempter, "The Roots of Nationalism: Nonverbal Behavior and Xenophobia," *Ethnology and Sociobiology* 13 (1992): 267–82.

24. S. Weitz, ed., *Nonverbal Communication: Readings with Commentary* (New York: Oxford University Press, 1974).

25. For a comparison of Japanese and Arab nonverbal communication norms, see D.G. Leathers, *Successful Nonverbal Communication* (New York: Macmillan, 1986): 258–61.

26. M. Booth-Butterfield and F. Jordan, "'Act Like Us': Communication Adaptation among Racially Homogeneous and Heterogeneous Groups." Paper presented at the Speech Communication Association meeting, New Orleans (1988).

27. J.A. Hall, "Male and Female Nonverbal Behavior," in A.W. Siegman and S. Feldstein, eds, *Multichannel Integrations of Nonverbal Behavior* (Hillsdale, NJ: Erlbaum, 1985).

28. J.A. Hall, J.D. Carter, and T.G. Horgan, "Status Roles and Recall of Nonverbal Cues," *Journal of Nonverbal Behavior* 25 (2001): 79–100.

29. For a comprehensive summary of male–female differences and similarities in nonverbal communication, see P.A. Andersen, *Nonverbal Communication: Forms and Functions* (Mountain View, CA: Mayfield, 1999): 107. For a detailed summary of similarities and differences, see D.J. Canary and T.M. Emmers-Sommer, *Sex and Gender Differences in Personal Relationships* (New York: Guilford, 1997).

30. Andersen, *op. cit.*, 107.

31. E.S. Cross and E.A. Franz, "Talking Hands: Observation of Bimanual Gestures as a Facilitative Working Memory Mechanism." Paper presented at the Cognitive Neuroscience Society 10th Annual Meeting, New York (30 March–1 April 2003).

32. J. Butler, *Gender Trouble* (New York: Routledge: 1990): 3.

33. Hall, op. cit.

34. C.R. Kleinke, "Compliance to Requests Made by Gazing and Touching Experi-

menters in Field Settings," *Journal of Experimental Social Psychology* 13 (1977): 218–33.

35. M.F. Argyle, F. Alkema, and R. Gilmour, "The Communication of Friendly and Hostile Attitudes: Verbal and Nonverbal Signals," *European Journal of Social Psychology* 1 (1971): 385–402.

36. D.B. Buller and J.K. Burgoon, "Deception: Strategic and Nonstrategic Communication," in J. Daly and J.M. Wiemann, eds, *Interpersonal Communication* (Hillsdale, NJ: Erlbaum, 1994).

37. J.K. Burgoon, D.B. Buller, L.K. Guerrero, and C.M. Feldman, "Interpersonal Deception: VI Effects on Preinteractional and International Factors on Deceiver and Observer Perceptions of Deception Success," *Communication Studies* 45 (1994): 263–80; and J.K. Burgoon, D.B. Buller, and L.K. Guerrero, "Interpersonal Deception: IX Effects of Social Skill and Nonverbal Communication on Deception Success and Detection Accuracy," *Journal of Language and Social Psychology* 14 (1995): 289–311.

38. R.G. Riggio and H.S. Freeman, "Individual Differences and Cues to Deception," *Journal of Personality and Social Psychology* 45 (1983): 899–915.

39. N.E. Dunbar, A. Ramirez Jr, and J.K. Burgoon, "The Effects of Participation on the Ability to Judge Deceit," *Communication Reports* 16 (2003): 23–33.

40. A. Vrig, L. Akehurst, S. Soukara, and R. Bull, "Detecting Deceit Via Analyses of Verbal and Nonverbal Behavior in Children and Adults," *Human Communication Research* 30 (2004): 8–41.

41. M.G. Millar and K.U. Millar, "The Effects of Suspicion on the Recall of Cues to Make Veracity Judgments," *Communication Reports* 11 (1998): 57–64.

42. T.R. Levine and S.A. McCornack, "Behavior Adaptation, Confidence, and Heuristic-Based Explanations of the Probing Effect," *Human Communication Research* 27 (2001): 471–502. See also D.B. Buller, J. Comstock, R.K. Aune, and K.D. Stryzewski, "The Effect of Probing on Deceivers and Truth-Tellers," *Journal of Nonverbal Behavior* 13 (1989): 155–70; and D.B. Buller, K.D. Stryzewski, and J. Comstock, "Interpersonal Deception: I. Deceivers' Reactions to Receivers' Suspicions and Probing," *Communication Monographs* 58 (1991): 1–24.

43. T.H. Feely and M.J. Young, "Self-Reported Cues about Deceptive and Truthful Communication: The Effects of Cognitive Capacity and Communicator Veracity," *Communication Quarterly* 48 (2000): 101–19.

44. P. Rockwell, D.B. Buller, and J.K. Burgoon, "The Voice of Deceit: Refining and Expanding Vocal Cues to Deception," *Communication Research Reports* 14 (1997): 451–9.

45. P. Kalbfleisch, "Deceit, Distrust, and Social Milieu: Applications of Deception Research in a Troubled World," *Journal of Applied Communication Research* (1992): 308–34.

46. J. Hale and J.B. Stiff, "Nonverbal Primacy in Veracity Judgments," *Communication Reports* 3 (1990): 75–83; and J.B. Stiff, J.L. Hale, R. Garlick, and R.G. Rogan, "Effect of Cue Incongruence and Social Normative Influences on Individual Judgments of Honesty and Deceit," *Southern Speech Communication Journal* 55 (1990): 206–29.

47. J.K. Burgoon, T. Birk, and M. Pfau, "Nonverbal Behaviors, Persuasion, and Credibility," *Human Communication Research* 17 (1990): 140–69.

48. M.A. deTurck, T.H. Feeley, and L.A. Roman, "Vocal and Visual Cue Training in Behavior Lie Detection," *Communication Research Reports* 14 (1997): 249–59.

49. Kalbfleisch, op. cit.

50. S.A. McCornack and M.R. Parks, "What Women Know that Men Don't: Sex Differences in Determining the Truth behind Deceptive Messages," *Journal of Social and Personal Relationships* 7 (1990): 107–18.

51. S.A. McCornack and T.R. Levine, "When Lovers Become Leery: The Relationship between Suspicion and Accuracy in Detecting Deception," *Communication Monographs* 7 (1990): 219–30.

52. M.A. deTurck, "Training Observers to Detect Spontaneous Deception: Effects of Gender," *Communication Reports* 4 (1991): 81–9.

53. J. Pavlidis, N.L. Eberhardt, and J.A. Levine, "Seeing through the Face of Deception," *Nature* 415 (2002).

54. R.E. Maurer and J.H. Tindall, "Effect of Postural Congruence on Client's Perception of Counselor Empathy," *Journal of Counseling Psychology* 30 (1983): 158–63.

55. V. Manusov, "Reacting to Changes in Nonverbal Behaviors: Relational Satisfaction and Adaptation Patterns in Romantic Dyads," *Human Communication Research* 21 (1995): 456–77.

56. M.B. Myers, D. Templer, and R. Brown, "Coping Ability of Women Who Become Victims of Rape," *Journal of Consulting and Clinical Psychology* 52 (1984): 73–8. See also C. Rubenstein, "Body Language That Speaks to Muggers," *Psychology Today* 20 (August 1980): 20; and J. Meer, "Profile of a Victim," *Psychology Today* 24 (May 1984): 76.

57. J.M. Iverson, "How to Get to the Cafeteria: Gesture and Speech in Blind and Sighted Children's Spatial Descriptions," *Developmental Psychology* 35 (1999): 1132–42.

58. P. Ekman, *Telling Lies: Clues to Deceit in the Marketplace, Politics, and Marriage* (New York: Norton, 1985): 109–110.

59. W. Donaghy and B.F. Dooley, "Head Movement, Gender, and Deceptive Communication," *Reports* 7 (1994): 67–75.

60. P. Ekman and W.V. Friesen, "Nonverbal Behavior and Psychopathology," in R.J. Friedman and M.N. Katz, eds, *The Psychology of Depression: Contemporary Theory and Research* (Washington, DC: J. Winston, 1974).

61. R. Sutton and A. Rafaeli, "Untangling the Relationship between Displayed Emotions and Organizational Sales: The Case of Convenience Stores," *Academy of Management Journal* 31 (1988): 463.

62. P. Ekman and W.V. Friesen, *Unmasking the Face*.

63. P. Ekman, W.V. Friesen, and P. Ellsworth, *Emotion in the Human Face: Guidelines for Research and an Integration of Findings* (Elmsford, NY: Pergamon, 1972).

64. J.A. Starkweather, "Vocal Communication of Personality and Human Feeling," *Journal of Communication* II (1961): 69; and K.R. Scherer, J. Koiwunaki, and R. Rosenthal, "Minimal Cues in the Vocal Communication of Affect: Judging Emotions from Content-Masked Speech," *Journal of Psycholinguistic Speech* I (1972): 269–85. See also F.S. Cox and C. Olney, "Vocalic Communication of Relational Messages." Paper delivered at annual meeting of the Speech Communication Association, Denver (1985).

65. K.L. Burns and E.G. Beier, "Significance of Vocal and Visual Channels for the Decoding of Emotional Meaning," *The Journal of Communication* 23 (1973): 118–30. See also Timothy G. Hegstrom, "Message Impact: What Percentage Is Nonverbal?" *Western Journal of Speech Communication* 43 (1979): 134–43; and E.M. McMahan, "Nonverbal Communication as a Function of Attribution in Impression Formation," *Communication Monographs* 43 (1976): 287–94.

66. A. Mehrabian and M. Weiner, "Decoding of Inconsistent Communications," *Journal of Personality and Social Psychology* 6 (1967): 109–14.

67. D. Buller and K. Aune, "The Effects of Speech Rate Similarity on Compliance:

Application of Communication Accommodation Theory," *Western Journal of Communication* 56 (1992): 37–53. See also D. Buller, B.A. LePoire, K. Aune, and S.V. Eloy, "Social Perceptions as Mediators of the Effect of Speech Rate Similarity on Compliance," *Human Communication Research* 19 (1992): 286–311; and J. Francis and R. Wales, "Speech a la Mode: Prosodic Cues, Message Interpretation, and Impression Formation," *Journal of Language and Social Psychology* 13 (1994): 34–44.

68. M.S. Remland and T.S. Jones, "The Influence of Vocal Intensity and Touch on Compliance Gaining," *Journal of Social Psychology* 134 (1994): 89–97.

69. Ekman, op. cit., 93.

70. C.E. Kimble and S.D. Seidel, "Vocal Signs of Confidence," *Journal of Nonverbal Behavior* 15 (1991): 99–105.

71. K.J. Tusing and J.P. Dillard, "The Sounds of Dominance: Vocal Precursors of Perceived Dominance during Interpersonal Influence," *Human Communication Research* 26 (2000): 148–71.

72. M. Zuckerman and R.E. Driver, "What Sounds Beautiful Is Good: The Vocal Attractiveness Stereotype," *Journal of Nonverbal Behavior* 13 (1989): 67–82.

73. A. Montagu, *Touching: The Human Significance of the Skin* (New York: Harper & Row, 1972): 93.

74. *ibid.*, 244–9.

75. L.J. Yarrow, "Research in Dimension of Early Maternal Care," *Merrill-Palmer Quarterly* 9 (1963): 101–22.

76. For a review of research on this subject, see S. Thayer, "Close Encounters," *Psychology Today* 22 (March 1988): 31–6.

77. See, for example, C. Segrin, "The Effects of Nonverbal Behavior on Outcomes of Compliance Gaining Attempts," *Communication Studies* 11 (1993): 169–87.

78. C.R. Kleinke, "Compliance to Requests Made by Gazing and Touching Experimenters in Field Settings," *Journal of Experimental Social Psychology* 13 (1977): 218–23.

79. F.N. Willis and H.K. Hamm, "The Use of Interpersonal Touch in Securing Compliance," *Journal of Nonverbal Behavior* 5 (1980): 49–55.

80. A.H. Crusco and C.G. Wetzel, "The Midas Touch: Effects of Interpersonal Touch on Restaurant Tipping," *Personality and Social Psychology Bulletin* 10 (1984): 512–17.

81. S.E. Jones and E. Yarbrough, "A Naturalistic Study of the Meanings of Touch," *Communication Monographs* 52 (1985): 221–31.

82. R. Heslin and T. Alper, "Touch: The Bonding Gesture," in J.M. Wiemann and R.P. Harrison, eds, *Nonverbal Interaction* (Beverly Hills, CA: Sage, 1983).

83. D.K. Fromme, W.E. Jaynes, D.K. Taylor, E.G. Hanold, J. Daniell, J.R. Rountree, and M. Fromme, "Nonverbal Behavior and Attitudes toward Touch," *Journal of Nonverbal Behavior* 13 (1989): 3–14.

84. For a summary, see M.L. Knapp and J.A. Hall, *Nonverbal Communication in Human Interaction*, 3rd edn (New York: Holt, Rinehart and Winston, 1992): 93–132. See also W. Hensley, "Why Does the Best Looking Person in the Room Always Seem to Be Surrounded by Admirers?" *Psychological Reports* 70 (1992): 457–69.

85. V. Ritts, M.L. Patterson, and M.E. Tubbs, "Expectations, Impressions, and Judgments of Physically Attractive Students: A Review," *Review of Educational Research* 62 (1992): 413–26.

86. L. Bickman, "The Social Power of a Uniform," *Journal of Applied Social Psychology* 4 (1974): 47–61.

87. S.G. Lawrence and M. Watson, "Getting Others to Help: The Effectiveness of Professional Uniforms in Charitable Fund Raising," *Journal of Applied Communication Research* 19 (1991): 170–85.

88. J.H. Fortenberry, J. Maclean, P. Morris, and M. O'Connell, "Mode of Dress as a Perceptual Cue to Deference," *The Journal of Social Psychology* 104 (1978).

89. L. Bickman, "Social Roles and Uniforms: Clothes Make the Person," *Psychology Today* 7 (April 1974): 48–51.

90. M. Lefkowitz, R.R. Blake, and J.S. Mouton, "Status of Actors in Pedestrian Violation of Traffic Signals," *Journal of Abnormal and Social Psychology* 51 (1955): 704–6.

91. L.E. Temple and K.R. Loewen, "Perceptions of Power: First Impressions of a Woman Wearing a Jacket," *Perceptual and Motor Skills* 76 (1993): 339–48.

92. T.F. Hoult, "Experimental Measurement of Clothing as a Factor in Some Social Ratings of Selected American Men," *American Sociological Review* 19 (1954): 326–7.

93. Y.K. Chan, "Density, Crowding, and Factors Intervening in Their Relationship: Evidence from a Hyper-Dense Metropolis," *Social Indicators Research* 48 (1999): 103–24.

94. E.T. Hall, op. cit., 113–30.

95. M. Hackman and K. Walker, "Instructional Communication in the Televised Classroom: The Effects of System Design and Teacher Immediacy," *Communication Education* 39 (1990): 196–206. See also J.C. McCroskey and V.P. Richmond, "Increasing Teacher Influence through Immediacy," in V.P. Richmond and J.C. McCroskey, eds, *Power in the Classroom: Communication, Control, and Concern* (Hillsdale, NJ: Erlbaum, 1992).

96. C. Conlee, J. Olvera, and N. Vagim, "The Relationships among Physician Nonverbal Immediacy and Measures of Patient Satisfaction with Physician Care," *Communication Reports* 6 (1993): 25–33.

97. D.I. Ballard and D.R. Seibold, "Time Orientation and Temporal Variation across Work Groups: Implications for Group and Organizational Communication," *Western Journal of Communication* 64 (2000): 218–42.

98. R. Levine, *A Geography of Time: The Temporal Misadventures of a Social Psychologist* (New York: Basic Books, 1997).

99. See, for example, O.W. Hill, R.A. Block, and S.E. Buggie, "Culture and Beliefs about Time: Comparisons among Black Americans, Black Africans, and White Americans," *Journal of Psychology* 134 (2000): 443–57.

100. R. Levine and E. Wolff, "Social Time: The Heartbeat of Culture," *Psychology Today* 19 (March 1985): 28–35. See also R. Levine, "Waiting Is a Power Game," *Psychology Today* 21 (April 1987): 24–33.

101. Burgoon, Buller, and Woodall, op. cit., 148.

102. Mehrabian, op. cit., 69.

103. E. Sadalla, "Identity and Symbolism in Housing," *Environment and Behavior* 19 (1987): 569–87.

104. A.H. Maslow and N.L. Mintz, "Effects of Esthetic Surroundings," *Journal of Psychology* 41 (1956): 247–54.

105. L. Festinger, S. Schachter, and K. Back, *Social Pressures in Informal Groups: A Study of Human Factors in Housing* (New York: Harper & Row, 1950).

106. Sommer, op. cit., 78.

107. *ibid.*, 35.

108. M. Dewing, "Social Media: Who Uses Them?" (Parliament of Canada, 20 November 2012). Accessed 25 June 2014 at www.parl.gc.ca/Content/LOP/ResearchPublications/2010-05-e.htm

Chapter 5

1. L. Barker, R. Edwards, C. Gaines, K. Gladney, and F. Holley, "An Investigation of Proportional Time Spent in Various Communication Activities by College Students," *Journal of Applied Communication Research* 8 (1981): 101–9.

2. Research summarized in A.D. Wolvin and C.G. Coakley, "A Survey of the Status of Listening Training in Some Fortune 500 Corporations," *Communication Education*

40 (1991): 152–64.

3. Conference Board of Canada. 2000. "Employability Skills 2000+." Accessed 25 June 2014 at www.conferenceboard.ca/education/learning-tools/pdfs/esp2000.pdf

4. B.D. Sypher, R.N. Bostrom, and J.H. Seibert, "Listening Communication Abilities and Success at Work," *Journal of Business Communication* 26 (1989): 293–303.

5. K.W. Hawkins and B.P. Fullion, "Perceived Communication Skill Needs for Work Groups," *Communication Research Reports* 16 (1999): 167–74.

6. S.D. Johnson and C. Bechler, "Examining the Relationship between Listening Effectiveness and Leadership Emergence," *Small Group Research* 29 (1998): 452–71.

7. A.L. Vangelisti, "Couples' Communication Problems: The Counselor's Perspective," *Journal of Applied Communication Research* 22 (1994): 106–26.

8. A.D. Wolvin, "Meeting the Communication Needs of the Adult Learner," *Communication Education* 33 (1984): 267–71.

9. K.J. Prage and D. Buhrmester, "Intimacy and Need Fulfillment in Couple Relationships," *Journal of Social and Personal Relationships* 15 (1998): 435–69.

10. K.K. Hjalone and L.L. Pecchioni, "Relational Listening: A Grounded Theoretical Model," *Communication Reports* 14 (2001): 59–71.

11. R.G. Nichols, "Factors in Listening Comprehension," *Speech Monographs* 15 (1948): 154–63.

12. M.H. Lewis and N.L. Reinsch, Jr, "Listening in Organizational Environments," *Journal of Business Communication* 25 (1988): 49–67.

13. T.L. Thomas and T.R. Levine, "Disentangling Listening and Verbal Recall: Related but Separate Constructs?" *Human Communication Research* 21 (1994): 103–27.

14. Nichols, op. cit.

15. J. Brownell, "Perceptions of Effective Listeners: A Management Study," *Journal of Business Communication* 27 (1990): 401–15.

16. N. Spinks and B. Wells, "Improving Listening Power: The Payoff," *Bulletin of the Association for Business Communication* 54 (1991): 75–7.

17. Reported by R. Nichols and L. Stevens, "Listening to People," *Harvard Business Review* 35 (September–October 1957): 85–92.

18. W. Winter, A. Ferreira, and N. Bowers, "Decision-Making in Married and Unrelated Couples," *Family Process* 12 (1973): 83–94.

19. A.L. Vangelisti, M.L. Knapp, and J.A. Daly, "Conversational Narcissism,"

20. G. Barr, "International Negotiations and Cross-Cultural Communication—A Study in Thailand," unpublished MBA project, Royal Roads University, British Columbia (1998).

21. K.B. McComb and F.M. Jablin, "Verbal Correlates of Interviewer Empathic Listening and Employment Interview Outcomes," *Communication Monographs* 51 (1984): 367.

22. R.G. Nichols, "Listening Is a Ten-Part Skill," *Nation's Business* 75 (September 1987): 40.

23. R. Drullman and G.F. Smoorenburg, "Audio-Visual Perception of Compressed Speech by Profoundly Hearing-Impaired Subjects," *Audiology* 36 (1997): 165–77.

24. N. Kline, *Time to Think: Listening to Ignite the Human Mind* (London: Ward Lock, 1999): 21.

25. A. Mulac, J.M. Wiemann, S.J. Widenmann, and T.W. Gibson, "Male/Female Language Differences and Effects in Same-Sex and Mixed-Sex Dyads: The Gender-Linked Language Effect," *Communication Monographs* 55 (1988): 315–35.

26. C. Kiewitz, J.B. Weaver III, B. Brosius, and G. Weimann, "Cultural Differences in Listening Styles Preferences: A Comparison of Young Adults in Germany, Israel, and the United States," *International Journal of Public Opinion Research* 9 (1997): 233–48.

27. L.L. Barker and K.W. Watson, *Listen Up* (New York: St. Martin's Press, 2000).

28. J.L. Chesebro, "The Relationship between Listening Styles and Conversational Sensitivity," *Communication Research Reports* 16 (1999): 233–8.

29. K.W. Watson, L.L. Barker, and J.B. Weaver, "The Listening Styles Profile" (New Orleans: SPECTRA, 1995).

30. For a brief summary of ancient rhetoric, see E. Griffin, *A First Look at Communication Theory*, 4th edn (New York: McGraw-Hill, 2000).

31. R. Remer and P. De Mesquita, "Teaching and Learning the Skills of Interpersonal Confrontation," in D. Cahn, ed., *Intimates in Conflict: A Communication Perspective* (Norwood, NJ: Erlbaum, 1991): 242.

32. Adapted from D.A. Infante, *Arguing Constructively* (Prospect Heights, IL: Waveland, 1988): 71–5.

33. J. Sprague and D. Stuart, *The Speaker's Handbook*, 3rd edn (Fort Worth, TX: Harcourt Brace Jovanovich, 1992): 172.

34. For a detailed look at empathic listening, see S. Spacapan and S. Oskamp, *Helping and Being Helped: Naturalistic Studies* (Newbury Park, CA: Sage, 1992).

35. Research summarized in J. Pearson,

Communication in the Family (New York: Harper & Row, 1989): 272–5.

36. J.B. Weaver and M.D. Kirtley, "Listening Styles and Empathy," *Southern Communication Journal* 60 (1995): 131–40.

37. C.E. Currona, J.A. Suhr, and R. MacFarlane, "Interpersonal Transactions and the Psychological Sense of Support," in S. Duck, ed., *Personal Relationships and Social Support* (London: Sage, 1990).

38. D.J. Goldsmith and K. Fitch, "The Normative Context of Advice as Social Support," *Human Communication Research* 23 (1997): 454–76.

39. D.J. Goldsmith and K. Fitch, "The Normative Context of Advice as Social Support," *Human Communication Research* 23 (1997): 454–76. See also D.J. Goldsmith and E.L. MacGeorge, "The Impact of Politeness and Relationship on Perceived Quality of Advice about a Problem," *Human Communication Research* 26 (2000): 234–63; and B.R. Burleson, "Social Support," in M.L. Knapp and J.A. Daly, eds, *Handbook of Interpersonal Communication*, 3rd edn (Thousand Oaks, CA: Sage, 2002).

40. D.J. Goldsmith, "The Sequential Placement of Advice." Paper presented at the annual convention of the Speech Communication Association (New Orleans, November 1994).

41. D.J. Goldsmith, "Soliciting Advice: The Role of Sequential Placement in Mitigating Face Threat," *Communication Monographs* 67 (2000): 1–19.

42. D.J. Goldsmith and E.L. MacGeorge, "The Impact of Politeness and Relationship on Perceived Quality of Advice about a Problem," *Human Communication Research* 26 (2000): 234–63.

43. For a summary of the findings, see B.R. Burleson's review in this issue: "Psychological Mediators of Sex Differences in Emotional Support: A Reflection on the Mosaic," *Communication Reports* 15 (Winter 2002): 71–9.

44. See research cited in B. Burleson, "Comforting Messages: Their Significance and Effects," in J.A. Daly and J.M. Wiemann, eds, *Communicating Strategically: Strategies in Interpersonal Communication* (Hillside, NJ: Erlbaum, 1990).

45. D.J. Goldsmith and K. Fitch, "The Normative Context of Advice as Social Support," *Human Communication Research* 23 (1997): 454–76.

46. M. Davidowitz and R.D. Myricm, "Responding to the Bereaved: An Analysis of 'Helping' Statements," *Death Education* 8 (1984): 1–10.

47. "Helping Adults, Children Cope with

Grief," *Washington Post* (13 September 2001).

48. Adapted from B.R. Burleson, "Comforting Messages: Features, Functions, and Outcomes," in J.A. Daly and J.M. Wiemann, eds, *Strategic Interpersonal Communication* (Hillsdale, NJ: Erlbaum, 1994): 140.

49. J.M. Gottman, J. Coan, S. Carrere, and C. Swanson, "Predicting Marital Happiness and Stability from Newlywed Interactions," *Journal of Marriage & the Family* 60 (1998): 5–22.

50. C.R. Rogers, "Reflection of Feelings," *Person-Centered Review* 1 (1986): 375–7.

51. L.A. Hosman, "The Evaluational Consequences of Topic Reciprocity and Self-Disclosure Reciprocity," *Communication Monographs* 54 (1987): 420–35.

52. R.A. Clark and J.G. Delia, "Individuals' Preferences for Friends' Approaches to Providing Support in Distressing Situations," *Communication Reports* 10 (1997): 115–21.

53. See, for example, R. Silver and C. Wortman, "Coping with Undesirable Life Events," in J. Garber and M. Seligman, eds, *Human Helplessness: Theory and Applications* (New York: Academic Press, 1981): 279–340; and C.R. Young, D.E. Giles, and M.C. Plantz, "Natural Networks: Help-Giving and Help-Seeking in Two Rural Communities," *American Journal of Community Psychology* 10 (1982): 457–69.

54. Clark and Delia, *op. cit.*

55. Burleson, *op. cit.*

Chapter 6

1. For further discussion of the characteristics of impersonal and interpersonal communication, see A.P. Bochner, "The Functions of Human Communication in Interpersonal Bonding," in C.C. Arnold and J.W. Bowers, eds, *Handbook of Rhetorical and Communication Theory* (Boston: Allyn and Bacon, 1984): 550; S. Trenholm and A. Jensen, *Interpersonal Communication* (Belmont, CA: Wadsworth, 1987): 37; and J. Stewart and C. Logan, *Together: Communicating Interpersonally*, 5th edn (New York: McGraw-Hill, 1998).

2. K. O'Toole, "Study Takes Early Look at Social Consequences of Net Use," *Stanford Online Report* (16 February 2000). As cited in *Encyclopedia of Virtual Communities and Technologies* (Hershey, PA, 2006).

3. R. Kraut, M. Patterson, V. Lundmark, S. Kiesler, T. Mukophadhyay, and W. Scherlis, "Internet Paradox: A Social Technology That Reduces Social Involvement

and Psychological Well-Being?" *American Psychologist* 53 (1998): 1017–31.

4. See J.B. Walther, "Computer-Mediated Communication: Impersonal, Interpersonal, and Hyperpersonal Interaction," *Communication Research* 23 (1996): 3–43.

5. B.G. Chenault, "Developing Personal and Emotional Relationships via Computer-Mediated Communication," *CMC Magazine* (May 1998). Accessed 25 June 2014 at www.december.com/cmc/mag/1998/may/chenault.html

6. B. Veenhof, B. Wellman, C. Quell, and B. Hogan, "How Canadians' Use of the Internet Affects Social Life and Civic Participation," Connectedness Series (December 2008). Statistics Canada Catalogue no. 56F0004M.

7. B. Veenhof, "The Internet Experience of Younger and Older Canadian," *Innovation Analysis Bulletin* 8, 1 (February 2006).

8. UCLA Center for Communication Policy, "Surveying the Digital Future." UCLA Center for Communications Policy. Accessed 14 July 2014 at www.ccp.ucla.edu/internetreport

9. See J.P. Dillard, D.H. Solomon, and M.T. Palmer, "Structuring the Concept of Relational Communication," *Communication Monographs* 66 (1999): 46–55.

10. T.S. Lim and J.W. Bowers, "Facework: Solidarity, Approbation, and Tact," *Human Communication Research* 17 (1991): 415–50.

11. J.R. Frei and P.R. Shaver, "Respect in Close Relationships: Prototype, Definition, Self-Report Assessment, and Initial Correlates," *Personal Relationships* 9 (2002): 121–39.

12. See C.M. Rossiter, Jr, "Instruction in Metacommunication," *Central States Speech Journal* 25 (1974): 36–42; and W.W. Wilmot, "Metacommunication: A Reexamination and Extension," in *Communication Yearbook* 4 (New Brunswick, NJ: Transaction Books, 1980).

13. L.M. Register and T.B. Henley, "The Phenomenology of Intimacy," *Journal of Social and Personal Relationships* 9 (1992): 467–81.

14. D. Morris, *Intimate Behavior* (New York: Bantam, 1973): 7.

15. K. Floyd, "Meanings for Closeness and Intimacy in Friendship," *Journal of Social and Personal Relationships* 13 (1996): 85–107.

16. L.A. Baxter, "A Dialogic Approach to Relationship Maintenance," in D. Canar and L. Stafford, eds, *Communication and Relational Maintenance* (San Diego: Academic Press, 1994).

17. J.T. Wood and C.C. Inman, "In a Different Mode: Masculine Styles of

Communicating Closeness," *Applied Communication Research* 21 (1993): 279–95.

18. See, for example, K. Dindia and M. Allen, "Sex Differences in Self-Disclosure: A Meta-Analysis," *Psychological Bulletin* 112 (1992): 106–24; I. and P. Backlund, *Exploring GenderSpeak* (New York: McGraw-Hill, 1994): 219; and J.C. Pearson, L.H. Turner and W. Todd-Mancillas, *Gender and Communication*, 2nd edn (Dubuque, IA: W.C. Brown, 1991): 170–1.

19. See, for example, K. Floyd, "Gender and Closeness among Friends and Siblings," *Journal of Psychology* 129 (1995): 193–202; and K. Floyd, "Communicating Closeness among Siblings: An Application of the Gendered Closeness Perspective," *Communication Research Reports* 13 (1996): 27–34.

20. E.L. MacGeorge, A.R. Graves, B. Feng, S.J. Gillihan, and B.R. Burleson, "The Myth of Gender Cultures: Similarities Outweigh Differences in Men's and Women's Provision of and Responses to Supportive Communication," *Sex Roles* 50 (2004): 143–75.

21. C. Inman, "Friendships among Men: Closeness in the Doing," in J.T. Wood, ed., *Gendered Relationships* (Mountain View, CA: 1996). See also S. Swain, "Covert Intimacy in Men's Friendships: Closeness in Men's Friendships," in B.J. Risman and P. Schwartz, eds, *Gender in Intimate Relationships: A Microstructural Approach* (Belmont, CA: Wadsworth, 1989).

22. C.K. Reissman, *Divorce Talk: Women and Men Make Sense of Personal Relationships* (New Brunswick: Rutgers University Press, 1990).

23. J.A. Vandello, D. Cohen, R. Grandon, and R. Franiuk, "Stand by Your Man: Indirect Prescriptions for Honorable Violence and Feminine Loyalty in Canada, Chile, and the United States," *Journal of Cross-Cultural Psychology* 40, 1 (January 2009): 81–104.

24. For a useful survey of cultural differences in interpersonal communication, see W.B. Gudykunst, S. Ting-Toomey, and T. Nishida, eds, *Communication in Personal Relationships across Cultures* (Thousand Oaks, CA: Sage, 1996).

25. M. Argyle and M. Henderson, "The Rules of Relationships," in S. Duck and D. Perlman, eds, *Understanding Personal Relationships* (Beverly Hills, CA: Sage, 1985).

26. W.B. Gudykunst, "The Influence of Cultural Variability on Perceptions of Communication Behavior Associated with Relationship Terms," *Human Communication Research* 13 (1986): 147–66.

27. Z. Hong Li, J. Connolly, D. Jiang, D. Pepler, and W. Craig, "Adolescent Romantic

Relationships in China and Canada: A Cross-National Comparison," *International Journal of Behavioral Development* 34, 2 (March 2010): 113–20.

28. H.C. Triandis, *Culture and Social Behavior* (New York: McGraw-Hill, 1994): 230.

29. K. Lewin, *Principles of Topological Psychology* (New York: McGraw-Hill, 1936).

30. M.L. Knapp and A.L. Vangelisti, *Interpersonal Communication and Human Relationships*, 4th edn (Boston: Allyn and Bacon, 2003).

31. D.J. Canary and L. Stafford, eds, *Communication and Relational Maintenance* (San Diego: Academic Press, 1994). See also J. Lee, "Effective Maintenance Communication in Superior-Subordinate Relationships," *Western Journal of Communication* 62 (1998): 181–208.

32. For a discussion of relational development in non-intimate relationships, see A. Jensen and S. Trenholm, "Beyond Intimacy: An Alternative Trajectories Model of Relationship Development." Paper presented at the Speech Communication Association annual meeting, New Orleans, LA (1988).

33. B.W. Scharlott and W.G. Christ, "Overcoming Relationship-Initiation Barriers: The Impact of a Computer-Dating System on Sex Role, Shyness, and Appearance Inhibitions," *Computers in Human Behavior* 11 (1995): 191–204.

34. W.B. Gudykunst and S. Ting-Toomey, *Culture and Interpersonal Communication* (Newbury Park, CA: Sage, 1988): 193.

35. J.H. Tolhuizen, "Communication Strategies for Intensifying Dating Relationships: Identification, Use and Structure," *Journal of Social and Personal Relationships* 6 (1989): 413–34.

36. L.K. Guerrero and P.A. Andersen, "The Waxing and Waning of Relational Intimacy: Touch as a Function of Relational Stage, Gender and Touch Avoidance," *Journal of Social and Personal Relationships* 8 (1991): 147–65.

37. L.A. Baxter, "Symbols of Relationship Identity in Relationship Culture," *Journal of Social and Personal Relationships* 4 (1987): 261–80.

38. C.J. Bruess and J.C. Pearson, "Like Sands through the Hour Glass: These Are the Rituals Functioning in Day-to-Day Married Lives." Paper delivered at the Speech Communication Association convention, San Antonio, TX (November 1995).

39. H. Giles and P.F. Poseland, *Speech Style and Social Evaluation* (London: Academic Press, 1975).

40. M. Roloff, C.A. Janiszewski, M.A. McGrath, C.S. Burns, and L.A. Manrai, "Acquiring Resources from Intimates: When Obligation Substitutes for Persuasion," *Human Communication Research* 14 (1988): 364–96.

41. J.K. Burgoon, R. Parrott, B.A. LePoire, D.L. Kelley, J.B. Walther, and D. Perry, "Maintaining and Restoring Privacy through Different Types of Relationships," *Journal of Social and Personal Relationships* 6 (1989): 131–58.

42. J.A. Courtright, F.E. Millar, L.E. Rogers, and D. Bagarozzi, "Interaction Dynamics of Relational Negotiation: Reconciliation versus Termination of Distressed Relationships," *Western Journal of Speech Communication* 54 (1990): 429–53.

43. D.M. Battaglia, F.D. Richard, D.L. Datteri, and C.G. Lord, "Breaking Up Is (Relatively) Easy to Do: A Script for the Dissolution of Close Relationships," *Journal of Social and Personal Relationships* 15 (1998): 829–45.

44. See, for example, L.A. Baxter and B.M. Montgomery, "A Guide to Dialectical Approaches to Studying Personal Relationships," in B.M. Montgomery and L.A. Baxter, eds, *Dialectical Approaches to Studying Personal Relationships* (New York: Erlbaum, 1998) and L.A. Ebert and S.W. Duck, "Rethinking Satisfaction in Personal Relationships from a Dialectical Perspective," in R.J. Sternberg and M. Hojjatr, eds, *Satisfaction in Close Relationships* (New York: Guilford, 1997).

45. Summarized by L.A. Baxter, "A Dialogic Approach to Relationship Maintenance," in D.J. Canary and L. Stafford, eds, *Communication and Relational Maintenance* (San Diego: Academic Press, 1994).

46. Morris, *op. cit.*, 21–9.

47. D. Barry, *Dave Barry Turns 40* (New York: Fawcett, 1990): 47.

48. C.A. VanLear, "Testing a Cyclical Model of Communicative Openness in Relationship Development," *Communication Monographs* 58 (1991): 337–61.

49. Adapted from Baxter and Montgomery, op. cit., 185–206.

50. R.L. Conville, *Relational Transitions: The Evolution of Personal Relationships* (New York: Praeger, 1991): 80.

51. L.B. Rosenfeld and W.L. Kendrick, "Choosing to Be Open: Subjective Reasons for Self-Disclosing," *Western Journal of Speech Communication* 48 (Fall 1984): 326–43.

52. I. Altman and D.A. Taylor, *Social Penetration: The Development of Interpersonal Relationships* (New York: Holt, Rinehart and Winston, 1973).

53. J. Luft, *Of Human Interaction* (Palo Alto, CA: National Press, 1969).

54. W.B. Gudykunst and S. Ting-Toomey, *Culture and Interpersonal Communication* (Newbury Park, CA: Sage, 1988): 197–8; and S. Ting-Toomey, "A Comparative Analysis of the Communicative Dimensions of Love, Self-Disclosure, Maintenance, Ambivalence, and Conflict in Three Cultures: France, Japan, and the United States." Paper presented at the International Communication Association convention, Montreal, QC, 1987.

55. S. Duck and D.E. Miell, "Charting the Development of Personal Relationships," in R. Gilmour and S. Duck, eds, *Studying Interpersonal Interaction* (Hillsdale, NJ: Erlbaum, 1991).

56. S. Duck, "Some Evident Truths about Conversations in Everyday Relationships: All Communications Are Not Created Equal," *Human Communication Research* 18 (1991): 228–67.

57. J.C. Pearson, *Communication in the Family*, 2nd edn (Needham, MA: Allyn & Bacon, 1993): 292–6.

58. Summarized in J. Pearson, *Communication in the Family* (New York: Harper & Row, 1989): 252–7.

59. E.M. Eisenberg and M.G. Witten, "Reconsidering Openness in Organizational Communication," *Academy of Management Review* 12 (1987): 418–28.

60. L.B. Rosenfeld and J.R. Gilbert, "The Measurement of Cohesion and Its Relationship to Dimensions of Self-Disclosure in Classroom Settings," *Small Group Behavior* 20 (1989): 291–301.

61. G. Bach and Ronald Deutsch, *Stop! You're Driving Me Crazy* (New York: Putnam, 1979).

62. D. O'Hair and M.J. Cody, "Interpersonal Deception: The Dark Side of Interpersonal Communication?" in B.H. Spitzberg and W.R. Cupach, eds, *The Dark Side of Interpersonal Communication* (Hillsdale, NJ: Erlbaum, 1993).

63. M.E. Kaplar and A.K. Gordon, "The Enigma of Altruistic Lying: Perspective Differences in What Motivates and Justifies Lie Telling within Romantic Relationships," *Personal Relationships* 11 (2004).

64. R.E. Turner, C. Edgley, and G. Olmstead, "Information Control in Conversation: Honesty Is Not Always the Best Policy," *Kansas Journal of Sociology* 11 (1975): 69–89.

65. K.L. Bell and B.M. DePaulo, "Liking and Lying," *Basic and Applied Social Psychology* 18 (1996): 243–66.

66. R.S. Feldman, J.A. Forrest, and B.R. Happ, "Self-Presentation and Verbal Deception: Do Self-Presenters Lie More?" *Basic*

and Applied Social Psychology 24 (2002): 163–70.

67. S.A. McCornack and T.R. Levine, "When Lies Are Uncovered: Emotional and Relational Outcomes of Discovered Deception," *Communication Monographs* 57 (1990): 119–138.

68. See M.A. Hamilton and P.J. Mineo, "A Framework for Understanding Equivocation," *Journal of Language and Social Psychology* 17 (1998): 3–35.

69. S. Metts, W.R. Cupach, and T.T. Imahori, "Perceptions of Sexual Compliance-Resisting Messages in Three Types of Cross-Sex Relationships," *Western Journal of Communication* 56 (1992): 1–17.

70. J.B. Bavelas, A. Black, N. Chovil, and J. Mullett, *Equivocal Communication* (Newbury Park, CA: Sage, 1990): 171.

71. *ibid.*

72. See, for example, W.P. Robinson, A. Shepherd, and J. Heywood, "Truth, Equivocation/Concealment, and Lies in Job Applications and Doctor-Patient Communication," *Journal of Language & Social Psychology* 17 (1998): 149–64.

73. Several of the following examples were offered by M.T. Motley, "Mindfulness in Solving Communicators' Dilemmas," *Communication Monographs* 59 (1992): 306–14.

74. D.B. Buller and J.K. Burgoon, "Deception," in *Communicating Strategically: Strategies in Interpersonal Communication* (Hillsdale, NJ: Erlbaum, 1994).

75. S. Bok, *Lying: Moral Choice in Public and Private Life* (New York: Pantheon, 1978).

Chapter 7

1. K.N.L. Cissna and E. Seiburg, "Patterns of Interactional Confirmation and Disconfirmation," in M.V. Redmond, ed., *Interpersonal Communication: Readings in Theory and Research* (Fort Worth, TX: Harcourt Brace, 1995).

2. *ibid.*

3. M.W. Allen, "Communication Concepts Related to Perceived Organizational Support," *Western Journal of Communication* 59 (1995): 326–46.

4. B. Bower, "Nice Guys Look Better in Women's Eyes," *Science News* (18 March 1995): 165.

5. See, for example, J. Veroff Douvan, T.L. Orbuch, and L.K. Acitelli, "Happiness in Stable Marriages: The Early Years," in T.N. Bradbury, ed., *The Development Course of Marital Dysfunction* (New York: Cambridge University Press, 1999): 152–79.

6. D.J. Canary and T.M. Emmers-Sommer, *Sex and Gender Differences in Personal Relationships* (New York: Guildford, 1997).

7. J.J. Teven, M.M. Martin, and N.C. Neupauer, "Sibling Relationships: Verbally Aggressive Messages and Their Effect on Relational Satisfaction," *Communication Reports* 11 (1998): 179–86.

8. K. Ellis, "The Impact of Perceived Teacher Confirmation on Receiver Apprehension, Motivation, and Learning," *Communication Education* 53 (2004): 1–20.

9. For a discussion of reactions to disconfirming responses, see A.L. Vangelisti and L.P. Crumley, "Reactions to Messages That Hurt: The Influence of Relational Contexts," *Communication Monographs* 64 (1998): 173–96. See also L.M. Cortina, V.J. Magley, J.H. Williams, and R.D. Langhout, "Incivility in the Workplace: Incidence and Impact," *Journal of Occupational Health Psychology* 6 (2001): 64–80.

10. A.L. Vangelisti, "Messages That Hurt," in W.R. Cupach and B.H. Spitzberg, eds, *The Dark Side of Interpersonal Communication* (Hillsdale, NJ: Erlbaum, 1994).

11. See W.W. Wilmot, *Dyadic Communication* (New York: Random House, 1987): 149–58, and L.M. Andersson and C.M. Pearson, "Tit for Tat? The Spiraling Effect of Incivility in the Workplace," *Academy of Management Review* 24 (1999): 452–71. See also L.N. Olson and D.O. Braithwaite, "'If You Hit Me Again, I'll Hit You Back': Conflict Management Strategies of Individuals Experiencing Aggression during Conflicts," *Communication Studies* 55 (2004): 271–86.

12. C. Burggraf and A.L. Sillars, "A Critical Examination of Sex Differences in Marital Communication," *Communication Monographs* 54 (1987): 276–94. See also D.A. Newton and J.K. Burgoon, "The Use and Consequences of Verbal Strategies during Interpersonal Disagreements," *Human Communication Research* 16 (1990): 477–518.

13. J.L. Hocker and W.W. Wilmot, *Interpersonal Conflict*, 6th edn (New York: McGraw-Hill, 2001): 33.

14. *ibid.*, 37.

15. J. Gibb, "Defensive Communication," *Journal of Communication* 11 (1961): 141–8. See also W.F. Eadie, "Defensive Communication Revisited: A Critical Examination of Gibb's Theory," *Southern Speech Communication Journal* 47 (1982): 163–77.

16. For a review of research supporting the effectiveness of "I" language, see R.F. Proctor II and J.R. Wilcox, "An Exploratory Analysis of Responses to Owned Messages in Interpersonal Communication," *Et Cetera: A Review of General Semantics* 50 (1993): 201–20. See also R.F. Proctor II, "Responsibility or Egocentrism? The Paradox of Owned Messages," *Speech Association of Minnesota Journal* 16 (1989): 59–60.

17. T.C. Sabourin and G.H. Stamp, "Communication and the Experience of Dialectical Tensions in Family Life: An Examination of Abusive and Nonabusive Families," *Communication Monographs* 62 (1995): 213–43.

18. R. Vonk, "The Slime Effect: Suspicion and Dislike of Likeable Behavior toward Superiors," *Journal of Personality and Social Psychology* 74 (1998): 849–64.

19. P. Sullivan and D. Feltz, "The Relationship between Intrateam Conflict and Cohesion within Hockey Teams," *Small Group Research* 32, 3 (2001): 342–55.

20. J.L. Hocker and W.W. Wilmot, *Interpersonal Conflict*, 6th edn (New York: McGraw-Hill, 2001): 23.

21. See, for example, L.A. Baxter, W.W. Wilmot, C.A. Simmons, and A. Swartz, "Ways of Doing Conflict: A Folk Taxonomy of Conflict Events in Personal Relationships," in P.J. Kalbfleisch, ed., *Interpersonal Communication: Evolving Interpersonal Relationships* (Hillsdale, NJ: Erlbaum, 1993).

22. P.J. Lannutti and J.I. Monahan, "'Not Now, Maybe Later': The Influence of Relationship Type, Request Persistence, and Alcohol Consumption on Women's Refusal Strategies," *Communication Studies* 55 (2004): 362–77.

23. G.R. Birchler, R.L. Weiss, and J.P. Vincent, "Multimethod Analysis of Social Reinforcement Exchange between Maritally Distressed and Nondistressed Spouse and Stranger Dyads," *Journal of Personality and Social Psychology* 31 (1975): 349–60.

24. J.R. Meyer, "Effect of Verbal Aggressiveness on the Perceived Importance of Secondary Goals in Messages," *Communication Studies* 55 (2004): 168–84.

25. G.R. Bach and H. Goldberg, *Creative Aggression* (Garden City, NY: Doubleday, 1974).

26. See K. Kellermann and B.C. Shea, "Threats, Suggestions, Hints, and Promises: Gaining Compliance Efficiently and Politely," *Communication Quarterly* 44 (1996): 145–65.

27. J. Jordan and M.E. Roloff, "Acquiring Assistance from Others: The Effect of Indirect Requests and Relational Intimacy on Verbal Compliance," *Human Communication Research* 16 (1990): 519–55.

28. Research summarized by D. Tannen in *You Just Don't Understand: Women and*

Men in Conversation (New York: William Morrow, 1989): 152–7, 162–5.

29. N. Crick, "Relational and Overt Forms of Peer Victimization: A Multi-informant Approach," *Journal of Consulting and Clinical Psychology* 66 (1998): 337–47.

30. J.F. Benenson, S.A. Ford, and N.H. Apostoleris, "Girls' Assertiveness in the Presence of Boys," *Small Group Research* 29 (1998): 198–211.

31. M.J. Collier, "Conflict Competence within African, Mexican, and Anglo American Friendships," in S. Ting-Toomey and F. Korzenny, eds, *Cross-Cultural Interpersonal Communication* (Newbury Park, CA: Sage, 1991).

32. The information in this paragraph is drawn from research summarized by J.T. Wood in *Gendered Lives*, 6th edn (Belmont, CA: Wadsworth, 2005).

33. N.A. Klinetob and D.A. Smith, "Demand–Withdraw Communication in Marital Interaction: Tests of Interpersonal Contingency and Gender Role Hypotheses," *Journal of Marriage & the Family* 58 (1996): 945–57.

34. See M.J. Papa and E.J. Natalle, "Gender, Strategy Selection, and Discussion Satisfaction in Interpersonal Conflict," *Western Journal of Speech Communication* 52 (1989): 260–72.

35. See, for example, J.C. Pearson, *Gender and Communication*, 2nd edn (Dubuque, IA: W.C. Brown, 1991): 183–4.

36. For a more detailed discussion of culture, conflict, and context, see W.B. Gudykunst and S. Ting-Toomey, *Culture and Interpersonal Communication* (Newbury Park, CA: Sage, 1988): 153–60.

37. D. Wright and J. Bricker, *What Canadians Think . . . About Almost Everything* (Toronto: Doubleday, 2005): 287

38. S. Ting-Toomey, K.K. Yee-Jung, R.B. Shapiro, W. Garcia, and T. Wright, "Ethnic Identity Salience and Conflict Styles in Four Ethnic Groups: African Americans, Asian Americans, European Americans, and Latino Americans." Paper presented at the annual conference of the Speech Communication Association, New Orleans (November 1994).

39. See, for example, S. Ting-Toomey, "Rhetorical Sensitivity Style in Three Cultures: France, Japan, and the United States," *Central States Speech Journal* 39 (1988): -28–36.

40. K. Okabe, "Indirect Speech Acts of the Japanese," in L. Kincaid, ed., *Communication Theory: Eastern and Western Perspectives* (San Diego: Academic Press, 1987): 127–36.

41. The following research is summarized in Tannen, *op. cit.*, 160.

42. J. Voyer, "A Special Edition on Child Development," *Applied Research Bulletin* (Fall 1999): 20–1.

43. A.C. Filley, *Interpersonal Conflict Resolution* (Glenview, IL: Scott Foresman, 1975): 3.

44. S. Gravestock, *Goon*. Accessed 25 June 2014 at http://thecinematheque.ca/canadas-top-ten-2012/goon

Chapter 8

1. Rikia Saddy, "Social media revolutions," *Journal of Professional Communication* 1(1), (2011): 31–33.

2. J. Halliday, "Boston 'Witchhunt' on Social Media Sites—and a Bad Week for the Old Guard," *The Guardian* (22 April 2013). Accessed 25 June 2014 at www.theguardian.com/world/2013/apr/22/boston-bombings-witchhunt-social-media

3. E. Hueypriest, "Reflections on the Recent Boston Crisis," BLOG.reddit, 22 April 2013. Accessed 25 June 2014 at http://blog.reddit.com/2013/04/reflections-on-recent-boston-crisis.html

4. M. Geist, "How Canada Avoided the Latest Net Neutrality Battle," *Ottawa Citizen* (12 May 2014). Accessed 25 June 2014 at www.ottawacitizen.com/technology/Canada+avoided+latest+neutrality+battle/9832602/story.html

5. Government of Canada, Telecommunications Act (S.C. 1993, c. 38), Part III: Rates, Facilities and Services, Provision of Services. Accessed 25 June 2014 at http://laws-lois.justice.gc.ca/eng/acts/t-3.4/page-8.html

6. S. Duncombe, *Zines and the Politics of Alternative Culture* (London: Verso, 2001).

7. E. Ringmar, *A Blogger's Manifesto: Free Speech and Censorship in the Age of the Internet* (London: Anthem Press, 2007).

8. Sidney Eve Matrix Faculty Profile, Queen's University Film and Media. Accessed 25 June 2014 at www.film.queensu.ca/Matrix.html

9. Z. Fox, "Goodbye, 'Gossip Girl,' Mashable (18 December 2012). Accessed 25 June 2014 at http://mashable.com/2012/12/18/gossip-girl-goodbye/

10. CBC, "Marshall McLuhan: The Global Village," CBC Digital Archives (23 January 2012). Accessed 25 June 2014 at www.cbc.ca/archives/categories/arts-entertainment/media/marshall-mcluhan-the-man-and-his-message/world-is-a-global-village.html

11. B. Heil and M. Piskorski, "New Twitter Research: Men Follow Men and Nobody Tweets," *Harvard Business Review* (1 June 2009). Accessed 25 June 2014 at blogs.hbr.org/cs/2009/06/new_twitter_research_men_follo.html

12. *ibid.*

13. I. Paul, "It's Quit Facebook Day, Are You Leaving?" *PC World* (31 May 2010). Accessed 25 June 2014 at www.pcworld.com/article/197621/its_quit_facebook_day_are_you_leaving.html

14. d. boyd, "MySpace vs. Facebook: A Digital Enactment of Class-Based Social Categories Amongst American Teenagers." Paper presented at the International Communications Association Conference, Chicago (23 May 2009). Accessed 14 June 2014 at www.danah.org/papers/talks/ICA2009.html

15. A. Baulcomb, "Science Sunday Making Waves on Google+," *Daily News,* (23 July 2012). Accessed 25 June 2014 at http://dailynews.mcmaster.ca/article/science-sunday-making-waves-on-google/

16. C.L. Toma, "Affirming the Self through Online Profiles: Beneficial Effects of Social Networking Sites." Proceedings of the 28th International Conference on Human Factors in Computing Systems (2010): 1749–52.

17. S. Zhao, S. Grasmuch, and J. Martin, "Identity Construction on Facebook: Digital Empowerment in Anchored Relationships," *Computers in Human Behavior* 24, 5 (2008): 1816–36.

18. V. Barash, N. Ducheneaut, E. Isaacs, and V. Bellotti, "Faceplant: Impression (Mis)management in Facebook Status Updates," Proceedings of the Fourth International AAAI Conference on Weblogs and Social Media (2010). Accessed 25 June 2014 at www.aaai.org/ocs/index.php/ICWSM/ICWSM10/paper/viewPDFInterstitial/1465/1858

19. A.N. Joinson, "Looking At, Looking Up or Keeping Up with People? Motives and Use of Facebook," Proceeding of the 26th Annual SIGCHI Conference on Human Factors in Computing Systems (2008): 1027–36.

20. K. Duong and S. Adamo, "2013 Canada Digital Future in Focus," comScore (4 March 2013). Accessed 25 June 2014 at www.comscore.com/Insights/Presentations_and_Whitepapers/2013/2013_Canada_Digital_Future_in_Focus

21. J. Baudrillard (trans. Sheila Glaser), *Simulations and Simulacra* (Ann Arbor: University of Michigan Press, 1996).

22. R. Myles, "Facebook Use Declining among Canadian and US Teens," *Digital Journal* (29 April 2013). Accessed 25 June 2014 at http://digitaljournal.com/article/349087

23. Personal communication with Alexandre Sèvigny. Chris Farias is the Creative Director at KITESTRING, a strategic

branding consultancy who was the first in its region to creatively leverage the power of conversation on social media for its clients' brands. Together with a small team of strategic thinkers, creators, and communicators, Chris and his business partner, Jenn Hudder, have led KITESTRING to become an industry leader with its philosophy on how brands should interact in the social sphere.

24. Z. Kleinman, "Google Boss Eric Schmidt Warns on Social Use of Media," *BBC News Technology* (18 August 2010.) Accessed 25 June 2014 at www.bbc.co.uk/news/technology-11009700

25. P.B. O'Sullivan, "Bridging the Mass–Interpersonal Divide: Synthesis Scholarship," *Human Communication Research* 25 (1999): 569–88.

26. H. Innis, "Minerva's Owl," Project Gutenberg Canada (4 March 2007). Accessed 25 June 2014 at www.gutenberg.ca/ebooks/innis-minerva/innis-minerva-00-h.html

27. *McLuhan's Wake.* Dir. Kevin McMahon, 2002.

28. The name "bullet theory," also referred to as "hypodermic needle theory" or "transmission belt theory," was used not by the early researchers who performed these studies but rather by later theorists. See M.L. DeFleur and S. Ball-Rokeach, *Theories of Mass Communication*, 5th edn (New York: Longman, 1989): 145–66. See also W.J. Severin and J.W. Tankard, Jr, *Communication Theories: Origins, Methods, and Uses in the Mass Media*, 4th edn (New York: Longman, 1997): 322.

29. See, for example, P.M. Sandman, D.M. Rubin, and D.B. Sachsman, *Media: An Introductory Analysis of American Mass Communications*, 3rd edn (Englewood Cliffs, NJ: Prentice Hall, 1982): 4–5.

30. These and other social learning experiments are reported in Bandura's seminal book, *Social Learning Theory* (Englewood Cliffs, NJ: Prentice Hall, 1977). For more on this study and social learning and modelling theory see DeFleur and Ball-Rokeach, *op. cit.*, 112–16.

31. See, for example, S.J. Baran and D.K. Davis, *Mass Communication Theory: Foundations, Ferment, and Future* (Belmont, CA: Wadsworth, 1995): 206.

32. DeFleur and Ball-Rokeach, *op. cit.*, 172–86.

33. Diffusion of innovations theory is attributed primarily to E. Rogers, *Diffusion of Innovations*, 3rd edn (New York: Free Press, 1983). See also Severin and Tankard, *op. cit.*, 238–9. This research perspective continues to be the foundation for important research. See, for example, T.W.

Valents, "Diffusion of Innovations and Policy Decision-Making," *Journal of Communication* 43, 1 (Winter 1993): 30–45; or M. Meyer, J.D. Johnson, and C. Ethington, "Contrasting Attributes of Preventive Health Innovations," *Journal of Communication* 47, 2 (Spring 1997): 112–31.

34. See, for example, L. Jeffres and D. Atkin, "Prediction Use of Technologies for Communication and Consumer Needs," *Journal of Broadcasting and Electronic Media* 40, 3 (Summer 1996): 318–30. See also T. Adams, "Follow the Yellow Brick Road: Using Diffusion of Innovations Theory to Enrich Virtual Organization in Cyberspace," *Southern Communication Journal* 62, 2 (Winter 1997): 133–48.

35. G. Gerbner, L. Gross, M. Morgan, and N. Signorelli, "Living with Television: The Cultivation Perspective," in J. Bryant and D. Zillmann, eds, *Media Effects: Advances in Theory and Research* (Hillsdale, NJ: Lawrence Erlbaum, 1994): 17–41. See also Severin and Tankard, *op. cit.*, 299–303.

36. D. Shaw and M. McCombs, *The Emergence of American Political Issues: The Agenda-Setting Function of the Press* (St Paul, MN: West Publishing Co., 1977): 7.

37. The way these theories converge can be seen in studies such as H.B. Brosius and G. Weimann, "Who Sets the Agenda? Agenda-Setting as a Two-Step Glow," *Communication Research* 23, 5 (October 1996): 561–80. This research examined news items on German television and found that issues tend to flow from the public to the media and within the public.

38. See, for example, J.W. Dearing and E.M. Rogers, *Agenda-Setting* (Thousand Oaks, CA: Sage, 1996): Ch. 5.

Chapter 9

1. M.V. Redmond, "A Plan for the Successful Use of Teams in Design Education," *Journal of Architectural Education* 17 (May 1986): 27–49.

2. "Professional Occupations in Multimedia," *California Occupational Guide* 2006 (Sacramento, CA: California State Employment Division, 1995): 4. See also "A Labor Market Analysis of the Interactive Digital Media Industry: Opportunities in Multimedia" (San Francisco: Reagan & Associates, 1997): 15–29.

3. L. Thompson, E. Peterson, and S.E. Brodt, "Team Negotiation: An Examination of Integrative and Distributive Bargaining," *Journal of Personality and Social Psychology* 70 (1996): 66–78.

4. For a more detailed discussion of the advantages and disadvantages of working in groups, see S.A. Beebe and J.T. Masterson, *Communicating in Small Groups: Principles and Practices*, 7th edn (Needham Heights: Allyn & Bacon, 2003).

5. See, for example, S. Barnes and L.M. Greller, "Computer-Mediated Communication in the Organization," *Communication Education* 43 (1994): 129–42.

6. S.L. Herndon, "Theory and Practice: Implications for the Implementation of Communication Technology in Organizations," *Journal of Business Communication* 34 (January 1997): 121–9.

7. E.A. Marby, "The Systems Metaphor in Group Communication," in L.R. Frey, ed., *Handbook of Group Communication Theory and Research* (Thousand Oaks, CA: Sage, 1999).

8. J.D. Rothwell, *In Mixed Company: Small Group Communication*, 5th edn (Belmont, CA: Wadsworth, 2004): 29–31.

9. See, for example, J.R. Katzenbach and D.K. Smith, "The Discipline of Teams," *Harvard Business Review* 86 (March–April 1993): 111–20.

10. J. Hackman, "The Design of Work Teams," in J. Lorsch, ed., *Handbook of Organizational Behavior* (Englewood Cliffs, NJ: Prentice Hall, 1987): 315–42.

11. Rothwell, *op. cit.*, 42–7.

12. For a discussion of the relationship between individual and group goals, see L. Frey, "Individuals in Groups," in L.R. Frey and J.K. Barge, eds, *Managing Group Life: Communicating in Decision-Making Groups* (Boston: Houghton Mifflin, 1997).

13. J. Krakauer, *Into Thin Air* (New York: Anchor, 1997): 212–13.

14. See D. Scheerhorn and P. Geist, "Social Dynamics in Groups," in Frey and Barge, *op. cit.*

15. S.B. Shimanoff, "Group Interaction via Communication Rules," in R.S. Cathcart and L.A. Samovar, eds, *Small Group Communication: A Reader*, 5th edn (Dubuque, IA: W.C. Brown, 1988): 50–64.

16. D.S. Gouran, R.Y. Hirokawa, K.M. Julian, and G.B. Leatham, "The Evolution and Current Status of the Functional Perspective on Communication in Decision-Making and Problem-Solving Groups," in S.A. Deetz, ed., *Communication Yearbook* 16 (Newbury Park, CA: Sage, 1992). See also G.M. Wittenbaum, A.B. Hollingshead, P.B. Paulus, R.Y. Hirokawa, D.G. Ancona, R.S. Peterson, K.A. Jehn, and K. Yoon, "The Functional Perspective as a Lens for Understanding Groups," *Small Group Research* 35 (2004): 17–43.

17. M.E. Mayer, "Behaviors Leading to More Effective Decisions in Small Groups Embedded in Organizations," *Communication Reports* 11 (1998): 123–32.

18. R.F. Bales and P.L. Strodbeck, "Phases in Group Problem Solving," *Journal of Abnormal and Social Psychology* 46 (1951): 485–95.

19. E. Bormann, *Small Group Communication: Theory and Practice* (New York: Harper & Row, 1990).

20. N. Postman, *Crazy Talk, Stupid Talk* (New York: Dell, 1976).

21. B. Steinzor, "The Spatial Factor in Face-to-Face Discussion Groups," *Journal of Abnormal and Social Psychology* 45 (1950): 522–55.

22. P.L. Strodtbeck and L.H. Hook, "The Social Dimensions of a Twelve-Man Jury Table," *Sociometry* 24 (1961): 397–415.

23. N.F. Russo, "Connotations of Seating Arrangements," *Cornell Journal of Social Relations* 2 (1967): 37–44.

24. Adapted from D.W. Johnson and F.P. Johnson, *Joining Together: Group Theory and Group Skills*, 8th edn (Boston: Allyn and Bacon, 2003).

25. R. Hastle, *Inside the Jury* (Cambridge, MA: Harvard University Press, 1983).

26. B. Day, "The Art of Conducting International Business," *Advertising Age* (6 October 1990): 48.

27. Adapted from R.B. Adler and J.M. Elmhorst, *Communicating at Work: Principles and Practices for Business and the Professions*, 8th edn (New York: McGraw-Hill, 2005): 269.

28. Statistics Canada, 2011. "Immigration and Ethno-Cultural Diversity in Canada." Ottawa: Government of Canada.

29. S.G. Barsade and D.E. Gibson, "Group Emotion: A View from Top and Bottom," in D.H. Gruenfeld, ed., *Composition* (Greenwich, CT: JAI Press, 1998). See also K.Y. Williams and C.A. O'Reilly, "Demography and Diversity in Organizations: A Review of 40 Years of Research," in B. Staw and R. Sutton, eds, *Research in Organizational Behavior* 20 (1998): 77–140.

30. Williams and O'Reilly, *op. cit.*

31. S.B. Paletz, K. Peng, M. Erez, and C. Maslach, "Ethnic Composition and Its Differential Impact on Group Processes in Diverse Teams," *Small Group Research* 35 (2004): 128–57.

32. G. Hofstede, *Cultures and Organizations: Software of the Mind* (New York: McGraw-Hill, 1997): 158.

33. See H.C. Triandis, R. Bontempo, M. Villareal, M. Asai, and N. Lucca, "Individualism and Collectivism: Cross-Cultural Perspectives of Self-Ingroup Relationships," *Journal of Personality and Social Psychology* 54 (1988): 323–38.

34. Research supporting these differences is summarized in S. Ting-Toomey, "Identity and Interpersonal Bonding," in M.K. Asante and W.B. Gudykunst, eds, *Handbook of International and Intercultural Communication* (Newbury Park, CA: Sage, 1989): 351–73.

35. Hofstede, *op. cit.*, 65–109.

36. *ibid.*, 110–47.

37. *ibid.*, 189–210.

Chapter 10

1. L. Tuck, "Meeting Madness," *Presentations* (May 1995): 20.

2. C. Downs, D.M. Berg, and W.A. Linkugel, *The Organizational Communicator* (New York: Harper & Row, 1977): 127.

3. G.L. Wilson, *Groups in Context: Leadership and Participation in Small Groups* (New York: McGraw-Hill, 2005): 12–13.

4. See, for example, C. Pavitt, "Do Interacting Groups Perform Better than Aggregates of Individuals?" *Human Communication Research* 29 (2003): 592–9; G.M. Wittenbaum, "Putting Communication into the Study of Group Memory," *Human Communication Research* 29 (2004): 616–23; and M.G. Frank, T.H. Feely, N. Paolantonio, and T.J. Servoss, "Individual and Small Group Accuracy in Judging Truthful and Deceptive Communication," *Group Decision and Negotiation* 13 (2004): 45–54.

5. R.B. Adler and J.M. Elmhorst, *Communicating at Work: Principles and Practices for Business and the Professions*, 8th edn (New York: McGraw-Hill, 2005): 289–90.

6. K.A. Graetz, E.S. Boyle, C.E. Kimble, P. Thompson, and J.L. Garloch, "Information Sharing in Face-to-Face, Teleconferencing, and Electronic Chat Groups," *Small Group Research* 29 (1998): 714–43.

7. M. Zey, ed., *Decision Making: Alternatives to Rational Choice Models* (Newbury Park, CA: Sage, 1992). For a discussion of how groups "muddle through" in organizational decision-making, see H. Mintzberg and A. McHugh, "Strategy Formation in an Adhocracy," *Administrative Science Quarterly* 30 (1985): 160–97.

8. See, for example, A.L. Salazar, R.Y. Hirokawa, K.M. Propp, K.M. Julian, and G.B. Leatham, "In Search of True Causes: Examination of the Effect of Group Potential and Group Interaction on Decision Performance," *Human Communication Research* 20 (1994): 529–99.

9. J. Dewey, *How We Think* (New York: Heath, 1910).

10. M.S. Poole, "Procedures for Managing Meetings: Social and Technological Innovation," in R.A. Swanson and B.O. Knapp, eds, *Innovative Meeting Management* (Austin, TX: 3M Meeting Management Institute, 1991). See also M.S. Poole and M.E. Holmes, "Decision Development in Computer-Assisted Group Decision Making," *Human Communication Research* 22 (1995): 90–127.

11. K. Lewin, *Field Theory in Social Science* (New York: Harper & Row, 1951): 30–59.

12. See S. Jarboe, "Group Communication and Creativity Processes," in L.R. Frey, ed., *Handbook of Group Communication Theory and Research* (Thousand Oaks, CA: Sage, 1999).

13. A. Osborn, *Applied Imagination* (New York: Scribner's, 1959).

14. See, for example, M. Diehl and W. Strobe, "Productivity Loss in Brainstorming Groups: Toward the Solution of a Riddle," *Journal of Personality and Social Psychology* 53 (1987): 497–509; and V. Brown, M. Tumero, T.S. Larey, and P.B. Paulus, "Modeling Cognitive Interactions during Group Brainstorming," *Small Group Research* 29 (1998): 495–526.

15. B.A. Fisher, "Decision Emergence: Phases in Group Decision Making," *Speech Monographs* 37 (1970): 53–66.

16. C.R. Frantz and K.G. Jin, "The Structure of Group Conflict in a Collaborative Work Group during Information Systems Development," *Journal of Applied Communication Research* 23 (1995): 108–27.

17. M. Poole and J. Roth, "Decision Development in Small Groups IV: A Typology of Group Decision Paths," *Human Communication Research* 15 (1989): 323–56. See also M. Poole and J. Roth, "Decision Development in Small Groups V: Test of a Contingency Model," *Human Communication Research* 15 (1989): 549–89.

18. S.A. Wheelan, D. Murphy, E. Tsumaura, and S.F. Kline, "Member Perceptions of Internal Group Dynamics and Productivity," *Small Group Research* 29 (1998): 371–93.

19. S.M. Farmer and J. Roth, "Conflict-Handling Behavior in Work Groups: Effects of Group Structure, Decision Process, and Time," *Small Group Research* 29 (1998): 669–713.

20. B. Mullen and C. Cooper, "The Relation between Group Cohesiveness and Performance: An Integration," *Psychological Bulletin* 115 (1994): 210–27.

21. R.T. Keller, "Predictors of the Performance of Project Groups in R & D Organizations,"

Academy of Management Journal 29 (1986): 715–26. See also B.A. Welch, K.W. Mossholder, R.P. Stell, and N. Bennett, "Does Work Group Cohesiveness Affect Individuals' Performance and Organizational Commitment?" *Small Group Research* 29 (1998): 472–94.

22. The following types of power are based on the categories developed by J.R. French and B. Raven, "The Basis of Social Power," in D. Cartright and A. Zander, eds, *Group Dynamics* (New York: Harper & Row, 1968): 565.

23. For a detailed discussion of leadership emergence, see E.G.G. Bormann and N.C. Bormann, *Effective Small Group Communication*, 6th edn (New York: Pearson Custom Publishing, 1997).

24. C. Conrad, *Strategic Organizational Communication: An Integrated Perspective*, 2nd edn (Fort Worth, TX: Holt, Rinehart and Winston, 1990): 139.

25. J.D. Rothwell, *In Mixed Company: Small Group Communication*, 5th edn (Belmont, CA: Wadsworth, 2004): 247–82.

26. Aristotle, *Politics* 7 (New York: Oxford University Press, 1958).

27. See B.L. Kelsey, "The Dynamics of Multicultural Groups," *Small Group Research* 29 (1998): 602–23.

28. W. Bennis and B. Nanus, *Leaders: The Strategies for Taking Charge* (New York: Harper & Row, 1985): 164.

29. K. Lewin, R. Lippitt, and R.K. White, "Patterns of Aggressive Behavior in Experimentally Created Social Climates," *Journal of Social Psychology* 10 (1939): 271–99.

30. G. Cheney, "Democracy in the Workplace: Theory and Practice from the Perspective of Communication," *Journal of Applied Communication Research* 23 (1995): 167–200.

31. L.L. Rosenbaum and W.B. Rosenbaum, "Morale and Productivity Consequences of Group Leadership Style, Stress, and Type of Task," *Journal of Applied Psychology* 55 (1971): 343–58.

32. J. Hall and S. Donnell, "Managerial Achievement: The Personal Side of Behavioral Theory," *Human Relations* 32 (1979): 77–101.

33. R.R. Blake and A.A. McCanse, *Leadership Dilemmas—Grid Solutions* (Houston: Gulf Publishing Co., 1991).

34. For a discussion of situational theories, see G.L. Wilson, *Groups in Context*, 6th edn (New York: McGraw-Hill, 2002): 190–4.

35. F.E. Fiedler, *A Theory of Leadership Effectiveness* (New York: McGraw-Hill, 1967).

36. P. Hersey and K. Blanchard, *Management of Organizational Behavior: Utilizing Human Resources*, 8th edn (Upper Saddle River, NJ: Prentice Hall, 2001).

37. Rothwell, *op. cit.*, 139–42.

38. M.E. Mayer, "Behaviors Leading to More Effective Decisions in Small Groups Embedded in Organizations," *Communication Reports* 11 (1998): 123–32.

39. L.R. Hoffman and N.R.F. Maier, "Valence in the Adoption of Solutions by Problem-Solving Groups: Concept, Method, and Results," *Journal of Abnormal and Social Psychology* 69 (1964): 264–71.

40. E.P. Torrence, "Some Consequences of Power Differences on Decision Making in Permanent and Temporary Three-Man Groups," *Research Studies, Washington State College* 22 (1954): 130–40.

41. R.F. Bales, F.L. Strodtbeck, T.M. Mills, and M.E. Roseborough, "Channels of Communication in Small Groups," *American Sociological Review* 16 (1951): 461–8.

42. S.E. Asch, "Studies of Independence and Conformity: A Minority of One Against a Unanimous Majority," *Psychological Monographs* (1956): 70.

43. I. Janis, *Groupthink: Psychological Studies of Policy Decisions and Fiascoes* (Boston: Houghton Mifflin, 1982).

44. Adapted from Rothwell, *op. cit.*, 223–6.

Chapter 11

1. For an explanation of social judgment theory, see E. Griffin, *A First Look at Communication Theory*, 5th edn (New York: McGraw-Hill, 2003).

2. C. Lasch, "Journalism, Publicity and the Lost Art of Argument," *Gannett Center Journal* (Spring 1990): 1–11.

3. See, for example, J.A. Jaska and M.S. Pritchard, *Communication Ethics: Methods of Analysis*, 2nd edn (Belmont, CA: Wadsworth, 1994).

4. Speech made by Justine Zaleschuk, winner of the Canadian Association of Former Parliamentarians essay competition for undergraduate students at Canadian colleges and universities. "How to Improve Canada's Health Care System." (No date available.)

5. There are, of course, other classifications of logical fallacies than those presented here. See, for example, B. Warnick and E. Inch, *Critical Thinking and Communication: The Use of Reason in Argument*, 2nd edn (New York: Macmillan, 1994): 137–61.

6. J.M. Burger, "The Foot-in-the-Door Compliance Procedure: A Multiple-Process Analysis and Review," *Personality and Social Psychology Review* 3, 4 (November 1999): 303–25.

7. R.B. Cialdini, J.E. Vincent, S.K. Lewis, J. Catalan, D. Wheeler, and B.L. Darby, "Reciprocal Concessions Procedure for Inducing Compliance: The Door-in-the-Face Technique," *Journal of Personality and Social Psychology* 31, 2 (February 1975): 206–15.

Chapter 12

1. See, for example, L. Stern, *The Structures and Strategies of Human Memory* (Homewood, IL: Dorsey Press, 1985). See also C. Turner, "Organizing Information: Principles and Practices," *Library Journal* (15 June 1987).

2. J. Buckley, *Fit to Print: The Canadian Students' Guide to Essay Writing*, 6th edn (Scarborough, ON: Nelson Education Ltd, 2004).

3. C. Koehler, "Mending the Body by Lending an Ear: The Healing Power of Listening," *Vital Speeches of the Day* (15 June 1998): 543; as cited in S. Metcalfe, *Building a Speech* 7th edn (Boston: Wadworth, 2010).

4. L. Johnson, "Poverty in Liberia." Student speech presented for "Celebrate Africa," McMaster University, Dundas, ON (25 November 2006).

5. A.H. Monroe, *Principles and Types of Speech* (Glenview, IL: Scott, Foresman, 1935).

6. The examples of the steps of the motivated sequence are adapted from Elizabeth Marshal Thomas, "Canine Liberation," *The New York Times* (1 May 1996): A19.

7. H.M. Weston, "Announcement of the Lieutenant Governor's Community Volunteer Award for Graduating Students" (Emery Collegiate Institute, Toronto, 11 April 2000).

8. P.E. Trudeau, "First Among Equals: Notes for a National Broadcast" (16 October 1970). Accessed 25 June 2014 at www .collectionscanada.ca/2/4/h4-4000-e.html

9. B. Neil, "Social Media and Corporate Trust." Speech presented to the Empire Club of Canada, Toronto, ON, 7 May 2009. Accessed 25 June 2014 at www.speeches .empireclub.org/69578/data?n=18

10. Trudeau, *op. cit.*

11. R. Hansen, Speech to University of Ottawa, Distinguished Canadian Leadership Awards (2005). Accessed 25 June 2014 at www.canadianleadership.uottawa.ca/ recipients_details-10-e-html

12. S. Haydu, "Briefing Note: 2006 Premier's TV Address" (2006). Accessed 25 June 2014 at www.uofaweb.ualberta.ca/govrel//pdfs/ Premier's2006TVAddressGRBrief.pdf

13. T.C. Douglas and L.H. Thomas, *The Making of a Socialist: The Recollections of T.C. Douglas* (Edmonton, University of Alberta Press, 1984): 60.

14. J. Chrètien, "A Tribute to the Right Honourable Pierre Elliott Trudeau." Speech presented at the Paul Sauvé Arena, Montreal (May 14, 1980). Accessed 25 June 2014 at www.collectionscanada.gc.ca/primeministers/h4-4082-e.html

15. General R. Hillier, "The Men and Women of the Canadian Armed Forces." Speech presented to the Empire Club of Canada, Toronto (11 April 2006). Accessed 25 June 2014 at speeches.empireclub.org/62933/data?n=8.

16. *ibid.*

17. C. Boris, "3 Simple and Creative Alternatives to Using PowerPoint for Presentations," *Entrepreneur* (2013). Accessed 25 June 2014 at www.entrepreneur.com/article/226612

18. J.T. Cacioppo and R.E. Petty, "Effects of Message Repetition and Position on Cognitive Response, Recall, and Persuasion," *Journal of Personality and Social Psychology* 37 (1979): 97–109.

19. For an example of how demographics have been taken into consideration in great speeches, see G. Stephens, "Frederick Douglass' Multiracial Abolitionism: 'Antagonistic Cooperation' and 'Redeemable Ideals' in the 5 July 1852 speech," *Communication Studies* 48 (Fall 1997): 175–94. On 5 July 1852, Douglass gave a speech entitled "What to the Slave Is the 4th of July," attacking the hypocrisy of Independence Day in a slaveholding republic. It was one of the greatest anti-slavery speeches ever given, and part of its success stemmed from the way Douglass sought common ground with his multiracial audience.

20. Aristotle (trans. W. Rhys Roberts and I. Bywater), *The Rhetoric and Poetics of Aristotle* (New York: Modern Library College Ed., 1984): Book 2, Section 12.

21. For example, see J.E. Kopfman and S. Smith, "Understanding the Audiences of a Health Communication Campaign: A Discriminant Analysis of Potential Organ Donors Based on Intent to Donate," *Journal of Applied Communication Research* 24 (February 1996): 33–49.

22. R.K. Stutman and S.E. Newell, "Beliefs versus Values: Silent Beliefs in Designing a Persuasive Message," *Western Journal of Speech Communication* 48, 4 (Fall 1984): 364.

23. J.A. DeVito, *The Communication Handbook: A Dictionary* (New York: Harper & Row, 1986): 84–6.

24. Speeches are also easier to understand than written text. See, for example, D.L. Rubin, T. Hafer, and K. Arata, "Reading and Listening to Oral-Based versus Literate-Based Discourse," *Communication Education* 49, 2 (April 2000): 121. An interesting study in this area is D.P. Hayes's "Speaking and Writing: Distinct Patterns of Word Choice," *Journal of Memory and Language* 27 (October 1988): 572–85. This extensive study of written/spoken language differences found these differences so pronounced that "conversations between college graduates more closely resemble a preschool child's speech to its parents than texts from newspapers."

25. See, for example, L.R. Rosenfeld and J.M. Civikly, *With Words Unspoken* (New York: Holt, Rinehart and Winston, 1976): 62. Also see S. Chaiken, "Communicator Physical Attractiveness and Persuasion," *Journal of Personality and Social Psychology* 37 (1979): 1387–97.

26. A study demonstrating this stereotype is R.L. Street, Jr, and R.M. Brady, "Speech Rate Acceptance Ranges as a Function of Evaluative Domain, Listener Speech Rate, and Communication Context," *Speech Monographs* 49 (December 1982): 290–308.

27. See, for example, A. Mulac and M.J. Rudd, "Effects of Selected American Regional Dialects upon Regional Audience Members," *Communication Monographs* 44 (1977): 184–95. Some research, however, suggests that non-standard dialects do not have the detrimental effects on listeners that were once believed. See, for example, F.L. Johnson and R. Buttny, "White Listener's Responses to 'Sounding Black' and 'Sounding White': The Effect of Message Content on Judgments about Language," *Communication Monographs* 49 (March 1982): 33–9.

28. J.S. Hinton and M.W. Kramer, "The Impact of Self-Directed Videotape Feedback on Students' Self-Reported Levels of Communication Competence and Apprehension," *Communication Education* 47, 2 (April 1998): 151–61. Significant increases in competency and decreases in apprehension were found using this method.

29. See, for example, J. Borhis and M. Allen, "Meta-analysis of the Relationship between Communication Apprehension and Cognitive Performance," *Communication Education* 41, 1 (January 1992): 68–76.

30. J.A. Daly, A.L. Vangelisti, and D.J. Weber, "Speech Anxiety Affects How People Prepare Speeches: A Protocol Analysis of the Preparation Process of Speakers,"

Communication Monographs 62 (December 1995).

31. Researchers generally agree that speech anxiety has three causes: genetics, social learning, and inadequate skills acquisition. See, for example, M.J. Beatty and K.M. Valencic, "Context-Based Apprehension versus Planning Demands: A Communibiological Analysis of Anticipatory Public Speaking Anxiety," *Communication Education* 49, 1 (January 2000): 58.

32. See, for example, C.R. Sawyer and R.R. Behnke, "Communication Apprehension and Implicit Memories of Public Speaking State Anxiety," *Communication Quarterly* 45, 3 (Summer 1997): 211–22.

33. Adapted from A. Ellis, *A New Guide to Rational Living* (North Hollywood, CA: Wilshire Books, 1977). G.M. Philips listed a different set of beliefs that he believed contributes to reticence. The beliefs are: "(1) an exaggerated sense of self-importance (Reticent people tend to see themselves as more important to others than others see them.); (2) Effective speakers are born, not made; (3) Skilful speaking is manipulative; (4) Speaking is not that important; (5) I can speak whenever I want to; I just choose not to; (6) It is better to be quiet and let people think you are a fool than prove it by talking (they assume they will be evaluated negatively); and (7) What is wrong with me requires a (quick) cure." See J.A. Keaten, L. Kelly, and C. Finch, "Effectiveness of the Penn State Program in Changing Beliefs Associated with Reticence," *Communication Education* 49, 2 (April 2000): 134.

34. R.R. Behnke, C.R. Sawyer, and P.E. King, "The Communication of Public Speaking Anxiety," *Communication Education* 36 (April 1987): 138–41.

35. See, for example, J. Ayres and B.L. Heuett, "The Relationship between Visual Imagery and Public Speaking Apprehension," *Communication Reports* 10, 1 (Winter 1997): 87–94. Besides visualization, treatments for speech anxiety include skills training (such as a public speaking class); systematic desensitization (such as having practice sessions until you feel more comfortable with the real thing); rational-emotive therapy (recognizing irrational beliefs, as discussed earlier in this chapter); interpersonal support (such as coaching); and physical exercise. Students tend to do best when selecting their own treatment. See, for example, K. Kangas Dwyer, "The Multidimensional Model: Teaching Students to Self-Manage High Communication Apprehension by

Self-Selecting Treatments," *Communication Education* 49, 1 (January 2000): 72.

36. R.R. Behnke and C.R. Sawyer, "Milestones of Anticipatory Public Speaking Anxiety," *Communication Education* 48, 2 (April 1999): 165.

37. J. Chrètien, "Speech at the Treaty-Signing Conference for the Global Ban on Anti-Personnel Landmines," Ottawa, 3 December 1997.

Appendix I

1. There is more detail on a similar process in C. Meyer, *Communicating for Results: A Canadian Student's Guide* (Toronto: Oxford University Press, 2007): 23–37. Meyer also has specific tools for preparing business communications (e.g., letters, e-mails, memos, and reports) that students would find helpful.

2. In working on major writing projects, both at CBC and elsewhere, I would most often work with other writers in a team. Part of the value of the PAE approach is that you set out the common planning goals among a team of contributors, thus avoiding duplication or even counter-productive writing communication.

3. When I did formal CBC reporting to groups like the CRTC, I often used this outlining method, which is also the basis for the briefing notes in this chapter.

4. Some people use a form of free-writing before they make the outline, or at least partly at that point.

5. Also check for accuracy, completeness, structure, and coherence.

6. Some organizations have their own internal "house style" for certain types of documents (always follow those first). Otherwise, you may choose to use an academic publication, such as *The Chicago Manual of Style* (now available online at www.chicagomanualofstyle.org). I prefer using a journalist's style guide for professional writing; both *The Globe and Mail* and the *Canadian Press* publish guides suitable for Canadian contexts and spellings.

7. Some believe this is how they get their name: [op]posite the [ed]itorial. Other think of them as opinion-editorials.

8. McGill University Newsroom, "Op-Ed Writing Tips." Accessed 25 June 2014 at www.mcgill.ca/newsroom/facstaffresources/op-ed/

Appendix II

1. A. Pease and B. Pease, *The Definitive Book on Body Language* (New York: Bantam, 2006): 10.

Credits

Photos

Page 1: Courtesy of Rikia Saddy; page 3: © Tim Hale Photography/Corbis; page 7: © apomares/iStockphoto; page 8: © canada/Alamy; page 10: Photo credit: Matt Llewellyn ; page 15: © gpointstudio/iStockphoto; page 16: Norman James/GetStock.com; page 17: © Maartje van Caspel/iStockphoto; page 25: © iStockphoto.com/Sean Locke; page 33: © iStockphoto/Tatiana Gladskikh; page 39: © Tino Soriano/National Geographic Society/Corbis; page 42: © AF archive/Alamy; page 45: © michellegibson/iStockphoto; page 46: © killerb10/iStockphoto; page 49: © Chris Schmidt/iStockphoto; page 50: © bo1982/iStockphoto; page 54: Julie Oliver/Ottawa Citizen. Reprinted by permission.; page 55: © MarcusPhoto1/iStockphoto; page 57: © digitalskillet/iStockphoto; "page 61: Sergeibach/Dreamstime.com; "page 62: Sangiorzboy/Dreamstime.com; page 68: © Maartje van Caspel/iStockphoto; page 72: © Chris Schmidt/iStockphoto; page 73: Courtesy of Bianca Freedman; page 85: © Stevens Fremont/Corbis; page 89: © Arief Priyono/Alamy; page 92: © hartcreations/iStockphoto; page 98: © Nikada/iStockphoto; page 99: © MOF/iStockphoto; page 109: Courtesy of Melonie Fullick; page 110: © MarcusPhoto1/iStockphoto; page 112: © digitalskillet/iStockphoto; page 121: © 2010 Anthony Asael and World of Stock; page 129: © Chris Crisman/Corbis; page 132: AP Photo/Kevin Rivoli/CP; page 134: Used with the permission of The Come Up Show.; page 137: © iStockphoto.com/Shelly Perry; page 143: © kevinruss/iStockphoto; page 156: François Pesant; page 158: © humonia/iStockphoto; page 167: © moodboard/Alamy; page 170: © echo1/iStockphoto; page 171: © GlobalStock/iStockphoto; page 176: © Chris Schmidt/iStockphoto; page 178: © Pali Rao/iStockphoto; page 186: Lite/Dreamstime.com; page 193: Courtesy of Emily Maurice; page 197: © bo1982/iStockphoto; page 203: © Chris Schmidt/iStockphoto; page 209: Courtesy of Heather Pullen; page 211: © Oliver Rossi/Corbis; page 220: © Izabela Habur/iStockphoto; page 221: © Lokibaho/iStockphoto; page 223: © nano/iStockphoto; page 226: © XiXinXing/iStockphoto; page 231: © -ilkeryuksel-/iStockphoto; page 245: © ranplett/iStockphoto; page 249: Courtesy of Joey Coleman; page 261: © Dean Mitchell/iStockphoto; page 263: © monkeybusinessimages/iStockphoto; page 268: © MarcusPhoto1/iStockphoto; page 269: Courtesy of Steve Dolson; "page 270: Mocker/Dreamstime.com; "page 273: Photo by Dave Sandford/Getty Images); page 283: © Yuri/iStockphoto; page 286: © Nigel Carse/iStockphoto; page 293: Courtesy of Andrew Laing; page 295: © Curi Hyvrard/Corbis; page 297: © pagadesign/iStockphoto; page 298: © dynasoar/iStockphoto; page 299: © Chris Schmidt/iStockphoto; page 303: © krie/iStockphoto; page 308: © arekmalang/iStockphoto; page 316: Courtesy of Chris Farias; page 323: © webphotographeer/iStockphoto; page 339: © Rick Gomez/Corbis; page 341: © bedo/iStockphoto; page 343: © urbancow/iStockphoto; page 349: © Jason Lugo/iStockphoto; page 354: Courtesy of Christopher Tuckwood; page 357: © francisblack/iStockphoto; page 361: © George Clerk/iStockphoto; page 369: © Steve Prezant/Corbis; page 372: iStockPhoto; page 374: Courtesy of Jessica Martin; page 379: © Steve Debenport/iStockphoto; page 383: © DaveBolton/iStockphoto; page 391: © Kronick/iStockphoto; page 392: © RelaxFoto.de/iStockphoto; page 407: Courtesy of Donald T. Smith; page 409: © Jim Purdum/Blend Images/Corbis; page 410: THE CANADIAN PRESS/Graham Hughes; page 413: © Chris Schmidt/iStockphoto; page 418: © diego_cervo/iStockphoto; page 421: Courtesy of Gurdeep Ahluwalia; page 423: © Brainsil/iStockphoto; page 431: © Hero Images Inc./Alamy; page 433: © GlobalStock/iStockphoto; page 435: © GlobalStock/iStockphoto; page 440: © Viorika/iStockphoto; page 455: © urbancow/iStockphoto; page 459: © Cimmerian/iStockphoto; page 461: David Schnokking; page 465: © iStockphoto.com/René Mansi; page 468: © Sean_Warren/iStockphoto.

Cartoons

Page 5: David Malki !; page 19: www.octopuspie.com; page 22: David Malki !; page 27: CALVIN AND HOBBES © 2014 Watterson. Reprinted with permission of UNIVERSAL UCLICK. All rights reserved.; page 41: Harry Bliss The New Yorker Collection/The Cartoon Bank; page 52: Cartoonstock/Chris Wildt; page 65: Cartoonstock/Aaron Bacall; page 76: Robert Weber The New Yorker Collection/The Cartoon Bank; page 86: Eric Lewis The New Yorker Collection/The Cartoon Bank; page 93: Cartoonstock/Aaron Bacall; page 102: Cartoonstock/Marty Bucella; page 107: David Malki !; page 108: Leo Cullum The New Yorker Collection/The Cartoon Bank; page 117: (c)2006-2011 Kate Beaton; page 133: The estate of Michael ffolkes.; page 139: CALVIN AND HOBBES © 2013 Watterson. Reprinted with permission of UNIVERSAL UCLICK. All rights reserved.; page 188: CALVIN AND HOBBES © 1995 Watterson. Reprinted with permission of UNIVERSAL UCLICK. All rights reserved.; page 195: ZITS © 2004 Zits Partnership, Dist. By King Features; page 212: Bruce Eric Kaplan The New Yorker Collection/The Cartoon Bank; page 232: Cartoonstock/Marty Bucella; page 235: © The New Yorker Collection J. Dator from cartoonbank.com. All Rights Reserved.; page 251: David Malki !; page 277: Bruce Eric Kaplan The New Yorker Collection/The Cartoon Bank; page 280: © The New Yorker Collection BEK from cartoonbank.com. All Rights Reserved.; page 284: CALVIN AND HOBBES © 1995 Watterson. Reprinted with permission of UNIVERSAL UCLICK. All rights reserved.; page 306: David Malki !; page 309: John Atkinson; page 314: David Malki !; page 359: DILBERT © Scott Adams/Dist. by United Feature Syndicate, Inc.; page 399: Cartoonstock/Ralph Hagen; page 419: Cartoonstock/Jerry King; page 450: Cartoonstock/Bradford Veley.

Literary

Pages 4–5: "The Many Meanings of Communication" by Brent Rubin, *Communication and Human Behavior*, 2/e, Allyn & Bacon, 1988; pages 54–5: "The Biggest Thing in Aboriginal Art in Ottawa", material reprinted with the express permission of *Ottawa Citizen*, a division of Postmedia Network Inc.; pages 120–1: "Loyalists to Loonies: A Very Short History of Canadian English" from Katherine Barber, *Six Words You Never Knew Had Something To Do With Pigs*. Copyright © 2006 Oxford University Press Canada. Reprinted by permission of the publisher; pages 140–1: "An Expert Speaks Man to Mane", reprinted with permission – Torstar Syndication Services; pages 152–3: "Computer Can Judge Human Attractiveness" by Andrea Janus, CTV.ca News Staff Date: Sat. Jul. 18 2009 7:10 AM ET http://www.ctv.ca/servlet/ArticleNews/story/CTVNews/20090717/computer_attractiveness_090718/20090718?hub=TopStories; pages 154–5: "New Generation Of Opera Singers Slimming Down Before Belting Out", reprinted with permission – Torstar Syndication Services; pages 198–9: "Digital Distraction" reprinted with permission of Terence Day; page 201: "School's Playground Planning Includes Hearing-Impaired Kids", material reprinted with the express permission of *The StarPhoenix*, a division of Postmedia Network Inc.; pages 224–5: "Immigrant Parents Are Gradually Accepting Interracial Relationships" by Nirushan Sivagnanasuntharam, July 16, 2012 http://canadianimmigrant.ca/family/immigrant-parents-are-gradually-accepting-interracial-relationships; page 232: "What do you think qualifies as cheating?" by Trish McAlaster, *The Globe and Mail*, 3 July 2009. © The Globe and Mail Inc. All Rights Reserved; "pages 236–7: ""Six Web Design Tips Based on Brain Science"" by Andy Crestodina, Orbit Media, 1 May 2013 http://www.orbitmedia.com/blog/web-design-tips/; pages 238–9: "Mapping Her Musical Landscape" by Robert Everett-Green, *The Globe and Mail*, 6 February 2010. © The Globe and Mail Inc. All Rights Reserved.; page 252:

"University Of Toronto Study Shows That Toddlers Can Lie", reprinted with permission – Torstar Syndication Services; page 267: "A Comparison of Dialogue and Debate", adapted from R. Poliner and J. Benson, *Dialogue: Turning Controversy into Community* (Cambridge, MA: Educators for Social Responsibility, 1997); page 272: "Whether Attack Ads 'Work' Is the Wrong Question" by Ken Gallinger, *Toronto Star*, 26 Apr 2013, http://www.thestar.com/life/2013/04/26/whether_attack_ads_work_is_the_wrong_question.html; pages 318–9: "How to Use Social Media to Find a Job" by Krystal Yee, *Toronto Star*, 1 December 2011, http://www.thestar.com/business/personal_finance/2011/12/01/how_to_use_social_media_to_find_a_job.html; pages 320–1: "Royalties Deal Breaks Barrier to Entry in Canada's Digital Music Streaming Market" © The Globe and Mail Inc. All Rights Reserved; pages 324–5: "The Internet Dilemma: Do People Have a Right to Be Forgotten?" by Drew Nelles, *The Globe and Mail*, 3 May 2013, http://www.theglobeandmail.com/life/the-internet-dilemma-do-people-have-a-right-to-be-forgotten/article11715854/?page=all; pages 344–5: "Search Engine Optimization (SEO)" by Victoria Edwards, 31 December 2013 http://searchenginewatch.com/article/2259693/SEO-Basics-8-Essentials-When-Optimizing-Your-Site; pages 346–7: "Memo to Abercrombie & Fitch: Anger Those Millennials at Your Peril" © The Globe and Mail Inc. All Rights Reserved; page 350: William Golding quote used by permission of Faber & Faber; pages 386–7: "Ten Tips for Running a Successful Crowdfunding Campaign", used by permission of Michelle Shemilt, www.michelleshemilt.com; page 400: "Justin Trudeau's Feminine Mystique" by John Geddes, *Macleans*, 2 May 2013, http://adinnovation.rogersmedia.com/news/canada/the-feminine-mystique/; page 401: "What Can We Learn About Leadership From Mark Carney?" © The Globe and Mail Inc. All Rights Reserved; pages 424–5: "How to Persuade Anyone: Four Timeless Strategies" by Dan Roitman, *Huffington Post*, May 20, 2013, http://www.huffingtonpost.com/dan-roitman/how-to-persuade-anyone-fo_b_3288023.html.

Index

Abercrombie & Fitch, 346–7
Aboriginal peoples: art, 54–5; education, 58–9; endangered languages, 90–1; language and communication style, 117, 118–19; news for, 12–13; non-verbal communication, 131
abstraction ladder, 104
abstract language, 103–5
action-oriented listening, 184
activating, 417, 419
active learning, 198–9
active listening, 188–9, 201–4
Adam, Betty Ann, 201
ad hominem fallacy, 420
advice, in listening, 194–5
affect blends, 148
affinity, 218
afiliation, and language, 99–100
agenda-setting theory, 332–3
aggression, direct and passive, 271, 273–4
Ahluwalia, Gurdeep, 421
Akkad, Omar, 320–1
all-channel network, 356
altruistic lies, 250
ambushing, 173
analogy, in speeches, 450
anchor, 411–12
anecdotes, in speeches, 450–1
Anglo-North American culture: communication style, 116–17; intimacy, 227; language, 123; self-concept, 61–2; self-disclosure, 245. *see also* English Canadians
animals, communication, 5
apologies, 115
appearance, 74, 464. *see also* clothing
approval, fallacy of, 468
apps, for health, 378
Arabic language, 117–18
Arab Spring, 298
Argo, 42
argumentatum ad populum fallacy, 421–3
argumentatum ad verecundiam fallacy, 421
articulation, in speeches, 466
Asian cultures: communication style, 116, 117; intimacy, 227; perceptions, 50; self-concept, 61–2
assertion and assertive message, 271, 275–9

associative conditioning, 416
assumptions, 45
asynchronous discussion, 376
attack ads, 272
attitudes, 91–100, 132, 461, 469
attribution, 42
audience: analysis, 457–60; attention of, 441–4, 454–7; attitudes, beliefs, and values, 460–1; involvement, 456–7; in public communication, 8–9; type and purpose, 458; of writing, 479
authoritarian leadership style, 396
authority rule, 360
autonomy–connection dialectic, 233–5
avatars, use of, 174–5
avoiding stage, in relationships, 232

Balser, Erin, 300–1
Barber, Katherine, 120–1
bar charts, 453
Bauman, Martin, 134–5
beauty, in non-verbal communication, 151, 152–3, 154–5
behaviour, and self-concept, 63–6
behavioural descriptions, 104–5
behavioural interviews, 496–7
Being Erica, 75
belief, 460–1
Benson, J., 267
Berners-Lee, Tim, 76–7
Besner, Linda, 156–7
"black" as identification, 123
BlackBerry, museum app, 88
Blackwell, Richard, 401
blogs and blogging: blogosphere community, 306; dangers of, 306–7; definition, 303; microblogs, 307–9; as social media, 303–9; tips for success, 274–5; types, 304–6; writing of, 484–5
body of speeches, 436, 438–9, 441–8, 470–1
Bon Cop, Bad Cop, 51
bonding stage, 230
Boston, Dawn, 58–9
brain, and web design, 236–7
brainstorming, 382
branding, 416
breakout groups, 375

briefing notes, 485–9
buildings, and non-verbal communication, 157–9
bullet theory, 330
Burke, Brian, 306–7
business, 144–5, 180–1

Canadian Constitution, 370–1
Canadian English, 94–5, 120–1
Canadian Museum of Civilization, 88
Canadian Press, 96–7, 306–7
Canadian Radio-television and Telecommunications Commission (CRTC), 299–300
Carney, Mark, 401
catastrophic failure, fallacy of, 468
Catfish, 302
cause-effect patterns, 440–1
CBC, Native news, 12–13
certainty in communication climates, 268
chain network, 356
channels of communication, 15–16
Chapman, Julia, 378
Charette, Robert N., 174–5
charisma, 462
charts, in speeches, 453
cheating in relationships, 232
children: and communication, 20–1, 33, 52, 120–1; and conflict, 279–80; empathy, 52; immigrant *vs.* Canadian-born, 282; and immigration, 182–3; lies, 252; physical attractiveness, 151; physical contact, 150
Chinook Jargon, 121
chronemics, 155
circumscribing stage, in relationships, 231
citations, 437, 452
Ciulla, Joanne B., 254–5
Clark, Christy, 44
climates. *see* communication climates
climax patterns, 439
Clone High, 434
clothing, 152–3
"Coach's Corner", 273
coercive power, 391–2, 394
cognitive complexity, 25–6
cognitive dissonance, 424, 426
cohesiveness in groups, 388–90

Coleman, Joey, 249, 304
collectivistic cultures, 61–2, 227, 281, 361–2, 363
column charts, 453
communication: definition and meanings, 4–6; feedback, 18; functions of and human needs, 9–15; misconceptions, 26–34; models, 15–21; non-verbal (*see* non-verbal communication); as process, 6; theory (*see* communication theory); types, 6–9; verbal (*see* verbal communication)
communication climates: confirming and disconfirming responses, 262–5; description, 262; development, 264–5; positive climates, 265–9
communication theory: agenda-setting theory, 332–3; cultivation theory, 332; cumulative effects theory, 333; flow theories, 330–1; individual differences theory, 331–2; key theories, 326–33; McLuhan's theories, 328–30; social learning theory, 331; time- and space binding media, 326–8
community media, 299
competence in communication, 14, 21–6, 462
compromise, in conflict, 283–4, 285
computer-mediated communication (CMC), 75–8, 296, 376–7
conclusion, to speech, 436, 439, 446–8, 471
confirming responses, 262–5
conflict: definition, 270; existence and nature of, 269–71; and language, 106–8
conflict management in interpersonal relationships: assertion and assertive message, 271, 275–9; and culture, 281–2; dialogue *vs.* debate, 267; distancing tactics, 264; and gender, 279–81; overview, 269–70; resolution methods, 282–8; styles of expression, 271–6
conflict resolution, 282–8
conflict stage, 384–5
conformity, in groups, 400–2
connection–autonomy dialectic, 233–5
consensus, 357, 370–1
constructive criticism, 196
content messages, 217–22
content-oriented listening, 181
control, in relationships, 219
controlling message, 266
conventionalism, 326
conversation, hogging, 173, 179
convincing, 416–17, 419
cool media, 330
coordinated communication, 27–8
corporate blogs, 305
counterfeit questions, 187
covergence, in language, 99
Cowley, Madeleine, 113
Crawford, Trish, 154–5
crazymaking, 271, 273–4
credibility, 92–3, 192, 462
Crestodina, Andy, 236–7

Cribb, Robert, 140–1
critical listening, 190–4
crowdfunding, 386–7
Cube, 373
cultivation theory, 332
cultural norms, 349
culture: and communication, 22–3; and conflict, 281–2; and decision-making, 360; and groups, 360–4; and intimacy, 226–7; and language, 115–23; and listening, 179; and non-verbal communication, 136–7; and perception, 49–51; and self-concept, 60–2; and self-disclosure, 245; and time, 156
cumulative effects theory, 333
cyberbullying, 20–1
cyberstalking, 307

dating, 224–5, 234
Day, Terence, 198–9
deafness, 155–6, 201
debate, *vs.* dialogue, 267
debilitative stage fright, 467–70
deception: by children, 252; and gender, 146; in non-verbal communication, 142–3; reasons for, 250; right and wrong of, 254–5; and self-disclosure, 250–1, 254
decision-making, 357–60, 372, 378
defensive listening, 172
definitions, in speeches, 449
delivery of speech, 462–7; types, 462–4; visual and auditory aspects, 464–6
democratic leadership style, 396
demographics of audience, 458–9
description, 434
descriptive communication, 266
developmental model of relationships, 228–33
diagrams, in speeches, 453
dialectical model of relationships, 233–40
dialectical tensions, 233
dialects, 94–5
dialogue, 267, 296–7
differentiating stage, in relationships, 230–1
diffusion of innovations theory, 331–2
digital divide, 213
digital memory, 324–5
direct aggression, 271, 273
direct–indirect verbal style, 115–17
direct persuasion, 418
disclosure of information, 224, 226, 237–8. *see also* self-disclosure
disconfirming responses, 263–5
disfluencies, 149
distance, in non-verbal communication, 137, 153–5
distancing tactics, 264
divergence, in language, 99–100
doctors' communication, 174–5
dogmatism, 268
Dolson, Steve, 269
Domansky, Jeff, 30–1
door-in-the-face, 423
Downtown Abbey, 364

drafting, in writing, 480–1
dress, 152–3
Dr Fox hypothesis, 92
dyadic communication. *see* interpersonal relationships
dysfunctional roles, 352–3, 354

earphones, 191
editing, 481
Edwards, Victoria, 344–5
either–or fallacy, 420
elaborate–succinct verbal style, 117–19
El Akkad, Omar, 320–1
e-mail, 28–9, 75, 216–17, 219
emblem, 140
emergence stage, 385
emoticons, 159–60
emotions, 132–3, 194
emotive language, 107–8
empathy: in communication climates, 268; dimensions of, 51–3; and listening, 194–205; and perception, 51–6; *vs.* sympathy, 52
endangered languages, 90–1
English Canadians: accents and idioms, 94–5; communication style, 117; language, 89, 102; non-verbal communication, 137; perceptions, 50–1; self-disclosure, 245
English language: in Canada, 94–5, 120–1; influence of worldviews, 120–2; informal nature, 119–20; sexism in, 93–5; slang and jargon, 102–3; and status, 93; variations and technical versions, 89
environment (physical), 17, 157–9
environments, in communication, 17–18
equality in communication climates, 268
equivocal language, 101, 251
equivocal words, 101
equivocation, 109–10, 251–3, 254
ethical persuasion, 413–14
euphemisms, 108
evaluative communication, 265–6
evaluative listening, 190–4
Everett-Green, Robert, 238–9
evidence, as supporting material, 192–3
examples, in speeches, 449–50
experimenting stage, in relationships, 229
expert opinion, 358
expert power, 392, 394
explanations, 434
extemporaneous speech, 462–3
eyes and eye contact, 148, 465

Facebook: age of users, 76–8; and non-verbal communication, 159; privacy, 218; and relationships, 234; and the self, 313; as social networking site, 310, 311
face-to-face interaction, 74–5, 214, 376–7
facework, 67
facial attractiveness, 152–3
facial expression, 147–8, 465
facilitative stage fright, 467
factual statements, 106–7

fallacies, 419–23, 468–9
families, communication in, 20–1
Farias, Chris, 315, 316–17
fear-then-relief technique, 425
feedback, 18
fidgeting, 147
Firefly, 103
first impressions, 44–5
flow theories, 330–1
focus groups, 375
foot-in-the-door, 423
Foran, Charles, 94–5
force field analysis, 381
foreign-born residents, 361
formal–informal verbal style, 119–20
formal outline, 436
formal roles, 350
forum, 376
Foursquare, 314
Freedman, Bianca, 73
French Canadians, 50–1, 89, 117, 137
Frost/Nixon, 264
Fullick, Melonie, 109, 118–19, 274–5
functional roles, 350–2

Gallinger, Ken, 272
gatekeeper, 357
gaze direction, 136
Gdyczynski, Caroline, 10
Geddes, John, 400
gender: in audiences, 458; and conflict,
    279–81; conversational style, 112–13;
    and deception, 146; equivocal
    misunderstandings, 101; interruptions
    in conversation, 178–9; and intimacy,
    224–7; and language, 93–5, 110–15; non-
    gender factors, 113–15; and non-verbal
    communication, 133, 138–9; and physical
    attractiveness, 151; physical contact, 151;
    reasons for communicating, 110–12; topics
    of conversation, 110
GeoCities, 302
geo-tagging, 314–15
gesture, 146–7, 148
Ghost Pine, 300–1
Gibb categories, 265–6
global village, 330
goals: groups, 342–6; individuals, 343–5
Good God, 347
Google+ and Google Glass, 160, 311
Google Maps, 314–15
Google News, 318
Goon, 287
Gossip Girl, 305
Grenier, Éric, 305
groups: characteristics, 348–60; cohesiveness,
    388–90; communication networks, 355–7;
    conformity in, 400–2; and culture, 360–4;
    dangers in, 398–402; decision-making
    methods, 357–60; definition, 340–2; goals
    in, 342–6; importance, 340; interaction
    in, 340–1, 355–7; interdependence, 341;

leadership in, 393–8; participation equality,
    399–400; positive relationships in, 386–90;
    power distance, 362–3; power in, 390–4;
    roles, 350–4; rules and norms, 348–50;
    short- and long-term orientation, 362, 364;
    size, 342; small groups, 8, 356; task and
    social orientation, 343, 362, 364; and time,
    342; types, 346–8; uncertainty avoidance,
    362, 363–4; virtual, 341. *see also* problem-
    solving groups
groupthink, 402
growth groups, 348

hair, in non-verbal communication, 140–1
Hall, Chris, 70–1
Hall, Joseph, 252
Harris, Kathleen, 218
hashtags, 308–9
hate speech and Hatebase, 138
health, 10–11, 191, 216, 378
HealthCorpus, 174–5
hearing, 169–70, 178, 191, 201
Hersey and Blanchard's leadership model,
    398
high-context cultures, 116–17, 281–2
hinting, and self-disclosure, 253–4
hip-hop, 134–5
"hold me tight," "put me down," and "leave
    me alone" stages, 233–5
honesty, 248–51
Hopi, worldviews and language, 121–2
hot media, 329
Housley, Sharon, 442–3
human brain, and web design, 236–7
humour, 11, 14
hypothetical examples, 449–50

identity: and communication, 11–13; and
    language, 123; multiplicity, 68; public and
    private selves, 66–7; and social media, 313.
    see also self-concept
identity management: characteristics, 68–72;
    in computer-mediated communication,
    75–8; conscious and unconscious, 69–72;
    degree of, 72; face-to-face, 74–5; and
    honesty, 78; methods, 74–8; and non-verbal
    communication, 132; and photographs,
    70–1; public and private selves, 66–7;
    reasons for, 73–4
"I" language, 266
illustrators, 141
I Love You, Man, 111
immediacy, 219
immigrants: in Canada, 360–1; and conflict,
    282; culture and values, 182–3; interracial
    relationships, 224–5; soft skills, 168–9
impersonal communication, 212–13
impression management, 66
impromtu speech, 463
indifference, 267–8
indirect communication in conflict, 271,
    274–5

indirect–direct verbal style, 115–17
indirect persuasion, 418
individual differences theory, 331–2
individualistic cultures, 61–2, 227, 281, 361–2,
    363
inferential statements, 106–7
influence, 390–4
informal–formal verbal style, 119–20
informal roles, 350–2
informational listening, 185–90
information power, 393, 394
information underload and overload, 398–9
informative speech, 433–4
initiating stage, in relationships, 228–9
Innis, Harold, and theory of time- and space-
    binding media, 326–8
insensitive listening, 173
instant messaging, 309
instructions, 434
insulated listening, 173
integrating stage, in relationships, 230
intensifying stage, in relationships, 229–30
interaction, in groups, 355–7
internet: activities online, 220; Canadian
    speeches on, 466; collaborations, 358–9,
    376–7; dangers of, 218; devices used,
    213; future of, 76–7; and health, 216;
    and identity management, 75–8; and
    interpersonal relationships, 213–17; and
    mass communication, 9; net neutrality,
    299–300; personal information, 218,
    324–5; positive impact, 217; use and access,
    213–16, 219, 220
interpersonal communication, description, 7
interpersonal persuasion, 423–5
interpersonal relationships: change in, 240–1;
    characteristics, 212–22; communication
    climates, 262–9; conflict management (*see*
    conflict management in interpersonal
    relationships); content messages, 217–18;
    and context, 212; description, 7, 212–13;
    developmental perspective, 228–33;
    dialectical perspective, 233–40; and
    internet, 213–17; intimacy in, 222–7;
    metacommunication, 222; qualitatively
    interpersonal communication, 212–13;
    relational development and maintenance,
    228–41; relational messages, 217–22; self-
    disclosure, 241–54
interpretation, 196–7
interracial relationships, 224–5
interruptions, in conversation, 173, 178–9
interview for a position. *see* selection
    interview
intimacy: and culture, 226–7; definition,
    222–3; and gender, 224–7; in multicultural
    Canada, 224–5; types of, 222–4
intimate distance, 153–4
intrapersonal communication, 6–7
introduction, in speeches, 436, 438, 441–6,
    470
Inuit and Inuktitut, 122

Invention of Lying, The, 251
Isaac, Elisapie, 238–9
It's a Guy Girl Thing, 141

Janus, Andrea, 152–3
Japan and Japanese language, 99, 116, 281–2
jargon, 102–3
job interview. *see* selection interview
Johari Window, 243–4
Jones, Miles, 134–5
judging responses, 195–6

Kawasaki, Guy, 422
Keynote, 454
kinesics, 147
King's Speech, The, 184
Knapp's 10 stages of relationships, 228–33
Korean language, 119–20

Laing, Andrew, 293
laissez-faire leadership style, 396
Langtry, David, 46–7
language: abstract, 103–5; accents and
   idioms, 94–5; and affiliation, 99–100; in
   Anglo-North American culture, 123–4; and
   attitudes, 91–100; behavioural descriptions,
   104–5; conflict in, 106–8; and culture,
   115–23; emotive, 107–8; endangered,
   90–1; equivocation, 109–10; euphemisms,
   108; evasiveness of, 108–10; and gender,
   93–5, 110–15; and identity, 123; meaning
   of words, 87; and misunderstandings,
   101–5; and naming, 91–2; nature of, 86–90;
   and politeness, 98–9; and power, 97–9;
   power of, 91–100; racism and sexism in,
   93–6; rules, 87–90; and self-concept,
   60; slang and jargon, 102–3; symbolism
   of, 86–7; verbal communication styles,
   115–20; and worldview, 120–2. *see also*
   specific languages
laptops, use in classrooms, 198–9
Lars and the Real Girl, 229
latitudes of acceptance, rejection, and non-
   commitment, 411–12
leadership, in groups, 393–8
Leadership Grid, 396–7
learning groups, 346–7
"leave me alone" stage, 233–5
LeBlanc, John C., 20–1
legitimate power, 390–1, 394
lies. *see* deception
linear communication model, 15–18
line charts, 453
linguistic determinism, 120–2
linguistic relativism, 122
LinkedIn, 311, 422
listening: action-oriented, 184; and advice,
   194–5; challenges to, 172–80; content-
   oriented, 181; critical, 190–4; and culture,
   179; and distractions, 198–9; effort in,
   171, 174–8; emotional appeals, 194;
   and empathy, 194–205; evidence and

reasoning in, 192–3; faulty assumptions,
   178; faulty behaviours, 172–3; and health,
   191; *vs.* hearing, 169–70; importance,
   168; informational, 185–90; judging
   responses, 195–6; key ideas in, 186–7; and
   making judgments, 185, 191–2; media and
   social media, 179–80; message overload,
   175–6; misconceptions, 169–72; and note
   taking, 190; opportunism in, 186–9; and
   paraphrase, 188–9, 201–4; people-oriented,
   184; poor listening, 174–80; psychological
   and physical noise, 176–7; and questions,
   187, 197–8; remembering and residual
   message, 170; responsiveness to, 170; as
   skill, 170–1; speaker credibility, 192; stages,
   170; statements analysis, 196–7; styles,
   180–5; and support, 198–201; *vs.* talking,
   178–9; time-oriented, 184–5
logical fallacies, 419–23, 468–9
lose–lose problem-solving, 283
low-balling, 424
low-context cultures, 115–17, 281
lying. *see* deception

McCue, Duncan, 12–13
McLuhan, Marshall, 16, 328–30
McLuhan's Wake, 329
Mcquigge, Michelle, 358–9
majority rule, 357
manipulation, 267
manipulators, 147
manners, 74
Man on Wire, 420
manuscript speech, 463
marketing, and social media, 315
Martin, Clancy, 254–5
Martin, Jessica, 374
mass communication, 9
mass media: effect, theories of, 326–33; and
   listening, 179; *vs.* social media, 297–300,
   315–21
Maurice Richard/The Rocket, 355
media convergence, 299
mediated communication, 75–8, 296, 376–7
"the medium is the message," 328–9
meetings, online, 358–9, 376–7
memorized speech, 463–4
men. *see* gender
*Merchants of Cool: Where Does Cool Come
   From,* 376
message, and persuasion, 412, 419–23
message overload, 175–6
metacommunication, 222
microblogging and microblogs, 307–9
Mi'kmaq language, 90–1, 99
Miller, Jeff, 300–1
minority control, 358
mixed messages, 142
mobile solutions, for health, 378
mobility, and social media, 314–15
models, in speeches, 452
Mohawk College, 58–9

Monsieur Lazhar, 147
Morrice, Emily, 193
motivated sequence, 441
motives, 43
MP3 players, 191
multi-step flow theory, 330–1
Murphy, Brian, 148
music streaming and royalties, 320–1
MySpace, 310–11

names, and attitudes, 91–2
narration, in speeches, 451–2
National Arts Centre (Ottawa), 54–5
Native people. *see* Aboriginal peoples
Nelles, Drew, 324–5
net neutrality, 299–300
networks, in groups, 355–7
neutrality in communication climates, 267–8
Newfoundland, language, 95, 123
newspapers, and social media, 318–19
news releases, 481–2
noise: in communication, 16–17, 176–8;
   hearing damage, 191
nominal group technique, 382
nominal leader, 391, 393–8
non-assertion in conflict, 271–3
non-verbal communication: ambiguity in,
   132–3; in business, 144–5; characteristics,
   130–6; and clothing, 152–3; and culture,
   136–7; distance in, 137, 153–5; and
   emotions, 132–3; and environment, 157–9;
   face and eyes, 147–8; functions, 140–6;
   and gender, 133, 138–9; hair in, 140–1; and
   identity management, 132; importance,
   131, 135–6; influences on, 136–9; overview
   and definition, 130–1; and physical
   attractiveness, 151, 152–3, 154–5; posture
   and gesture, 146–7, 148; and relational
   messages, 221–2; relational nature of,
   132; and relationships, 132; social media,
   159–60; and territory, 157; and time, 155–6;
   and touch, 150–1; types, 131, 146–60; value,
   131; and verbal communication, 134, 136,
   140–6; voice in, 148–9
Noorani, Nick, 168–9
norms, 348–9
note taking, 190
novelty–predictability dialectic, 235–6
number charts, 453

occasion, in speeches, 460–1
Office québécois de la langue française, 96–7
online communications. *see* specific aspects
   and technologies
online meetings, 358–9, 376–7
online presence, 324–5
Onstad, Katrina, 346–7
Oonark, Jessie, 54–5
op-eds, 482–4
openness–privacy dialectic, 237–8
opinion statements, 106
organizational blogs, 305

orientation stage, 384
others, perception of, 41–56
outlining, in writing, 480
overgeneralization, fallacy of, 468–9

panel discussion, 375
paralanguage, 148–9
paraphrase, and listening, 188–9, 201–4
parents, 20–1, 52, 120–1, 182–3
parliamentary procedure, 375
Parsons, Rehtaeh, 324–5
participation in groups, 399–400
participative decision-making, 372
passive aggression, 271, 273–4
pattern recognition, 322
people-oriented listening, 184
perceived self, 66–7
perception: checks, 53–6; common tendencies
    and errors, 42–7; and communication,
    40–1; and culture, 49–51; and empathy,
    51–6; and narratives, 41–2; of others,
    41–56; of the self, 56–66; and self-concept,
    49; situational factors, 47–9; and social
    roles, 48
perception-checking, 53–6
perfection, fallacy of, 468
personal blogs, 304
personal distance, 154
personal information, on internet, 218, 324–5
personality, and self-concept, 62–3
Persuaders, The, 377
persuasion: characteristics, 410–14; ethics
    in, 413–14; example, 416–17; as goal, 185;
    interpersonal, 423–5; and message, 412,
    419–23; strategies, 424–5; types, 414–18;
    and writing, 478–9
phonological rules, 87–8
photography, and identity management, 70–1
photo sharing websites, 312–13
physical attractiveness, in non-verbal
    communication, 151, 152–3, 154–5
physical contact, 150–1
physical intimacy, 223
physical noise, 177
pie charts, 453
pitch, in voice, 466
podcasting tips, 442–3
pointing, 140
police, racial data, 47
Poliner, R., 267
politeness, 98–9
politics, attack ads, 272
Pontypool, 32
position power, 390–1, 394
post hoc fallacy, 420–1
posture, 146–7, 464–5
power, in groups, 390–4
power distance in groups, 362–3
PowerPoint, 454
pragmatic rules, 89–90
predictability–novelty dialectic, 235–6
presenting self, 67

pre-writing, 480
Prezi, 454
privacy, on internet, 218
privacy–openness dialectic, 237–8
private self, 66–7
problem census, 375
problem/options/solutions (POS) approach,
    481
problem orientation, 266
problem-solution patterns, 440
problem-solving: in conflict resolution, 282–8;
    creativity in, 381–2
problem-solving groups: advantages, 371–2;
    approaches, 377–84; brainstorming, 382;
    cohesiveness in groups, 388–90; computer-
    mediated groups, 376–7; description,
    347–8; formats, 374–7; nominal group
    technique, 382; positive relationships in,
    386–90; situations for, 372–4; stages, 384–6;
    structured approach, 378–84; types, 375–6
procedural norms, 348–9
professional blogs, 304–5
prompting, 200–1
propositions of fact, of value, and of policy,
    414–16
provisionalism in communication climates,
    269
proxemics, 153
pseudo-listening, 172
psychological noise, 176–7
public communication, 8–9
public distance, 154–5
public relations, and social media, 315
public self, 66–7
public speaking. *see* speeches
Pullen, Heather, 209
purpose, 433–5
purpose statement, 434–5
"put me down" stage, 233–5

qualitatively interpersonal communication,
    212–13
Quebec, language, 96–7
question-and-answer period, 457
questions, 187, 197–8
quotations, 451

racial discrimination, 46–7
racial identification, 123
racial profiling, 46–7
racism, and language, 95–6
radical ideas and conventionalism, 326
radio, and social media, 320–1
rate, in voice, 465–6
reductio ad absurdum fallacy, 420
referent power, 393, 394
reflected appraisals, 58
reinforcement stage, 385
relational messages, 218–22
relationships. *see* interpersonal relationships
relative words, 101–2
repetition, 456

Reppler, 318
residual message, 170
Re:Sound, 320–1
respect, 219
responsiveness, to listening, 170
resume, for employment, 491–2
reward power, 392, 394
"right to be forgotten", 324–5
Roitman, Dan, 424–5
roles: emergence, 352–3; problems and
    solutions in, 353–4; sex roles, 114–15;
    social, 48, 73–4, 352; types, 350–2
Rose, Emily, 182–3
royalty rates, 320–1
Ruben, Brent, 4–5
rules, 348, 349

Saddy, Rikia, 1
Sapir-Whorf hypothesis, 121–2
Sass, Erik, 234
Savage, Philip, 478
Schokking, David, 417, 461
Scott Pilgrim vs. the World, 281
search engine optimization (SEO), 344–5
selection interview: during the interview, 494,
    495–7; legal aspects, 497–8; preparation,
    490–5
selective listening, 172
the self, 56–66, 313, 314
self-concept: acquisition, 58–9; and
    behaviour, 63–6; and communication,
    58–60, 62–3; and culture, 60–2; definition,
    56–7; and perception, 49; personality and
    communication, 62–3; public and private
    selves, 66–7; and relationships, 59–60; as
    self-fulfilling prophecy, 64–6; and social
    media, 313. *see also* identity
self-disclosure: characteristics, 245–6;
    and culture, 245; deception, hinting,
    and equivocation, 248–54; definition,
    241; guidelines, 246–8; in interpersonal
    relationships, 241–54; Johari Window,
    243–4; level and criteria, 246, 247; models,
    242–4; one-way, 248; reasons for, 241–2;
    risks, 246–7; social penetration, 242–3
self-esteem, 57
self-fulfilling prophecy, 64–6
self-monitoring, 26, 72
self-serving bias, 42–3
semantic rules, 89
Semantic Web, 76–7, 302–3
setting, and identity management, 74–5
sexism, and language, 93–5
sex roles, 114–15
Shemilt, Michelle, 386–7
Sheridan College, 58–9
significant others, 59–60
sign languages, 86, 155–6
signposts, 456
Silver Linings Playbook, 240
Simpson, Peter, 54–5
sincere questions, 187

situational leadership, 397–8
Sivagnanasuntharam, Nirushan, 225
slang, 102
small-group communication, 8, 356
smartphones, 70–1, 88, 179–80, 314
Smith, Donald, 407
Smith, Todd, 180–1
Snapchat, 325
snap judgments, 185
social activities, traditional *vs.* online, 216–17
social bookmarking websites, 312
social currency, 315
social distance, 154
social exchange, 424
social groups, 348
social judgment theory, 411–12
social learning theory, 331
social media: advantages, 321–2;
    characteristics, 297–9; dangers of, 306–7,
    322–3; dating and romance, 234; definition,
    297; and groups, 358–9, 376–7; and identity,
    313; and job hunting, 318–19; and listening,
    179–80; and mobility, 314–15; newness
    of, 300–3; and newspapers, 318–19; and
    non-verbal communication, 159–60;
    overview, 296–7; personal information,
    218, 324–5; personal protection, 323–4;
    public relation and marketing, 315; and
    radio, 320–1; and the self and society, 313,
    314; social networking websites, 309–11;
    and television, 319; *vs.* traditional media,
    297–300, 315–21; types, 303–13; use of,
    216–17, 219, 228, 318–19, 321–2; Vancouver
    riot, 30–1. *see also* specific social media
social networking websites, 309–11
social news aggregators, 312
social norms, 348
social orientation, 343, 362, 364
social penetration, 242–3
social roles, 48, 73–4, 352
social support and isolation, 10–11
society, and social media, 313
sociograms, 355–6
soft skills, 168–9
Solomon, Robert C., 254–5
Songza, 320–1
space-binding media theory, 326–8
space patterns, 439
speeches: attention of audience, 441–4,
    454–7; audience analysis, 457–60; auditory
    and visual aspects, 464–6; body of, 436,
    438–9, 441–8, 470–1; conclusion, 436, 439,
    446–8, 471; credibility of communicator,
    462; delivery, 462–7; introduction, 436,
    438, 441–6, 470; occasion analysis, 460–1;
    online, 442–3, 466; outlines of, 436–7,
    438; practice, 467; purpose and purpose
    statement, 433–5; resources, 466; samples,
    438–9, 470–3; software, 454–5; stage fright,
    467–70; structure, 435–41; supporting

materials, 449–54; topic selection, 432;
    visual aids, 452–4
spirals, 265
spontaneity, 267
stage fright, 467–70
stage hogging, 173, 179
stagnating stage, in relationships, 231
Star Trek, 391
statistics, in speeches, 450
status, and language, 93
stereotypes, 104
straightforwardness, 267
Straker, David, 426
strategy in communication climates, 267
superiority in communication climates, 268
supporting materials: functions, 449;
    narration and citation, 451–2; of speakers,
    192–3; for speeches, 449–54; types, 449–51;
    visual aids, 452–4
supporting responses, 198–200
symbols, 6, 86–7, 326
sympathy, *vs.* empathy, 52
symposium, 375–6
syntactic rules, 88–9

talking, *vs.* listening, 178–9
task norms, 349
task orientation, 343, 362, 364
task roles, 352
teams. *see* groups
television, and social media, 319
terminating stage, in relationships, 232–3
territory, in non-verbal communication, 157
terrorism, and racial profiling, 46–7
testimony, 451
tetrad, 328–9
texting, 28, 180–1
Thank You for Smoking, 419
that's-not-all technique, 425
theory of communication. *see* communication
    theory
thesis statement, 435
time, in non-verbal communication, 155–6
time-binding media theory, 326–8
time-oriented listening, 184–5
time patterns, 438
toddlers, lies, 252
topic patterns, 440
topic selection, in speeches, 432
touch, 150–1
traditional media, *vs.* social media, 297–300,
    315–21
Trailer Park Boys, 117
trait theories of leadership, 394–6
transactional communication model, 18–21
transitions, in speeches, 448
Trotsky, The, 14
Trudeau, 451
Trudeau, Justin, 400
Tuckwood, Christopher, 138, 354

Tumblr, 160, 304
Twitter, 118–19, 159–60, 308–9, 318
two-step flow theory, 330

uncertainty avoidance, 362, 363–4
uniforms, influence, 152
user-generated content, 297

value, 460–1
Vancouver riot, 30–1
Vancouver Sun, 31
verbal communication: and non-verbal
    communication, 134, 136, 140–6; styles,
    115–20; types, 131
video blogs, 305
video sharing websites, 312–13
Vine, 159–60
virtual teams, 341
visible minorities, 360–1
visual aids, to speeches, 452–4
visualization technique, 469
vlogs, 305
vocal messages, 148–9
voice, 148–9, 465–6
volume, in speeches, 465

Web 2.0 and 3.0, 76–7, 302–3
web design and marketing, 144–5, 236–7
web sources, 437
Wessman, Lars, 76–7
Western cultures, 61–2, 123. *see also* Anglo-
    North American culture
wheel network, 356–7
white lies, 250
Whiting, Robert, 363
Who's on First, 190
Wikipedia, 312, 358–9
wikis, 311–12
win–lose problem-solving, 282–3
win–win problem-solving, 284–8
Wizard of Oz, The, 361
women. *see* gender
word charts, 453
WordPress, 304
words, 87, 101–2
work, and environment, 158
working outline, 436
writing: forms of, 481–6; and persuasion,
    478–9; process and stages, 480–1; purpose,
    479; samples, 483, 487–9
Ws, five (Who, What, When, Where, and
    Why), 481

Yee, Krystal, 318–19
"you" language, 266
YouTube, 312–13
Yowching, Donna, 58–9

zines, 301–2